Data Structures and Algorithms in Java

Second Edition

Michael T. Goodrich
Department of Computer Science
Johns Hopkins University

Roberto Tamassia
Department of Computer Science
Brown University

John Wiley & Sons, Inc.
New York • Chichester • Weinheim • Brisbane • Singapore • Toronto

EXECUTIVE EDITOR	Bill Zobrist
EDITOR	Paul Crockett
MARKETING MANAGER	Katherine Hepburn
ASSOCIATE PRODUCTION DIRECTOR	Lucille Buonocore
SENIOR PRODUCTION EDITOR	Monique Calello
SENIOR DESIGNER	Dawn Stanley
PREPRESS SERVICES	Color Associates
COVER DESIGNER	Dawn Stanley
COVER ART	Anatjari Tjampitjinpa, "Snake Dreaming," 1988. Reproduced courtesy of Patrick Corbally Stourton of Corbally Stourton Contemporary Art Ltd.

Java is a trademark of Sun Microsystems, Inc.
UNIX® is a registered trademark in the United States and other countries, licensed through X/Open Company, Ltd.
All other product names mentioned herein are the trademarks of their respective owners.

This book was set in 10/12 Times Roman by Roberto Tamassia and Michael Goodrich and printed and bound by Quebecor World, Fairfield. The cover was printed by Phoenix Color Corporation.

This book is printed on acid-free paper. ∞

The paper in this book was manufactured by a mill whose forest management programs include sustained yield harvesting of its timberlands. Sustained yield harvesting principles ensure that the numbers of trees cut each year does not exceed the amount of new growth.

Library of Congress Cataloging-in-Publication Data
Goodrich, Michael T
Data structures and algorithms in Java / Michael T. Goodrich, Roberto Tamassia.-2nd ed.
    p. cm.
Includes bibliographical references and index.
ISBN 0-471-38367-8 (cloth : alk. Paper)
    1. Java (Computer program language) 2. Data Structures (Computer science)
    3.Computer algorithms. I. Tamassia, Roberto II. Title.

QA76.76.J38 G66 1997
005.7'3-dc21   00-043294

To order books or for customer service call 1-800-CALL-WILEY (225-5945).

Printed in the United States of America

10 9 8 7 6 5 4 3

To Karen, Paul, and Anna
  – *Michael T. Goodrich*

To Isabel
  – *Roberto Tamassia*

Preface to the Second Edition

This second edition is designed to provide a comprehensive introduction to data structures and algorithms, including their design, analysis, and implementation. In terms of the computer science and computer engineering curricula, we have written this book to be primarily focused on the Freshman-Sophomore level Data Structures (CS2) course.

Note: The first edition of this book contained additional material more suitable for a Junior-Senior level Data Structures and Algorithms (CS7) course. Readers interested in a text for this course are invited to consider augmenting it with the supplementary material at the accompanying Web site or using the companion text, *Algorithm Engineering*, by the same authors.

Several changes have been incorporated into this second edition. The introductory Chapters 1 and 2 were added to provide a stronger background in object-oriented programming, and to make the text more self-contained. In addition, the following changes were made:

- Expanded discussion of object-oriented design and the Java programming language, including the Java Collections Framework and design patterns
- Expanded coverage of Internet-related algorithmic topics, including hashing and text processing
- Revised and expanded exercises and Java code examples
- Expanded accompanying Web site (http://www.wiley.com/college/goodrich/)
- More focused attention on the most-used data structures, including vectors, lists, hash tables, and search trees.

With the ever-increasing influence of the World Wide Web (WWW) and the Internet, the importance of data structure design principles has actually increased in the three years since we wrote the first edition. Given the powerful influence this medium is having on all areas of software engineering, we expect the central role of data structure design in the computer science and computer engineering curricula to remain strong, and even increase, in the years ahead. Indeed, we have revised and expanded our previous discussions on hashing and text processing to focus more on Internet applications of efficient data structures.

About the Authors

Professors Goodrich and Tamassia are well-recognized researchers in data structures and algorithms, having published many papers in this field, with applications to internet computing, information visualization, geographic information systems, computer security, and computer-aided layout. They have an extensive record of research collaboration and have served as principal investigators in several joint projects sponsored by the National Science Foundation, the Army Research Office, and the Defense Advanced Research Projects Agency. They are also active in educational technology research, with special emphasis on algorithm visualization systems and infrastructure support for distance learning.

Michael Goodrich received his Ph.D. in Computer Science from Purdue University in 1987. He is currently a professor in the Department of Computer Science at Johns Hopkins University, and codirector of the Johns Hopkins Center for Algorithm Engineering. He is an editor for the *International Journal of Computational Geometry & Applications*, *Journal of Computational and System Sciences*, and *Journal of Graph Algorithms and Applications*.

Roberto Tamassia received his Ph.D. in Electrical and Computer Engineering from the University of Illinois at Urbana-Champaign in 1988. He is currently a professor in the Department of Computer Science at Brown University. He is also an editor for *Computational Geometry: Theory and Applications*, and the *Journal of Graph Algorithms and Applications*, and previously served on the editorial board of IEEE *Transactions on Computers*.

In addition to their research accomplishments, the authors also have extensive experience in the classroom. For example, Dr. Goodrich has taught data structures and algorithms courses at Johns Hopkins University since 1987, including Data Structures as a freshman-sophomore level course and Introduction to Algorithms as a upper level course. He has earned several teaching awards in this capacity. His teaching style is to involve the students in lively interactive classroom sessions that bring out the intuition and insights behind data structuring and algorithmic techniques, as well as in formulating solutions whose analysis is mathematically rigorous. Dr. Tamassia has taught Data Structures and Algorithms as an introductory freshman-level course at Brown University since 1988. He has also attracted many students (including several undergraduates) to his advanced course on Computational Geometry, which is a popular graduate-level CS course at Brown. One thing that has set his teaching style apart is his effective use of interactive hypermedia presentations, continuing the tradition of Brown's "electronic classroom." The carefully designed Web pages of the courses taught by Dr. Tamassia have been used as reference material by students and professionals worldwide.

Use as a Textbook

The design and analysis of efficient data structures has long been recognized as a key subject in computing, for the study of data structures is part of the core of every collegiate computer science and computer engineering major program we are familiar with. Typically, in programs based upon semesters, elementary data structures are briefly introduced in the first programming or introduction to computer science course (CS1), and this is followed by a more in-depth introduction to data structures (CS2) course. Furthermore, this introductory course is typically listed as a prerequisite for a host of other courses, and is often followed at a later point in the curriculum by a more in-depth study of data structures and algorithms (CS7). Curricula based upon the quarter system follow a similar approach, but divide the subject matter into more courses. In either case, however, we feel that the central role of data structure design and analysis in the curriculum is fully justified, given the importance of efficient data structures in most software systems, including operating systems, databases, compilers, and scientific simulation systems.

With the emergence of the object-oriented paradigm as the framework of choice for the implementation of robust and reusable software, we have tried to take a consistent object-oriented viewpoint throughout this text. One of the main ideas of the object-oriented approach is that data should be presented as being encapsulated with the methods that access and modify them. That is, rather than simply viewing data as a collection of bytes and addresses, we think of data as instances of an ***abstract data type*** (***ADT***) that includes a repertory of methods for performing operations on the data. Likewise, object-oriented solutions are often organized utilizing common ***design patterns***, which facilitate software reuse and robustness. Thus, we present each data structure using ADTs and their respective implementations and we introduce important design patterns as means to organize those implementations into classes, methods, and objects.

Prerequisites

We have written this book assuming that the reader comes to it with certain knowledge. Namely, we assume that the reader is at least vaguely familiar with a high-level programming language, such as C, C++, Pascal, or Java, and that he or she understands the main constructs from such a high-level language, including:

- Variables and expressions
- Methods (also known as functions or procedures)
- Decision structures (such as if-statements and switch-statements)
- Iteration structures (for-loops and while-loops).

For readers who are familiar with these concepts, but not with how they are expressed in Java, we provide a primer on the Java language in Chapter 1. We do not assume, however, that the reader is necessarily familiar with object-oriented design or with linked structures, such as linked lists, for these topics are covered in the core chapters of this book.

In terms of mathematical background, we assume the reader is somewhat familiar with topics from high-school mathematics, including exponents, logarithms, and elementary probability. Even so, we review most of these facts in Chapter 3, including exponents, logarithms, and summations, and we give a summary of other useful mathematical facts, including elementary probability, in Appendix A.

For the Instructor

As mentioned above, the second edition of this book is intended primarily as a textbook for a Freshman-Sophomore Data Structures (CS2) course. This book contains many Java-code and pseudo-code fragments, and over five hundred exercises, which are divided with roughly 40% being reinforcement exercises, 40% being creativity exercises, and 20% being projects.

This book is also structured to allow the instructor a great deal of freedom in how to organize and present the material. For example, we include in several chapters optional material that is somewhat mathematically more advanced. Such optional sections are indicated with a star ($\star$). In Table 0.1, we illustrate some possible uses of this book for an intermediate-paced CS2 course.

Chapter	Possible Options
1. Java Programming	skip if students know it already
2. Object-Oriented Design	skip if students know it already
3. Analysis Techniques	omit justification methods
4. Stacks, Queues & Deques	provide alternate case study
5. Vectors, Lists, and Sequences	omit amortized analysis
6. Trees	visit the tree drawing applet
7. Priority Queues	omit bottom-up heap construction, locators
8. Dictionaries	omit skip lists, locators
9. Search Trees	omit (2,4) and red-black trees
10. Sorting, Sets, and Selection	omit sorting lower bound
11. Text Processing	omit tries, compression, & LCS
12. Graphs	omit directed graphs

Table 0.1: Options for a Freshman-Sophomore Data Structures (CS2) course.

Web Added-Value Education

This book comes accompanied by an extensive Web site:

- **http://www.wiley.com/college/goodrich/**

Included on this Web site is an extensive collection of educational aids that augment the topics of this book, for both students and instructors. Specifically for students we include:

- All the Java source code presented in this book
- Four-per-page overhead transparencies for topics covered in this book
- A database of hints on selected assignments, indexed by problem number
- Java animations and interactive applets for data structures and algorithms
- Hyper-links to other data structures and algorithms resources.

We feel that the Java animations and interactive applets should be of particular interest, since they allow readers to interactively "play" with different data structures, which leads to better understanding of the different ADTs and the way they can be implemented.

For instructors using this book, there is a dedicated portion of the Web site just for them, which includes the following additional teaching aids:

- A keyword-searchable database of exercises, with additional exercises and projects
- Solutions to selected exercises
- One-per-page overhead transparencies
- Self-contained special-topic supplements, including discussions on splay trees, range trees, partition trees, convex hulls, and orthogonal segment intersection.

Data Structures in Java

As mentioned earlier, the implementation language used in this book is Java. There are several important reasons for this. First, Java is object-oriented; hence, it incorporates the important software-engineering concepts that allow for code reuse. In addition, Java has a concise syntax like C, but it avoids a number of mechanisms that typically confuse beginning programmers, such as pointer arithmetic, unions and structs, and loosely typed expressions. In addition, it builds in mechanisms for easily performing several tasks that are difficult to implement using C and C++, including window and mouse management, memory management and garbage collection, socket communication, and multiprogramming via threads. More importantly, unlike C and C++, Java is designed to be platform-independent, which is a feature that can greatly simplify class project implementation. Moreover, Java is supported by all modern Web browsers. By using Java as our implementation language, we are using a language that is simple, versatile, and fun.

Our use of Java is inspired by more than just the language itself, however. We present fundamental data structure interfaces in this book so as to conform to application programmer interfaces (APIs) of data structures libraries in Java, including the *Java Collections Framework*, introduced in the Java 2 platform, and *JDSL*, the data structures library in Java developed by the authors and their collaborators. Our use of terms such as "container," "sequence," and "iterator" are consistent with terminology used by these libraries, with "container" being synonymous with "collection." Thus, in addition to conveying the essentials of data structure design and implementation, this book also implicitly provides an introduction to data structure software libraries.

Acknowledgments

There are a number of individuals who have made contributions to this book. Many students at Brown University and Johns Hopkins University have used prepublication versions of chapters of this text, and their experiences and responses have helped shape it. There are also a number of collaborators who made specific contributions to the book. Ryan Baker, Edward Bross, Natasha Gelfand, Mark Handy, Matthew Harris, Benoit Hudson, David Jackson, John Kloss, Russell Schwager, Amit Sobti, and Luca Vismara, developed Java code examples and animations. Also, Ryan, Natasha, Mark, Matthew, Benoit, and Luca provided valuable feedback and useful suggestions on drafts of book chapters. Lubomir Bourdev, Mike Demmer, Mark Handy, Michael Horn, and Scott Speigler developed a basic Java tutorial, which ultimately led to Chapter 1, Java Programming.

We are grateful to all our former teaching assistants who helped us in developing exercises, programming assignments, and algorithm animation systems, and in particular to James Baker, Stina Bridgeman, Robert Cohen, Yi-Jen Chiang, Ashim Garg, Jeff Achter, Benjamin Boer, Lubomir Bourdev, Bryan Cantrill, Jody Fanto, Michael Horn, Jovanna Ignatowicz, Seth Padowitz, Michael Shapiro, and Galina Shubina.

There have been a number of friends and colleagues whose comments have lead to improvements in the text. We are particularly thankful to Karen Goodrich, Art Moorshead, and Scott Smith for their insightful comments. We are also truly indebted to the outside reviewers and readers for their copious comments, emails, and constructive criticism, which were extremely useful in writing the second edition. We specifically thank the following reviewers for their comments and suggestions: Divy Agarwal, University of California, Santa Barbara; Bobby Blumofe, University of Texas, Austin; Michael Clancy, University of California, Berkeley; Larry Davis, University of Maryland; Scott Drysdale, Dartmouth College; Stan Kwasny, Washington University; Ken Slonneger, University of Iowa; C.V. Ravishankar, University of Michigan; Val Tannen, University of Pennsylvania; and Paul Van Arragon, Messiah College.

We are grateful to our editors, Regina Brooks, Paul Crocket, and Bill Zobrist for their enthusiastic support of this project. The production team at Wiley has been great. Many thanks go to Lilian Brady, Monique Calello, Katherine Hepburn, Jay Kirsch, Madelyn Lesure, Charity Robey, Dawn Stanley, Jeri Uzzo, and Jennifer Welter.

The advanced computing environments and excellent technical staff in the Computer Science Departments at Brown and Hopkins gave us a reliable working environment. This manuscript was prepared primarily with LaTeX for the text and Adobe FrameMaker® and Visio® for the figures.

Finally, we would like to warmly thank Isabel Cruz, Karen Goodrich, Giuseppe Di Battista, Franco Preparata, Ioannis Tollis, and our parents for providing advice, encouragement, and support at various stages of the preparation of this book. We also thank them for reminding us that there are things in life beyond writing books.

Michael T. Goodrich
Roberto Tamassia

Contents

Chapter

1

Java Programming

Contents

The first digital computer, ENIAC, did not use any data structures to speak of. Its primary function was to quickly perform long sequences of mathematical calculations at speeds that were truly remarkable for its time. As important an achievement as this was, the major impact of ENIAC is not in the actual calculations it performed, but in the computational era it ushered in.

Computers are utilized today in a myriad of different ways. For consumers, computers provide real-time control of washing machines, automobiles, and ovens. For scientists and engineers, computers are used to design new airplanes, to model complex molecules, and to simulate galaxies. And computers are essential for modern-day commerce, as they are employed to perform most financial transactions and to facilitate a host of different modes of communication, including the Internet. Indeed, we have come a long way since 1945 when ENIAC was first built.

Modern computers routinely have memory capacities that are tens of millions of times larger than ENIAC ever had,[1] and memory capacities continue to grow at astonishing rates. This growth in capacity has brought with it a new and exciting role for computers. Rather than simply being fast calculators, modern computers are ***information processors***. They store, analyze, search, transfer, and update huge collections of complex data. Quickly performing these tasks requires that data be well organized and that the methods for accessing and maintaining data be fast and efficient. In short, modern computers need good data structures and algorithms.

Specifying these data structures and algorithms requires that we communicate instructions to a computer, and an excellent way to perform such communication is using a high-level computer language, such as Java. In this chapter, we give a brief overview of the Java programming language, assuming the reader is somewhat familiar with an existing high-level language, such as Pascal, C, or C++.

Java possesses a number of features that make it an excellent tool for exploring the implementation of data structures and algorithms. It was designed to allow for secure, platform-independent software execution, which is a big advantage in heterogeneous educational computing environments. Java allows us to use pointers for implementing sophisticated linked structures, but it restricts potentially dangerous programming styles, such as pointer arithmetic and arbitrary array indexing. In addition, it provides for several levels of data protection (such as public and private variables and methods), and it has an extensive collection of meaningfully named error conditions. It has a simple built-in mechanism for memory management and garbage collection, which can be used transparently by the novice programmer, but which has several "behind-the-scenes" hooks for expert programmers. And, finally, it contains simple constructs for performing fairly sophisticated kinds of computing, such as multiprocessing, network computing, and graphical user interfaces.

---

[1]ENIAC's memory was upgraded around 1952 to be able to store a program of 1,800 two-digit instructions and a data set of 100 ten-digit numbers.

The specific topics of the Java language we focus on in this chapter, and the next, are those that are directly related to the implementation of data structures and algorithms, including the following:

- Classes and objects (Section 1.1)
- Methods (Section 1.2)
- Variables and expressions (Section 1.3)
- Control flow (Section 1.4)
- Arrays (Section 1.5)
- Input and Output (Section 1.6)
- Packages (Section 1.8)
- Exceptions (Section 2.3)
- Interfaces (Section 2.4)
- Casting (Section 2.5).

This book does not provide a complete description of the Java language, however. There are major aspects of the language that are not directly relevant to data structure and algorithm design. These language features are therefore not included here, but are nevertheless fundamental parts of the language. These include graphical user interfaces, threads, JavaBeans, and sockets. For the reader interested in learning more about these topics, please see the notes at the end of this chapter.

1.1 Classes, Types, and Objects

We begin by discussing Java classes and objects, which are central to Java programming. The main "actors" in a Java program are *objects*. Objects store data and provide methods for accessing and modifying this data. Every object is an instance of a *class*, which defines the *type* of data that the object stores, as well as the kinds of operations that can act on that data. In particular, the allowable *members* of a class in Java are the following:

- Data of Java objects are stored in *instance variables* (also called *fields*). Therefore, if an object from some class is to store data, then its class must specify the instance variables for such objects. Instance variables can either come from base types (such as integers, floating-point numbers, or Booleans) or they can refer to objects of other classes.
- The operations that can act on data, and which express the "messages" that objects respond to, are called *methods*. The methods of a class consist of constructors, procedures, and functions. They define the behavior of objects from that class.

In short, an object is a specific combination of data and the methods that can process and communicate that data. Classes define the *types* for objects; hence, objects are sometimes referred to as instances of their defining class, for they take on the name of that class as their type.

How Classes Are Declared

The syntax for a Java class definition is as follows:

```
[⟨class_modifiers⟩] class ⟨class_name⟩
               [extends ⟨superclass_name⟩]
               [implements ⟨interface_1⟩, ⟨interface_2⟩, . . . ] {

       // class methods and instance variable definitions go here . . .

   }
```

where we use a syntax shorthand where optional material is enclosed in square brackets ("[" and "]") and identifiers and keywords are indicated by words inside angle brackets ("⟨" and "⟩"). In Java, identifiers, such as ⟨class_name⟩, must begin with a letter and be a string of letters, numbers, and underscore characters (where "letter" and "number" can be from any written language defined in the Unicode character set). We list the exceptions to this general rule for Java identifiers in Table 1.1. We discuss the optional **extends** and **implements** clauses in Sections 2.2.1 and 2.4, respectively.

A simple example template for a class definition without these optional clauses is as follows:

```
class Gnome {

    // instance variable definitions would go here...

    // method definitions would go here...

}
```

In this example, we do not use any class modifiers (which we discuss next). Notice that the class definition is delimited by braces, that is, it begins with a "{" and ends with a "}." In Java, any set of statements between the braces "{" and "}" define a program *block*.

Reserved Words			
abstract	else	interface	switch
boolean	extends	long	synchronized
break	false	native	this
byte	final	new	throw
case	finally	null	throws
catch	float	package	transient
char	for	private	true
class	goto	protected	try
const	if	public	void
continue	implements	return	volatile
default	import	short	while
do	instanceof	static	
double	int	super	

Table 1.1: A listing of the reserved words in Java. These names cannot be used as method or variable names in Java.

Class Modifiers

Class modifiers are optional keywords that precede the **class** keyword. They modify a class's scope and status in a program in the following ways:

- The **abstract** class modifier describes a class that has abstract methods. Abstract methods are declared with the **abstract** keyword and are empty (that is, they have no block defining a body of code for this method). A class that has nothing but abstract methods and no instance variables is more properly called an interface (see Section 2.4), so an **abstract** class usually has a mixture of abstract methods and actual methods. (We discuss abstract classes and their uses in Section 2.4.)

- The **final** class modifier describes a class that can have no subclasses.

- The **public** class modifier describes a class that can be instantiated or extended by anything in the same package or by anything that *imports* the class. (This is explained in more detail in Section 1.8.) All public classes are declared in their own separate file called ⟨classname⟩.java. There can only be one public class per file.

- If the **public** class modifier is not used, the class is considered *friendly*. This means that it can be used and instantiated by all classes in the same *package*. This is the default class modifier.

1.1.1   Base Types

The types of objects are determined by the class they come from. For the sake of efficiency and simplicity, Java also has the following *base types* (also called *primitive types*), which are not objects:

boolean	Boolean value: true or false
char	16-bit Unicode character
byte	8-bit signed two's complement integer
short	16-bit signed two's complement integer
int	32-bit signed two's complement integer
long	64-bit signed two's complement integer
float	32-bit floating-point number (IEEE 754-1985)
double	64-bit floating-point number (IEEE 754-1985)

A variable declared to have one of these types simply stores a value of that type, rather than a reference to some object. Integer constants, like 14 or 195, are of type **int**, unless followed immediately by an 'L' or 'l', in which case they are of type **long**. Floating-point constants, like 3.1415 or 2.158*e*5, are of type **double**, unless followed immediately by an 'F' or 'f', in which case they are of type **float**.

Even though they themselves do not refer to objects, base-type variables are useful in the context of objects, for they often make up the instance variables (or fields) inside an object. They also provide an additional safety feature of Java, in that such instance variables are always given an initial value whenever an object containing them is created.

1.1.2   Objects

In Java, a new object is created from a defined class by using the **new** operator. The **new** operator creates a new object from a specified class and returns a *reference* to that object. Here is the syntax for using the **new** operator in an expression:

> **new** ⟨class_type⟩([param, param, . . .])

Typically, such an expression would appear in an assignment statement, having the following form:

> ⟨variable_name⟩ = **new** ⟨class_type⟩([param, param, . . .]);

We use ⟨variable_name⟩ here to denote an identifier that is the name of an object variable, which is a reference to the object just created. The ⟨class_type⟩ name refers to a special *constructor* method (with the same name as the class), which initializes the object being created. (We say more about constructor methods in Section 1.2.) The ⟨class_type⟩ is an identifier defining the name of the class, and the list of parameters is optional. Calling the **new** operator on a class type as shown above causes three events to occur:

- A new object is dynamically allocated in memory, and all instance variables are initialized to standard default values. The default values are **null** for object variables and 0 for all base types except **boolean** variables (which are **false** by default).
- The constructor for the new object is called with the parameters specified. The constructor fills in meaningful values for the instance variables and performs any additional computations that must be done to create this object.
- After the constructor returns, the **new** operator returns a reference (that is, a memory address) to the newly created object. If the expression is in the form of an assignment statement, then this address is stored in the object variable, so the object variable *refers* to this newly created object.

In the following statement, a new object of class Point is instantiated with a constructor that takes the coordinates of the point as arguments, and variable my-Point becomes a reference to that object:

myPoint = **new** Point (3,6);

Number Objects

We sometimes want to store numbers as objects, but base type numbers are not themselves objects, as we have noted. To get around this obstacle, Java defines a special class for each numeric base type. We call these classes *number classes*. In Table 1.2, we show the numeric base types and their corresponding number class, along with examples of how number objects are created and accessed.

Base Type	*Class Name*	*Creation Example*	*Access Example*
byte	Byte	n = **new** Byte((**byte**)34)	n.byteValue()
short	Short	n = **new** Short((**short**)100)	n.shortValue()
int	Integer	n = **new** Integer(1045)	n.intValue()
long	Long	n = **new** Long(10849L)	n.longValue()
float	Float	n = **new** Float(3.934F)	n.floatValue()
double	Double	n = **new** Double(3.934)	n.doubleValue()

Table 1.2: Java number classes. Each class is given with its corresponding base type and example expressions for creating and accessing such objects. For each row, we assume the variable n is declared with the corresponding class name.

String Objects

A string is a sequence of characters that come from some **alphabet**, which is a set Σ of **characters**. Each character c that makes up a string s can be referenced by its index in the string, which is equal to the number of characters that come before c in s (so the first character is at index 0). In Java, the alphabet Σ used to define strings is the Unicode international character set, a 16-bit character encoding that covers the most used written languages. Other programming languages tend to use the smaller ASCII character set (which is a proper subset of the Unicode alphabet based on a 7-bit encoding). In addition, Java defines a special built-in class of objects called String objects.

Let $P = P[0]P[1]P[2]\dots P[m-1]$ be a string of m characters. For example, P could be the string `"hogs and dogs"`, which has length 13 and could have come from someone's Web page. In this case, $P[2] = $ 'g' and $P[5] = $ 'a'. Alternately, P could be the string `"CGTAATAGTTAATCCG"`, which has length 16 and could have come from a scientific application for DNA sequencing.

String processing involves dealing with both large strings and smaller ones. It also involves combining smaller strings into larger ones. The primary operation for combining strings is called **concatenation**, which takes a string

$$P = P[0]P[1]\dots P[m-1]$$

and a string

$$Q = Q[0]Q[1]\dots Q[n-1]$$

and combines them into a new string, denoted $P + Q$, with the following sequence of characters:

$$P[0]P[1]\dots P[m-1]Q[0]Q[1]\dots Q[n-1].$$

In Java, the "+" operation works exactly like this when acting on two strings. Thus, it is legal (and even useful) in Java to write an assignment statement like

```
String s = "kilo" + "meters";
```

This statement defines a variable s that references objects of the String class, and assigns it the string `"kilometers"`. (We will discuss assignment statements and expressions such as that above in more detail later in this chapter.) Every object in Java is assumed to have a built-in method toString() that returns a string associated with the object. This description of the String class should be sufficient for most uses; we discuss the String class and its "relative" the StringBuffer class in more detail in Section 11.1.

Instance Variables

Java classes can define ***instance variables***, also called ***fields***. These variables represent the data associated with the objects of a class. Instance variables must have a ***type***, which can either be a ***base type*** (such as **int, float, double**) or a ***reference type***, that is, a class, such as String, an interface (see Section 2.4), or an array (see Section 1.5). The syntax for declaring an instance variable is as follows:

$$[\langle variable\_modifier \rangle] \; \langle variable\_type \rangle \; \langle variable\_name \rangle \; [=\langle initial\_value \rangle];$$

The syntax of the ⟨variable_name⟩ parameter is the same as any other Java identifier. The ⟨variable_type⟩ parameter is either a base type, indicating that this variable stores values of this type, or a class name, indicating that this variable is a ***reference*** to an object from this class. The optional ⟨initial_value⟩ must match the variable's type. Our running example, the Gnome class, with some definitions of instance variables, could look like the following:

```java
class Gnome {
    // Instance variables:
    protected String name;
    protected int age;
    protected Gnome gnome_buddy;
    private boolean magical;
    public double height = 2.6;             // an initialization
    public static final int MAX_HEIGHT = 3; // a constant

    // Method definitions would go here...

}
```

Note the use of comments in this and other examples. These comments are annotations provided for human readers and are not processed by a Java compiler. Java allows for two kinds of comments—block comments and inline comments—which define text ignored by the compiler. Java uses a /* to begin a block comment and a */ to close it. In addition, Java uses a // to begin inline comments and ignores everything else on the line. For example:

```java
/*
 * This is a block comment.
 */

// This is an inline comment.
```

Also note the use of instance variables in the Gnome example. The variables age, magical, and height are base types, the variable name is a reference to an instance of the built-in class String, and the variable gnome_buddy is a reference to an object of the class we are now defining. Our declaration of the instance variable MAX_HEIGHT is taking advantage of a number of variable modifiers to define a "variable" that has a fixed constant value. Next, we describe the precise meaning of these and other variable modifiers that can be used in Java.

Variable Modifiers

The scope (visibility) of instance variables can be controlled through the use of the following *variable modifiers*:

- **public**: Anyone can access public instance variables.
- **protected**: Only methods of the same package or of subclasses can access protected instance variables.
- **private**: Only methods of the same class (not methods of a subclass) can access private instance variables.
- If none of the above modifiers are used, the instance variable is considered friendly. Friendly instance variables can be accessed by any class in the same package. Packages are discussed in more detail in Section 1.8.

In addition to scope variable modifiers, there are also the following usage modifiers:

- **static**: A static variable is used to declare a variable that is associated with the class, not with individual instances of that class. Static variables are used to store "global" information about a class (for example, a static variable could be used to maintain the total number of Gnome objects created). Static variables exist even if no instance of their class is created.
- **final**: A final instance variable is one that *must* be assigned an initial value, and then can never be assigned a new value after that. If it is a base type, then it is a constant (like the MAX_HEIGHT constant in the Gnome class above). If an object variable is **final**, then it will always refer to the same object (even if that object changes its internal state).

Constant values associated with a class should be declared to be both **static** and **final**. Before we go into more detail about instance variables and their uses, however (which we do in Section 1.3), let us discuss the methods that can act on instance variables in a class.

1.2 Methods

Methods in Java are conceptually similar to functions and procedures in other high-level languages. In general, they are "chunks" of code that can be called on a particular object (from some class). Methods can accept parameters as arguments, and their behavior depends on the object they belong to and the values of any parameters that are passed. Every method in Java is specified in the body of some class. A method definition has two parts: the *signature*, which defines the name and parameters for a method, and the *body*, which defines what the method actually does.

Declaring Methods

The syntax for defining a method is as follows:

```
[⟨method_modifiers⟩] ⟨return_type⟩ ⟨method_name⟩ ([⟨params⟩]) {
    // method body . . .
}
```

where ⟨params⟩ is an optional comma-separated list of parameter declarations that has the following syntax:

```
⟨param_type⟩ ⟨param_name⟩ [, ⟨param_type⟩ ⟨param_name⟩ [, ...] ]
```

Methods in a class are associated with a specific instance of that class (unless they are **static**), and can be used to change the state of that object. Here is a simple example:

```
public void renameGnome (String s) {
    name = s;     // Reassign the name instance variable of this gnome.
}
```

The syntax rule for the return type of a method is the same as for instance variables, and this rule also applies to parameter names. In the example above, we use the keyword **void** to indicate that this method has no return value. Parameters that are passed to a method can be either base types or object references. These variables and the instance variables of the class can be referenced inside the body of the method. Likewise, other methods of this class can be called from inside the body of a method. We discuss each of the components of a method declaration in more detail below.

Method Modifiers

As with instance variables, method modifiers can restrict the scope of a method as follows:

- **public**: Anyone can call public methods.
- **protected**: Only methods of the same package or of subclasses can call a protected method.
- **private**: Only methods of the same class (not methods of a subclass) can call a private method.
- If none of the above modifiers are used, then the method is friendly. Friendly methods can only be called by objects of classes in the same package.

The above method modifiers may be preceded by the following additional modifiers, which further restrict a method:

- **abstract**: A method declared as **abstract** will have no code. The parameter list of an abstract method is followed by a semicolon with no method body. For example:

  public abstract void setHeight (**double** newHeight);

  Abstract methods may only appear within an abstract class. We discuss the usefulness of this construct in Section 2.4.
- **final**: This is a method that cannot be overridden by a subclass.
- **static**: This is a method that is associated with the class itself, and not with a particular instance of the class. Static methods can also be used to change the state of static variables associated with a class (provided these variables are not declared to be **final**).

Return Types

A method definition must specify the type of value the method will return. If the method does not return a value, then the keyword **void** must be used. If the return type is **void**, the method is called a *procedure*; otherwise, it is called a *function*. To return a value in Java, a method must use the **return** keyword (and the type returned must match the return type of the method). Here is an example of a method (from inside the Gnome class) that is a function:

```
public boolean isMagical () {
    return magical;
}
```

As soon as a **return** is performed in a Java function, the method invocation ends.

Java functions can return only one value. To return multiple values in Java, we should instead combine all the values we wish to return in a ***compound object***, whose instance variables include all the values we want to return, and then return a reference to that compound object. In addition, we can change the internal state of an object that is passed to a method as another way of "returning" multiple results.

Parameters

A method's parameters are defined in a comma-separated list enclosed in parentheses after the name of the method. A parameter consists of two parts, the parameter type and the parameter name. If a method has no parameters, then only an empty pair of parentheses is used.

All parameters in Java are passed ***by value***, that is, any time we pass a parameter to a method, a copy of that parameter is made for use within the method body. So if we pass an **int** variable to a method, then that variable's integer value is copied. The method can change the copy but not the original. If we pass an object reference as a parameter to a method, then the reference is copied as well. Remember that we can have many different variables that all refer to the same object. Changing the internal reference inside a method will not change the reference that was passed in. For example, if we pass a Gnome reference g to a method that calls this parameter h, then this method can change the reference h to point to a different object, but g will still refer to the same object it did before. Of course, the method can use the reference h to change the internal state of the object, and this will change g's object as well (since g and h are currently referring to the same object).

Constructor Methods

A ***constructor*** is a special kind of method that is used to initialize newly created objects. Java has a special way to declare the constructor and a special way to invoke the constructor. First, let's look at the syntax for declaring a constructor:

```
[constructor_modifiers] ⟨constructor_name⟩ ([⟨params⟩]) {
    // Constructor body . . .
}
```

Thus, its syntax is essentially the same as that of any other method. The name of the constructor must be the same as the name of the class it constructs, however. So, if the class is called Fish, the constructor must be called Fish as well. In addition, a constructor has no return value. So its return type is implicitly void. The constructor modifier follows the same rules as for normal methods. An **abstract**, **static**, or **final** constructor is not allowed, however.

Here is an example:

```java
public Fish (int w, String n) {
   weight = w;
   name = n;
}
```

The body of a constructor is like a normal method's body (with one exception that we discuss in the next chapter). This body is intended to be used to initialize the data associated with objects of this class so that they may be in a stable initial state when first created.

Constructor methods are invoked in a unique way: they ***must*** be called using the **new** operator. So, upon invocation, a new instance of this class is automatically created and its constructor is then called (to initialize its instance variables and perform other setup tasks). For example, consider the following constructor invocation (which is also a declaration for the myFish variable):

```java
Fish myFish = new Fish (7, "Wally");
```

A class can have many constructors, but each must have a different *signature*, that is, each must be distinguished by the type and number of the parameters it takes.

The main Method

Some Java classes are meant to be utilized by other classes, others are meant to define stand-alone programs. Classes that define stand-alone programs must contain one other special kind of method for a class—the main method. When we wish to execute a stand-alone Java program, we reference the name of the class that defines this program, say, by issuing the following command (in DOS or UNIX):

```
java Aquarium
```

In this case, the Java run-time system looks for a compiled version of the Aquarium class, and then invokes the special main method in that class. This method must be declared as follows:

```java
public static void main(String[] args) {
   // main method body . . .
}
```

The arguments passed as the parameter args to the main method are the command-line arguments given when the program is called. The args variable is an array of String objects; that is, a collection of indexed strings, with the first string being args[0], the second being args[1], and so on. (We say more about arrays in Section 1.5.) For example, we may have defined the Aquarium program to take an optional argument that specifies the number of fish in the aquarium. We could then invoke the program by typing

java Aquarium 45

to specify that we want an aquarium with 45 fish in it. In this case, args[0] refers to the string "45". One nice feature of the main method is that it allows each class to define a stand-alone program, and one of the uses for this method is to test all the other methods in a class. Thus, thorough use of the main method is an effective tool for debugging collections of Java classes.

Statement Blocks and Local Variables

The body of a method is a ***statement block***, which is a sequence of statements and declarations to be performed between the braces "{" and "}". Method bodies and other statement blocks can themselves have statement blocks nested inside of them. In addition to statements that perform some action, like calling the method of some object, statement blocks can contain declarations of ***local variables***. These variables are declared inside the statement body, usually at the beginning (but between the braces "{" and "}"). Local variables are similar to instance variables, but they only exist while the statement block is being executed. As soon as control flow exits out of that block, all local variables inside it can no longer be referenced. A local variable can be either a ***base type*** (such as **int**, **float**, **double**) or a ***reference*** to an instance of some class. Single statements and declarations in Java are always terminated by a semicolon, that is, a ";".

Here is the syntax for declaring local variables:

⟨variable_type⟩ ⟨variable_name⟩ [= ⟨initial_value⟩];

where the rules for the type, name, and initial value are the same as for instance variables. Here are some examples of local variable declarations:

```
{
  double r;
  Point p1 = new Point (3, 4);
  Point p2 = new Point (8, 2);
  int i = 512;
  double e = 2.71828;
}
```

Notice that we can assign an initial value to a variable when we declare it.

We show a complete example definition of the Gnome class in Code Fragment 1.1.

```java
public class Gnome {
  // Instance variables:
  protected String name;
  protected int age;
  protected Gnome gnome_buddy;
  private boolean magical = false;
  public double height = 2.6;              // in feet
  public static final int MAX_HEIGHT = 3; // maximum height

  // Constructors:
  Gnome(String nm, int ag, Gnome bud, double hgt) { // fully parameterized
    name = nm;
    age = ag;
    gnome_buddy = bud;
    height = hgt;
  }
  Gnome() { // Default constructor
    name = "Rumple";
    age = 204;
    gnome_buddy = null;
    height = 2.1;
  }

  // Methods:
  public static void makeKing (Gnome h) {
    h.name = "King " + h.getRealName();
    h.magical = true;  // Only the Gnome class can reference this field.
  }
  public void makeMeKing () {
    name = "King " + getRealName();
    magical = true;
  }
  public boolean isMagical() { return magical; }
  public void setHeight(int newHeight) { height = newHeight; }
  public String getName() { return "I won't tell!"; }
  public String getRealName() { return name; }
  public void renameGnome(String s) { name = s; }
}
```

Code Fragment 1.1: The Gnome class.

1.3   Expressions

Variables and constants are used in *expressions* to define new values and to modify variables. In this section, we discuss how expressions work in Java in more detail. Expressions involve the use of *literals*, *variables*, and *operators*. Since we have already discussed variables, let us briefly focus on literals and then discuss operators in some detail.

1.3.1   Literals

A *literal* is any "constant" value that can be used in an assignment or other expression. Java allows the following kinds of literals:

- The **null** object reference (this is the only object literal, and it is defined to be from the general Object class).
- Boolean: **true** and **false**.
- Integer: The default for an integer like 176 or -52 is that it is of type **int**, which is a 32-bit integer. A long integer literal must end with an "L" or "l," for example, 176L or -52l, and defines a 64-bit integer.
- Floating Point: The default for floating point numbers, such as 3.1415 and 10035.23, is that they are **double**. To specify that a literal is a **float**, it must end with an "F" or "f." Floating-point literals, in exponential notation, are also allowed, such as 3.14E2 or .19e10; the base is assumed to be 10.
- Character: In Java character constants are assumed to be taken from the Unicode alphabet. Typically, a character is defined as an individual symbol enclosed in single quotes, for example, 'a' and '?'. In addition, Java defines the following special character constants:

'\n'	(newline)	'\t'	(tab)
'\b'	(backspace)	'\r'	(return)
'\f'	(form feed)	'\\'	(backslash)
'\''	(single quote)	'\"'	(double quote).

- Strings: A string is a sequence of characters enclosed in double quotes, for example, "dogs all around" or "jump".

1.3.2   Operators

Java expressions involve composing literals and variables with operators. We survey the operators in Java in this section.

The Assignment Operator

The standard assignment operator in Java is " =". It is used to assign a value to an instance variable or local variable. Its syntax is as follows:

⟨variable⟩ = ⟨expression⟩

Where ⟨variable⟩ refers to a variable that can be referenced by the statement block containing this expression. The value of an assignment operation is the value of the expression that was assigned. Thus, if i and j are both declared as type **int**, it is correct to have an assignment statement like the following:

i = j = 25;

The Dot Operator

As we have mentioned above, creating a new object in Java involves the use of the **new** operator to allocate space for the object, and then the use of a constructor of the object to initialize this space. The location (or **address**) of this space is then assigned to a **reference** variable. Therefore, a reference variable can be viewed as a link or "pointer" to some object. Every object reference variable must refer to some object, even if it is the null object. There can, in fact, be many references to the same object, and each reference to a specific object can be used to call methods on that object.

One of the primary uses of an object reference variable is to access the members of the class for this object, an instance of its class. That is, an object reference variable is useful for accessing the methods and instance variables associated with an object. This access is performed with the dot (".") operator. We call a method associated with an object by using the following syntax:

⟨object_reference⟩.⟨method_name⟩([⟨param⟩,⟨param⟩, ...]);

This calls the method with the specified name for the object referred to by this object reference. It can optionally be passed multiple parameters. If there are several methods with this same name defined for this object, then the Java run-time system uses the one that matches the number of parameters and most closely matches their respective types. A method's name combined with the number and types of its parameters is called a method's **signature**, for it takes all of these parts to determine the actual method to perform for a certain method call. Consider the following examples:

```
oven.cookDinner();
oven.cookDinner(food);
oven.cookDinner(food,seasoning);
```

Each of these method calls is actually referring to a different method with the same name defined in the class that oven belongs to. Note, however, that the signature of a method in Java does not include the type that the method returns, so Java does not allow two methods with the same signature to return different types.

We refer to the instance variables associated with an object using the dot operator, with the following syntax:

$$\langle object\_reference \rangle . \langle variable\_name \rangle$$

Assuming, of course, that the scope specification for such a variable allows access, then this use can appear anywhere in an expression. Nevertheless, the name $\langle variable\_name \rangle$ must be a member of the object to which $\langle object\_reference \rangle$ refers.

If an object reference is not **final**, then it can appear on the left-hand side of an assignment as well. Consider the following examples:

```
gnome.name = "Professor Smythe";
gnome.age = 132;
```

The $\langle object\_reference \rangle$ can also be any expression that returns an object reference. So the following is also syntactically correct:

```
Gnome g = new Gnome();
String buddyName = (g.gnome_buddy).name;
```

Arithmetic Operators

The following are binary arithmetic operators in Java:

+	addition
−	subtraction
*	multiplication
/	division
%	the modulo operator

All of these but the last should be clear. The modulo operator is also known as the "remainder" operator, for it is the remainder left after an integer division. We often use "mod" to denote the modulo operator, and we defined it formally as

$$n \bmod m = n - \lfloor n/m \rfloor m.$$

Java also provides a unary minus ($-$), which can be placed in front of an arithmetic expression to invert its sign. Parentheses can be used in any expression to define the order of evaluation. Java also uses a fairly intuitive operator precedence rule to determine the order of evaluation when parentheses are not used. Unlike C++, Java does not allow operator overloading.

Increment and Decrement Operators

Like C and C++, Java provides increment and decrement operators. Specifically, it provides the plus-one increment (++) and decrement (−−) operators. If such an operator is used in front of a variable reference, then 1 is added to (or subtracted from) the variable and its value is read into the expression. If it is used after a variable reference, then the value is first read and then the variable is incremented or decremented by 1. So, for example, the code fragment

```
int i = 8;
int j = i++;
int k = ++i;
int m = i--;
int n = i++ + --i;
```

assigns 8 to j, 10 to k, 10 to m, 18 to n, and leaves *i* with value 9.

Logical Operators

Java allows for the standard comparison operators between numbers:

<	less than
<=	less than or equal to
==	equal to
!=	not equal to
>=	greater than or equal to
>	greater than

The operators == and != can also be used for object references. The type of the result of a comparison is a **boolean**.

Operators that operate on **boolean** values are the following:

!	not (prefix)
&&	conditional and
||	conditional or

The Boolean operators && and || will not evaluate the second operand in their expression if it is not needed to determine the value of the expression. This feature is useful, for example, for constructing Boolean expressions where we first test that a certain condition holds (such as a reference not being null) and then we test a condition that could have otherwise generated an error condition had the prior test not succeeded.

Bitwise Operators

Java also provides the following bitwise operators for integers and Booleans:

~	bitwise complement (prefix unary operator)
&	bitwise and
|	bitwise or
^	bitwise exclusive-or
<<	shift bits left, filling in with zeros
>>	shift bits right, filling in with sign bit
>>>	shift bits right, filling in with zeros

Operational Assignment Operators

Besides the standard assignment operator (=), Java also provides a number of other assignment operators that have operational side effects. These other kinds of operators are of the following form:

⟨variable⟩ ⟨op⟩= ⟨expression⟩;

This is equivalent to

⟨variable⟩ = ⟨variable⟩ ⟨op⟩ ⟨expression⟩;

except that if ⟨variable⟩ contains an expression (for example, an array index), the expression is evaluated only once. Thus, the code fragment

```
a[5] = 10;
i = 5;
a[i++] += 2;
```

leaves a[5] with value 12 and i with value 6.

String Concatenation

Strings can be composed using the ***concatenation*** operator (+), so that the code

```
String rug = "carpet";
String dog = "spot";
String mess = rug + dog;
String answer = mess + " will cost me dollars!";
```

would have the effect of making answer refer to the string

```
"carpetspot will cost me dollars!"
```

This example also shows how Java converts nonstring constants into strings, when they are involved in a string concatenation operation.

Operator Precedence

Operators in Java are given preferences, or precedence, that determine the order in which operations are performed when the absence of parentheses brings up evaluation ambiguities.

We show the precedence of the operators in Java (which, incidentally, is the same as in C) in Table 1.3.

	Type	Symbols
	Operator Precedence	
	Type	**Symbols**
1	postfix ops	$\langle$exp$\rangle$ ++ $\langle$exp$\rangle$ −−
	prefix ops	++$\langle$exp$\rangle$ −−$\langle$exp$\rangle$ +$\langle$exp$\rangle$ −$\langle$exp$\rangle$ ˜$\langle$exp$\rangle$!$\langle$exp$\rangle$
	cast	($\langle$type$\rangle$)$\langle$exp$\rangle$
2	mult./div.	* / %
3	add./subt.	+ −
4	shift	<< >> >>>
5	comparison	< <= > >= **instanceof**
6	equality	== !=
7	bitwise-and	&
8	bitwise-xor	ˆ
9	bitwise-or	|
10	and	&&
11	or	||
12	conditional	$\langle$bool_exp$\rangle$? $\langle$true_val$\rangle$: $\langle$false_val$\rangle$
13	assignment	= += −= *= /= %= >>= <<= >>>= &= ˆ= |=

Table 1.3: The Java precedence rules. Operators in Java are evaluated according to the above ordering, if parentheses are not used to determine the order of evaluation. Operators on the same line are evaluated in left-to-right order (except for assignment and prefix operations, which are evaluated right-to-left), subject to the conditional evaluation rule for Boolean **and** and **or** operations. The operations are listed from highest to lowest precedence (we use $\langle$exp$\rangle$ to denote an atomic or parenthesized expression). Without parenthesization, higher precedence operators are performed before lower precedence operators.

We have now discussed almost all of the operators listed in Table 1.3. A notable exception is the conditional operator, which involves evaluating a Boolean expression and then taking on the appropriate value depending on whether this Boolean expression is true or false. (We discuss the use of the **instanceof** operator in the next chapter.)

1.3.3 Casting in Expressions

Casting is an operation that allows us to change the type of a variable. In essence, we can take a variable of one type and *cast* it into an equivalent variable of another type. Casting can be useful for doing certain numerical and input/output operations.

The syntax for casting a variable to a desired type is as follows:

$$(\langle \text{desired\_type}\rangle)\langle \text{variable}\rangle;$$

There are two fundamental types of casting that can be done in Java. We can either cast with respect to the base numerical types or we can cast with respect to objects. We discuss here how to perform casting of numerical and string types, and we discuss object casting in Section 2.5. For instance, it might be helpful to cast an **int** to a **double** in order to perform operations like division.

Ordinary Casting

When casting from a **double** to an **int**, we may lose precision. This means that the resulting double value will be rounded down. But we can cast an **int** to a **double** without this worry. For example, consider the following:

```
double d1 = 3.2;
double d2 = 3.9999;
int i1 = (int)d1;          // i1 has value 3
int i2 = (int)d2;          // i2 has value 3
double d3 = (double)i2;    // d3 has value 3.0
```

Casting with Operators

Certain binary operators, like division, will have different results depending on the variable types they are used with. We must take care to make sure operations perform their computations on values of the intended type. When used with integers, division does not keep track of the fractional part, for example. When used with doubles, division keeps this part, as is illustrated in the following example:

```
int i1 = 3;
int i2 = 6;
dresult = (double)i1 / (double)i2;    // dresult has value 0.5
dresult = i1 / i2;                    // dresult has value 0.0
```

Notice that when i1 and i2 were cast to doubles, regular division for real numbers was performed. When i1 and i2 were not cast, the " /" operator performed an integer division and the result of i1 / i2 was the **int** 0. Java then did an *implicit cast* to assign an **int** value to the **double** result. We discuss implicit casting next.

Implicit Casting

If an *explicit cast*, that is, a cast that is syntactically included in the code, is not specified, then there are cases where Java will need to perform an *implicit cast*. This means that Java will go ahead and change the types of variables, even though the programmer did not explicitly include the cast. Java will perform a cast according to the type of the assignment variable, provided there is no loss of precision.

For example:

```
int iresult, i = 3;
double dresult, d = 3.2;

dresult = i / d;          // dresult has value 0.9375. i was
                          // cast to a double because dresult is a double.
iresult = i / d;          // this results in a compilation error;
                          // an explicit cast is needed where
                          // precision will be lost.
```

Java will not perform implicit casts where precision is lost. In the above example, the line

```
    iresult = i / d;
```

needs an explicit cast to an **int**. In this case, casting the **double** d to an **int** would loose d's decimal precision.

The general rule with casting then is to *play it safe*. If unsure about whether the compiler will be implicitly casting our variables, it is better to spell it out. Explicitly casting variables guarantees the right results.

Implicit Casting with String Objects

There is one situation in Java when only implicit casting is allowed, and that is in string concatenation. Any time a string is concatenated with any object or base type, that object or base type is automatically converted to a string. Explicit casting of an object or base type to a string is not allowed, however. Thus, the following assignments are incorrect:

```
String s = (String) 4.5;          // this is wrong!
String t = "Value = " + (String) 13;   // this is wrong!
String u = 22;                    // this is wrong!
```

To perform conversions to string, we must instead use the appropriate toString method or perform an implicit cast via the concatenation operation.

Thus, the following statements are correct:

```
String s = "" + 4.5;          // correct, but poor style
String t = "Value = " + 13;   // this is good
String u = Integer.toString(22);  // this is good
```

As noted above, every object in Java supports a toString() method (with no arguments), which converts that object to a string. In addition, the Integer, Long, Short, Byte, Float, and Double classes each have a built-in static toString(x) method for converting the analogous base type to a string.

1.4 Control Flow

Control flow in Java is similar to that of other high-level languages. We review the basic structure and syntax of control flow in Java in this section, including method returns, if statements, switch statements, loops, and restricted forms of "jumps" (the **break** and **continue** statements).

1.4.1 The If and Switch Statements

In Java, conditionals work the same as in other languages. They provide a way of making a decision and then executing one or more different statement blocks based on the outcome of that decision.

The If Statement

The syntax of an if statement is as follows:

```
if (⟨boolean_expr⟩)
    ⟨true_statement⟩
[else if (⟨boolean_expr⟩)
    ⟨else_if_statement⟩]
[else
    ⟨else_statement⟩]
```

where each statement can be a block of statements enclosed in braces ("{" and "}"). In addition, the "else if" and "else" parts are optional; either or both may be omitted from a valid if statement.

Unlike C and C++, the expression in an if statement in Java *must* be a Boolean expression.

This requirement helps us avoid a common programming error, for the following bug will be caught by the compiler:

```
i = 5;
// intermediate code ...
if (i = 5)                      // (THIS IS WRONG!)
    // ...
```

In this case, the "condition" is really an assignment, which is of type **int**. Thus, this is not a syntactically correct if statement. The following is correct, however:

```
if (snowLevel < 2) {
    goToClass();
    comeHome();
}
else if (snowLevel < 5) {
    goSledding();
    haveSnowballFight();
}
else
    stayAtHome();
```

Switch Statements

Java provides for multiple-value control flow using the **switch** statement. The following is an indicative example:

```
public Candy getCandy (int money) {
    Candy candy;
    int tax=1;
    switch (money+tax) {
      case 5:
        candy = new Gumball ();
        break;
      case 25:
        candy = new Peanuts ();
        break;
      case 50:
        candy = new Candybar ();
        break;
      default:
        candy = new EmptyWrapper();
        break;
    }
    return candy;
}
```

The **switch** statement evaluates an integer expression (such as " money+tax") and causes control flow to jump to the code location labeled with the value of this expression. If there is no such label, then control flow jumps to the location labeled "**default**." This is the only explicit jump performed by the **switch** statement, however, so flow of control "falls through" to other cases if the code for each case is not ended with a **break** statement (which causes control flow to jump to the next line after the **switch** statement).

1.4.2 Loops

Another important control flow mechanism in a programming language is looping. Java provides for three types of loops.

For Loops

In their simplest form, **for** loops provide for repeated code based on an integer index. In Java, we can do that and much more. The functionality of a **for** loop is significantly more flexible. In particular, the usage of a **for** loop is split into four sections; the initialization, the condition, the increment, and the body. Here is the syntax for a Java **for** loop:

```
for ([⟨initialization⟩];[⟨condition⟩];[⟨increment⟩])
    ⟨body_statement⟩
```

In the ⟨initialization⟩ section, we can declare an index variable that will only be in the scope of the **for** loop. For example, if we want a loop that indexes on a counter, and we have no need for the counter variable outside of the **for** loop, then declaring

```
for (int counter = 0; ⟨condition⟩; ⟨increment⟩)
```

will declare a variable counter whose scope is the loop body only.

In the ⟨condition⟩ section, we specify the repeat (while) condition of the loop. This must be a Boolean expression. The body of the **for** loop will be executed each time the ⟨condition⟩ is **true** when evaluated at the beginning of a potential iteration. As soon as ⟨condition⟩ evaluates to **false**, then the loop body is not executed, and, instead, the program executes the next statement after the **for** loop.

In the ⟨increment⟩ section, we declare the incrementing statement for the loop. The incrementing statement can be any legal statement, allowing for significant flexibility in coding.

The following example shows a simple **for** loop in Java:

```java
public void eatApples (Apples apples) {
   numApples = apples.getNumApples ();
   for (int x = 0; x < numApples; x++) {
      eatApple (apples.getApple (x));
      spitOutCore ();
   }
}
```

In the Java example above, the loop variable x was declared as **int** x = 0. Before each iteration, the loop tests the condition " x < numApples" and executes the loop body only if this is true. Finally, at the end of each iteration the loop uses the statement x++ to increment the loop variable x before again testing the condition.

Java has two other kinds of loops besides **for** loops, the standard **while** loop and the **do-while** loop. One loop tests a Boolean condition before performing an iteration of the loop body and the other tests a condition after.

While Loops

The syntax for testing a condition before a loop body is executed is as follows:

```
while (⟨boolean_expression⟩)
   ⟨loop_body_statement⟩
```

At the beginning of each iteration, the loop tests the Boolean expression and then executes the loop body only if this expression evaluates to true. As with the **for** loop, the loop body statement can also be a block of statements.

Consider, for example, a gnome that is trying to water all of the carrots in his carrot patch, which he does until his watering can is empty. Since his can might be empty to begin with, we would write the code to perform this task as follows:

```java
public void waterCarrots () {
   Carrot current = garden.findNextCarrot ();

   while (!waterCan.isEmpty ()) {
      water (current, waterCan);
      current = garden.findNextCarrot ();
   }
}
```

Recall that "!" in Java is the "not" operator.

Do-While Loops

The syntax for a **while** loop that tests a condition after the loop body is as shown below:

> **do**
> ⟨loop_body_statement⟩
> **while** (⟨boolean_expression⟩)

Again, the loop body statement will typically be a block of statements, and the conditional must be a Boolean expression. In a **do-while** loop, we repeat the loop body for as long as the condition is true each time it is evaluated.

Consider, for example, that we want to prompt the user for input and then do something useful with that input. (We discuss Java input and output in more detail in Section 1.6.) A possible condition, in this case, for exiting the loop is when the user enters an empty string. However, even in this case, we may want to handle that input and inform the user that she has quit. The following example illustrates this case:

```java
public void getUserInput() {
    String input;
    do {
        input = getInputString();
        handleInput(input);
    } while (input.length()>0);
}
```

Notice the exit condition for the above example. Specifically, it is written to be consistent with the rule in Java that **do-while** loops exit when the condition is *not* true (unlike the repeat-until construct used in other languages).

1.4.3 Explicit Control-Flow Statements

Java also provides statements that allow for explicit change in the flow of control of a program.

Returning from a Method

If a Java method is declared with return type of **void**, then flow of control returns when it reaches the last line of code in the method or when it encounters a **return** statement with no argument. If a method is declared with a return type, however, the method is a function and it must exit by returning the function's value as an argument to a **return** statement. The following (correct) example illustrates returning from a function:

```java
// Check for a specific birthday
public boolean checkBDay (int date) {
   if (date == BirthdayList.MIKES_BDAY)
      return true;
   }
   return false;
}
```

It follows that the **return** statement *must* be the last statement executed in a function, as the rest of the code will never be reached.

Note that there is a significant difference between a statement being the last line of code that is *executed* in a method and the last line of code in the method itself. In the example above, the line **return true;** is clearly not the last line of code that is written in the function, but it may be the last line that is executed (if the condition involving date is **true**). Such a statement explicitly interrupts the flow of control in the method. There are two other such explicit control-flow statements, which are used in conjunction with loops and switch statements.

The break Statement

The typical use of a **break** statement has the following simple syntax:

> **break**;

It is used to "break" out of the innermost **switch, for, while,** or **do-while** statement body. When it is executed, a break statement causes the flow of control to jump to the next line after the statement body containing the **break**.

The **break** statement can also be used in a labeled form to jump out of an outer-nested loop or **switch** statement. In this case, it has the syntax

> **break** ⟨label⟩;

where ⟨label⟩ is a Java identifier that is used to label a loop or **switch** statement. Such a label can only appear at the beginning of the declaration of a loop; there are no other kinds of "go to" statements in Java.

We illustrate the use of a label with a **break** statement in the following example:

```
public static boolean hasZeroEntry (int[][] a) {
    boolean foundFlag = false;

zeroSearch:
    for (int i=0; i<a.length; i++) {
        for (int j=0; j<a[i].length; j++) {
            if (a[i][j] == 0) {
                foundFlag = true;
                break zeroSearch;
            }
        }
    }
    return foundFlag;
}
```

The above example also uses arrays, which are covered in Section 1.5.

The continue Statement

The other statement to explicitly change the flow of control in a Java program is the **continue** statement, which has the following syntax:

```
continue [⟨label⟩];
```

where ⟨label⟩ is a Java identifier that is used to label a loop. As mentioned above, there are no explicit "go to" statements in Java. Likewise, the **continue** statement can only be used inside loops (**for**, **while**, and **do-while**). The **continue** statement causes the execution to skip over the remaining steps of the loop in the current iteration. We show below an example use of the **continue** statement.

```
// count times an integer x appears in an array a
public static int countInteger (int[] a, int x) {
    int count = 0;
    for (int i=0; i<a.length; i++) {
        if (a[i] != x) continue;
        count++;
    }
    return count;
}
```

This example also makes use of an array, which is a structure we discuss next.

1.5 Arrays

An *array* is a numbered collection of variables all of the same type. Each variable, or *cell*, in an array has an *index*, and the cells in an array are numbered consecutively starting with 0 and going to $N - 1$, where N is the *length* of the array, which is also known as its *capacity*. Any index not in the range from 0 to $N - 1$ is said to be *out of bounds*.

As a safety feature, array indices are always checked in Java to see if they are ever out of bounds. If an array index is out of bounds, the run-time Java environment signals an error condition. This check helps Java avoid a number of security problems that other languages must cope with. We never need to guess the length of an array, however, to avoid the out-of-bounds error. The size of an array is stored in an instance variable length, which can be accessed as follows:

⟨array_name⟩.length

We can avoid out-of-bounds errors by carefully using the early termination feature of Boolean operations in Java. For example, a statement like the following will never generate an index out-of-bounds error:

```
if (((i >= 0) && (i < a.length)) && (a[i] > 0.5) )
    x = a[i];
```

for the comparison " $a[i] > 0.5$" will only be performed if the first two comparisons succeed.

The syntax for declaring an array is as follows:

⟨array_type⟩[] ⟨array_name⟩ [=
{⟨init_val_0⟩,⟨init_val_1⟩,...,⟨init_val_N−1⟩}];

where the first set of brackets, " []", are part of the syntax, and the second denotes an optional array initialization. The ⟨array_type⟩ can be any Java base type or class name, and ⟨array_name⟩ can be any value Java identifier. We can create the collection of cells for an array using the following syntax:

new ⟨array_type⟩[⟨length⟩]

where ⟨length⟩ is a positive integer denoting the length of the array created, and the brackets "[" and "]" are a nonoptional part of the syntax. Typically this expression appears in an assignment statement with an array name on the left-hand side of the assignment operator. So, for example, the following statement defines an array variable named a, and assigns it an array of 10 cells, each of type **int**:

> **int**[] a = **new int**[10];

The cells of the new array "a" are indexed using the integer set $\{0, 1, 2, \ldots, 9\}$ (note that arrays in Java always start indexing at 0).

Arrays in Java are similar to objects, which explains our use of the dot operator to find an array's length, and are defined to be one-dimensional. Nevertheless, we can compose arrays to define multi-dimensional arrays. That is, a two-dimensional array is actually an array of arrays, which can be created with a declaration statement like the following:

> **float**[][] x = **new float**[8][10];

This statement creates a two-dimensional "array of arrays." The following are then valid uses of the above arrays a and x:

> i = 5;
> a[i] = 138;
> x[i][i+1] = 2.189 + x[i][i];
> i = a.length;
> j = x[4].length;

1.6 Simple Input and Output

Java provides a rich set of classes and methods for performing input and output. There are classes for doing graphical user interface design, complete with pop-up windows and pull-down menus, as well as methods for the display and input of text and numbers. Java also provides methods for dealing with graphical objects, images, sounds, Web pages, and mouse events (such as clicks, mouse overs, and dragging). Moreover, many of these input and output methods can be used in either stand-alone programs or in applets. Unfortunately, going into the details on how all of these methods work for constructing sophisticated graphical user interfaces is beyond the scope of this book. Still, for the sake of completeness, we describe how simple input and output can be done in Java in this section.

Simple input and output in Java occurs within the Java console window. Depending on the Java environment we are using, this window is either a special pop-up window that can be used for displaying and inputting text, or it is a window used to issue commands to our operating system (such windows are referred to as shell windows, DOS windows, or terminal windows).

Output Methods

Java provides a built-in static object, called System.out, that performs output to the "standard output" device. Operating systems, such as Unix/Linux allow users to redirect standard output to files or even as input to other programs, but the default output is to the Java console window. The System.out object is an instance of the java.io.PrintStream class. This class defines methods for a buffered output stream, meaning that characters are put in a temporary location, called a **buffer**, which is then emptied when the console window is ready to print characters. This class also provides the following methods for performing simple output (we use ⟨base_type⟩ here to refer to any of the possible base types):

- print(Object *o*): print the object *o* using its toString method.
- print(String *s*): print the string *s*.
- print(⟨base_type⟩ *b*): print the base type value *b*.
- println(String *s*): print the string *s*, followed by the newline character.
- flush(): print and empty the contents of the print buffer.

Consider, for example, the following code fragment:

```
System.out.print("Java values: ");
System.out.print(3.1415);
System.out.print(',');
System.out.print(15);
System.out.println(" (double,char,int).");
```

When executed, this fragment produces the following output:

```
Java values: 3.1415,15 (double,char,int).
```

This output will appear, of course, in the Java console window.

Input Methods

Just as there is a special object for performing output to the Java console window, there is also a special object, called System.in, for performing input from the Java console window. Technically, the input is actually coming from the "standard input" device, which by default is the computer keyboard echoing its characters in the Java console. The System.in object is an instance of the java.io.InputStream class, which is defined to proceed one character at time. This form of input is typically too primitive to be convenient, but it can be used to define another input object that processes input in a streaming and buffered way, using the java.io.BufferedReader and java.io.InputStreamReader classes.

For example, we can use the following template:

```
java.io.BufferedReader stndin;  // Standard input (buffered)
stndin=new java.io.BufferedReader(new java.io.InputStreamReader(System.in));
```

The class java.io.BufferedReader supports the following methods:

- **int** read(): read a single character. If the input stream is at its end, this method returns −1. This method raises an error condition, "java.io.IOException," if an input error occurs.
- String readLine(): read a line of text, that is, a string of characters up to the next newline character. The newline character is read, but it is not included in the string. If the input stream is at its end, this method returns **null**. This method raises the error condition "java.io.IOException" if an input error occurs.

Consider, for example, the following code fragment that combines input and output:

```
java.io.BufferedReader stndin;  // Standard input (buffered)
String line;                    // A line of input text
double sum, d = 0.0;
int i = 0;
stndin=new java.io.BufferedReader(new
java.io.InputStreamReader(System.in));
System.out.print("Input a double: ");
System.out.flush();
if ((line = stndin.readLine()) != null)
  d = Double.valueOf(line).doubleValue();
System.out.print("Input an int: ");
System.out.flush();
if ((line = stndin.readLine()) != null)
  i = Integer.valueOf(line).intValue();
sum = d + i;
System.out.println("Their sum is " + sum + ".");
```

When executed, this code fragment could produce the following combination of input and output:

```
Input a double: 6.1078
Input an int: 209
Their sum is 215.1078.
```

1.7   An Example Program

In this section, we describe a simple example Java program that illustrates many of the constructs defined above. Our example consists of two classes, one, CreditCard, that defines credit card objects, and another, Test, that tests the functionality of CreditCard class. The credit card objects defined by the CreditCard class are simplified versions of traditional credit cards. They have identifying numbers, identifying information about their owners and their issuing bank, and information about their current balance and credit limit. They do not charge interest or late payments, however, but they do restrict charges that would cause a card's balance to go over its spending limit.

The CreditCard Class

We show the CreditCard class in Code Fragment 1.2. Note that the CreditCard class defines five instance variables, all of which are private to the class, and it provides a simple constructor that initializes these instance variables.

It also defines five *accessor methods* that provide access to the current values of these instance variables. Of course, we could have alternatively defined the instance variables as being public, which would have made the accessor methods moot. The disadvantage with this direct approach, however, is that it allows users to modify an object's instance variables directly, whereas in many cases such as this, we prefer to restrict the modification of instance variables to special *update methods*. We include two such update methods, chargeIt and makePayment in Code Fragment 1.2.

In addition, it is often convenient to include *action methods*, which define specific actions for that object's behavior. To demonstrate, we have defined such an action method, the printCard method, as a static method, which is also included in Code Fragment 1.2.

The Test Class

We test the CreditCard class in a Test class. Note the use of an array of CreditCard objects here, and how we are using iteration to make charges and payments. We show the complete code for the Test class in Code Fragment 1.3. For simplicity's sake, the Test class does not do any fancy graphical output, but simply sends its output to the Java console. We show this output in Code Fragment 1.4. Note the difference between the way we utilize the nonstatic chargeIt and makePayment methods and the static printCard method.

```java
public class CreditCard {
  // Instance variables:
  private String number;
  private String name;
  private String bank;
  private double balance;
  private int limit;
  // Constructor:
  CreditCard(String no, String nm, String bk, double bal, int lim) {
    number = no;
    name = nm;
    bank = bk;
    balance = bal;
    limit = lim;
  }
  // Accessor methods:
  public String getNumber() { return number; }
  public String getName() { return name; }
  public String getBank() { return bank; }
  public double getBalance() { return balance; }
  public int getLimit() { return limit; }
  // Action methods:
  public boolean chargeIt(double price) { // Make a charge
    if (price + balance > (double) limit)
      return false; // There is not enough money left to charge it
    balance += price;
    return true; // The charge goes through in this case
  }
  public void makePayment(double payment) { // Make a payment
    balance -= payment;
  }
  public static void printCard(CreditCard c) { // Print a card's information
    System.out.println("Number = " + c.getNumber());
    System.out.println("Name = " + c.getName());
    System.out.println("Bank = " + c.getBank());
    System.out.println("Balance = " + c.getBalance()); // Implicit cast
    System.out.println("Limit = " + c.getLimit()); // Implicit cast
  }
}
```

Code Fragment 1.2: The CreditCard class.

```
public class Test {
  public static void main(String[] args) {
    CreditCard wallet[] = new CreditCard[10];
    wallet[0] = new CreditCard("5391 0375 9387 5309",
                        "John Bowman", "Calfornia Savings", 0.0, 2500);
    wallet[1] = new CreditCard("3485 0399 3395 1954",
                        "John Bowman", "Calfornia Federal", 0.0, 3500);
    wallet[2] = new CreditCard("6011 4902 3294 2994",
                        "John Bowman", "Calfornia Finance", 0.0, 5000);
    for (int i=1; i<=16; i++) {
      wallet[0].chargeIt((double)i);
      wallet[1].chargeIt(2.0*i);          // implicit cast
      wallet[2].chargeIt((double)3*i);    // explicit cast
    }
    System.out.println("Card payments:");
    for (int i=0; i<3; i++) {
      CreditCard.printCard(wallet[i]);
      while (wallet[i].getBalance() > 100.0) {
        wallet[i].makePayment(100.0);
        System.out.println("New balance = " + wallet[i].getBalance());
      }
      System.out.println();
    }
  }
}
```

Code Fragment 1.3: The Test class.

```
Card payments:
Number = 5391 0375 9387 5309
Name = John Bowman
Bank = Calfornia Savings
Balance = 136.0
Limit = 2500
New balance = 36.0

Number = 3485 0399 3395 1954
Name = John Bowman
Bank = Calfornia Federal
Balance = 272.0
Limit = 3500
New balance = 172.0
New balance = 72.0

Number = 6011 4902 3294 2994
Name = John Bowman
Bank = Calfornia Finance
Balance = 408.0
Limit = 5000
New balance = 308.0
New balance = 208.0
New balance = 108.0
New balance = 8.0
```

Code Fragment 1.4: Output from the Test class.

1.8   Packages

The Java language takes a general and useful approach to the organization of classes into programs. Every public class defined in Java must be given in a separate file. The file name is the name of the class with a *.java* extension. So a class, **public class** SmartBoard, is defined in a file, *SmartBoard.java*. A set of related classes, all defined in a common subdirectory, can be a Java **package**. Every file in a package starts with the line:

> **package** ⟨package_name⟩;

The subdirectory containing the package must be named the same as the package. We can also define a package in a single file that contains several class definitions, but when it is compiled, all the classes will be compiled into separate files in the same subdirectory.

Using Other Packages

In Java, we can use classes that are defined in other packages by prefixing class names with dots (that is, using the '.' character) that correspond to the other packages' directory structure.

```
public boolean Temperature(TA.Measures.Thermometer thermometer,
                           int temperature) {
    // . . .
}
```

Here, the function Temperature takes a class Thermometer as a parameter. Thermometer is defined in the TA package in a subpackage called Measures. The dots in TA.Measures.Thermometer correspond directly to the directory structure in the TA package.

The Import Command

All the extra typing needed to refer to a class outside of the current package can get tiring. In Java, we can use the **import** keyword to include external classes or entire packages in the current file. To import an individual class from a specific package, we type the following at the beginning of the file:

> **import** ⟨packageName⟩.⟨classNames⟩;

For example, we could type

```
package Project;

import TA.Measures.Thermometer;
import TA.Measures.Scale;
```

at the beginning of a Project package to indicate that we are importing the classes named TA.Measures.Thermometer and TA.Measures.Scale. The Java run-time environment will now search these classes to match identifiers to classes, methods, and instance variables that we use in our program.

Importing a Whole Package

We can also import an entire package, by using the following syntax:

```
import ⟨packageName⟩.*;
```

For example:

```
package student;

import TA.Measures.*;

public boolean Temperature(Thermometer thermometer, int temperature) {
    // . . .
}
```

In the case where two packages have classes of the same name, we **must** specifically reference the package that contains a class. For example, suppose both the package Gnomes and package Cooking have a class named Mushroom.

If we provide an **import** statement for both packages, then we must specify which class we mean as follows:

```
Gnomes.Mushroom shroom = new Gnomes.Mushroom ("purple");
Cooking.Mushroom topping = new Cooking.Mushroom ();
```

If we do not specify the package (that is, in the previous example we just use a variable of type Mushroom), the compiler will give an "ambiguous class" error.

To sum up the structure of a Java program, we can have instance variables and methods inside a class, and classes inside a package.

1.9 Writing a Java Program

The process of writing a Java program involves three fundamental steps:

1. Design
2. Coding
3. Testing and Debugging.

We briefly discuss each of these steps in this section.

1.9.1 Design

The design step is perhaps the most important step in the process of writing a program. For it is in the design step that we decide how to divide the workings of our program into classes, we decide how these classes will interact, what data each will store, and what actions each will perform. Indeed, one of the main challenges that beginning Java programmers face is deciding what classes to define to do the work of their program. While general prescriptions are hard to come by, there are some general rules of thumb that we can apply when determining how to define our classes:

- *Responsibilities*: divide the work into different *actors*, each with a different responsibility. Try to describe responsibilities using action verbs. These actors will form the classes for the program.
- *Independence*: define the work for each class to be as independent from other classes as possible. Subdivide responsibilities between classes so that each class has autonomy over some aspect of the program. Give data (as instance variables) to the class that has jurisdiction over the actions that require access to this data.
- *Behaviors*: so that the consequences of each action performed by a class will be well understood by other classes that interact with it, define the behaviors for each class carefully and precisely. These behaviors will define the methods that this class performs. The set of behaviors for a class is sometimes referred to as a *protocol*, for we expect the behaviors for a class to hold together as a cohesive unit.

Defining the classes, together with their instance variables and methods, determines the design of a Java program. A good programmer will naturally develop greater skill in performing these tasks over time, as experience teaches him or her to notice patterns in the requirements of a program that match patterns that he or she has seen before.

In order to accelerate the development of this skill, we discuss, at various points throughout this text, various *design patterns* for designing object-oriented programs. These patterns provide templates for defining classes and the interactions between these classes.

Several programmers do their initial designs using *CRC cards*. Component-responsibility-collaborator, or CRC, cards are simple index cards that subdivide the work required of a program. The use of such cards allows a programmer to iteratively refine his or her organizational structure so as to ultimately arrive at a coherent set of classes. The main idea behind this tool is to have each card represent a component, which will ultimately become a class in our program. We write the name of each component on the top of its index card. On the left-hand side of its card we begin writing the responsibilities for this component. On the right-hand side, we list the collaborators for this component, that is, the other components that this component will have to interact with to perform its duties. The design process iterates through an action/actor cycle, where we first identify an action (that is, a responsibility), and we then determine an actor (that is, a component) that is best suited to perform that action. The design is complete when we have assigned all actions to actors.

By the way, in using index cards to perform our design, we are of course assuming that each component will have a small set of responsibilities and collaborators. This assumption is no accident, for it helps keep our programs manageable, even when they must necessarily be large.

An alternative to CRC cards is the use of UML (Unified Modeling Language) diagrams to express the design of a program. UML diagrams are a standard visual notation to express object-oriented software designs. Several computer-aided tools are available to build UML diagrams.

1.9.2 Coding

Once we have decided on the classes for our program, together with their responsibilities, we are ready to begin coding. We create the actual code for the classes in our program by using either an independent text editor (e.g., emacs, notepad, vi), or the editor embedded in an *integrated development environment* (IDE), such as IBM VisualAge, Microsoft J++, or Symantec Visual Cafe.

Once we have completed coding for a class (or package) we then compile this file into working code by invoking a compiler. If we are not using an IDE, then we compile our program by calling a program, such as javac, on our file. If we are using an IDE, then we compile our program by clicking the appropriate compilation button. If we are fortunate, and our program has no syntax errors, then this compilation process will create files with a ".class" extension.

If our program contains syntax errors, then these will be identified, and we will have to go back into our editor to fix the offending lines of code. Once we have eliminated all syntax errors, and created the appropriate compiled code, we then run our program by either invoking a command, such as "java" (outside an IDE) or clicking on the appropriate "run" button (within an IDE). When a Java program is run in this way, the run-time environment locates the directories containing the named class and any other classes that are referenced from this class according to a special operating system environment variable. This variable is named "CLASS-PATH," and the ordering of directories to search in is given as a list of directories, which are separated by colons in Unix/Linux or semicolons in DOS/Windows. An example CLASSPATH assignment in the DOS/Windows operating system could be the following:

```
SET CLASSPATH=.;C:\java;C:\Program Files\Java\
```

Whereas an example CLASSPATH assignment in the Unix/Linux operating system could be the following:

```
setenv  CLASSPATH ".:/usr/local/java/lib:/usr/netscape/classes"
```

where, in both cases, the dot (".") refers to the current directory in which the run-time environment is invoked.

Javadoc

In order to encourage good use of block comments and the automatic production of documentation, the Java programming environment comes with a documentation production program called *javadoc*. This program takes a collection of Java source files that have been commented using certain keywords, called *tags*, and it produces a series of HTML documents that describe the classes, methods, variables, and constants contained in these files. For space reasons, we have not used javadoc-style comments in all the example programs included in this book, but we include a javadoc example in Code Fragment 1.5 as well as other examples at the Web site that accompanies this book.

Each javadoc comment is a block comment that starts with "/**," ends with "*/," and has each line between these two begin with a single asterisk, "*." The block comment is assumed to start with a descriptive sentence, followed by a blank line, which is followed by special lines that begin with javadoc tags. A block comment that comes just before a class definition, instance variable declaration, or method definition, is processed by javadoc into a comment about that class, variable, or method.

```
/**
 * This class defines an immutable (x,y) point in the plane.
 *
 * @author Michael Goodrich
 */
public class XYPoint {
  private double x,y; // private instance variables for the coordinates

  /**
   * Construct an (x,y) point at a specified location.
   *
   * @param xCoor The x-coordinate of the point
   * @param yCoor The y-coordinate of the point
   */
  public XYPoint(double xCoor, double yCoor) {
    x = xCoor;
    y = yCoor;
  }

  /**
   * Return x-coordinate value.
   *
   * @return x-coordinate
   */
  public double getX() { return x; }

  /**
   * Return y-coordinate value.
   *
   * @return y-coordinate
   */
  public double getY() { return y; }
}
```

Code Fragment 1.5: An example class definition using javadoc-style comments. Note that this class includes only two instance variables, one constructor, and two accessor methods.

The primary javadoc tags are the following:

- `@author` *text*: identifies each author (one per line) for a class
- `@exception` *exception-name description*: identifies an error condition that is signaled by this method (see Section 2.3)
- `@param` *parameter-name description*: identifies a parameter accepted by this method
- `@return` *description*: describes the return type and its range of values for a method.

There are other tags as well; the interested reader is referred to on-line documentation for javadoc for further discussion.

Readability and Style

Programs should be made easy to read and understand. Good programmers should therefore be mindful of their coding style, and develop a style that communicates the important aspects of a program's design for both humans and computers.

Much has been written about good coding style, with some of the main principles being the following:

- Use meaningful names for identifiers. Try to choose names that can be read aloud, and choose names that reflect the action, responsibility, or data each identifier is naming. The tradition in most Java circles is to capitalize the first letter of each word in an identifier, except for the first word in an identifier for a variable or method. So, in this tradition, "Date," "Vector," "DeviceManager" would identify classes, and 'isFull()," "insertItem()," "studentName," and "studentHeight" would respectively identify methods and variables.
- Use named constants instead of embedded values. Readability, robustness, and modifiability are enhanced if we include a series of definitions of named constant values in a class definition. These can then be used within this class and others to refer to special values for this class. The tradition in Java is to fully capitalize such constants, as shown below:

```java
public class Student {
    public static final int MIN_CREDITS = 12;  // min. credits in a term
    public static final int MAX_CREDITS = 24;  // max. credits in a term
    public static final int FRESHMAN = 1;      // code for freshman
    public static final int SOPHOMORE = 2;     // code for sophomore
    public static final int JUNIOR = 3;        // code for junior
    public static final int SENIOR = 4;        // code for senior

    // Instance variables, constructors, and method definitions go here...
}
```

- Indent statement blocks. Typically programmers indent each statement block by 4 spaces; in this book we typically use 2 spaces, however, to avoid having our code overrun the book's margins.
- Organize each class in the following order:
  1. constants
  2. instance variables
  3. constructors
  4. methods.

We note that some Java programmers prefer to put instance variable definitions last; we put them earlier so that we can read each class sequentially and understand the data each method is working with.

- Use comments that add meaning to a program and explain ambiguous or confusing constructs. In-line comments are good for quick explanations and do not need to be sentences. Block comments are good for explaining the purpose of a method and complex code sections.

1.9.3 Testing and Debugging

Testing is the process of verifying the correctness of a program, while debugging is the process of tracking the execution of a program and discovering the errors in it. Testing and debugging are often the most time-consuming activity in the development of a program.

Testing

A careful testing plan is an essential part of writing a program. While verifying the correctness of a program over all possible inputs is usually infeasible, we should aim at executing the program on a representative subset of inputs. At the very minimum, we should make sure that every method in the program is tested at least once (method coverage). Even better, each code statement in the program should be executed at least once (statement coverage).

Programs often tend to fail on *special cases* of the input. Such cases need to be carefully identified and tested. For example, when testing a method that sorts (that is, puts in order) an array of integers, we should consider the following inputs:

- the array has zero length (no elements)
- the array has one element
- all the elements of the array are the same
- the array is already sorted
- the array is reverse sorted.

In addition to special inputs to the program, we should also consider special conditions for the structures used by the program. For example, if we use an array to store data, we should make sure that boundary cases, such as inserting/removing at the beginning or end of the subarray holding data, are properly handled.

While it is essential to use hand-crafted test suites, it is also advantageous to run the program on a large collection of randomly generated inputs. The Random class in the java.util package provides several methods to generate random numbers.

There is a hierarchy among the classes and methods of a program induced by the caller-callee relationship. Namely, a method *A* is above a method *B* in the hierarchy if *A* calls *B*. There are two main testing strategies, ***top-down*** and ***bottom-up***, which differ in the order in which methods are tested.

Bottom-up testing proceeds from lower-level methods to higher-level methods. Namely, bottom-level methods, which do not invoke other methods, are tested first, followed by methods that call only bottom-level methods, and so on. This strategy ensures that errors found in a method are not likely to be caused by lower-level methods nested within it.

Top-down testing proceeds from the top to the bottom of the method hierarchy. It is typically used in conjunction with ***stubbing***, a boot-strapping technique that replaces a lower-level method with a ***stub***, a replacement for the method that simulates the output of the original method. For example, if method *A* calls method *B* to get the first line of a file, when testing *A* we can replace *B* with a stub that returns a fixed string.

Debugging

The simplest debugging technique consists of using ***print statements*** (using method System.out.println($\langle$string$\rangle$)) to track the values of variables during the execution of the program. A problem with this approach is that the print statements need to be eventually removed or commented out before the program can be executed.

A better approach is to run the program within a ***debugger***, which is a specialized environment for controlling and monitoring the execution of a program. The basic functionality provided by a debugger is the insertion of ***breakpoints*** within the code. When the program is executed within the debugger, it stops at each breakpoint. While the program is stopped, the current value of variables can be inspected. In addition to fixed breakpoints, advanced debuggers allow for specification of ***conditional breakpoints***, which are triggered only if a given expression is satisfied.

The standard Java tools include a basic debugger called jdb, which is command-line oriented. IDEs for Java programming provide advanced debugging environments with graphical user interfaces.

1.10 Utilities in the java.lang Package

The java.lang package provides classes that are fundamental to the Java language. It also includes a number of static methods and predefined special classes that provide several useful utilities. We have already mentioned several classes that are defined in this package, including the String class and the number classes (Integer, Float, etc.). This package also includes *exceptions*, which are classes associated with error conditions in a Java program; we discuss exceptions in more detail in Section 2.3.

In this section, we list a few static methods and constants that are a part of some of the classes in the java.lang package. A complete listing of all utility classes in the java.lang package and other useful packages in Java can be found in a full reference work on Java or at a Java documentation Web site.

The Math Class

The java.lang package includes a useful Math class that provides a number of fundamental mathematical functions and constants, including the following (we use ⟨number⟩ to refer to any of the possible numeric base types):

- **double** E: The **double** number closest to e, the base of the natural logarithm function, ln.
- **double** PI: The **double** number closest to π, the ratio of the circumference of a circle to its diameter.
- ⟨number⟩ abs(⟨number⟩ x): The absolute value of x, unless x is the smallest negative integer that can be represented.
- **double** acos(**double** x): The arc cosine of the value x in radians.
- **double** asin(**double** x): The arc sine of the value x in radians.
- **double** atan(**double** x): The arc tangent of the value x in radians.
- **double** cos(**double** a): The cosine of the angle a.
- **double** exp(**double** x) The exponential function e^x.
- **double** log(**double** x) The natural logarithm (base e) ln x.
- ⟨number⟩ max(⟨number⟩ x, ⟨number⟩ y): The greater of x and y.
- ⟨number⟩ min(⟨number⟩ x, ⟨number⟩ y): The smaller of x and y.
- **double** pow(**double** x, **double** y): The power function, x^y.
- **double** random(): A (pseudo-)random number in the range $[0.0, 1.0)$.
- **long** round(**double** x): The **long** integer closest to x.
- **double** sin(**double** a): The sine of the angle a.
- **double** sqrt(**double** x): The value $\sqrt{x}$.
- **double** tan(**double** a): The tangent of the angle a.

All of the above methods and constants are static; hence, we reference them directly from the Math class. For example, the absolute value function is referenced as Math.abs.

String Conversions

Every class in Java has a method toString, which converts instances of that class to a string. Indeed, each of the number classes even has a static version of toString, which takes a base type of the corresponding number class as an argument, and returns a string representing that value. For example, Integer.toString(i) returns a string representation of the **int** i. Additionally, to provide for the same functionality in a uniform way, the String class includes a valueOf method, which can take any base type value as an argument and convert it to a string. This method is static; hence, we can call String.valueOf(i) to convert an **int** i to a string representing i's value.

For input functions, on the other hand, we desire methods for converting a string in the appropriate syntax to each of the various base types. To provide for this functionality, Java includes a method valueOf in each of the number classes, which takes a string as its argument and returns an object of the corresponding number class that represents that string. So, for example, to convert the string "3.1415F" to its corresponding **float** value, we would call Float.valueOf("3.1415F").floatValue().

Big Numbers

There are some numbers that are too big to fit in the standard number types defined in Java. Since it often is necessary to process such numbers, Java provides two arbitrary precision number types, which are both kinds of number classes. These are the java.math.BigDecimal and java.math.BigInteger classes. In addition to the usual operations provided by a number class, these classes also provide methods for performing various mathematical operations on big numbers. We do not list all the methods here, however, and instead refer the interested reader to a Java reference.

1.11   Exercises

Reinforcement

R-1.1 Rewrite each of the following statements to achieve the intended result without a syntax error:

```
String s = 49.5;
String t = "Pi = " + (String) 3.1415;
String u = 22;
```

R-1.2 Consider the following (*incorrect*) example for changing the state of an object reference passed to a method called makeKing:

```
public static void makeKing (Gnome h) {
    Gnome k = new Gnome("King "+h.name,h.age,null,h.height);
    h = k;
    k.magical = true;
}
```

Rewrite the above code fragment so that it correctly updates the Gnome reference by variable h so that its name has the title "King" and its magical flag is set to **true**.

R-1.3 Modify the CreditCard class from Code Fragment 1.2 to check that the price argument passed to method chargeIt and the payment argument passed to method makePayment are positive.

R-1.4 Modify the CreditCard class from Code Fragment 1.2 to charge interest on each payment.

R-1.5 Modify the CreditCard class from Code Fragment 1.2 to charge a late fee for any payment that is past its due date.

R-1.6 Modify the CreditCard class from Code Fragment 1.2 to include *modifier methods*, which allow a user to modify internal variables in a CreditCard class in a controlled manner.

R-1.7 Modify the declaration of the first **for** loop in the Test class in Code Fragment 1.3 so that its charges will eventually cause exactly one of the three credit cards to go over its credit limit. Which credit card is it?

R-1.8 Write a short Java function, isASCII, that takes a **char** c as input and returns **true** if and only if c is an ASCII character, that is, c is represented using only the seven least significant bits of c.

R-1.9 Write a Java class, AllKinds, that has three instance variables of type **int**, **long**, and **float**, respectively. Your class must include a constructor method that initializes each variable to a nonzero value, and your class should include methods for setting the value of each type, getting the value of each type, and adding each possible combination of types.

R-1.10 Write a short Java function, isMultiple, that takes two **long** values, n and m, and returns true if and only if n is a multiple of m, that is, $n = mi$ for some integer i.

R-1.11 Write a short Java function, isTwoPower, that takes an **int** i and returns true if and only if i is a power of 2. Your function cannot use multiplication or division, however.

R-1.12 Write a short Java function that takes an integer n and returns the sum of all the integers smaller than n.

R-1.13 Write a short Java function that takes an integer n and returns the sum of all the odd integers smaller than n.

R-1.14 Write a short Java function that takes a positive **double** value x and returns the number of times we can divide x by 2 before we get a number less than 2.

Creativity

C-1.1 Write a short Java program that prints its own source code when executed, but does not perform any input or file reading.

C-1.2 Write a Java method that takes an array of **int** values and prints all the odd numbers in the array.

C-1.3 Write a Java method that takes an array containing the set of all integers in the range 1 to 52 and shuffles it into random order. Your method should output each possible order with equal probability.

C-1.4 Write a short Java program that outputs all possible strings formed by using the characters 'a', 'b', 'c', 'd', 'e', and 'f' exactly once.

C-1.5 Write a short Java program that takes all the lines input to standard input and writes them to standard output in reverse order. That is, each line is output in the correct order, but the ordering of the lines is reversed.

C-1.6 Write a short Java program that takes two arrays a and b of length n storing **double** values, and returns the dot product of a and b. That is, it returns an array c of length n such that $c[i] = a[i] \cdot b[i]$, for $i = 0, \ldots, n - 1$.

C-1.7 Write a fast Java function that can take any int value, i, and return 2^i, as a long value. Your method should **not** multiply 2 by itself i times; there are much faster ways of computing 2^i.

C-1.8 The **greatest common divisor**, or GCD, of two positive integers n and m is the largest number j, such that n and m are both multiples of j. Euclid proposed a simple algorithm for computing $GCD(n, m)$, where $n > m$, which is based on a concept known as the Chinese Remainder Theorem. The main idea of the algorithm is to repeatedly perform modulo computations of consecutive pairs of the sequence that starts $(n, m, \ldots)$, until reaching zero. The last nonzero number in this sequence is the GCD of n and m. For example, for $n = 80,844$ and $m = 25,320$, the sequence is as follows:

$$
\begin{aligned}
80,844 \bmod 25,320 &= 4,884 \\
25,320 \bmod 4,884 &= 900 \\
4,884 \bmod 900 &= 384 \\
900 \bmod 384 &= 132 \\
384 \bmod 132 &= 120 \\
132 \bmod 120 &= 12 \\
120 \bmod 12 &= 0
\end{aligned}
$$

So, GCD of $80,844$ and $25,320$ is 12. Write a short Java function to compute $GCD(n, m)$ for two integers n and m.

Projects

P-1.1 A common punishment for schoolchildren is to write out the same sentence multiple times. Write a Java stand-alone program that will write out the following sentence one hundred times: "I will always use object-oriented design." Your program should number each of the sentences and it should "accidentally" make eight different random-looking typos at various points in the listing, so that it looks like a human typed it all by hand.

P-1.2 (For those who know Java graphical user interface methods) Define a GraphicalTest class that tests the functionality of the CreditCard class from Code Fragment 1.2 using text fields and buttons.

P-1.3 The ***birthday paradox*** says that the probability that two people in a room will have the same birthday is more than half as long as *n*, the number of people in the room, is more than 23. This property is not really a paradox, but many people find it surprising. Design a Java program that can test this paradox by a series of experiments on randomly generated birthdays, which test this paradox for $n = 5, 10, 15, 20, \ldots, 100$. You should run at least 10 experiments for each value of *n* and it should output, for each *n*, the number of experiments for that *n*, such that two people in that test have the same birthday.

Chapter Notes

For more detailed information about the Java programming language, we refer the reader to some of the fine books about Java, including the books by Arnold and Gosling [7], Campione and Walrath [19], Cornell and Horstmann [26], Flanagan [34], and Horstmann [50], as well as the Javasoft Web site (http://www.javasoft.com).

Chapter 2

Object-Oriented Design

Contents

In the early days of the information age, computers were expensive and large, but had slow processors and small memories. It should come as no surprise then, that early computers had a limited number of applications, most of which dealt with numeric processing, not information management. Modern computers, on the other hand, are continually becoming cheaper and smaller, while also coming equipped with faster processors and larger memories. Consequently, modern computers are used for a myriad of different applications. Indeed, many modern toys, such as singing dolls and talking action figures, have embedded processors with more speed and memory than the first digital computer, ENIAC, which was the size of a large room. In addition, computing researchers of a couple decades ago used the term "supercomputers" to refer to computing devices that were slower and had smaller memories than today's personal computers. Thus, modern computers are significantly smaller, cheaper, faster, and higher-capacity than their predecessors. Yet these advances bring higher expectations for software.

Creating software has become a complex enterprise. Designing and implementing a new software application typically involves the interaction of pieces of software written by many different people in several different organizations. These people may not know each other and may not even be willing to share the source code for their respective software pieces. In addition, over time, there is a natural tendency to want to upgrade old software, adding new features for applications in new environments. The challenge for software engineers is to create software that is itself complex, but nevertheless appears conceptually simple, so as to easily integrate with other software and allow for future modifications.

Thus, a driving force in research in software engineering and programming languages has been the development of methodologies that can produce designs that are conceptually *simple* enough to be understandable while being *powerful* enough to solve hard problems efficiently. Achieving such a balance is not easy, but a methodology that is showing considerable promise is *object-oriented design*.

2.1   Goals and Principles

As the name implies, the main "actors" in the object-oriented design paradigm are called *objects*. An object comes from a *class*, which is a specification of the data *fields*, also called *instance variables*, that the object contains, as well as the *methods* (operations) that the object can execute. Each class presents to the outside world a concise and consistent view of the objects that are instances of this class, without going into too much unnecessary detail or giving others access to the inner workings of the objects. This view of computing is intended to fulfill several goals and incorporate several design principles, which we discuss in this section.

2.1.1   Object-Oriented Design Goals

The fundamental goal of dealing with the complexity of building modern software naturally gives rise to several subgoals. These subgoals are directed at the production of quality software, including quality data structure and algorithm implementations. In particular, software implementations should achieve ***robustness***, ***adaptability***, and ***reusability***. (See Figure 2.1.)

Robustness   Adaptability   Reusability

Figure 2.1: Goals of object-oriented design.

Robustness

Every good programmer wants to produce software that is correct, which means that a program produces the right output for all the anticipated inputs in the program's application. In addition, we want software to be ***robust***, that is, capable of handling unexpected inputs that are not explicitly defined for its application. For example, if a program is expecting a positive integer (e.g., representing the price of an item) and instead is given a negative integer, then the program should be able to recover gracefully from this error. A program that does not gracefully handle such unexpected-input errors can be embarrassing for the programmer.

More importantly, in ***life-critical applications***, where a software error can lead to injury or loss of life, software that is not robust is deadly. This importance was driven home in the late 1980s in accidents involving Therac-25, a radiation-therapy machine, which severely overdosed six patients between 1985 and 1987, some of whom died from complications resulting from their radiation overdoses [64]. All six accidents were traced to software errors, with one of the most troubling being a user-interface error involving unexpected inputs (a fast-typing radiologist could backspace over a radiation dosage on the screen without the previous characters actually being deleted from the input).

The goal of robustness goes beyond the need to handle unexpected inputs, however. Software should produce correct solutions, even given the well-known limitations of computers. For example, if a user wishes to store more elements in a data structure than originally expected, then the software should expand the capacity of this structure to handle more elements. This philosophy of robustness is present, for example, in the java.util.Vector class in Java, which defines an expandable array. In addition, if an application calls for numerical computations, those numbers should be represented fully and should not overflow or underflow. Indeed, software should achieve **correctness** for its full range of possible inputs, including boundary cases, such as when an integer value is 0 or 1 or the maximum or minimum possible values. Robustness and correctness do not come automatically, however, they must be designed in from the start.

Adaptability

Modern software projects, such as word processors, Web browsers, and Internet search engines, typically involve large programs that are expected to last for many years. Software, therefore, needs to be able to evolve over time in response to changing conditions in its environment. These changes can be expected, such as the need to adapt to an increase in CPU or network speed, or they can be unexpected, such as the need to add new functionality because of new market demands. Software should also be able to adapt to unexpected events that, in hindsight, really should have been expected, such as the coming of a new millennium and its effects on date calculations (the "year 2000" problem). Thus, another important goal of quality software is that it achieve **adaptability** (also called **evolvability**). Related to this concepts is **portability**, which is the ability of software to run with minimal change on different hardware and operating system platforms. An advantage of writing software in Java is the portability provided by the language itself.

Reusability

Going hand in hand with adaptability is the desire that software be reusable, that is, code should be usable as a component of different systems in various applications. Developing quality software can be an expensive enterprise, and its cost can be offset somewhat if the software is designed in a way that makes it easily reusable in future applications. Such reuse should be done with care, however, for one of the major sources of software errors in the Therac-25 came from inappropriate reuse of software from the Therac-20 (which was not designed for the hardware platform used with the Therac-25). So, for software to be truly reusable, we must be clear about what it does and does not do. Given this clarity, however, software reuse can be a significant cost-saving and time-saving technique.

2.1.2 Object-Oriented Design Principles

Chief among the principles of the object-oriented approach, which are intended to facilitate the goals outlined above, are the following (see Figure 2.2):

- Abstraction
- Encapsulation
- Modularity.

Abstraction   Encapsulation   Modularity

Figure 2.2: Principles of object-oriented design.

Abstraction

The notion of ***abstraction*** is to distill a complicated system down to its most fundamental parts and describe these parts in a simple, precise language. Typically, describing the parts of a system involves naming them and describing their functionality. For example, a typical text-editor graphical user interface (GUI) provides an abstraction of an "edit" menu that offers several text-editing operations, including cutting and pasting portions of text or other graphical objects. Without going into details about the ways a GUI represents and displays text and graphical objects, the concepts of cutting and pasting are simple and precise. A cut operation deletes the selected text and graphics and places them into an external storage buffer. A paste operation inserts the contents of the external storage buffer at a specific location in the text. Thus, the abstract functionality of an "edit" menu and its cutting and pasting operations is specified in a language precise enough to be clear, but simple enough to "abstract away" unnecessary details. This combination of clarity and simplicity benefits robustness, since it leads to understandable and correct implementations.

Applying this paradigm to the design of data structures gives rise to *abstract data types* (ADTs). An ADT is a mathematical model of a data structure that specifies the type of data stored, the operations supported on them, and the types of parameters of the operations. An ADT specifies *what* each operation does, but not *how* it does it. In Java, an ADT can be expressed by an *interface*, which is simply a list of method declarations. (We say more about Java interfaces in Section 2.4.)

An ADT is realized by a concrete data structure, which is modeled in Java by a *class*. A class defines the data being stored and the operations supported by the objects that are instances of the class. Also, unlike interfaces, classes specify *how* the operations are performed. A Java class is said to *implement an interface* if its methods give life to all of those of the interface.

Encapsulation

Another important principle of object-oriented design is the concept of *encapsulation*, or *information hiding*, which states that different components of a software system should not reveal the internal details of their respective implementations. Consider again our example of an edit menu with cutting and pasting functionality in a text-editor graphical user interface (GUI). One of the main reasons an edit menu is so useful is that we can completely understand how to use it without understanding exactly how it is implemented. For example, we do not need to know how the menu is drawn, how selected text to be cut or pasted is represented, how selected portions of text are stored in an external buffer, or how various graphical objects, such as graphs, images, or drawings, are identified, stored, and copied in and out of the external buffer. Indeed, the code associated with the edit menu should not depend on all of these details to work correctly. Instead, the edit menu should provide an interface that is sufficiently specified for other software components to use its methods effectively, while also requiring well-defined interfaces from other software components that it needs. In general terms, the principle of encapsulation states that all the different components of a large software system should operate on a strictly need-to-know basis.

One of the main advantages of encapsulation is that it gives the programmer freedom in implementing the details of a system. The only constraint on the programmer is to maintain the abstract interface that outsiders see. For example, the programmer of the edit menu code in a text-editor GUI might at first implement the cut and paste operations by copying actual screen images in and out of an external buffer. Later, he or she may be dissatisfied with this implementation, since it does not allow compact storage of the selection, and it does not distinguish text and graphic objects. If the programmer has designed the cut and paste interface with encapsulation in mind, switching the underlying implementation to one that stores text as text and graphic objects in an appropriate compact format should not cause any problems to methods that need to interface with this GUI. Thus, encapsulation yields adaptability, for it allows the implementation details of parts of a program to change without adversely affecting other parts.

Modularity

In addition to abstraction and encapsulation, a principle fundamental to object-oriented design is ***modularity***. Modern software systems typically consist of several different components that must interact correctly in order for the entire system to work properly. Keeping these interactions straight requires that these different components be well organized. In the object-oriented approach, this structure centers around the concept of ***modularity***. Modularity refers to an organizing structure in which different components of a software system are divided into separate functional units. For example, a house or apartment can be viewed as consisting of several interacting units: electrical, heating and cooling, plumbing, and structural. Rather than viewing these systems as one giant jumble of wires, vents, pipes, and boards, the organized architect designing a house or apartment will view them as separate modules that interact in well-defined ways. In so doing, he or she is using modularity to bring a clarity of thought that provides a natural way of organizing functions into distinct manageable units. In like manner, using modularity in a software system can also provide a powerful organizing framework that brings clarity to an implementation.

The structure imposed by modularity helps to enable software reusability. If software modules are written in an abstract way to solve general problems, then modules can be reused when instances of these same general problems may arise in other contexts. For example, the structural definition of a wall is the same from house to house, typically being defined in terms of 2- by 4-inch studs, spaced a certain distance apart, etc. Thus, an organized architect can reuse his or her wall definitions from one house to another. In reusing such a definition, some parts may require redefinition, for example, a wall in a commercial building may be similar to that of a house, but the electrical system might be different. Thus, our architect may wish to organize the various structural components, such as electrical and structural, in a ***hierarchical*** fashion, which groups similar abstract definitions together in a level-by-level manner that goes from specific to more general as one traverses up the hierarchy. A common use of such hierarchies is in an organizational chart, where each link going up can be read as "is a," as in "a ranch is a house is a building." (See Figure 2.3.) Likewise, this kind of hierarchy is useful in software design, for it groups together common functionality at the most general level, and views specialized behavior as an extension of the general one.

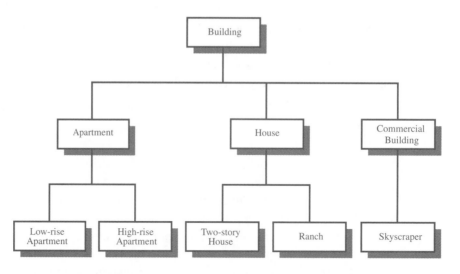

Figure 2.3: An example of an "is a" hierarchy involving architectural buildings.

2.2   Inheritance and Polymorphism

To take advantage of hierarchical relationships, which are common in software projects, the object-oriented design approach provides ways of reusing code in a software system. Reusing software saves programming time and reduces the probability of errors. Indeed, once a software component is completely debugged, it is better to reuse it than to copy it and slightly modify it at several different locations, for all this copying and modifying can introduce new errors into a program.

2.2.1   Inheritance

To avoid redundant code, the object-oriented paradigm provides a modular and hierarchical organizing structure for reusing code, through a technique called ***inheritance***. This technique allows the design of generic classes that can be specialized to more particular classes, with the specialized classes reusing the code from the generic class. For example, the Java Number class is specialized into the Float, Integer, and Long classes. The general class, which is also known as a ***base class*** or ***superclass***, can define "generic" instance variables and methods that apply in a multitude of situations. A class that ***specializes***, or ***extends***, or ***inherits from***, a superclass need not give new implementations for the general methods, for it inherits them. It should only define those methods that are specialized for this particular ***subclass*** (which is also known as a ***derived*** class).

Let us consider an example to illustrate these concepts.

Example 2.1: Consider a class S *that defines objects with a field,* x, *and three methods,* a(), b(), *and* c(). *(The particular type of* x *and the functionality of* a(), b(), *and* c() *are not important for this example.) Suppose we were to define a class* T *that extends* S *and includes an additional field,* y, *and two methods,* d() *and* e(). *This would imply that objects of the class* T *have two fields,* x *and* y, *and five methods,* a(), b(), c(), d(), *and* e(). *The class* T **inherits** *the instance variable* x *and the methods* a(), b(), *and* c() *from* S. *We illustrate the relationships between the class* S *and the class* T *in a* **class inheritance diagram** *in Figure 2.4. Each box in such a diagram denotes a class, with its name, fields (or instance variables), and methods included as subrectangles. An arrow from one box* T *to another box* S *indicates that class* T *extends (or inherits from) class* S.

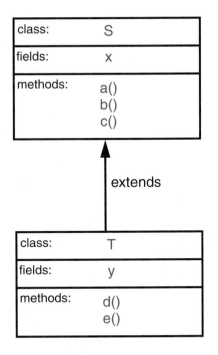

Figure 2.4: A class inheritance diagram. Each box denotes a class, with its name, fields, and methods. Some of these entries can be omitted if they are denoting unnecessary details. Likewise, as shown, we can optionally annotate the arrow between the two boxes to denote an inheritance relation.

Object Creation and Referencing

When an object o is created, memory is allocated for its data fields, and these same fields are initialized to specific beginning values. Typically, one associates the new object o with a variable, which serves as a "link" to object o, and is said to **reference** o. When we wish to access object o (for the purpose of getting at its fields or executing its methods), we can either request the execution of one of o's methods (defined by the class that o belongs to), or look up one of the fields of o. Indeed, the primary way that an object p interacts with another object o is for p to send a "message" to o that invokes one of o's methods, for example, for o to print a description of itself, for o to convert itself to a string, or for o to return the value of one of its data fields. The secondary way that p can interact with o is for p to access one of o's fields directly, but only if o has given other objects like p permission to do so. For example, an instance of the Java class Integer stores, as an instance variable, an integer, and it provides several operations for accessing this data, including methods for converting it into other number types, for converting it to a string of digits, and for converting strings of digits to a number. It does not allow for direct access of its instance variable, however, for such details are hidden.

Dynamic Dispatch

When a program wishes to invoke a certain method a() of some object o, it sends a message to o, which is usually denoted, using the dot-operator syntax (Section 1.3.2), as "o.a()." In the compiled version of this program, the code corresponding to this invocation directs the run-time environment to examine o's class T to determine if the class T supports an a() method, and, if so, to execute it. Specifically, the run-time environment examines the class T to see if it defines an a() method itself. If it does, then this method is executed. If T does not define an a() method, then the run-time environment examines the superclass S of T. If S defines a(), then this method is executed. If S does not define a(), on the other hand, then the run-time environment repeats the search at the superclass of S. This search continues up the hierarchy of classes until it either finds an a() method, which is then executed, or it reaches a topmost class (for example, the Object class in Java) without an a() method, which generates a run-time error. The algorithm that processes the message o.a() to find the specific method to invoke is called the **dynamic dispatch** (or **dynamic binding**) algorithm. This dynamic dispatch algorithm for finding a method a() to process the message "o.a()" provides an effective mechanism for locating reused software. It also allows for another powerful technique of object-oriented programming—**polymorphism**.

2.2.2 Polymorphism

Literally, "polymorphism" means "many forms." In the context of object-oriented design, it refers to the ability of an object variable to take different forms. Object-oriented languages, such as Java, address objects using reference variables. The reference variable o must define which class of objects it is allowed to refer to, in terms of some class S. But this implies that o can also refer to any object belonging to a class T that extends S. Now consider what happens if S defines an a() method and T also defines an a() method. The dynamic dispatch algorithm for method invocation always starts its search from the most restrictive class that applies. When o refers to an object from class T, then it will use T's a() method when asked for o.a(), not S's. In this case, T is said to *override* method a() from S. Alternatively, when o refers to an object from class S (that is not also a T object), it will execute S's a() method when asked for o.a(). Polymorphism such as this is useful because the caller of o.a() does not have to know whether the object o refers to an instance of T or S in order to get the a() method to execute correctly. Thus, the object variable o can be *polymorphic*, or take many forms, depending on the specific class of the objects it is referring to. This kind of functionality allows a specialized class T to extend a class S, inherit the "generic" methods from S, and redefine other methods from S to account for specific properties of objects of T.

Some object-oriented languages, such as Java, also provide a "watered down" kind of polymorphism, which is more accurately called method *overloading*. Overloading occurs when a single class T has multiple methods with the same name, provided each one has a different *signature*. The signature of a method is a combination of its name and the type and number of arguments that are passed to it. Thus, even though multiple methods in a class can have the same name, they can be distinguished by a compiler, provided they have different signatures, that is, are different in actuality. In languages that allow for method overloading, the run-time environment determines which actual method to invoke for a specific method call by searching up the class hierarchy to find the first method with a signature matching the method being invoked. For example, suppose a class T, which defines a method a(), extends a class U, which defines a method a(x, y). If an object o from class T receives the message "o.a(x, y)," then it is U's version of method a that is invoked (with the two parameters x and y). Thus, true polymorphism applies only to methods that have the same signature, but are defined in different classes.

Inheritance, polymorphism, and method overloading support the development of reusable software. We can define classes that inherit the generic instance variables and methods and can then define new more-specific instance variables and methods that deal with special aspects of objects of the new class.

2.2.3   Using Inheritance in Java

There are two primary ways of using the inheritance of classes in Java, **specialization** and **extension**. In using specialization we are specializing a general class to particular subclasses. Such subclasses typically possess an "is a" relationship to their superclass. Such subclasses then inherit all methods of the superclass. For each inherited method, if that method operates correctly independent of whether it is operating for a specialization, no additional work is needed. If, on the other hand, a general method of the superclass would not work correctly on the subclass, then we should override the method to have the correct functionality for the subclass. For example, we could have a general class, Dog, which has a method drink and a method sniff. Specializing this class to a Bloodhound class would probably not require that we override the drink method, as all dogs drink pretty much the same way. But it could require that we override the sniff method, as a Bloodhound has a much more sensitive sense of smell than a "generic" dog. In this way, the Bloodhound class specializes the methods of its superclass, Dog.

In using extension, on the other hand, we utilize inheritance to reuse the code written for methods of the superclass, but we then add new methods that are not present in the superclass, so as to extend its functionality. For example, returning to our Dog class, we might wish to create a subclass, BorderCollie, which inherits all the generic methods of the Dog class, but then adds a new method, herd, since Border Collies have a herding instinct that is not present in generic dogs. By adding the new method, we are extending the functionality of a generic dog.

Class Inheritance in Java

In Java, each class can extend exactly one other class. Even if a class definition makes no explicit use of the **extends** clause, it still inherits from exactly one other class, which in this case is java.lang.Object. Because of this property, Java is said to allow only for **single inheritance** among classes.

Types of Method Overriding

Inside the declaration of a new class, Java uses two kinds of method overriding, **refinement** and **replacement**. In the replacement type of overriding, a method completely replaces the method of the superclass that it is overriding (as in the sniff method of Bloodhound mentioned above). In Java, all regular methods of a class utilize this type of overriding behavior.

In the refinement type of overriding, however, a method does not replace the method of its superclass, but instead adds additional code to that of its superclass. In Java, all constructor methods utilize the refinement type of overriding, a scheme called **constructor chaining**. Namely, a constructor begins its execution by calling a constructor of the superclass. This call can be made explicitly or implicitly. To call a constructor of the superclass explicitly, we use the keyword **super** to refer to the superclass. (For example, super() calls the constructor of the superclass with no arguments.) If no explicit call is made in the body of a constructor, however, the compiler automatically inserts, as the first line of the constructor, a call to the super() method. (Note that there is an exception to this general rule, which is discussed in the next section.) Summarizing, in Java, constructors use the refinement type of method overriding whereas regular methods use replacement.

The Keyword **this**

Sometimes in a Java class it is convenient to reference the current instance of that class that a certain method is operating on. Java provides such a reference, which is called **this**. Using such a construct is useful, for example, if we would like to reference a field inside the current object that has a name clash with a variable defined in the current block, as shown in the following program:

```java
public class ThisTester {
    // instance variable
    public int dog = 2;
    // constructor
    ThisTester() {
        /* null constructor */
    }
    public void clobber() {
        double dog=5.0;
        this.dog = (int) dog;  // two different dogs!
    }
    public static void main(String args[]) {
        ThisTester t = new ThisTester();
        System.out.println("The dog field = " + t.dog);
        t.clobber();
        System.out.println("After clobbering, dog = " + t.dog);
    }
}
```

When this program is executed it prints the following:

```
The dog field = 2
After clobbering, dog = 5
```

An Illustration of Inheritance in Java

To make some of the above notions about inheritance and polymorphism more concrete, let us consider some simple examples in Java.

In particular, we consider some examples of several classes for stepping through and printing out numeric progressions. A numeric progression is a sequence of numbers, where the value of each number depends on one or more of the previous values. For example, an arithmetic progression determines a next number by addition and a geometric progression determines a next number by multiplication. In any case, a progression requires a way of defining its first value and it needs a way of identifying the current value as well.

We begin by defining a class, Progression, shown in Code Fragment 2.1, which defines the "generic" fields and methods of a numeric progression. Specifically, it defines the following two long-integer fields:

- first: first value of the progression;
- cur: current value of the progression;

and the following three methods:

> firstValue(): Reset the progression to the first value, and return that value.
> *Input:* None; *Output:* Long Integer.

> nextValue(): Step the progression to the next value and return that value.
> *Input:* None; *Output:* Long Integer.

> printProgression(n): Reset the progression and print the first n values of the progression.
> *Input:* Integer; *Output:* None.

We say that the method printProgression has no output in the sense that it does not return any value, whereas the methods firstValue and nextValue both return long-integer values. That is, firstValue and nextValue are functions, and printProgression is a procedure.

The Progression class also includes a method Progression(), which is a **constructor** method. Recall that constructor methods set up all the instance variables at the time an object of this class is created. The Progression class is meant to be a generic superclass from which specialized classes inherit, so this constructor is code that will be included in the constructors for each class that extends the Progression class.

```java
/**
 * A class for numeric progressions.
 */
public class Progression {

  /** First value of the progression. */
  protected long first;

  /** Current value of the progression. */
  protected long cur;

  /** Default constructor. */
  Progression() {
    cur = first = 0;          // initializes both of them to 0
  }

  /** Resets the progression to the first value.
   *
   * @return first value
   */
  protected long firstValue() {
    cur = first;
    return cur;
  }

  /** Advances the progression to the next value.
   *
   * @return next value of the progression
   */
  protected long nextValue() {
    return ++cur; // default next value
  }

  /** Prints the first n values of the progression.
   *
   * @param n number of values to print
   */
  public void printProgression(int n) {
    System.out.print(firstValue());
    for (int i = 2; i <= n; i++)
      System.out.print(" " + nextValue());
    System.out.println(); // ends the line
  }
}
```

Code Fragment 2.1: Generic numeric progression class.

An Arithmetic Progression Class

Next, we consider the class ArithProgression, which we present in Code Fragment 2.2.

This class defines a progression where each value is determined by adding a fixed increment, inc, to the previous value. That is, ArithProgression defines an arithmetic progression.

Class ArithProgression inherits the fields first and cur and methods firstValue() and printProgression(n) from the Progression class. It adds a new field, inc, to store the increment, and two constructors for setting the increment. Finally, it overrides the nextValue() method to conform to the way we get a next value for an arithmetic progression.

Polymorphism is at work here. When a Progression reference is pointing to an ArithProgression object, then it is the ArithProgression methods firstValue() and nextValue() that will be used. This polymorphism is also true inside the inherited version of printProgression(n), for the calls to the firstValue() and nextValue() methods here are implicitly for the "current" object (called this in Java), which in this case will be of the ArithProgression class.

In the definition of the ArithProgression class, we have added two constructor methods, a default method, which takes no parameters, and a parametric method, which takes an integer parameter as the increment for the progression. The default constructor actually calls the parametric one, using the keyword **this** and passing 1 as the value of the increment parameter. These two constructors illustrate method overloading, where a method name can have multiple versions inside the same class, since a method is actually specified by its name, the class of the object that calls it, and the types of arguments that are passed to it—its signature. In this case, the overloading is for constructor methods (a default constructor and a parametric constructor).

The call **this**(1) to the parametric constructor as the first statement of the default constructor triggers an exception to the general constructor chaining rule discussed in Section 2.2.3. Namely, whenever the first statement of a constructor C' calls another constructor C'' of the same class using the **this** reference, the superclass constructor is not implicitly called for C'. Note that a superclass constructor will be eventually called along the chain, however, either explicitly or implicitly. In particular, for our ArithProgression class, the default constructor of the superclass (Progression) is implicitly called as the first statement of the parametric constructor of ArithProgression.

We discuss constructors in more detail in Section 1.2.

```
/**
 * Arithmetic progression.
 */
class ArithProgression extends Progression {

  /** Increment. */
  protected long inc;

  // Inherits variables first and cur.

  /** Default constructor setting a unit increment. */
  ArithProgression() {
    this(1);
  }

  /** Parametric constructor providing the increment. */
  ArithProgression(long increment) {
    inc = increment;
  }

  /** Advances the progression by adding the increment to the current value.
   *
   * @return next value of the progression
   */
  protected long nextValue() {
    cur += inc;
    return cur;
  }

  // Inherits methods firstValue() and printProgression(int).
}
```

Code Fragment 2.2: Class for arithmetic progressions.

A Geometric Progression Class

Let us next define a class, GeomProgression, shown in Code Fragment 2.3, which steps through and prints out a geometric progression, determined by multiplying the previous value by a base b. A geometric progression is like a generic progression, except for the way we determine the next value. Hence, GeomProgression is declared as a subclass of the Progression class. As with the ArithProgression class, the GeomProgression class inherits the fields first and cur, and the methods firstValue and printProgression from the Progression class.

```
/**
 * Geometric Progression
 */
class GeomProgression extends Progression {

  // Inherits variables first and cur.

  /** Default constructor setting base 2. */
  GeomProgression() {
    this(2);
  }

  /** Parametric constructor providing the base.
   *
   * @param base base of the progression.
   */
  GeomProgression(long base) {
    first = base;
    cur = first;
  }

  /** Advances the progression by multiplying the base with the current value.
   *
   * @return next value of the progression
   */
  protected long nextValue() {
    cur *= first;
    return cur;
  }

  //  Inherits methods firstValue() and printProgression(int).
}
```

Code Fragment 2.3: Class for geometric progressions.

A Fibonacci Progression Class

As a further example, we define a FibonacciProgression class that represents another kind of progression, the *Fibonacci progression*, where the next value is defined as the sum of the current and previous values. We show the Fibonacci Progression class in Code Fragment 2.4. Note our use of a parameterized constructor in the FibonacciProgression class to provide a different way of starting the progression.

```java
/**
 * Fibonacci progression.
 */
class FibonacciProgression extends Progression {
  /** Previous value. */
  long prev;
  // Inherits variables first and cur.

  /** Default constructor setting 0 and 1 as the first two values. */
  FibonacciProgression() {
    this(0, 1);
  } constructor (w/ arguments)
  /** Parametric constructor providing the first and second values.
   *
   * @param value1 first value.
   * @param value2 second value.
   */
  FibonacciProgression(long value1, long value2) {
      first = value1;
      prev = value2 — value1; // fictitious value preceding the first
  }

  /** Advances the progression by adding the previous value to the current value.
   *
   * @return next value of the progression
   */
  protected long nextValue() {
    long temp = prev;
    prev = cur;
    cur += temp;
    return cur;
  }
  // Inherits methods firstValue() and printProgression(int).
}
```

Code Fragment 2.4: Class for the Fibonacci progression.

In order to visualize how the three different progression classes are derived from the generic Progression class, we give their inheritance diagram in Figure 2.5.

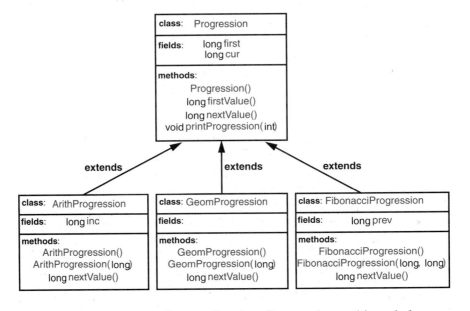

Figure 2.5: Inheritance diagram for class Progression and its subclasses.

To complete our example, we define a class Tester, shown in Code Fragment 2.5, which performs a simple test of each of the three classes. In this class, variable prog is polymorphic during the execution of the main method, since it references objects of class ArithProgression, GeomProgression, and FibonacciProgression in turn. When the main method of the Tester class is invoked by the Java run-time system, the output shown in Code Fragment 2.6 is produced.

The example presented in this section is admittedly small, but it provides a simple illustration of inheritance in Java. The Progression class, its subclasses, and the tester program have a number of shortcomings, however, which might not be immediately apparent. One problem is that the geometric and Fibonacci progressions grow quickly, and there is no provision for handling the inevitable overflow of the long integers involved. For example, since $3^{40} > 2^{63}$, a geometric progression with base $b = 3$ will overflow a long integer after 40 iterations. Likewise, the 94th Fibonacci number is greater than 2^{63}; hence, the Fibonacci progression will overflow a long integer after 94 iterations. Another problem is that we may not allow arbitrary starting values for a Fibonacci progression. For example, do we allow a Fibonacci progression starting with 0 and -1? Dealing with input errors or error conditions that occur during the running of a Java program requires that we have some mechanism for handling them. We discuss this topic next.

```
/** Test program for the progression classes */
class Tester {
  public static void main(String[] args) {
    Progression prog;
    // test ArithProgression
    System.out.println("Arithmetic progression with default increment:");
    prog = new ArithProgression();
    prog.printProgression(10);
    System.out.println("Arithmetic progression with increment 5:");
    prog = new ArithProgression(5);
    prog.printProgression(10);
    // test GeomProgression
    System.out.println("Geometric progression with default base:");
    prog = new GeomProgression();
    prog.printProgression(10);
    System.out.println("Geometric progression with base 3:");
    prog = new GeomProgression(3);
    prog.printProgression(10);
    // test FibonacciProgression
    System.out.println("Fibonacci progression with default start values:");
    prog = new FibonacciProgression();
    prog.printProgression(10);
    System.out.println("Fibonacci progression with start values 4 and 6:");
    prog = new FibonacciProgression(4,6);
    prog.printProgression(10);
  }
}
```

Code Fragment 2.5: Program for testing the progression classes.

```
Arithmetic progression with default increment:
0 1 2 3 4 5 6 7 8 9
Arithmetic progression with increment 5:
0 5 10 15 20 25 30 35 40 45
Geometric progression with default base:
2 4 8 16 32 64 128 256 512 1024
Geometric progression with base 3:
3 9 27 81 243 729 2187 6561 19683 59049
Fibonacci progression with default start values:
0 1 1 2 3 5 8 13 21 34
Fibonacci progression with start values 4 and 6:
4 6 10 16 26 42 68 110 178 288
```

Code Fragment 2.6: Output of the Tester program shown in Code Fragment 2.5.

2.3   Exceptions

Exceptions are unexpected events that occur during the execution of a program. An exception can be the result of an error condition or simply an unanticipated input. In any case, in an object-oriented language, such as Java, exceptions can be thought of as being objects themselves.

2.3.1   Throwing Exceptions

In Java, exceptions are objects that are "***thrown***" by code that encounters some sort of unexpected condition. They can also be thrown by the Java run-time environment should it encounter an unexpected condition, like running out of object memory. A thrown exception is *caught* by other code that "handles" the exception somehow, or the program is terminated unexpectedly. (We will say more about catching exceptions shortly.)

Exceptions originate when a piece of Java code finds some sort of problem during execution and *throws* an exception object, which is identified with a descriptive name. For instance, if we try to delete the tenth element from a sequence that has only five elements, the code may throw a BoundaryViolationException. This action could be done, for example, using the following code fragment:

```
if (insertIndex > size()) {
   throw new
      BoundaryViolationException("No element at index " + insertIndex);
}
```

It is often convenient to instantiate an exception object at the time the exception has to be thrown. Thus, a **throw** statement is typically written as follows:

```
throw new ⟨exception_constructor⟩([⟨param⟩,⟨param⟩,...]);
```

Exceptions are also thrown by the Java run-time environment itself. For example, the counterpart to the example above is ArrayIndexOutOfBoundsException. If we have a six-element array and ask for the 9th element, then this exception will be thrown by the Java run-time system.

The Throws Clause

When a method is declared, it is appropriate to specify the exceptions it might throw. This convention has both a functional and courteous purpose. For one, it lets users know what to expect. It also lets the Java compiler know which exceptions to prepare for. The following is an example of such a method definition:

```
public void goShopping() throws ShoppingListTooSmallException,
                                OutOfMoneyException {
    // method body . . .
}
```

By specifying all the exceptions that might be thrown by a method, we prepare others to be able to handle all of the exceptional cases that might arise from using this method. Another benefit of declaring exceptions is that we do not need to catch those exceptions in our method. Sometimes this is appropriate in the case where other code is responsible for causing the circumstances leading up to the exception.

The following illustrates an exception that is "passed through":

```
public void getReadyForClass() throws ShoppingListTooSmallException,
                                      OutOfMoneyException {
    goShopping();    // I don't have to try or catch the exceptions
                     // which goShopping() might throw because
                     // getReadyForClass() will just pass these along.

    makeCookiesForTA();
}
```

A function can declare that it throws as many exceptions as it likes. Such a listing can be simplified somewhat if all exceptions that can be thrown are subclasses of the same exception. In this case, we only have to declare that a method throws the appropriate superclass.

Kinds of Throwables

As illustrated in Figure 2.6, Java defines classes Exception and Error as subclasses of Throwable, which denotes any object that can be thrown and caught. Also, it defines class RuntimeException as a subclass of Exception.

The Error class is used for abnormal conditions occurring in the run-time environment, such as running out of memory. Errors can be caught, but they probably should not be, because they usually signal problems that cannot be handled gracefully. An error message or a sudden program termination is about as much grace as we can expect.

The Exception class is the root of the exception hierarchy. Specialized exceptions (for example, BoundaryViolationException) should be defined by subclassing from either Exception or RuntimeException. Note that exceptions that are not subclasses of RuntimeException must be declared in the **throws** clause of any method that can throw them.

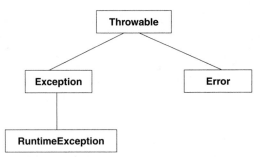

Figure 2.6: The class hierarchy of throwable objects.

2.3.2 Catching Exceptions

When an exception is thrown, it must be *caught* or the program will terminate. In any particular method, an exception in that method can be passed through to the calling method or it can be caught in that method. When an exception is caught, it can be analyzed and dealt with. The general methodology for dealing with exceptions is to "*try*" to execute some fragment of code that might throw an exception. If it does throw an exception, then that exception is *caught* by having the flow of control jump to a predefined **catch** block. Within the catch block we can then deal with the exceptional circumstance.

The general syntax for a *try-catch block* in Java is as follows:

```
try
    ⟨block_of_statements_1⟩
catch (⟨exception_type⟩ ⟨identifier⟩)
    ⟨block_of_statements_2⟩
[catch (⟨exception_type⟩ ⟨identifier⟩)
    ⟨block_of_statements_3⟩]
    . . .
[finally
    ⟨block_of_statements_n⟩]
```

The Java environment begins by executing ⟨block_of_statements_1⟩. If this execution generates no exceptions, then the flow of control continues with the first statement after the last line of the entire **try-catch** block, unless the **try-catch** block includes an optional **finally** block. The **finally** block, if it exists, is executed regardless of whether any exceptions are thrown or caught. Thus, in this case, if no exception is thrown, execution progresses through the **try** block, jumps to the **finally** block, and then continues with the first statement after the last line of the **try** block.

If, on the other hand, ⟨block_of_statements_1⟩ generates an exception, then execution in the **try** block terminates at that point and execution jumps to the **catch** block most closely matching the exception thrown. The ⟨identifier⟩ for this catch statement identifies the exception object itself, which can be referenced in the block of the matching **catch** statement. Once execution of that **catch** block completes, control flow is passed to the optional **finally** block, if it exists, or immediately to the first statement after the last line of the entire **try-catch** block if there is no **finally** block. Otherwise, if there is no **catch** block matching the exception thrown, then control is passed to the optional **finally** block, if it exists, and then the exception is thrown back to the calling method.

Consider the following example code fragment:

```
int index = Integer.MAX_VALUE;    // 2.14 Billion
try                               // This code might have a problem...
{
    String toBuy = shoppingList[index];
}
catch (ArrayIndexOutOfBoundsException aioobx)
{
    System.out.println("The index "+index+" is outside the array.");
}
```

If this code does not catch a thrown exception, the flow of control will immediately exit the method and return to the code that called our method. There, the Java run-time environment will look again for a catch block. If there is no catch block in the code that called this method, the flow of control will jump to the code that called this, and so on. Eventually, if no code catches the exception, the Java run-time system (the origin of our program's flow of control) will catch the exception. At this point, an error message and a stack trace is printed to the screen and the program is terminated.

The following is an actual (hopefully unfamiliar) run-time error message:

```
java.lang.NullPointerException: Returned a null locator
    at java.awt.Component.handleEvent(Component.java:900)
    at java.awt.Component.postEvent(Component.java:838)
    at java.awt.Component.postEvent(Component.java:845)
    at sun.awt.motif.MButtonPeer.action(MButtonPeer.java:39)
    at java.lang.Thread.run(Thread.java)
```

Once an exception is caught, there are several things a programmer might want to do. One possibility is to print out an error message and terminate the program. There are also some interesting cases in which the best way to handle an exception is to ignore it (this can be done by having an empty **catch** block).

Ignoring an exception is usually done, for example, when the programmer does not care whether there was an exception or not. Another legitimate way of handling exceptions is to create and throw another exception, possibly one that specifies the exceptional condition more precisely. The following is an example of this approach:

```
catch (ArrayIndexOutOfBoundsException aioobx) {
    throw new ShoppingListTooSmallException(
                "Product index is not in the shopping list");
}
```

Perhaps the best way to handle an exception (although this is not always possible) is to find the problem, fix it, and continue execution.

2.4 Interfaces and Abstract Classes

In order for two objects to interact, they must "know" about the various messages that each will accept, that is, the methods each object supports. To enforce this "knowledge," the object-oriented design paradigm asks that classes specify the *application programming interface* (API), or simply *interface*, that their objects present to other objects. In the *ADT-based* approach (see Section 2.1.2) to data structures followed in this book, an interface defining an ADT is specified as a type definition and a collection of methods for this type, with the arguments for each method being of specified types. This specification is, in turn, enforced by the compiler or run-time system, which requires that the types of parameters that are actually passed to methods rigidly conform with the type specified in the interface. This requirement is known as *strong typing*. Having to define interfaces and then having those definitions enforced by strong typing admittedly places a burden on the programmer, but this burden is offset by the rewards it provides, for it enforces the encapsulation principle and often catches programming errors that would otherwise go unnoticed.

2.4.1 Implementing Interfaces

The main structural element in Java that enforces an API is the *interface*. An interface is a collection of method declarations with no data and no bodies. That is, the methods of an interface are always empty. When a class implements an interface, it must implement all of the methods declared in the interface. In this way, interfaces enforce a kind of inheritance called *specification*, where we require that each method inherited be specified in full.

Suppose, for example, that we want to create an inventory of antiques we own, categorized as objects of various types and with various properties. We might, for instance, wish to identify some of our objects as sellable, in which case they could implement the Sellable interface shown in Code Fragment 2.7.

```
/** Interface for objects that can be sold. */
public interface Sellable {

  /** description of the object */
  public String description();

  /** list price in cents */
  public int listPrice();

  /** lowest price in cents we will accept */
  public int lowestPrice();
}
```

Code Fragment 2.7: Interface Sellable.

We can then define a concrete class, Photograph, shown in Code Fragment 2.8, that implements the Sellable interface, indicating that we would be willing to sell any of our Photograph objects: This class defines an object that implements each of the methods of the Sellable interface, as required. In addition, it adds a method, isColor, which is specialized for Photograph objects.

```
/** Class for photographs that can be sold */
public class Photograph implements Sellable {
  private String descript;      // description of this photo
  private int price;            // the price we are setting
  private boolean color;        // true if photo is in color

  public Photograph(String desc, int p, boolean c) { // constructor
    descript = desc;
    price = p;
    color = c;
  }

  public String description() { return descript; }
  public int listPrice() { return price; }
  public int lowestPrice() { return price/2;  }
  public boolean isColor() { return color; }
}
```

Code Fragment 2.8: Class Photograph implementing the Sellable interface.

Another kind of object in our collection might be something we could transport. For such objects, we define the interface shown in Code Fragment 2.9.

```java
/** Interface for objects that can be transported. */
public interface Transportable {
  /** weight in grams */
  public int weight();
  /** whether the object is hazardous */
  public boolean isHazardous();
}
```

Code Fragment 2.9: Interface Transportable.

We could then define the class BoxedItem, shown in Code Fragment 2.10, for miscellaneous antiques that we can sell, pack, and ship. Thus, the class BoxedItem implements the methods of the Sellable interface and the Transportable interface.

```java
/** Class for objects that can be sold, packed, and shipped. */
public class BoxedItem implements Sellable, Transportable {
  private String descript;     // description of this item
  private int price;           // list price in cents
  private int weight;          // weight in grams
  private boolean haz;         // true if object is hazardous
  private int height=0;        // box height in centimeters
  private int width=0;         // box width in centimeters
  private int depth=0;         // box depth in centimeters
  /** Constructor */
  public BoxedItem(String desc, int p, int w, boolean h) {
    descript = desc;
    price = p;
    weight = w;
    haz = h;
  }
  public String description() { return descript; }
  public int listPrice() { return price; }
  public int lowestPrice() { return price/2;   }
  public int weight() { return weight; }
  public boolean isHazardous() { return haz; }
  public int insuredValue() { return price*2; }
  public void setBox(int h, int w, int d) {
    height = h;
    width = w;
    depth = d;
  }
}
```

Code Fragment 2.10: Class BoxedItem.

The class BoxedItem shows another feature of classes and interfaces in Java, as well—a class can implement multiple interfaces—which allows us a great deal of flexibility when defining classes that should conform to multiple APIs.

2.4.2 Multiple Inheritance in Interfaces

The ability of extending from more than one class is known as ***multiple inheritance***. In Java, multiple inheritance is allowed for interfaces but not for classes. The reason for this rule is that the methods of an interface never have bodies, while methods in a class always do. Thus, if Java were to allow for multiple inheritance for classes, there could be a confusion if a class tried to extend from two classes that contained methods with the same signatures. This confusion does not exist for interfaces, however, since their methods are empty. So, since no confusion is involved, and there are times when multiple inheritance of interfaces is useful, Java allows for interfaces to use multiple inheritance.

One use for multiple inheritance of interfaces is to approximate a multiple inheritance technique called the ***mixin***. Unlike Java, some object-oriented languages, such as Smalltalk and C++, allow for multiple inheritance of concrete classes, not just interfaces. In such languages, it is common to define classes, called ***mixin*** classes, that are never intended to be created as stand-alone objects, but are instead meant to provide additional functionality to existing classes. That is, the mixin class "mixes" new methods that provide richer abilities into an existing class. Such inheritance is not allowed in Java, however, so programmers must approximate it with interfaces. In particular, we can use multiple inheritance of interfaces as a mechanism for "mixing" the methods from two or more unrelated interfaces to define an interface that combines their functionality, possibly adding more methods of its own. Returning to our example of the antique objects, we could define an interface for insurable items as follows:

```
public interface InsurableItem extends Transportable, Sellable {
    public int insuredValue();      // Return insured Value in cents
}
```

This interface mixes the methods of the Transportable interface with the methods of the Sellable interface, and adds an extra method, insuredValue. Such an interface could allow us to define the BoxedItem alternately as follows:

```
public class BoxedItem implements InsurableItem {
    // ... rest of code exactly as before
}
```

In this case, note that the method insuredValue is not optional, whereas it was optional in the declaration of BoxedItem given previously.

Java interfaces that approximate the mixin include java.lang.Cloneable, which adds a copy feature to a class, java.lang.Comparable, which adds a comparability feature to a class (imposing a natural order on its instances), and java.util.Observer, which adds an update feature to a class that wishes to be notified when certain "observable" objects change state.

2.4.3   Abstract Classes

An abstract class is a class that contains empty method declarations (that is, declarations of methods without bodies) as well as concrete definitions of methods and/or instance variables. Thus, an abstract class lies between an interface and a complete concrete class. Like an interface, an abstract class may not be instantiated, that is, no object can be created from an abstract class. A subclass of an abstract class must provide an implementation for the abstract methods of its superclass, unless it is itself abstract. But, like a concrete class, an abstract class *A* can extend another abstract class, and abstract and concrete classes can further extend *A*, as well. Ultimately, we must define another class that is not abstract and extends (subclasses) the abstract superclass, and this new class must fill in code for all abstract methods. Thus, an abstract class uses the specification style of inheritance, but also allows for the specialization and extension styles as well.

It turns out that we have already seen an example of an abstract class. Namely, the Java number classes (shown in Table 1.2) specialize an abstract class called java.lang.Number. Each concrete number class, such as java.lang.Integer and java.lang.Double, extends the java.lang.Number class and fills in the details for the abstract methods of the superclass. In particular, the methods intValue, floatValue, doubleValue, and longValue are all abstract in java.lang.Number. Each concrete number class must specify the details of these methods.

2.5   Casting

An object variable can be viewed as being of various types, but it can be declared as only one type (either a class or an interface). Moreover, the type in which a variable is declared determines how it is used, and even determines how certain methods will act on it. By enforcing that all variables be typed and that operations declare the types they expect, Java uses the technique of **strong typing** to help prevent bugs. But with such strong types, it is sometimes necessary to explicitly change, or **cast**, a variable from one type to another. We have already discussed, in Section 1.3.3, how casting works for base types. We discuss in this section how it works for object variables.

2.5.1 Casting in an Inheritance Hierarchy

In Java, we can cast an object reference o of type T into a type S, provided the object o is referring to is actually of type S. If, on the other hand, o is referring to a T object that is not also of type S, then attempting to cast o to type S will throw an exception called "ClassCastException." We illustrate this rule in the following example code fragment:

```
Number n;
Integer i;
n = new Integer(3);
i = (Integer) n;      // This is legal
n = new Double(3.1415);
i = (Integer) n;      // This is illegal!
```

To help avoid potentially embarrassing problems such as this, and to avoid peppering our code with **try-catch** blocks every time we wish to perform a cast, Java provides a simple way to make sure an object cast will be correct. Namely, it provides an operator, **instanceof**, which allows us to test whether an object variable is referring to an object of a certain class (or implementing a certain interface). The syntax for using this operator is as follows:

⟨object_reference⟩ **instanceof** ⟨reference_type⟩

where ⟨object_reference⟩ is an expression that evaluates to an object reference, and ⟨reference_type⟩ is the name of some existing class or interface. If ⟨object_reference⟩ is indeed an instance of ⟨class_type⟩, then the above expression returns **true**. Otherwise, it returns **false**. Thus, we can avoid a class-cast exception from being raised in the above code fragment by modifying it as follows:

```
Number n;
Integer i;
n = new Integer(3);
if (n instanceof Integer)
  i = (Integer) n;    // This is legal
n = new Double(3.1415);
if (n instanceof Integer)
  i = (Integer) n;    // This will not be attempted
```

In addition to being simpler than surrounding each cast by a **try-catch** block, using the **instanceof** in this way is also more efficient.

2.5.2   Casting with Interfaces

In Java, we can define generic data structures that organize elements of a common class or a common interface. We can use these data structures to hold elements of any class we like, as long as the class extends the common class or implements the common interface. Suppose, for example, we want to declare a Person interface for all classes that are associated with persons. We could specify this as shown in Code Fragment 2.11.

```
/** Interface for a person. */
public interface Person {

    /** Compare if this Person is equal to another */
    public boolean equalTo (Person other);

    /** Return the name of this Person */
    public String getName();

    /** Return the age of this Person */
    public int getAge();
}
```

Code Fragment 2.11: Interface Person.

Thus, the Person interface declares three functions. The first of these functions takes one parameter of type Person. So, any class implementing the Person comparison function is passed another object from a class implementing the Person interface to compare to.

Now, suppose we want to build a directory database for objects of class Student, shown in Code Fragment 2.12, which implements the Person interface. But a Student object only knows how to compare itself to other Student objects, since the comparison is based on student IDs that only students have. To resolve this difficulty, we must cast a Person object into a Student. We can do this because we know that only Student objects are in our directory; hence, we know that a reference to a given Person object in this case is also a reference to a Student. This knowledge assures us that the run-time environment will let us perform the cast in method equalTo.

In order to compare two student names, we did an explicit cast of the Person parameter other into a Student. This cast is allowed in this case, but, in general, there are limited circumstances when we can perform a cast to a concrete class S of an object variable v that is declared as an interface type U. In particular, such a cast is allowed only if v is referring an object taken from a concrete class T such that T extends S (or $T = S$) and S implements U.

```
/** Class for a student. */
public class Student implements Person {
  String id;
  String name;
  int age;
  /** Constructor. */
  public Student (String i, String n, int a) {
    id = i;
    name = n;
    age = a;
  }

  /** Number of hours spent studying weekly */
  protected int studyHours() {
    return age/2;       // guessing it is proportional to the age
  }

  //** ID of the student. */
  public String getID () {
    return id;
  }

  // The next three methods are for implementing the Person interface.
  public String getName() {
    return name;
  }
  public int getAge() {
    return age;
  }
  public boolean equalTo (Person other) {
    Student otherStudent = (Student) other;   // cast Person to Student
    return (id.equals (otherStudent.getID()));   // compare IDs
  }
}
```

Code Fragment 2.12: Class Student implementing interface Person.

This type of generic casting also allows us to write general kinds of data structures, which only make minimal assumptions about the elements they store. In Code Fragment 2.13, we sketch how to build a person-pair directory storing pairs of objects implementing the Person interface. This directory contains pairs of elements implementing the interface Person. The remove method performs a search on the directory contents and removes the specified person pair, if it exists, and, like the findOther method, it uses the equalTo method to do this.

```java
/** Class for a directory storing pairs pf Person objects. */
public class PersonPairDirectory {

  // instance variables...

  public PersonPairDirectory() {
    // constructor code body...
  }

  public void insert (Person person, Person other) {
    // insertion code for a person pair...
  }

  public Person findOther (Person person) {
    // code for finding a pair containing person... (uses equalTo)
    return null; // stub to make this class compile successfully
  }

  public void remove (Person person, Person other) {
    // code for removing a specified person pair...
  }
}
```

Code Fragment 2.13: Class PersonPairDirectory.

Now, suppose we have filled a directory, myDirectory, full of pairs of Student objects that represent roommate pairs. In order to find the roommate of a given Student object, smart_one, we may try to do the following (which is wrong):

```java
// THIS IS WRONG:
Student cute_one = myDirectory.findOther(smart_one);
```

The above statement causes an "explicit-cast-required" compilation error. The problem here is that we are trying to assign something of type Person to something of type Student. To solve this problem, we write something like the following:

```java
// THIS IS RIGHT:
Student cute_one = (Student) (myDirectory.findOther(smart_one));
```

We cast the Person return value of method findOther to the Student type. This works fine as long as we are sure that myDirectory.findOther is really giving us a Student object. In general, interfaces can be a valuable tool for the design of general data structures, which can then be specialized by other programmers through the use of casting.

2.6 Design Patterns

As mentioned earlier, one of the main advantages of the object-oriented design paradigm is that it encourages organized code development for building software that is reusable, robust, and adaptable. Designing quality object-oriented code takes more than simply understanding the object-oriented design methodologies, however. It requires the effective use of these and other object-oriented techniques in powerful and elegant ways.

Computing researchers and practitioners have developed a variety of organizational concepts and methodologies for designing quality object-oriented software that is concise, correct, and reusable. Of special relevance to this book is the concept of a *design pattern*, which describes a solution to a "typical" software design problem. A pattern provides a general template for a solution that can be applied in many different situations. It describes the main elements of a solution in an abstract way that can be specialized for the specific problem at hand. It consists of a name, which identifies the pattern, a context, which describes the scenarios for which this pattern can be applied, a template, which describes how the pattern is applied, and a result, which describes and analyzes what the pattern produces. Design patterns are important but sometimes neglected in the discussion of data structures and algorithms.

We present several design patterns in this book, and we show how they can be consistently applied to design quality implementations of data structures and algorithms. These design patterns naturally fall into two groups—patterns for solving algorithm engineering problems and patterns for solving software engineering problems. Some of the algorithm engineering design patterns we discuss include the following:

- Amortization (Section 5.1.3)
- Divide-and-conquer (Section 10.1.1)
- Prune-and-search, also known as decrease-and-conquer (Section 10.7.1)
- Brute force (Section 11.2.1)
- The greedy method (Section 11.4.2)
- Dynamic programming (Section 11.5.2).

Likewise, some of the software engineering design patterns we discuss include:

- Position (Section 5.2.2)
- Iterator (Section 5.5)
- Template method (Section 6.3.5)
- Composition (Section 7.1.4)
- Comparator (Section 7.1.4)
- Locator (Section 7.4)
- Decorator (Section 12.3.1).

Rather than explain each of these concepts here, we introduce them throughout the text as noted above. For each pattern, be it for algorithm engineering or software engineering, we explain its general use and we illustrate it with at least one concrete example. For instance, in this section we include a brief discussion of a software engineering object-oriented design pattern that requires no prior experience with data structures or algorithms.

2.6.1   The Adapter Pattern

Classes are often written to provide similar functionality to other classes, but with slight differences. For example, we may have a class that performs insertion and removal operations on a directory of Person objects, whereas we might wish to have a directory that operates exclusively on Student objects. We could, of course, rewrite a complete directory program for processing Student objects, but that would be a waste. Instead, we could use the ***adapter pattern*** to adapt the similar functionality of the existing class to that of the class we would like to build.

In general, the adapter pattern applies to any context where we want to modify an existing class so that its methods match those of a related, but different, class or interface. The general rule for applying the adapter pattern is to define the new class in such a way that it contains an instance of the old class as a hidden field, and implement each method of the new class using methods of this hidden instance variable.

In the example of a Person directory adapted so that it operates exclusively on Student objects, we can define an adapter class that uses the existing generic directory as a protected instance variable in such a way that it guarantees only objects of the correct type go in and out of our directory. In particular, to adapt a directory designed to handle Person objects, we can write a simple StudentPairDirectory class guaranteeing that only Student pairs go into our directory, as shown in Code Fragment 2.14. Such an adapter class ***specializes***, or "adapts," the generic directory data structure to only work for pairs of Student objects. Note that it performs casting inside its implementation of the findOther method.

```
/** Class for a directory storing pairs of Student objects. */
public class StudentPairDirectory {

  protected PersonPairDirectory directory;

  public StudentPairDirectory() {
    directory = new PersonPairDirectory ();
  }

  public void insert(Student s, Student t) {
    directory.insert(s,t);
  }

  public Student findOther(Student s) {
    return (Student) directory.findOther(s);
  }

  public void remove(Student s, Student t) {
    directory.remove(s, t);
  }
}
```

Code Fragment 2.14: Class StudentPairDirectory adapting class PersonPairDirectory of Code Fragment 2.13.

The result of applying the adapter pattern is that a new class that performs almost the same functions as a previous class, but in a more convenient way, has been created. Analyzing this solution, we see that it adds to the length of an existing program, and performs two method calls in the place of one (one to the method with the desired signature and one to the method inside this method to do the actual computation). Thus, if our directory data structure is to be used infrequently in another program, then it is probably reasonable to do the casting explicitly with each use, and not use the above adapter class. If our directory data structure is to be used extensively, however, it saves typing time and eases readability to design an adapter class such as that above, which hides the casting inside its internal methods.

We study further applications of the adapter pattern in Section 4.4.4.

2.7   Exercises

Reinforcement

R-2.1 Give three examples of life-critical software applications.

R-2.2 Give an example of a software application where adaptability can mean the difference between a prolonged sales lifetime and bankruptcy.

R-2.3 Describe a component from a text-editor GUI (other than an "edit" menu) and the methods that it encapsulates.

R-2.4 Draw a class inheritance diagram for the following set of classes:

- Class Dog extends Object and adds an instance variable tail and methods bark() and jump().
- Class Cat extends Object and adds an instance variable nose and methods purr() and jump().
- Class Sheep extends Object and adds instance variables length and color, and methods clip() and clone() (which overrides the Object clone() method).
- Class Poodle extends Dog and adds a method groom().
- Class Puppy extends Dog and adds an instance variable weight and methods sleep() and isTrained().

R-2.5 Give a short fragment of Java code that uses the progression classes from Section 2.2.3 to find the 7th value of a Fibonacci progression that starts with 3 and 4 as its first two values.

R-2.6 If we choose inc = 128, how many calls to the nextValue method from the ArithProgression class of Section 2.2.3 can we make before we cause a long-integer overflow?

R-2.7 Suppose we have an instance variable p that is declared of type Progression, using the classes of Section 2.2.3. Suppose further that p actually refers to an instance of the class GeomProgression that was created with the default constructor. If we cast p to type Progression and call p.firstValue(), what will be returned? Why?

R-2.8 Consider the inheritance of classes from Exercise R-2.4, and let d be an object variable of type Dog. If d refers to an actual object of type Poodle, can it be cast to the class Puppy? Why or why not?

R-2.9 Give an example of a Java code fragment that performs an array reference that is possibly out of bounds, and if it is out of bounds, the program catches that exception and prints the string
Don't try buffer overflow attacks in Java!

R-2.10 Consider the following code fragment, taken from some package:

```java
public class Maryland extends State {
  Maryland() { /* null constructor */ }
  public void printMe() { System.out.println("Read it."); }
  public static void main(String[] args) {
    Region mid = new State();
    State md = new Maryland();
    Object obj = new Place();
    Place usa = new Region();
    md.printMe();
    mid.printMe();
    ((Place) obj).printMe();
    obj = md;
    ((Maryland) obj).printMe();
    obj = usa;
    ((Place) obj).printMe();
    usa = md;
    ((Place) usa).printMe();
  }
}
class State  extends Region {
  State() { /* null constructor */ }
  public void printMe() { System.out.println("Ship it."); }
}
class Region extends Place {
  Region() { /* null constructor */ }
  public void printMe() { System.out.println("Box it."); }
}
class Place extends Object {
  Place() { /* null constructor */ }
  public void printMe() { System.out.println("Buy it."); }
}
```

What is the output from calling the main() method of the Maryland class?

Creativity

C-2.1 Explain why the Java dynamic dispatch algorithm that looks for the specific method to invoke for a message $o.a()$ will never get into an infinite loop.

C-2.2 Write a Java class that extends the Progression class to produce a progression where each value is the absolute value of the difference between the previous two values. You should include a default constructor that starts with 2 and 200 as the first two values and a parametric constructor that starts with a specified pair of numbers as the first two values.

C-2.3 Write a Java class that extends the Progression class to produce a progression where each value is the square root of the previous value. (Note that you can no longer represent each value with an integer.) You should include a default constructor that starts with $65,536$ as the first value and a parametric constructor that starts with a specified (**double**) number as the first value.

C-2.4 Rewrite all the classes in the Progression hierarchy so that all values are from the BigInteger class, in order to avoid overflows all together.

Projects

P-2.1 Fill in code for the PersonPairDirectory class of Code Fragment 2.13, assuming that you will store person pairs in an array with capacity $1,000$. Your directory should keep track of how many person pairs are actually in the directory.

P-2.2 Write a Java program that can take a positive integer greater than 2 as input and write out the number of times one must repeatedly divide this number by 2 before getting a value less than 2.

P-2.3 Write a Java program that can "make change." Your program should take two numbers as input, one that is a monetary amount charged and the other that is a monetary amount given. It should then return the number of each kind of bill and coin to give back as change for the difference between the amount given and the amount charged. The values assigned to the bills and coins can be based on the monetary system of any current or former government. Try to design your program so that it returns the fewest number of bills and coins as possible.

Chapter Notes

The reader interested in learning more about the contribution to computing that was made by ENIAC and other historical computing devices is referred to the book by Williams [99] or the Web site (`http://ftp.arl.mil/~mike/comphist/`) for the Army Research Laboratory's "History of Computing Information." For a broad overview of recent developments in computer science and engineering, we refer the reader to *The Computer Science and Engineering Handbook* [93].

The reader interested in further studying object-oriented programming is referred to the books by Booch [14], Budd [18], and Liskov and Guttag [68]. Liskov and Guttag [68] also provide a nice discussion of abstract data types, as does the survey paper by Cardelli and Wegner [20] and the book chapter by Demurjian [28] in the *The Computer Science and Engineering Handbook* [93]. Design patterns are described in the book by Gamma, *et al.* [38]. The class inheritance diagram notation we use is derived from the book by Gamma, *et al.*

Chapter

3

Analysis Tools

Contents

In a classic story, the famous mathematician Archimedes was asked to determine if a golden crown commissioned by the king was indeed pure gold, and not part silver, as an informant had claimed. Archimedes discovered a way to determine this while stepping into a (Greek) bath. He noted that water spilled out of the bath in proportion to the amount of him that went in. Realizing the implications of this fact, he immediately got out of the bath and ran naked through the city shouting, "Eureka, eureka!," for he had discovered an analysis tool (displacement), which, when combined with a simple scale, could determine if the king's new crown was good or not. This discovery was unfortunate for the goldsmith, however, for when Archimedes did his analysis, the crown displaced more water than an equal-weight lump of pure gold, indicating that the crown was not, in fact, pure gold.

In this book, we are interested in the design of "good" data structures and algorithms. Simply put, a ***data structure*** is a systematic way of organizing and accessing data, and an ***algorithm*** is a step-by-step procedure for performing some task in a finite amount of time. These concepts are central to computing, but to be able to classify some data structures and algorithms as "good," we must have precise ways of analyzing them. The primary analysis tool we will use in this book involves characterizing the running times of algorithms and data structure operations, with space usage also being of interest. Running time is a natural measure of "goodness," since time is a precious resource. But focusing on running time as a primary measure of goodness raises an interesting question.

3.1 What Is Running Time Anyway?

The running time of an algorithm or data structure operation typically depends on a number of factors, so what should be the proper way of measuring it? If an algorithm has been implemented, we can study its running time by executing it on various test inputs and recording the actual time spent in each execution. Such measurements can be taken in an accurate manner by using system calls that are built into the language or operating system for which the algorithm is written (for example, by using the System.currentTimeMillis() method or calling the run-time environment with profiling enabled). In general, we are interested in determining the dependency of the running time on the size of the input. In order to determine this, we can perform several experiments on many different test inputs of various sizes. We can then visualize the results of such experiments by plotting the performance of each run of the algorithm as a point with x-coordinate equal to the input size, n, and y-coordinate equal to the running time, t. (See Figure 3.1.) To be meaningful, this analysis requires that we choose good sample inputs and test enough of them to be able to make sound statistical claims about the algorithm.

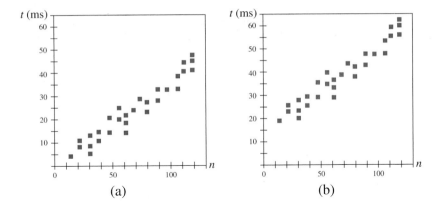

Figure 3.1: Results of an experimental study on the running time of an algorithm. A dot with coordinates (n,t) indicates that on an input of size n, the running time of the algorithm is t milliseconds (ms). (a) The algorithm executed on a fast computer; (b) the algorithm executed on a slow computer.

In general, the running time of an algorithm or data structure method increases with the input size, although it may also vary for distinct inputs of the same size. Also, the running time is affected by the hardware environment (processor, clock rate, memory, disk, etc.) and software environment (operating system, programming language, compiler, interpreter, etc.) in which the algorithm is implemented, compiled, and executed. All other factors being equal, the running time of the same algorithm on the same input data will be smaller if the computer has, say, a much faster processor or if the implementation is done in a program compiled into native machine code instead of an interpreted implementation run on a virtual machine.

3.1.1 Requirements for a General Analysis Methodology

While experimental studies on running times are useful, they have three major limitations:

- Experiments can be done only on a limited set of test inputs, and may not be indicative of the running time on other inputs that were not included in the experiment.
- It is difficult to compare the efficiency of two algorithms unless experiments on their running times have been performed in the same hardware and software environments.
- It is necessary to implement and execute an algorithm in order to study its running time experimentally.

In the rest of this chapter, we develop a general methodology for analyzing the running time of algorithms that:

- Takes into account all possible inputs
- Allows us to evaluate the relative efficiency of any two algorithms in a way that is independent from the hardware and software environment
- Can be performed by studying a high-level description of the algorithm without actually implementing it or running experiments on it.

This methodology aims at associating with each algorithm a function $f(n)$ that characterizes the running time of the algorithm as a function of the input size n. Typical functions that will be encountered include n and n^2. For example, we will write statements of the type "Algorithm A runs in time proportional to n," meaning that if we were to perform experiments, we would find that the actual running time of algorithm A on *any* input of size n never exceeds cn, where c is a constant that depends on the hardware and software environment used in the experiment. Given two algorithms A and B, where A runs in time proportional to n and B runs in time proportional to n^2, we will prefer A to B, since function n grows at a smaller rate than function n^2. These, of course, are intuitive notions of the growth of two familiar functions, but our methodology will make such notions precise.

Before we "roll up our sleeves" and start developing our methodology for algorithm analysis, we present a high-level notation for describing algorithms (Section 3.2) and review fundamental mathematical concepts (Section 3.3) as well as techniques for formal reasoning (Section 3.4).

3.2   Pseudo-Code

Programmers are often asked to describe algorithms in a way that is intended for human eyes only. Such descriptions are not computer programs, but are more structured than usual prose. In particular, these "high-level" descriptions combine natural language and familiar structures from a programming language, in a way that is both clear and informative. Such descriptions also facilitate the high-level analysis of a data structure or algorithm. We call these descriptions ***pseudo-code***.

3.2.1   An Example of Pseudo-Code

The array-maximum problem is the simple problem of finding the maximum element in an array A storing n integers. To solve this problem, we can use an algorithm called arrayMax, which scans through the elements of A using a **for** loop.

The pseudo-code description of algorithm arrayMax is shown in Code Fragment 3.1, while a complete Java implementation is shown in Code Fragment 3.2.

Algorithm arrayMax(A, n):

   Input: An array A storing $n \geq 1$ integers.

   Output: The maximum element in A.

   $currentMax \leftarrow A[0]$

   for $i \leftarrow 1$ **to** $n - 1$ **do**

     if $currentMax < A[i]$ **then**

       $currentMax \leftarrow A[i]$

   return $currentMax$

Code Fragment 3.1: Algorithm arrayMax.

```
/**
 *Test program for an algorithm that finds the maximum element in an array.
 */
public class ArrayMaxProgram {
  /** Finds the maximum element in array A of n integers. */
  static int arrayMax(int[] A, int n) {
    int currentMax = A[0];      // executed once
    for (int i=1; i < n; i++)   // executed once; n times; n-1 times, resp.
      if (currentMax < A[i])    // executed n-1 times
        currentMax = A[i];      // executed at most n-1 times
    return currentMax;          // executed once
  }
  /** Testing method called when the program is executed. */
  public static void main(String args[ ]) {
    int[ ] num = { 10, 15, 3, 5, 56, 107, 22, 16, 85 };
    int n = num.length;
    System.out.print("Array:");
    for (int i=0; i < n; i++)
      System.out.print(" " + num[i]);  // prints one element of the array
    System.out.println(".");
    System.out.println("The maximum element is " + arrayMax(num,n) + ".");
  }
}
```

Code Fragment 3.2: Algorithm arrayMax within a complete Java program. The comments indicate how many times some statements are executed when the program is run.

Note that the pseudo-code is more compact than the Java code and is easier to read and understand. By inspecting the pseudo-code, we can argue about the correctness of algorithm arrayMax with a simple argument. Variable *currentMax* starts out being equal to the first element of *A*. We claim that at the beginning of the *i*th iteration of the loop, *currentMax* is equal to the maximum of the first *i* elements in *A*. Since we compare *currentMax* to $A[i]$ in iteration *i*, if this claim is true before this iteration, it will be true after it for $i + 1$ (which is the next value of counter *i*). Thus, after $n - 1$ iterations *currentMax* will equal the maximum element in *A*.

3.2.2   What Is Pseudo-Code?

Pseudo-code is a mixture of natural language and high-level programming constructs to describe the main ideas behind a generic implementation of a data structure or algorithm. There really is no precise definition of the ***pseudo-code*** language, however, because of its reliance on natural language. At the same time, to help achieve clarity, pseudo-code mixes natural language with standard programming language constructs, such as:

- Expressions: We use standard mathematical symbols to express numeric and Boolean expressions. We use the left arrow sign ($\leftarrow$) as the assignment operator in assignment statements (equivalent to the Java = operator) and we use the equal sign (=) as the equality relation in Boolean expressions (which is equivalent to the "==" relation in Java).
- Method declarations: **Algorithm** name($param1, param2, \ldots$) declares a new method "name" and its parameters.
- Decision structures: **if** condition **then** true-actions [**else** false-actions]. We use indentation to indicate what actions should be included in the true-actions and false-actions.
- While-loops: **while** condition **do** actions. We use indentation to indicate what actions should be included in the loop actions.
- Repeat-loops: **repeat** actions **until** condition. We use indentation to indicate what actions should be included in the loop actions.
- For-loops: **for** variable-increment-definition **do** actions. We use indentation to indicate what actions should be included among the loop actions.
- Array indexing: $A[i]$ represents the *i*th cell in the array *A*. The cells of an *n*-celled array *A* are indexed from $A[0]$ to $A[n - 1]$ (consistent with Java).
- Method calls: object.method(args) (object is optional if it is understood).
- Method returns: **return** value. This operation returns the value specified to the method that called this one.

When we write pseudo-code, we must keep in mind that we are writing for a human reader, not a computer. Thus, we should strive to communicate high-level ideas, not low-level implementation details. At the same time, we should not gloss over important steps. Like many forms of human communication, finding the right balance is an important skill that is refined through practice. We provide several opportunities for such practice in the exercises included in this book.

In addition, to better communicate the essence of an algorithm or data structure operation, it is useful to begin an algorithm description with a brief abstract explaining the input/output behavior of the algorithm, as well as what it does and the main ideas it uses.

3.3 A Quick Mathematical Review

In this section, we briefly review some of the fundamental concepts from discrete mathematics that will arise in several of our discussions. In addition to these fundamental concepts, we include in Appendix A a list of other useful mathematical facts that apply in the context of data structure and algorithm analysis.

3.3.1 Logarithms and Exponents

One of the interesting and sometimes even surprising aspects of the analysis of data structures and algorithms is the ubiquitous presence of logarithms and exponents, where we say

$$\log_b a = c \qquad \text{if} \qquad a = b^c.$$

As is the custom in the computing literature, we omit writing the base b of the logarithm when $b = 2$. For example, $\log 1024 = 10$.

There are a number of important rules for logarithms and exponents, including the following:

Proposition 3.1: *Let a, b, and c be positive real numbers. We have:*

1. $\log_b ac = \log_b a + \log_b c$
2. $\log_b a/c = \log_b a - \log_b c$
3. $\log_b a^c = c \log_b a$
4. $\log_b a = (\log_c a)/\log_c b$
5. $b^{\log_c a} = a^{\log_c b}$
6. $(b^a)^c = b^{ac}$
7. $b^a b^c = b^{a+c}$
8. $b^a/b^c = b^{a-c}$

Also, as a notational shorthand, we use $\log^c n$ to denote the function $(\log n)^c$ and we use $\log \log n$ to denote $\log(\log n)$. Rather than show how we could derive each of the above identities, which all follow from the definition of logarithms and exponents, let us instead illustrate these identities with a few examples of their usefulness.

Example 3.2: *We illustrate some interesting cases when the base of a logarithm or exponent is 2. The rules cited refer to Proposition 3.1.*

- $\log(2n \log n) = 1 + \log n + \log \log n$, *by rule 1 (twice)*
- $\log(n/2) = \log n - \log 2 = \log n - 1$, *by rule 2*
- $\log \sqrt{n} = \log(n)^{1/2} = (\log n)/2$, *by rule 3*
- $\log \log \sqrt{n} = \log(\log n)/2 = \log \log n - 1$, *by rules 2 and 3*
- $\log_4 n = (\log n)/\log 4 = (\log n)/2$, *by rule 4*
- $\log 2^n = n$, *by rule 3*
- $2^{\log n} = n$, *by rule 5*
- $2^{2 \log n} = (2^{\log n})^2 = n^2$, *by rules 5 and 6*
- $4^n = (2^2)^n = 2^{2n}$, *by rule 6*
- $n^2 2^{3 \log n} = n^2 \cdot n^3 = n^5$, *by rules 5, 6, and 7*
- $4^n/2^n = 2^{2n}/2^n = 2^{2n-n} = 2^n$, *by rules 6 and 8*

One additional comment concerning logarithms is in order. The value of a logarithm is typically not an integer, yet the running time of an algorithm is typically expressed by means of an integer quantity, such as the number of operations performed. Thus, an algorithm analysis may sometimes involve the use of the so-called "floor" and "ceiling" functions, which are defined respectively as follows:

- $\lfloor x \rfloor$ = the largest integer less than or equal to x.
- $\lceil x \rceil$ = the smallest integer greater than or equal to x.

These functions give us a way to convert real-valued functions into integer-valued functions. Even so, functions used to analyze data structures and algorithms are often expressed simply as real-valued functions (for example, $n \log n$ or $n^{3/2}$). We should read such a running time as having a "big" ceiling function surrounding it.[1]

---

[1] Real-valued running-time functions are almost always used in conjunction with the asymptotic notation described in Section 3.6, for which the use of the ceiling function would usually be redundant anyway. (See Exercise R-3.18.)

3.3.2 Summations

Another notation that appears again and again in the analysis of data structures and algorithms is the **summation**, which is defined as follows:

$$\sum_{i=a}^{b} f(i) = f(a) + f(a+1) + f(a+2) + \cdots + f(b).$$

Summations arise in data structure and algorithm analysis because the running times of loops naturally give rise to summations. For example, a summation that often arises in data structure and algorithm analysis is the geometric summation.

Proposition 3.3: *For any integer $n \geq 0$ and any real number $0 < a \neq 1$, consider*

$$\sum_{i=0}^{n} a^i = 1 + a + a^2 + \cdots + a^n$$

(remembering that $a^0 = 1$ if $a > 0$). This summation is equal to

$$\frac{1 - a^{n+1}}{1 - a}.$$

Summations as shown in Proposition 3.3 are called **geometric** summations, because each term is geometrically larger than the previous one if $a > 1$. That is, the terms in such a geometric summation exhibit exponential growth. For example, everyone working in computing should know that

$$1 + 2 + 4 + 8 + \cdots + 2^{n-1} = 2^n - 1,$$

for this is the largest integer that can be represented in binary notation using n bits.

Another summation that arises in several contexts is

$$\sum_{i=1}^{n} i = 1 + 2 + 3 + \cdots + (n-2) + (n-1) + n.$$

This summation often arises in the analysis of loops in cases where the number of operations performed inside the loop increases by a fixed, constant amount with each iteration. This summation also has an interesting history. In 1787, a German elementary schoolteacher decided to keep his 9- and 10-year-old pupils occupied with the task of adding up all the numbers from 1 to 100. But almost immediately after giving this assignment, one of the children claimed to have the answer! The teacher was suspicious, for the student had only the answer on his slate, with no calculations. But the answer was correct—5,050. That student was none other than Karl Gauss, who would grow up to be one of the greatest mathematicians of the 19th century. It is widely suspected that young Gauss derived the answer to his teacher's assignment using the following identity.

Proposition 3.4: *For any integer $n \geq 1$, we have:*

$$\sum_{i=1}^{n} i = \frac{n(n+1)}{2}.$$

We give two "visual" justifications of Proposition 3.4 in Figure 3.2.

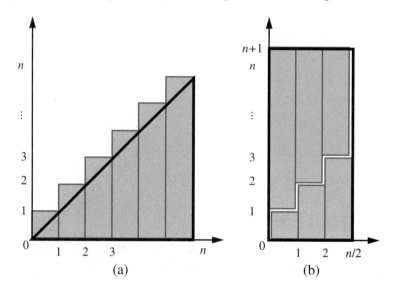

(a)   (b)

Figure 3.2: Visual justifications of Proposition 3.4. Both illustrations visualize the identity in terms of the total area covered by n unit-width rectangles with heights $1, 2, \ldots, n$. In (a) the rectangles are shown to cover a big triangle of area $n^2/2$ (base n and height n) plus n small triangles of area $1/2$ each (base 1 and height 1). In (b), which applies only when n is even, the rectangles are shown to cover a big rectangle of base $n/2$ and height $n+1$.

3.4 Simple Justification Techniques ⋆

We will sometimes wish to make strong claims about a certain data structure or algorithm. We may, for example, wish to show that our algorithm is correct or that it runs fast. In order to rigorously make such claims, we must use mathematical language, and in order to back up such claims, we must justify or ***prove*** our statements. Fortunately, there are several simple ways to do this.

⋆We use a star (⋆) to indicate sections containing material more advanced than the material in the rest of the chapter; this material can be considered optional in a first reading.

3.4.1   By Example

Some claims are of the generic form, "There is an element x in a set S that has property P." To justify such a claim, we need only produce a particular $x \in S$ that has property P. Likewise, some hard-to-believe claims are of the generic form, "Every element x in a set S has property P." To justify that such a claim is false, we need to only produce a particular x from S that does not have property P. Such an instance is called a ***counterexample***.

Example 3.5: *A certain Professor Amongus claims that every number of the form $2^i - 1$ is a prime, when i is an integer greater than 1. Professor Amongus is wrong.*

Justification: *To prove Professor Amongus is wrong, we need to find a counter-example. Fortunately, we need not look too far, for $2^4 - 1 = 15 = 3 \cdot 5$.*   ∎

3.4.2   The "Contra" Attack

Another set of justification techniques involves the use of the negative. The two primary such methods are the use of the ***contrapositive*** and the ***contradiction***. The use of the contrapositive method is like looking through a negative mirror. To justify the statement "if p is true, then q is true" we instead establish that "if q is not true, then p is not true." Logically, these two statements are the same, but the latter, which is called the ***contrapositive*** of the first, may be easier to think about.

Example 3.6: *If ab is odd, then a is odd or b is even.*

Justification: *To justify this claim, consider the contrapositive, "If a is even and b is odd, then ab is even." So, suppose $a = 2i$, for some integer i. Then $ab = (2i)b = 2(ib)$; hence, ab is even.*   ∎

Besides showing a use of the contrapositive justification technique, the previous example also contains an application of ***DeMorgan's Law***. This law helps us deal with negations, for it states that the negation of a statement of the form "p or q" is "not p and not q." Likewise, it states that the negation of a statement of the form "p and q" is "not p or not q."

Another negative justification technique is justification by ***contradiction***, which also often involves using DeMorgan's Law. In applying the justification by contradiction technique, we establish that a statement q is true by first supposing that q is false and then showing that this assumption leads to a contradiction (such as $2 \neq 2$ or $1 > 3$). By reaching such a contradiction, we show that no consistent situation exists with q being false, so q must be true. Of course, in order to reach this conclusion, we must be sure our situation is consistent before we assume q is false.

Example 3.7: *If ab is odd, then a is odd or b is even.*

Justification: *Let ab be odd. We wish to show that a is odd or b is even. So, with the hope of leading to a contradiction, let us assume the opposite, namely, suppose a is even and b is odd. Then a = 2i for some integer i. Hence, ab = (2i)b = 2(ib), that is, ab is even. But this is a contradiction: ab cannot simultaneously be odd and even. Therefore a is odd or b is even.* ∎

3.4.3   Induction and Loop Invariants

Most of the claims we make about a running time or a space bound involve an integer parameter n (usually denoting an intuitive notion of the "size" of the problem). Moreover, most of these claims are equivalent to saying some statement $q(n)$ is true "for all $n \geq 1$." Since this is making a claim about an infinite set of numbers, we cannot justify this exhaustively in a direct fashion.

Induction

We can often justify claims such as those above as true, however, by using the technique of **induction**. This technique amounts to showing that, for any particular $n \geq 1$, there is a finite sequence of implications that starts with something known to be true and ultimately leads to showing that $q(n)$ is true. Specifically, we begin a justification by induction by showing that $q(n)$ is true for $n = 1$ (and possibly some other values $n = 2, 3, \ldots, k$, for some constant k). Then we justify that the inductive "step" is true for $n > k$, namely, we show "if $q(i)$ is true for $i < n$, then $q(n)$ is true." The combination of these two pieces completes the justification by induction.

Example 3.8: *Consider the Fibonacci sequence: $F(1) = 1$, $F(2) = 2$, and $F(n) = F(n-1) + F(n-2)$ for $n > 2$. We claim that $F(n) < 2^n$.*

Justification: *We will show our claim is right by induction.*
Base cases: *($n \leq 2$). $F(1) = 1 < 2 = 2^1$ and $F(2) = 2 < 4 = 2^2$.*
Induction step: *($n > 2$). Suppose our claim is true for $n' < n$. Consider $F(n)$. Since $n > 2$, $F(n) = F(n-1) + F(n-2)$. Moreover, since $n - 1 < n$ and $n - 2 < n$, we can apply the inductive assumption (sometimes called the "inductive hypothesis") to imply that $F(n) < 2^{n-1} + 2^{n-2}$. But*

$$2^{n-1} + 2^{n-2} < 2^{n-1} + 2^{n-1} = 2 \cdot 2^{n-1} = 2^n.$$

This completes the justification. ∎

Let us do another inductive argument, this time for a fact we have seen before.

Proposition 3.9: *(which is the same as Proposition 3.4)*

$$\sum_{i=1}^{n} i = \frac{n(n+1)}{2}.$$

Justification: We will justify this equality by induction.
Base case: $n = 1$. Trivial, for $1 = n(n+1)/2$, if $n = 1$.
Induction step: $n \geq 2$. Assume the claim is true for $n' < n$. Consider n.

$$\sum_{i=1}^{n} i = n + \sum_{i=1}^{n-1} i.$$

By the induction hypothesis, then

$$\sum_{i=1}^{n} i = n + \frac{(n-1)n}{2},$$

which we can simplify as

$$n + \frac{(n-1)n}{2} = \frac{2n + n^2 - n}{2} = \frac{n^2 + n}{2} = \frac{n(n+1)}{2}.$$

This completes the justification. ∎

We may sometimes feel overwhelmed by the task of justifying something true for *all* $n \geq 1$. We should remember, however, the concreteness of the inductive technique. It shows that, for any particular n, there is a finite step-by-step sequence of implications that starts with something true and leads to the truth about n. In short, the inductive argument is a formula for building a sequence of direct justifications.

Loop Invariants

The final justification technique we discuss in this section is the ***loop invariant***, which is used to analyze and prove the correctness of loops:

> To prove some statement S about a loop is correct, define S in terms of a series of smaller statements $S_0, S_1, \ldots, S_k$, where:
>
> 1. The ***initial*** claim, S_0, is true before the loop begins.
> 2. If S_{i-1} is true before iteration i begins, then one can show that S_i will be true after iteration i is over.
> 3. The final statement, S_k, implies the statement S that we wish to justify as being true.

We have, in fact, already seen the loop-invariant justification technique at work in Section 3.2 (for arguing the correctness of Algorithm arrayMax), but let us nevertheless give one more example of its usage here. In particular, let us consider applying the loop invariant method to justify the correctness of Algorithm arrayFind, shown in Code Fragment 3.3, which solves the problem of finding an element x in an array A.

Algorithm arrayFind(x, A):
  Input: An element x and an n-element array, A.
  Output: The index i such that $x = A[i]$ or -1 if no element of A is equal to x.
Abstract: This method uses a simple **while** loop to search through A from the beginning.
  $i \leftarrow 0$
  while $i < n$ **do**
    if $x = A[i]$ **then**
      return i
    else
      $i \leftarrow i + 1$
  return -1

Code Fragment 3.3: Algorithm arrayFind.

To show that Algorithm arrayFind is correct, we use a loop invariant argument. That is, we inductively define a series of statements, S_i, that lead to the correctness of our algorithm. Specifically, we claim the following is true at the beginning of iteration i:

S_i: x is not equal to any of the first i elements of A.

This claim is true at the beginning of the first iteration of the loop, since there are no elements among the first 0 in A (this kind of a trivially-true claim is said to hold **vacuously**). In iteration i, we compare element x to element $A[i]$ and return the index i if these two elements are equal, which is clearly correct and completes the algorithm in this case. If the two elements x and $A[i]$ are not equal, then we have found one more element not equal to x and we increment the index i. Thus, the claim S_i will be true for this new value of i; hence, it is true at the beginning of the next iteration. If the while-loop terminates without ever returning an index in A, then it must be true that $i = n$. That is, S_n is true—there are no elements of A equal to x. Therefore, the algorithm is correct to return the nonindex value -1, as required.

3.5 Analysis of Algorithms

Now that we have developed a high-level way of describing algorithms, let us address the different ways we can analyze algorithms.

3.5.1 Primitive Operations

As we noted above, experimental analysis is valuable, but it has its limitations. If we wish to analyze a particular algorithm without performing experiments on its running time, we can take the following more analytical approach:

1. Code up the algorithm in some high-level computer language (like Java).
2. Compile the program into some low-level executable language (like the byte-code language of the Java Virtual Machine).
3. Determine, for each instruction i of the low-level language, the time t_i needed to execute the instruction.
4. Determine, for each instruction i of the low-level language, the number of times n_i that instruction i gets executed when the algorithm is run.
5. Sum up the products $n_i \cdot t_i$ over all the instructions, which yields the running time of the algorithm.

This approach can often give us an accurate estimate of the running time, but it is very complicated to pursue since it requires a detailed understanding of the low-level language generated by a program's compilation and the environment in which it is to run.

So, instead, we perform our analysis directly on the high-level code or pseudo-code. We define a set of high-level *primitive operations* that are largely independent from the programming language used and can be identified also in the pseudo-code. Primitive operations include the following:

- Assigning a value to a variable
- Calling a method
- Performing an arithmetic operation (for example, adding two numbers)
- Comparing two numbers
- Indexing into an array
- Following an object reference
- Returning from a method.

Specifically, a primitive operation corresponds to a low-level instruction with an execution time that depends on the hardware and software environment but is nevertheless constant. Instead of trying to determine the specific execution time of each primitive operation, we will simply ***count*** how many primitive operations are executed, and use this number t as a high-level estimate of the running-time of the algorithm. This operation count will correlate to an actual running time in a specific hardware and software environment, for each primitive operation corresponds to a constant-time instruction, and there are only a fixed number of primitive operations. The implicit assumption in this approach is that the running times of different primitive operations will be fairly similar. Thus, the number, t, of primitive operations an algorithm performs will be proportional to the actual running time of that algorithm.

Counting Primitive Operations

We now show how to count the number of primitive operations executed by an algorithm, using as an example algorithm arrayMax, whose pseudo-code and Java implementation are given in Code Fragments 3.1 and 3.2, respectively, on page 101. The following analysis can be carried out looking either at the pseudo-code or at the Java implementation.

- Initializing variable *currentMax* to $A[0]$ corresponds to two primitive operations (indexing into an array and assigning a value to a variable) and is executed only once at the beginning of the algorithm. Thus, it contributes two units to the count.
- At the beginning of the for loop, counter i is initialized to 1. This action corresponds to executing one primitive operation (assigning a value to a variable).
- Before entering the body of the for loop, condition $i < n$ is verified. This action corresponds to executing one primitive instruction (comparing two numbers). Since counter i starts at 0 and is incremented by 1 at the end of each iteration of the loop, the comparison $i < n$ is performed n times. Thus, it contributes n units to the count.
- The body of the for loop is executed $n - 1$ times (for values $1, 2, \ldots, n - 1$ of the counter). At each iteration, $A[i]$ is compared with *currentMax* (two primitive operations, indexing and comparing), $A[currentMax]$ is possibly assigned to *currentMax* (two primitive operations, indexing and assigning), and the counter i is incremented (two primitive operations, summing and assigning). Hence, at each iteration of the loop, either four or six primitive operations are performed, depending on whether $A[i] \leq currentMax$ or $A[i] > currentMax$. Therefore, the body of the loop contributes between $4(n - 1)$ and $6(n - 1)$ units to the count.
- Returning the value of variable *currentMax* corresponds to one primitive operation, and is executed only once.

To summarize, the number of primitive operations $t(n)$ executed by algorithm arrayMax is at least

$$2 + 1 + n + 4(n - 1) + 1 = 5n$$

and at most

$$2 + 1 + n + 6(n - 1) + 1 = 7n - 2.$$

The best case ($t(n) = 5n$) occurs when $A[0]$ is the maximum element, so that variable *currentMax* is never reassigned. The worst case ($t(n) = 7n - 2$) occurs when the elements are sorted in increasing order, so that variable *currentMax* is reassigned at each iteration of the for loop.

3.5.2 Average-Case and Worst-Case Analysis

Like the arrayMax method, an algorithm may run faster on some inputs than it does on others. In such cases we may wish to express the running time of such an algorithm as an average taken over all possible inputs. Unfortunately, such an *average case* analysis is typically quite challenging. It requires us to define a probability distribution on the set of inputs, which is typically a difficult task. Figure 3.3 schematically shows how, depending on the input distribution, the running time of an algorithm can be anywhere between the worst-case time and the best-case time. For example, what if inputs are really only of types "A" or "D"?

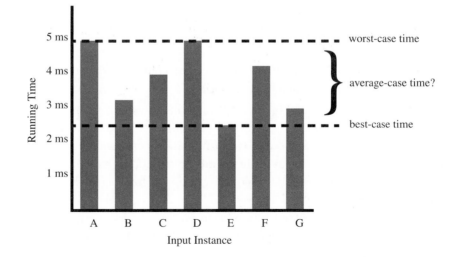

Figure 3.3: The difference between best-case and worst-case time. Each bar represents the running time of some algorithm on a different possible input.

An average-case analysis also typically requires that we calculate expected running times based on a given input distribution. Such an analysis often requires heavy mathematics and probability theory.

Therefore, for the remainder of this book, unless we specify otherwise, we will characterize running times in terms of the ***worst case***. We shall say that algorithm arrayMax executes $t(n) = 7n - 2$ primitive operations ***in the worst case***, meaning that the maximum number of primitive operations executed by the algorithm, taken over all inputs of size n, is $7n - 2$.

This type of analysis is much easier than an average case analysis, as it does not require probability theory; it just requires the ability to identify the worst-case input, which is often straightforward. In addition, taking a worst-case approach can actually lead to better algorithms. Making the standard of success that of having an algorithm perform well in the worst case necessarily requires that it perform well on ***every*** input. That is, designing for the worst case leads to stronger algorithmic "muscles," much like a track star who always practices by running up hill.

3.6   Asymptotic Notation

We have clearly gone into laborious detail for evaluating the running time of such a simple algorithm as the arrayMax algorithm. There are a number of questions that this analysis raises:

- Is this level of detail really needed?
- How important is it to figure out the exact number of primitive operations performed by an algorithm?
- How carefully must we define the set of primitive operations? For example, how many primitive operations are used in the statement y = a∗x + b? (We may argue that two arithmetic operations and one assignment are executed, but we may be disregarding the additional "hidden" assignment of the result of a∗x to a temporary variable before performing the sum.)

In general, each step in a pseudo-code description and each statement in a high-level language implementation corresponds to a small number of primitive operations that does not depend on the input size. Thus, we can perform a simplified analysis that estimates the number of primitive operations executed up to a constant factor, by counting the steps of the pseudo-code or the statements of the high-level language executed. Going back to algorithm arrayMax, our simplified analysis indicates that between $5n$ and $7n - 2$ steps are executed on an input of size n.

Simplifying the Analysis Further

It is useful in algorithm analysis to focus on the growth rate of the running time as a function of the input size n, taking a "big-picture" approach, rather than being bogged down with small details. It is often enough just to know that the running time of an algorithm such as arrayMax **grows proportionally to** n, with its true running time being n times a small constant factor that depends on the hardware and software environment and varies in a certain range depending on the specific input.

We formalize our method for analyzing data structures and algorithms using a mathematical notation for functions that disregards constant factors. Namely, we characterize the running time and memory requirements of an algorithm by using functions that map integers to real numbers in a way that focuses attention on the primary "big-picture" aspects in a running time or space requirement function.

3.6.1 The "Big-Oh" Notation

Let $f(n)$ and $g(n)$ be functions mapping nonnegative integers to real numbers. We say that $f(n)$ is $O(g(n))$ if there is a real constant $c > 0$ and an integer constant $n_0 \geq 1$ such that $f(n) \leq cg(n)$ for every integer $n \geq n_0$. This definition is often referred to as the "big-Oh" notation, for it is sometimes pronounced as "$f(n)$ is **big-Oh** of $g(n)$." Alternatively, we can also say "$f(n)$ is **order** $g(n)$." (This definition is illustrated in Figure 3.4.)

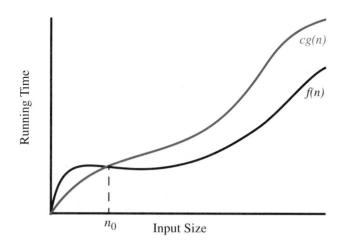

Figure 3.4: Illustrating the "big-Oh" notation. The function $f(n)$ is $O(g(n))$, for $f(n) \leq c \cdot g(n)$ when $n \geq n_0$.

Example 3.10: *$7n - 2$ is $O(n)$.*

Justification: *By the big-Oh definition, we need to find a real constant $c > 0$ and an integer constant $n_0 \geq 1$ such that $7n - 2 \leq cn$ for every integer $n \geq n_0$. It is easy to see that a possible choice is $c = 7$ and $n_0 = 1$. Indeed, this is one of infinitely many choices available because any real number greater than or equal to 7 will work for c, and any integer greater than or equal to 1 will work for n_0.*   ■

The big-Oh notation allows us to say that a function of n is "less than or equal to" another function (by the inequality "$\leq$" in the definition), up to a constant factor (by the constant c in the definition) and in the ***asymptotic*** sense as n grows toward infinity (by the statement "$n \geq n_0$" in the definition).

The big-Oh notation is used widely to characterize running times and space bounds in terms of some parameter n, which varies from problem to problem, but is usually defined as an intuitive notion of the "size" of the problem. For example, if we are interested in finding the largest element in an array of integers (see arrayMax given in Code Fragments 3.1 and 3.2), it would be most natural to let n denote the number of elements of the array. The big-Oh notation allows us to ignore constant factors and lower order terms and focus on the main components of a function that affect its growth.

Using the big-Oh notation, we can write the following mathematically precise statement on the running time of algorithm arrayMax (see Code Fragment 3.1 and Code Fragment 3.2) in ***any*** hardware and software environment.

Proposition 3.11: *The running time of algorithm arrayMax for computing the maximum element in an array of n integers is $O(n)$.*

Justification: As shown in Section 3.5.1, the number of primitive operations executed by algorithm arrayMax is at most $7n - 2$. Hence, there is a positive constant a that depends on the time unit and on the hardware and software environment where the algorithm is implemented, compiled, and executed such that the running time of algorithm arrayMax on an input of size n is at most $a(7n - 2)$. We apply the big-Oh definition with $c = 7a$ and $n_0 = 1$ and conclude that the running time of algorithm arrayMax is $O(n)$.   ■

Let us consider a few additional examples that illustrate the big-Oh notation.

Example 3.12: *$20n^3 + 10n \log n + 5$ is $O(n^3)$.*

Justification: $20n^3 + 10n \log n + 5 \leq 35n^3$, *for $n \geq 1$.*   ■

In fact, any polynomial $a_k n^k + a_{k-1} n^{k-1} + \cdots + a_0$ will always be $O(n^k)$.

Example 3.13: $3\log n + \log\log n$ is $O(\log n)$.

Justification: $3\log n + \log\log n \leq 4\log n$, for $n \geq 2$. *Note that* $\log\log n$ *is not even defined for* $n = 1$. *That is why we use* $n \geq 2$.   ■

Example 3.14: 2^{100} is $O(1)$.

Justification: $2^{100} \leq 2^{100} \cdot 1$, for $n \geq 1$. *Note that variable* n *does not appear in the inequality, since we are dealing with constant-valued functions.*   ■

Example 3.15: $5/n$ is $O(1/n)$.

Justification: $5/n \leq 5(1/n)$, for $n \geq 1$ *(even though this is actually a* **decreasing** *function).*   ■

In general, we should use the big-Oh notation to characterize a function as closely as possible. While it is true that the function $f(n) = 4n^3 + 3n^{4/3}$ is $O(n^5)$ or even $O(n^3 \log n)$, it is more accurate to say that $f(n)$ is $O(n^3)$. Consider, by way of analogy, a scenario where a hungry traveler driving along a long country road happens upon a local farmer walking home from a market. If the traveler asks the farmer how much longer he must drive before he can find some food, it may be truthful for the farmer to say, "certainly no longer than 12 hours," but it is much more accurate (and helpful) for him to say, "you can find a market just a few minutes drive up this road." Thus, even with the big-Oh notation, we should strive as much as possible to tell the *whole* truth.

Instead of always applying the big-Oh definition directly to obtain a big-Oh characterization, we can use the following rules to simplify notation.

Proposition 3.16: *Let* $d(n)$, $e(n)$, $f(n)$ *and* $g(n)$ *be functions mapping nonnegative integers to nonnegative reals. Then*

1. *If* $d(n)$ *is* $O(f(n))$, *then* $ad(n)$ *is* $O(f(n))$, *for any constant* $a > 0$.
2. *If* $d(n)$ *is* $O(f(n))$ *and* $e(n)$ *is* $O(g(n))$, *then* $d(n) + e(n)$ *is* $O(f(n) + g(n))$.
3. *If* $d(n)$ *is* $O(f(n))$ *and* $e(n)$ *is* $O(g(n))$, *then* $d(n)e(n)$ *is* $O(f(n)g(n))$.
4. *If* $d(n)$ *is* $O(f(n))$ *and* $f(n)$ *is* $O(g(n))$, *then* $d(n)$ *is* $O(g(n))$.
5. *If* $f(n)$ *is a polynomial of degree* d *(that is,* $f(n) = a_0 + a_1 n + \cdots + a_d n^d$*), then* $f(n)$ *is* $O(n^d)$.
6. n^x *is* $O(a^n)$ *for any fixed* $x > 0$ *and* $a > 1$.
7. $\log n^x$ *is* $O(\log n)$ *for any fixed* $x > 0$.
8. $\log^x n$ *is* $O(n^y)$ *for any fixed constants* $x > 0$ *and* $y > 0$.

It is considered poor taste to include constant factors and lower order terms in the big-Oh notation. For example, it is not fashionable to say that the function $2n^2$ is $O(4n^2 + 6n \log n)$, although this is completely correct. We should strive instead to describe the function in the big-Oh in *simplest terms*.

Example 3.17: $2n^3 + 4n^2 \log n$ is $O(n^3)$.

Justification: *We apply the rules of Proposition 3.16 as follows:*

- $\log n$ is $O(n)$ *(Rule 8).*
- $4n^2 \log n$ is $O(4n^3)$ *(Rule 3).*
- $2n^3 + 4n^2 \log n$ is $O(2n^3 + 4n^3)$ *(Rule 2).*
- $2n^3 + 4n^3$ is $O(n^3)$ *(Rule 5 or Rule 1).*
- $2n^3 + 4n^2 \log n$ is $O(n^3)$ *(Rule 4).*

■

Some functions appear often in the analysis of algorithms and data structures, and we often use special terms to refer to them. The term *linear* is often used, for example, to refer to the class of functions that are $O(n)$. Table 3.1 shows this and other related terms commonly used in algorithm analysis.

logarithmic	linear	quadratic	polynomial	exponential
$O(\log n)$	$O(n)$	$O(n^2)$	$O(n^k)$ $(k \geq 1)$	$O(a^n)$ $(a > 1)$

Table 3.1: Terminology for classes of functions.

3.6.2 "Relatives" of the Big-Oh

Just as the big-Oh notation provides an asymptotic way of saying that a function is "less than or equal to" another function, the following notations provide asymptotic ways of making other types of comparisons.

Let $f(n)$ and $g(n)$ be functions mapping integers to real numbers. We say that $f(n)$ is $\Omega(g(n))$ (pronounced "$f(n)$ is big-Omega of $g(n)$") if $g(n)$ is $O(f(n))$; that is, there is a real constant $c > 0$ and an integer constant $n_0 \geq 1$ such that $f(n) \geq cg(n)$, for $n \geq n_0$. This definition allows us to say asymptotically that one function is greater than or equal to another, up to a constant factor. Likewise, we say that $f(n)$ is $\Theta(g(n))$ (pronounced "$f(n)$ is big-Theta of $g(n)$") if $f(n)$ is $O(g(n))$ and $f(n)$ is $\Omega(g(n))$; that is, there are real constants $c' > 0$ and $c'' > 0$, and an integer constant $n_0 \geq 1$ such that $c'g(n) \leq f(n) \leq c''g(n)$, for $n \geq n_0$.

The big-Theta allows us to say that two functions are asymptotically equal, up to a constant factor. We consider some examples of these notations below.

Example 3.18: $3\log n + \log\log n$ *is* $\Omega(\log n)$.

Justification: $3\log n + \log\log n \geq 3\log n$, *for* $n \geq 2$. ∎

This example shows that lower order terms are not dominant in establishing lower bounds, with the big-Omega notation. Thus, as the next example sums up, lower order terms are not dominant in the big-Theta notation either.

Example 3.19: $3\log n + \log\log n$ *is* $\Theta(\log n)$.

Justification: *This follows from Examples 3.13 and 3.18.* ∎

"Distant Cousins" of the Big-Oh

There are also some ways of saying that one function is strictly less than or strictly greater than another asymptotically, but these are not used as often as the big-Oh, big-Omega, and big-Theta. Nevertheless, for the sake of completeness, we give their definitions as well.

Let $f(n)$ and $g(n)$ be functions mapping integers to real numbers. We say that $f(n)$ is $o(g(n))$ (pronounced "$f(n)$ is little-oh of $g(n)$") if, for any constant $c > 0$, there is a constant $n_0 > 0$ such that $f(n) \leq cg(n)$ for $n \geq n_0$. Likewise, we say that $f(n)$ is $\omega(g(n))$ (pronounced "$f(n)$ is little-omega of $g(n)$") if $g(n)$ is $o(f(n))$, that is, if, for any constant $c > 0$, there is a constant $n_0 > 0$ such that $g(n) \leq cf(n)$ for $n \geq n_0$. Intuitively, $o(\cdot)$ is analogous to "less than" in an asymptotic sense, and $\omega(\cdot)$ is analogous to "greater than" in an asymptotic sense.

Example 3.20: *The function* $f(n) = 12n^2 + 6n$ *is* $o(n^3)$ *and* $\omega(n)$.

Justification: *Let us first show that* $f(n)$ *is* $o(n^3)$. *Let* $c > 0$ *be any constant. If we take* $n_0 = (12+6)/c$, *then, for* $n \geq n_0$, *we have*

$$cn^3 \geq 12n^2 + 6n^2 \geq 12n^2 + 6n.$$

Thus, $f(n)$ *is* $o(n^3)$.

To show that $f(n)$ *is* $\omega(n)$, *let* $c > 0$ *again be any constant. If we take* $n_0 = c/12$, *then, for* $n \geq n_0$, *we have*

$$12n^2 + 6n \geq 12n^2 \geq cn.$$

Thus, $f(n)$ *is* $\omega(n)$. ∎

For the reader familiar with limits, we note that $f(n)$ is $o(g(n))$ if and only if

$$\lim_{n \to \infty} \frac{f(n)}{g(n)} = 0,$$

provided this limit exists. The main difference between the little-oh and big-Oh notions is that $f(n)$ is $O(g(n))$ if *there exist* constants $c > 0$ and $n_0 \geq 1$ such that $f(n) \leq cg(n)$, for $n \geq n_0$; whereas $f(n)$ is $o(g(n))$ if *for all* constants $c > 0$ there is a constant n_0 such that $f(n) \leq cg(n)$, for $n \geq n_0$. Intuitively, $f(n)$ is $o(g(n))$ if $f(n)$ becomes insignificant compared to $g(n)$ as n grows toward infinity. As previously mentioned, asymptotic notation is useful because it allows us to concentrate on the main factor determining a function's growth.

3.7   Asymptotic Analysis

Suppose two algorithms solving the same problem are available: an algorithm A, which has a running time of $\Theta(n)$, and an algorithm B, which has a running time of $\Theta(n^2)$. Which one is better? The little-oh notation says that n is $o(n^2)$, which implies that algorithm A is *asymptotically better* than algorithm B, although for a given (small) value of n, it is possible for algorithm B to have lower running time than algorithm A.

We can use the little-oh notation to order classes of functions by asymptotic growth rate. The following list of functions is ordered by increasing growth rate, that is, if a function $f(n)$ precedes a function $g(n)$ in the list, then $f(n)$ is $o(g(n))$:

$$\log n \quad \log^2 n \quad \sqrt{n} \quad n \quad n \log n \quad n^2 \quad n^3 \quad 2^n.$$

We illustrate the difference in the growth rate of the above functions in Table 3.2.

n	$\log n$	$\sqrt{n}$	n	$n \log n$	n^2	n^3	2^n
2	1	1.4	2	2	4	8	4
4	2	2	4	8	16	64	16
8	3	2.8	8	24	64	512	256
16	4	4	16	64	256	4,096	65,536
32	5	5.7	32	160	1,024	32,768	4,294,967,296
64	6	8	64	384	4,096	262,144	1.84×10^{19}
128	7	11	128	896	16,384	2,097,152	3.40×10^{38}
256	8	16	256	2,048	65,536	16,777,216	1.15×10^{77}
512	9	23	512	4,608	262,144	134,217,728	1.34×10^{154}
1,024	10	32	1,024	10,240	1,048,576	1,073,741,824	1.79×10^{308}

Table 3.2: Growth of several functions.

We further illustrate the importance of the asymptotic viewpoint in Table 3.3. This table explores the maximum size allowed for an input instance for various running times to be solved in 1 second, 1 minute, and 1 hour, assuming each operation can be processed in 1 microsecond (1 μs). It also shows the importance of good algorithm design, because an algorithm with an asymptotically slow running time (for example, one that is $O(n^2)$) is easily beaten in the long run by an algorithm with an asymptotically faster running time (for example, one that is $O(n \log n)$), even if the constant factor for the asymptotically faster algorithm is worse.

Running	Maximum Problem Size (n)		
Time	1 second	1 minute	1 hour
$400n$	2,500	150,000	9,000,000
$20n\lceil \log n \rceil$	4,096	166,666	7,826,087
$2n^2$	707	5,477	42,426
n^4	31	88	244
2^n	19	25	31

Table 3.3: Maximum size of a problem that can be solved in one second, one minute, and one hour, for various running times measured in microseconds.

The importance of good algorithm design goes beyond just what can be solved effectively on a given computer, however. As shown in Table 3.4, even if we achieve a dramatic speed-up in hardware, we still cannot overcome the handicap of an asymptotically slow algorithm. This table shows the new maximum problem size achievable for any fixed amount of time, assuming algorithms with the given running times are now run on a computer 256 times faster than the previous one.

Running	New Maximum
Time	Problem Size
$400n$	$256m$
$20n\lceil \log n \rceil$	approx. $256((\log m)/(7 + \log m))m$
$2n^2$	$16m$
n^4	$4m$
2^n	$m + 8$

Table 3.4: Increase in the maximum size of a problem that can be solved in a certain fixed amount of time, by using a computer that is 256 times faster than the previous one, for various running times of the algorithm. Each entry is given as a function of m, the previous maximum problem size.

3.7.1   Using the Big-Oh Notation

It is considered poor taste, in general, to say "$f(n) \leq O(g(n))$," since the big-Oh already denotes the "less-than-or-equal-to" concept. Likewise, although common, it is not completely correct to say "$f(n) = O(g(n))$" (with the usual understanding of the "=" relation), and it is actually wrong to say "$f(n) \geq O(g(n))$" or "$f(n) > O(g(n))$." It is best to say "$f(n)$ *is* $O(g(n))$." For the more mathematically inclined, it is also correct to say,

$$\text{``}f(n) \in O(g(n)),\text{''}$$

for the big-Oh notation is, technically speaking, denoting a whole collection of functions.

Even with this interpretation, there is considerable freedom in how we can use arithmetic operations with the big-Oh notation, provided the connection to the definition of the big-Oh is clear. For example, we can say,

$$\text{``}f(n) \text{ is } g(n) + O(h(n)),\text{''}$$

which would mean that there are constants $c > 0$ and $n_0 \geq 1$ such that $f(n) \leq g(n) + ch(n)$ for $n \geq n_0$. In fact, we may sometimes wish to give the exact leading term in an asymptotic characterization, in which case we would say that "$f(n)$ is $g(n) + O(h(n))$," where $h(n)$ grows slower than $g(n)$. For example, we could say that $2n \log n + 4n + 10\sqrt{n}$ is $2n \log n + O(n)$.

Some Words of Caution

A few words of caution about asymptotic notation are in order at this point. First, note that the use of the big-Oh and related notations can be somewhat misleading should the constant factors they "hide" be very large. For example, while it is true that the function $10^{100}n$ is $\Theta(n)$, if this is the running time of an algorithm being compared to one whose running time is $10n \log n$, we should prefer the $\Theta(n \log n)$ time algorithm, even though the linear-time algorithm is asymptotically faster. This preference is because the constant factor, 10^{100}, which is called "one googol," is believed by many astronomers to be an upper bound on the number of atoms in the observable universe. So we are unlikely to ever have a real-world problem that has this number as its input size. Thus, even when using the big-Oh notation, we should at least be somewhat mindful of the constant factors and lower order terms we are "hiding."

The above observation raises the issue of what constitutes a "fast" algorithm. Generally speaking, any algorithm running in $O(n \log n)$ time (with a reasonable constant factor) should be considered efficient. Even an $O(n^2)$ time method may be fast enough in some contexts, that is, when n is small. But an algorithm running in $\Theta(2^n)$ time should never be considered efficient.

There is a famous story about the inventor of the game of chess. He asked only that his king pay him 1 grain of rice for the first square on the board, 2 grains for the second, 4 grains for the third, 8 for the fourth, and so on. It is an interesting test of programming skills to write a program to exactly compute the number of grains of rice the king would have to pay. In fact, any Java program written to compute this number in a single integer value will cause an integer overflow to occur (although the run-time machine will probably not complain). To represent this number exactly as an integer requires using a BigInteger class.

If we must draw a line between efficient and inefficient algorithms, therefore, it is natural to make this distinction be that between those algorithms running in polynomial time and those requiring exponential time. That is, make the distinction between algorithms with a running time that is $O(n^k)$, for some constant $k \geq 1$, and those with a running time that is $\Theta(c^n)$, for some constant $c > 1$. Like so many notions we have discussed in this section, this too should be taken with a "grain of salt," for an algorithm running in $\Theta(n^{100})$ time should probably not be considered "efficient." Even so, the distinction between polynomial-time and exponential-time algorithms is considered a robust measure of tractability.

To summarize, the asymptotic notations of big-Oh, big-Omega, and big-Theta provide a convenient language for us to analyze data structures and algorithms. As mentioned earlier, these notations provide convenience because they let us concentrate on the "big picture" rather than low-level details.

3.7.2 Examples of Asymptotic Algorithm Analysis

We conclude this chapter by analyzing two algorithms that solve the same problem but have rather different running times. The problem we are interested in is the one of computing the so-called ***prefix averages*** of a sequence of numbers. Namely, given an array X storing n numbers, we want to compute an array A such that $A[i]$ is the average of elements $X[0], \ldots, X[i]$, for $i = 0, \ldots, n-1$, that is,

$$A[i] = \frac{\sum_{j=0}^{i} X[j]}{i+1}.$$

Computing prefix averages has many applications in economics and statistics. For example, given the year-by-year returns of a mutual fund, an investor will typically want to see the fund's average annual returns for the last year, the last three years, the last five years, and the last ten years.

A Quadratic-Time Algorithm

Our first algorithm for the prefix averages problem, called prefixAverages1, is shown in Code Fragment 3.4. It computes every element of A separately, following the definition.

Algorithm prefixAverages1(X):

    Input: An n-element array X of numbers.

    Output: An n-element array A of numbers such that $A[i]$ is
        the average of elements $X[0], \ldots, X[i]$.

  Let A be an array of n numbers.
  for $i \leftarrow 0$ **to** $n-1$ **do**
    $a \leftarrow 0$
    for $j \leftarrow 0$ **to** i **do**
      $a \leftarrow a + X[j]$
    $A[i] \leftarrow a/(i+1)$
  return array A

Code Fragment 3.4: Algorithm prefixAverages1.

Let us analyze the prefixAverages1 algorithm.

- Initializing and returning array A at the beginning and end can be done with a constant number of primitive operations per element, and takes $O(n)$ time.
- There are two nested **for** loops, which are controlled by counters i and j, respectively. The body of the outer loop, controlled by counter i, is executed n times, for $i = 0, \ldots, n-1$. Thus, statements $a = 0$ and $A[i] = a/(i+1)$ are executed n times each. This implies that these two statements, plus the incrementing and testing of counter i, contribute a number of primitive operations proportional to n, that is, $O(n)$ time.
- The body of the inner loop, which is controlled by counter j, is executed $i+1$ times, depending on the current value of the outer loop counter i. Thus, statement $a = a + X[j]$ in the inner loop is executed $1 + 2 + 3 + \cdots + n$ times. By recalling Proposition 3.4, we know that $1 + 2 + 3 + \cdots + n = n(n+1)/2$, which implies that the statement in the inner loop contributes $O(n^2)$ time. A similar argument can be done for the primitive operations associated with incrementing and testing counter j, which also take $O(n^2)$ time.

The running time of algorithm prefixAverages1 is given by the sum of three terms. The first and the second term are $O(n)$, and the third term is $O(n^2)$. By a simple application of Proposition 3.16, the running time of prefixAverages1 is $O(n^2)$.

A Linear-Time Algorithm

In order to compute prefix averages more efficiently, we can observe that two consecutive averages $A[i-1]$ and $A[i]$ are similar:

$$
\begin{aligned}
A[i-1] &= (X[0]+X[1]+\cdots+X[i-1])/i \\
A[i] &= (X[0]+X[1]+\cdots+X[i-1]+X[i])/(i+1).
\end{aligned}
$$

If we denote with S_i the **prefix sum** $X[0]+X[1]+\cdots+X[i]$, we can compute the prefix averages as $A[i] = S_i/(i+1)$. It is easy to keep track of the current prefix sum while scanning array X with a loop. We are now ready to present Algorithm prefixAverages2 in Code Fragment 3.5.

Algorithm prefixAverages2(X):
  Input: An n-element array X of numbers.
  Output: An n-element array A of numbers such that $A[i]$ is
    the average of elements $X[0],\ldots,X[i]$.

Let A be an array of n numbers.
$s \leftarrow 0$
for $i \leftarrow 0$ **to** $n-1$ **do**
  $s \leftarrow s + X[i]$
  $A[i] \leftarrow s/(i+1)$
return array A

Code Fragment 3.5: Algorithm prefixAverages2.

The analysis of the running time of algorithm prefixAverages2 follows:

- Initializing and returning array A at the beginning and end can be done with a constant number of primitive operations per element, and takes $O(n)$ time.
- Initializing variable s at the beginning takes $O(1)$ time.
- There is a single **for** loop, which is controlled by counter i. The body of the loop is executed n times, for $i = 0,\ldots,n-1$. Thus, statements $s = s + X[i]$ and $A[i] = s/(i+1)$ are executed n times each. This implies that these two statements plus the incrementing and testing of counter i contribute a number of primitive operations proportional to n, that is, $O(n)$ time.

The running time of algorithm prefixAverages2 is given by the sum of three terms. The first and the third term are $O(n)$, and the second term is $O(1)$. By a simple application of Proposition 3.16, the running time of prefixAverages2 is $O(n)$, which is much better than the quadratic-time algorithm prefixAverages1.

3.8   Exercises

Most of the following exercises are designed to build the reader's comfort with using asymptotic notation and the other analysis tools developed in this chapter. For some additional mathematical tools, refer to Appendix A.

Reinforcement

R-3.1   Graph the functions $12n$, $6n\log n$, n^2, n^3, and 2^n using a logarithmic scale for the x- and y-axes; that is, if the function value $f(n)$ is y, plot this as a point with x-coordinate at $\log n$ and y-coordinate at $\log y$.

R-3.2   Algorithm A uses $10n\log n$ operations, while algorithm B uses n^2 operations. Determine the value n_0 such that A is better than B for $n \geq n_0$.

R-3.3   Repeat the previous problem assuming B uses $n\sqrt{n}$ operations.

R-3.4   Show that $\log^3 n$ is $o(n^{1/3})$.

R-3.5   Show that the following two statements are equivalent:

(a) The running time of algorithm A is $O(f(n))$.

(b) In the worst case, the running time of algorithm A is $O(f(n))$.

R-3.6   Order the following list of functions by the big-Oh notation. Group together (for example, by underlining) those functions that are big-Theta of one another.

$$\begin{array}{ccccc} 6n\log n & 2^{100} & \log\log n & \log^2 n & 2^{\log n} \approx n \\ 2^{2^n} & \lceil\sqrt{n}\rceil & n^{0.01} & 1/n & 4n^{3/2} \\ 3n^{0.5} & 5n & \lfloor 2n\log^2 n\rfloor & 2^n & n\log_4 n \\ 4^n & n^3 & n^2\log n & 4^{\log n} & \sqrt{\log n} \end{array}$$

(Hint: When in doubt about two functions $f(n)$ and $g(n)$, consider $\log f(n)$ and $\log g(n)$ or $2^{f(n)}$ and $2^{g(n)}$.)

R-3.7   Bill has an algorithm, find2D, to find an element x in an $n \times n$ array A. The algorithm find2D iterates over the rows of A, and calls the algorithm arrayFind, of Code Fragment 3.3, on each one, until x is found or it has searched all rows of A. What is the worst-case running time of find2D in terms of n? Is this a linear-time algorithm? Why or why not?

R-3.8 For each function $f(n)$ and time t in the following table, determine the largest size n of a problem that can be solved in time t assuming that the algorithm to solve the problem takes $f(n)$ microseconds. Recall that $\log n$ denotes the logarithm in base 2 of n. Some entries have already been completed to get you started.

	1 Second	1 Hour	1 Month	1 Century
$\log n$	$\approx 10^{300000}$			
$\sqrt{n}$				
n				
$n \log n$				
n^2				
n^3				
2^n				
$n!$		12		

R-3.9 Show that if $f(n)$ is $O(g(n))$ and $d(n)$ is $O(h(n))$, then $f(n) + d(n)$ is $O(g(n) + h(n))$.

R-3.10 Show that $O(\max\{f(n), g(n)\}) = O(f(n) + g(n))$.

R-3.11 Show that $f(n)$ is $O(g(n))$ if and only if $g(n)$ is $\Omega(f(n))$.

R-3.12 Show that if $p(n)$ is a polynomial in n, then $\log p(n)$ is $O(\log n)$.

R-3.13 Show that $(n+1)^5$ is $O(n^5)$.

R-3.14 Show that 2^{n+1} is $O(2^n)$.

R-3.15 Show that n is $o(n \log n)$.

R-3.16 Show that n^2 is $\omega(n)$.

R-3.17 Show that $n^3 \log n$ is $\Omega(n^3)$.

R-3.18 Show that $\lceil f(n) \rceil$ is $O(f(n))$ if $f(n)$ is a positive nondecreasing function that is always greater than 1.

R-3.19 Justify the fact that if $d(n)$ is $O(f(n))$ and $e(n)$ is $O(g(n))$, then $d(n)e(n)$ is $O(f(n)g(n))$.

R-3.20 Give a big-Oh characterization, in terms of *n*, of the running time of the Ex1 method shown in Code Fragment 3.6.

R-3.21 Perform a similar analysis for method Ex2 shown in Code Fragment 3.6.

R-3.22 Perform a similar analysis for method Ex3 shown in Code Fragment 3.6.

R-3.23 Perform a similar analysis for method Ex4 shown in Code Fragment 3.6.

R-3.24 Perform a similar analysis for method Ex5 shown in Code Fragment 3.6.

```java
class Reinforcable {

  public void Ex1(int n) {
    int a;
    for (int i=0; i < n; i++)
      a = i;
  }
  public void Ex2(int n) {
    int a;
    for (int i=0; i < n; i+=2)
      a = i;
  }
  public void Ex3(int n) {
    int a;
    for (int i=0; i < n*n; i++)
      a = i;
  }
  public void Ex4(int n) {
    int a;
    for (int i=0; i < n; i++)
      for (int j=0; j <= i; j++)
        a = i;
  }
  public void Ex5(int n) {
    int a;
    for (int i=0; i < n*n; i++)
      for (int j=0; j <= i; j++)
        a = i;
  }
}
```

Code Fragment 3.6: A collection of Java methods.

Creativity

C-3.1 Al and Bill are arguing about the performance of their sorting algorithms. Al claims that his $O(n \log n)$-time algorithm is *always* faster than Bill's $O(n^2)$-time algorithm. To settle the issue, they implement and run the two algorithms on many randomly generated data sets. To Al's dismay, they find that if $n < 100$, the $O(n^2)$-time algorithm actually runs faster, and only when $n \geq 100$ is the $O(n \log n)$-time one better. Explain why this scenario is possible. You may give numerical examples.

C-3.2 Communication security is extremely important in computer networks, and one way many network protocols achieve security is to encrypt messages. Typical *cryptographic* schemes for the secure transmission of messages over such networks are based on the fact that no efficient algorithms are known for factoring large integers. Hence, if we can represent a secret message by a large prime number p, we can transmit over the network the number $r = p \cdot q$, where $q > p$ is another large prime number that acts as the *encryption key*. An eavesdropper who obtains the transmitted number r on the network would have to factor r in order to figure out the secret message p.

Using factoring to figure out a message is very difficult without knowing the encryption key q. To understand why, consider the following naive factoring algorithm:

> For every integer p such that $1 < p < r$, check if p divides r. If so, print "The secret message is p!" and stop; if not, continue.

a. Suppose that the eavesdropper uses the above algorithm and has a computer that can carry out in 1 microsecond (1 millionth of a second) a division between two integers of up to 100 bits each. Give an estimate of the time that it will take in the worst case to decipher the secret message if r has 100 bits.

b. What is the worst-case time complexity of the above algorithm? Since the input to the algorithm is just one large number r, assume that the input size n is the number of bytes needed to store r, that is, $n = (\log_2 r)/8$, and that each division takes time $O(n)$.

C-3.3 Give an example of a positive function $f(n)$ such that $f(n)$ is neither $O(n)$ nor $\Omega(n)$.

C-3.4 Show that $\sum_{i=1}^{n} i^2$ is $O(n^3)$.

C-3.5 Show that $\sum_{i=1}^{n} i/2^i < 2$.   (Hint: Try to bound this sum term by term with a geometric progression.)

C-3.6 Show that $\log_b f(n)$ is $\Theta(\log f(n))$ if $b > 1$ is a constant.

C-3.7 Describe a method for finding both the minimum and maximum of n numbers using fewer than $3n/2$ comparisons.   (Hint: First construct a group of candidate minimums and a group of candidate maximums.)

C-3.8 Given a set $A = \{a_1, a_2, \ldots, a_n\}$ of n integers, describe in pseudo-code an efficient method for computing each of partial sums

$$s_k = \sum_{i=1}^{k} a_i,$$

for $k = 1, 2, \ldots, n$. (Note: remember that we are assuming that arrays begin indexing from 0.) What is the running time of this method?

C-3.9 An n-degree **polynomial** $p(x)$ is an equation of the form

$$p(x) = \sum_{i=0}^{n} a_i x^i,$$

where x is a real number and each a_i is a constant.

   a. Describe a simple $O(n^2)$ time method for computing $p(x)$ for a particular value of x.

   b. Consider now a rewriting of $p(x)$ as

$$p(x) = a_0 + x(a_1 + x(a_2 + x(a_3 + \cdots + x(a_{n-1} + x a_n)\cdots))),$$

which is known as **Horner's method**. Characterize, using the big-Oh notation, the number of multiplications and additions this method of evaluation uses.

C-3.10 Consider the following induction "justification" that all sheep in a flock are the same color:

Base case: One sheep. It is clearly the same color as itself.

Induction step: A flock of n sheep. Take a sheep, a, out of the flock. The remaining $n-1$ are all the same color by induction. Now put sheep a back in the flock, and take out a different sheep, b. By induction, the $n-1$ sheep (now with a in their group) are all the same color. Therefore, a is the same color as all the other sheep; hence, all the sheep in the flock are the same color.

What is wrong with this "justification"?

C-3.11 Consider the following "justification" that the Fibonacci function, $F(n)$, defined as $F(1) = 1$, $F(2) = 2$, $F(n) = F(n-1) + F(n-2)$, is $O(n)$:
Base case ($n \leq 2$): $F(1) = 1$, which is $O(1)$, and $F(2) = 2$, which is $O(2)$.
Induction step ($n > 2$): Assume the claim is true for $n' < n$. Consider n. $F(n) = F(n-1) + F(n-2)$. By induction, $F(n-1)$ is $O(n-1)$ and $F(n-2)$ is $O(n-2)$. Then, $F(n)$ is $O((n-1) + (n-2))$, by the identity presented in Exercise R-3.9. Therefore, $F(n)$ is $O(n)$, since $O((n-1) + (n-2))$ is $O(n)$.
What is wrong with this "justification"?

C-3.12 Consider the Fibonacci function, $F(n)$, from the previous exercise. Show by induction that $F(n)$ is $\Omega((3/2)^n)$.

C-3.13 Draw a visual justification of Proposition 3.4 analogous to that of Figure 3.2(b) for the case when n is odd.

C-3.14 An array A contains $n-1$ unique integers in the range $[0, n-1]$; that is, there is one number from this range that is not in A. Design an $O(n)$-time algorithm for finding that number. You are allowed to use only $O(1)$ additional space besides the array A itself.

C-3.15 An evil king has a cellar containing n bottles of expensive wine, and his guards have just caught a spy trying to poison the king's wine. Fortunately, the guards caught the spy after he succeeded in poisoning only one bottle. Unfortunately, they don't know which one. To make matters worse, the poison the spy used was very deadly; just one drop diluted even a billion to one will still kill someone. Even so, the poison works slowly; it takes a full month for the person to die. Design a scheme that allows the evil king to determine exactly which one of his wine bottles was poisoned in just one month's time while expending at most $O(\log n)$ of his taste testers.

C-3.16 Show that the summation $\sum_{i=1}^{n} \lceil \log_2 i \rceil$ is $O(n \log n)$.

C-3.17 Show that the summation $\sum_{i=1}^{n} \lceil \log_2 i \rceil$ is $\Omega(n \log n)$.

C-3.18⋆ Show that the summation $\sum_{i=1}^{n} \lceil \log_2(n/i) \rceil$ is $O(n)$. You may assume that n is a power of 2. (Hint: Use induction to reduce the problem to that for $n/2$.)

C-3.19 Let S be a set of n lines such that no two are parallel and no three meet in the same point. Show by induction that the lines in S determine $\Theta(n^2)$ intersection points.

C-3.20 Suppose that each row of an $n \times n$ array A consists of 1's and 0's such that, in any row of A, all the 1's come before any 0's in that row. Assuming A is already in memory, describe a method running in $O(n)$ time (not $O(n^2)$ time) for finding the row of A that contains the most 1's.

C-3.21 Suppose that each row of an $n \times n$ array A consists of 1's and 0's such that, in any row i of A, all the 1's come before any 0's in that row. Suppose further that the number of 1's in row i is at least the number in row $i+1$, for $i = 0, 1, \ldots, n-2$. Assuming A is already in memory, describe a method running in $O(n)$ time (not $O(n^2)$ time) for counting the number of 1's in the array A.

C-3.22 Describe in pseudo-code a method for multiplying an $n \times m$ matrix A and an $m \times p$ matrix B. Recall that the product $C = AB$ is defined so that $C[i][j] = \sum_{k=1}^{m} A[i][k] \cdot B[k][j]$. What is the running time of your method?

Projects

P-3.1 Program the two algorithms, prefixAverages1 and prefixAverages2 from Section 3.7.2, and perform a careful experimental analysis of their running times. Plot their running times as a function of their input sizes as scatter plots on both a linear-linear scale and a linear-log scale. Choose representative values of the size n, and run at least 5 tests for each size value n in your tests.

P-3.2 Perform a careful experimental analysis that compares the relative running times of the methods shown in Code Fragment 3.6.

P-3.3 A Java program is limited by the amount of memory allocated to its run-time environment.

a. Modify the main method of Code Fragment 3.2 to call the array-Max method on a series of randomly generated arrays with rapidly increasing size (say, doubling at each iteration).
b. Find out for which value of the array size, the program terminates because it runs out of memory, using various values of the maximum memory allocated to the Java run-time environment. In the JDK, this value can be set with the -mx option of the java command.
c. Perform a similar experiment for algorithms prefixAverages1 and prefixAverages2 from Section 3.7.2.

Chapter Notes

The methodology for analyzing algorithms is traditionally within a model of computation called the ***RAM***, or ***random access machine*** (not to be confused with "random access memory"). Within this model, a computer consists of a ***central processing unit*** (or ***CPU***) and a ***memory***. The CPU performs elementary operations, such as loads, stores, additions, and comparisons, and the memory stores the program and data in ***cells*** that have integer addresses. The term "random access" refers to the ability of the CPU to access an arbitrary memory cell with one primitive operation. Each primitive operation executed by an algorithm corresponds to a constant number of elementary computations of the RAM. Our approach of counting primitive operations is equivalent to this approach theoretically, but does not require the conceptual burden of an abstract model like the RAM.

Our use of the big-Oh notation is consistent with most authors' usage, but we have taken a slightly more conservative approach than some. The big-Oh notation has prompted several discussions in the algorithms and computation theory community over its proper use [17, 47, 61]. Knuth [59, 61], for example, defines it using the notation $f(n) = O(g(n))$, but he refers to this "equality" as being only "one way," even though he mentions that the big-Oh is actually defining a set of functions. We have chosen to take a more standard view of equality and view the big-Oh notation truly as a set, following the suggestions of Brassard [17]. The reader interested in studying average-case analysis is referred to the book chapter by Vitter and Flajolet [96].

We include a number of useful mathematical facts in Appendix A. The reader interested in further study into the analysis of algorithms is referred to the books by Graham, Knuth, and Patashnik [45], and Sedgewick and Flajolet [87]. The reader interested in learning more about the history of mathematics is referred to the book by Boyer and Merzbach [15]. Our version of the famous story about Archimedes is taken from [77].

Chapter

4

Stacks, Queues, and Deques

Contents

Stacks and queues are among the simplest of all data structures, but are also among the most important. Stacks and queues are used in a host of different applications that include many more sophisticated data structures. In addition, stacks and queues are among the few kinds of data structures that are often implemented in the hardware microinstructions inside a CPU. They are central to some important features of modern computing environments, like the Java run-time environment called the Java Virtual Machine.

In this chapter, we define stack and queue abstract data types in a general way and we give two alternative implementations for them: arrays and linked lists. To illustrate the usefulness of stacks and queues, we present examples of their application to realizations of the Java Virtual Machine. We also present a generalization of stacks and queues, called the double-ended queue, and show how it can be implemented using a doubly linked list. In addition, this chapter includes discussions of several programming concepts, including interfaces, casting, sentinels, and the adapter pattern. We conclude this chapter with a case study that uses the stack data structure to build a simple stock analysis application.

4.1   Stacks

A *stack* is a container of objects that are inserted and removed according to the ***last-in first-out*** (***LIFO***) principle. Objects can be inserted into a stack at any time, but only the most-recently inserted (that is, "last") object can be removed at any time. The name "stack" is derived from the metaphor of a stack of plates in a spring-loaded, cafeteria plate dispenser. In this case, the fundamental operations involve the "pushing" and "popping" of plates on the stack. When we need a new plate from the dispenser, we "pop" the top plate off the stack, and when we add a plate, we "push" it down on the stack to become the new top plate. Perhaps an even more amusing metaphor would be a PEZ® candy dispenser, which stores mint candies in a spring-loaded container that "pops" out the top-most candy in the stack when the top of the dispenser is lifted. (See Figure 4.1.) Stacks are a fundamental data structure. They are used in many applications, including the following.

Example 4.1: *Internet Web browsers store the addresses of recently visited sites on a stack. Each time a user visits a new site, that site's address is "pushed" onto the stack of addresses. The browser then allows the user to "pop" back to previously visited sites using the "back" button.*

Example 4.2: *Text editors usually provide an "undo" mechanism that cancels recent editing operations and reverts to former states of a document. This undo operation can be accomplished by keeping text changes in a stack.*

Figure 4.1: A schematic drawing of a PEZ® dispenser; a physical implementation of the stack ADT. (PEZ® is a registered trademark of PEZ Candy, Inc.)

4.1.1 The Stack Abstract Data Type

A stack S is an abstract data type (ADT) that supports the following two fundamental methods:

> push(o): Insert object o at the top of the stack.
> *Input:* Object; ***Output:*** None.

> pop(): Remove from the stack and return the top object on the stack; an error occurs if the stack is empty.
> *Input:* None; ***Output:*** Object.

Additionally, let us also define the following supporting methods:

> size(): Return the number of objects in the stack.
> *Input:* None; ***Output:*** Integer.

> isEmpty(): Return a Boolean indicating if the stack is empty.
> *Input:* None; ***Output:*** Boolean.

> top(): Return the top object on the stack, without removing it; an error occurs if the stack is empty.
> *Input:* None; ***Output:*** Object.

Example 4.3: *The following table shows a series of stack operations and their effects on an initially empty stack S of integer objects. For simplicity, we use integers instead of integer objects as arguments of the operations.*

Operation	Output	S
push(5)	–	(5)
push(3)	–	(5,3)
pop()	3	(5)
push(7)	–	(5,7)
pop()	7	(5)
top()	5	(5)
pop()	5	()
pop()	"error"	()
isEmpty()	true	()
push(9)	–	(9)
push(7)	–	(9,7)
push(3)	–	(9,7,3)
push(5)	–	(9,7,3,5)
size()	4	(9,7,3,5)
pop()	5	(9,7,3)
push(8)	–	(9,7,3,8)
pop()	8	(9,7,3)
pop()	3	(9,7,3)

A Stack Interface in Java

Because of its importance, the stack data structure is included as a "built-in" class in the java.util package of Java. Class java.util.Stack is a data structure that stores generic Java objects and includes, among others, the methods push(obj), pop(), peek() (equivalent to top()), size(), and empty() (equivalent to isEmpty()). Methods pop() and peek() throw exception StackEmptyException if they are called on an empty stack. While it is convenient to just use the built-in class java.util.Stack, it is instructive to learn how to design and implement a stack "from scratch."

Implementing an abstract data type in Java involves two steps. The first step is the definition of a Java *Application Programming Interface* (API), or simply *interface*, which describes the names of the methods that the ADT supports and how they are to be declared and used. A complete Java interface for the stack ADT is given in Code Fragment 4.1. Note that this interface is very general since it specifies that objects of arbitrary, and possibly heterogeneous, classes can be inserted into the stack.

```
/**
 * Interface for a stack: a collection of objects
 * that are inserted and removed according to the
 * last-in first-out principle.
 *
 * @author Roberto Tamassia
 * @author Michael Goodrich
 * @see StackEmptyException
 */

public interface Stack {
 /**
  * @return number of elements in the stack.
  */
 public int size();
 /**
  * @return true if the stack is empty, false otherwise.
  */
 public boolean isEmpty();
 /**
  * @return top element in the stack.
  * @exception StackEmptyException if the stack is empty.
  */
 public Object top()
   throws StackEmptyException;
 /**
  * Insert an element at the top of the stack.
  * @param element element to be inserted.
  */
 public void push (Object element);
 /**
  * Remove the top element from the stack.
  * @return element removed.
  * @exception StackEmptyException if the stack is empty.
  */
 public Object pop()
   throws StackEmptyException;
}
```

Code Fragment 4.1: Interface Stack documented with comments in Javadoc style. (See Section 1.9.2.)

The error condition that occurs when calling method pop() or top() on an empty stack is signaled by throwing an exception of type StackEmptyException, which is defined in Code Fragment 4.2.

```
/**
 * Runtime exception thrown when one tries to perform operation top or
 * pop on an empty stack.
 */

public class StackEmptyException extends RuntimeException {
  public StackEmptyException(String err) {
    super(err);
  }
}
```

Code Fragment 4.2: Exception thrown by methods pop() and top() of the Stack interface when called on an empty stack.

For a given ADT to be of any use, we need to provide a concrete class that implements the methods of the interface associated with that ADT. We give a simple implementation of the Stack interface in the following subsection.

4.1.2 A Simple Array-Based Implementation

In this subsection, we show how to realize a stack by storing its elements in an array. Since an array's size needs to be determined when it is created, one of the important details of our implementation is that we specify some maximum size N for our stack, say, $N = 1,000$ elements. Our stack then consists of an N-element array S plus an integer variable t that gives the index of the top element in array S. (See Figure 4.2.)

Figure 4.2: Realization of a stack by means of an array S. The top element in the stack is stored in the cell $S[t]$.

Recalling that arrays start at index 0 in Java, we initialize t to -1, and we use this value for t to identify when the stack is empty. Likewise, we can use this variable to determine the number of elements in a stack $(t + 1)$. We also introduce a new type of exception, called StackFullException, to signal the error condition that arises if we try to insert a new element and the array S is full. Exception StackFullException is specific to our implementation of a stack and is not defined in the stack ADT. Given this new exception, we can then implement the stack ADT methods as described in Code Fragment 4.3.

Algorithm size():
    return $t + 1$

Algorithm isEmpty():
    return $(t < 0)$

Algorithm top():
    if isEmpty() **then**
        throw a StackEmptyException
    return $S[t]$

Algorithm push(o):
    if size() $= N$ **then**
        throw a StackFullException
    $t \leftarrow t + 1$
    $S[t] \leftarrow o$

Algorithm pop():
    if isEmpty() **then**
        throw a StackEmptyException
    $e \leftarrow S[t]$.
    $S[t] \leftarrow$ **null**
    $t \leftarrow t - 1$
    return e

Code Fragment 4.3: Implementation of a stack by means of an array.

The correctness of these methods follows immediately from the definition of the methods themselves. There is, nevertheless, a mildly interesting point in this implementation involving the implementation of the pop method. Note that we could have avoided resetting the old $S[t]$ to **null** and we would still have a correct method. There is a trade-off in being able to avoid this assignment in Java, however. The trade-off involves the Java *garbage collection* mechanism that searches memory for objects that are no longer referenced by active objects, and reclaims their space for future use. Let $e = S[t]$ be the top element before the pop method is called. By making $S[t]$ a null reference, we indicate that the stack no longer needs to hold a reference to object e. Indeed, if there are no other active references to e, then the memory space taken by e will be reclaimed by the garbage collector. A concrete Java implementation of the above pseudo-code specification, by means of Java class ArrayStack implementing the Stack interface, is given in Code Fragments 4.4 and 4.5.

```java
/**
 * Implementation of the Stack interface using a fixed-length array.
 * An exception is thrown if a push operation is attempted when the size of
 * the stack is equal to the length of the array.
 *
 * @author Natasha Gelfand
 * @author Roberto Tamassia
 * @see StackFullException
 */
public class ArrayStack implements Stack {
  /**
   * Default length of the array used to implement the stack.
   */
  public static final int CAPACITY = 1000;
  /**
   * Lenght of the array used to implement the stack.
   */
  private int capacity;
  /**
   * Array used to implement the stack.
   */
  private Object S[];
  /**
   * Index of the top element of the stack in the array.
   */
  private int top = -1;
  /**
   * Initialize the stack to use an array of default length CAPACITY.
   */
  public ArrayStack() {
    this(CAPACITY);
  }
  /**
   * Initialize the stack to use an array of given length.
   *
   * @param cap length of the array.
   */
  public ArrayStack(int cap) {
    capacity = cap;
    S = new Object[capacity];
  }
```

Code Fragment 4.4: Array-based Java implementation of the Stack interface. (Continues in Code Fragment 4.5.)

```
/**
 * O(1) time.
 */
public int size() {
  return (top + 1);
}
/**
 * O(1) time.
 */
public boolean isEmpty() {
  return (top < 0);
}
/**
 * O(1) time.
 * @exception StackFullException if the array is full.
 */
public void push(Object obj) throws StackFullException {
  if (size() == capacity)
    throw new StackFullException("Stack overflow.");
  S[++top] = obj;
}
/**
 * O(1) time.
 */
public Object top() throws StackEmptyException {
  if (isEmpty())
    throw new StackEmptyException("Stack is empty.");
  return S[top];
}
/**
 * O(1) time.
 */
public Object pop() throws StackEmptyException {
  Object elem;
  if (isEmpty())
    throw new StackEmptyException("Stack is Empty.");
  elem = S[top];
  S[top--] = null; // dereference S[top] for garbage collection.
  return elem;
}
}
```

Code Fragment 4.5: Array-based Java implementation of the Stack interface. (Continued from Code Fragment 4.4.) Note that the Javadoc comments on methods of the Stack interface provide only class-specific information (e.g., the running time of the method) that is not already contained in Code Fragment 4.1.

Table 4.1 shows the running times for methods in a realization of a stack by an array. Each of the stack methods in the array realization executes a constant number of statements involving arithmetic operations, comparisons, and assignments. Thus, in this implementation of the Stack ADT, each method runs in constant time, that is, they each run in $O(1)$ time.

Method	Time
size	$O(1)$
isEmpty	$O(1)$
top	$O(1)$
push	$O(1)$
pop	$O(1)$

Table 4.1: Performance of a stack realized by an array. The space usage is $O(N)$, where N is the size of the array, determined at the time the stack is instantiated. Note that the space usage is independent from the number $n \leq N$ of elements that are actually in the stack.

The array implementation of a stack is both simple and efficient, and is widely used in a variety of computing applications. Nevertheless, this implementation has one negative aspect; it must assume a fixed upper bound N on the ultimate size of the stack. In Code Fragment 4.4 we chose the capacity value $N = 1,000$ more or less arbitrarily. An application may actually need much less space than this, in which case we would be wasting memory. Alternatively, an application may need more space than this, in which case our stack implementation may "crash" the application with an error as soon as it tries to push its $(N+1)$st object on the stack. Thus, even with its simplicity and efficiency, the array-based stack implementation is not necessarily ideal. Fortunately, there are other implementations, discussed later in this chapter, that do not have a size limitation and use space proportional to the actual number of elements stored in the stack. In cases where we have a good estimate on the number of items needing to go in the stack, however, the array-based implementation is hard to beat. Stacks serve a vital role in a number of computing applications, so it is helpful to have a fast stack ADT implementation, such as the simple array-based implementation.

Casting with a Generic Stack

One of the strong points of our realization of the stack ADT by means of a Java class that implements the Stack interface is that we can store generic objects in the stack, each belonging to an arbitrary class. (See again Code Fragments 4.1

and 4.4–4.5.) Namely, an ArrayStack can store Integer objects, Student objects, or even Planet objects.

We must take care, however, that we are consistent in how we use our generic stack, because any elements that are stored in it are viewed as instances of the Java Object class. This causes no trouble when we are adding elements to the stack, because every class in Java inherits from the Object class. However, when we retrieve an object from the stack (with either the top or pop method), we always get back a reference of type Object, no matter what the specific class of the object is. Thus, in order to use the retrieved element as an instance of the specific class it really belongs to, we must perform a *cast*, which forces the object to be viewed as a member of a specific class rather than a more general superclass Object. (Casting in Java is discussed in more detail in Section 2.5.)

In the example of Code Fragment 4.6, we illustrate the need for casting in a simple application that uses a stack.

```java
public static Integer[] reverse(Integer[] a) {
    ArrayStack S = new ArrayStack(a.length);
    Integer[] b = new Integer[a.length];
    for (int i=0; i < a.length; i++)
        S.push(a[i]);
    for (int i=0; i < a.length; i++)
        b[i] = (Integer) (S.pop());
    return b;
}
```

Code Fragment 4.6: A method that reverses the ordering of the elements in an array using an auxiliary ArrayStack. Casting is performed to force the object returned by pop to be viewed as an Integer object. Note that a Java array has a field length that stores the size of the array.

The reverse method, shown in Code Fragment 4.6, illustrates a small application of the stack data structure, but this data structure has many more important applications than this. In fact, the stack data structure plays an important role in the implementation of the Java language itself.

4.1.3 Stacks in the Java Virtual Machine

A Java program is typically compiled into a sequence of byte codes that are defined as "machine" instructions for a well-defined machine model—the *Java Virtual Machine*. The definition of the Java Virtual Machine is at the heart of the definition of the Java language itself. By compiling Java code into the Java Virtual Machine byte codes, rather than the machine language of a specific CPU, a Java program can be run on any computer, such as a PC or UNIX workstation, that can emulate the Java Virtual Machine. Interestingly, the stack data structure plays a central role in the definition of the Java Virtual Machine.

The Java Method Stack

Stacks are an important application to the run-time environment of Java programs. A running Java program (more precisely, a running Java thread) has a private stack, called the ***Java method stack*** or just ***Java stack*** for short, which is used to keep track of local variables and other important information on methods, as they are invoked during execution. (See Figure 4.3.)

More specifically, during the execution of a Java program, the Java Virtual Machine maintains a stack whose elements are descriptors of the currently active (that is, nonterminated) invocations of methods. These descriptors are called ***frames***. A frame for some invocation of method "cool" stores the current values of the local variables and parameters of method cool, as well as information on the method that called cool and on what needs to be returned to this method.

The Java Virtual Machine keeps in a special register, called the ***program counter***, the address of the statement the Java Virtual Machine is currently executing in the program. When a method "cool" invokes another method "fool", the current value of the program counter is recorded in the frame of the current invocation of cool (so the Java Virtual Machine will know where to return to when method fool is done). At the top of the Java stack is the frame of the ***running method***, that is, the method that currently has control of the execution. The remaining elements of the stack are frames of the ***suspended methods***, that is, methods that have invoked another method and are currently waiting for it to return control to them upon its termination. The order of the elements in the stack corresponds to the chain of invocations of the currently active methods. When a new method is invoked, a frame for this method is pushed onto the stack. When it terminates, its frame is popped from the stack and the Java Virtual Machine resumes the processing of the previously suspended method.

The Java stack performs parameter passing to methods. Specifically, Java uses the ***call-by-value*** parameter passing protocol. This means that the current ***value*** of a variable (or expression) is what is passed as an argument to a called method.

In the case of a variable x of a primitive type, such as an int or float, the current value of x is simply the number that is associated with x. When such a value is passed to the called method, it is assigned to a local variable in the called method's frame. (This simple assignment is also illustrated in Figure 4.3.) Note that if the called method changes the value of this local variable, it will ***not*** change the value of the variable in the calling method.

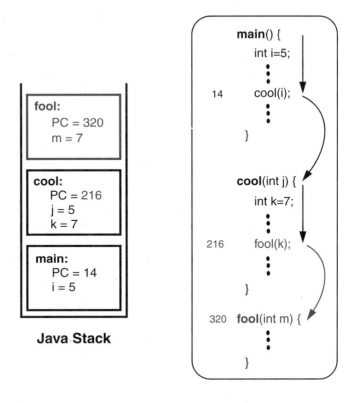

Java Stack

Java Program

Figure 4.3: An example of a Java stack: Method fool has just been called by method cool, which itself was previously called by method main. Note the values of the program counter, parameters, and local variables stored in the stack frames. When the invocation of method fool terminates, the invocation of method cool will resume its execution at instruction 217, which is obtained by incrementing the value of the program counter stored in the stack frame.

In the case of a variable x that refers to an object, however, the current value of x is the memory address of object x. (We will say more about where in memory this address actually is in Section 4.2.3.) Thus, when object x is passed as a parameter to some method, the address of x is actually passed. When this address is assigned to some local variable y in the called method, y will refer to the same object that x refers to. Therefore, if the called method changes the internal state of the object that y refers to, it will simultaneously be changing the internal state of the object that x refers to (which is the same object). Nevertheless, if the called program changes y to refer to some other object, x will remain unchanged—it will still refer to the same object it was referencing before.

Thus, the Java Method Stack is used by the Java Virtual Machine to implement method calls and parameter passing. Incidentally, method stacks are not a specific feature of Java. They are used in the run-time environment of most modern programming languages, including C and C++.

Recursion

One of the benefits of using a stack to implement method invocation is that it allows programs to use **recursion**. That is, it allows a method to call itself as a subroutine. For example, we can use recursion to compute the classic factorial function, $n! = n(n-1)(n-2)\cdots 1$, as shown in Code Fragment 4.7.

```java
public static long factorial(long n) {
  if (n <= 1)
    return 1;
  else
    return n*factorial(n−1);
}
```

Code Fragment 4.7: Recursive method factorial.

The method factorial calls itself recursively to compute the factorial of $n-1$. When the recursive call terminates, it returns $(n-1)!$, which is then multiplied by n to compute $n!$. In turn, the recursive invocation calls itself to compute the factorial of $n-2$, etc. The chain of recursive invocations, and thus the Java stack, grows only up to size n, because calling factorial(1) returns 1 immediately without invoking itself recursively. The Java stack in the Java Virtual Machine allows for the method factorial to exist simultaneously in several active frames (as many as n at some point). Each frame stores the value of its parameter n as well as the value to be returned.

This example also illustrates an important property that a recursive method should always possess—the method terminates. We ensured this property in method factorial by writing nonrecursive statements for the case $n \leq 1$, and always performing the recursive call on a smaller value of the parameter $(n-1)$ than that which we were given (n), so that, at some point (at the "bottom" of the recursion) we will perform the nonrecursive part of the computation (returning 1). We must always design a recursive method so that it is guaranteed to terminate at some point (for example, by always making recursive calls for "smaller" instances of the problem and handling the "smallest" instances nonrecursively as special cases). We note that if we design an "infinitely recursive" method, it will not actually run forever. It will instead, at some point, use up all the memory available for the Java stack and generate an out-of-memory error. If we use recursion with care, however, the method stack will implement recursive methods without any trouble. Recursion can be very powerful, as it often allows us to design simple and efficient programs for fairly difficult problems.

The Operand Stack

Interestingly, there is actually another place where the Java Virtual Machine uses a stack. An ***operand stack*** is used to evaluate arithmetic expressions, such as the expression $((a+b)*(c+d))/e$. A simple binary operation, such as $a+b$, is computed by pushing a on the operand stack, pushing b on the operand stack, and then calling an instruction that pops the top two items from the operand stack, performs the binary operation on them, and pushes the result back onto the operand stack. Likewise, instructions for writing and reading elements to and from memory involve the use of pop and push methods for the operand stack.

In Chapter 6 we discuss the evaluation of arithmetic expressions in a more general framework. For now, however, let us simply note that the operand stack plays a crucial role in this computation. Thus, the operand stack and the Java (method) stack are fundamental components of the Java Virtual Machine.

4.2 Queues

Another fundamental data structure is the ***queue***. It is a close "cousin" of the stack, as a queue is a container of objects that are inserted and removed according to the ***first-in first-out*** (**FIFO**) principle. That is, elements can be inserted at any time, but only the element that has been in the queue the longest can be removed at any time. We usually say that elements enter the queue at the ***rear*** and are removed from the ***front***. The metaphor for this terminology is a line of people waiting to get on an amusement park ride. People enter at the rear of the line and get on the ride from the front of the line.

4.2.1 The Queue Abstract Data Type

Formally, the queue abstract data type defines a container that keeps objects in a sequence, where element access and deletion are restricted to the first element in the sequence, which is called the ***front*** of the queue, and element insertion is restricted to the end of the sequence, which is called the ***rear*** of the queue. This restriction enforces the rule that items are inserted and deleted in a queue according to the first-in first-out (FIFO) principle.

The *queue* abstract data type (ADT) supports the following two fundamental methods:

enqueue(*o*): Insert object *o* at the rear of the queue.
Input: Object; *Output:* None.

dequeue(): Remove and return from the queue the object at the front; an error occurs if the queue is empty.
Input: None; *Output:* Object.

Additionally, similar to the case with the Stack ADT, the queue ADT includes the following supporting methods:

size(): Return the number of objects in the queue.
Input: None; *Output:* Integer.

isEmpty(): Return a Boolean value that indicates whether the queue is empty.
Input: None; *Output:* Boolean.

front(): Return, but do not remove, the front object in the queue; an error occurs if the queue is empty.
Input: None; *Output:* Object.

Example 4.4: *The following table shows a series of queue operations and their effects on an initially empty queue Q of integer objects. For simplicity, we use integers instead of integer objects as arguments of the operations.*

Operation	Output	front $\leftarrow$ Q $\leftarrow$ rear
enqueue(5)	–	(5)
enqueue(3)	–	(5,3)
dequeue()	5	(3)
enqueue(7)	–	(3,7)
dequeue()	3	(7)
front()	7	(7)
dequeue()	7	()
dequeue()	"error"	()
isEmpty()	true	()
enqueue(9)	–	(9)
enqueue(7)	–	(9,7)
size()	2	(9,7)
enqueue(3)	–	(9,7,3)
enqueue(5)	–	(9,7,3,5)
dequeue()	9	(7,3,5)

A Queue Interface in Java

A Java interface for the queue ADT is given in Code Fragment 4.8. This generic interface specifies that objects of arbitrary classes can be inserted into the queue. Thus, we may need to use casting when removing elements.

```java
public interface Queue {
/**
 * @return number of elements in the queue.
 */
 public int size();
/**
 * @return true if the queue is empty, false otherwise.
 */
 public boolean isEmpty();
/**
 * Inspect the element at the front of the queue.
 *
 * @return element at the front of the queue.
 * @exception QueueEmptyException if the queue is empty.
 */
 public Object front() throws QueueEmptyException;
/**
 * Insert an element at the rear of the queue.
 *
 * @param element new element to be inserted.
 */
 public void enqueue (Object element);
/**
 * Remove the element at the front of the queue.
 *
 * @return element removed.
 * @exception QueueEmptyException if the queue is empty.
 */
 public Object dequeue() throws QueueEmptyException;
}
```

Code Fragment 4.8: Interface Queue documented with comments in Javadoc style. (See Section 1.9.2.)

Note that the size and isEmpty methods have the same meaning as their counterparts in the Stack ADT. These two methods, as well as the front method, are known as *accessor* methods, for they return a value and do not change the contents of the data structure. Also note the use of the QueueEmptyException to indicate the error state of an empty queue.

Example Applications

There are several possible applications for queues. Stores, theaters, public of-fices, reservation centers, and other similar service organizations typically serve customers according to the FIFO principle.[1] A queue would therefore be a logical choice for a data structure to handle transaction processing for such applications. For example, it would be a natural choice for handling incoming calls to an au-tomated airline reservation center, where callers are requesting seats on flights for a particular airline. Likewise, it would be an excellent choice for an automated system for selling concert or theater tickets.

4.2.2   A Simple Array-Based Implementation

We present a simple realization of a queue by means of an array, Q, with capacity N, for storing its elements, say, with $N = 1,000$. Since the main rule with the queue ADT is that we insert and delete objects according to the FIFO principle, we must decide how we are going to keep track of the front and rear of the queue.

One possibility would be to adapt the approach we used for the stack imple-mentation, letting $Q[0]$ be the front of the queue and then letting the queue grow from there. This is not an efficient solution, however, for it requires that we move all the elements forward one array cell each time we perform a dequeue operation. Such an implementation would therefore require $\Theta(n)$ time to perform the dequeue method, where n is the current number of objects in the queue. Thus, if we want to achieve constant time for each queue method, we need a different approach.

To avoid moving objects once they are placed in Q, we define two variables f and r, which have the following meanings:

- f is an index to the cell of Q storing the first element of the queue (which is the next candidate to be removed by a dequeue operation), unless the queue is empty (in which case $f = r$).

- r is an index to the next available array cell in Q.

Initially, we assign $f = r = 0$, which indicates that the queue is empty. Now, when we remove an element from the front of the queue, we can simply increment f to index the next cell. Likewise, when we add an element, we can simply increment r to index the next available cell in Q. This scheme allows us to implement the enqueue and dequeue methods in constant time, that is, $O(1)$ time. However, there is still a problem with this approach.

---

[1]This policy is true in most Western countries, such as France, Germany, the UK, and the U.S.A., with the notable exception of Italy, where customers at a post office usually loathe to form a line, and instead typically choose more creative arrangements.

Consider, for example, what happens if we repeatedly enqueue and dequeue a single element N different times. We would have $f = r = N$. If we were then to try to insert the element just one more time, we would get an array-out-of-bounds error (since the N valid locations in Q are from $Q[0]$ to $Q[N-1]$), even though there is plenty of room in the queue in this case. To avoid this problem and be able to utilize all of the array Q, we let the f and r indices "wrap around" the end of Q. That is, we now view Q as a "circular array" that goes from $Q[0]$ to $Q[N-1]$ and then immediately back to $Q[0]$ again. (See Figure 4.4.)

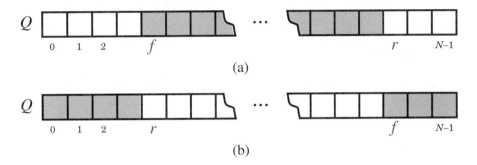

Figure 4.4: Using array Q in a circular fashion: (a) the "normal" configuration with $f \le r$; (b) the "wrapped around" configuration with $r < f$. The cells storing queue elements are highlighted.

Implementing this circular view of Q is actually pretty easy. Each time we increment f or r, we simply need to compute this increment as "$(f+1)$ mod N" or "$(r+1)$ mod N," respectively, where the operator "mod" is the **modulo** operator, computed by taking the remainder after an integral division, so that, if y is nonzero, then

$$x \bmod y = x - \lfloor x/y \rfloor y.$$

Java uses "%" to denote the modulo operator. By using the modulo operator, we can view Q as a circular array and implement each queue method in a constant amount of time (that is, $O(1)$ time). Thus, we can solve the array-overflow problem by using the modulo operator, but one small problem yet remains with this approach.

Consider now the situation that occurs if we enqueue N objects into Q without dequeuing any of them. We would have $f = r$, which is the same condition that occurs when the queue is empty. Hence, we would not be able to tell the difference between a full queue and an empty one in this case. Fortunately, this is not a big problem, and a number of ways for dealing with it exist. The solution we describe here is to insist that Q can never hold more than $N-1$ objects. (We explore another solution in an exercise.)

The above simple rule for handling a full queue takes care of the final problem with our implementation, and leads to the pseudo-coded descriptions of the queue methods given in Code Fragment 4.9. Note our introduction of an implementation-specific exception, called QueueFullException, to signal that no more elements can be inserted in the queue. Also note the way we compute the size of the queue by means of the expression $(N - f + r) \bmod N$, which gives the correct result both in the "normal" configuration (when $f \leq r$) and in the "wrapped around" configuration (when $r < f$). The Java implementation of a queue by means of an array is similar to that of a stack, and is left as an exercise.

Algorithm size():
    return $(N - f + r) \bmod N$

Algorithm isEmpty():
    return $(f = r)$

Algorithm front():
    if isEmpty() **then**
        throw a QueueEmptyException
    return $Q[f]$

Algorithm dequeue():
    if isEmpty() **then**
        throw a QueueEmptyException
    $temp \leftarrow Q[f]$
    $Q[f] \leftarrow$ **null**
    $f \leftarrow (f + 1) \bmod N$
    return $temp$

Algorithm enqueue(o):
    if size() $= N - 1$ **then**
        throw a QueueFullException
    $Q[r] \leftarrow o$
    $r \leftarrow (r + 1) \bmod N$

Code Fragment 4.9: Implementation of a queue by means of an array, which is viewed circularly. The implementation uses the modulo operator to "wrap" indices around the end of the array and it also includes two instance variables, f and r, which respectively index the front of the queue and first empty cell after the rear of the queue.

Table 4.2 shows the running times of methods in a realization of a queue by an array. As with our array-based stack implementation, each of the queue methods in the array realization executes a constant number of statements involving arithmetic operations, comparisons, and assignments. Thus each method in this implementation runs in $O(1)$ time.

Method	Time
size	$O(1)$
isEmpty	$O(1)$
front	$O(1)$
enqueue	$O(1)$
dequeue	$O(1)$

Table 4.2: Performance of a queue realized by an array. The space usage is $O(N)$, where N is the size of the array, determined at the time the queue is created. Note that the space usage is independent from the number $n < N$ of elements that are actually in the queue.

As with the array-based stack implementation, the only real disadvantage of the array-based queue implementation is that we artificially set the capacity of the queue to be some number N. In a real application, we may actually need more or less queue capacity than this, but if we have a good estimate of the number of elements that will be in the queue at the same time, then the array-based implementation is quite efficient. One such possible application of a queue is dynamic memory allocation in Java.

4.2.3 Memory Allocation in Java

We have already discussed (in Section 4.1.3) how the Java Virtual Machine allocates a method's local variables in that method's frame on the Java stack. The Java stack is not the only kind of memory available for program data in Java, however. Memory for an object can also be allocated dynamically during a method's execution, by having that method utilize the special **new** operator built into Java. For example, we can create a new 12-element Vector object in Java using the statement

Vector items = **new** Vector(12);

A Vector object can be treated much like an array, except that its capacity grows and shrinks as necessary. Moreover, this object continues to exist even after the method that created it terminates. Thus, the memory for this object cannot be allocated on the Java stack.

Instead of using the Java stack for this object's memory, Java uses memory from another area of storage—the ***memory heap*** (which should not be confused with the "heap" data structure we will discuss in Chapter 7). We illustrate this memory area, together with the other memory areas, in a Java Virtual Machine in Figure 4.5. The storage available in the memory heap is divided into ***blocks***, which are contiguous array-like "chunks" of memory that may be of variable or fixed sizes.

To simplify the discussion, let us assume that blocks in the memory heap are of a fixed size, say, $1,024$ bytes, and that one block is big enough for any object we might want to create. (Efficiently handling the more general case is actually an interesting research problem.)

Figure 4.5: A schematic view of the layout of memory addresses in a Java Virtual Machine.

The Java Virtual Machine definition requires that the memory heap be able to quickly allocate memory blocks for new objects, but it does not specify the algorithm that we should use to do this. So each implementor of a Java Virtual Machine is free to choose the implementation thought to be best. We therefore exercise this freedom and choose to use a queue to manage the unused blocks in the memory heap. When a method uses the **new** operator to request a block of memory for some new object, we will perform a dequeue operation on the queue of unused blocks to provide a free block of memory in the memory heap. Likewise, when the Java Virtual Machine determines (by means of its "garbage collector") that a block of memory previously allocated is no longer being used, then the Java Virtual Machine performs an enqueue operation to return this block to the queue of available blocks.

As long as there are enough blocks available in the memory heap, this scheme is guaranteed to efficiently allocate memory for newly created objects. Thus, the queue data structure can be applied in the implementation of Java itself.

There are other applications for queues in Java, as well.

4.2.4 Java Threads ⋆

Multiprogramming is a way of achieving a limited form of parallelism, even on a computer that has only one CPU. This mechanism allows us to have multiple tasks or computational ***threads*** running at the same time, with each thread being responsible for some specific computation. Multiprogramming is useful in graphical applications. For example, one thread can be responsible for catching mouse clicks while several others are responsible for moving parts of an animation around in a screen canvas. Even if the computer has only one CPU, these different computational threads can all seem to be running at the same time because:

1. The CPU is so fast relative to our perception of time.
2. The operating system is providing each thread with a different "slice" of the CPU's time.

The time slices given to each different thread occur with such rapid succession that the different threads appear to be running simultaneously, in parallel.

Java has a built-in mechanism for achieving multiprogramming—Java threads. Java threads are computational objects that can cooperate and communicate with one another to share other objects in memory, the computer's screen, or other kinds of resources and devices. Switching between different threads in a Java program occurs rapidly because each thread has its own Java stack stored in the memory of the Java Virtual Machine. The Java stack for each thread contains the local variables and the frames for the methods that that thread is currently running. Thus, to switch from a thread T to another thread U, all the CPU needs to do is to "remember" where it left off in the thread T before it switches to the thread U. We have already discussed a way for this to be done, namely, by storing the current value of T's program counter, which is a reference to the next instruction T is to perform, at the top of T's Java stack. By saving the program counter for each active thread in the top of its Java stack, the CPU can pick up where it left off in some other thread U, by restoring the value of the program counter to the value that was stored at the top of U's Java stack (and using U's stack as the "current" Java stack).

A Java thread will always be in one of four different states:

- New
- Runnable
- Blocked
- Dead

⋆We use a star (⋆) to indicate sections containing material more advanced than the material in the rest of the chapter; this material can be considered optional in a first reading.

When a thread is first created, it is in a *new* state, and it remains in this state until the thread that created it sends it a start message. Once it starts, a Java thread becomes *runnable*, which means that it is a candidate to perform computations when given a slice of the CPU's time. When a thread is in the runnable state and it becomes the active thread, then it executes its instructions. These instructions can be regular primitive operations, or they can be special operations that put the thread into a *blocked* state so that it is no longer runnable (until some event or thread puts it back in the runnable state). These blocking operations include calls to sleep, suspend, and wait methods or any instruction that causes the thread to have to wait for some input-output (I/O) action. A thread can be brought back into the runnable state by having its sleep event terminate (that is, it "wakes up"), having some other thread send it a resume or notify message, or having an I/O it was waiting for complete. Finally, when a thread is done performing its computations, it enters a *dead* state.

When designing a program that uses multiple threads, we must be careful not to allow an individual thread to monopolize the CPU. Such CPU monopolization can lead to an application or applet *hanging*, where it is technically running, but not actually doing anything.

However, in some operating systems, CPU monopolizing by threads is not an issue. These operating systems utilize a queue to allocate CPU time to the runnable threads in the *round-robin* protocol. The main idea of this protocol is to store all runnable threads in a queue Q. When the CPU is ready to provide a time slice to a thread, it performs a dequeue operation on the queue Q to get the next available runnable thread; let's call it T. Before the CPU actually begins executing instructions for T, however, it starts a timer running in hardware that is set to expire a fixed amount of time later. The CPU now waits until either (i) thread T blocks itself (by one of the blocking methods mentioned above), or (ii) the timer expires. In the latter case, the CPU stops the execution of T and and performs an enqueue operation to place T at the end of the line of currently runnable threads. In either case, the CPU saves the current value of T's program counter at the top of T's Java stack and processes the next available runnable thread by extracting it from Q with a dequeue operation. In this way, the CPU ensures that each runnable thread is given its fair share of time. Thus, by using a simple queue data structure and a hardware stopwatch, the operating system can avoid CPU monopolization.

While this queue-based solution solves the multiprogramming problem, we should mention that this solution is actually an oversimplification of the protocol used by most operating systems that do round-robin time slicing, as most systems give threads priorities. Thus, they use a *priority queue* to implement time slicing. We discuss priority queues in Chapter 7.

4.3   Linked Lists

In the previous sections, we presented the stack and queue ADTs and discussed some important applications of them. We also showed how to implement these abstract data types with concrete data structures based on arrays. While these implementations are quite simple, they have the drawback of not being very adaptable, since the size *N* of the array must be fixed in advance. There are other ways to implement these data structures, however, that do not have this drawback. In this section, we explore an important alternate implementation, which is known as the singly linked list.

4.3.1   Singly Linked Lists

A **linked list** in its simplest form is a collection of **nodes** that together form a linear ordering. The ordering is determined as in the children's game "Follow the Leader," in that each node is a compound object that stores a reference to an element and a reference, called **next**, to another node. (See Figure 4.6.)

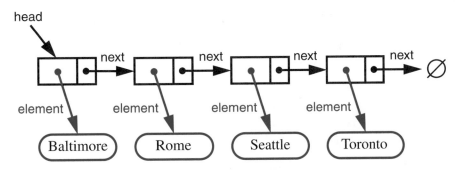

Figure 4.6: A singly linked list. References to elements are shown with blue arrows; next references are shown with black arrows. The **null** object is denoted as ∅. The head reference is a single instance variable.

It might seem like circular reasoning to have a node reference another node, but such a scheme easily works. The **next** reference inside a node can be viewed as a **link** or **pointer** to another node. Likewise, moving from one node to another by following a **next** reference is known as **link hopping** or **pointer hopping**. The first and last node of a linked list usually are called the **head** and **tail** of the list, respectively. We can identify the tail as the node having a null **next** reference, which indicates the termination of the list. A linked list defined in this way is known as a **singly linked list**.

Like an array, a singly linked list keeps the elements in a certain linear order, which is determined by the chain of ***next*** references between the nodes. Unlike an array, a singly linked list does not have a predetermined fixed size, and uses space proportional to the number of its elements.

More precisely, the space usage of a singly linked list with n elements is $O(n)$, since it has n nodes and each node uses $O(1)$ space to store references to an element and to the next node. To implement a singly linked list in Java, we define a Node class, as shown in Code Fragment 4.10, which specifies the format of the objects associated with the nodes of the list, and a LinkedList class (not shown), which keeps a reference to the head node of the list and other information for the list, such as the number of elements. Note that to save space, Javadoc comments are not included in Code Fragment 4.10 and in most Java code fragments shown in the rest of this book, but instead are replaced by inline comments.

Caution

```java
public class Node {
  // Instance variables:
  private Object element;
  private Node next;
  // Simple constructors:
  public Node() {
    this(null, null);
  }
   public Node(Object e, Node n) {
    element = e;
    next = n;
  }
  // Accessor methods:
  Object getElement() {
    return element;
  }
  Node getNext() {
    return next;
  }
  // Modifier methods:
  void setElement(Object newElem) {
    element = newElem;
  }
  void setNext(Node newNext) {
    next = newNext;
  }
}
```

Code Fragment 4.10: Implementation of a node of a singly linked list. To save space, Javadoc comments have been replaced by inline comments.

With a singly linked list, we can easily insert or delete an element at the head of the list in $O(1)$ time, as shown in Figure 4.7. We create a new node, set its ***next*** pointer to refer to the same object as the head, and then set the head to point to the new node. Note that this simple procedure works even when the linked list is empty and the head refers to the null object.

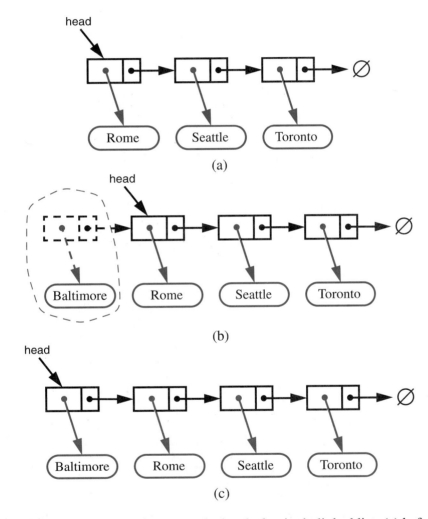

Figure 4.7: Insertion of an element at the head of a singly linked list: (a) before the insertion; (b) creation of a new node; (c) after the insertion. Deleting an element from the head of the list is a symmetric operation, which can be visualized by looking first at (c), then (b), and finally (a).

We can also insert an element at the tail of the list in $O(1)$ time, provided we keep a reference to the tail node, as shown in Figure 4.8. In this case, we create a new node, assign its next reference to point to the null object, set the next reference of the tail to point to this new object, and then assign the tail reference itself to this new node.

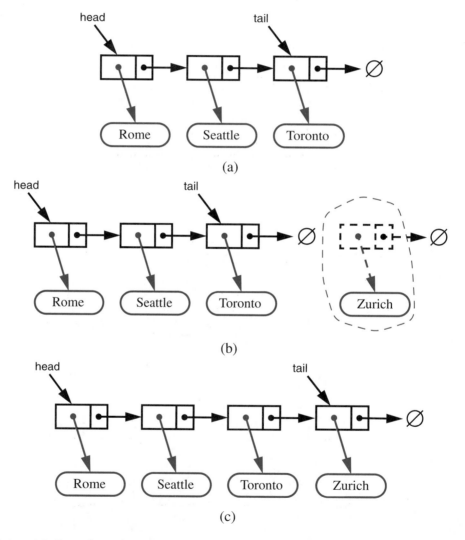

Figure 4.8: Insertion of an element at the tail of a singly linked list: (a) before the insertion; (b) creation of a new node; (c) after the insertion. Note that it is crucial that we set the next pointer for the tail in (b) before we assign the tail variable to point to the new node in (c).

We cannot delete the tail node of a singly linked list in $O(1)$ time, however. Even if we have a tail reference directly to the last node of the list, we must be able to access the node ***before*** the last node, in order to remove the last node. This is one time when it is appropriate to say, "you can't get there from here," for we cannot reach the node before a node v by following next links from v. The only way to access the node before v is to start from the head of the list and search all the way through the list until coming to a node whose ***next*** reference points to v. But if v is the last node, such link hopping takes an amount of time proportional to the number of elements in the list, that is, $\Theta(n)$ time.

We next consider how one could use a singly linked to implement an ADT described earlier in this chapter.

4.3.2 Implementing a Stack with a Singly Linked List

Let us explore using a singly linked list to implement the stack ADT. In principle, the top of the stack could be either at the head or at the tail of the list. However, since we can insert and delete elements in $O(1)$ time only at the head, it is more efficient to have the top of the stack at the head. Also, in order to perform operation size in $O(1)$ time, we keep track of the current number of elements in an instance variable. A Java implementation of a stack, by means of a singly linked list, is given in Code Fragment 4.11. All the methods of the Stack interface are therefore executed in $O(1)$ time.

In addition to being time efficient, this linked list implementation has a space requirement that is $O(n)$, where n is the current number of elements in the stack. That is, its space usage depends on the number of elements in the stack and not on any artificial capacity constraint. Likewise, this implementation does not require that a new exception be created to handle any size overflow problems. It instead implicitly has the run-time environment deal with the general issue of whether our implementation will run out of memory, which involves the OutOfMemoryError error (see Section 2.3 for the difference between exceptions and errors). Thus, this implementation of a stack, by means of a singly linked list, has an important advantage over the array-based one: it does not require that we place an explicit upper bound on the size of the stack.

We use a reference variable top to refer to the head of the list (which points to the null object if the list is empty). When we push a new element e on the stack, we simply create a new node v for e, reference e from v, and insert v at the head of the list. Likewise, when we pop an element from the stack, we simply remove the node at the head of the list and return its element. Thus, we perform all insertions and removals of elements at the head of the list.

```java
public class LinkedStack implements Stack {
  private Node top;              // reference to the head node
  private int size;             // number of elements in the stack
  public LinkedStack() {        // initializes an empty stack
    top = null;
    size = 0;
  }
  public int size() {
    return size;
  }
  public boolean isEmpty() {
    if (top == null)
      return true;
    return false;
  }
  public void push(Object elem) {
    Node v = new Node();        // create a new node
    v.setElement(elem);
    v.setNext(top);             // link-in the new node
    top = v;
    size++;
  }
  public Object top() throws StackEmptyException {
    if (isEmpty())
      throw new StackEmptyException("Stack is empty.");
    return top.getElement();
  }
  public Object pop() throws StackEmptyException {
    if (isEmpty())
      throw new StackEmptyException("Stack is empty.");
    Object temp = top.getElement();
    top = top.getNext();        // link-out the former top node
    size--;
    return temp;
  }
}
```

Code Fragment 4.11: Class LinkedStack, which implements the Stack interface using a singly linked list. The nodes of the list are objects of class Node shown in Code Fragment 4.10.

4.3.3 Implementing a Queue with a Singly Linked List

We can efficiently implement the queue ADT using a singly linked list, as well. For efficiency reasons, we choose the front of the queue, where we delete only, to be at the head of the list, and the rear of the queue, where we insert only, to be at the tail of the list. (Why would it be bad to insert at the head and remove at the tail?) Note that we need to maintain references to both the head and tail nodes of the list. Rather than go into every detail of this implementation, we simply give a Java implementation for the fundamental queue methods in Code Fragment 4.12.

```java
public void enqueue(Object obj) {
    Node node = new Node();
    node.setElement(obj);
    node.setNext(null); // node will be new tail node
    if (size == 0)
        head = node; // special case of a previously empty queue
    else
        tail.setNext(node); // add node at the tail of the list
    tail = node; // update the reference to the tail node
    size++;
}

    ...

public Object dequeue() throws QueueEmptyException {
    Object obj;
    if (size == 0)
        throw new QueueEmptyException("Queue is empty.");
    obj = head.getElement();
    head = head.getNext();
    size--;
    if (size == 0)
    tail = null; // the queue is now empty
    return obj;
}
```

Code Fragment 4.12: Methods enqueue and dequeue in the implementation of the queue ADT by means of a singly linked list.

Each of the methods of the singly linked list implementation of the queue ADT runs in $O(1)$ time. We also avoid the need to specify a maximum size for the queue, as was done in the array-based queue implementation, but this benefit comes at the expense of increasing the amount of space used per element. Still, the methods in the singly linked list queue implementation are more complicated than we might like, for we must take extra care in how we deal with special cases where the queue is empty before an enqueue or where the queue becomes empty after a dequeue.

4.4　Double-Ended Queues

Consider now a queue-like data structure that supports insertion and deletion at both the front and the rear of the queue. Such an extension of a queue is called a ***double-ended queue***, or ***deque***, which is usually pronounced "deck" to avoid confusion with the dequeue method of the regular queue ADT, which is pronounced like the abbreviation "D.Q."

4.4.1　The Deque Abstract Data Type

The deque abstract data type is richer than both the stack and the queue ADTs. The fundamental methods of the deque ADT are as follows (where we use D to denote the deque):

insertFirst(e): Insert a new element e at the beginning of D.
Input: Object; *Output:* None.

insertLast(e): Insert a new element e at the end of D.
Input: Object; *Output:* None.

removeFirst(): Remove and return the first element of D; an error occurs if D is empty.
Input: None; *Output:* Object.

removeLast(): Remove and return the last element of D; an error occurs if D is empty.
Input: None; *Output:* Object.

Additionally, the deque ADT may also include the following support methods:

first(): Return the first element of D; an error occurs if D is empty.
Input: None; *Output:* Object.

last(): Return the last element of D; an error occurs if D is empty.
Input: None; *Output:* Object.

size(): Return the number of elements of D.
Input: None; *Output:* Integer.

isEmpty(): Determine if D is empty.
Input: None; *Output:* Boolean.

We illustrate a series of deque operations performed on an initially empty deque in the following example.

Example 4.5: *The following table shows a series of operations and their effects on an initially empty deque D of integer objects. For simplicity, we use integers instead of integer objects as arguments of the operations.*

Operation	*Output*	*D*
insertFirst(3)	–	(3)
insertFirst(5)	–	(5,3)
removeFirst()	5	(3)
insertLast(7)	–	(3,7)
removeFirst()	3	(7)
removeLast()	7	()
removeFirst()	"error"	()
isEmpty()	true	()

4.4.2 Implementing a Deque with a Doubly Linked List

Since the deque requires insertion and removal at both ends of a list, using a singly linked list would be inefficient. (See Section 4.3.1.) There is a type of linked list, however, that allows for a great variety of operations, including insertion and removal at both ends, to run in $O(1)$ time—the **doubly linked** list. A node in a doubly linked list stores two references—a **next** link, which points to the next node in the list, and a **prev** link, which points to the previous node in the list. A Java implementation of a node of a doubly linked list is shown in Code Fragment 4.13.

To simplify programming, it is convenient to add special nodes at both ends of the list; a **header** node just before the head of the list, and a **trailer** node just after the tail of the list. These "dummy" or **sentinel** nodes do not store any element. The header has a valid *next* reference but a null *prev* reference, while the trailer has a valid *prev* reference but a null *next* reference. A doubly linked list with these sentinels is shown in Figure 4.9. Note that a linked list object would simply need to store these two sentinels and a size counter that keeps track of the number of elements (not counting sentinels) in the list.

Inserting or removing elements at either end of a doubly linked list is straightforward to do in $O(1)$ time. (See Figure 4.10.) Indeed, the *prev* links eliminate the need to traverse the list to get to the node just before the tail.

For any insertion of a new element *e*, we can therefore assume we have access to the node *p* before the place *e* should go and the node *q* after the place *e* should go. To insert a new element between the two nodes *p* and *q* (either or both of which could be sentinels), we create a new node *t*, have *t*'s prev and next pointers respectively refer to *p* and *q*, and then have *p*'s next pointer refer to *t*, and have *q*'s prev pointer refer to *t*.

Likewise, if we wish to remove an element stored at a node *t*, we can again assume we have access to the nodes *p* and *q* on either side of *t* (and these nodes must exist, since we are using sentinels). To remove a node *t* between two nodes *p* and *q*, we simply have *p* and *q* point to each other instead of *t*. We do not need to change any of the fields in *t*, for now *t* can be reclaimed by the garbage collector, since no one is pointing to *t*.

```
class DLNode {
  private Object element;
  private DLNode next, prev;
  DLNode() { this(null, null, null); }
  DLNode(Object e, DLNode p, DLNode n) {
    element = e;
    next = n;
    prev = p;
  }
  void setElement(Object newElem) { element = newElem; }
  void setNext(DLNode newNext) { next = newNext; }
  void setPrev(DLNode newPrev) { prev = newPrev; }
  Object getElement() { return element; }
  DLNode getNext() { return next; }
  DLNode getPrev() { return prev; }
}
```

Code Fragment 4.13: Implementation of a node of a doubly linked list.

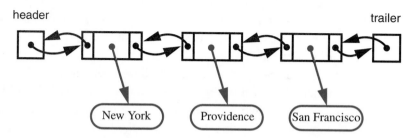

Figure 4.9: A doubly linked list with sentinels, header and trailer, marking the ends of the list. An empty list would have these sentinels pointing to each other. We do not show the null prev pointer for the header nor do we show the null next pointer for the trailer.

(a)

(b)

(c)

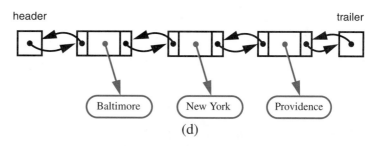

(d)

Figure 4.10: Update operations for a doubly linked list with header and trailer sentinels: (a) inserting at the head; (b) after the insertion and before deleting at the tail; (c) deleting at the tail; (d) after the deletion.

```java
public class MyDeque implements Deque {
  DLNode header, trailer;  // sentinels
  int size;     // number of elements
  public MyDeque() {  // initialize an empty deque
    header = new DLNode();
    trailer = new DLNode();
    header.setNext(trailer);  // make header point to trailer
    trailer.setPrev(header);  // make trailer point to header
    size = 0;
  }
...
  public Object first() throws DequeEmptyException {
    if (isEmpty())
      throw new DequeEmptyException("Deque is empty.");
    return header.getNext().getElement();
  }
...
  public void insertFirst(Object o) {
    DLNode second = header.getNext();
    DLNode first = new DLNode(o, header, second);
    second.setPrev(first);
    header.setNext(first);
    size++;
  }
...
  public Object removeLast() throws DequeEmptyException {
    if (isEmpty())
      throw new DequeEmptyException("Deque is empty.");
    DLNode last = trailer.getPrev();
    Object o = last.getElement();
    DLNode secondtolast = last.getPrev();
    trailer.setPrev(secondtolast);
    secondtolast.setNext(trailer);
    size--;
    return o;
  }
...
```

Code Fragment 4.14: Portions of the implementation of the deque ADT by means of a doubly linked list. Note that thanks to the use of sentinels, we do not need to check for "special cases" of an empty, or about to become empty, list. Methods insertFirst and removeLast are illustrated in Figure 4.10.

Thus, a doubly linked list can be used to implement all the methods of the deque ADT in $O(1)$ time. We show in Code Fragment 4.14 portions of a Java implementation of a deque by means of a doubly linked list. Note the use of sentinels and the way we initialize them in the constructor for the class MyDeque.

Table 4.3 shows the running times of methods in a realization of a deque by a doubly linked list. Note that every method of the deque ADT has $O(1)$ worst-case running time in this implementation.

Method	Time
size	$O(1)$
isEmpty	$O(1)$
first	$O(1)$
last	$O(1)$
insertFirst	$O(1)$
insertLast	$O(1)$
removeFirst	$O(1)$
removeLast	$O(1)$

Table 4.3: Performance of a deque realized by a doubly linked list. The space usage is $O(n)$, where n is number of elements in the deque.

4.4.3 Implementing Stacks and Queues with Deques

There is a simple mapping that takes the methods of the stack and queue ADTs and implements them using deque operations. Specifically, there are the following simple correspondences for the stack ADT:

Stack Method	*Deque Implementation*
size()	size()
isEmpty()	isEmpty()
top()	last()
push(e)	insertLast(e)
pop()	removeLast()

Likewise, we have the following simple correspondences for the queue ADT:

Queue Method	*Deque Implementation*
size()	size()
isEmpty()	isEmpty()
front()	first()
enqueue(e)	insertLast(e)
dequeue()	removeFirst()

With an implementation MyDeque of the deque ADT, we can easily implement the Stack interface with the class DequeStack shown in Code Fragment 4.15.

```java
public class DequeStack implements Stack {
  private Deque D;
  public DequeStack() {
    D = new MyDeque();
  }
  public int size() {
    return D.size();
  }
  public boolean isEmpty() {
    return D.isEmpty();
  }
  public void push(Object obj) {
    D.insertLast(obj);
  }
  public Object top() throws StackEmptyException {
    try {
      return D.last();
    }
    catch (DequeEmptyException ece) {
      throw new StackEmptyException("Stack is empty!");
    }
  }
  public Object pop() throws StackEmptyException {
    try {
      return D.removeLast();
    }
    catch (DequeEmptyException ece) {
      throw new StackEmptyException("Stack is empty!");
    }
  }
}
```

Code Fragment 4.15: Implementation of the Stack interface by means of a deque. Note that since the deque throws its own DequeEmptyException, methods top and pop catch it and throw a StackEmptyException instead.

All the methods of DequeStack are essentially one-line calls to methods of the Deque interface. Note that some methods of Deque throw a DequeEmptyException when we try to access or delete elements in an empty deque.

4.4.4   The Adapter Pattern

The DequeStack methods shown in Code Fragment 4.15 also illustrate an important design pattern—the **adapter** pattern defined in Section 2.6.1. This pattern adjusts methods from one class so they can be used to implement methods of another class. There are several situations for which the adapter pattern comes in handy. One is the situation illustrated in the DequeStack class, where we want to specialize a general class and simplify its usage by changing the names of some of its methods. In the case of the DequeStack class, we adapt class MyDeque, which implements the more complex Deque interface, so that it can be used to implement the simpler Stack interface. Another useful application of the adapter pattern is to specialize the types of objects that are used by a general class. We can use this kind of adapter, for example, to define an IntegerArrayStack class that adapts the ArrayStack class (see Code Fragments 4.4–4.5) so that the stack only stores Integer objects. Class IntegerArrayStack can then be used in a method, such as the reverse method of Code Fragment 4.6, to avoid the extra typing and possible confusion associated with casting, since the casting would be done internally by the class.

4.5   Sample Case Study Application

Given a series of n daily price quotes for a stock, we call the **span** of the stock's price on a certain day the maximum number of consecutive days up to the current day that the price of the stock has been less than or equal to its price on that day. (See Figure 4.11.) More formally, assume that price quotes begin with day 0 and that p_i denotes the price on day i. The span s_i on day i is equal to the maximum integer k such that $k \leq i+1$ and $p_j \leq p_i$ for $j = i-k+1, \ldots, i$. Given the prices $p_0, p_1, \ldots, p_{n-1}$, consider the problem of computing the spans $s_0, s_1, \ldots, s_{n-1}$.

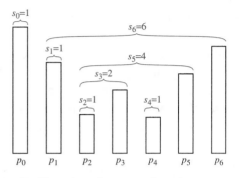

Figure 4.11: Daily prices for a stock and span on each day.

4.5.1   A Quadratic-Time Algorithm

We show a straightforward solution to our problem in Code Fragment 4.16.

Algorithm computeSpans1(P):

    Input: An n-element array P of numbers

    Output: An n-element array S of numbers such that $S[i]$ is the largest integer k
        such that $k \leq i+1$ and $P[j] \leq P[i]$ for $j = i-k+1, \ldots, i$

    for $i = 0$ **to** $n-1$ **do**
        $k \leftarrow 0$
        done $\leftarrow$ **false**
        repeat
            if $P[i-k] \leq P[i]$ **then**
                $k \leftarrow k+1$
            else
                done$\leftarrow$**true**
        until $(k > i)$ **or** *done*
        $S[i] \leftarrow k$
    return array S

Code Fragment 4.16: Algorithm computeSpans1.

We analyze the running time of algorithm computeSpans1 as follows.

- Initializing the array S at the beginning and returning it at the end requires a constant number of primitive operations per element; hence, takes $O(n)$ time.
- There is a **repeat** loop nested within a **for** loop. The **for** loop, controlled by counter i, is executed n times, for $i = 0, \ldots, n-1$. The statements inside the **for** loop but outside the **repeat** loop are executed n times. That is, these statements, plus the incrementing and testing of counter i, contribute $O(n)$ primitive operations to the total running time.
- In iteration i of the outer **for** loop, the body of the inner **repeat** loop is executed at most $i+1$ times. Indeed, in the worst case, element $S[i]$ is larger than all the preceding elements. Thus, testing for the **if** condition $(S[i-k] \leq S[i])$, executing one of the ensuing statements, and testing for the **until** condition is performed $i+1$ times during iteration i of the outer loop ($i = 0, \ldots, n-1$). Therefore, the worst-case running time is proportional to $1 + 2 + 3 + \cdots + n$. Recalling Proposition 3.4, the total time contributed by the statements in the inner loop is $O(n(n+1)/2)$, which is $O(n^2)$.

The running time of computeSpans1 is therefore given by the sum of three terms. The first and the second term are $O(n)$, and the third term is $O(n^2)$. Thus, the running time of algorithm computeSpans1 is $O(n^2)$.

4.5.2 A Linear-Time Algorithm

To compute spans more efficiently, we observe that the span s_i on a certain day i can be easily computed if we know the closest day preceding i, such that the price on that day is higher than the price on day i. (See Figure 4.12.) If such a preceding day exists for a day i, let us denote it with $h(i)$, and otherwise let us define $h(i) = -1$. The span on day i is given by $s_i = i - h(i)$.

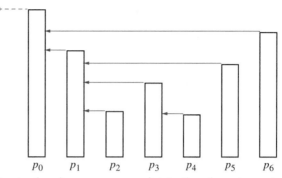

p_0 p_1 p_2 p_3 p_4 p_5 p_6

Figure 4.12: Daily stock prices; arrows point to the closest previous higher price.

Our second algorithm, computeSpans2, shown in Code Fragment 4.17, uses a stack as an auxiliary data structure to store days $i, h(i), h(h(i))$, etc. When going from day $i - 1$ to day i, we repeatedly pop days with prices less than or equal to p_i, and then push day i.

An example run of algorithm computeSpans2 is shown in Figure 4.13.

We assume that stack D is implemented so that each method of the stack ADT takes $O(1)$ time. With this assumption, our analysis of the running time of algorithm computeSpans2 is as follows:

- Initializing the array S at the beginning and returning it at the end can be done with $O(1)$ primitive operations per element, and takes $O(n)$ time.

- There is a **while** loop nested within a **for** loop. The **for** loop, controlled by counter i, is executed n times, for $i = 0, \ldots, n - 1$. Thus, the statements in the **for** loop outside the **while** loop are executed at most n times, that is, such statements (plus the incrementing and testing of counter i) take $O(n)$ time.

- Consider now the execution of the inner **while** loop during iteration i of the **for** loop. Statement *done*←**true** is executed at most once, since this causes a subsequent exit from the loop. Let t_i be the number of times statement D.pop() is executed. Conditions (**not** (D.isEmpty() **or** *done*)) and ($P[i] \geq P[D$.top()]$) are each tested at most $t_i + 1$ times.

Algorithm computeSpans2(P):

    Input: An n-element array P of numbers, and an empty stack D

    Output: An n-element array S of numbers such that $S[i]$ is the largest integer k
      such that $k \leq i+1$ and $P[j] \leq P[i]$ for $j = i-k+1, \ldots, i$

    for $i = 0$ **to** $n-1$ **do**

      done $\leftarrow$ **false**

      while not (D.isEmpty() **or** *done*) **do**

        if $P[i] \geq P[D.\text{top}()]$ **then**

          D.pop()

        else

          done$\leftarrow$**true**

      if D.isEmpty() **then**

        $h \leftarrow -1$

      else

        $h \leftarrow D$.top()

      $S[i] \leftarrow i - h$

      D.push(i)

    return array S

Code Fragment 4.17: Algorithm computeSpans2.

Thus, the total running time contribution of the statements in the **while** loop is

$$O\left(\sum_{i=0}^{n-1} (t_i + 1) \right).$$

Once an element is popped out from stack D, it is never pushed in again by the algorithm. Hence,

$$\sum_{i=0}^{n-1} t_i \leq n.$$

In other words, the total time spent performing statements in the **while** loop is $O(n)$. The running time of algorithm computeSpans2 is given by the sum of three terms, each of which is $O(n)$. Therefore, the running time of computeSpans2 is $O(n)$.

4.5.3 Java Implementation

Method computeDailyHighSpan, shown in Code Fragment 4.18, is a Java implementation of algorithm computeSpans2. An array of objects of class Quote, shown in Code Fragment 4.19, is used by method computeDailyHighSpan to access the price information and to store the computed spans.

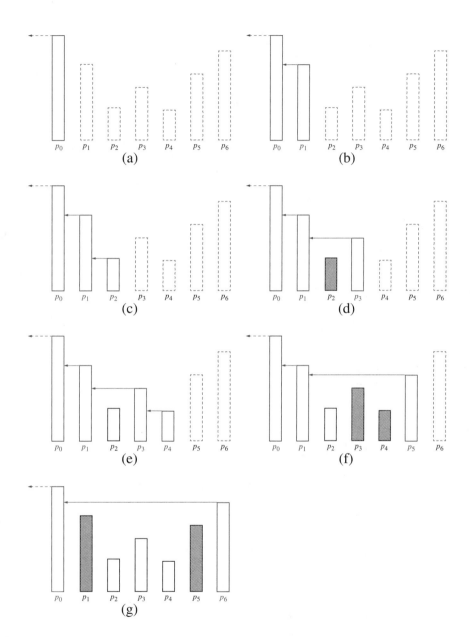

Figure 4.13: A sample run of algorithm computeSpans2. The contents of the stack D at the end of each iteration of the **for** loop are visualized by highlighting and connecting with arrows the bars associated with the days stored in D. The dashed bars denote days not yet examined by the algorithm. The shaded bars denote days popped from D in the current iteration.

```
public void computeDailyHighSpan (Quote Q[]) {
   // compute the span of the stock price on each day by means of a
   // stack, and store the information in the Quote objects
   int prevHigh; // closest preceding day when the stock price was higher
   Stack D = new ArrayStack();
   for (int i = 0 ; i < Q.length ; i++) {   // process the current day i
      while ( !D.isEmpty() &&
              Q[i].getPrice() >= ((Quote) D.top()).getPrice() )
         // note that if the first condition !D.empty() evaluates to
         // false, then the second condition is not evaluated
         D.pop();
      if (D.isEmpty())
         prevHigh = −1; // day i is a new high for the stock price
      else
         prevHigh = ((Quote) D.top()).getDay();
      Q[i].setSpan(i − prevHigh); // compute and store the span
      D.push(Q[i]); // add to the stack the current quote
   }
}
```

Code Fragment 4.18: Java implementation of algorithm computeSpans2.

```
public class Quote {
   private int day, price, span;
   public Quote(int d, int p) {
      setDay(d);
      setPrice(p);
   }
   public void setDay(int d) { day = d; }

   public int getDay() { return day; }

   public void setPrice(int p) { price = p; }

   public int getPrice() { return price; }

   public void setSpan(int s) { span = s; }

   public int getSpan() { return span; }
}
```

Code Fragment 4.19: Class of objects used by method computeDailyHighSpan to access the stock price information and to store the computed spans.

4.6   Exercises

Reinforcement

R-4.1 Describe the output of the following series of stack operations: push(5), push(3), pop(), push(2), push(8), pop(), pop(), push(9), push(1), pop(), push(7), push(6), pop(), pop(), push(4), pop(), pop().

R-4.2 Describe the output for the following sequence of queue operations: enqueue(5), enqueue(3), dequeue(), enqueue(2), enqueue(8), dequeue(), dequeue(), enqueue(9), enqueue(1), dequeue(), enqueue(7), enqueue(6), dequeue(), dequeue(), enqueue(4), dequeue(), dequeue().

R-4.3 Describe the output for the following sequence of deque operations: insertFirst(3), insertLast(8), insertLast(9), insertFirst(5), removeFirst(), removeLast(), first(), insertLast(7), removeFirst(), last(), removeLast().

R-4.4 Describe in pseudo-code, how to insert an element at the beginning of a singly linked list, assuming that the list does *not* have a sentinel header node, and instead uses a reference variable head to reference the first node in the list.

R-4.5 Give an algorithm for finding the penultimate node in a singly linked list where the last element is indicated by a null *next* reference.

R-4.6 Give an algorithm for determining, just by link hopping, whether a doubly linked list with header and trailer sentinels is empty (that is, do not make use of a *size* instance variable).

R-4.7 Describe a recursive algorithm for finding the maximum element in an array A of n elements. What is the running time and space usage of your method?

Creativity

C-4.1 Describe in pseudo-code, a method for finding by link hopping the middle node of a doubly linked list with header and trailer sentinels, and an odd number of real nodes between them. (Note: This method must only use link hopping; it cannot use a counter.) What is the running time of this method?

C-4.2 Describe how to implement the queue ADT using two stacks. What is the running time of the enqueue() and dequeue() methods in this case?

C-4.3 Give an algorithm for concatenating two singly linked lists L and M, with header sentinel nodes, into a single list L' that contains all the nodes of L (in their original order) followed by all the nodes of M (also in their original order). What is the running time of this method, if we let n denote the number of nodes in L and we let m denote the number of nodes in M?

C-4.4 Give an algorithm for concatenating two doubly linked lists L and M, with header and trailer sentinel nodes, into a single list L', as in the previous exercise. What is the running time of this method?

C-4.5 Describe in pseudo-code how to swap two nodes x and y in a singly linked list L given references only to x and y. Repeat this exercise for the case when L is a doubly linked list. What are the running times of each of these methods in terms of n, the number of nodes in L?

C-4.6 In most programming languages, parenthetic symbols (), [], and {} must be balanced and properly nested. We define a *parenthetically correct* string of characters as a string that matches one of the following patterns, where S denotes a (possibly empty) string without any parenthetic symbols, and P, P', and P'' recursively denote parenthetically correct strings:

- S
- $P'(P)P''$
- $P'[P]P''$
- $P'\{P\}P''$

Design an algorithm that checks whether a string is parenthetically correct in time proportional to the size of the string using a stack as an auxiliary data structure.

C-4.7 Describe in pseudo-code a linear-time algorithm for reversing a queue Q. To access the queue, you are only allowed to use the methods of queue ADT.

C-4.8 Describe in pseudo-code a linear-time algorithm for reversing a singly linked list L, so that the ordering of the nodes becomes exactly opposite of what it was before.

C-4.9★ Describe in pseudo-code an algorithm for reversing a singly linked list L using only a constant amount of additional space and not using any recursion. What is the running time of this method?

C-4.10 Give a pseudo-code description for an array-based implementation of the double-ended queue ADT. What is the running time for each operation?

C-4.11 Describe how to implement the stack ADT using two queues. What is the running time of the push() and pop() methods in this case?

C-4.12 Describe a recursive algorithm for enumerating all permutations of the numbers $\{1, 2, \ldots, n\}$. What is the running time of your method?

C-4.13 Describe a recursive algorithm that counts the number of nodes in a singly linked list.

C-4.14 Give a recursive algorithm to compute the product of two positive integers m and n using only addition.

Projects

P-4.1 When a share of common stock of some company is sold, the ***capital gain*** (or, sometimes, loss) is the difference between the share's selling price and the price originally paid to buy it. This rule is easy to understand for a single share, but if we sell multiple shares of stock bought over a long period of time, then we must identify the shares actually being sold. A standard accounting principle for identifying which shares of a stock were sold in such a case is to use a FIFO protocol—the shares sold are the ones that have been held the longest (indeed, this is the default method built into several personal finance software packages). For example, suppose we buy 100 shares at $20 each on day 1, 20 shares at $24 on day 2, 200 shares at $36 on day 3, and then sell 150 shares on day 4 at $30 each. Then applying the FIFO protocol means that of the 150 shares sold, 100 were bought on day 1, 20 were bought on day 2, and 30 were bought on day 3. The capital gain in this case would therefore be $100 \cdot 10 + 20 \cdot 6 + 30 \cdot (-6)$, or $940. Write a program that takes as input a sequence of transactions of the form

buy x share(s) at $$y$ each

or

sell x share(s) at $$y$ each,

assuming that the transactions occur on consecutive days and the values x and y are integers. Given this input sequence, the output should be the total capital gain (or loss) for the entire sequence, using the FIFO protocol to identify shares.

P-4.2 Design an ADT for a two-color, double-stack ADT that consists of two stacks—one "red" and one "blue"—and has as its operations color-coded versions of the regular stack ADT operations. For example, this ADT should allow for both a red push operation and a blue push operation. Give an efficient implementation of this ADT using a single array whose capacity is set at some value N that is assumed to always be larger than the sizes of the red and blue stacks combined.

P-4.3 Implement the stack ADT with a simply linked list (without using the built-in Java Stack class).

P-4.4 Implement the stack ADT using the Java Vector class.

P-4.5 Implement the queue ADT using an array.

P-4.6 Implement the queue ADT using a simply linked list.

P-4.7 Complete the implementation of class MyDeque.

P-4.8 Implement the deque ADT with an array used in a circular fashion.

P-4.9 Implement the Stack and Queue interfaces with a unique class that extends class MyDeque (Code Fragment 4.14).

Chapter Notes

The fundamental data structures of stacks, queues, and linked lists discussed in this chapter belong to the folklore of computer science. They were first chronicled by Knuth in his seminal book on *Fundamental Algorithms* [58]. In this chapter, we have taken the approach of defining the fundamental data structures of stacks, queues, and deques, first in terms of their ADTs and then in terms of concrete implementations. This approach to data structure specification and implementation is an outgrowth of software engineering advances brought on by the object-oriented design approach, and is now considered a standard approach for teaching data structures. We were introduced to this approach to data structure design by the classic books by Aho, Hopcroft, and Ullman on data structures and algorithms [4, 5]. For further study of abstract data types, please see the book by Liskov and Guttag [68], the survey paper by Cardelli and Wegner [20], or the book chapter by Demurjian [28]. The naming conventions we use for the methods of the stack, queue, and deque ADTs are taken from JDSL [43]. JDSL is a data structures library in Java that builds on approaches taken for C++ in the libraries STL [80] and LEDA [75]. We shall use this convention throughout this text. In this chapter, we motivated the study of stacks and queues from implementation issues in Java. The reader interested in learning more about the Java runtime environment known as the Java Virtual Machine (JVM) is referred to the book by Lindholm and Yellin [67] that defines the JVM.

Chapter

5

Vectors, Lists, and Sequences

Contents

The concept of a sequence, where each object comes before or after another, is fundamental. We see it in a line-by-line listing of the code of a computer program, where the order of instructions determines the computation that the program represents. We also see it in the sequence of network packets that together comprise an e-mail message, which, if it is to make sense, requires that the packets be assembled in the same order in which they are sent. Sequences are interesting, then, for they represent the important relationships of "next" and "previous" between related objects. In addition, sequences are widely used to realize and implement other data structures; hence, they are foundational building blocks for data structure design.

In this chapter, we present the *vector*, *list*, and *sequence* ADTs, each of which represents a collection of linearly arranged elements and provides methods for accessing, inserting, and removing arbitrary elements. The different types of sequences are distinguished from one another by the specific ways in which these operations are defined. Stacks, queues, and deques, studied in Chapter 4, can be viewed as restricted types of sequences that access only the first and/or last elements. An important property of a sequence is that, just as with stacks, queues, and deques, the order of the elements in a sequence is determined by the operations in the abstract data type specification, and not by the values of the elements.

The vector ADT is an extension of the concrete array data structure. It provides accessor methods that can index into the middle of a sequence and it also provides update methods for adding and removing elements by their indices. To avoid confusion with the way items are accessed in the concrete array data structure, we typically use the term *rank* to refer to the index of an element in a vector.

The list ADT, on the other hand, is an object-oriented extension of the concrete linked list data structure. It provides accessor and update methods based on an object-oriented encapsulation of the node objects used by linked lists. We call these abstract node objects *positions*, for they provide an object-oriented way of referring to "places" where elements are stored, independent of the specific implementation of the list.

Finally, the full sequence ADT is a unification of the vector and list concepts. Therefore, it is useful in contexts where we desire a generic data structure that can be implemented naturally using either an array or a linked list. We show, however, that this generality comes at a cost, for we give two basic ways of implementing a sequence, with an array and with a doubly linked list, and we point out performance trade-offs between these two implementations.

We illustrate the use of the sequence ADT through the implementation of a well-known (though inefficient) sorting algorithm known as *bubble-sort*. We also discuss the *iterator* (or *enumeration*) design pattern and mention its realization by means of a vector or list.

5.1 Vectors

Caution

Suppose we are given a linear sequence S that contains n elements. We can uniquely refer to each element e of S using an integer in the range $[0, n-1]$ that is equal to the number of elements of S that precede e in S. We therefore define the **rank** of an element e in S to be the number of elements that are before e in S. Hence, the first element in a sequence has rank 0 and the last element has rank $n-1$. This definition is consistent with the way arrays are indexed in Java and other programming languages (including C and C++).

Note that we do **not** imply that an array should be used to implement a sequence in such a way that the element at rank 0 is stored at index 0 in the array, although that is one possibility. The rank definition offers us a way to refer to the "index" of an element in a sequence without having to worry about the exact implementation of that list. So, in general, if an element is the rth element in a sequence, then it has rank $r-1$. Also, if an element of the sequence has rank r, its previous element (if it exists) has rank $r-1$, and its next element (if it exists) has rank $r+1$. The rank of an element may change whenever the sequence is updated, however. For example, if we insert a new element at the beginning of the sequence, the rank of each of the other elements increases by one.

A linear sequence that supports access to its elements by their ranks is called a **vector**. Rank is a simple yet powerful notion, since it can be used to specify where to insert a new element into a vector or where to remove an old element. For example, we can give the rank that a new element will have after it is inserted (for example, insert at rank 2). We could also use rank to specify an element to be removed (for example, remove the element at rank 2).

Example 5.1: *In the following, we show a series of rank-based operations on an initially empty vector S.*

Operation	Output	S
insert 7 *at rank* 0	–	(7)
insert 4 *at rank* 0	–	$(4,7)$
return the element at rank 1	7	$(4,7)$
insert 2 *at rank* 2	–	$(4,7,2)$
return the element at rank 3	"error"	$(4,7,2)$
remove the element at rank 1	7	$(4,2)$
insert 5 *at rank* 1	–	$(4,5,2)$
insert 3 *at rank* 1	–	$(4,3,5,2)$
insert 9 *at rank* 4	–	$(4,3,5,2,9)$
return the element at rank 2	5	$(4,3,5,2,9)$

5.1.1   The Vector Abstract Data Type

A *vector S* is an ADT that supports the following fundamental methods.

elemAtRank(r): Return the element of S with rank r; an error condition occurs if $r < 0$ or $r > n - 1$, where n is the current number of elements.
Input: Integer; *Output:* Object.

replaceAtRank(r, e): Replace with e the element at rank r and return it; an error condition occurs if $r < 0$ or $r > n - 1$, where n is the current number of elements.
Input: Integer r and object e; *Output:* Object.

insertAtRank(r, e): Insert a new element e into S to have rank r; an error condition occurs if $r < 0$ or $r > n$, where n is the number of elements before the insertion.
Input: Integer r and object e; *Output:* None.

removeAtRank(r): Remove from S the element at rank r; an error condition occurs if $r < 0$ or $r > n - 1$, where n is the current number of elements.
Input: Integer; *Output:* Object.

In addition, a vector supports the usual methods size() and isEmpty().

The repertory of methods we have given for the vector is small, but it is sufficient for us to define an adapter class (see Section 4.4.4) that realizes the deque ADT. One possible adaptation is given in Table 5.1. (See Exercise C-5.13.)

Deque Method	*Realization with Vector Methods*
size()	size()
isEmpty()	isEmpty()
first()	elemAtRank(0)
last()	elemAtRank(size() -1)
insertFirst(e)	insertAtRank(0, e)
insertLast(e)	insertAtRank(size(), e)
removeFirst()	removeAtRank(0)
removeLast()	removeAtRank(size() -1)

Table 5.1: Realization of a deque by means of a vector.

5.1.2 A Simple Array-Based Implementation

An obvious choice for implementing the vector ADT is to use an array A, where $A[i]$ stores (a reference to) the element with rank i. We choose the size N of array A sufficiently large, and we maintain in an instance variable the number $n < N$ of elements in the vector. The details of the implementation of the methods of the vector ADT are reasonably simple. To implement the elemAtRank(r) operation, for example, we just return $A[r]$. Implementations of methods insertAtRank(r, e) and removeAtRank(r) are given in Code Fragment 5.1. An important (and time-consuming) part of this implementation involves the shifting of elements up or down to keep the occupied cells in the array contiguous. These shifting operations are required to maintain our rule of always storing an element of rank i at index i in A. (See Figure 5.1 and also Exercise R-5.10.)

Algorithm insertAtRank(r, e):

    for $i = n - 1, n - 2, \ldots, r$ **do**

        $A[i+1] \leftarrow A[i]$ {make room for the new element}

    $A[r] \leftarrow e$

    $n \leftarrow n + 1$

Algorithm removeAtRank(r):

    $e \leftarrow A[r]$ {e is a temporary variable}

    for $i = r, r+1, \ldots, n-2$ **do**

        $A[i] \leftarrow A[i+1]$ {fill in for the removed element}

    $n \leftarrow n - 1$

    return e

Code Fragment 5.1: Methods in an array implementation of the vector ADT.

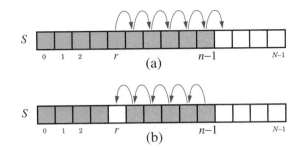

Figure 5.1: Array-based implementation of a vector S storing n elements: (a) shifting up for an insertion at rank r; (b) shifting down for a removal at rank r.

Table 5.2 shows the running times of the methods of a vector realized by means of an array. The methods isEmpty, size, and elemAtRank clearly run in $O(1)$ time, but the insertion and removal methods can take much longer than this. In particular, insertAtRank(r, e) runs in time $\Theta(n)$ in the worst case. Indeed, the worst case for this operation occurs when $r = 0$, since all the existing n elements have to be shifted forward. A similar argument applies to the method removeAtRank(r), which runs in $O(n)$ time, because we have to shift backward $n - 1$ elements in the worst case $(r = 0)$. In fact, assuming that each possible rank is equally likely to be passed as an argument to these operations, their average running time is $\Theta(n)$, for we will have to shift $n/2$ elements on average.

Method	Time
size()	$O(1)$
isEmpty()	$O(1)$
elemAtRank(r)	$O(1)$
replaceAtRank(r, e)	$O(1)$
insertAtRank(r, e)	$O(n)$
removeAtRank(r)	$O(n)$

Table 5.2: Performance of a vector with n elements realized by an array. The space usage is $O(N)$, where N is the size of the array.

Looking more closely at insertAtRank(r, e) and removeAtRank(r), we note that they each run in time $O(n - r + 1)$, for only those elements at rank r and higher have to be shifted up or down. Thus, inserting or removing an item at the end of a vector, using the methods insertAtRank(n, e) and removeAtRank$(n - 1)$, respectively take $O(1)$ time each. Moreover, this observation has an interesting consequence for the adaptation of the vector ADT to the deque ADT given in Section 5.1.1. If the vector ADT in this case is implemented by means of an array as described above, then methods insertLast and removeLast of the deque each run in $O(1)$ time. However, methods insertFirst and removeFirst of the deque each run in $O(n)$ time.

Actually, with a little effort, we can produce an array-based implementation of the vector ADT that achieves $O(1)$ time for insertions and removals at rank 0, as well as insertions and removals at the end of the vector. Achieving this requires that we give up on our rule that an element at rank i is stored in the array at index i, however, as we would have to use a circular array approach like we used in Section 4.2 to implement a queue. We leave the details of this implementation for an exercise (C-5.14).

5.1.3 An Extendable Array Implementation

A major weakness of the simple array implementation for the vector ADT given in Section 5.1.2 is that it requires advance specification of a fixed capacity, N, for the total number of elements that may be stored in the vector. If the actual number of elements, n, of the vector is much smaller than N, then this implementation will waste space. Worse, if n increases past N, then this implementation will crash. Fortunately, there is a simple way to fix this major drawback.

Let us provide a means to grow the array A that stores the elements of a vector S. Of course, in Java (and other programming languages) we cannot actually grow the array A; its capacity is fixed at some number N, as we have already observed. Instead, when an *overflow* occurs, that is, when $n = N$ and method insertAtRank is called, we perform the following steps:

1. Allocate a new array B of capacity $2N$

2. Copy $A[i]$ to $B[i]$, for $i = 0, \ldots, N - 1$

3. Let $A = B$, that is, we use B as the array supporting S.

This array replacement strategy is known as an *extendable array*, for it can be viewed as extending the end of the underlying array to make room for more elements. (See Figure 5.2.) Intuitively, this strategy is much like that of the hermit crab, which moves into a larger shell when it outgrows its previous one.

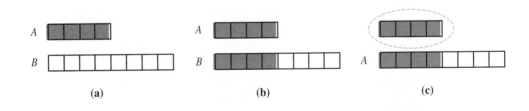

Figure 5.2: An illustration of the three steps for "growing" an extendable array: (a) create new array B; (b) copy elements from A to B; (c) reassign reference A to the new array. Not shown is the future garbage collection of the old array.

We give an implementation of the vector ADT using an extendable array in Code Fragment 5.2.

```
public class ArrayVector {
  private Object[] a;           // Array storing the elements of the vector
  private int capacity = 16;    // Length of array a
  private int size = 0;         // Number of elements stored in the vector
  // Constructor
  public ArrayVector() { a = new Object[capacity]; } // O(1) time
  // Accessor methods
  public Object elemAtRank(int r) { return a[r]; }    // O(1) time
  public int size() { return size; }
  public boolean isEmpty() { return size() == 0; }    // O(1) time
  // Modifier methods
  public Object replaceAtRank(int r, Object e) {       // O(1) time
    Object temp = a[r];
    a[r] = e;
    return temp;
  }
  public Object removeAtRank(int r) {                  // O(n) time
    Object temp = a[r];
    for (int i=r; i<size−1; i++)       // Shift elements down
      a[i] = a[i+1];
    size−−;
    return temp;
  }
  public void insertAtRank(int r, Object e) {          // O(n) time
    if (size == capacity) {           // An overflow
      capacity *= 2;
      Object[] b = new Object[capacity];
      for (int i=0; i<size; i++)
        b[i] = a[i];
      a = b;
    }
    for (int i=size−1; i>=r; i−−)      // Shift elements up
      a[i+1] = a[i];
    a[r] = e;
    size++;
  }
}
```

Code Fragment 5.2: Class ArrayVector realizing the vector ADT by means of an extendable array. For the sake of simplicity, we are not performing any checks for error conditions. In addition, this code only provides means for the array to grow; there is no corresponding means to shrink the array. We leave the details for dealing with these weaknesses as exercises (C-5.1 and C-5.3).

In terms of efficiency, this array replacement strategy might at first seem slow, for performing a single array replacement required by some element insertion takes $O(n)$ time, which is not so good. Still, notice that after we perform an array replacement, our new array allows us to add n new elements to the vector before the array must be replaced again. This simple fact allows us to show that the running time of a series of operations performed on an initially empty vector is actually quite efficient. As a shorthand notation, let us refer to the insertion of an element to be the last element in a vector as a "push" operation. We can show, using a design pattern called **amortization**, that performing a sequence of such push operations on a vector implemented with an extendable array is actually quite efficient.

Proposition 5.2: *Let S be a vector implemented by means of an extendable array A, as described above. The total time to perform a series of n push operations in S, starting from S being empty and A having size $N = 1$, is $O(n)$.*

Justification: We justify this proposition using a simple accounting trick known as **amortization**. To perform this analysis, we view the computer as a coin-operated appliance that requires the payment of one **cyber-dollar** for a constant amount of computing time. When an operation is executed, we should have enough cyber-dollars available in our current "bank account" to pay for that operation's running time. Thus, the total amount of cyber-dollars spent for any computation will be proportional to the total time spent on that computation. The beauty of using this analysis method is that we can over charge some operations in order to save up cyber-dollars to pay for others.

Let us assume that one cyber-dollar is enough to pay for the execution of each push operation in S, excluding the time spent for growing the array. Also, let us assume that growing the array from size k to size $2k$ requires k cyber-dollars for the time spent copying the elements. We shall charge each push operation three cyber-dollars. Thus, we over charge each push operation that does not cause an overflow by two cyber-dollars. Think of the two cyber-dollars profited in an insertion that does not grow the array as being "stored" at the element inserted. An overflow occurs when the vector S has 2^i elements, for some integer $i \geq 0$, and the size of the array used by the vector representing S is 2^i. Thus, doubling the size of the array will require 2^i cyber-dollars. Fortunately, these cyber-dollars can be found at the elements stored in cells 2^{i-1} through $2^i - 1$. (See Figure 5.3.) Note that the previous overflow occurred when the number of elements became larger than 2^{i-1} for the first time, and thus the cyber-dollars stored in cells 2^{i-1} through $2^i - 1$ were not previously spent. Therefore, we have a valid amortization scheme in which each operation is charged three cyber-dollars and all the computing time is paid for. That is, we can pay for the execution of n push operations using $3n$ cyber-dollars.

■

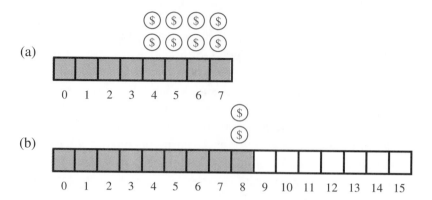

Figure 5.3: Illustration of a series of push operations on a vector: (a) an 8-cell array is full, with two cyber-dollars "stored" at cells 4 through 7; (b) a push operation causes an overflow and a doubling of capacity. Copying the eight old elements to the new array is paid for by the cyber-dollars already stored in the table; inserting the new element is paid for by one of the cyber-dollars charged to the push operation; and two cyber-dollars profited are stored at cell 8.

5.1.4   The java.util.ArrayList and java.util.Vector Classes

Java has built-in classes, java.util.ArrayList and java.util.Vector, that provide similar functionality to the vector ADT. Moreover, the standard implementations of these two classes use extendable arrays as described in the previous subsection. The correspondence between these classes and our vector ADT is given in Table 5.3. Note that methods of the java.util classes have short names. This feature speeds up coding, at the slight expense of readability, since the exact meaning of how the vector is being accessed or updated must be inferred, in this case, from a method's complete signature, not just its name.

Vector ADT Methods	java.util.Vector Methods
size(), isEmpty()	size(), isEmpty()
elemAtRank(r)	get(r)
replaceAtRank(r,e)	set(r,e)
insertAtRank(r,e)	add(r,e)
removeAtRank(r)	remove(r)

Table 5.3: Correspondence between similar methods in the vector ADT and the java.util.Vector class. The corresponding methods in the java.util.ArrayList class are the same as in the java.util.Vector class.

The Java classes, java.util.ArrayList and java.util.Vector have features and methods in addition to those of our simplified vector ADT. For example, the class java.util.Vector provides an integer capacityIncrement parameter, which determines how the underlying extendable array grows. If the capacityIncrement parameter is set to 0, then the array doubles when it grows (like in our class ArrayVector). If this parameter is set to a positive value, k, however, then the array adds k new cells when it grows. We must utilize this parameter with caution, however. For most applications, leaving the capacityIncrement parameter set to 0 is the right choice, as the following proposition shows.

Proposition 5.3: *If we create an initially empty* java.util.Vector *object with a fixed positive* capacityIncrement *value, then performing a series of n push operations on this vector takes* $\Omega(n^2)$ *time.*

Justification: Let $c > 0$ be the capacityIncrement value, and let $c_0 > 0$ denote the initial size of the array. An overflow will be caused by an add operation when the current number of elements in the table is $c_0 + ic$, for $i = 0, \ldots, m-1$, where $m = \lfloor (n - c_0)/c \rfloor$. Hence, by Proposition 3.4, the total time for handling the overflows is proportional to

$$\sum_{i=0}^{m-1} (c_0 + ci) = c_0 m + c \sum_{i=0}^{m-1} i = c_0 m + c \frac{m(m-1)}{2},$$

which is $\Omega(n^2)$. Thus, performing the n push operations takes $\Omega(n^2)$ time. ∎

Figure 5.4 compares the running times of a series of push operations on an initially empty java.util.Vector, for two initial values of capacityIncrement.

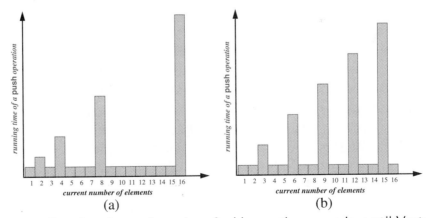

Figure 5.4: Running times of a series of add operations on a java.util.Vector instantiated with capacityIncrement equal to 0 in (a) and 3 in (b).

5.2   Lists

Using a rank is not the only means of referring to the place where an element
appears in a list. If we have a list S implemented with a (singly or doubly) linked
list, then it could possibly be more natural and efficient to use a **node** instead of a
rank as a means of identifying where to access and update a list. In this section, we
explore a way of abstracting the node concept of "place" in a list without revealing
the details of how the list is implemented.

5.2.1   Node-Based Operations

Let S be a linear list implemented using a doubly linked list. We would like to define
methods for S that take nodes of the list as parameters and provide nodes as return
types. Such methods could provide significant speedups over rank-based methods,
for finding the rank of an element in a linked list requires searching through the list
incrementally from its beginning or end, counting elements as we go.

For instance, we could define a hypothetical method removeAtNode(v) that
removes the element of S stored at node v of the list. Using a node as a parameter
allows us to remove an element in $O(1)$ time by simply going directly to the place
where that node is stored and then "linking out" this node through an update of the
next and *prev* links of its neighbors. Similarly, we could insert, in $O(1)$ time, a new
element e into S with an operation such as insertAfterNode(v, e), which specifies
the node v after which the node of the new element should be inserted. In this case,
we simply "link in" the new node.

Defining methods of a list ADT by adding such node-based operations raises
the issue of how much information we should be exposing about the implementation of our list. Certainly, it is desirable for us to be able to use either a singly or
doubly linked list without revealing this detail to a user. Likewise, we do not wish
to allow a user to modify the internal structure of a list without our knowledge.
Such modification would be possible, however, if we provided to a user a reference
to a node in our list in a form that allowed the user to access internal data in that
node (such as a *next* or *prev* field).

To abstract and unify the different ways of storing elements in the various implementations of a list, we introduce the concept of **position** in a list, which formal-
izes the intuitive notion of "place" of an element relative to others in the list.

5.2.2 Positions

So as to safely expand the set of operations for lists, we abstract a notion of "position" that allows us to enjoy the efficiency of doubly or singly linked list implementations without violating object-oriented design principles. In this framework, we view a list as a container of elements that stores each element at a position and that keeps these positions arranged in a linear order. A position is itself an abstract data type that supports the following simple method:

element(): Return the element stored at this position.
Input: None; *Output:* Object.

A position is always defined *relatively*, that is, in terms of its neighbors. In a list, a position p will always be "after" some position q and "before" some position s (unless p is the first or last position). A position p, which is associated with some element e in a list S, does not change, even if the rank of e changes in S, unless we explicitly remove e (and, hence, destroy position p). Moreover, the position p does not change even if we replace or swap the element e stored at p with another element. These facts about positions allow us to define a rich set of position-based list methods that take position objects as parameters and also provide position objects as return values.

5.2.3 The List Abstract Data Type

Using the concept of position to encapsulate the idea of "node" in a list, we can define another type of sequence ADT, called simply the *list* ADT. This ADT supports the following methods for a list S:

first(): Return the position of the first element of S; an error occurs if S is empty.
Input: None; *Output:* Position.

last(): Return the position of the last element of S; an error occurs if S is empty.
Input: None; *Output:* Position.

isFirst(p): Return a boolean value indicating whether the given position is the first one in the list.
Input: Position p; *Output:* Boolean.

isLast(p): Return a boolean value indicating whether the given position is the last one in the list.
Input: Position p; *Output:* Boolean.

before(p): Return the position of the element of S preceding the one at position p; an error occurs if p is the first position. *Input:* Position; *Output:* Position.

after(p): Return the position of the element of S following the one at position p; an error occurs if p is the last position. *Input:* Position; *Output:* Position.

The above methods allow us to refer to relative positions in a list, starting at the beginning or end, and to be able to move incrementally up or down the list. These positions can intuitively be thought of as nodes in the list, but note that there are no specific references to node objects and their *prev* and *next* links in these methods. In addition to the above methods and the generic methods size and isEmpty, we also include the following update methods for the list ADT.

replaceElement(p,e): Replace the element at position p with e, returning the element formerly at position p. *Input:* Position p and object e; *Output:* Object.

swapElements(p,q): Swap the elements stored at positions p and q, so that the element that is at position p moves to position q and the element that is at position q moves to position p. *Input:* Two positions; *Output:* None.

insertFirst(e): Insert a new element e into S as the first element. *Input:* Object e; *Output:* Position of the newly inserted element e.

insertLast(e): Insert a new element e into S as the last element. *Input:* Object e; *Output:* Position of the newly inserted element e.

insertBefore(p,e): Insert a new element e into S before position p in S; an error occurs if p is the first position. *Input:* Position p and Object e; *Output:* Position of the newly inserted element e.

insertAfter(p,e): Insert a new element e into S after position p in S; an error occurs if p is the last position. *Input:* Position p and Object e; *Output:* Position of the newly inserted element e.

remove(p): Remove from S the element at position p. *Input:* Position; *Output:* The removed element.

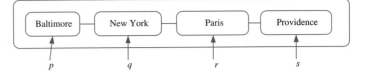

Figure 5.5: An illustration of a list. The positions in the current order are p, q, r, and s. E.g., q is defined as the position after position p and before position r.

The list ADT allows us to view an ordered collection of objects in terms of their places, without worrying about the exact way those places are represented. (See Figure 5.5.)

Also, note that there is some redundancy in the above repertory of operations for the list ADT. Namely, we can perform operation isFirst(p) by checking whether p is equal to the position returned by first(). Similarly, operation isLast(p) reduces to calling last(). We can also perform operation insertFirst(e) by performing the operation insertBefore(first(), e), and operation insertLast(e) can be replaced with insertAfter(last(), e). The redundant methods can be viewed as shortcuts for common operations that help code readability.

Note that an error condition occurs if a position passed as argument to one of the list operations is invalid. Reasons for a position p to be invalid include:

- $p = $ **null**
- p was previously deleted from the list
- p is a position of a different list.

We use an exception called InvalidPositionException in the above cases.

We illustrate the operations of the list ADT in the following example.

Example 5.4: *We show below a series of operations for an initially empty list S. We use variables p_1, p_2, and so on, to denote different positions, and we show the object currently stored at such a position in parentheses.*

Operation	Output	S
insertFirst(8)	$p_1(8)$	(8)
insertAfter(p_1,5)	$p_2(5)$	(8,5)
insertBefore(p_2,3)	$p_3(3)$	(8,3,5)
insertFirst(9)	$p_4(9)$	(9,8,3,5)
before(p_3)	$p_1(8)$	(9,8,3,5)
last()	$p_2(5)$	(9,8,3,5)
remove(p_4)	9	(8,3,5)
swapElements(p_1,p_2)	–	(5,3,8)
replaceElement(p_3,7)	3	(5,7,8)
insertAfter(first(),2)	$p_5(2)$	(5,2,7,8)

The list ADT, with its built-in notion of position, is useful in a number of settings. For example, a program that models several people playing a game of cards could model each person's hand as a list. Since most people like to keep cards of the same suit together, inserting and removing cards from a person's hand could be implemented using the methods of the list ADT, with the positions being determined by a natural ordering of the suits. Likewise, a simple text editor embeds the notion of positional insertion and removal, since such editors typically perform all updates relative to a *cursor*, which represents the current position in the list of characters of text being edited.

There are a number of different ways to implement the list ADT. Probably the most natural and efficient way is to use a doubly linked list. Next, we discuss how to achieve this common implementation using object-oriented design principles.

5.2.4 Doubly Linked List Implementation

Suppose we wish to implement the list ADT using a doubly linked list. We can simply make the nodes of the linked list implement the position ADT. That is, we have each node implement the Position interface and therefore define a method element(), which returns the element stored at the node. Thus, the nodes themselves act as positions. They are viewed internally by the linked list as nodes, but from the outside, they are viewed only as generic positions. In the internal view, we can give each node v instance variables prev and next that respectively refer to predecessor and successor nodes of v (which could in fact be header or trailer sentinel nodes marking the beginning and end of the list). Then, given a position p in S, we can "unwrap" p to reveal the node v. This is accomplished by *casting* the position to a node. Once we have node v, we can, for example, implement method before(p) by returning v.prev (unless v.prev is the header, in which case we signal an error). Therefore, positions in a doubly linked list implementation can be supported in an object-oriented way without any additional time or space overhead. Moreover, this approach has the advantage of hiding the implementation details of the list from a user, which aids in code reuse, since the user will not know that the position objects given as parameters and return values are actually node objects as well.

In Code Fragment 5.3, we show a Java class DNode for the nodes of a doubly linked list that implements the position ADT. This class is similar to class DLNode shown in Code Fragment 4.13. Note that the prev and next instance variables in this class are private references to other DNode objects. By making these fields private we achieve a degree of encapsulation, for we are hiding the details of how our nodes are implemented. Moreover, using these simple instance variables, we can use the doubly linked list to perform all the methods of the list ADT in $O(1)$ time. Thus, a doubly linked list is an efficient implementation of the list ADT.

```
class DNode implements Position {
  private DNode prev, next;    // References to the nodes before and after
  private Object element;      // Element stored in this position
  // Constructor
  public DNode(DNode newPrev, DNode newNext, Object elem) {
    prev = newPrev;
    next = newNext;
    element = elem;
  }
  // Method from interface Position
  public Object element() throws InvalidPositionException {
    if ((prev == null) && (next == null))
      throw new InvalidPositionException("Position is not in a list!");
    return element;
  }
  // Accessor methods
  public DNode getNext() { return next; }
  public DNode getPrev() { return prev; }
  // Update methods
  public void setNext(DNode newNext) { next = newNext; }
  public void setPrev(DNode newPrev) { prev = newPrev; }
  public void setElement(Object newElement) { element = newElement; }
}
```

Code Fragment 5.3: Class DNode realizing a node of a doubly linked list and implementing the Position interface (ADT). Note how accessor and update methods are used to access and update the instance variables.

Method element of the DNode class throws an InvalidPositionException when both its prev and next fields refer to the null object. The code for this exception is shown in Code Fragment 5.4.

```
// A run-time exception for invalid positions
public class InvalidPositionException extends RuntimeException {
  public InvalidPositionException(String err) {
    super(err);
  }
}
```

Code Fragment 5.4: Class InvalidPositionException for positions used incorrectly at run time. Note, in particular, that this class extends the RuntimeException class for error conditions that occur at run time.

Consider how we might implement the insertAfter(p, e) method, for inserting an element e after position p. We create a new node v to hold the element e, link v into its place in the list, and then update the next and prev references of v's two new neighbors. This method is given in pseudo-code in Code Fragment 5.5, and is illustrated in Figure 5.6. Recalling the use of header and trailer sentinels (Section 4.4.2), note that this algorithm works even if p is the last real position.

Algorithm insertAfter(p, e):

    Create a new node v

    v.setElement(e)

    v.setPrev(p)   {link v to its predecessor}

    v.setNext(p.getNext())   {link v to its successor}

    (p.getNext()).setPrev(v)   {link p's old successor to v}

    p.setNext(v)   {link p to its new successor, v}

    return v {the position for the element e}

Code Fragment 5.5: Inserting an element e after a position p in a linked list.

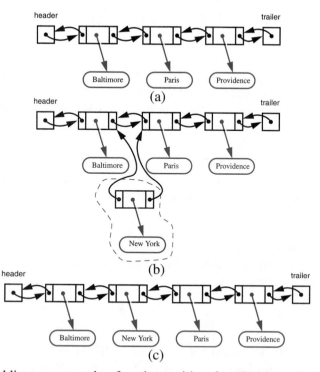

Figure 5.6: Adding a new node after the position for "Baltimore": (a) before the insertion; (b) creating node v and linking it in; (c) after the insertion.

The algorithms for methods insertBefore, insertFirst, and insertLast are similar to that for method insertAfter; we leave their details as an exercise (R-5.4). Next, consider the remove(p) method, which removes the element e stored at position p. To perform this operation we link the two neighbors of p to refer to one another as new neighbors—linking out p. Note that after p is linked out, no nodes will be pointing to p; hence, the garbage collector can reclaim the space for p. This algorithm is given in Code Fragment 5.6 and is illustrated in Figure 5.7. Recalling our use of sentinels, note that this algorithm works even if p is the first, last, or only real position in the list.

Algorithm remove(p):

    $t \leftarrow p.$element   {a temporary variable to hold the return value}

    ($p.$getPrev()).setNext($p.$getNext())   {linking out p}

    ($p.$getNext()).setPrev($p.$getPrev())

    $p.$setPrev(**null**)   {invalidating the position p}

    $p.$setNext(**null**)

    return t

Code Fragment 5.6: Removing an element e stored at a position p in a linked list.

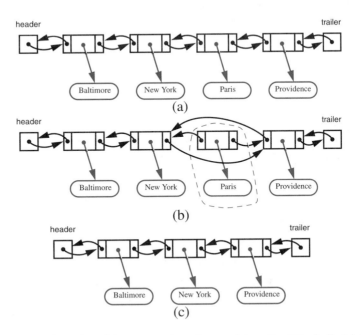

Figure 5.7: Removing the object stored at the position for "Paris:" (a) before the removal; (b) linking out the old node; (c) after the removal (and garbage collection).

Portions of the Java class NodeList, which implements the list ADT using a doubly linked list, are shown in Code Fragments 5.8–5.10. The specific List interface implemented is given in Code Fragment 5.7.

```java
public interface List {
  public int size();
  public boolean isEmpty();
  public boolean isFirst(Position p) throws InvalidPositionException;
  public boolean isLast(Position p) throws InvalidPositionException;
  public Position first() throws EmptyContainerException;
  public Position last() throws EmptyContainerException;
  public Position before (Position p)
    throws InvalidPositionException, BoundaryViolationException;
  public Position after (Position p)
    throws InvalidPositionException, BoundaryViolationException;
  public Position insertBefore (Position p, Object element)
    throws InvalidPositionException;
  public Position insertAfter (Position p, Object element)
    throws InvalidPositionException;
  public Position insertFirst(Object element);
  public Position insertLast(Object element);
  public Object remove(Position p) throws InvalidPositionException;
  public Object replaceElement (Position p, Object element)
    throws InvalidPositionException;
  public void swapElements (Position a, Position b)
    throws InvalidPositionException;
}
```

Code Fragment 5.7: A List interface.

Error conditions are signaled by the following exceptions:

EmptyContainerException: thrown if the list is empty and an attempt is made at accessing an element of it (for example, via the first method).

BoundaryViolationException: thrown if an attempt is made at accessing an element whose position is outside the range of positions of the list.

InvalidPositionException: thrown if a position provided as argument is not valid (for example, it is a null reference or it has no associated list).

Code Fragment 5.8 shows NodeList's instance variables, its constructor, some accessor methods, and a "convenience" method, checkPosition, which performs some safety checks and "unwraps" a position, casting it back to a DNode object. Code Fragment 5.9 shows additional accessor and update methods. Code Fragment 5.10 shows additional update methods.

```
public class NodeList implements List {
  protected int numElts;                // Number of items in the list
  protected DNode header, trailer;      // Special sentinels
  // Constructor; O(1) time
  public NodeList() {
    numElts = 0;
    header = new DNode(null, null, null);     // create header
    trailer = new DNode(header, null, null);  // create trailer
    header.setNext(trailer);       // make header and trailer point to each other
  }
  // Convenience function; O(1) time
  protected DNode checkPosition(Position p)
        throws InvalidPositionException {
    if (p == null)
      throw new InvalidPositionException
        ("Null Position passed to NodeList.");
    if (p == header)
      throw new InvalidPositionException
        ("The header node is not a valid position");
    if (p == trailer)
      throw new InvalidPositionException
        ("The trailer node is not a valid position");
    try {
      DNode temp = (DNode)p;
      if ((temp.getPrev() == null) || (temp.getNext() == null))
        throw new InvalidPositionException
          ("Position does not belong to a valid NodeList");
      return temp;
    } catch (ClassCastException e) {
      throw new InvalidPositionException
        ("Position is of wrong type for this container.");
    }
  }
  // Simple accessor methods:
  public int size() {  return numElts; }              // O(1) time
  public boolean isEmpty() { return (numElts < 1); } // O(1) time
  public boolean isFirst(Position p)                  // O(1) time
      throws InvalidPositionException {
    DNode v = checkPosition(p);
    return v.getPrev() == header;
  }
```

Code Fragment 5.8: Portions of the NodeList class: variables, constructor, a convenience function, and some simple accessor methods. (See Code Fragments 5.9 and 5.10.)

```java
public Position first()                                  // O(1) time
    throws EmptyContainerException {
  if (isEmpty())
    throw new EmptyContainerException("List is empty");
  return header.getNext();
}
public Position last()                                   // O(1) time
    throws EmptyContainerException {
  if (isEmpty())
    throw new EmptyContainerException("List is empty");
  return trailer.getPrev();
}
public Position before(Position p)                       // O(1) time
    throws InvalidPositionException, BoundaryViolationException {
  DNode v = checkPosition(p);
  DNode prev = v.getPrev();
  if (prev == header)
    throw new BoundaryViolationException
      ("Cannot advance past the beginning of the list");
  return prev;
}
public Position insertBefore(Position p, Object element)
    throws InvalidPositionException {                    // O(1) time
  DNode v = checkPosition(p);
  numElts++;
  DNode newNode = new DNode(v.getPrev(), v, element);
  v.getPrev().setNext(newNode);
  v.setPrev(newNode);
  return newNode;
}
public Position insertFirst(Object element) {            // O(1) time
  numElts++;
  DNode newNode = new DNode(header, header.getNext(), element);
  header.getNext().setPrev(newNode);
  header.setNext(newNode);
  return newNode;
}
```

Code Fragment 5.9: Additional accessor and insert methods of the NodeList class. (See also Code Fragments 5.8 and 5.10.)

```
        public Object remove(Position p)                      // O(1) time
            throws InvalidPositionException {
          DNode v = checkPosition(p);
          numElts--;
          DNode vPrev = v.getPrev();
          DNode vNext = v.getNext();
          vPrev.setNext(vNext);
          vNext.setPrev(vPrev);
          Object vElem = v.element();
          // unlink the position from the list and make it invalid
          v.setNext(null);
          v.setPrev(null);
          return vElem;
        }

        public Object replaceElement(Position p, Object element)
            throws InvalidPositionException {                 // O(1) time
          DNode v = checkPosition(p);
          Object oldElt = v.element();
          v.setElement(element);
          return oldElt;
        }

        public void swapElements(Position a, Position b)
            throws InvalidPositionException {                 // O(1) time
          DNode pA = checkPosition(a);
          DNode pB = checkPosition(b);
          Object temp = pA.element();
          pA.setElement(pB.element());
          pB.setElement(temp);
        }
```

Code Fragment 5.10: Additional remove and update methods in the NodeList class. Note that the mechanism used to invalidate a position in the remove method is consistent with one of the checks performed in the checkPosition convenience function. (See Code Fragments 5.8 and 5.9.)

5.3 Sequences

In this section, we define a generalized sequence ADT that includes all the methods of the vector and list ADTs. This ADT therefore provides access to its elements using both ranks and positions, and is a versatile data structure for a wide variety of applications.

5.3.1 The Sequence Abstract Data Type

A *sequence* is an ADT that supports all the methods of both the vector ADT (discussed in Section 5.1) and the list ADT (discussed in Section 5.2), plus the following two "bridging" methods that provide connections between ranks and positions:

> atRank(r): Return the position of the element with rank r.
> *Input:* Integer; *Output:* Position.

> rankOf(p): Return the rank of the element at position p.
> *Input:* Position; *Output:* Integer.

The definition of the sequence ADT is an example of ***multiple inheritance***, since the sequence inherits methods from two other "super" ADTs. Therefore, its methods include the union of the methods of its super ADTs. See Code Fragment 5.11 for a Java specification.

```
interface Sequence extends List, Vector {
  // Additional "bridging" methods:
  public Position atRank(int rank) throws BoundaryViolationException;
  public int rankOf(Position position) throws InvalidPositionException;
}
```

Code Fragment 5.11: The sequence interface defined via multiple inheritance.

5.3.2 Implementing a Sequence with a Doubly Linked List

One possible implementation of a sequence, of course, is with a doubly linked list. Then, all of the methods of the list ADT can be easily implemented to run in $O(1)$ time each. But the methods from the vector ADT can also be implemented with a doubly linked list, though in a less efficient manner. In particular, if we want the methods from the list ADT to run efficiently (using position objects to indicate where accesses and updates should occur), then we can no longer explicitly store the ranks of elements in the sequence. Hence, to perform the operation elemAtRank(r), we must perform link "hopping" from one of the ends of the list until we locate the node storing the element with rank r. As a slight optimization, we can start hopping from the closest end of the sequence, achieving a running time that is

$$O(\min(r+1, n-r)),$$

which is $O(n)$. The worst case occurs when

$$r = \lfloor n/2 \rfloor.$$

Operations insertAtRank(r, e) and removeAtRank(r) also perform link hopping to locate the node storing the element with rank r, and then insert or delete a node, as shown in Figures 5.6. and 5.7. The running time of this implementation of insertAtRank(r, e) and removeAtRank(r) is

$$O(\min(r+1, n-r+1)),$$

which is $O(n)$. One advantage of this approach is that, if $r = 0$ or $r = n-1$, as is the case in the adaptation of the vector ADT to the deque ADT given in Section 5.1.1, then insertAtRank and removeAtRank run in $O(1)$ time.

In Code Fragment 5.12, we show selected portions of a Java implementation of the Sequence interface by means of a doubly linked list. Note that this implementation is a class, NodeSequence, that extends (through class inheritance) the implementation of a list given in Section 5.3.2. Like its parent class, NodeList, the class NodeSequence uses class DNode for the implementation of the nodes of a doubly linked list. It also uses an internal convenience method, checkRank(r) that throws a BoundaryViolationException when its argument r is an invalid rank, that is, if

$$r < 0 \quad \textbf{or} \quad r > n-1.$$

The worst-case running times of the methods of a vector implemented by means of a doubly linked list are the same as those of the implementation with an array (see Table 5.2), except for the method elemAtRank. The doubly linked list implementation has the advantage that it requires space $O(n)$, proportional to the number of elements effectively present in the sequence, whereas the array implementation needs space proportional to the size of the array. The trade-off is that operation elemAtRank is more efficient in the array implementation, since this operation requires $O(n)$ time in the worst case when we use a doubly linked list. Still, implementing a sequence with a doubly linked list allows other kinds of insertion and deletion operations to be performed very quickly; namely, the methods of the list ADT.

```
public class NodeSequence extends NodeList implements Sequence {
  // Check that rank is in the range [0,numElts-1]; O(1) time
  protected void checkRank(int rank)
      throws BoundaryViolationException {
    if (rank < 0 || rank >= numElts)
      throw new BoundaryViolationException("Rank " + rank +
        " is invalid for this sequence of " + numElts + " elements.");
  }
  public Position atRank (int rank) {              // O(1) time
    DNode node;
    checkRank(rank);
    if (rank <= size()/2) { // scan forward from the head
      node = header.getNext();
      for (int i=0; i < rank; i++)
        node = node.getNext();
    }
    else { // scan backward from the tail
      node = trailer.getPrev();
      for (int i=1; i < size()-rank; i++)
        node = node.getPrev();
    }
    return node;
  }
  // . . . (skipping methods elemAtRank(r) and rankOf(p))
  public void insertAtRank (int rank, Object element)
      throws BoundaryViolationException {    // O(n) time
    if (rank == size()) // we shouldn't checkRank in this case
      insertLast(element);
    else {
      checkRank(rank);
      insertBefore(atRank(rank), element);
    }
  }
  public Object removeAtRank (int rank)        // O(n) time
    throws BoundaryViolationException {
    checkRank(rank);
    return remove(atRank(rank));
  }
  public Object replaceAtRank (int rank, Object element)
      throws BoundaryViolationException {    // O(n) time
    checkRank(rank);
    return replaceElement(atRank(rank),element);
  }
}
```

Code Fragment 5.12: Excerpts from a linked-list Sequence implementation.

5.3.3 Implementing a Sequence with an Array

Suppose we want to implement a sequence S by storing each element e of S in a cell $A[i]$ of an array A. We can define a position object p to hold an index i and a reference to array A, as instance variables. We can then implement method element(p) by simply returning $A[i]$. A major drawback with this approach, however, is that the cells in A have no way to reference their corresponding positions. Thus, after performing an insertFirst operation, we have no way of informing the existing positions in S that their ranks each went up by 1 (remember that positions in a sequence are always defined relative to their neighboring positions, not their ranks). Hence, if we are going to implement a general sequence with an array, we need a different approach.

Consider an alternate solution in which, instead of storing the elements of S in array A, we store a new kind of position object in each cell of A, and we store elements in positions. The new position object p holds the index i and the element e associated with p. With this data structure, illustrated in Figure 5.8, we can easily scan through the array to update the i variable for each position whose rank changes because of an insertion or deletion.

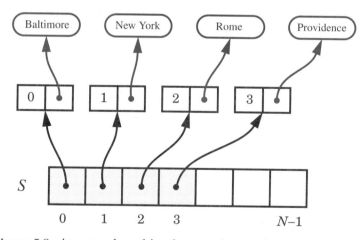

Figure 5.8: An array-based implementation of the sequence ADT.

In this array implementation of a sequence, methods insertFirst, insertBefore, insertAfter, and remove take $O(n)$ time because we have to shift position objects to make room for the new position or to fill in the hole created by the removal of the old position (just as in the insert and remove methods based on rank). All the other position-based methods take $O(1)$ time.

Note that we can use an array in a circular fashion like we used for implementing a queue (see Section 4.2.2). With a little work, we can then perform method insertFirst in $O(1)$ time. Note that methods insertBefore, insertAfter, and remove still take $O(n)$ time. Now, the worst case occurs when the element to be inserted or removed has rank $\lfloor n/2 \rfloor$.

5.3.4 Comparing Sequence Implementations

Table 5.4 compares the running times of the implementations of the general sequence ADT, by means of an array (used in a circular fashion) and by means of a doubly linked list.

Operations	Array	List
size, isEmpty	$O(1)$	$O(1)$
atRank, rankOf, elemAtRank	$O(1)$	$O(n)$
first, last, before, after	$O(1)$	$O(1)$
replaceElement, swapElements	$O(1)$	$O(1)$
replaceAtRank	$O(1)$	$O(n)$
insertAtRank, removeAtRank	$O(n)$	$O(n)$
insertFirst, insertLast	$O(1)$	$O(1)$
insertAfter, insertBefore,	$O(n)$	$O(1)$
remove	$O(n)$	$O(1)$

Table 5.4: Comparison of the running times of the methods of a sequence implemented with either an array (used in a circular fashion) or a doubly linked list. We denote with n the number of elements in the sequence at the time the operation is performed. The space usage is $O(n)$ for the doubly linked list implementation, and $O(N)$ for the array implementation, where N is the size of the array.

Summarizing this table, we see that the array-based implementation is superior to the linked-list implementation on the rank-based access operations (atRank, rankOf, and elemAtRank), and it is equal in performance to the linked-list implementation on all the other access operations. Regarding update operations, the linked-list implementation beats the array-based implementation in the position-based update operations (insertAfter, insertBefore, and remove). Even so, the array-based and linked-list implementations have the same worst-case performance on the rank-based update methods (insertAtRank and removeAtRank), though for different reasons. In update operations insertFirst and insertLast, the two implementations have comparable performance.

Considering space usage, note that an array requires $O(N)$ space, where N is the size of the array (unless we utilize an extendable array), while a doubly linked list uses $O(n)$ space, where n is the number of elements in the sequence. Since n is less than or equal to N, this implies that the asymptotic space usage of a linked-list implementation is superior to that of a fixed-size array, although there is a small constant factor overhead that is larger for linked lists, since arrays do not need links to maintain the ordering of their cells.

The array and linked-list implementations each have their advantages and disadvantages. The correct one for a particular application depends on the kinds of operations that are to be performed and the memory space available. Designing the sequence ADT in a way that does not depend on the way it is implemented allows us to easily switch between implementations, enabling the use of the implementation that best suits our applications with few changes to our program.

5.4   Case Study: Bubble-Sort on a Sequence

In this section, we illustrate the use of the sequence ADT and its implementation trade-offs with sample Java methods, using the well-known ***bubble-sort*** algorithm.

5.4.1   The Bubble-Sort Algorithm

Consider a sequence of n elements such that any two elements in the sequence can be compared according to an order relation (for example, companies compared by revenue, states compared by population, or words compared lexicographically). The ***sorting*** problem is to reorder the sequence so that the elements are in nondecreasing order. The ***bubble-sort*** algorithm (see Figure 5.9) solves this problem by performing a series of ***passes*** over the sequence. In each pass, the elements are scanned by increasing rank, from rank 0 to the end of the sequence. At each position in a pass, an element is compared with its neighbor, and if these two consecutive elements are found to be in the wrong relative order (that is, the preceding element is larger than the succeeding one), then the two elements are swapped. The sequence is sorted by completing n such passes.

The bubble-sort algorithm has the following property:

- In the first pass, once the largest element is reached, it will keep on being swapped until it gets to the last position of the sequence.
- In the second pass, once the second largest element is reached, it will keep on being swapped until it gets to the second-to-last position of the sequence.
- And so on.

pass	swaps	sequence
		$(5,7,2,6,9,3)$
1st	$7 \leftrightarrow 2$ $7 \leftrightarrow 6$ $9 \leftrightarrow 3$	$(5,2,6,7,3,9)$
2nd	$5 \leftrightarrow 2$ $7 \leftrightarrow 3$	$(2,5,6,3,7,9)$
3rd	$6 \leftrightarrow 3$	$(2,5,3,6,7,9)$
4th	$5 \leftrightarrow 3$	$(2,3,5,6,7,9)$

Figure 5.9: The bubble-sort algorithm on a sequence of integers. For each pass, the swaps performed and the sequence after the pass are shown.

Thus, at the end of the ith pass, the right-most i elements of the sequence (that is, those with ranks from $n-1$ down to $n-i$) are in final position. This observation implies that it is correct to limit the number of passes made by a bubble-sort on an n-element sequence to n. Moreover, it allows the ith pass to be limited to the first $n-i+1$ elements of the sequence.

5.4.2 A Sequence-Based Analysis of Bubble-Sort

Assume that the implementation of the sequence is such that the accesses to elements and the swaps of elements performed by bubble-sort take $O(1)$ time each. That is, the running time of the ith pass is $O(n-i+1)$. We have that the overall running time of bubble-sort is

$$O\left(\sum_{i=1}^{n}(n-i+1) \right).$$

We can rewrite the above sum as

$$O\left(n + (n-1) + \cdots + 2 + 1\right).$$

That is, it is

$$O\left(\sum_{i=1}^{n} i \right).$$

By Proposition 3.4, we have

$$\sum_{i=1}^{n} i = \frac{n(n+1)}{2}.$$

Thus, bubble-sort runs in $O(n^2)$ time provided that accesses and swaps can each be implemented in $O(1)$ time.

```java
// Bubble-sort using ranks
public static void bubbleSort1(Sequence S) {
  int n = S.size();
  for (int i=0; i < n; i++)    // i-th pass
    for (int j=1; j < n−i; j++)
      if ( valAtRank(S, j−1) > valAtRank(S, j) )
        S.swapElements(S.atRank(j−1), S.atRank(j));
}
// Bubble-sort using positions
public static void bubbleSort2(Sequence S) {
  Position prec, succ;
  int n = S.size();
  for (int i=0; i < n; i++) { // i-th pass
    prec = S.first();
    for (int j=1; j < n−i; j++) {
      succ = S.after(prec);
      if ( valAtPos(prec) > valAtPos(succ) )
        S.swapElements(prec, succ);
      prec = succ;
    }
  }
}
private static int valAtRank(Sequence S, int i) {
  return ((Integer) S.elemAtRank(i)).intValue();
}
private static int valAtPos(Position p) {
  return ((Integer) p.element()).intValue();
}
```

Code Fragment 5.13: A class containing two Java implementations of bubble-sort on a sequence of Integer objects.

Code Fragment 5.13 contains two Java implementations of bubble-sort on a sequence of Integer objects. The two implementations differ in the preferred choice of methods to access and modify the sequence.

Note that method BubbleSort1 accesses the elements only through the rank-based interface methods atRank and elemAtRank. It is a rank-based implementation of the bubble-sort algorithm, and it is suitable only for the array implementation of the sequence, where atRank and elemAtRank take $O(1)$ time. Given such an array-based implementation, this method will run in $O(n^2)$ time. On the other hand, if we implement the sequence used by this algorithm using a doubly linked list, then each atRank call takes $O(n)$ time in the worst case; hence, the entire algorithm would actually run in $O(n^3)$ worst-case time with a linked-list implementation.

Method BubbleSort2 accesses the elements only through the position-based interface methods first and after. It is a position-based implementation of the bubble-sort algorithm, and it is suitable for both the array and the linked-list implementation of the sequence. Indeed, both implementations support constant-time performance for the first and after methods. Thus, BubbleSort2 runs in $\Theta(n^2)$ time, no matter which implementation is used for the sequence.

The two bubble-sort implementations given above show the importance of providing efficient implementations of ADTs. Nevertheless, in spite of its implementation simplicity, computing researchers generally feel that the bubble-sort algorithm is not a good sorting method, because, even if implemented in the best possible way, it still takes quadratic time. Indeed, there are sorting algorithms that run in $O(n \log n)$ time, and are thus much more efficient than bubble-sort. We explore some of them in Chapters 7 and 10.

5.5 Iterators

A typical computation on a vector, list, or sequence is to march through its elements in order, one at a time, for example, to look for a specific element.

An *iterator* is a software design pattern that abstracts the process of scanning through a collection of elements one element at a time. An iterator consists of a sequence S, a current position in S, and a way of stepping to the next position in S and making it the current position. Thus, an iterator extends the concept of the position ADT we introduced in Section 5.2. In fact, a position can be thought of as an iterator that doesn't go anywhere. An iterator encapsulates the concepts of "place" and "next" in a collection of objects.

We define the ObjectIterator ADT as supporting the following two methods:

hasNext: Test whether there are elements left in the iterator.
               Input: None; *Output:* Boolean.

nextObject: Return and remove the next element in the iterator.
               Input: None; *Output:* Object.

Note that this ADT has the notion of the "current" element in a traversal through a sequence. The first element in an iterator is returned by the first call to the method nextObject, assuming of course that the iterator contains at least one element.

An iterator provides a unified scheme to access all the elements of a container (a collection of objects) in a way that is independent from the specific organization of the collection. An iterator for a sequence should return the elements according to their linear ordering.

Java provides an iterator through its java.util.Iterator interface. This interface uses the terser name next instead of nextObject and supports an additional method to remove the previously returned element from the collection. The latter functionality (removing elements through an iterator) is somewhat controversial from an object-oriented viewpoint, and it is not surprising that its implementation by classes is optional. Incidentally, Java also provides the java.util.Enumeration interface, which is historically older than the iterator interface and uses names hasMoreElements and nextElement.

In order to provide a unified generic mechanism for scanning through a container, ADTs storing collections of objects should support a method elements() that returns an iterator of the elements in the collection. This method is supported by the java.util.Vector interface. In Code Fragment 5.14, we show an example of using a java.util.Iterator for printing the elements of a java.util.Vector.

```
public static void printVector(java.util.Vector vec) {
  java.util.Iterator iter = vec.iterator();
  while (iter.hasNext()) {
    System.out.println(iter.next());
  }
}
```

Code Fragment 5.14: Example of a Java iterator used to print the elements of a vector.

For ADTs that support the notion of position, such as the list and sequence ADTs, we can also provide a method positions() that returns an iterator of the positions in the container. To avoid the need to cast the object returned by the method nextObject into a position, we conveniently define the Java interface PositionIterator that extends ObjectIterator and supports the additional method:

nextPosition: Return and remove the next position in the iterator.
Input: None; ***Output:*** Object.

We can use many of the data structures presented in this and the previous chapter to implement an iterator. For example, we can implement an iterator by inserting all the elements of the collection into a stack. Method hasNext() corresponds to isEmpty(), while method nextObject corresponds to pop(). In case there is a given order in which the elements should be returned by the iterator, we should insert the elements into the stack in reverse order. Alternatively, we can realize an iterator with a queue, which allows us to insert the elements in order.

The iterator methods given above define a restricted type of iterator that allows only one pass through the elements. More powerful iterators can also be defined, which allow one to move forward and backward over a certain ordering of the elements, and that provide repeated access to the current element. An important application of a sequence is to realize such iterators: namely, an iterator can be implemented with a sequence S and a position *cur* that keeps track of the current element.

A new iterator may or may not be a copied "snapshot" of its container. It is therefore generally considered dangerous practice to use an iterator while modifying the contents of its container. Indeed, many of the concrete implementations of the java.util.Iterator have a "fail-fast" feature that crashes the iterator if its underlying container is modified unexpectedly. Of course, this danger is not shared by position objects, which are used in the list ADT to specify update locations, since position objects do not move.

5.6   A Hierarchy of Sequence ADTs

In this chapter, we have presented three ADTs for sequences: vector, list, and sequence. These ADTs can be further refined, by grouping methods with similar purpose, and can be organized in a coherent inheritance hierarchy.

5.6.1   Methods of a Container

A *container* is a data structure that stores and organizes a collection of objects, called the elements of the container, and provides access to them through the methods of an abstract data type. Some people use the term *collection* instead of container with essentially the same meaning.

Stacks, queues, deques, vectors, lists, and sequences, which we studied in this chapter and the previous one, are all examples of containers. However, a position is not a container, since it stores a single element and not a collection of elements.

The methods of a container specified by its ADT can be grouped in four main categories:

- *Query methods* that return information on the container or specific elements of it (for example, method size). These methods typically have a Boolean or integer return type.
- *Accessor methods* that return elements or positions of the container (for example, method first in a sequence).
- *Update methods* that change the container by adding elements (for example, the insertAtRank method of a vector), removing elements (for example, the dequeue method of a queue), or altering the relation between elements (for example, the swapElements method of a list).

In addition, a concrete implementation of a container must also provide:

- *Constructor methods* that generate an instance of the container. For example, the NodeList class has a constructor returning an empty list (see Code Fragment 5.8).

5.6.2 Inspectable Containers

Containers that do not provide update methods are called *inspectable containers*. Once instantiated via a constructor, these containers support "read-only" access and cannot be modified. Thus, they protect their elements from erroneous or malicious update attempts by other objects. Note that some authors use the term "immutable" instead of "inspectable" for inspectable containers.

An obvious limitation of inspectable containers is that they cannot be used when their elements are subject to updates during the life of the container. However, by exploiting inheritance, we can actually get all the protection provided by inspectable containers while at the same time retaining the flexibility of update methods. Consider, for example, the vector ADT defined in Section 5.1.1. We can restructure this ADT as follows (see Figure 5.10):

- We introduce a new ADT, called *inspectable vector*, that contains only the query methods size and isEmpty, and the accessor method elemAtRank.
- We redefine a vector as an ADT that *extends* the inspectable vector ADT and *adds* the update methods replaceAtRank, insertAtRank, and removeAtRank.

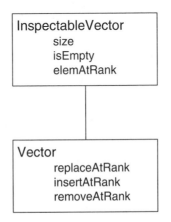

Figure 5.10: Java inheritance hierarchy where interface Sequence inherits from Sequence.

The revised vector ADT is functionally equivalent to the original one, that is, it provides the same methods. However, we now have a simple and powerful way to protect instances of the vector ADT. Namely, we can reference a vector instance vect with a variable of type inspectable vector, thus allowing only the query and accessor methods to be executed on vect. Likewise, we can restructure the list and sequence ADTs by introducing inspectable versions of them.

5.6.3   Inheritance Structure of Sequence ADTs

After separating the update methods from the other methods, we need to restructure the simple hierarchical organization of the vector, list, and sequence ADTs given in Section 5.3.1. For this purpose, we introduce a super-interface, InspectableContainer, that provides the generic methods size, isEmpty, and elements. By exploiting the power of multiple inheritance, we finally obtain the organization shown in Figure 5.11. In Exercise C-5.16 we explore how to extend the ADT hierarchy to include the stack, queue, and deque ADTs given in Chapter 4.

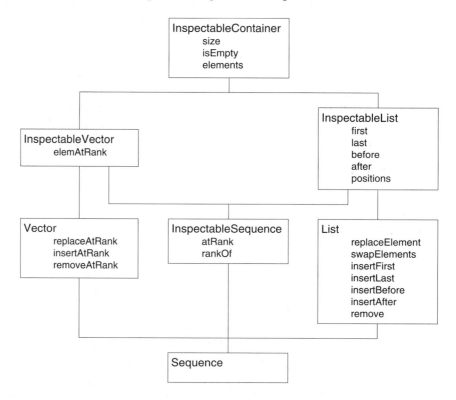

Figure 5.11: Inheritance hierarchy for ADTs representing sequences.

5.7 Exercises

Reinforcement

R-5.1 Give a detailed justification of the running times shown in Table 5.2 for the methods of a vector implemented with an array that does not expand in size.

R-5.2 Give an adapter class to support the Stack interface using the methods of the vector ADT.

R-5.3 Rewrite the justification of Proposition 5.2 under the assumption that the the cost of growing the array from size k to size $2k$ is $3k$ cyber-dollars. How much should each push operation be charged to make the amortization work?

R-5.4 Give pseudo-code descriptions of algorithms for performing the methods insertBefore(p, e), insertFirst(e), and insertLast(e) of the list ADT, assuming the list is implemented using a doubly linked list.

R-5.5 Draw pictures illustrating each of the major steps in the algorithms given in the previous exercise.

R-5.6 Draw a picture illustrating the final state of a doubly linked list after performing the algorithm for insertAfter(p, e), but with the order of the last two assignment statements in Code Fragment 5.5 reversed, so that the pseudo-code (which is now incorrect) would become:

> Create a new node v
> v.setElement(e)
> v.setPrev(p)
> v.setNext$(p$.getNext$())$
> p.setNext(v)
> $(p$.getNext$())$.setPrev(v)
> **return** v

R-5.7 Provide the details of an array implementation of the list ADT. In particular, describe how the index fields of the position objects are updated after an insertion or deletion of an element.

R-5.8 Provide Java code fragments for the methods of the List interface of Code Fragment 5.7 that are not included in Code Fragments 5.8–5.10.

R-5.9 Let MySequence be a sequence of 99 Dalmatian puppies, and let Boiler be a Dalmatian puppy. Give the value returned or the exception thrown by each of the following statements that make calls to methods of the MySequence object:

    a. size()
    b. isEmpty()
    c. rankOf(first())
    d. rankOf(last())
    e. rankOf(atRank(0))
    f. rankOf(atRank(99))
    g. rankOf(atRank(100))
    h. rankOf(atRank(size()))
    i. rankOf(before(last()))
    j. rankOf(after(before(first())))
    k. rankOf(insertFirst(Boiler))
    l. rankOf(insertBefore(first(), Boiler))
    m. remove(first())
    n. remove(insertAtRank(1, Boiler))

R-5.10 Give pseudo-code describing how to implement all the operations in the sequence ADT using an array used in a circular fashion. What is the running time for each of these methods?

R-5.11 Using the Sequence interface methods, describe a recursive method for determining if a sequence S of n integer objects contains a given integer k. Your method should not contain any loops. How much space does your method use in addition to the space used for S?

R-5.12 Give a short fragment of pseudo-code describing a new sequence method makeFirst(p) that moves the element of a sequence S at position p to be the first element in S while keeping the relative ordering of the remaining elements in S unchanged. Your method should run in $O(1)$ time if S is implemented with a doubly linked list.

R-5.13 Describe how to use a list and a position in that list to implement an iterator. Include pseudo-code fragments describing the methods hasNext() and nextObject().

R-5.14 Describe how to use a vector and an integer rank index to implement an iterator. Include pseudo-code fragments describing the methods hasNext() and nextObject().

Creativity

C-5.1 Describe what changes need to be made to the extendable array implementation given in Code Fragment 5.2 in order to avoid unexpected termination due to an error. Specify the new types of exceptions you would add, and when and where they should be thrown.

C-5.2 Give complete Java code for a new class, ShrinkingVector, that extends the ArrayVector class shown in Code Fragment 5.2 and adds a method, shrinkToFit(), which replaces the underlying array with an array whose capacity is exactly equal to the number of elements currently in the vector.

C-5.3 Describe what changes need to be made to the extendable array implementation given in Code Fragment 5.2 in order to shrink by half the size N of the array any time the number of elements in the vector goes below $N/4$.

C-5.4★ Show that using an extendable array that grows and shrinks as described in the previous exercise implies that a sequence of n insertions and removals at the end of a vector with initial capacity $N = 1$ takes $O(n)$ time.

C-5.5 Show how to improve the implementation of method insertAtRank in Code Fragment 5.2 so that, in case of an overflow, the elements are copied into their final place in the new array.

C-5.6★ Consider an implementation of the vector ADT using an extendable array, but instead of copying the elements of the vector into an array of double the size (that is, from N to $2N$) when its capacity is reached, we copy the elements into an array with $\lceil \sqrt{N} \rceil$ additional cells, going from capacity N to $N + \lceil \sqrt{N} \rceil$. Show that performing a sequence of n push operations (that is, insertions at the end) runs in $\Theta(n^{3/2})$ time in this case.

C-5.7 The NodeList implementation given in Code Fragments 5.8–5.10 does not do any error checks to test if a given position p is actually a member of this particular list. For example, if p is a position in list S and we call T.insertAfter(p, e) on a different list T, then we actually will add the element to S just after p. Describe how to change the NodeList implementation in an efficient manner to disallow such misuses.

C-5.8 Describe an implementation of the methods insertLast and insertBefore realized by using combinations of only the methods isEmpty, checkPosition, insertAfter, and insertFirst.

C-5.9 Compare the methods of the java.util.Vector class with the methods of the Sequence interface, presented in this chapter, by answering the following questions:

a. Why are indices in the Vector class not equivalent to positions in the Sequence class? Show your answer with an example.

b. Which methods of Vector and Sequence are completely equivalent?

c. Which methods of Vector do not have an equivalent in Sequence?

d. Which methods of Sequence do not have an equivalent in Vector?

C-5.10 Suppose we want to extend the Sequence abstract data type with methods rankOfElement(e) and positionOfElement(e), which respectively return the rank and the position of the (first occurrence of) element e in the sequence. Show how to implement these methods by expressing them in terms of other methods of the Sequence interface.

C-5.11 Consider the following fragment of Java code, assuming that the constructor MySequence() creates an empty sequence of integer objects. Recall that "/" denotes integer division (for example, $7/2 = 3$):

```
Sequence seq = new MySequence();
for (int i=0; i<n; i++)
    seq.insertAtRank((i/2, Integer(i));
```

a. Assume that the **for** loop is executed 10 times, that is, n=10, and show the sequence after each iteration of the loop.

b. Draw a schematic illustration of the sequence at the end of the **for** loop, for a generic number n of iterations.

(Hint: Consider separately the cases of n being even and n being odd.)

C-5.12 Design algorithms for reversing a sequence that access the sequence only through a restricted set of methods, as indicated below. Each algorithm should rearrange the elements of the sequence. Returning a new sequence is not allowed. However, using other sequences for auxiliary storage is allowed.

a. Reverse a sequence using only methods size, first, last, remove, and insertFirst.

b. Reverse a sequence using only size, first, remove, and insertFirst.

C-5.13 Give an adaptation of the vector ADT to the deque ADT that is different from that given in Table 5.1.

C-5.14 Describe the structure and pseudo-code for an array-based implementation of the vector ADT that achieves $O(1)$ time for insertions and removals at rank 0, as well as insertions and removals at the end of the vector. Your implementation should also provide for a constant time elemAtRank method. (Hint: Think about how to extend the circular array implementation of the queue ADT given in the previous chapter.)

C-5.15 Give a Java code fragment for the method rankOf(p), which is missing from the implementation given in Code Fragment 5.12.

C-5.16 Extend the inheritance hierarchy shown in Figure 5.10 to include the stack, queue, and deque ADTs.

C-5.17 In the children's game "hot potato," a group of n children sit in a circle passing an object, called the "potato," around the circle (say in a clockwise direction). The children continue passing the potato until a leader rings a bell, at which point the child holding the potato must leave the game, and the other children close up the circle. This process is then continued until there is only one child remaining, who is declared the winner. Using the sequence ADT, describe an efficient method for implementing this game. Suppose the leader always rings the bell immediately after the potato has been passed k times. (Determining the last child remaining in this variation of hot potato is known as the *Josephus problem*.) What is the running time of your method, in terms of n and k, assuming the sequence is implemented with a doubly linked list? What if the sequence is implemented with an array?

C-5.18★ Using the Sequence ADT, describe an efficient way of putting a sequence representing a deck of n cards into random order. You may use a function, randomInteger(n), which returns a random number between 0 and $n - 1$, inclusive. Your method should guarantee that every possible ordering is equally likely. What is the running time of your method, if the sequence is implemented with an array? What if it is implemented with a linked list?

C-5.19 Using the Enumeration ADT, describe an algorithm for finding the minimum and maximum of a sequence of integer elements using, at most, $3n/2$ comparisons between elements. (Hint: Consider the elements in pairs.)

C-5.20 Show that only $n - 1$ passes are needed in the execution of bubble-sort on a sequence with n elements.

C-5.21 Give a pseudo-code description of an implementation of the bubble-sort algorithm that uses only two stacks and, at most, five additional variables to sort a collection of objects stored initially in one of the stacks. You may operate on the stacks using only methods of the stack ADT. The final output should be one of the stacks containing all the elements so that a sequence of pop operations would list the elements in order.

C-5.22 Give a pseudo-code description of an implementation of the bubble-sort algorithm that uses only one queue and, at most, five additional variables to sort a collection of objects stored initially in the queue. You may operate on the queue using only methods of the queue ADT. The final output should be the queue containing all the elements so that a sequence of dequeue operations would list the elements in order.

Projects

P-5.1 Implement the vector ADT by means of an extendable array used in a circular fashion, so that insertions and deletions at the beginning and end of the vector run in constant time.

P-5.2 Write a simple text editor, which stores a string of characters using the list ADT, together with a cursor object that highlights the position of some character in the string (or possibly the position before the first character). Your editor should support the following operations and redisplay the current text (that is, the list) after performing any one of them.

- left: move cursor left one character (or do nothing if at end of the text).
- right: move cursor right one character (or do nothing if at end of the text).
- delete: delete the character to the right of the cursor (or do nothing if at end of the text).
- insert c: insert the character c just after the cursor.

P-5.3 Implement the sequence ADT by means of an extendable array used in a circular fashion, so that insertions and deletions at the beginning and end of the sequence run in constant time.

P-5.4 Implement the sequence ADT by means of a singly linked list.

P-5.5 Write a complete adapter class that implements the sequence ADT using a java.util.Vector object.

P-5.6 Write a simulator for a person arranging a group of cards in his or her hand. The simulator should represent the sequence of cards using the list ADT so that cards of the same suit are kept together. Implement this strategy by means of four "fingers" into the hand, one for each of the suits of hearts, clubs, spades, and diamonds, so that adding a new card to the person's hand or playing a correct card from the hand can be done in constant time. Your simulator should have a graphical or ASCII output that shows the person's hand of cards and the "finger" positions in the hand after each play. The possible plays should include the following:

- newCard(c, s): add the new card c of suit s to the hand.
- playDown(s): remove a card of suit s from the player's hand; if there is no card of suit s, then remove an arbitrary card from the hand.

Chapter Notes

Sequences and iterators are pervasive concepts in the C++ Standard Template Library (STL) [80], and they play fundamental roles in JDSL, the data structures library in Java. The sequence ADT is a generalization and extension of the Java java.util.Vector API (for example, see the book by Arnold and Gosling [7]) and the list ADTs proposed by several authors, including Aho, Hopcroft, and Ullman [5], who introduce the "position" abstraction, and Wood [100], who defines a list ADT similar to ours. Implementations of sequences via arrays and linked lists are discussed in Knuth's seminal book, *Fundamental Algorithms* [59]. Knuth's companion volume, *Sorting and Searching* [60], describes the bubble-sort method and the history of this and other sorting algorithms.

Chapter

6

Trees

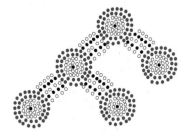

Contents

Productivity experts say that breakthroughs come by thinking "nonlinearly." In this chapter, we discuss one of the most important nonlinear data structures in computing—*trees*. Tree structures are indeed a breakthrough in data organization, for they allow us to implement a host of algorithms much faster than when using linear data structures, such as list, vectors, and sequences. Trees also provide a natural organization for data, and consequently have become ubiquitous structures in file systems, graphical user interfaces, databases, Web sites, and other computer systems.

It is not always clear what productivity experts mean by "nonlinear" thinking, but when we say that trees are "nonlinear," we are referring to an organizational relationship that is richer than the simple "before" and "after" relationships between objects in sequences. The relationships in a tree are *hierarchical*, with some objects being "above" and some "below" others. Actually, the main terminology for tree data structures comes from family trees, with the terms "parent," "child," "ancestor," and "descendent" being the most common words used to describe relationships. We show an example of a family tree in Figure 6.1.

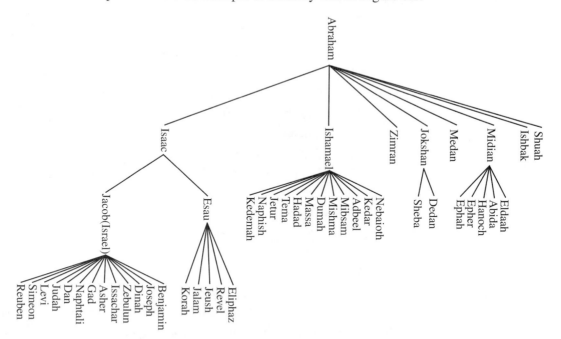

Figure 6.1: A family tree showing some descendents of Abraham, as recorded in Genesis, chapters 25–36.

6.1 The Tree Abstract Data Type

A *tree* is an abstract data type that stores elements hierarchically. With the exception of the top element, each element in a tree has a *parent* element and zero or more *children* elements. A tree is usually visualized by placing elements inside ovals or rectangles, and by drawing the connections between parents and children with straight lines. (See Figure 6.2.) We typically call the top element the *root* of the tree, but it is drawn as the highest element, with the other elements being connected below (just the opposite of a botanical tree).

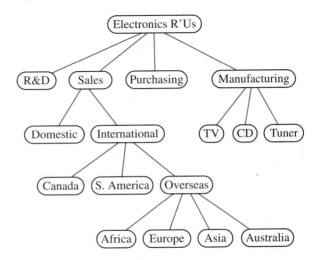

Figure 6.2: A tree with 17 nodes representing the organizational structure of a fictitious corporation. *Electronics R'Us* is stored at the root. The children of the root store *R&D*, *Sales*, *Purchasing*, and *Manufacturing*. The internal nodes store *Sales*, *International*, *Overseas*, *Electronics R'Us*, and *Manufacturing*. The other nodes are external nodes.

6.1.1 Terminology and Basic Properties

A *tree* T is a set of *nodes* storing elements in a *parent-child* relationship with the following properties:

- T has a special node r, called the *root* of T.
- Each node v of T different from r has a *parent* node u.

Caution

Note that according to the above definition, a tree cannot be empty, since it must have at least one node, the root. One could also allow the definition to include empty trees, but we adopt the convention that a tree always has a root so as to keep our presentation simple and to avoid having to always deal with the special case of an empty tree in our algorithms.

If node u is the parent of node v, then we say that v is a ***child*** of u. Two nodes that are children of the same parent are ***siblings***. A node is ***external*** if it has no children, and it is ***internal*** if it has one or more children. External nodes are also known as ***leaves***. The ***subtree*** of T ***rooted*** at a node v is the tree consisting of all the descendents of v in T (including v itself). An ***ancestor*** of a node is either the node itself or an ancestor of the parent of the node. Conversely, we say that a node v is a ***descendent*** of a node u if u is an ancestor of v. For example, in Figure 6.2, *Sales* is an ancestor of *Europe*, and *Europe* is a descendent of *Sales*.

Example 6.1: *The inheritance relation between classes in a Java program forms a tree. The class* java.lang.Object *is an ancestor of all other classes.*

Example 6.2: *In most operating systems, files are organized hierarchically into nested directories (also called folders), which are presented to the user in the form of a tree. (See Figure 6.3.) More specifically, the internal nodes of the tree are associated with directories and the external nodes are associated with regular files. In the UNIX operating system, the root of the tree is appropriately called the "root directory," and is represented by the symbol "/." It is the ancestor of all directories and files in a UNIX file system.*

A tree is ***ordered*** if there is a linear ordering defined for the children of each node; that is, we can identify children of a node as being the first, second, third, and so on. Such an ordering is determined by the use we wish to make for the tree, and it is usually indicated in a drawing of a tree by arranging siblings left to right, corresponding to their linear relationship. Ordered trees typically indicate the linear order relationship existing between siblings by listing them in a sequence or iterator in the correct order.

Example 6.3: *A structured document, such as a book, is hierarchically organized as a tree whose internal nodes are chapters, sections, and subsections, and whose external nodes are paragraphs, tables, figures, the bibliography, and so on. (See Figure 6.4.) The root of the tree corresponds to the book itself. We could in fact consider expanding the tree further to show paragraphs consisting of sentences, sentences consisting of words, and words consisting of characters. In any case, such a tree is an example of an ordered tree, because there is a well-defined ordering among the children of each node.*

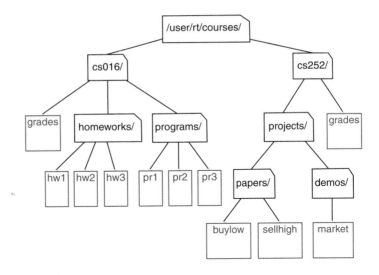

Figure 6.3: Tree representing a portion of a file system. Note that the subtree rooted at cs016/ contains 10 nodes.

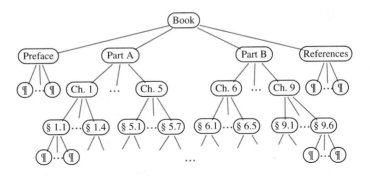

Figure 6.4: A tree associated with a book.

A **binary tree** is an ordered tree in which every node has at most two children. A binary tree is **proper** if each node has either zero or two children. Thus, in a proper binary tree, every internal node has exactly two children. For each internal node in a binary tree, we label each child as either being a **left child** or a **right child**. These children are ordered so that a left child comes before a right child. The subtree rooted at a left or right child of an internal node v is called a **left subtree** or **right subtree**, respectively, of v. We make the convention in this book that, unless otherwise stated, every binary tree is a proper binary tree. Of course, even an improper binary tree is still a general tree, with the property that each internal node has at most two children.

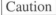

Binary trees have a number of useful applications. We discuss two common uses in the examples below.

Example 6.4: *An important class of binary trees arises in contexts where we wish to represent a number of different outcomes that can result from answering a collection of yes-or-no questions. Each internal node is associated with a question. Starting at the root, we go to the left or right child of the current node, depending on whether the answer to the question is "Yes" or "No." Such trees are known as* **decision** *trees, because each external node v in such a tree represents a decision of what to do if the questions associated with v's ancestors are answered in a way that leads to v. Figure 6.5 illustrates a binary decision tree that provides recommendations to a prospective investor. Each external node contains a recommended investment based on the answers provided.*

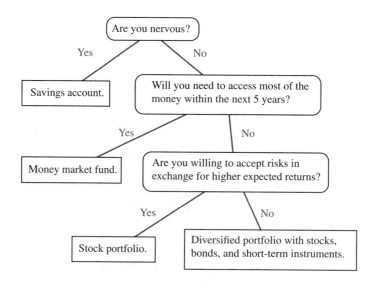

Figure 6.5: A binary decision tree providing investment advice.

Example 6.5: *An arithmetic expression can be represented by a tree whose external nodes are associated with variables or constants, and whose internal nodes are associated with one of the operators* $+$, $-$, $\times$, *and* $/$. *(See Figure 6.6.) Each node in such a tree has a value associated with it.*

- *If a node is external, then its value is that of its variable or constant.*
- *If a node is internal, then its value is defined by applying its operation to the values of its children.*

Such an arithmetic expression tree is a proper binary tree, since each of the operators +, −, ×, and / take exactly two operands. Of course, if we were to allow for unary operators, like negation (−), as in "−x," then we could have an improper binary tree.

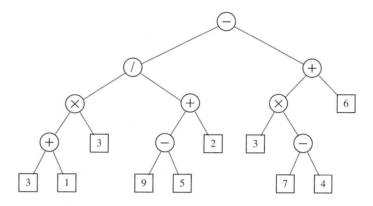

Figure 6.6: A binary tree representing an arithmetic expression. This tree represents the expression $((((3+1) \times 3)/((9-5)+2)) - ((3 \times (7-4)) + 6))$. The value associated with the internal node labeled "/" is 2.

6.1.2 Tree Methods

The tree ADT stores elements at positions, which, as with positions in a list, are defined relative to neighboring positions. The **positions** in a tree are its **nodes**, and neighboring positions satisfy the parent-child relationships that define a valid tree. Therefore we use the terms "position" and "node" interchangeably for trees. As with a list position, a position object for a tree supports the method:

element(): Return the object at this position.
Input: None; **Output:** Object.

The real power of node positions in a tree, however, comes from the **accessor methods** of the tree ADT that return and accept positions, such as the following:

root(): Return the root of the tree.
Input: None; **Output:** Position.

parent(v): Return the parent of node v; an error occurs if v is root.
Input: Position; **Output:** Position.

children(v): Return an iterator of the children of node v.
Input: Position; **Output:** Iterator of positions.

If a tree T is ordered, then the iterator children(v) provides access to the children of v in order. If v is an external node, then children(v) is an empty iterator.

In addition to the above fundamental accessor methods, we also include the following *query methods*:

isInternal(v): Test whether node v is internal.
                   Input: Position; *Output:* Boolean.

isExternal(v): Test whether node v is external.
                   Input: Position; *Output:* Boolean.

isRoot(v): Test whether node v is the root.
                   Input: Position; *Output:* Boolean.

These methods make programming with trees easier and more readable, since we can use them in the conditionals of if-statements and while-loops, rather than using a nonintuitive conditional or trying to catch an error condition. For instance, isInternal(v) and isExternal(v) can be performed by checking whether or not the iterator returned by method children(v) has elements.

There are also a number of methods a tree should probably support that are not necessarily related to its tree structure. Such *generic methods* for a tree include the following:

size(): Return the number of nodes in the tree.
                   Input: None; *Output:* Integer.

elements(): Return an iterator of all the elements stored at nodes of the tree.
                   Input: None; *Output:* Iterator of objects.

positions(): Return an iterator of all the nodes of the tree.
                   Input: None; *Output:* Iterator of positions.

swapElements(v, w): Swap the elements stored at the nodes v and w.
                   Input: Two positions; *Output:* None.

replaceElement(v, e): Replace with e and return the element stored at node v.
                   Input: A position and an object; *Output:* Object.

We do not define any specialized update methods for a tree here. Instead, we prefer to describe different tree update methods in conjunction with specific applications of trees in subsequent chapters. In fact, we can imagine several kinds of tree update operations beyond those given in this book. Even though we are not including any update operations here, we nevertheless consider how we might organize this collection of tree ADT methods into a set of Java interfaces in the next section.

6.1.3 A Tree Interface in Java

We can use the tree ADT to define a Java interface that defines the methods every tree should implement. Rather than include all of the above tree methods directly, however, we divide the tree-specific methods from the generic methods, and further separate the query and accessor methods from the update methods. The resulting set of interfaces are shown in Code Fragments 6.1–6.2. Since we extend InspectableContainer (see Figure 5.11), we also include method isEmpty(). However, according to our definition of a tree, this method should always return "false" since a tree cannot be empty (it has at least one node, the root).

```
public interface InspectablePositionalContainer
        extends InspectableContainer {
  // accessor methods
  /** return the positions in the container */
  public PositionIterator positions();
}
public interface PositionalContainer
        extends InspectablePositionalContainer {
  // update methods
  /** swap the elements at two nodes */
  public void swapElements(Position v, Position w);
  /** replace with and return the element at a node */
  public Object replaceElement(Position v, Object e);
}
public interface InspectableTree extends InspectablePositionalContainer {
  // accessor methods
  /** return the root of the tree */
  public Position root();
  /** return the parent of a node */
  public Position parent(Position v);
  /** return the children of a node */
  public PositionIterator children(Position v);
  // query methods
  /** test whether a node is internal */
  public boolean isInternal(Position v);
  /** test whether a node is external */
  public boolean isExternal(Position v);
  /** test whether a node is the root of the tree */
  public boolean isRoot(Position v);
}
```

Code Fragment 6.1: Interfaces InspectablePositionalContainer, PositionalContainer, and InspectableTree. Note that InspectablePositionalContainer inherits from InspectableContainer methods size(), isEmpty(), and elements().

```
public interface Tree extends InspectableTree, PositionalContainer {
}
```

Code Fragment 6.2: Interface Tree. Additional update methods may be added, depending on the application. We do not include any such methods in the interface, however, so the interface is a simple mixing of two other interfaces.

6.2   Basic Algorithms on Trees

In this section, we present algorithms for performing computations on a tree by accessing it through the tree ADT methods, which correspond to the methods of the InspectableTree interface.

6.2.1   Assumptions

In order to analyze the running time of the algorithms presented throughout Section 6.2, we make the following assumptions on the running times of the methods of the tree ADT.

- The accessor methods root() and parent(v) take $O(1)$ time.
- The query methods isInternal(v), isExternal(v), and isRoot(v) take $O(1)$ time, as well.
- The accessor method children(v) takes $O(c_v)$ time, where c_v is the number of children of v.
- The generic methods swapElements(v, w) and replaceElement(v, e) take $O(1)$ time.
- The generic methods elements() and positions(), which return iterators, take $O(n)$ time, where n is the number of nodes in the tree.
- For the iterators returned by methods elements(), positions(), and children(v), the methods hasNext(), nextObject() or nextPosition() take $O(1)$ time each.

In Section 6.4, we will present data structures for trees that satisfy the above assumptions. Before we describe how to implement the tree ADT using a concrete data structure, however, let us describe how we can use the methods of the tree ADT to solve some interesting problems for trees.

6.2.2 Depth and Height

Let v be a node of a tree T. The **depth** of v is the number of ancestors of v, excluding v itself. For example, in the tree of Figure 6.2, the node storing *International* has depth 2. Note that this definition implies that the depth of the root of T is 0.

The depth of a node v can also be recursively defined as follows:

- If v is the root, then the depth of v is 0.
- Otherwise, the depth of v is one plus the depth of the parent of v.

Based on the above definition, the recursive algorithm depth, shown in Code Fragment 6.3, computes the depth of a node v of T by calling itself recursively on the parent of v, and adding 1 to the value returned. Thus, each ancestor of v is visited by a recursive call, and contributes a value of 1 to the depth, as it should.

Algorithm depth(T, v):
   if T.isRoot(v) **then**
      return 0
   else
      return $1 +$ depth$(T, T$.parent$(v))$

Code Fragment 6.3: Algorithm depth for computing the depth of a node v in a tree T.

A simple Java implementation of algorithm depth is shown in Code Fragment 6.4.

```java
public static int depth (InspectableTree T, Position v) {
  if (T.isRoot(v))
    return 0;
  else
    return 1 + depth(T, T.parent(v));
}
```

Code Fragment 6.4: Method depth written in Java.

The running time of algorithm depth(T, v) is $O(1 + d_v)$, where d_v denotes the depth of the node v in the tree T, because the algorithm performs a constant-time recursive step for each ancestor of v. Thus, in the worst case, the depth algorithm runs in $O(n)$ time, where n is the total number of nodes in the tree T, since some nodes may have this depth in T. Although such a running time is a function of the input size, it is more accurate to characterize the running time in terms of the parameter d_v, since this will often be much smaller than n.

The *height* of a node v in a tree T is also defined recursively:

- If v is an external node, then the height of v is 0.
- Otherwise, the height of v is one plus the maximum height of a child of v.

The *height* of a tree T is the height of the root of T. For example, the tree of Figure 6.2 has height 4. In addition, height can also be viewed as follows.

Proposition 6.6: *The height of a tree T is equal to the maximum depth of an external node of T.*

We leave the justification of this fact to an exercise (R-6.4). We present here an algorithm, height1, shown in Code Fragment 6.5 and implemented in Java in Code Fragment 6.6, for computing the height of a tree T based on the above proposition. This algorithm utilizes an iterator of all the nodes in the tree to aid the computation of the depth of each external node by using algorithm depth (Code Fragment 6.3) as a subroutine, keeping track of the maximum depth seen so far.

Algorithm height1(T):
  $h = 0$
  for each $v \in T$.positions() **do**
    if T.isExternal(v) **then**
      $h = \max(h, \text{depth}(T, v))$
  return h

Code Fragment 6.5: Algorithm height1 for computing the height a tree T. Note that algorithm depth (Code Fragment 6.3) is used as a subroutine.

```java
public static int height1 (InspectableTree T) {
    int h = 0;
    PositionIterator positer = T.positions();
    while (positer.hasNext()) {
        Position v = positer.nextPosition();
        if (T.isExternal(v))
            h = Math.max(h, depth(T, v));
    }
    return h;
}
```

Code Fragment 6.6: Method height1 written in Java. Note the use of the max method of class java.lang.Math.

Unfortunately, algorithm height1 is not very efficient. Since height1 calls algorithm depth(v) on each external node v of T, the running time of height1 is given by $O(n + \sum_{v \in E}(1 + d_v))$, where n is the number of nodes of T, d_v is the depth of a node v, and E is the set of external nodes of T. Since $d_v \leq h \leq n - 1$ for each node v, and $|E| \leq n - 1$ (the upper bound is attained when the root has $n - 1$ children), algorithm height1 runs in time $O(n + \sum_{v \in E} n)$, which is $O(n^2)$ in the worst case. (See Exercise C-6.5.)

Algorithm height2, shown in Code Fragment 6.7 and implemented in Java in Code Fragment 6.8, computes the height of tree T in a more efficient manner by using the recursive definition of height. The algorithm is expressed by a recursive method height2(T, v) that computes the height of the subtree of T rooted at a node v. If the node v is external, then the algorithm returns 0. Otherwise, it gets an iterator of the children of v, recursively computes the height of each child, and returns 1 plus the maximum height returned from a recursive call. The height of tree T is obtained by calling height2$(T, T.\text{root}())$.

Algorithm height2(T, v):
  if $T.\text{isExternal}(v)$ **then**
    return 0
  else
    $h = 0$
    for each $w \in T.\text{children}(v)$ **do**
      $h = \max(h, \text{height2}(T, w))$
    return $1 + h$

Code Fragment 6.7: Algorithm height2 for computing the height of the subtree of tree T rooted at a node v.

```java
public static int height2 (InspectableTree T, Position v) {
    if (T.isExternal(v))
        return 0;
    else {
        int h = 0;
        PositionIterator children = T.children(v);
        while (children.hasNext())
            h = Math.max(h, height2(T, children.nextPosition()));
        return 1 + h;
    }
}
```

Code Fragment 6.8: Method height2 written in Java.

Algorithm height2 is much more efficient than Algorithm height1 (from Code Fragment 6.5). The algorithm is recursive, and if it is initially called on the root of T, it will eventually be called once on each node of T. Thus, we can determine the running time of this method by first determining the amount of time spent at each node (on the nonrecursive part), and then summing this time bound over all the nodes. The computation of an iterator children(v) takes $O(c_v)$ time, where c_v denotes the number of children of node v. Also, the **while** loop has c_v iterations, and each iteration of the loop takes $O(1)$ time plus the time for the recursive call on a child of v. Thus, algorithm height2 spends $O(1+c_v)$ time at each node v, and its running time is $O(\sum_{v \in T}(1+c_v))$. In order to complete the analysis, we make use of the following property.

Proposition 6.7: *Let T be a tree with n nodes, and let c_v denote the number of children of a node v of T. Then*

$$\sum_{v \in T} c_v = n - 1.$$

Justification: Each node of T, with the exception of the root, is a child of another node, and thus contributes one unit to the above sum.   ■

By Proposition 6.7, the running time of algorithm height2, when called on the root of T, is $O(n)$, where n is the number of nodes of T.

6.2.3 Preorder Traversal

A *traversal* of a tree T is a systematic way of accessing, or "visiting," all the nodes of T. In this section, we present a basic traversal scheme for trees, called preorder traversal. In the next section, we will study another basic traversal scheme, called postorder traversal.

In a *preorder* traversal of a tree T, the root of T is visited first and then the subtrees rooted at its children are traversed recursively. If the tree is ordered, then the subtrees are traversed according to the order of the children. The specific action associated with the "visit" of a node v depends on the application of this traversal, and could involve anything from incrementing a counter to performing some complex computation for v. The pseudo-code for the preorder traversal of the subtree rooted at a node v is shown in Code Fragment 6.9. We initially call this routine as preorder(T, T.root()).

The preorder traversal algorithm is useful for producing a linear ordering of the nodes of a tree where parents must always come before their children in the ordering. Such orderings have several different applications; we explore a simple instance of such an application in the next example.

Algorithm preorder(T, v):

    perform the "visit" action for node v

    for each child w of v **do**

        recursively traverse the subtree rooted at w by calling preorder(T, w)

Code Fragment 6.9: Algorithm preorder.

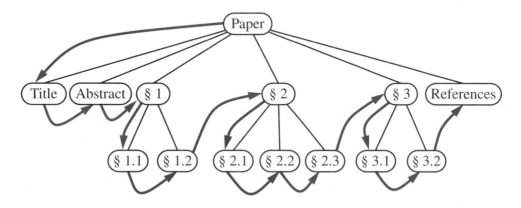

Figure 6.7: Preorder traversal of an ordered tree, where the children of each node are ordered from left to right.

Example 6.8: *The preorder traversal of the tree associated with a document, as in Example 6.3, examines an entire document sequentially, from beginning to end. If the external nodes are removed before the traversal, then the traversal examines the table of contents of the document. (See Figure 6.7.)*

    The preorder traversal is also an efficient way to access all the nodes of a tree. To justify this, let us consider the running time of the preorder traversal of a tree T with n nodes under the assumption that visiting a node takes $O(1)$ time. The analysis of the preorder traversal algorithm is actually similar to that of algorithm height2 (Code Fragment 6.8), given in Section 6.2.2. At each node v, the nonrecursive part of the preorder traversal algorithm requires time $O(1 + c_v)$, where c_v is the number of children of v. Thus, by Proposition 6.7, the overall running time of the preorder traversal of T is $O(n)$.

    Algorithm preorderPrint(T, v), implemented in Java in Code Fragment 6.10, performs a preorder printing of the subtree of a node v of T, that is, it performs the preorder traversal of the subtree rooted at v and prints the element stored at a node when the node is visited. Recall that, for an ordered tree T, method T.children(v) returns an iterator that accesses the children of v in order.

```
public static String preorderPrint(InspectableTree T, Position v) {
  String s = v.element().toString(); // elements must implement toString
  PositionIterator children = T.children(v);
  while (children.hasNext())
    s += " " + preorderPrint(T, children.nextPosition());
  return s;
}
```

Code Fragment 6.10: Method preorderPrint(T,v) that performs a preorder print-ing of the elements in the subtree of node v of T. The method implicitly calls the standard Java method toString to return a string associated with an element, that is, its "name" or "label." Method toString has a default implementation in java.lang.Object, which is typically overridden by subclasses to print useful infor-mation about instances of each such subclass.

There is an interesting variation of the preorderPrint method that produces a string representation of an entire tree. Let us assume again that for each element e stored in tree T, calling e.toString() returns a string associated with e. The ***paren-thetic string representation*** $P(T)$ of tree T is recursively defined as follows. If T consists of a single node v, then

$$P(T) = v.\text{element}().\text{toString}().$$

Otherwise,

$$P(T) = v.\text{element}().\text{toString}() + "(" + P(T_1) + P(T_2) + \cdots + P(T_k) + ")",$$

where v is the root of T and $T_1, T_2, \ldots, T_k$ are the subtrees rooted at the children of v, which are given in order if T is an ordered tree. Note that the definition of $P(T)$ is recursive. Also, we are using "+" here to denote string concatenation. (See Section 1.3.2 for details.) The parenthetic representation of the tree of Figure 6.2 is shown in Figure 6.8.

> *Electronics R'Us (R&D*
> *Sales (Domestic*
> *International (Canada S.America*
> *Overseas (Africa Europe Asia Australia)))*
> *Purchasing*
> *Manufacturing (TV CD Tuner))*

Figure 6.8: Parenthetic representation of the tree of Figure 6.2. Indentation, line breaks and spaces have been added for clarity.

Note that, technically speaking, there are some computations that occur between and after the recursive calls at a node's children in the above algorithm. We still consider this algorithm to be a preorder traversal, however, since the primary action of printing a node's contents occurs prior to the recursive calls.

The Java method parentheticRepresentation, shown in Code Fragment 6.11, is a variation of method preorderPrint (Code Fragment 6.10). It implements the definition given above to output a parenthetic string representation of a tree T. As with the method preorderPrint, the method parentheticRepresentation makes use of the toString method that is defined for every Java object. In fact, we can view this method as a kind of toString() method for tree objects.

```java
public static String parentheticRepresentation(InspectableTree T, Position v) {
    String s = v.element().toString(); // elements must implement toString
    if (T.isInternal(v)) {
        PositionIterator children = T.children(v);
        // open parenthesis and recursively process the first subtree
        s += " ( " + parentheticRepresentation(T, children.nextPosition());
        while (children.hasNext())
            // recursively process the remaining subtrees
            s += ", " + parentheticRepresentation(T, children.nextPosition());
        s += " )"; // close parenthesis
    }
    return s;
}
```

Code Fragment 6.11: Algorithm parentheticRepresentation. Note the use of the $+$ operator to concatenate two strings.

We explore a modification to Code Fragment 6.11 in Exercise R-6.7, to display a tree in a fashion more closely matching that given in Figure 6.8.

Preorder traversal is useful for solving a tree problem where we must perform a computation for each node before performing any computations for its descendents.

6.2.4 Postorder Traversal

Another important tree traversal algorithm is the ***postorder*** traversal. This algorithm can be viewed as the opposite of the preorder traversal, because it recursively traverses the subtrees rooted at the children of the root first, and then visits the root. Still, as with the preorder traversal, if the tree is ordered, we make recursive calls for the children of a node v according to their specified order. Pseudo-code for the postorder traversal is given in Code Fragment 6.12.

Algorithm postorder(T,v):

   for each child w of v **do**

      recursively traverse the subtree rooted at w by calling postorder(T,w)

    perform the "visit" action for node v

Code Fragment 6.12: Method postorder.

The name of the postorder traversal comes from the fact that this traversal method will visit a node v after it has visited all the other nodes in the subtree rooted at v. (See Figure 6.9.)

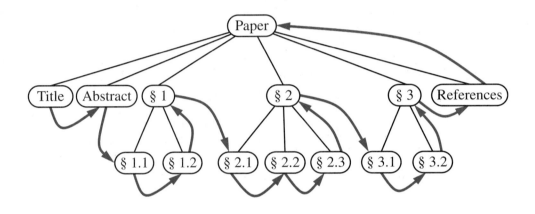

Figure 6.9: Postorder traversal of the ordered tree of Figure 6.7.

The analysis of the running time of a postorder traversal is analogous to that of a preorder traversal. (See Section 6.2.3.) The total time spent in the nonrecursive portions of the algorithm is proportional to the time spent visiting the children of each node in the tree. Thus, a postorder traversal of a tree T with n nodes takes $O(n)$ time, assuming that visiting each node takes $O(1)$ time. That is, the postorder traversal runs in linear time.

As an example instance of a postorder traversal, we show a Java method postorderPrint in Code Fragment 6.13, which performs a postorder traversal of a tree T. This method prints the element stored at a node when it is visited.

The postorder traversal method is useful for solving problems where we wish to compute some property for each node v in a tree, but computing that property for v requires that we have already computed that same property for v's children. Such an application is illustrated in the following example.

```
public static String postorderPrint(InspectableTree T, Position v) {
  String s = "";
  PositionIterator children = T.children(v);
  while (children.hasNext())
    s += postorderPrint(T, children.nextPosition()) + " ";
  s += v.element();              // elements must implement toString
  return s;
}
```

Code Fragment 6.13: Method postorderPrint(T, v) that performs a postorder print-ing of the elements in the subtree of node v of T. The method implicitly calls toString on elements, when they are involved in a string concatenation operation.

Example 6.9: *Consider a file system tree T, where external nodes represent files and internal nodes represent directories (Example 6.2). Suppose we want to com-pute the disk space used by a directory, which is recursively given by the sum of:*

- *The size of the directory itself*
- *The sizes of the files in the directory*
- *The space used by the children directories.*

(See Figure 6.10.) This computation can be done with a postorder traversal of tree T. After the subtrees of an internal node v have been traversed, we compute the space used by v by adding the sizes of the directory v itself and of the files contained in v, to the space used by each internal child of v, which was computed by the recursive postorder traversals of the children of v.

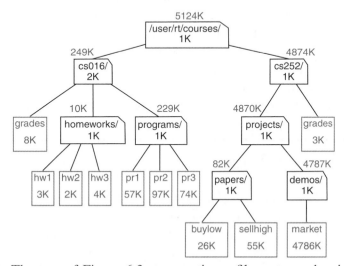

Figure 6.10: The tree of Figure 6.3 representing a file system, showing the name and size of the associated file/directory inside each node, and the disk space used by the associated directory above each internal node.

Motivated by Example 6.9, algorithm diskSpace, shown in Code Fragment 6.14, performs a postorder traversal of a file-system tree T, printing the name and disk space used by the directory associated with each internal node of T. When called on the root of tree T, diskSpace runs in time $O(n)$, where n is the number of nodes of the tree, provided the auxiliary methods name and size take $O(1)$ time.

```
public static int diskSpace (InspectableTree T, Position v) {
    int s = size(v);          // start with the size of the node itself
    PositionIterator children = T.children(v);
    while (children.hasNext())
        // add the recursively computed space used by the children of v
        s += diskSpace(T, children.nextPosition());
    if (T.isInternal(v))
        // print name and disk space used
        System.out.print(name(v) + ": " + s);
    return s;
}
```

Code Fragment 6.14: Method diskSpace prints the name and disk space used by the directory associated with v, for each internal node v of a file-system tree T. This method calls the auxiliary methods name and size, which should be defined to return the name and size of the file/directory associated with a node.

Although the preorder and postorder traversals are common ways of visiting the nodes of a tree, we can also imagine other traversals. For example, we could traverse a tree so that we visit all the nodes at depth d before we visit the nodes at depth $d + 1$. Such a traversal could be implemented, for example, using a queue, whereas the preorder and postorder traversals use a stack (this stack is implicit in our use of recursion to describe these methods, but we could make this use explicit, as well, to avoid recursion). In addition, binary trees, which we discuss next, support an additional traversal method, known as the inorder traversal.

6.3 Binary Trees

One kind of tree that is of particular interest is the binary tree. As we mentioned in Section 6.1.1, a proper *binary tree* is an ordered tree in which each internal node has two children. Moreover, we make the convention that, unless otherwise stated, binary trees are assumed to be proper. Note that our convention for binary trees is made without loss of generality, for we can easily convert any improper binary tree into a proper one, as we explore in Exercise R-6.3. Even without such a conversion, we can consider an improper binary tree as proper, simply by viewing missing external nodes as "null nodes" or place holders that still count as nodes.

Binary trees arise naturally in many different applications. For example, an arithmetic expression tree (Example 6.5) is a binary tree, since each of the operators used to define this tree is a binary operator. Also, a decision tree (see Example 6.4) is a binary tree, since the outcome of a decision is always "yes" or "no." We discuss some of the specialized topics for binary trees below.

6.3.1 The Binary Tree ADT

As an abstract data type, a binary tree is a specialization of a tree that supports three additional accessor methods:

leftChild(v): Return the left child of v; an error condition occurs if v is an external node.
Input: Position; *Output:* Position.

rightChild(v): Return the right child of v; an error condition occurs if v is an external node.
Input: Position; *Output:* Position.

sibling(v): Return the sibling of node v; an error condition occurs if v is the root.
Input: Position; *Output:* Position.

Note that these methods have additional error conditions if we are dealing with improper binary trees. For example, in an improper binary tree, an internal node may not have the left child or right child. Even so, just as done in Section 6.1.2 for the tree ADT, we do not define specialized update methods for binary trees here.

6.3.2 A Binary Tree Interface in Java

We model a binary tree as an abstract data type with the Java interfaces InspectableBinaryTree and BinaryTree, shown in Code Fragment 6.15. The relationships between these and related interfaces are shown in Figure 6.11. By the way, since binary trees are ordered trees, the iterator returned by method children(v) (inherited from interface InspectableTree) accesses the left child of v before the right child of v.

We make the following assumptions on the running time of the methods of any class that implements the BinaryTree interface.

- All the assumptions on the running time of the tree ADT methods made in Section 6.2 hold. In particular, for a binary tree, method children(v) takes $O(1)$ time, because each node has either zero or two children.
- Methods leftChild(v), rightChild(v), and sibling(v) each take $O(1)$ time.

```
public interface InspectableBinaryTree
    extends InspectableTree {
  // accessor methods
  /** return the left child of a node */
  public Position leftChild(Position v);
  /** return the right child of a node */
  public Position rightChild(Position v);
  /** return the sibling of a node */
  public Position sibling(Position v);
}
public interface BinaryTree
  extends InspectableBinaryTree, PositionalContainer {
}
```

Code Fragment 6.15: Interfaces InspectableBinaryTree, which extends interface InspectableTree (Code Fragment 6.1), and Interface BinaryTree, which extends interfaces InspectableBinaryTree (Code Fragment 6.15) and PositionalContainer (Code Fragment 6.1).

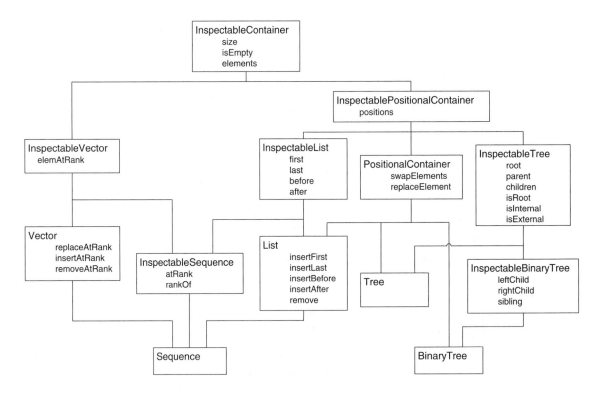

Figure 6.11: Inheritance hierarchy for ADTs representing sequences and trees.

6.3.3 Properties of Binary Trees

Binary trees have several interesting properties dealing with relationships between their heights and number of nodes. We denote the set of all nodes of a tree T at the same depth d as the **level** d of T. In a binary tree, level 0 has one node (the root), level 1 has at most two nodes (the children of the root), level 2 has at most four nodes, and so on. (See Figure 6.12.) In general, level d has at most 2^d nodes.

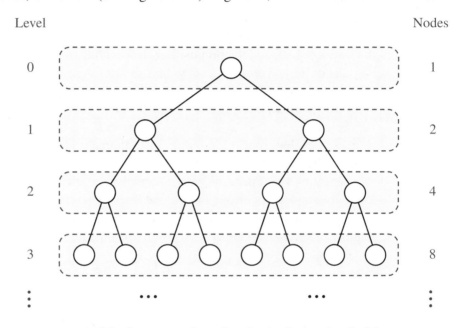

Figure 6.12: Maximum number of nodes in the levels of a binary tree.

We can see that the maximum number of nodes on the levels of a binary tree grows exponentially as we go down the tree. From this simple observation, we can derive the following properties relating the height of a binary T with its number of nodes. A detailed justification of these properties is left as an exercise (R-6.13).

Proposition 6.10: *Let T be a (proper) binary tree with n nodes, and let h denote the height of T. Then T has the following properties:*

1. *The number of external nodes in T is at least $h + 1$ and at most 2^h.*
2. *The number of internal nodes in T is at least h and at most $2^h - 1$.*
3. *The total number of nodes in T is at least $2h + 1$ and at most $2^{h+1} - 1$.*
4. *The height of T is at least $\log(n+1) - 1$ and at most $(n-1)/2$, that is,* $\log(n+1) - 1 \le h \le (n-1)/2$.

In addition, we also have the following relationship between the number of internal nodes and external nodes in a binary tree.

Proposition 6.11: *In a (proper) binary tree T, the number of external nodes is 1 more than the number of internal nodes.*

Justification: We justify this proposition by dividing up the nodes of a binary tree into two "piles": an internal-node pile and an external-node pile, as if we were dividing pieces of candy between two preschoolers. If T itself has only one node v, then v is external, and the proposition clearly holds.

Otherwise, we remove from T an (arbitrary) external node w and its parent v, which is an internal node. We imagine placing w on the external-node pile and v on the internal-node pile. If v has a parent u, then we reconnect u with the former sibling z of w, as shown in Figure 6.13. This operation, which we call removeAboveExternal(w), removes one internal node and one external node, and it leaves the tree being a proper binary tree.

Repeating this operation, we eventually are left with a single external node. Since the same number of external and internal nodes are removed and placed on their respective piles by the sequence of operations leading to this final tree, the number of external nodes of T is 1 more than the number of internal nodes. ∎

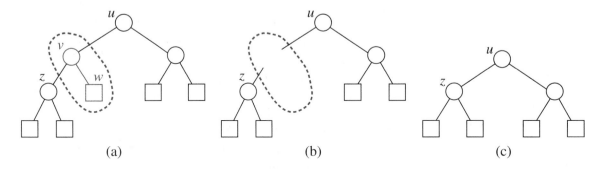

(a)   (b)   (c)

Figure 6.13: Operation removeAboveExternal(w), which removes an external node and its parent node, used in the justification of Proposition 6.11.

Note that the above relationship does not hold, in general, for nonbinary trees, although there are other interesting relationships that can hold, as we explore in an exercise (C-6.6).

In subsequent chapters, we explore some important applications of the above facts. Before we can discuss such applications, however, we should first understand more about how binary trees are traversed and represented.

6.3.4 Traversals of a Binary Tree

As with general trees, computations performed on binary trees often involve tree traversals. In this section, we present algorithms that perform traversal computations on binary trees. The algorithms will be expressed using the binary tree ADT methods, and will work even for improper binary trees, assuming the visit action for a null external node is to do nothing.

Preorder Traversal of a Binary Tree

Since any binary tree can also be viewed as a general tree, the preorder traversal for general trees (Code Fragment 6.9) can be applied to any binary tree. We can simplify the algorithm in the case of a binary tree traversal, however, as we show in Code Fragment 6.16.

Algorithm binaryPreorder(T, v):
    perform the "visit" action for node v
    if v is an internal node **then**
        binaryPreorder(T, T.leftChild(v))   {recursively traverse left subtree}
        binaryPreorder(T, T.rightChild(v))   {recursively traverse right subtree}

Code Fragment 6.16: Algorithm binaryPreorder that performs the preorder traversal of the subtree of a binary tree T rooted at node v.

As is the case for general trees, there are many applications of the preorder traversal for binary trees.

Postorder Traversal of a Binary Tree

Analogously, the postorder traversal for general trees (Code Fragment 6.12) can be specialized for binary trees, as shown in Code Fragment 6.17.

Algorithm binaryPostorder(T, v):
    if v is an internal node **then**
        binaryPostorder(T, T.leftChild(v))   {recursively traverse left subtree}
        binaryPostorder(T, T.rightChild(v))   {recursively traverse right subtree}
    perform the "visit" action for the node v

Code Fragment 6.17: Algorithm binaryPostorder for performing the postorder traversal of the subtree of a binary tree T rooted at node v.

The postorder traversal of a binary tree can be used to solve the expression evaluation problem. In this problem, we are given an arithmetic expression tree, that is, a binary tree where each external node has a value associated with it and each internal node has an arithmetic operation associated with it (see Example 6.5), and we want to compute the value of the arithmetic expression represented by the tree.

Algorithm evaluateExpression, given in Code Fragment 6.18, evaluates the expression associated with the subtree rooted at a node v of an arithmetic expression tree T by performing a postorder traversal of T starting at v. In this case, the "visit" action consists of performing a single arithmetic operation.

Algorithm evaluateExpression(T, v):

    if v is an internal node storing operator $\circ$ **then**
        $x \leftarrow$ evaluateExpression(T, T.leftChild(v))
        $y \leftarrow$ evaluateExpression(T, T.rightChild(v))
        return $x \circ y$
    else
        return the value stored at v

Code Fragment 6.18: Algorithm evaluateExpression for evaluating the expression represented by the subtree of an arithmetic expression tree T rooted at node v.

The expression-tree evaluation application of the postorder traversal provides an $O(n)$-time algorithm for evaluating an arithmetic expression represented by a binary tree with n nodes. Indeed, like the general postorder traversal, the postorder traversal for binary trees can be applied to other "bottom-up" evaluation problems (such as the size computation given in Example 6.9) as well. The specialization of the postorder traversal for binary trees simplifies that for general trees, however, because we use the leftChild and rightChild methods to avoid a loop that iterates through the children of an internal node.

Interestingly, the specialization of the general preorder and postorder traversal methods to binary trees suggests a third traversal in a binary tree that is different from both the preorder and postorder traversals.

Inorder Traversal of a Binary Tree

An additional traversal method for a binary tree is the ***inorder*** traversal. In this traversal, we visit a node between the recursive traversals of its left and right subtrees. The inorder traversal of the subtree rooted at a node v in a binary tree T is given in Code Fragment 6.19.

Algorithm inorder(T, v):

    if v is an internal node **then**

        inorder(T, T.leftChild(v))   {recursively traverse left subtree}

    perform the "visit" action for node v

    if v is an internal node **then**

        inorder(T, T.rightChild(v))   {recursively traverse right subtree}

Code Fragment 6.19: Algorithm inorder for performing the inorder traversal of the subtree of a binary tree T rooted at a node v.

The inorder traversal of a binary tree T can be informally viewed as visiting the nodes of T "from left to right." Indeed, for every node v, the inorder traversal visits v after all the nodes in the left subtree of v and before all the nodes in the right subtree of v. (See Figure 6.14.)

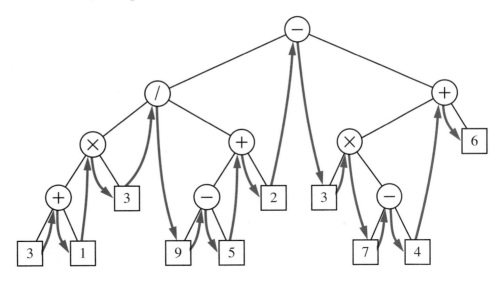

Figure 6.14: Inorder traversal of a binary tree.

The inorder traversal algorithm also has several applications. One of the most important ones arises when we store an ordered sequence of elements in a binary tree, defining a structure we call a *binary search tree*. Specifically, let us define a binary search tree so that each internal node v stores an element e such that the elements stored in the left subtree of v are less than or equal to e, and the elements stored in the right subtree of v are greater than or equal to e. Furthermore, let us assume that external nodes store no elements; hence, they could in fact be null or references to a NULL_NODE object.

An inorder traversal of a binary search tree visits the elements stored in such a tree in nondecreasing order. A binary search tree can be viewed as a binary decision tree (recall Example 6.4) that supports searching, where the question asked at each internal node is whether the element at that node is less than, equal to, or larger than the element being searched for.

We can use a binary search tree T to locate an element with a certain value x by traversing down the tree T. At each internal node we compare the value of the current node to our search element x. If the answer to the question is "smaller," then the search continues in the left subtree. If the answer is "equal," then the search terminates successfully. If the answer is "greater," then the search continues in the right subtree. Finally, if we reach an external node (which is empty), then the search terminates unsuccessfully. (See Figure 6.15.)

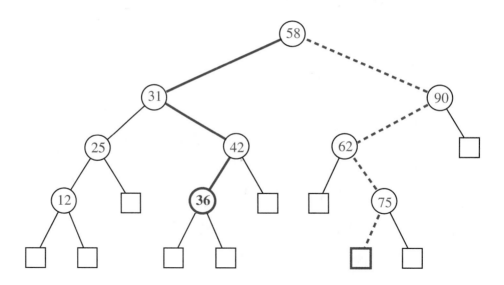

Figure 6.15: A binary search tree storing integers. The blue solid path is traversed when searching (successfully) for 36. The blue dashed path is traversed when searching (unsuccessfully) for 70.

Note that the running time of searching in a binary search tree T is proportional to the height of T. Recall from Propositition 6.10 that the height of a tree with n nodes can be as small as $O(\log n)$ or as large as $\Omega(n)$. Thus, binary search trees are most efficient when they have small height. We illustrate an example search operation in a binary search tree in Figure 6.15, and we study binary search trees in more detail in Section 9.1.

Using Inorder Traversal for Tree Drawing

The inorder traversal can also be applied to the problem of computing a drawing of a binary tree. We can draw a binary tree T with an algorithm that assigns x- and y-coordinates to a node v of T using the following two rules (see Figure 6.16):

- $x(v)$ is equal to the number of nodes visited before v in the inorder traversal of T.
- $y(v)$ is equal to the depth of v in T.

In this application, we take the convention common in computer graphics that x-coordinates increase left to right and y-coordinates increase top to bottom. So the origin is in the upper left corner of the computer screen.

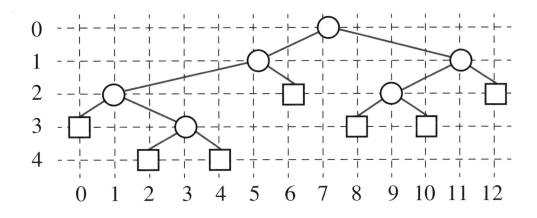

Figure 6.16: The inorder drawing algorithm for a binary tree.

A Unified Tree Traversal Framework

Viewed in an object-oriented framework, the tree-traversal algorithms we have discussed so far are all forms of iterators. Each traversal visits the nodes of a tree in a certain order, and is guaranteed to visit each node exactly once. We can unify the tree-traversal algorithms given above into a single framework, however, by relaxing the requirement that each node be visited exactly once. The resulting traversal method is called the ***Euler tour traversal***, which we study next. The advantage of this traversal is that it allows for more general kinds of algorithms to be expressed easily.

The Euler Tour Traversal of a Binary Tree

The Euler tour traversal of a binary tree T can be informally defined as a "walk" around T, where we start by going from the root toward its left child, viewing the edges of T as being "walls" that we always keep to our left. (See Figure 6.17.) Each node v of T is encountered three times by the Euler tour:

- "On the left" (before the Euler tour of v's left subtree)
- "From below" (between the Euler tours of v's two subtrees)
- "On the right" (after the Euler tour of v's right subtree).

If v is external, then these three "visits" actually all happen at the same time.

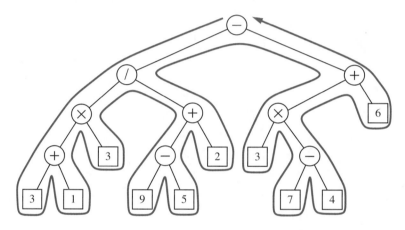

Figure 6.17: Euler tour traversal of a binary tree.

We give pseudo-code for the Euler tour of the subtree rooted at a node v in Code Fragment 6.20.

The preorder traversal of a binary tree is equivalent to an Euler tour traversal such that each node has an associated "visit" action occur only when it is encountered on the left. Likewise, the inorder and postorder traversals of a binary tree are equivalent to an Euler tour such that each node has an associated "visit" action occur only when it is encountered from below or on the right, respectively.

The Euler tour traversal extends the preorder, inorder, and postorder traversals, but it can also perform other kinds of traversals. For example, suppose we wish to compute the number of descendents of each node v in an n node binary tree T. We start an Euler tour by initializing a counter to 0, and then increment the counter each time we visit a node on the left. To determine the number of descendents of a node v, we compute the difference between the values of the counter when v is

Algorithm eulerTour(T, v):

perform the action for visiting node v on the left

if v is an internal node **then**

recursively tour the left subtree of v by calling eulerTour(T, T.leftChild(v))

perform the action for visiting node v from below

if v is an internal node **then**

recursively tour the right subtree of v by calling eulerTour(T, T.rightChild(v))

perform the action for visiting node v on the right

Code Fragment 6.20: Algorithm eulerTour for computing the Euler tour traversal of the subtree of a binary tree T rooted at a node v.

visited on the left and when it is visited on the right, and add 1. This simple rule gives us the number of descendents of v, because each node in the subtree rooted at v is counted between v's visit on the left and v's visit on the right. Therefore, we have an $O(n)$-time method for computing the number of descendents of each node in T.

The running times of the Euler tour traversal is easy to analyze, assuming a node takes $O(1)$ time. Namely, in each traversal, we spend a constant amount of time at each node of the tree during the traversal, so the overall running time is $O(n)$ for an n node tree.

Another application of the Euler tour traversal is to print a fully parenthesized arithmetic expression from its expression tree (Example 6.5). Algorithm printExpression, shown in Code Fragment 6.21, accomplishes this task by performing the following actions in an Euler tour:

- "On the left" action: if the node is internal, print "("
- "From below" action: print the value or operator stored at the node
- "On the right" action: if the node is internal, print ")".

Algorithm printExpression(T, v):

if T.isExternal(v) **then**

print the value stored at v

else

print "("

printExpression(T, T.leftChild(v))

print the operator stored at v

printExpression(T, T.rightChild(v))

print ")"

Code Fragment 6.21: An algorithm for printing the arithmetic expression associated with the subtree of an arithmetic expression tree T rooted at v.

6.3.5   The Template Method Pattern

The tree traversal methods described above are actually examples of an interesting object-oriented software design pattern, the ***template method pattern***. The template method pattern describes a generic computation mechanism that can be specialized for a particular application by redefining certain steps.

Euler Tour with the Template Method Pattern

Following the template method pattern, we can design an algorithm, templateEuler-Tour, that implements a generic Euler tour traversal of a binary tree. When called on a node v, method templateEulerTour calls several other auxiliary methods at different phases of the traversal. First of all, it creates a three-element array r to store the result of the computation calling auxiliary method initResult. Next, if v is an external node, templateEulerTour calls auxiliary method visitExternal, else (v is an internal node) templateEulerTour executes the following steps:

- Calls auxiliary method visitLeft, which performs the computations associated with encountering the node on the left
- Recursively calls itself on the left child
- Calls auxiliary method visitBelow, which performs the computations associated with encountering the node from below
- Recursively calls itself on the right subtree
- Calls auxiliary method visitRight, which performs the computations associated with encountering the node on the right.

Finally, templateEulerTour returns the result of the computation by calling auxiliary method returnResult. Method templateEulerTour can be viewed as a ***template*** or "skeleton" of an Euler tour. (See Code Fragment 6.22.)

In an object-oriented context, we can then write a class EulerTour that:

- Contains method templateEulerTour
- Contains all the auxiliary methods called by templateEulerTour as empty place holders (that is, with no instructions or returning null)
- Contains a method execute that calls templateEulerTour$(T, T.root())$.

Class EulerTour itself does not perform any useful computation. However, we can extend it with the inheritance mechanism and override the empty methods to do useful tasks.

Algorithm templateEulerTour(T, v):
  $r =$ initResult()
  if T.isExternal(v) **then**
    $r[0] =$ visitExternal(T, v, r)
  else
    visitLeft(T, v, r)
    $r[1] =$ templateEulerTour(T, T.leftChild(v))
    visitBelow(T, v, r)
    $r[2] =$ templateEulerTour(T, T.rightChild(v))
    visitRight(T, v, r)
  return returnResult(r)

Code Fragment 6.22: Method templateEulerTour for computing a generic Euler tour traversal of the subtree of a binary tree T rooted at a node v, following the template method pattern. This method calls the methods initResult, visitExternal, visitLeft, visitBelow, visitRight, and returnResult.

Template Method Examples

As a first example, we can evaluate the expression associated with an arithmetic expression tree (see Example 6.5) by writing a new class EvaluateExpression that:

- Extends class EulerTour
- Overrides method initResult by returning an array of three numbers
- Overrides visitExternal by returning the value stored at the node
- Overrides visitRight by combining $r[1]$ and $r[2]$ with the operator stored at the node, and setting $r[0]$ equal the result of the operation
- Overrides returnResult by returning $r[0]$.

This approach should be compared with the direct implementation of the algorithm shown in Code Fragment 6.18.

As a second example, we can print the expression associated with an arithmetic expression tree (see Example 6.5) using a new class PrintExpression that:

- Extends class EulerTour
- Overrides visitExternal by printing the value of the variable or constant associated with the node
- Overrides visitLeft by printing "("
- Overrides visitBelow by printing the operator associated with the node
- Overrides visitRight by printing ")".

This approach should be compared with the direct implementation of the algorithm shown in Code Fragment 6.21.

Java Implementation

A complete Java implementation of the generic EulerTour class and of its specializations EvaluateExpressionTour and PrintExpressionTour is shown in Code Fragments 6.23–6.25. Note that we use an object of class TraversalResult with fields
finalResult, leftResult, and rightResult instead of an array of length 3.

```java
/**
 * Template for algorithms traversing a binary tree using an Euler
 * tour. The subclasses of this class will redefine some of the
 * methods of this class to create a specific traversal.
 */
public abstract class EulerTour {
  protected InspectableBinaryTree tree;
  public Object execute(BinaryTree T) {
    tree = T;
    return null;  // nothing interesting to return
  }
  protected Object eulerTour(Position p) {
    TraversalResult r = initResult();
    if (tree.isExternal(p)) {
      visitExternal(p, r);
    } else {
      visitLeft(p, r);
      r.leftResult = eulerTour(tree.leftChild(p)); // recursive traversal
      visitBelow(p, r);
      r.rightResult = eulerTour(tree.rightChild(p)); // recursive traversal
      visitRight(p, r);
    }
    return result(r);
  }
  // methods that can be redefined by the subclasses
  protected void visitExternal(Position p, TraversalResult r) {}
  protected void visitLeft(Position p, TraversalResult r) {}
  protected void visitBelow(Position p, TraversalResult r) {}
  protected void visitRight(Position p, TraversalResult r) {}
  protected TraversalResult initResult() { return new TraversalResult(); }
  protected Object result(TraversalResult r) { return r.finalResult; }
}
```

Code Fragment 6.23: Class EulerTour defining a generic Euler tour of a binary tree.
This class realizes the template method pattern and must be specialized in order to
get an interesting computation.

```
/**
 * This traversal specializes EulerTour to compute the
 * value of an arithmetic expression stored in the tree. It assumes
 * that the elements stored at the external nodes are Integer objects
 * and that the elements stored at the internal nodes are of type
 * OperatorInfo, supporting method operation(Integer x, Integer y), which
 * returns the result of applying an arithmetic operation to x and y.
 */
public class EvaluateExpressionTour extends EulerTour {

  public Object execute(BinaryTree T) {
      super.execute(T); // calls method of superclass
    System.out.print("The value is: ");
    System.out.println(eulerTour(tree.root()));
    return null;  // nothing interesting to return
  }

  protected void visitExternal(Position p, TraversalResult r) {
    r.finalResult = (Integer) p.element();
  }

  protected void visitRight(Position p, TraversalResult r) {
    OperatorInfo op = (OperatorInfo) p.element();
    r.finalResult = op.operation((Integer) r.leftResult,
                                 (Integer) r.rightResult);
  }

}
```

Code Fragment 6.24: Class EvaluateExpressionTour that specializes EulerTour to evaluate the expression associated with an arithmetic expression tree.

```
/**
 * This traversal specializes EulerTour to print out the
 * arithmetic expression stored in the tree. It assumes that the
 * elements stored in the nodes of the tree support a toString
 * method that prints the value at an external node or the
 * operator at an internal node.
 */
public class PrintExpressionTour extends EulerTour {
  public Object execute(BinaryTree T) {
    super.execute(T);
    System.out.print("Expression: ");
    eulerTour(T.root());
    System.out.println();
    return null;    // nothing interesting to return
  }
  protected void visitExternal(Position p, TraversalResult r) {
    System.out.print(p.element());
  }
  protected void visitLeft(Position p, TraversalResult r) {
    System.out.print("(");
  }
  protected void visitBelow(Position p, TraversalResult r) {
    System.out.print(p.element());
  }
  protected void visitRight(Position p, TraversalResult r) {
    System.out.print(")");
  }
}
```

Code Fragment 6.25: Class PrintExpressionTour that specializes EulerTour to print the expression associated with an arithmetic expression tree.

Having presenting these code fragments, we describe in the next section a number of efficient ways of realizing the tree abstract data type by concrete data structures, such as sequences and linked structures.

6.4 Data Structures for Representing Trees

In this section, we describe concrete data structures for representing trees.

6.4.1 A Vector-Based Structure for Binary Trees

A simple structure for representing a binary tree T is based on a way of numbering the nodes of T. For every node v of T, let $p(v)$ be the integer defined as follows.

- If v is the root of T, then $p(v) = 1$.
- If v is the left child of node u, then $p(v) = 2p(u)$.
- If v is the right child of node u, then $p(v) = 2p(u) + 1$.

The numbering function p is known as a **level numbering** of the nodes in a binary tree T, for it numbers the nodes on each level of T in increasing order from left to right, although it may skip some numbers. (See Figure 6.18.)

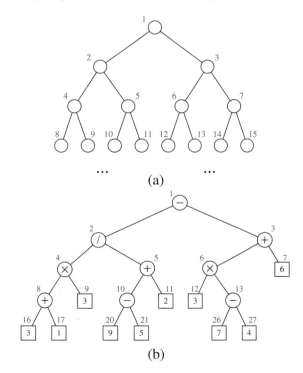

Figure 6.18: Binary tree level numbering: (a) general scheme; (b) an example.

The level numbering function p suggests a representation of a binary tree T by means of a vector S such that node v of T is associated with the element of S at rank $p(v)$. (See Figure 6.19.) Typically, we realize the vector S by means of an extendable array. (See Section 5.1.3.) Such an implementation is simple and efficient, for we can use it to easily perform the methods root, parent, leftChild, rightChild, sibling, isInternal, isExternal, and isRoot by using simple arithmetic operations on the numbers $p(v)$ associated with each node v involved in the operation. That is, each position object v is simply a "wrapper" for the index $p(v)$ into the vector S. We leave the details of such implementations as a simple exercise (R-6.24).

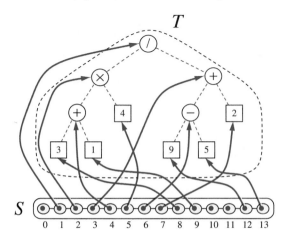

Figure 6.19: Representation of a binary tree T by means of a vector S.

Let n be the number of nodes of T, and let p_M be the maximum value of $p(v)$ over all the nodes of T. Vector S has size $N = p_M + 1$ since the element of S at rank 0 is not associated with any node of T. Also, vector S will have, in general, a number of empty elements that do not refer to existing nodes of T. These empty slots could, for example, correspond to empty external nodes or even slots where descendents of such nodes would go. In fact, in the worst case, $N = 2^{(n+1)/2}$, the justification of which is left as an exercise (R-6.20). In Section 7.3, we will see a class of binary trees, called "heaps" for which $N = n + 1$. Moreover, if all external nodes are empty, as will be the case in our heap implementation, then we can save additional space by not even extending the size of the vector S to include external nodes whose index is past that of the last internal node in the tree. Thus, in spite of the worst-case space usage, there are applications for which the vector representation of a binary tree is space efficient. Still, for general binary trees, the exponential worst-case space requirement of this representation is prohibitive.

Table 6.1 summarizes the running times of the methods of a binary tree implemented with a vector. We do not include in this table any methods for updating a binary tree; we instead explore such operations in an exercise (C-6.18).

Operation	Time
positions, elements	$O(n)$
swapElements, replaceElement	$O(1)$
root, parent, children	$O(1)$
leftChild, rightChild, sibling	$O(1)$
isInternal, isExternal, isRoot	$O(1)$

Table 6.1: Running times of the methods of a binary tree T implemented with a vector S, where S is realized by means of an array. We denote with n the number of nodes of T, and N denotes the size of S. Methods hasNext(), nextObject(), and nextPosition() of the iterators elements(), positions(), and children(v) take $O(1)$ time. The space usage is $O(N)$, which is $O(2^{(n+1)/2})$ in the worst case.

The vector implementation of a binary tree is a fast and easy way of realizing the binary tree ADT, but it can be very space inefficient if the height of the tree is large. The next data structure we discuss for representing binary trees does not have this drawback.

6.4.2 A Linked Structure for Binary Trees

A natural way to realize a binary tree T is to use a ***linked structure***. In this approach we represent each node v of T by an object with references to the element stored at v and to the position objects associated with the children and parent of v. (See Figure 6.20.)

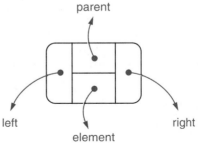

Figure 6.20: A node in a linked data structure for representing a binary tree.

We show a linked structure representation of a binary tree in Figure 6.21.

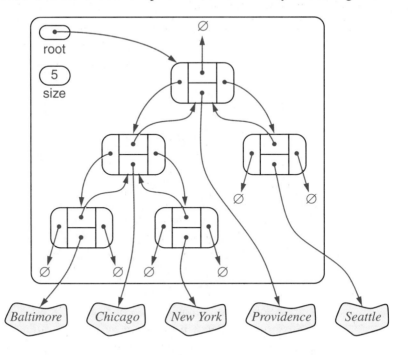

Figure 6.21: An example linked data structure for representing a binary tree.

If v is the root of T, then the reference to the parent node is null, and if v is an external node, then the references to the children of v are null. If we wish to save space for cases when external nodes are empty, then we can have references to empty external nodes be null. That is, we can allow a reference from an internal node to an external node child to be null. Even better, from an object-oriented

Caution   viewpoint, is that we could use a specially-created object, NULL_NODE, so that every missing external node reference is instead a reference to this object. Such an object can implement the Position interface. Of course, if we use such place holders for external nodes, then we may have to be prepared for the parent method throwing an exception should it be given such a place-holder external node.

Class BTNode (Code Fragment 6.26) represents a node v by an object implementing the position ADT and having instance variables element, left, right, and parent, which reference the element stored at v, the left child of v, the right child of v, and the parent of v, respectively. Class BTNode also has methods that return and set these variables.

```
/** Node of a binary tree */
public class BTNode implements Position {
  private Object element;
  private BTNode left, right, parent;
  /** default constructor */
  public BTNode() { }
  /** constructor with parameters */
  public BTNode(Object o, BTNode u, BTNode v, BTNode w) {
    setElement(o);
    setParent(u);
    setLeft(v);
    setRight(w);
  }
  public Object element() { return element; }
  public void setElement(Object o) { element=o; }
  public BTNode getLeft() { return left; }
  public void setLeft(BTNode v) { left=v; }
  public BTNode getRight() { return right; }
  public void setRight(BTNode v) { right=v; }
  public BTNode getParent() { return parent; }
  public void setParent(BTNode v) { parent=v; }
}
```

Code Fragment 6.26: Auxiliary class BTNode for implementing binary tree nodes.

In Code Fragments 6.27 and 6.28, we show class LinkedBinaryTree that implements the BinaryTree interface (Code Fragment 6.15) using a linked data structure. This class stores the size of the tree and a reference to the BTNode object associated with the root of the tree in internal variables. In addition to the BinaryTree interface methods, LinkedBinaryTree includes also the following update methods:

expandExternal(v): Transform v from an external node into an internal node by creating two new external nodes and making them the left and right children of v, respectively; an error condition occurs if v is an internal node.
Input: Position; *Output:* None.

removeAboveExternal(w): Remove the external node w together with its parent v, replacing v with the sibling of w (see Figure 6.13); this operation generates an error condition if w is an internal node or w is the root.
Input: Position; *Output:* None.

Class LinkedBinaryTree has a constructor with no arguments that returns a binary tree consisting of a single node. Starting from this single-node tree, we can
build any binary tree by repeatedly applying the expandExternal method. Likewise,
we can dismantle any binary tree T using the removeAboveExternal operation, ultimately reducing such a tree T to a single external node.

```
public class LinkedBinaryTree implements BinaryTree {
  private Position root; // reference to the root
  private int size; // number of nodes
  public LinkedBinaryTree() {
    root = new BTNode(null,null,null,null);
    size = 1;
  }

  public int size() { return size; }
  public boolean isEmpty() { return (size==0); }
  public boolean isInternal(Position v) {
    return (((BTNode) v).getLeft()!=null && ((BTNode) v).getRight()!=null);
  }
  public boolean isExternal(Position v) {
    return (((BTNode) v).getLeft()==null && ((BTNode) v).getRight()==null);
  }
  public boolean isRoot(Position v) { return (v==root()); }

  public Position root() { return root; }
  public PositionIterator positions() {
    Position[] positions = new Position[size()];
    inorderPositions(root(), positions, 0);
    return new ArrayPositionIterator(positions);
  }
  public Position leftChild(Position v) { return ((BTNode) v).getLeft(); }
  public Position rightChild(Position v) { return ((BTNode) v).getRight(); }
  public Position sibling(Position v) {
    Position p = parent(v);
    Position lc = leftChild(p);
    if (v == lc)
      return rightChild(p);
    else
      return lc;
  }
  public Position parent(Position v) { return ((BTNode) v).getParent(); }
```

Code Fragment 6.27: Class LinkedBinaryTree, implementing the BinaryTree interface. (Continues in Code Fragment 6.28.)

```java
public Object replaceElement(Position v, Object o) {
    Object temp = ((BTNode) v).element();
    ((BTNode) v).setElement(o);
    return temp;
}
public void swapElements(Position v, Position w) {
    Object temp = w.element();
    ((BTNode) w).setElement(v.element());
    ((BTNode) v).setElement(temp);
}
public void expandExternal(Position v) {
    if (isExternal(v)) {
        ((BTNode) v).setLeft(new BTNode(null,(BTNode) v, null, null));
        ((BTNode) v).setRight(new BTNode(null,(BTNode) v, null, null));
        size += 2;
    }
}
public void removeAboveExternal(Position v) {
    if (isExternal(v)) {
        BTNode p = (BTNode) parent(v);
        BTNode s = (BTNode) sibling(v);
        if (isRoot(p)) {
            s.setParent(null);
            root = s;
        }
        else {
            BTNode g = (BTNode) parent(p);
            if (p == leftChild(g))
                g.setLeft(s);
            else
                g.setRight(s);
            s.setParent(g);
        }
        size -= 2;
    }
}
```

Code Fragment 6.28: Class LinkedBinaryTree, implementing the BinaryTree interface. (Continued from Code Fragment 6.27.)

Note that the update methods expandExternal(v) and removeAboveExternal(v) work properly only when the external nodes are regular nodes, that is, they are not null nor the special NULL_NODE object. We explore alternate binary tree update methods in Exercise C-6.7.

Another example use of method expandExternal is to "clone" a binary tree T, to construct an exact copy T' of T. We do this recursively, starting with T' being a single external node v'. We call the recursive algorithm shown in Code Fragment 6.29 on the root v of T, which clones T using a preorder traversal. In Java, every object implementing the java.lang.Cloneable interface must be able to duplicate itself using the clone() method. The default implementation of clone() is simply to copy the instance variables for an object. Thus, an implementation of an algorithm like that given in Code Fragment 6.29 should be used for cloning a binary tree.

Algorithm clone(T, T', v, v'):

  Input: A binary tree T containing a node v and a binary tree T' containing an external node v'

  Output: An augmentation of T' so that the subtree rooted at v' is an exact copy of the subtree of T rooted at v

T'.replaceElement(v', v.element())
if T.isInternal(v) **then**
   T'.expandExternal(v')
   clone(T, T', T.leftChild(v), T'.leftChild(v'))
   clone(T, T', T.rightChild(v), T'.rightChild(v'))

Code Fragment 6.29: Algorithm clone.

Let us now analyze the running times of the methods of class LinkedBinary-Tree, which uses a linked structure representation:

- Methods size() and isEmpty() use an instance variable storing the number of nodes of T, and each take $O(1)$ time.
- Method swapElements(v, w) just swaps the element references of v and w, and also takes $O(1)$ time. Likewise, the method replaceElement(v, e) takes $O(1)$ time.
- Method positions() is implemented by performing an inorder traversal. Note any one of the three traversals discussed in Section 6.3.4 (preorder, inorder, and postorder) will serve the purpose. The nodes visited by the traversal are stored in an array and the output iterator is generated via an adapter class ArrayPositionIterator. Method elements() is similar. Thus, methods positions() and elements() take $O(n)$ time each.
- The adapter class ArrayPositionIterator supports hasNext(), nextObject(), and nextPosition() methods of iterators elements() and positions(), as well as the iterator children(v), in $O(1)$ time.

Considering the space required by this data structure, note that there is an object of class BTNode (Code Fragment 6.26) for every node of tree T. Thus, the overall space requirement is $O(n)$.

Table 6.2 summarizes the performance of this implementation of a binary tree.

Operation	Time
positions, elements	$O(n)$
swapElements, replaceElement	$O(1)$
root, parent, children	$O(1)$
leftChild, rightChild, sibling	$O(1)$
isInternal, isExternal, isRoot	$O(1)$
expandExternal, removeAboveExternal	$O(1)$

Table 6.2: Running times for the methods of an n-node binary tree implemented with a linked structure. The space usage is $O(n)$.

6.4.3 A Linked Structure for General Trees

We can extend the linked structure for binary trees to represent general trees. Since there is no limit on the number of children that a node v in a general tree can have, we use a container (for example, a list or vector) to store the children of v, instead of using instance variables. This structure is schematically illustrated in Figure 6.22.

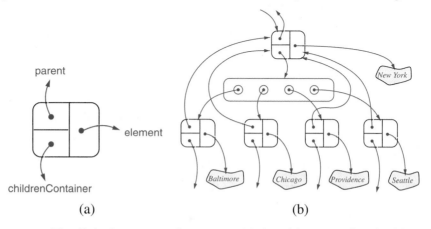

Figure 6.22: The linked structure for a tree: (a) the object associated with a node; (b) the portion of the data structure associated with a node and its children.

Table 6.3 summarizes the performance of the implementation of a tree by means of a linked structure. The analysis is left as an exercise, but we note that, by using a container to store the children of each node v, we can implement the children(v) method simply by calling the elements() method of the children container that v stores.

Operation	Time
size, isEmpty	$O(1)$
positions, elements	$O(n)$
swapElements, replaceElement	$O(1)$
root, parent	$O(1)$
children(v)	$O(c_v)$
isInternal, isExternal, isRoot	$O(1)$

Table 6.3: Running times of the methods of an n-node tree implemented with a linked structure. We let c_v denote the number of children of a node v. The space usage is $O(n)$.

6.4.4 Representing General Trees with Binary Trees

An alternative representation of a general tree T is obtained by transforming T into a binary tree T'. (See Figure 6.23.) We assume that either T is ordered or that it has been arbitrarily ordered. The transformation is as follows:

- For each node u of T, there is an internal node u' of T' associated with u.

- If u is an external node of T and does not have a sibling immediately following it, then the children of u' in T' are external nodes.

- If u is an internal node of T and v is the first child of u in T, then v' is the left child of u' in T.

- If node v has a sibling w immediately following it, then w' is the right child of v' in T'.

Note that the external nodes of T' are not associated with nodes of T and serve only as place holders (hence, may even be null).

It is easy to maintain the correspondence between T and T', and to express operations in T in terms of corresponding operations in T'. Intuitively, we can think of the correspondence in terms of a conversion of T into T' that takes each set of siblings $\{v_1, v_2, \ldots, v_k\}$ in T with parent v and replaces it with a chain of right children rooted at v_1, which then becomes the left child of v.

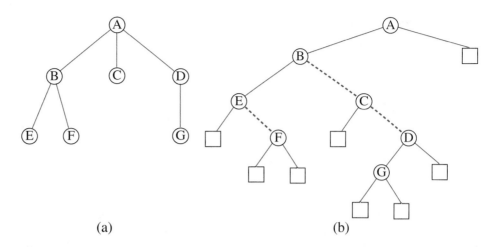

Figure 6.23: Representation of a tree by means of a binary tree: (a) tree T; (b) binary tree T' associated with T. The dashed edges connect nodes of T' associated with sibling nodes of T.

Table 6.4 summarizes the performance of the implementation of a tree by means of a binary tree. The analysis is left as an exercise (C-6.20).

Operation	Time
size, isEmpty	$O(1)$
positions, elements	$O(n)$
swapElements, replaceElement	$O(1)$
root	$O(1)$
parent(v)	$O(s_v)$
children(v)	$O(c_v)$
isInternal, isExternal, isRoot	$O(1)$

Table 6.4: Running times of the methods of a tree represented by means of a binary tree, which is in turn implemented with a linked structure. We denote with n the number of nodes of the tree, with c_v the number of children of a node v, and with s_v the number of siblings of v. The methods hasNext() and nextObject() of the iterators returned by elements(), positions(), and children(v) take $O(1)$ time. The space usage is $O(n)$.

6.5 Exercises

Reinforcement

R-6.1 The following questions refer to the tree of Figure 6.3.

    a. Which node is the root?

    b. What are the internal nodes?

    c. How many descendents does node cs016/ have?

    d. How many ancestors does node cs016/ have?

    e. What are the siblings of node homeworks/?

    f. Which nodes are in the subtree rooted at node projects/?

    g. What is the depth of node papers/?

    h. What is the height of the tree?

R-6.2 Find the value of the arithmetic expression associated with each subtree of the binary tree of Figure 6.6.

R-6.3 Let T be an n-node improper binary tree (that is, each internal node has one or two children). Describe how to represent T by means of a ***proper*** binary tree T' with $O(n)$ nodes.

R-6.4 Give a justification of Proposition 6.6.

R-6.5 What is the running time of algorithm height2(T, v) (Code Fragment 6.7) when called on a node v distinct from the root of T?

R-6.6 Let T be the tree of Figure 6.3.

    a. Give the output of algorithm preorderPrint$(T, T.\text{root}())$ (Code Fragment 6.10).

    b. Give the output of algorithm parentheticRepresentation$(T, T.\text{root}())$ (which is shown in Code Fragment 6.11).

R-6.7 Describe a modification to the parentheticRepresentation method given in Code Fragment 6.11 so that it uses the length() method for String objects to output the parenthetic representation of a tree with line breaks and spaces added to display the tree in a text window that is 80 characters wide.

R-6.8★ Draw an expression tree that has four external nodes, storing the numbers 1, 5, 6, and 7 (with each number stored one per external node but not necessarily in this order), and has three internal nodes, each storing an operation from the set $\{+, -, \times, /\}$ of binary arithmetic operators, so that the value of the root is 21. The operators are assumed to return rational numbers (not integers), and an operator may be used more than once (but we only store one operator per internal node).

R-6.9 Let T be an ordered tree with more than one node. Is it possible that the preorder traversal of T visits the nodes in the same order as the postorder traversal of T? If so, give an example; otherwise, argue why this cannot occur. Likewise, is it possible that the preorder traversal of T visits the nodes in the reverse order of the postorder traversal of T? If so, give an example; otherwise, argue why this cannot occur.

R-6.10 Answer the previous question for the case when T is a proper binary tree with more than one node.

R-6.11 Let T be a tree with n nodes.

- What is the running time of parentheticRepresentation(T, T.root())? (See Code Fragment 6.11.)

R-6.12 Draw a (single) binary tree T such that

- Each internal node of T stores a single character
- A *preorder* traversal of T yields EXAMFUN
- An *inorder* traversal of T yields MAFXUEN.

R-6.13 Answer the following questions so as to justify Proposition 6.10.

a. Draw a binary tree with height 7 and maximum number of external nodes.
b. What is the minimum number of external nodes for a binary tree with height h? Justify your answer.
c. What is the maximum number of external nodes for a binary tree with height h? Justify your answer.
d. Let T be a binary tree with height h and n nodes. Show that

$$\log(n+1) - 1 \leq h \leq (n-1)/2.$$

e. For which values of n and h can the above lower and upper bounds on h be attained with equality?

R-6.14 Modify the Java method preorderPrint given in Code Fragment 6.10 so that it will print the strings associated with the nodes of a tree one per line, and indented proportionally to the depth of the node.

R-6.15 Let T be the tree of Figure 6.3. Draw, as best as you can, the output of the algorithm postorderPrint(T, T.root()) (see Code Fragment 6.13).

R-6.16 Let T be the tree of Figure 6.10. Compute, in terms of the values given in this figure, the output of algorithm diskSpace(T, T.root()) (see Code Fragment 6.14).

R-6.17 Let T be the binary tree of Figure 6.6.

    a. Give the output of algorithm preorderPrint(T, T.root()) (which is given in Code Fragment 6.10).
    b. Give the output of algorithm parentheticRepresentation(T, T.root()) (which is given in Code Fragment 6.11).

R-6.18 Let T be the binary tree of Figure 6.6.

    a. Give the output of algorithm postorderPrint(T, T.root()) (which is given in Code Fragment 6.13).
    b. Give the output of algorithm printExpression(T, T.root()) (which is given in Code Fragment 6.21).

R-6.19 Let T be a binary tree such that all the external nodes have the same depth. Let D_e be the sum of the depths of all the external nodes of T, and let D_i be the sum of the depths of all the internal nodes of T. Find constants a and b such that

$$D_e + 1 = aD_i + bn,$$

where n is the number of nodes of T. (Hint: Try to gain some intuition by drawing a few different binary trees such that all the external nodes have the same depth.)

R-6.20 Let T be a binary tree with n nodes, and let p be the level numbering of the nodes of T, as given in Section 6.4.1.

    a. Show that, for every node v of T, $p(v) \le 2^{(n+1)/2} - 1$.
    b. Show an example of a binary tree with at least five nodes that attains the above upper bound on the maximum value of $p(v)$ for some node v.

R-6.21 Show that the level numbering p of the nodes of a binary tree given in Section 6.4.1 assigns a unique integer to every node, that is, $p(u) \ne p(v)$ whenever $u \ne v$.

R-6.22 Draw the binary tree representation of the tree shown in Figure 6.2 using the binary-tree representation scheme described in Section 6.4.4.

R-6.23 Answer the following questions with reference to the following line of method isExternal from class LinkedBinaryTree (Code Fragment 6.27):

return ((BTNode) v).getLeft()==**null** && ((BTNode) v).getRight()==**null**;

    a. Can we replace the above line with

        return ((BTNode) v).getLeft()==**null**;

    and still get a correct behavior?

    b. Can we replace the above line with

        return ((BTNode) v).getRight()==**null**;

    and still get a correct behavior?

    c. Can we replace the above line with

        return ((BTNode) v).getParent()==**null**;

    and still get a correct behavior?

R-6.24 Let T be a binary tree with n nodes that is realized with a vector, S, and let p be the level numbering of the nodes in T, as given in Section 6.4.1. Give pseudo-code descriptions of each of the methods root, parent, leftChild, rightChild, isInternal, isExternal, and isRoot.

Creativity

C-6.1 Let T be a tree whose nodes store strings. Give an algorithm that computes and prints, for every internal node v of T, the string stored at v and the height of the subtree rooted at v.

C-6.2★ Design an algorithm for drawing general trees.

C-6.3 Design algorithms for the following operations for a binary tree T:

- preorderNext(v): return the node visited after node v in a preorder traversal of T
- inorderNext(v): return the node visited after node v in an inorder traversal of T
- postorderNext(v): return the node visited after node v in a postorder traversal of T.

What are the worst-case running times of your algorithms?

C-6.4 Give an $O(n)$-time algorithm for computing the depth of all the nodes of a tree T, where n is the number of nodes of T.

C-6.5 Give an example of a tree T that causes Algorithm height1 (Code Fragment 6.6) to run in time $\Theta(n^2)$, where n is the number of nodes in T.

C-6.6 For a tree T, let $i(T)$ denote the number of its internal nodes, and let $e(T)$ denote the number of its external nodes. Show that if every internal node in T has exactly three (3) children, then $e(T) = 2i(T) + 1$.

C-6.7 The update operations expandExternal and removeAboveExternal do not permit the creation of an improper binary tree. Give pseudo-code descriptions for alternate update operations suitable for improper binary trees. You may need to define new query operations as well.

C-6.8 The **balance factor** of an internal node v of a binary tree is the difference between the heights of the right and left subtrees of v. Show how to specialize the Euler tour traversal of Section 6.3.5 to print the balance factors of all the nodes of a binary tree.

C-6.9 Two ordered trees T' and T'' are said to be **isomorphic** if one of the following holds:

- Both T' and T'' consist of a single node
- Both T' and T'' have the same number k of subtrees, and the ith subtree of T' is isomorphic to the ith subtree of T'', for $i = 1, \ldots, k$.

Design an algorithm that tests whether two given ordered trees are isomorphic. What is the running time of your algorithm?

C-6.10 Extend the concept of an Euler tour to an ordered tree that is not necessarily a binary tree, and design a generic traversal of an ordered tree.

C-6.11 Algorithm preorderDraw draws a binary tree T by assigning x- and y-coordinates to each node v as follows:

- Set $x(v)$ equal to the number of nodes preceding v in the preorder traversal of T.
- Set $y(v)$ equal to the depth of v in T.

a. Show that the drawing of T produced by algorithm preorderDraw has no pairs of crossing edges.

b. Redraw the binary tree of Figure 6.16 using algorithm preorderDraw.

c. Redraw the binary tree of Figure 6.16 using algorithm postorderDraw, which is similar to preorderDraw but assigns x-coordinates using a postorder traversal.

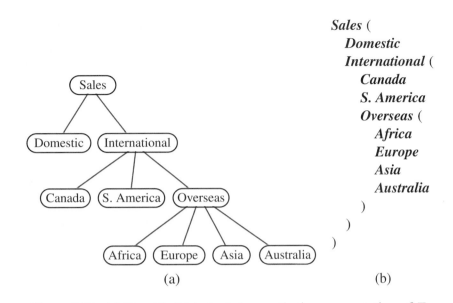

Sales (
Domestic
International (
   Canada
   S. America
   Overseas (
      Africa
      Europe
      Asia
      Australia
)
)
)

(a)   (b)

Figure 6.24: (a) Tree T; (b) indented parenthetic representation of T.

C-6.12 The *indented parenthetic representation* of a tree T is a variation of the parenthetic representation of T (see Figure 6.8) illustrated in Figure 6.24. Give an algorithm that prints the indented parenthetic representation of a tree.

C-6.13 Let a visit action in the Euler tour traversal be denoted by a pair (v, a), where v is the visited node and a is one of **left**, **below**, or **right**. Design an algorithm for performing operation tourNext(v, a), which returns the visit action (w, b) following (v, a). What is the worst-case running time of your algorithm?

C-6.14 Consider a variation of the linked data structure for binary trees where each node object has references to the node objects of the children but not to the node object of the parent. Describe an implementation of the methods of a binary tree with this data structure and analyze the time complexity for these methods.

C-6.15 Design an alternative implementation of the linked data structure for binary trees using a class for nodes that specializes into subclasses for an internal node, an external node, and the root node.

C-6.16 Justify the bounds in Table 6.1 by providing a detailed analysis of the running times of the methods of a binary tree T implemented with a vector S, where S is realized by means of an array.

C-6.17 Within the linked data structure for binary trees, explore an alternative design for implementing the iterators returned by methods elements(), nodes(), and children(v) such that each of these methods takes $O(1)$ time. Can you still achieve constant time implementations for the iterator methods hasNext(), nextObject(), and nextPosition() of the iterators returned?

C-6.18 Describe efficient implementations of the expandExternal and remove-AboveExternal binary tree update methods, described in Section 6.4.2, for the case when the binary tree is implemented using a vector S, where S is realized using an expandable array. Your methods should work even for null external nodes, assuming we represent such a node as a wrapper object storing an index to an empty or nonexistent cell in S. What are the worst-case running times of these methods? What is the running time of removeAboveExternal if the internal node removed has only external node children?

C-6.19 Justify Table 6.3, summarizing the running time of the methods of a tree represented with a linked structure, by providing, for each method, a description of its implementation, and an analysis of its running time.

C-6.20 Justify the bounds in Table 6.4 for the running times of the methods of a tree represented by means of a binary tree, which is in turn implemented with a linked structure, by providing, for each method, a description of its implementation and an analysis of its running time.

C-6.21 Let T be a binary tree with n nodes. Define a ***Roman node*** to be a node v in T, such that the number of descendents in v's left subtree differ from the number of descendents in v's right subtree by at most 5. Describe a linear-time method for finding each node v of T, such that v is not a Roman node, but all of v's descendents are Roman nodes.

C-6.22 Let T' be the binary tree representing a tree T (see Section 6.4.4).

   a. Is a preorder traversal of T' equivalent to a preorder traversal of T?
   b. Is a postorder traversal of T' equivalent to a postorder traversal of T?
   c. Is an inorder traversal of T' equivalent to some well-structured traversal of T?

C-6.23 Describe in pseudo-code a nonrecursive method for performing an Euler tour traversal of a binary tree that runs in linear time and does not use a stack. (Hint: You can tell which visit action to perform at a node by taking note of where you are coming from.)

C-6.24 Describe in pseudo-code a nonrecursive method for performing an inorder traversal of a binary tree in linear time. (Hint: Use a stack.)

C-6.25 Let T be a binary tree with n nodes (T may or may not be realized with a vector). Give a linear-time method that uses the methods of the Binary-Tree interface to traverse the nodes of T by increasing values of the level numbering function p given in Section 6.4.1. This traversal is known as the *level order traversal*. (Hint: Use a queue.)

C-6.26 The *path length* of a tree T is the sum of the depths of all the nodes in T. Describe a linear-time method for computing the path length of a tree T (which is not necessarily binary).

C-6.27 Define the *internal path length*, $I(T)$, of a tree T to be the sum of the depths of all the internal nodes in T. Likewise, define the *external path length*, $E(T)$, of a tree T to be the sum of the depths of all the external nodes in T. Show that if T is a binary tree with n internal nodes, then $E(T) = I(T) + 2n$. (Hint: Use the fact that we can build T from a single root node via a series of n expandExternal operations.)

C-6.28 Let T be a tree with n nodes. Define the *lowest common ancestor* (LCA) between two nodes v and w as the lowest node in T that has both v and w as descendents (where we allow a node to be a descendent of itself). Given two nodes v and w, describe an efficient algorithm for finding the LCA of v and w. What is the running time of your method?

C-6.29 Let T be a tree with n nodes, and, for any node v in T, let d_v denote the depth of v in T. The *distance* between two nodes v and w in T is $d_v + d_w - 2d_u$, where u is the LCA u of v and w (as defined in the previous exercise). The *diameter* of T is the maximum distance between two nodes in T. Describe an efficient algorithm for finding the diameter of T. What is the running time of your method?

Projects

P-6.1 Complete the implementation of class LinkedBinaryTree taking into account error conditions.

P-6.2 Implement the binary tree ADT using a vector.

P-6.3 Implement the binary tree ADT using a linked structure.

P-6.4 Write a program that draws a binary tree.

P-6.5★ Write a program that draws a general tree.

P-6.6 Write a program that can input and display a person's family tree.

P-6.7 Implement the binary tree representation of the tree ADT. You may reuse the LinkedBinaryTree implementation of a binary tree.

P-6.8 A *slicing floorplan* is a decomposition of a rectangle with horizontal and vertical sides using horizontal and vertical *cuts*. (See Figure 6.25a.) A slicing floorplan can be represented by a binary tree, called a *slicing tree*, whose internal nodes represent the cuts, and whose external nodes represent the *basic rectangles* into which the floorplan is decomposed by the cuts. (See Figure 6.25b.) The *compaction problem* is defined as follows. Assume that each basic rectangle of a slicing floorplan is assigned a minimum width w and a minimum height h. The compaction problem is to find the smallest possible height and width for each rectangle of the slicing floorplan that is compatible with the minimum dimensions of the basic rectangles. Namely, this problem requires the assignment of values $h(v)$ and $w(v)$ to each node v of the slicing tree such that:

$$w(v) = \begin{cases} w & \text{if } v \text{ is an external node whose basic rectangle has minimum width } w \\ \max(w(w), w(z)) & \text{if } v \text{ is an internal node associated with a horizontal cut with left child } w \text{ and right child } z \\ w(w) + w(z) & \text{if } v \text{ is an internal node associated with a vertical cut with left child } w \text{ and right child } z \end{cases}$$

$$h(v) = \begin{cases} h & \text{if } v \text{ is an external node whose basic rectangle has minimum height } h \\ h(w) + h(z) & \text{if } v \text{ is an internal node associated with a horizontal cut with left child } w \text{ and right child } z \\ \max(h(w), h(z)) & \text{if } v \text{ is an internal node associated with a vertical cut with left child } w \text{ and right child } z \end{cases}$$

Design a data structure for slicing floorplans that supports the operations:

- Create a floorplan consisting of a single basic rectangle.
- Decompose a basic rectangle by means of a horizontal cut.
- Decompose a basic rectangle by means of a vertical cut.
- Assign minimum height and width to a basic rectangle.
- Draw the slicing tree associated with the floorplan.
- Compact the floorplan.
- Draw the compacted floorplan.

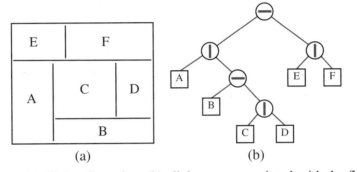

Figure 6.25: (a) Slicing floorplan; (b) slicing tree associated with the floorplan.

P-6.9 Write a program that takes as input a fully parenthesized, arithmetic expression and converts it to a binary expression tree. Your program should display the tree in some way and also print the value associated with the root. For an additional challenge, allow for the leaves to store variables of the form x_1, x_2, x_3, and so on, which are initially 0 and which can be updated interactively by your program, with the corresponding update in the printed value of the root of the expression tree.

Chapter Notes

The concept of viewing data structures as containers (and other principles of object-oriented design) can be found in object-oriented design books by Booch [14] and Budd [18]. The concept also exists under the name "collection class" in books by Golberg and Robson [40] and Liskov and Guttag [68]. Our use of the "position" abstraction derives from the "position" and "node" abstractions introduced by Aho, Hopcroft, and Ullman [5]. Discussions of the classic preorder, inorder, and postorder tree traversal methods can be found in Knuth's *Fundamental Algorithms* book [59]. The Euler tour traversal technique comes from the parallel algorithms community, as it is introduced by Tarjan and Vishkin [90] and is discussed by JáJá [52] and by Karp and Ramachandran [56]. The algorithm for drawing a tree is generally considered to be a part of the "folklore" of graph drawing algorithms. The reader interested in graph drawing is referred to works by Tamassia [89] and Di Battista *et al.* [29, 30]. The puzzler in Exercise R-6.7 was communicated by Micha Sharir.

Chapter

7

Priority Queues

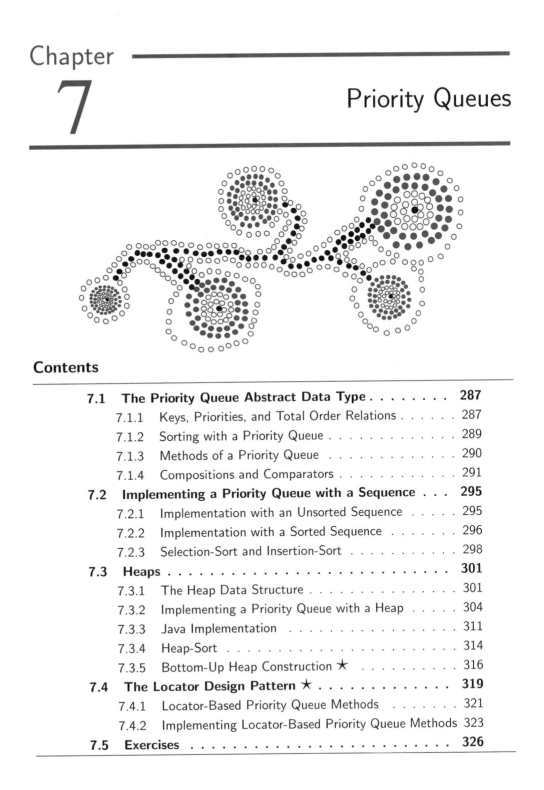

Contents

Having the right priorities is important to succeeding in life. On a quiet Saturday afternoon, presented with the opportunity of taking a nap, watching TV, playing soccer, or studying this chapter, the zealous student will certainly give first priority to the latter task. Outside of comfortable campus boundaries, priorities are an even more serious matter. Consider, for example, an air-traffic control center that has to decide which flight to clear for landing from among many approaching the airport. The priority of a flight may depend not only on the plane's distance from the runway, but also on the amount of fuel it has left. Choosing the next flight to land may be a life-critical decision. Another example is a standby passenger who, when she checks in, is told by the gate agent that she is "first" in line for a fully-booked flight. Thus, she thinks she has top priority if seats become available. Little does she know that the airline will give first priority to a standby passenger who has arrived later, if such a passenger is given a better priority by the agent (priority here is measured in terms of the fare paid, frequent-flyer status, and check-in time).

In this chapter, we study data structures that store "prioritized elements," that is, elements that have priorities assigned to them. Such a priority is typically a numerical value, and we take the view that the smallest numerical value should have first priority. However, as we show in this chapter, we can support the opposite viewpoint just as easily. More generally, priorities can be viewed as arbitrary objects, so long as there is a consistent way of comparing pairs of such objects to see if one is less than or equal to the other. This general viewpoint allows us to define a fairly generic ADT for storing prioritized elements.

A *priority queue* is an abstract data type for storing a collection of prioritized elements that supports arbitrary element insertion but supports removal of elements in order of priority; that is, the element with first priority can be removed at any time. This ADT is fundamentally different from the position-based data structures we discussed in previous chapters, such as stacks, queues, deques, sequences, and even trees. These other data structures store elements at specific positions, which are often positions in a linear arrangement of the elements determined by the insertion and deletion operations performed. The priority queue ADT stores elements according to their priorities, and has no notion of "position."

We present the priority queue ADT in Section 7.1. In Section 7.2, we present two implementations of a priority queue using sequences. These implementations are simple, but unfortunately not very efficient. Even so, they allow us to easily describe two well-known sorting algorithms, insertion-sort and selection-sort. In Section 7.3, we give a more efficient implementation of a priority queue, based on a concrete data structure known as a *heap*. A heap uses the hierarchical power of binary trees to support the priority queue operations in logarithmic time, which leads to a fast sorting algorithm known as heap-sort. We conclude this chapter with a discussion of a design pattern known as the locator.

7.1 The Priority Queue Abstract Data Type

In this section, we provide the framework for studying priority queues, based on the concepts of key and comparator, and we define the methods of a priority queue as an abstract data type (ADT).

7.1.1 Keys, Priorities, and Total Order Relations

Applications commonly require our comparing and ranking objects according to parameters or properties, called "keys," that are assigned for each object in a collection. Formally, we define a *key* to be an object that is assigned to an element as a specific attribute for that element, which can be used to identify, rank, or weight that element. Note that the key is assigned to an element, typically by a user or application; hence, a key might represent a property that an element did not originally possess.

The key an application assigns to an element is not necessarily unique, however, and an application may even change an element's key if it needs to. For example, we can compare companies by earnings or by number of employees; hence, either of these parameters can be used as a key for a company, depending on the information we wish to extract. Likewise, we can compare restaurants by a critic's food quality rating or by average entrée price. To achieve the most generality, then, we allow a key to be of any type that is appropriate for a particular application.

As in the above motivating examples from an airport, the key used for comparisons is often more than a single numerical value, such as price, length, weight, or speed. That is, a key can sometimes be a more complex property that cannot be quantified with a single number. For example, the priority of standby passengers is usually determined by taking into account a host of different factors, including frequent-flyer status, the fare paid, and check-in time. In some applications, the key for an object is part of the object itself (for example, it might be an instance variable storing the list price of a book, or the weight of a car). In other applications, the key is not part of the object but the object gets assigned its key by the application (for example, the quality rating given to a stock by a financial analyst, or the priority assigned to a standby passenger by a gate agent).

The concept of a key as an arbitrary object type is therefore quite general. But, in order to deal consistently with such a general definition for keys and still be able to discuss when one key has priority over another, we need a way of robustly defining a rule for comparing keys.

Comparing Keys with Total Orders

A priority queue needs a comparison rule that will never contradict itself. In order for a comparison rule, which we denote by $\leq$, to be robust in this way, it must define a ***total order*** relation, which is to say that the comparison rule is defined for every pair of keys and it must satisfy the following properties:

- **Reflexive property**: $k \leq k$.
- **Antisymmetric property**: if $k_1 \leq k_2$ and $k_2 \leq k_1$, then $k_1 = k_2$.
- **Transitive property**: if $k_1 \leq k_2$ and $k_2 \leq k_3$, then $k_1 \leq k_3$.

Any comparison rule, $\leq$, that satisfies these three properties will never lead to a comparison contradiction. In fact, such a rule defines a linear ordering relationship among a set of keys; hence, if a (finite) collection of elements has a total order defined for it, then the notion of a ***smallest*** key, $k_{\min}$, is well defined, as a key in which $k_{\min} \leq k$, for any other key k in our collection.

A ***priority queue*** is a container of elements, each having an associated key that is provided at the time the element is inserted. The name "priority queue" comes from the fact that keys determine the "priority" used to pick elements to be removed. The two fundamental methods of a priority queue P are as follows:

- insertItem(k, e): insert an element e with key k into P.
- removeMin(): return and remove from P an element with the smallest key, that is, an element whose key is less than or equal to that of every other element in P.

By the way, some people refer to the removeMin method as the "extractMin" method, so as to stress that this method simultaneously removes and returns a smallest element in P. There are many applications where the insertItem and removeMin operations play an important role. We consider one such application in the example that follows.

Example 7.1: *Suppose a certain flight is fully booked an hour prior to departure. Because of the possibility of cancellations the airline maintains a priority queue of standby passengers hoping to get a seat. The priority of each passenger is determined by the airline taking into account the fare paid, the standby passenger's frequent-flyer status, and the time when the passenger requested to fly standby. A standby passenger reference is inserted into the priority queue with an insertItem operation as soon as he or she requests to fly standby. Shortly before the flight departure, if seats become available (for example, due to no-shows or last-minute cancellations), the airline removes from the priority queue a standby passenger with first priority using a removeMin operation and lets this person board. This process is then repeated until all available seats have been filled or the priority queue becomes empty.*

7.1.2 Sorting with a Priority Queue

Another important application of a priority queue is sorting, where we are given a collection S of n elements that can be compared according to a total order relation, and we want to rearrange them in increasing order (or at least in nondecreasing order if there are ties). The algorithm for sorting S with a priority queue Q is quite simple and consists of the following two phases:

1. In the first phase, we put the elements of S into an initially empty priority queue P by means of a series of n insertItem operations, one for each element.

2. In the second phase, we extract the elements from P in nondecreasing order by means of a series of n removeMin operations, putting them back into S in order.

We give pseudo-code for this algorithm in Code Fragment 7.1, assuming that S is a sequence (pseudo-code for a different type of collection, such as a list or vector, would be similar). The algorithm works correctly for any priority queue P, no matter how P is implemented. However, the running time of the algorithm is determined by the running times of operations insertItem and removeMin, which do depend on how P is implemented. Indeed, PriorityQueueSort should be considered more a sorting "scheme" than a sorting "algorithm," because it does not specify how the priority queue P is implemented. The PriorityQueueSort scheme is the paradigm of several popular sorting algorithms, including selection-sort, insertion-sort, and heap-sort, which we discuss in this chapter.

Algorithm PriorityQueueSort(S, P):

    Input: A sequence S storing n elements, on which a total order relation is defined, and a priority queue, P, that compares keys using the same total order relation

    Output: The sequence S sorted by the total order relation

    while S is not empty **do**
        $e \leftarrow S.\text{removeFirst}()$ {remove an element e from S}
        $P.\text{insertItem}(e, e)$ {the key is the element itself}
    while P is not empty **do**
        $e \leftarrow P.\text{removeMin}()$ {remove a smallest element from P}
        $S.\text{insertLast}(e)$ {add the element at the end of S}

Code Fragment 7.1: Algorithm PriorityQueueSort. Note that the elements of the input sequence S serve both as keys and elements of the priority queue P.

7.1.3 Methods of a Priority Queue

Having described the priority queue abstract data type at an intuitive level, we now describe it in more detail. As an ADT, a priority queue P supports the following methods:

> size(): Return the number of elements in P.
> *Input:* None; *Output:* Integer.

> isEmpty(): Test whether P is empty.
> *Input:* None; *Output:* Boolean.

> insertItem(k,e): Insert a new element e with key k into P.
> *Input:* Objects k (key) and e (element); *Output:* None.

> minElement(): Return (but do not remove) an element of P with smallest key; an error condition occurs if the priority queue is empty.
> *Input:* None; *Output:* Object (element).

> minKey(): Return a smallest key in P; an error condition occurs if the priority queue is empty.
> *Input:* None; *Output:* Object (key).

> removeMin(): Remove from P and return an element with smallest key; an error condition occurs if the priority queue is empty.
> *Input:* None; *Output:* Object (element).

As mentioned above, the primary methods of the priority queue ADT are the insertItem and removeMin operations. The other operations are either secondary query methods (operations minElement and minKey) or are generic container methods (operations size and isEmpty).

One of the interesting aspects of the priority queue ADT, which should now be obvious, is that the priority queue ADT is much simpler than the sequence ADT. This simplicity is due to the fact that elements in a priority queue are inserted and removed based entirely on their keys, whereas elements are inserted and removed in a sequence based on their positions and ranks. Thus, only one insertion method and one deletion method are needed in the priority queue ADT, whereas the sequence ADT has many different methods for inserting and removing elements. We leave as an exercise (R-7.1) the writing of a Java interface for the priority queue ADT. The operations of the priority queue abstract data type are illustrated in the following example.

Example 7.2: *The following table shows a series of operations and their effects on an initially empty priority queue P, where an element e and its key k are indicated by the pair (k,e). The "Priority Queue" column is somewhat deceiving since it shows the items sorted by key. This is more than is required of a priority queue. A priority queue need only have the minimum pair available, while storing the remaining pairs in an implementation-dependent manner.*

Operation	Output	Priority Queue
insertItem$(5,A)$	–	$\{(5,A)\}$
insertItem$(9,C)$	–	$\{(5,A),(9,C)\}$
insertItem$(3,B)$	–	$\{(3,B),(5,A),(9,C)\}$
insertItem$(7,D)$	–	$\{(3,B),(5,A),(7,D),(9,C)\}$
minElement$()$	B	$\{(3,B),(5,A),(7,D),(9,C)\}$
minKey$()$	3	$\{(3,B),(5,A),(7,D),(9,C)\}$
removeMin$()$	B	$\{(5,A),(7,D),(9,C)\}$
size$()$	3	$\{(5,A),(7,D),(9,C)\}$
removeMin$()$	A	$\{(7,D),(9,C)\}$
removeMin$()$	D	$\{(9,C)\}$
removeMin$()$	C	$\{\}$
removeMin$()$	"error"	$\{\}$
isEmpty$()$	true	$\{\}$

There are still two important issues that we have left undetermined to this point:

- How do we keep track of the associations between keys and elements?
- How do we compare keys so as to determine a smallest key?

Answering these questions involves the use of two interesting design patterns.

7.1.4 Compositions and Comparators

The priority queue ADT implicitly makes use of two design patterns, compositions and comparators, which we discuss in this subsection.

The Composition Pattern

One such pattern is the **composition pattern**. In this pattern, we define a single object e that is a composition of other objects. We use this pattern in the priority queue ADT when we define the objects being stored in the priority queue to actually be **pairs**. A pair (k,e) is the simplest composition, for it composes two objects into a single **pair** object. To implement this concept, we define a class that stores two objects in its first and second instance variables, respectively, and which provides methods to access and update these variables. We show in Code Fragment 7.2 an example of Java implementation of the pair pattern as applied to key-element pairs used in a priority queue. Other kinds of compositions include triples, which store three objects, quadruples, which store four objects, and general compositions, which can store an arbitrary number of objects (using, say, a sequence).

```java
public class Item {
  private Object key, elem;
  protected Item (Object k, Object e) {
    key = k;
    elem = e;
  }
  public Object key() { return key; }
  public Object element() { return elem; }
  public void setKey(Object k) { key = k; }
  public void setElement(Object e) { elem = e; }
}
```

Code Fragment 7.2: Class for the key-element pairs stored in a priority queue.

We can also allow composition objects to store other composition objects as elements, which would give rise to a hierarchical tree relationship defined on compositions, but we will not explore this usage in this book.

The Comparator Pattern

Another important issue in the priority queue ADT that we have so far left undefined is how to specify the relation for comparing keys. We have a number of design choices concerning how to compare keys that we can make at this point.

One possibility, and the one that is the most concrete, is to implement a different priority queue for each key type we want to use and each possible way of comparing keys of such types. The problem with this approach is that it is not very general and it requires that we create a lot of similar code.

An alternative strategy is to require that keys be able to compare themselves to one another. This solution allows us to write a general priority queue class that can store instances of a key class that implements some kind of Comparable interface and encapsulates all the usual comparison methods. This solution is an improvement over the specialized approach, for it allows us to write a single priority queue class that can handle lots of different types of keys. But there are contexts in which this solution is asking too much of the keys, as keys often do not "know" how they ought to be compared. Two examples follow.

Example 7.3: *Given keys 4 and 11 we have that $4 \leq 11$ if the keys are integer objects (to be compared in the usual manner), but $11 \leq 4$ if the keys are string objects (to be compared lexicographically).*

Example 7.4: *A geometric algorithm may compare points p and q in the plane, by their x-coordinate (that is, $p \leq q$ if $x(p) \leq x(q)$), to sort them from left to right, while another algorithm may compare them by their y-coordinate (that is, $p \leq q$ if $y(p) \leq y(q)$), to sort them from bottom to top. In principle, there is nothing pertaining to the concept of a point that says whether points should be compared by x- or y-coordinate. Also, many other ways of comparing points can be defined (for example, we can compare the distances of p and q from the origin).*

Thus, for the most general and reusable form of a priority queue, we should not rely on the keys to provide their comparison rules. Instead, we use special *comparator* objects that are external to the keys to supply the comparison rules. A comparator is an object that compares two keys. We assume that a priority queue P is given a comparator when P is constructed, and we might also imagine the ability of a priority queue to be given a new comparator if its old one ever becomes "out of date." When P needs to compare two keys, it uses the comparator it was given to perform the comparison. Thus, a programmer can write a general priority queue implementation that can work correctly in a wide variety of contexts. Formally, a comparator object provides the following methods, each of which takes two keys and compares them (or reports an error if the keys are incomparable). The methods of the comparator ADT include:

isLessThan(a,b): True if and only if a is less than b.
Input: Pair of objects; ***Output:*** Boolean.

isLessThanOrEqualTo(a,b): True if and only if a is less than or equal to b.
Input: Pair of objects; ***Output:*** Boolean.

isEqualTo(a,b): True if and only if a and b are equal.
Input: Pair of objects; ***Output:*** Boolean.

isGreaterThan(a,b): True if and only if a is greater than b.
Input: Pair of objects; ***Output:*** Boolean.

isGreaterThanOrEqualTo(a,b): True if and only if a is greater than or equal to b.
Input: Pair of objects; ***Output:*** Boolean.

isComparable(a): True if and only if a can be compared.
Input: Object; ***Output:*** Boolean.

We provide an example of a comparator in Code Fragment 7.3.

```java
public class Lexicographic implements Comparator {
  int xa, ya, xb, yb;
  // Comparator for points in the plane with the standard lexicographic order.
  // Assumes a Point2D has getX() and getY() methods returning its coordinates.
  private void getXY(Object a, Object b) {
    if (a == null || b == null)
      throw new InvalidElementException("Null Argument");
    try{
      xa = ((Point2D) a).getX();
      ya = ((Point2D) a).getY();
      xb = ((Point2D) b).getX();
      yb = ((Point2D) b).getY();
    }
    catch (ClassCastException e)
      { throw new InvalidElementException("Argument not a Point2D"); }
  }
  public boolean isLessThan(Object a, Object b) {
    getXY(a, b);
    if (xa == xb)
      return (ya < yb);
    else
      return (xa < xb);
  }
  public boolean isLessThanOrEqualTo(Object a, Object b) {
    getXY(a, b);
    if (xa == xb)
      return (ya <= yb);
    else
      return (xa <= xb);
  }
  public boolean isEqualTo(Object a, Object b) {
    getXY(a, b);
    return (xa == xb) && (ya == yb);
  }
// constructor and some methods are omitted ...
  public boolean isComparable(Object a){
    if (a==null)
      return false;
    else {
      try{ Point2D p = (Point2D) a; }
      catch (ClassCastException e) { return false; }
      return true;
    }
  }
}
```

Code Fragment 7.3: Portions of a comparator for points in the plane.

The methods of the comparator ADT have admittedly long names, chosen for the sake of readability. Interestingly, the java.util package has an interface for the comparator pattern (from JDK version 1.2 onward), but with a streamlined comparison mechanism, based on a single method:

compare(a, b): Returns integer i, such that $i < 0$ if $a < b$, $i = 0$ if $a = b$, and $i > 0$ if $a > b$.
Input: Objects; ***Output:*** Integer.

Whether we use long names or short names, however, the comparator pattern offers a general, dynamic, reusable way to compare objects.

7.2 Implementing a Priority Queue with a Sequence

In this section, we show how to implement a priority queue by storing the elements and keys in a sequence S. (See Chapter 5.) We provide two realizations, depending on whether or not we keep the keys in S sorted.

7.2.1 Implementation with an Unsorted Sequence

As our first implementation of a priority queue P, let us consider storing the elements of P and their keys in a sequence S. For the sake of generality, let us say that S is a general sequence implemented with either an array or a doubly linked list (the choice of specific implementation will not affect performance, as we will see). Thus, the elements of S are pairs (k, e), where e is an element of P and k is its key. A simple way of implementing method insertItem(k, e) of P is to add the new pair object $p = (k, e)$ at the end of sequence S, by executing method insertLast(p) on S. This implementation of method insertItem takes $O(1)$ time, independent of whether the sequence is implemented using an array or a linked list (see Section 5.3). This choice means that S will be unsorted, for always inserting items at the end of S does not take into account the ordering of the keys. As a consequence, to perform operation minElement, minKey, or removeMin on P, we must inspect all the elements of sequence S to find an element $p = (k, e)$ of S with minimum k. Thus, no matter how the sequence S is implemented, these search methods on P all take $O(n)$ time, where n is the number of elements in P at the time the method is executed. Moreover, these methods run in $\Omega(n)$ time even in the best case, since they each require searching the entire sequence to find a minimum element. That is, these methods run in $\Theta(n)$ time. Thus, by using an unsorted sequence to implement a priority queue, we achieve constant-time insertion, but the removeMin operation takes linear time.

7.2.2   Implementation with a Sorted Sequence

An alternative implementation of a priority queue P also uses a sequence S, except that this time let us store items sorted by keys. We can implement methods minElement and minKey in this case simply by accessing the first element of the sequence with the first method of S. Likewise, we can implement the removeMin method of P as S.remove(S.first()). Assuming that S is implemented with a linked list or an array that supports constant-time, front-element removal (see Section 5.3), finding and removing the minimum in P takes $O(1)$ time. Thus, using a sorted sequence allows for simple and fast implementations of priority queue access and removal methods.

This benefit comes at a cost, however, for now the method insertItem of P requires that we scan through the sequence S to find the appropriate position to insert the new element and key. Thus, implementing the insertItem method of P now requires $O(n)$ time, where n is the number of elements in P at the time the method is executed. In summary, when using a sorted sequence to implement a priority queue, insertion runs in linear time whereas finding and removing the minimum can be done in constant time.

In Code Fragment 7.4, we show a priority queue implementation that uses a sorted sequence (and the key-element items of Code Fragment 7.2).

Comparing the Two Implementations

Table 7.1 compares the running times of the methods of a priority queue realized by means of a sorted and unsorted sequence, respectively. We see an interesting trade-off when we use a sequence to implement the priority queue ADT. An unsorted sequence allows for fast insertions but slow queries and deletions, while a sorted sequence allows for fast queries and deletions, but slow insertions.

Method	Unsorted Sequence	Sorted Sequence
size, isEmpty	$O(1)$	$O(1)$
insertItem	$O(1)$	$O(n)$
minElement, minKey, removeMin	$O(n)$	$O(1)$

Table 7.1: The running times of methods of a priority queue of size n, realized by means of a sorted or unsorted sequence, respectively. The bounds are independent of whether we use an array or a doubly linked list to implement the sequence.

```java
public class SortedSequencePriorityQueue implements PriorityQueue {
  protected Sequence S = new NodeSequence();
  protected Comparator comp;

  protected Object key (Position pos) {
    return ((Item) pos.element()).key();
  }
  protected Object elem (Position pos) {
    return ((Item) pos.element()).element();
  }
  protected Object elem (Object kep) {
    return ((Item) kep).element();
  }

  public SortedSequencePriorityQueue (Comparator c) { comp = c; }
  public int size () {return S.size(); }
  public boolean isEmpty () { return S.isEmpty(); }
  public void insertItem (Object k, Object e) throws InvalidKeyException {
    if (!comp.isComparable(k))
      throw new InvalidKeyException("The key is not valid");
    else if (S.isEmpty())
      S.insertFirst(new Item(k, e));
    else if (comp.isGreaterThan(k, key(S.last())))
      S.insertAfter(S.last(),new Item(k,e));
    else {
      Position curr = S.first();
      while (comp.isGreaterThan(k, key(curr)))
        curr = S.after(curr);
      S.insertBefore(curr,new Item(k,e));
    }
  }
  public Object removeMin() throws PriorityQueueEmptyException {
    if (S.isEmpty())
      throw new EmptyContainerException("The priority queue is empty");
    else
      return elem(S.remove(S.first()));
  }
}
```

Code Fragment 7.4: Portions of the Java class PriorityQueue, which implements a priority queue by means of a sorted sequence. Interface PriorityQueue defines the basic methods of the priority queue ADT.

7.2.3 Selection-Sort and Insertion-Sort

Recall the PriorityQueueSort scheme introduced in Section 7.1.2. We are given an unsorted sequence S containing n elements, which we sort using a priority queue P in two phases. In phase 1 we insert all the elements, one by one, and in phase 2 we repeatedly remove elements using the removeMin operation. In this section we consider two variations of this sorting algorithm.

Selection-Sort

If we implement the priority queue P with an unsorted sequence, then the first phase takes $O(n)$ time, for we can insert each element in constant time. In the second phase, assuming we can compare two keys in constant time, the running time of each removeMin operation is proportional to the number of elements currently in P. Thus, the bottleneck computation in this implementation is the repeated "selection" of the minimum element from an unsorted sequence in phase 2. For this reason, this algorithm is better known as ***selection-sort***. (See Figure 7.1.)

		Sequence S	**Priority Queue** P
Input		$(7,4,8,2,5,3,9)$	$()$
Phase 1	(a)	$(4,8,2,5,3,9)$	(7)
	(b)	$(8,2,5,3,9)$	$(7,4)$
	⋮	⋮	⋮
	(g)	$()$	$(7,4,8,2,5,3,9)$
Phase 2	(a)	(2)	$(7,4,8,5,3,9)$
	(b)	$(2,3)$	$(7,4,8,5,9)$
	(c)	$(2,3,4)$	$(7,8,5,9)$
	(d)	$(2,3,4,5)$	$(7,8,9)$
	(e)	$(2,3,4,5,7)$	$(8,9)$
	(f)	$(2,3,4,5,7,8)$	(9)
	(g)	$(2,3,4,5,7,8,9)$	$()$

Figure 7.1: An illustration of selection-sort run on sequence $S = (7,4,8,2,5,3,9)$. This algorithm follows the two-phase PriorityQueueSort scheme and uses a priority queue P implemented by means of an unsorted sequence. In the first phase we repeatedly remove the first element from S and insert it into P (as the last element of the sequence implementing P). Note that at the end of the first phase, P is a copy of what was initially S. In the second phase, we repeatedly perform removeMin operations on P (each of which requires that we scan the entire sequence implementing P) and we add the elements returned at the end of S.

Let us analyze the selection-sort algorithm. As noted above, the bottleneck is the second phase, where we repeatedly remove an element with smallest key from the priority queue P. The size of P starts at n and incrementally decreases with each removeMin until it becomes 0. Thus, the first removeMin operation takes time $O(n)$, the second one takes time $O(n-1)$, and so on, until the last (nth) operation takes time $O(1)$. Therefore, the total time needed for this second phase is

$$O\left(n+(n-1)+\cdots+2+1\right) = O\left(\sum_{i=1}^{n} i\right).$$

By Proposition 3.4 we have

$$\sum_{i=1}^{n} i = \frac{n(n+1)}{2}.$$

Thus, the second phase takes time $O(n^2)$, as does the entire selection-sort algorithm.

Insertion-Sort

If we implement the priority queue P using a sorted sequence, then we improve the running time of the second phase to $O(n)$, for each operation removeMin on P now takes $O(1)$ time. Unfortunately, the first phase now becomes the bottleneck for the running time. Indeed, in the worst case, the running time of each insertItem operation is proportional to the number of elements that are currently in the priority queue, which starts out having size zero and increases in size until it has size n. The first insertItem operation takes time $O(1)$, the second one takes time $O(2)$, and so on, until the last (nth) operation takes time $O(n)$, in the worst case. Thus, if we use a sorted sequence to implement P, then the first phase becomes the bottleneck phase. This sorting algorithm is therefore better known as ***insertion-sort*** (see Figure 7.2), for the bottleneck in this sorting algorithm involves the repeated "insertion" of a new element at the appropriate position in a sorted sequence.

Analyzing the running time of phase 1 of insertion-sort, we note that it is

$$O\left(\sum_{i=1}^{n} i\right),$$

in the worst case. Again, by recalling Proposition 3.4, the first phase runs in $O(n^2)$ time, and hence so does the entire algorithm.

In other words, the running time of the PriorityQueueSort scheme implemented with a sorted sequence is $O(n^2)$. Therefore, both selection-sort and insertion-sort have running time $O(n^2)$. That is, their worst-case performance is similar to that of bubble-sort (Section 5.4), which also runs in $O(n^2)$ time.

		sequence S	priority queue P
Input		$(7,4,8,2,5,3,9)$	$()$
Phase 1	(a)	$(4,8,2,5,3,9)$	(7)
	(b)	$(8,2,5,3,9)$	$(4,7)$
	(c)	$(2,5,3,9)$	$(4,7,8)$
	(d)	$(5,3,9)$	$(2,4,7,8)$
	(e)	$(3,9)$	$(2,4,5,7,8)$
	(f)	(9)	$(2,3,4,5,7,8)$
	(g)	$()$	$(2,3,4,5,7,8,9)$
Phase 2	(a)	(2)	$(3,4,5,7,8,9)$
	(b)	$(2,3)$	$(4,5,7,8,9)$
	$\vdots$	$\vdots$	$\vdots$
	(g)	$(2,3,4,5,7,8,9)$	$()$

Figure 7.2: Schematic visualization of the execution of insertion-sort on sequence $S = (7,4,8,2,5,3,9)$. This algorithm follows the two-phase PriorityQueueSort scheme and uses a priority queue P, implemented by means of a sorted sequence. In the first phase, we repeatedly remove the first element of S and insert it into P, by scanning the sequence implementing P, until we find the correct position for the element. In the second phase, we repeatedly perform removeMin operations on P, each of which returns the first element of the sequence implementing P, and we add the element at the end of S.

Although selection-sort and insertion-sort are similar, they actually have some interesting differences. For instance, note that selection-sort always takes $\Omega(n^2)$ time, for selecting the minimum in each step of the second phase requires scanning the entire priority-queue sequence. The running time of insertion-sort, on the other hand, varies depending on the input sequence. For example, if the input sequence S is in reverse order, then insertion-sort runs in $O(n)$ time, for we are always inserting the next element at the beginning of the priority-queue sequence in the first phase.

Alternately, we could change our definition of insertion-sort so that we insert elements starting from the end of the priority-queue sequence in the first phase, in which case performing insertion-sort on a sequence that is already sorted would run in $O(n)$ time. Indeed, the running time of insertion-sort in this case is $O(n+I)$, where I is the number of *inversions* in the sequence, that is, the number of pairs of elements that start out in the input sequence in the wrong relative order. The number of inversions in a small sequence is relatively small; hence, insertion-sort is fairly efficient for small sequences. Its $O(n^2)$ worst-case performance makes insertion-sort inefficient for sorting large sequences, however.

The two implementations of the PriorityQueueSort scheme presented in this section suggest a possible way of improving the running time for priority-queue sorting. For one algorithm (selection-sort) achieves a fast running time for the first phase, but has a slow second phase, whereas the other algorithm (insertion-sort) has a slow first phase, but achieves a fast running time for the second phase. If we can somehow balance the running times of the two phases, we might be able to significantly speed up the overall running time for sorting. This is, in fact, exactly what we can achieve using the priority-queue implementation discussed in the next section.

7.3 Heaps

An efficient realization of a priority queue uses a data structure called a ***heap***. This data structure allows us to perform both insertions and removals in logarithmic time, which is a significant improvement over the sequence-based implementations discussed in Section 7.2. The fundamental way the heap achieves this improvement is to abandon the idea of storing elements and keys in a sequence and take the approach of storing elements and keys in a binary tree instead.

7.3.1 The Heap Data Structure

A heap (see Figure 7.3) is a binary tree T that stores a collection of keys at its internal nodes and that satisfies two additional properties: a relational property defined in terms of the way keys are stored in T and a structural property defined in terms of the nodes of T itself. We assume that a total order relation on the keys is given, for example, by a comparator. Also, note that in our definition of a heap the external nodes of T do not store keys or elements and serve only as "place-holders."

The relational property of T, defined in terms of the way keys are stored, is the following:

Heap-Order Property: In a heap T, for every node v other than the root, the key stored at v is greater than or equal to the key stored at v's parent.

As a consequence of the heap-order property, the keys encountered on a path from the root to an external node of T are in nondecreasing order. Also, a minimum key is always stored at the root of T. This is the most important key and is informally said to be "at the top of the heap"; hence, the name "heap" for the data structure. By the way, the heap data structure defined here has nothing to do with the memory heap (Section 4.2.3) used in the run-time environment supporting a programming language like Java.

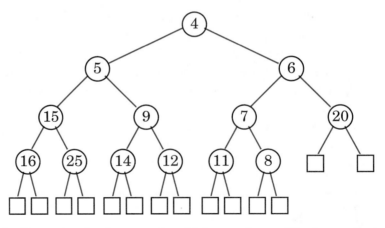

Figure 7.3: Example of a heap storing 13 integer keys. The last node is the one storing key 8, and external nodes are empty.

If we define our comparator to indicate the opposite of the standard total order relation between keys (so that isLessThan(3, 2) would, for example, return true), then the root of the heap stores the largest key. This versatility comes essentially "for free" from our use of the comparator pattern. By defining the minimum key in terms of the comparator, the "minimum" key with a "reverse" comparator is in fact the largest. Thus, without loss of generality, we assume that we are always interested in the minimum key, which will always be at the root of the heap.

> Caution

For the sake of efficiency, as will become clear later, we want the heap T to have as small a height as possible. We enforce this desire by insisting that the heap T satisfy an additional structural property: it must be **complete**. Recalling that level i of a binary tree T is the set of nodes that have depth i, we define this structural property as follows:

Complete Binary Tree: A binary tree T with height h is **complete** if the levels $0, 1, 2, \ldots, h-1$ have the maximum number of nodes possible (that is, level i has 2^i nodes, for $0 \le i \le h-1$) and in level $h-1$ all the internal nodes are to the left of the external nodes.

By saying that all the internal nodes on level $h-1$ are "to the left" of the external nodes, we mean that all the internal nodes on this level will be visited before any external nodes on this level in any standard tree traversal (for example, an inorder traversal). That is, in a standard drawing of a binary tree, all the internal nodes on level $h-1$ are drawn to the left of any of the external nodes on level $h-1$. (See Figure 7.3.) By insisting that a heap T be complete, we identify another important node in a heap T, other than the root, namely, the **last node** of T, which we define to be the right-most, deepest internal node of T. Insisting that T be complete also has an important consequence, as shown in Proposition 7.5.

Proposition 7.5: *A heap T storing n keys has height*

$$h = \lceil \log(n+1) \rceil.$$

Justification: From the fact that T is complete, we know the number of internal nodes of T is at least

$$
\begin{aligned}
1 + 2 + 4 + \cdots + 2^{h-2} + 1 &= 2^{h-1} - 1 + 1 \\
&= 2^{h-1}.
\end{aligned}
$$

This lower bound is achieved when there is only one internal node on level $h-1$. Alternately, but also following from T being complete, we can say that the number of internal nodes of T is at most

$$1 + 2 + 4 + \cdots + 2^{h-1} = 2^h - 1.$$

This upper bound is achieved when all the 2^{h-1} nodes on level $h-1$ are internal. Since the number of internal nodes is equal to the number n of keys,

$$2^{h-1} \le n$$

and

$$n \le 2^h - 1.$$

Thus, by taking logarithms of both sides of these two inequalities, we see that

$$h \le \log n + 1$$

and

$$\log(n+1) \le h,$$

which implies that

$$h = \lceil \log(n+1) \rceil.$$

■

Proposition 7.5 has an important consequence, for it implies that if we can perform update operations on a heap in time proportional to its height, then those operations will run in logarithmic time. Let us therefore turn to the problem of how to efficiently perform various priority queue methods using a heap.

7.3.2   Implementing a Priority Queue with a Heap

In this section, we show how to implement the priority queue ADT using a heap. Our heap-based data structure for a priority queue P consists of the following (see Figure 7.4):

- **heap**, a complete binary tree T whose elements are stored at internal nodes and have keys satisfying the heap-order property. We assume the binary tree T is implemented using a vector, as described in Section 6.4.1. For each internal node v of T, we denote the key of the element stored at v as $k(v)$.
- **last**, a reference to the last node of T. Given the vector implementation of T, we assume that the instance variable, last, is an integer index to the cell in the vector storing the last node of T.
- **comp**, a comparator that defines the total order relation among the keys.

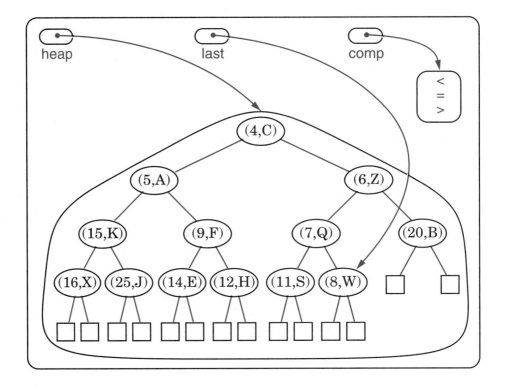

Figure 7.4: Heap-based implementation of a priority queue with integer keys and character elements. Each node of the heap stores a key-element pair. The heap-order property takes only the keys into account and ignores the elements.

The Vector Representation of a Heap

Note that when the heap T is implemented with a vector, the index of the last node w is always equal to n, and the first empty external node z has index equal to $n+1$. (See Figure 7.5.) Note that this index for z is valid even for the following cases:

- If the current last node w is the right-most node on its level, then z is the left-most node of the bottom-most level (see Figure 7.5b).
- If T has no internal nodes (that is, the priority queue is empty and the last node in T is not defined), then z is the root of T.

The simplifications that come from representing the heap T with a vector aid in our methods for implementing the priority queue ADT. For example, the update methods expandExternal(z) and removeAboveExternal(z) can also be performed in $O(1)$ time (assuming no vector expansion is necessary), for they simply involve allocating or deallocating a single cell in the vector. With this data structure, methods size and isEmpty take $O(1)$ time, as usual. In addition, methods minElement and minKey can also be easily performed in $O(1)$ time by accessing the element or key stored at the root of the heap (which is at rank 1 in the vector). Moreover, because T is a complete binary tree, the vector associated with heap T in a vector-based implementation of a binary tree has $2n+1$ elements, $n+1$ of which are place-holder external nodes by our convention. Indeed, since all the external nodes have indices higher that any internal node, we don't even have to explicitly store all the external nodes. (See Figure 7.5.)

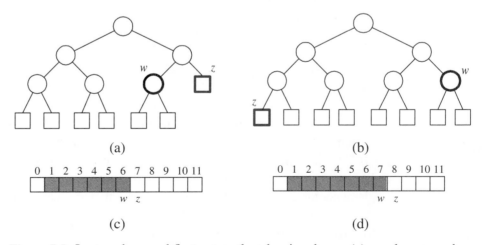

Figure 7.5: Last node w and first external node z in a heap: (a) regular case where z is right of w; (b) case where z is left-most on bottom level. The vector representation of (a) is shown in (c); similarly, the representation of (b) is shown in (d).

Insertion

Let us consider how to perform method insertItem of the priority queue ADT using the heap T. In order to store a new key-element pair (k,e) into T, we need to add a new internal node to T. In order to keep T as a complete binary tree, we must add this new node so that it becomes the new last node of T. That is, we must identify the correct external node z where we can perform an expandExternal(z) operation and insert the new element at z while keeping T complete. (See Figure 7.6a–b.) Node z is called the **insertion position**.

Usually, node z is the external node immediately to the right of the last node w (see Figure 7.5a). In any case, by our vector implementation of T, the insertion position z is stored at index $n+1$, where n is the current size of the heap. Thus, we can identify the node z in constant time in the vector implementing T. After then performing expandExternal(z), node z becomes the last node, and we store in it the new key-element pair (k,e), so that $k(z) = k$.

Up-Heap Bubbling after an Insertion

After this action, the tree T is complete, but it may violate the heap-order property. Hence, unless node z is the root of T (that is, the priority queue was empty before the insertion), we compare key $k(z)$ with the key $k(u)$ stored at the parent u of z. If $k(u) > k(z)$, then we need to restore the heap-order property, which can be locally achieved by swapping the key-element pairs stored at z and u. (See Figure 7.6c–d.) This swap causes the new key-element pair (k,e) to move up one level. Again, the heap-order property may be violated, and we continue swapping going up in T until no violation of heap-order property occurs. (See Figure 7.6e–h.)

The upward movement by means of swaps is conventionally called **up-heap bubbling**. A swap either resolves the violation of the heap-order property or propagates it one level up in the heap. In the worst case, up-heap bubbling causes the new key-element pair to move all the way up to the root of heap T. (See Figure 7.6.) Thus, in the worst case, the running time of method insertItem is proportional to the height of T, that is, it is $O(\log n)$ because T is complete.

If T is implemented with a vector, then we can find the new last node z immediately in $O(1)$ time. For example, we could use inheritance to extend a vector-based implementation of a binary tree, so as to add a method that returns the node with index $n+1$, that is, with level number $n+1$, as defined in Section 6.4.1. Alternately, we could even define an add method, which adds a new element at the first external node z, at rank $n+1$ in the vector. In Code Fragment 7.7, shown later in this chapter, we show how to use this method to efficiently implement the method insertItem. If, on the other hand, the heap T is implemented with a linked structure, then finding the insertion position z is a little more involved (see Exercise C-7.8).

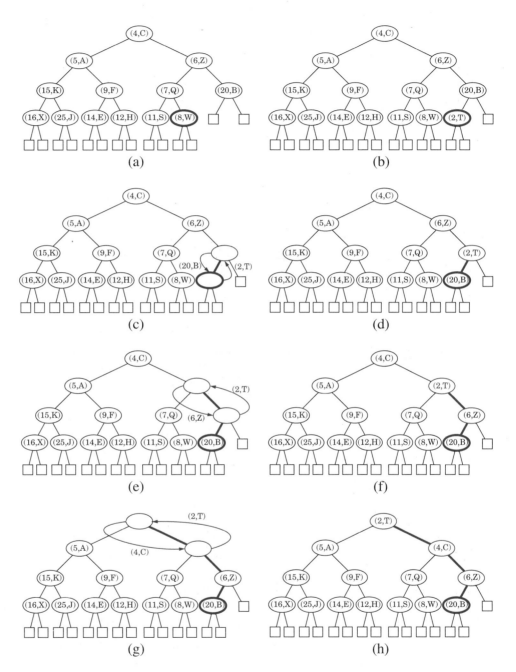

Figure 7.6: Insertion of a new element with key 2 into the heap of Figure 7.4: (a) initial heap; (b) adding a new last node to the right of the old last node; (c–d) swap to locally restore the partial order property; (e–f) another swap; (g–h) final swap.

Removal

Let us now turn to method removeMin of the priority queue ADT. The algorithm for performing method removeMin using heap T is illustrated in Figure 7.7.

We know that an element with the smallest key is stored at the root r of T (even if there is more than one smallest key). However, unless r is the only internal node of T, we cannot simply delete node r, because this action would disrupt the binary tree structure. Instead, we access the last node w of T, copy its key-element pair to the root r, and then delete the last node by performing operation removeAboveExternal(T.rightChild(w)) of the binary tree ADT. This operation removes w and its right child, and replaces w with its left child. (See Figure 7.7a–b.) After this constant-time action, we need to update our reference to the last node, which can be done simply by referencing the node at rank n (after the removal) in the vector implementing the tree T.

Down-Heap Bubbling after a Removal

We are not done, however, for, even though T is now complete, T may now violate the heap-order property. To determine whether we need to restore the heap-order property, we examine the root r of T. If both children of r are external nodes, then the heap-order property is trivially satisfied and we are done. Otherwise, we distinguish two cases:

- If the left child of r is internal and the right child is external, let s be the left child of r.
- Otherwise (both children of r are internal), let s be a child of r with the smallest key.

If the key $k(r)$ stored at r is greater than the key $k(s)$ stored at s, then we need to restore the heap-order property, which can be locally achieved by swapping the key-element pairs stored at r and s. (See Figure 7.7c–d.) (Note that we shouldn't swap r with s's sibling.) The swap we perform restores the heap-order property for node r and its children, but it may violate this property at s; hence, we may have to continue swapping down T until no violation of the heap-order property occurs. (See Figure 7.7e–h.) This downward swapping process is called ***down-heap bubbling***. A swap either resolves the violation of the heap-order property or propagates it one level down in the heap. In the worst case, a key-element pair moves all the way down to the level immediately above the bottom level. (See Figure 7.7.) Thus, the running time of method removeMin is, in the worst case, proportional to the height of heap T, that is, it is $O(\log n)$.

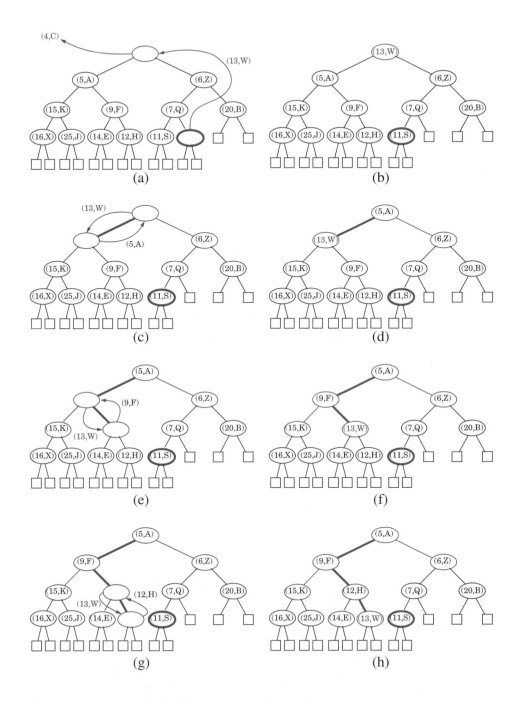

Figure 7.7: Removal of the element with the smallest key from a heap: (a–b) deletion of the last node, whose key-element pair gets stored into the root; (c–d) swap to locally restore the heap-order property; (e–f) another swap; (g–h) final swap.

Analysis

Table 7.2 shows the running time of the priority queue ADT methods for the heap implementation of a priority queue, assuming that the heap T is realized by a data structure for binary trees that supports the binary tree ADT methods (except for elements()) in $O(1)$ time. The linked structure and vector-based structure from Section 6.4 easily satisfy this requirement.

Operation	Time
size, isEmpty	$O(1)$
minElement, minKey	$O(1)$
insertItem	$O(\log n)$
removeMin	$O(\log n)$

Table 7.2: Performance of a priority queue realized by means of a heap, which is in turn implemented with a vector-based structure for binary trees. We denote with n the number of elements in the priority queue at the time a method is executed. The space requirement is $O(n)$ if the heap is realized with a linked structure, and is $O(N)$ if the heap is realized with a vector-based structure, where $N \geq n$ is the size of the array used to implement the vector.

In short, each of the priority queue ADT methods can be performed in $O(1)$ or in $O(\log n)$ time, where n is the number of elements at the time the method is executed. The analysis of the running time of the methods is based on the following:

- The height of heap T is $O(\log n)$, since T is complete.
- In the worst case, up-heap and down-heap bubbling take time proportional to the height of T.
- Finding the insertion position in the execution of insertItem and updating the last node position in the execution of removeMin takes constant time.
- The heap T has n internal nodes, each storing a reference to a key and a reference to an element, and $n + 1$ external nodes.

We conclude that the heap data structure is a very efficient realization of the priority queue ADT, independent of whether the heap is implemented with a linked structure or a sequence. The heap implementation achieves fast running times for both insertion and removal, unlike the sequence-based priority queue implementations. Indeed, an important consequence of the efficiency of the heap-based implementation is that it can speed up priority-queue sorting to be much faster than the sequence-based insertion-sort and selection-sort algorithms.

7.3.3 Java Implementation

A Java implementation of a heap-based priority queue is shown in Code Fragments 7.5–7.7. To aid in modularity, we delegate the maintenance of the structure of the heap itself to a data structure, called **heap-tree**, that extends a binary tree and provides the following additional specialized update methods:

> add(o): Performs the following sequence of operations:
> > expandExternal(z);
> > replaceElement(z, o);
> > return z;
>
> such that z becomes the last node of the tree at the end of the operation.
> *Input:* Object o; *Output:* Position.

> remove(): Performs the following sequence of operations:
> > $t \leftarrow z$.element();
> > removeAboveExternal(rightChild(z));
> > return t;
>
> where z is the last node at the beginning of the operation.
> *Input:* None; *Output:* Object.

That is, the add operation adds a new element at the first external node, and the remove operation removes the element at the last node. Using a vector-based implementation of a tree (see Section 6.4.1), operations add and remove take $O(1)$ time. The heap-tree ADT is represented by the Java interface HeapTree shown in Code Fragment 7.5. We assume that a Java class VectorHeapTree (not shown) implements the HeapTree interface with a vector and supports methods add and remove in $O(1)$ time.

```
public interface HeapTree extends InspectableBinaryTree, PositionalContainer {
    public Position add(Object elem);
    public Object remove();
}
```

Code Fragment 7.5: Interface HeapTree for a heap-tree. It extends the interface InspectableBinaryTree with methods replaceElement and swapElements, inherited from the PositionalContainer interface, and adds the specialized update methods add and remove.

Class HeapPriorityQueue implements the PriorityQueue interface using a heap. It is shown in Code Fragments 7.6 and 7.7. Note that we store key-element items of class Item (see Code Fragment 7.2) into the heap-tree.

```
public class HeapPriorityQueue implements PriorityQueue {
  HeapTree T;
  Comparator comp;

  public HeapPriorityQueue(Comparator c) {
    if ((comp = c) == null)
      throw new IllegalArgumentException("Null comparator passed");
    T = new VectorHeapTree();
  }

  public int size() {
    return (T.size() − 1) / 2;
  }

  public boolean isEmpty() {
    return T.size() == 1; }

  public Object minElement() throws PriorityQueueEmptyException {
    if (isEmpty())
      throw new PriorityQueueEmptyException("Empty Priority Queue");
    return element(T.root());
  }

  public Object minKey() throws PriorityQueueEmptyException {
    if (isEmpty())
      throw new PriorityQueueEmptyException("Empty Priority Queue");
    return key(T.root());
  }
```

  ⋮

Code Fragment 7.6: Instance variables, constructor, and methods size, isEmpty, minElement, and minKey of class HeapPriorityQueue, which implements a priority queue by means of a heap. Other methods of this class are shown in Code Fragment 7.7. The auxiliary methods key and element extract the key and element of an item of the priority queue stored at at given position of the heap-tree.

```
public void insertItem(Object k, Object e) throws InvalidKeyException {
  if (!comp.isComparable(k))
    throw new InvalidKeyException("Invalid Key");
  Position z = T.add(new Item(k, e));
  Position u;
  while (!T.isRoot(z)) { // up-heap bubbling
    u = T.parent(z);
    if (comp.isLessThanOrEqualTo(key(u), key(z)))
      break;
    T.swapElements(u, z);
    z = u;
  }
}

public Object removeMin() throws PriorityQueueEmptyException {
  if (isEmpty())
    throw new PriorityQueueEmptyException("Empty priority queue!");
  Object min = element(T.root());
  if (size() == 1)
    T.remove();
  else {
    T.replaceElement(T.root(), T.remove());
    Position r = T.root();
    while (T.isInternal(T.leftChild(r))) { // down-heap bubbling
      Position s;
      if (T.isExternal(T.rightChild(r)) ||
          comp.isLessThanOrEqualTo(key(T.leftChild(r)), key(T.rightChild(r))))
        s = T.leftChild(r);
      else
        s = T.rightChild(r);
      if (comp.isLessThan(key(s), key(r))) {
        T.swapElements(r, s);
        r = s;
      }
      else
        break;
    }
  }
  return min;
}
```

Code Fragment 7.7: Methods insertItem and removeMin of class HeapPriorityQueue. Other methods of this class are shown in Code Fragment 7.6.

7.3.4   Heap-Sort

As we have just observed, realizing a priority queue with a heap has the advantage that all the methods in the priority queue ADT run in logarithmic time or better. Hence, this realization is suitable for applications where fast running times are sought for all the priority queue methods. Therefore, let us again consider the PriorityQueueSort sorting scheme from Section 7.1.2, which uses a priority queue P to sort a sequence S.

If we implement the priority queue P with a heap, then, during the first phase, each of the n insertItem operations takes time $O(\log k)$, where k is the number of elements in the heap at the time. Likewise, during the second phase, each of the n removeMin operations also runs in time $O(\log k)$, where k is the number of elements in the heap at the time. Since we always have $k \le n$, each such operation runs in $O(\log n)$ time in the worst case. Thus, each phase takes $O(n \log n)$ time, so the entire priority-queue sorting algorithm runs in $O(n \log n)$ time when we use a heap to implement the priority queue. This sorting algorithm is better known as **heap-sort**, and its performance is summarized in the following proposition.

Proposition 7.6: *The heap-sort algorithm sorts a sequence S of n comparable elements in $O(n \log n)$ time.*

Recalling Table 3.3, we stress that the $O(n \log n)$ running time of heap-sort is considerably better than the $O(n^2)$ running time of bubble-sort (Section 5.4), selection-sort, and insertion-sort (Section 7.2.3).

Implementing Heap-Sort In-Place

If the sequence S to be sorted is implemented by means of an array, we can speed up heap-sort and reduce its space requirement by a constant factor using a portion of the sequence S itself to store the heap, thus avoiding the use of an external heap data structure. This is accomplished by modifying the algorithm as follows:

1. We use a reverse comparator, which corresponds to a heap where the largest element is at the top. At any time during the execution of the algorithm, we use the left portion of S, up to a certain rank $i - 1$, to store the elements in the heap, and the right portion of S, from rank i to $n - 1$ to store the elements in the sequence. Thus, the first i elements of S (at ranks $0, \ldots, i - 1$) provide the vector representation of the heap (with modified level numbers starting at 0 instead of 1), that is, the element at rank k is greater than or equal to its "children" at ranks $2k + 1$ and $2k + 2$.

2. In the first phase of the algorithm, we start with an empty heap and move the boundary between the heap and the sequence from left to right, one step at a time. In step i $(i = 1, \ldots, n)$, we expand the heap by adding the element at rank $i - 1$.

3. In the second phase of the algorithm, we start with an empty sequence and move the boundary between the heap and the sequence from right to left, one step at a time. At step i $(i = 1, \ldots, n)$, we remove a maximum element from the heap and store it at rank $n - i$.

The above variation of heap-sort is said to be **in-place** since we use only a constant amount of space in addition to the sequence itself. Instead of transferring elements out of the sequence and then back in, we simply rearrange them. We illustrate in-place heap-sort in Figure 7.8. In general, we say that a sorting algorithm is in-place if it uses only a constant amount of memory in addition to the memory needed for the objects being sorted themselves.

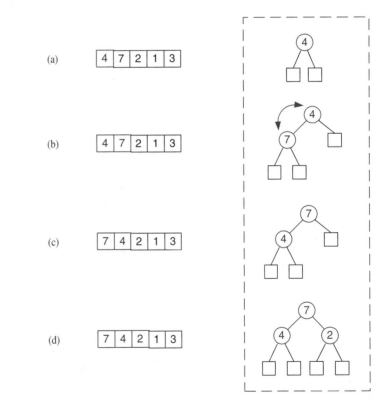

Figure 7.8: First three steps of Phase 1 of in-place heap-sort. The heap portion of the vector is highlighted in blue. We draw next to the vector a binary tree view of the heap, even though this tree is not actually constructed by the in-place algorithm.

7.3.5   Bottom-Up Heap Construction ⋆

The analysis of the heap-sort algorithm shows that we can construct a heap storing n key-element pairs in $O(n \log n)$ time, by means of n successive insertItem operations, and then use that heap to extract the elements in order. However, if all the keys to be stored in the heap are given in advance, there is an alternative ***bottom-up*** construction method that runs in $O(n)$ time.

We describe this method in this section, observing that it could be included as one of the constructors in a Heap class, instead of filling a heap using a series of n insertItem operations. For simplicity of exposition, we describe this bottom-up heap construction assuming the number n of keys is an integer of the type

$$n = 2^h - 1.$$

That is, the heap is a complete binary tree with every level being full, so the heap has height $h = \log(n+1)$.

Viewed nonrecursively, bottom-up heap construction consists of the following $h = \log(n+1)$ steps:

1. In the first step (see Figure 7.9a), we construct $(n+1)/2$ elementary heaps storing one key each.
2. In the second step (see Figure 7.9b–c), we form $(n+1)/4$ heaps, each storing three keys, by joining pairs of elementary heaps and adding a new key. The new key is placed at the root and may have to be swapped with the key stored at a child to preserve the heap-order property.
3. In the third step (see Figure 7.9d–e), we form $(n+1)/8$ heaps, each storing 7 keys, by joining pairs of 3-key heaps (constructed in the previous step) and adding a new key. The new key is placed initially at the root, but may have to move down with a down-heap bubbling to preserve the heap-order property.

$$\vdots$$

i. In the generic ith step, $2 \leq i \leq h$ (see Figure 7.9f–g, where $i = 4$), we form $(n+1)/2^i$ heaps, each storing $2^i - 1$ keys, by joining pairs of heaps storing $(2^{i-1} - 1)$ keys (constructed in the previous step) and adding a new key. The new key is placed initially at the root, but may have to move down with a down-heap bubbling to preserve the heap-order property.

We illustrate bottom-up heap construction in Figure 7.9 for $h = 4$.

⋆We use a star (⋆) to indicate sections containing material more advanced than the material in the rest of the chapter; this material can be considered optional in a first reading.

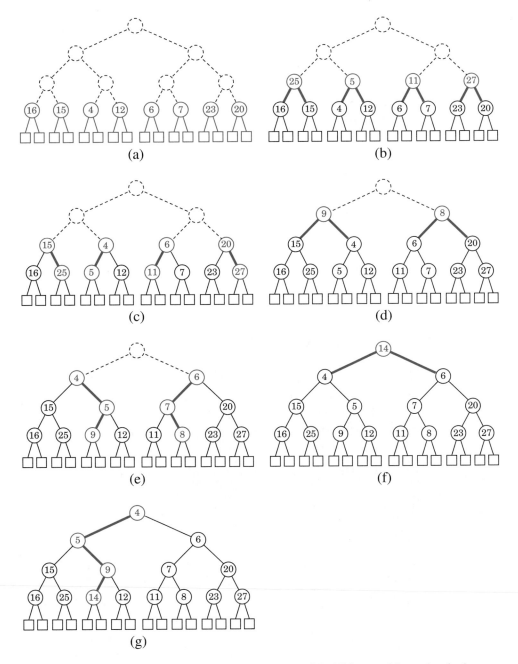

Figure 7.9: Bottom-up construction of a heap with 15 keys: (a) we begin by constructing 1-key heaps on the bottom level; (b–c) we combine these heaps into 3-key heaps and then (d–e) 7-key heaps, until (f–g) we create the final heap. The paths of the down-heap bubblings are highlighted in blue.

We can also describe bottom-up heap construction as a recursive algorithm, as shown in Code Fragment 7.8, which we call by passing a sequence storing the keys for which we wish to build a heap. We describe the construction algorithm as acting on keys, with the understanding that their elements accompany them.

Algorithm BottomUpHeap(S):

    Input: A sequence S storing $n = 2^h - 1$ keys

    Output: A heap T storing the keys in S.

    if S is empty **then**

        return an empty heap (consisting of a single external node).

    Remove the first key, k, from S.

    Split S into two sequences, S_1 and S_2, each of size $(n-1)/2$.

    $T_1 \leftarrow$ BottomUpHeap(S_1)

    $T_2 \leftarrow$ BottomUpHeap(S_2)

    Create binary tree T with root r storing k, left subtree T_1, and right subtree T_2.

    Perform a down-heap bubbling from the root r of T, if necessary.

    return T

Code Fragment 7.8: Recursive bottom-up heap construction.

Bottom-up heap construction is asymptotically faster than incrementally inserting n keys into an initially empty heap, as the following proposition shows.

Proposition 7.7: *Bottom-up heap construction with n keys takes $O(n)$ time.*

Justification: We analyze bottom-up heap construction using a "visual" approach, which is illustrated in Figure 7.10.

Let T be the final heap, let v be an internal node of T, and let $T(v)$ denote the subtree of T rooted at v. In the worst case, the time for forming $T(v)$ from the two recursively formed subtrees rooted at v's children is proportional to the height of $T(v)$. The worst case occurs when down-heap bubbling from v traverses a path from v all the way to a bottom-most external node of $T(v)$. Consider now the path $p(v)$ of T from node v to its inorder successor external node, that is, the path that starts at v, goes to the right child of v, and then goes down leftward until it reaches an external node. We say that path $p(v)$ is **associated with** node v. Note that $p(v)$ is not necessarily the path followed by down-heap bubbling when forming $T(v)$. Clearly, the length (number of edges) of $p(v)$ is equal to the height of $T(v)$. Hence, forming $T(v)$ takes time proportional to the length of $p(v)$, in the worst case. Thus, the total running time of bottom-up heap construction is proportional to the sum of the lengths of the paths associated with the internal nodes of T.

Note that for any two internal nodes u and v of T, paths $p(u)$ and $p(v)$ do not share edges, although they may share nodes. (See Figure 7.10.) Therefore, the sum of the lengths of the paths associated with the internal nodes of T is no more than the number of edges of heap T, that is, no more than $2n$. We conclude that the bottom-up construction of heap T takes $O(n)$ time. ∎

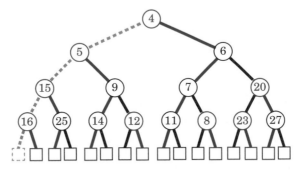

Figure 7.10: Visual justification of the linear running time of bottom-up heap construction, where the paths associated with the internal nodes have been highlighted with alternating colors. For example, the path associated with the root consists of the internal nodes storing keys 4, 6, 7, and 11, plus an external node.

To summarize, Proposition 7.7 states that the running time for the first phase of heap-sort can be reduced to be $O(n)$. Unfortunately, the running time of the second phase of heap-sort cannot be made asymptotically better than $O(n \log n)$ (that is, it will always be $\Omega(n \log n)$ in the worst case). We will not justify this lower bound until Chapter 10, however. Instead, we conclude this chapter by discussing a design pattern that allows us to extend the priority queue ADT to have additional functionality.

7.4 The Locator Design Pattern ⋆

As we saw with lists and binary trees, abstracting positional information in a container is a very powerful tool. The position ADT, described in Section 5.2.2, allows us to identify a specific "place" in a container that can store an element. A position can have its element changed, for example, as a consequence of a swapElements operation, but the position stays the same. In Section 5.4 we gave applications of the position abstraction to implementations of the bubble-sort algorithm.

There are also applications where we need to keep track of elements as they are being moved around inside a positional container, however. For example, suppose we want to remove an element e from a sequence S. The deletion methods of the sequence ADT require that we specify either the position or the rank of e in S. If sequence S is modified by a series of swapElements operations after the insertion of e, then element e is, in general, at a position and/or rank different from the one it had at the time it was inserted. Thus, in order to perform the deletion of element e, we would have to search for e inside S (spending time proportional to the size of S in the worst case), which is rather inefficient. Instead, we would like to have a mechanism for keeping track of the position of an element in a container.

A design pattern that fulfills this need is the ***locator***. A locator is a mechanism for maintaining the association between an element and its current position in a container. A locator "sticks" with a specific element, even if the element changes its position in the container. A locator is like a coat check; we can give our coat to a coat-room attendant, and we receive back a coat check, which is a "locator" for our coat. The position of our coat relative to the other coats can change, as other coats are added and removed, but our coat check can always be used to retrieve our coat. The important thing to remember about a locator is that it follows its item, even if it changes position.

Like a coat check, we can now imagine getting something back when we insert an element in a container—we can get back a locator for that element. This locator in turn can be used later to refer to the element within the container, for example, to specify that this element should be removed from the container. Thus, we can conveniently extend the repertory of operations of a positional container, such as a sequence or a binary tree, with methods that support the locator design pattern. For example, we can define insertion operations that return a locator to the element inserted, and deletion operations that take a locator as an argument.

Another important use of locators is to keep track of the items stored in a container whose operations do not refer to positions, but only to keys and elements, such as a priority queue. Indeed, the locator design pattern provides a generic mechanism for accessing an element, or key-element item, stored in a container in a way that abstracts from the concrete implementation of the container.

As an abstract data type, a locator ℓ supports the following methods:

element(): Return the element of the item associated with ℓ.
Input: None; ***Output:*** Object.

key(): Return the key of the item associated with ℓ.
Input: None; ***Output:*** Object.

For the sake of concreteness, we next discuss how we can use locators to extend the repertory of operations of the priority queue ADT to include methods that return locators and take locators as arguments.

7.4.1   Locator-Based Priority Queue Methods

We can use locators in a very natural way in the context of a priority queue. A locator in such a scenario stays attached to an item inserted in the priority queue, and allows us to access the item in a generic manner, independent of the specific implementation of the priority queue. This ability is important for a priority queue implementation, for there are no positions, *per se*, in a priority queue, since we do not refer to items by any notions of "rank," "index," or "node."

Although the implementations of the priority queue ADT that we have seen are based on underlying positional containers (sequences and trees), the position abstraction does not apply to the priority queue itself. Thus, we use locators to provide direct access to the items in a priority queue. A container class can give locators out when items are inserted and accept them as parameters to fast update methods.

Extending the Priority Queue ADT

By using locators, we can extend the priority queue ADT with the following methods that access and modify a priority queue P:

min(): Return the locator to an item of P with smallest key.
Input: None; *Output:* Locator.

insert(k,e): Insert a new item with element e and key k into P and return a locator to the item.
Input: Objects k (key) and e (element); *Output:* Locator.

remove(ℓ): Remove from P the item with locator ℓ.
Input: Locator; *Output:* None.

replaceElement(ℓ,e): Replace with e and return the element of the item of P with locator ℓ.
Input: Locator, object; *Output:* Object.

replaceKey(ℓ,k): Replace with k and return the key of the item of P with locator ℓ.
Input: Locator, object; *Output:* Object.

We explore the use of these methods in the example that follows.

Example 7.8: *Consider the following series of locator-based operations and their effects on an initially empty priority queue P.*

Operation	Output	P
insert(5,A)	ℓ_1	$\{(5,A)\}$
insert(3,B)	ℓ_2	$\{(3,B),(5,A)\}$
insert(7,C)	ℓ_3	$\{(3,B),(5,A),(7,C)\}$
min()	ℓ_2	$\{(3,B),(5,A),(7,C)\}$
key(ℓ_2)	3	$\{(3,B),(5,A),(7,C)\}$
remove(ℓ_1)	A	$\{(3,B),(7,C)\}$
replaceKey($\ell_2,9$)	3	$\{(7,C),(9,B)\}$
key(ℓ_2)	9	$\{(7,C),(9,B)\}$
replaceElement(ℓ_3,D)	C	$\{(7,D),(9,B)\}$

There are several applications in which the above locator-based methods are useful. For example, in a priority queue of standby airline passengers, a passenger with a pessimistic attitude may decide to leave ahead of the boarding time (requiring us to perform operation remove). At the same time, the priority of another passenger may have to be increased (requiring our performing operation replaceKey) after she pulls out her frequent-flyer gold card. If we are maintaining a database of standby passengers, we can implement these removal and replacement methods much faster if we access the items via their locators. The reason that such locator-based lookup methods are more efficient is that, as the implementers of the locators, we can encode in our locators information about our priority-queue implementation that provides for fast lookup. These locator-based lookups are often much faster than lookups using a key value, because key values are provided by the user, whereas we provide the locators. For example, if we implement the priority queue with an unsorted sequence, then the locator for our priority queue can store the position of the item in the sequence. In this case, a locator-based access runs in $O(1)$ time, while a key-based access, which must look for the element via a search in the sequence, runs in $O(n)$ time in the worst case.

Finally, we point out that locator-based methods can be used to implement nonlocator-based container methods. Some of the methods of the priority queue ADT given in Section 7.1.3, for instance, can be expressed by simple combinations of the locator-based methods given above. For example, operation minElement() is equivalent to min().element(), and operation removeMin() is equivalent to a combination of remove and min. In addition, some applications call for us to restrict the operation replaceKey so that it only increases or decreases the key. This restriction can be done by defining new methods increaseKey or decreaseKey, for example, which would take a locator as an argument. Further applications of priority queues extended with locator-based methods are given in Chapter 12.

7.4.2 Implementing Locator-Based Priority Queue Methods

We can easily extend the sequence-based and heap-based implementations of a priority queue to support locators. Specifically, we can take advantage of inheritance, recalling that sequences and binary trees are positional containers and we can use them to realize the priority queue ADT by storing key-element pairs (items) as their elements. We can realize a locator, therefore, by extending the key-element item of Code Fragment 7.2 to implement the locator ADT and adding as an instance variable a position reference, as shown in Code Fragment 7.9. With this implementation, the methods of the locator ADT are straightforward to implement, and each take $O(1)$ time. The most significant overhead is that, since the locators automatically stay attached to the items (indeed, they store the items) in this implementation, we must keep track of the positions where items are placed in the sequence or heap.

```
public class Item2 extends Item implements Locator {
  private Position pos;
  Item2 (Object k, Object e, Position p) {
    super(k, e);
    pos = p;
  }
  protected Position position() {return pos; }
  protected void setPosition(Position p) { pos = p; }
}
```

Code Fragment 7.9: Class Item2 realizing locators for the implementation of a priority queue with a sorted sequence.

In Table 7.3, we compare running times of the priority queue ADT methods defined in this section and in Section 7.1.3.

Method	Unsorted Sequence	Sorted Sequence	Heap
size, isEmpty, key, replaceElement	$O(1)$	$O(1)$	$O(1)$
minElement, min, minKey	$O(n)$	$O(1)$	$O(1)$
insertItem, insert	$O(1)$	$O(n)$	$O(\log n)$
removeMin	$O(n)$	$O(1)$	$O(\log n)$
remove	$O(1)$	$O(1)$	$O(\log n)$
replaceKey	$O(1)$	$O(n)$	$O(\log n)$

Table 7.3: Comparison of the running times of the priority queue ADT methods for the unsorted sequence, sorted sequence, and heap implementations. We denote with n the number of elements in the priority queue at the time a method is executed.

In Code Fragments 7.10 and 7.11, we show a Java implementation of a priority queue that supports locator-based methods. This implementation is obtained by extending class SortedSequencePriorityQueue shown in Code Fragment 7.4.

```java
public class SortedSequencePriorityQueue2
  extends SortedSequencePriorityQueue implements PriorityQueue2 {
    public SortedSequencePriorityQueue2 (Comparator comp) {
      super(comp);
    }
    protected Locator locInsert(Item2 locitem) throws InvalidKeyException {
      Position p, curr;
      Object k = locitem.key();
      if (!comp.isComparable(k))
        throw new InvalidKeyException("The key is not valid");
      else
        if (S.isEmpty())
          p = S.insertFirst(locitem);
        else if (comp.isGreaterThan(k, key(S.last())))
          p = S.insertAfter(S.last(),locitem);
        else {
          curr = S.first();
          while (comp.isGreaterThan(k, key(curr)))
            curr = S.after(curr);
          p = S.insertBefore(curr,locitem);
        }
      locitem.setPosition(p);
      return (Locator) locitem;
    }
    protected Item2 locRemove(Locator loc) {
      S.remove(((Item2) loc).position());
      return (Item2) loc;
    }
}
```

Code Fragment 7.10: Java implementation of a priority queue supporting locator-based methods by means of a sorted sequence. Class SortedSequencePriorityQueue2 extends class SortedSequencePriorityQueue (Code Fragment 7.4) and implements the Java interface PriorityQueue2, which includes the locator-based methods of the priority queue ADT given in Section 7.4.1. (Continues in Code Fragment 7.11.)

```
public Locator min () throws PriorityQueueEmptyException {
if (S.isEmpty())
  throw new PriorityQueueEmptyException("The priority queue is empty");
else
  return (Locator) S.first().element();
}
public void insert(Locator loc) throws InvalidKeyException {
  locInsert((Item2) loc);
}
public Locator insert(Object k, Object e) throws InvalidKeyException {
  Item2 locitem = new Item2(k, e, null);
  return locInsert(locitem);
}
public void insertItem (Object k, Object e) throws InvalidKeyException {
  insert(k, e);
}
public void remove(Locator loc) {
  locRemove(loc);
}
public Object removeMin () throws PriorityQueueEmptyException {
  Object toReturn = minElement();
  remove(min());
  return toReturn;
}
public Object replaceElement (Locator loc, Object newElement) {
  Object oldElement = ((Item2) loc).element();
  ((Item2) loc).setElement(newElement);
  return oldElement;
}
public Object replaceKey(Locator loc, Object newKey)
  throws InvalidKeyException {
    Item2 locitem = locRemove(loc);
    Object oldKey = ((Item2) loc).key();
    locitem.setKey(newKey);
    locInsert(locitem);
    return oldKey;
  }
}
```

Code Fragment 7.11: Java implementation of a priority queue supporting locator-based methods by means of a sorted sequence. (Continued from Code Fragment 7.10.)

7.5   Exercises

Reinforcement

R-7.1 Give a complete Java interface for the Priority Queue ADT, including appropriate comments in the javadoc style.

R-7.2 Rewrite the lexicographic comparison rule shown in Code Fragment 7.3 using the java.util.Comparator interface.

R-7.3 Although it is correct to use a "reverse" comparator with our priority queue ADT so that we retrieve and remove an element with the maximum key each time, it is confusing to have an element with maximum key returned by a method named "removeMin." Write a short adapter class that can take any priority queue P and an associated comparator C and implement a priority queue that concentrates on the element with maximum key, using methods with names like removeMax.   (Hint: Define a new comparator C' in terms of C.)

R-7.4 The implementation of a priority queue using a sequence S that is in turn implemented as an array only allows constant-time performance for the removeMin method if S's array is implemented in a circular fashion, so as to support constant-time removal of the first element. Describe an alternative approach that involves having the removeMin method always remove the last element in S, so that it runs in constant time even if S's array is not circular.

R-7.5 Illustrate the performance of the selection-sort algorithm on the following input sequence: $(22, 15, 36, 44, 10, 3, 9, 13, 29, 25)$.

R-7.6 Illustrate the performance of the insertion-sort algorithm on the input sequence of the previous problem.

R-7.7 Give an example of a worst-case sequence with n elements for insertion-sort, and show that insertion-sort runs in $\Omega(n^2)$ time on such a sequence.

R-7.8 Where may an item with largest key be stored in a heap?

R-7.9 Illustrate the performance of the heap-sort algorithm on the following input sequence: $(2, 5, 16, 4, 10, 23, 39, 18, 26, 15)$.

R-7.10 Suppose a binary tree T is implemented using a vector S, as described in Section 6.4.1. If n items are stored in S in sorted order, starting with index 1, is the tree T a heap?

R-7.11 Explain why the case where the right child of r is internal and the left child is external was not considered in the description of down-heap bubbling.

R-7.12 Is there a heap T storing seven distinct elements such that a preorder traversal of T yields the elements of T in sorted order? How about an inorder traversal? How about a postorder traversal?

R-7.13 Consider the numbering of the nodes of a binary tree defined in Section 6.4.1, and show that the insertion position in a heap with n keys is the node with number $n + 1$.

R-7.14 Show that the sum

$$\sum_{i=1}^{n} \log i,$$

which appears in the analysis of heap-sort, is $\Omega(n \log n)$.

R-7.15 An airport is developing a computer simulation of air-traffic control that handles events such as landings and takeoffs. Each event has a *time-stamp* that denotes the time when the event occurs. The simulation program needs to efficiently perform the following two fundamental operations:

- Insert a new event with a given time-stamp (that is, add a future event).
- Extract the event with smallest time-stamp (that is, determine the next event to process).

Which data structure would you use to support the above operations? Justify your answer.

R-7.16 A certain Professor Amongus claims that a preorder traversal of a heap will list out its keys in sorted order. Draw a small example of a heap that proves him wrong.

R-7.17 Show all the steps of the algorithm for removing key 16 from the heap of Figure 7.3.

R-7.18 Show all the steps of the algorithm for replacing 5 with 18 in the heap of Figure 7.3.

R-7.19 Draw an example of a heap whose keys are all the odd numbers from 1 to 59 (with no repeats), such that the insertion of an item with key 32 would cause up-heap bubbling to proceed all the way up to a child of the root (replacing that child's key with 32).

R-7.20 Complete Figure 7.8 by showing all the steps of the in-place heap-sort algorithm. Show both the sequence and the associated heap at the end of each step.

Creativity

C-7.1 Write a comparator for integer objects that determines order based on the number of 1's in each number's binary expansion, so that $i < j$ if the number of 1's in the binary representation of i is less than the number of 1's in the binary representation of j.

C-7.2 Show how to implement the stack ADT using only a priority queue and one additional instance variable.

C-7.3 Show how to implement the (standard) queue ADT using only a priority queue and one additional instance variable.

C-7.4 Assuming the input to the sorting problem is given in an array A, describe how to implement the selection-sort algorithm using only the array A and, at most, six additional (base-type) variables.

C-7.5 Assuming the input to the sorting problem is given in an array A, describe how to implement the insertion-sort algorithm using only the array A and, at most, six additional (base-type) variables.

C-7.6★ Assuming the input to the sorting problem is given in an array A, describe how to implement the heap-sort algorithm using only the array A and, at most, six additional (base-type) variables.

C-7.7 An alternative method for finding the last node during an insertion in a heap T is to store in the last node and each external node of T a reference to the external node immediately to its right (wrapping to the first node in the next lower level for the right-most external node). Show how to maintain such references in $O(1)$ time per operation of the priority queue ADT assuming T is implemented as a linked structure.

C-7.8 Suppose the binary tree T used to implement a heap can be accessed using only the methods of the binary tree ADT. That is, we cannot assume T is implemented as a vector. Given a reference to the current last node, v, describe an efficient algorithm for finding the insertion point (that is, the new last node) using just the methods of the binary tree interface. Be sure and handle all possible cases, as illustrated in Figure 7.11. What is the running time of this method?

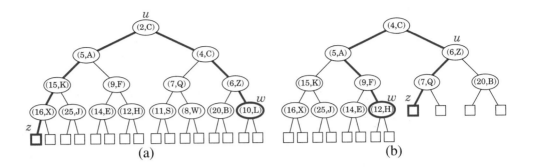

Figure 7.11: Finding the insertion position z in a heap: (a) the case when the current last node is the right-most node on its level; (b) an instance when this is not the case.

C-7.9 Show that, for any n, there is a sequence of insertions in a heap that requires $\Omega(n \log n)$ time to process.

C-7.10 We can represent a path from the root to a given node of a binary tree by means of a binary string, where 0 means "go to the left child" and 1 means "go to the right child." For example, the path from the root to the node storing 8 in the heap of Figure 7.3 is represented by the binary string 101. Design a logarithmic-time algorithm for finding the last node of a heap holding n elements based on the above representation.

C-7.11 Show that the problem of finding the kth smallest element in a heap takes at least $\Omega(k)$ time in the worst case.

C-7.12 Provide a justification of the time bounds in Table 7.3.

C-7.13 Tamarindo Airlines has the policy of giving generous rewards to their most loyal customers. In particular, at the end of each year, Tamarindo Airlines gives a booklet of first-class upgrade coupons to their top $\log n$ frequent flyers and a gift basket full of bananas and coconuts to the next $\sqrt{n}$ frequent flyers, based on the number of miles accumulated that year, where n is the total number of Tamarindo Airlines' frequent flyers. Since Tamarindo Airlines cannot afford an expensive computer, they need the fastest possible algorithm to determine which customers will receive the rewards. The algorithm they currently use first sorts the flyers by the number of miles flown, and then scans the sorted list to pick the top $\log n$ and the next $\sqrt{n}$ flyers. This algorithm has time-complexity $O(n \log n)$. Can you suggest a more efficient algorithm that runs in $O(n)$ time? Describe your algorithm informally and justify its running time.

C-7.14 Develop an algorithm that computes the kth smallest element of a set of n distinct integers in $O(n + k \log n)$ time.

C-7.15 Let T be a heap storing n keys. Give an efficient algorithm for reporting all the keys in T that are smaller than or equal to a given query key x (which is not necessarily in T). For example, given the heap of Figure 7.3 and query key $x = 7$, the algorithm should report 4, 5, 6, 7. Note that the keys do not need to be reported in sorted order. Ideally, your algorithm should run in $O(k)$ time, where k is the number of keys reported.

C-7.16 Suppose the internal nodes of two binary trees, T_1 and T_2 respectively, hold items that satisfy the heap-order property. Describe a method for combining these two trees into a tree T whose internal nodes hold the union of the items in T_1 and T_2 and also satisfy the heap-order property. Your algorithms should run in time $O(h_1 + h_2)$ where h_1 and h_2 are the respective heights of T_1 and T_2.

C-7.17 Show that the following summation, which arises in the analysis of bottom-up heap construction, is $O(1)$ for any positive integer h:

$$\sum_{i=1}^{h} \left(\frac{i}{2^i} \right).$$

Projects

P-7.1 Give a Java implementation of a priority queue based on an unsorted sequence.

P-7.2 Write an applet or stand-alone graphical program that animates both the insertion-sort and selection-sort algorithms. Your animation should clearly show the migration of elements to their correct locations in the insertion-sort and the migration of the selection process in selection-sort.

P-7.3 Develop a Java implementation of a priority queue that is based on a heap and supports the locator-based methods.

P-7.4 Write an applet or stand-alone graphical program that animates a heap. Your program should support all the priority queue operations and it should visualize the operations of the up-heap and down-heap bubbling procedures. (Extra: visualize bottom-up heap construction as well.)

P-7.5 Implement the in-place heap-sort algorithm. Compare its running time with that of the standard heap-sort that uses an external heap.

P-7.6 Implement a heap-based priority queue that supports the following additional operation in linear time:

replaceComparator(c): Replace the current comparator with c.
Input: Comparator; *Output:* None.

(Hint: Utilize the bottom-up heap construction algorithm.)

Chapter Notes

Knuth's book on sorting and searching [60] describes the motivation and history for the selection-sort, insertion-sort, and heap-sort algorithms. The heap-sort algorithm is due to Williams [98], and the linear-time heap construction algorithm is due to Floyd [36]. Additional algorithms and analyses for heaps and heap-sort variations can be found in papers by Bentley [13], Carlsson [21], Gonnet and Munro [42], McDiarmid and Reed [70], and Schaffer and Sedgewick [86]. The locator pattern (also described in [43]), appears to be new.

Chapter

8

Dictionaries

Contents

The familiar phrase, "Go look it up," might be heard when a lazy student asks for the definition of a word from an equally lazy teacher. This phrase is also the principle behind the ***dictionary*** abstract data type, which we discuss in this chapter.

As the name implies, the primary use of a dictionary is to store elements so that they can be located quickly using keys. The motivation for such searches is that each element in a dictionary typically stores additional useful information besides its search key, but the only way to get at that information is to use the search key. For example, a dictionary may hold bank accounts. Each account is an object that is identified by an account number and stores a wealth of additional information, including the current balance, the name and address of the account holder, and the history of deposits and withdrawals performed. An application wishing to operate on an account would have to provide the account number as a search key to get the account object from the dictionary.

As another example, a dictionary might hold a set of windows open in a graphical interface. The window objects are stored in the dictionary according to some identifier (like a process number), to determine a unique key value, but additional information is stored with each window object, including its dimensions, descriptions of its pull-down menus, its fonts, and its colors. A process wishing to send a message to a particular window object would need to be given a reference to this object, which it could request from the dictionary using the window's ID as a key.

Like a priority queue, a dictionary is a container of key-element pairs. However, although a total order relation on the keys is always required for a priority queue, it is optional for a dictionary. Indeed, the simplest form of a dictionary assumes only that we can determine whether two keys are equal. When a total order relation on the keys is defined, then we can talk about an ***ordered dictionary***, and we can specify additional ADT methods that refer to the ordering of the keys in such cases.

A computer dictionary is similar to a paper dictionary of words in the sense that both are used to look things up. The paper dictionary metaphor is not fully appropriate, however, for we typically desire a computer dictionary to be dynamic, so as to support element insertion and removal. Thus, the dictionary abstract data type has methods for the insertion, removal, and searching of elements with keys.

In this chapter, we describe several different techniques for realizing dictionaries. We show, for example, how to realize dictionaries using an unordered sequence. This implementation is simple, but not very efficient. So we introduce hash tables and skip lists, showing how these data structures can be used to realize dictionaries with fast query and update times. We conclude the chapter by discussing how the locator pattern presented in the previous chapter can be used to expand the collection of methods that are included in the dictionary ADT. Incidentally, we discuss other data structures for achieving fast dictionary-operation performance in Chapter 9, by using various kinds of balanced search trees.

8.1 The Dictionary Abstract Data Type

A dictionary stores key-element pairs (k,e), which we call *items*, where k is the key and e is the element. In order to achieve the highest level of generality, we allow both the keys and the elements stored in a dictionary to be of any object type. (See Figure 8.1.) For example, in a dictionary storing student records (such as the student's name, address, and course grades), the key might be the student's ID number. In some applications, the key may be the element itself. For example, if we had a dictionary storing prime numbers, we could use the numbers themselves as keys (and also as the elements).

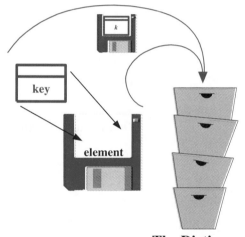

The Dictionary

Figure 8.1: A conceptual illustration of the dictionary ADT. Keys (labels) are assigned to elements (diskettes) by a user. The resulting items (labeled diskettes) are inserted into the dictionary (file cabinet). The keys can be used later to retrieve or remove the items.

We distinguish two types of dictionaries, the ***unordered dictionary*** and the ***ordered dictionary***. In either case, we use a ***key*** as an identifier that is assigned by an application or user to an associated element. In the ordered dictionary, we assume that a total order relation is defined on the keys, and we provide additional methods that refer to this ordering. An ordered dictionary determines the relative order of two keys by means of a comparator (see Section 7.1.4), which is provided to the dictionary as a parameter of the ordered dictionary constructor's method. In an unordered (generic) dictionary, however, no order relation is assumed on the keys, and only equality testing between keys is used.

For the sake of generality, our definition allows a dictionary to store multiple items with the same key. Nevertheless, there are applications in which we want to disallow items with the same key (for example, in a dictionary storing student records, we would probably want to disallow two students having the same ID). In such cases when keys are unique, then the key associated with an object can be viewed as an "address" for that object in memory. Indeed, such dictionaries are sometimes referred to as "associative stores," for the key associated with an object determines its "location" in the dictionary.

8.1.1 The Dictionary ADT

As an ADT, a *dictionary* D supports the following methods:

size(): Return the number of items in D.
Input: None; *Output:* Integer.

isEmpty(): Test whether D is empty.
Input: None; *Output:* Boolean.

elements(): Return the elements stored in D.
Input: None; *Output:* Iterator of objects (elements).

keys(): Return the keys stored in D.
Input: None; *Output:* Iterator of objects (keys).

findElement(k): If D contains an item with key equal to k, then return the element of such an item, else return a special element NO_SUCH_KEY.
Input: Object (key); *Output:* Object (element).

findAllElements(k): Return an iterator of all elements with keys equal to k.
Input: Object (key); *Output:* Iterator (of elements).

insertItem(k, e): Insert an item with element e and key k into D.
Input: Objects k (key) and e (element); *Output:* None.

removeElement(k): Remove from D an item with key equal to k, and return its element. If D has no such item, then return the special element NO_SUCH_KEY.
Input: Object (key); *Output:* Object (element).

removeAllElements(k): Remove from D the items with key equal to k, and return an iterator of their elements.
Input: Object (key); *Output:* Iterator (of elements).

When operations findElement(k) and removeElement(k) are unsuccessful (that is, the dictionary D has no item with key equal to k), we use the convention of returning a special element NO_SUCH_KEY. Such a special element is known as a *sentinel*. We could have used the alternative convention of returning a null element, but this would prevent us from storing in D an item whose element is null. Another choice, of course, would be to throw an exception when someone requests a key that is not in our dictionary. This would probably not be an appropriate use of an exception, however, since it is normal to ask for something that might not be in our dictionary. Moreover, throwing and catching an exception is typically slower than a test against a sentinel; hence, using a sentinel is more efficient (and, in this case, conceptually more appropriate).

Note that, as we have defined it, a dictionary D can contain different items with equal keys. In this case, operations findElement(k) and removeElement(k) return an *arbitrary* element whose associated key is equal to k. Also, if we wish to store an item e in a dictionary so that the item is itself its own key, then we would insert e with the method call insertItem(e, e).

Example 8.1: *In the following, we show the effect of a series of operations on an initially empty dictionary storing integer keys and single-character elements. The "Dictionary" column is somewhat deceiving since it shows the items sorted by key. This is not required for a dictionary. The way the items of a dictionary are stored is implementation-dependent.*

Operation	*Output*	*Dictionary*
insertItem$(5,A)$		$\{(5,A)\}$
insertItem$(7,B)$		$\{(5,A),(7,B)\}$
insertItem$(2,C)$		$\{(5,A),(7,B),(2,C)\}$
insertItem$(8,D)$		$\{(5,A),(7,B),(2,C),(8,D)\}$
insertItem$(2,E)$		$\{(5,A),(7,B),(2,C),(8,D),(2,E)\}$
findElement(7)	B	$\{(5,A),(7,B),(2,C),(8,D),(2,E)\}$
findElement(4)	NO_SUCH_KEY	$\{(5,A),(7,B),(2,C),(8,D),(2,E)\}$
findElement(2)	C	$\{(5,A),(7,B),(2,C),(8,D),(2,E)\}$
findAllElements(2)	C,E	$\{(5,A),(7,B),(2,C),(8,D),(2,E)\}$
size$()$	5	$\{(5,A),(7,B),(2,C),(8,D),(2,E)\}$
removeElement(5)	A	$\{(7,B),(2,C),(8,D),(2,E)\}$
removeAllElements(2)	C,E	$\{(7,B),(8,D)\}$
findElement(2)	NO_SUCH_KEY	$\{(7,B),(8,D)\}$

Equality Testers

Each of the standard dictionary operations given above requires that we have a mechanism for deciding whether two keys are equal. If the dictionary is ordered, then the areEqual method of the comparator (Section 7.1.4) associated with the dictionary serves the purpose. Otherwise, for a generic dictionary, we shall use an *equality tester* object that supports the operation areEqual on keys.

A comparator can be viewed as an extension of an equality tester, and can be used in lieu of an equality tester for an ordered dictionary. When a dictionary is instantiated, we associate it with an equality tester or a comparator, so that checking whether two keys are equal is a well-defined concept.

8.1.2   Dictionaries in the java.util Package

The standard Java package java.util also includes an interface for the dictionary ADT, called the java.util.Map. In addition, this package also includes an abstract class java.util.Dictionary, which also corresponds to the dictionary ADT given above, but this abstract class is now considered obsolete. Both java.util.Map and java.util.Dictionary are defined so that an implementing class has to enforce keys being unique. So, for example, there is no method in the java.util.Map interface corresponding to the findAllElements(k) method. Other than this issue about key

Caution

uniqueness, the java.util.Map interface corresponds closely to the dictionary ADT as defined above. Still, there are two subtle differences between our dictionary ADT and the java.util.Map interface, which are discussed below.

Testing for Equality in a java.util.Map

The first difference is that the java.util.Map interface assumes the use of the method equals, supported by any Java object, to decide whether two keys are equal. Thus, if we use a java.util.Map, we must "hard-code" method equals within the key class. This approach is not completely flexible, however, since there are contexts in which keys do not "know" when they are equal. For example, a geometric algorithm may consider points as "equal" if they have the same x-coordinate, while another algorithm may consider them equal if they have the same y-coordinate. (See the related discussion in Section 7.1.4.) Instead, we advocate the use of an equality tester (or a comparator) to test whether two keys in a dictionary are equal. This approach provides a general, reusable, and adaptive way of testing for object equality. Note that the equality tester can always use the equals method of the key class, if this use is appropriate.

Using **null** as an Element and Sentinel

The second difference between our dictionary ADT and the java.util.Map interface is that it uses the **null** object as the special element returned to denote the absence of an item with the given search key, while still allowing **null** as the element in a key-element item stored in the dictionary. Storing a **null** object as an element could arise, for example, if we wish to store a key without a "real" associated element. Incidentally, the obsolete java.util.Dictionary abstract class also uses the **null** object as the NO_SUCH_KEY value, but does not allow for **null** object elements. Thus, the **null** object is on the one hand a regular element and on the other hand the special element akin to the NO_SUCH_KEY object for our dictionary ADT. Choosing the **null** object as the NO_SUCH_KEY value allows for simple comparison tests, but it can also lead to some confusion. In particular, if **null** is a legitimate element, then there is no way of distinguishing between a search that returns a legitimate element, **null**, from the dictionary and one that cannot find the requested key. To help alleviate this confusion, java.util.Map also provides a Boolean method containsKey(k), which returns **true** if and only if the key k is present in the dictionary.

Corresponding Methods

Other than these subtle points and the issue about unique keys, the correspondences between the dictionary ADT and the java.util.Map interface are as shown in Table 8.1.

Dictionary ADT Methods	java.util.Map Methods
findElement(k)	get(k)
findAllElements(k)	n.a.
insertItem(k, e)	put(k, e)
removeElement(k)	remove(k)
removeAllElements(k)	n.a.

Table 8.1: Correspondences between methods of the dictionary ADT and the methods of the java.util.Map interface, which supports other methods as well.

Having defined the dictionary abstract data type, and its Java variants, let us now discuss different ways of implementing this ADT, pointing out the strengths and weaknesses of each approach.

8.2   Log Files

A simple way of realizing a dictionary uses an unordered vector, list, or general sequence to store the key-element pairs. Such an implementation is often called a *log file* or *audit trail*. The primary applications of such implementations are situations where we wish to archive structured data. For example, many financial database systems store a dictionary of all their transactions in this way. Likewise, many operating systems programs, such as Web servers and remote login programs, store log files of all requests they process over the Internet. The typical scenario in such applications is that there are many insertions into the dictionary but few searches. For example, searching such an operating system log file typically occurs only after something goes wrong, such as a system crash. Thus, log files should support simple and fast insertions, possibly at the expense of search time. Formally, we say that a *log file* is an implementation of a dictionary D using a sequence S (for full generality) to store the items of D in arbitrary order. (See Figure 8.2.)

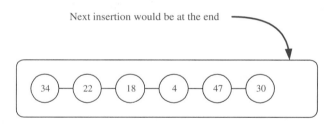

Next insertion would be at the end

Figure 8.2: Realization of a dictionary D by means of a log file. We show only the keys in this dictionary, so as to highlight its unordered sequence implementation.

We assume, in turn, that the sequence S used for a log file is implemented with either a vector or a doubly linked list (see Section 5.3). We also refer to the log file implementation of D as an *unordered sequence implementation*, since the keys have no influence on the linear arrangement of the items in S.

Analysis of the Log File Data Structure

The space required for a log file is $\Theta(n)$, since both the vector and linked list data structures can maintain their memory usage to be proportional to their size. In addition, with a log file implementation of the dictionary ADT, we can realize operation insertItem(k,e) easily and efficiently, just by a single call to the insertLast method on S, which simply adds the new item to the end of the sequence. Thus, we achieve $O(1)$ time for the insertItem(k,e) operation on D.

Unfortunately, this implementation does not allow for an efficient execution of the findElement method. A findElement(k) operation must be performed by scanning through the entire sequence S, examining each of its items. For example, we can iteratively use the after sequence operation until we either find an item with key equal to k or reach the end of the sequence. The worst case for the running time of this method clearly occurs when the search is unsuccessful, and we reach the end of the sequence having examined all of its n items. Thus, the findElement method runs in $O(n)$ time.

Similarly, a linear amount of time is needed in the worst case to perform a removeElement(k) operation on D, as well, for in order to remove an item with a given key, we must first find it by scanning through the entire sequence S. Thus the worst-case running time for performing removeElement(k) in a log file is $O(n)$.

The operations findAllElements and removeAllElements always require scanning through the entire sequence S, and hence their running time is $\Theta(n)$. That is, they run in linear time in both the best and worst case.

In conclusion, implementing a dictionary with a log file provides for fast insertions, but at the expense of slow searches and removals. Thus, we should only use a log file where we either expect the dictionary to always be small or we expect the number of insertions to be large relative to the number of searches and removals. Of course, archiving database and operating system transactions are precisely situations such as this. Nevertheless, there are many other scenarios where the number of insertions in a dictionary will be roughly proportional to the number of searches and removals, and in these cases the log file implementation is clearly inappropriate. The unordered dictionary implementation we discuss next can often be used, however, to achieve fast insertions, removals, and searches in many such cases.

8.3 Hash Tables

The keys associated with elements in a dictionary are often meant as "addresses" for those elements. Examples of such applications include a compiler's symbol table and a registry of environment variables. Both of these structures consist of a collection of symbolic names where each name serves as the "address" for properties about a variable's type and value. One of the most efficient ways to implement a dictionary in such circumstances is to use a **hash table**. Although, as we will see, the worst-case running time of the dictionary ADT operations is $O(n)$ when using a hash table where n is the number of items in the dictionary. A hash table can perform these operations in $O(1)$ expected time. It consists of two major components, the first of which is a bucket array.

8.3.1   Bucket Arrays

A ***bucket array*** for a hash table is an array A of size N, where each cell of A is thought of as a "bucket" (i.e., a container of key-element pairs) and the integer N defines the ***capacity*** of the array. If the keys are integers well distributed in the range $[0, N-1]$, this bucket array is all that is needed. An element e with key k is simply inserted into the bucket $A[k]$. Any bucket cells associated with keys not present in the dictionary are assumed to hold the special NO_SUCH_KEY object. (See Figure 8.3.)

Figure 8.3: An illustration of a bucket array.

Of course, if keys are not unique, then two different elements may be mapped to the same bucket in A. In this case, we say that a ***collision*** has occurred. Clearly, if each bucket of A can store only a single element, then we cannot associate more than one element with a single bucket, which is a problem in the case of collisions. To be sure, there are ways of dealing with collisions, which we will discuss later, but the best strategy is to try to avoid them in the first place.

Analysis of the Bucket Array Structure

If keys are unique, then collisions are not a concern, and searches, insertions, and removals in the hash table take worst-case time $O(1)$. This sounds like a great achievement, but it has two major drawbacks. The first is that it uses space $\Theta(N)$, which is not necessarily related to the number of items n actually present in the dictionary. Indeed, if N is large relative to n, then this implementation is wasteful of space. The second drawback is that the bucket array requires keys be unique integers in the range $[0, N-1]$, which is often not the case. Since these two drawbacks are so common, we define the hash table data structure to consist of a bucket array together with a "good" mapping from our keys to integers in the range $[0, N-1]$.

8.3.2 Hash Functions

The second part of a hash table structure is a function, h, called a ***hash function***, that maps each key k in our dictionary to an integer in the range $[0, N-1]$, where N is the capacity of the bucket array for this table. Equipped with such a hash function, h, we can apply the bucket array method to arbitrary keys. The main idea of this approach is to use the hash function value, $h(k)$, as an index into our bucket array, A, instead of the key k (which is most likely inappropriate for use as a bucket array index). That is, we store the item (k, e) in the bucket $A[h(k)]$.

We say that a hash function is "good" if it maps the keys in our dictionary so as to minimize collisions as much as possible. For practical reasons, we also would like the evaluation of a given hash function to be fast and easy to compute. Following the convention in Java, we view the evaluation of a hash function, $h(k)$, as consisting of two actions—mapping the key k to an integer, called the ***hash code***, and mapping the hash code to an integer within the range of indices of a bucket array, called the ***compression map***. (See Figure 8.4.)

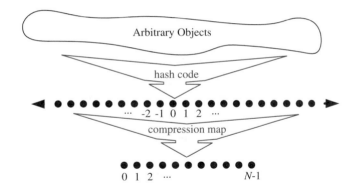

Figure 8.4: The two parts of a hash function: a hash code and a compression map.

8.3.3 Hash Codes

The first action that a hash function performs is to take an arbitrary key k in our dictionary and assign it an integer value. The integer assigned to a key k is called the ***hash code*** or ***hash value*** for k. This integer value need not be in the range $[0, N-1]$, and may even be negative, but we desire that the set of hash codes assigned to our keys should avoid collisions as much as possible. In addition, to be consistent with all of our keys, the hash code we use for a key k should be the same as the hash code for any key that is equal to k (as determined by the equality tester for our dictionary).

Hash Codes in Java

The generic Object class defined in a Java comes equipped with a default hash-Code() method for mapping each object instance to an integer that is a "representation" of that object. Specifically, the hashCode() method returns a 32-bit integer of type **int**. Unless specifically overridden, this method is inherited by every object used in a Java program. We should be careful in using the default Object version of hashCode(), however, as this could just be an integer interpretation of the object's location in memory (as is the case in many Java implementations). This type of hash code works poorly with character strings, for example, because two different string objects in memory might actually be equal, in which case we would like them to have the same hash code. Indeed, the Java String class overrides the hash-Code method of the Object class to be something more appropriate for character strings. Likewise, if we intend to use certain objects as keys in a dictionary, then we should override the built-in hashCode() method for these objects, replacing it with a mapping that assigns well-spread, consistent integers to these types of objects.

Caution

Let us consider, then, several common data types and some example methods for assigning hash codes to objects of these types.

Casting to an Integer

To begin, we note that, for any data type X that is represented using at most as many bits as our integer hash codes, we can simply take as a hash code for X an integer interpretation of its bits. Thus, for Java base types **byte**, **short**, **int**, and **char**, we can achieve a good hash code simply by casting this type to **int**. Likewise, for a variable x of base type **float**, we can covert x to an integer using a call to Float.floatToIntBits(x), and then use this integer as x's hash code.

Summing Components

For base types, such as **long** and **double**, whose bit representation is double that of a hash code, the above scheme is not immediately applicable. Still, one possible hash code, and indeed one that is used by many Java implementations, is to simply cast a (long) integer representation of the type down to an integer the size of a hash code. This hash code, of course, ignores half of the information present in the original value, and if many of the keys in our dictionary only differ in these bits, then they will collide using this simple hash code. An alternative hash code, then, which takes all the original bits into consideration, is to sum an integer representation of the high-order bits with an integer representation of the low-order bits. Such a hash code can be written in Java as follows:

```
static int hashCode(long i) {return (int)((i >> 32) + (int) i);}
```

Indeed, the approach of summing components can be extended to any object x whose binary representation can be viewed as a k-tuple $(x_0, x_1, \ldots, x_{k-1})$ of integers, for we can then form a hash code for x as $\sum_{i=0}^{k-1} x_i$. For example, given any floating-point number, we can sum its mantissa and exponent as long integers, and then apply a hash code for long integers to the result.

Polynomial Hash Codes

The summation hash code, described above, is not a good choice for character strings or other multiple-length objects that can be viewed as tuples of the form $(x_0, x_1, \ldots, x_{k-1})$, where the order of the x_i's is significant. For example, consider a hash code for a character string s that sums the ASCII (or Unicode) values of the characters in s. This hash code unfortunately produces lots of unwanted collisions for common groups of strings. In particular, "temp01" and "temp10" collide using this function, as do "stop", "tops", "pots", and "spot". A better hash code should somehow take into consideration the positions of the x_i's. An alternative hash code, which does exactly this, is to choose a nonzero constant, $a \neq 1$, and use as a hash code the value

$$x_0 a^{k-1} + x_1 a^{k-2} + \cdots + x_{k-2} a + x_{k-1},$$

which, by Horner's rule (see Exercise C-3.9), can be rewritten as

$$x_{k-1} + a(x_{k-2} + a(x_{k-3} + \cdots + a(x_2 + a(x_1 + a x_0)) \cdots)),$$

which, mathematically speaking, is simply a polynomial in a that takes the components $(x_0, x_1, \ldots, x_{k-1})$ of an object x as its coefficients. This hash code is therefore called a ***polynomial hash code***.

Intuitively, a polynomial hash code uses multiplication by the constant a as a way of "making room" for each component in a tuple of values while also preserving a characterization of the previous components. Of course, on a typical computer, evaluating a polynomial will be done using the finite bit representation for a hash code; hence, the value will periodically overflow the bits used for an integer. Since we are more interested in a good spread of the object x with respect to other keys, we simply ignore such overflows. Still, we should be mindful that such overflows are occurring and choose the constant a so that it has some nonzero, low-order bits, which will serve to preserve some of the information content even as we are in an overflow situation.

We have done some experimental studies that suggest that 33, 37, 39, and 41 are particularly good choices for a when working with character strings that are English words. In fact, in a list of over 50,000 English words formed as the union of the word lists provided in two variants of Unix, we found that taking a to be 33,

37, 39, or 41 produced less than 7 collisions in each case! It should come as no surprise, then, to learn that many Java implementations choose the polynomial hash function, using one of these constants for a, as a default hash code for strings. For the sake of speed, however, some Java implementations only apply the polynomial hash function to a fraction of the characters in long strings.

Cyclic Shift Hash Codes

A variant of the polynomial hash code replaces multiplication by a with a cyclic shift of a partial sum by a certain number of bits. Such a function, applied to character strings in Java could, for example, look like the following:

```java
static int hashCode(String s) {
  int h=0;
  for (int i=0; i<s.length(); i++) {
    h = (h << 5) | (h >>> 27); // 5-bit cyclic shift of the running sum
    h += (int) s.charAt(i);    // add in next character
  }
  return h;
}
```

As with the traditional polynomial hash code, using the cyclic-shift hash code requires some fine-tuning. In this case, we must wisely choose the amount to shift by for each new character. We show in Table 8.2 the results of some experiments run on a list of just over 25,000 English words, which compare the number of collisions for various shift amounts. These and our previous experiments show that if we choose our constant a or our shift value wisely, then either the polynomial hash code or its cyclic-shift variant are suitable for any object that can be written as a tuple $(x_0, x_1, \ldots, x_{k-1})$, where the order in tuples matters.

8.3.4 Compression Maps

The hash code for a key k will typically not be suitable for immediate use with a bucket array, because the range of possible hash codes for our keys will typically exceed the range of legal indices of our bucket array A. That is, incorrectly using a hash code as an index into our bucket array may result in an array out-of-bounds exception being thrown, either because the index is negative or it exceeds the capacity of A. Thus, once we have determined an integer hash code for a key object k, there is still the issue of mapping that integer into the range $[0, N-1]$. This compression step is the second action that a hash function performs.

Shift	Collisions	
	Total	**Max**
0	23739	86
1	10517	21
2	2254	6
3	448	3
4	89	2
5	4	2
6	6	2
7	14	2
8	105	2
9	18	2
10	277	3
11	453	4
12	43	2
13	13	2
14	135	3
15	1082	6
16	8760	9

Table 8.2: Comparison of collision behavior for the cyclic shift variant of the polynomial hash code as applied to a list of just over 25,000 English words. The "Total" column records the total number of collisions and the "Max" column records the maximum number of collisions for any one hash code. Note that with a cyclic shift of 0, this hash code reverts to the one that simply sums all the characters.

The Division Method

One simple *compression map* to use is

$$h(k) = |k| \bmod N,$$

which is called the *division method*. Additionally, if we take N to be a prime number, then this hash function helps "spread out" the distribution of hashed values. Indeed, if N is not prime, there is a higher likelihood that patterns in the distribution of keys will be repeated in the distribution of hash codes, thereby causing collisions. For example, if we hash the keys $\{200, 205, 210, 215, 220, \ldots, 600\}$ to a bucket array of size 100, then each hash code will collide with three others. But if this same set of keys is hashed to a bucket array of size 101, then there will be no collisions. If a hash function is chosen well, it should guarantee that the probability of two different keys getting hashed to the same bucket is at most $1/N$. Choosing N to be a prime number is not always enough, however, for if there is a repeated pattern of key values of the form $iN + j$ for several different i's, then there will still be collisions.

The MAD Method

A more sophisticated compression function, which helps eliminate repeated patterns in a set of integer keys is the ***multiply add and divide*** (or "MAD") method. In using this method we define the compression function as

$$h(k) = |ak + b| \bmod N,$$

where N is a prime number, and a and b are nonnegative integers randomly chosen at the time the compression function is determined so that $a \bmod N \neq 0$. This compression function is chosen in order to eliminate repeated patterns in the set of hash codes and get us closer to having a "good" hash function, that is, one such that the probability any two different keys collide is at most $1/N$. This good behavior would be the same as we would have if these keys were "thrown" into A uniformly at random.

With a compression function such as this, that spreads n integers fairly evenly in the range $[0, N - 1]$, and a mapping of the keys in our dictionary to integers, we have an effective hash function. Together, such a hash function and a bucket array define the key ingredients of a hash table implementation of the dictionary ADT.

But before we can give the details of how to perform such operations as findElement, insertItem, and removeElement, we must first resolve the issue of how we will be handling collisions.

8.3.5   Collision-Handling Schemes

Recall that the main idea of a hash table is to take a bucket array, A, and a hash function, h, and use them to implement a dictionary by storing each item (k, e) in the "bucket" $A[h(k)]$. This simple idea is challenged, however, when we have two distinct keys, k_1 and k_2, such that $h(k_1) = h(k_2)$. The existence of such ***collisions*** prevents us from simply inserting a new item (k, e) directly in the bucket $A[h(k)]$. They also complicate our procedure for performing the findElement(k) operation. To deal with collisions and come up with correct ways of fully implementing the methods of the dictionary ADT, we must have a consistent strategy for resolving collisions.

Separate Chaining

A simple and efficient way for dealing with collisions is to have each bucket $A[i]$ store a reference to a list, vector, or sequence, S_i, that stores all the items that our hash function has mapped to the bucket $A[i]$. The sequence S_i can be viewed as a miniature dictionary, implemented using the unordered sequence or *log file* method, but restricted to only hold items (k, e) such that $h(k) = i$. This *collision resolution* rule is known as *separate chaining*. Assuming that we implement each nonempty bucket in a miniature dictionary as a log file in this way, we can perform the fundamental dictionary operations as follows:

- findElement(k):
  > $B \leftarrow A[h(k)]$
  > **if** B is empty **then**
  > > **return** NO_SUCH_KEY
  >
  > **else**
  > > {search for the key k in the sequence for this bucket}
  > > **return** B.findElement(k)

- insertItem(k, e):
  > **if** $A[h(k)]$ is empty **then**
  > > Create a new initially empty, sequence-based dictionary B
  > > $A[h(k)] \leftarrow B$
  >
  > **else**
  > > $B \leftarrow A[h(k)]$
  > B.insertItem(k, e)

- removeElement(k):
  > $B \leftarrow A[h(k)]$
  > **if** B is empty **then**
  > > **return** NO_SUCH_KEY
  >
  > **else**
  > > **return** B.removeElement(k)

Thus, for each of the fundamental dictionary operations involving a key k, we delegate the handling of this operation to the miniature sequence-based dictionary stored at $A[h(k)]$. So, an insertion will put the new item at the end of this sequence, a find will search through this sequence until it reaches the end or finds an item with the desired key, and a remove will additionally remove an item after it is found. We can "get away" with using the simple log-file dictionary implementation in these cases, because the spreading properties of the hash function help keep each miniature dictionary small. Indeed, a good hash function will try to minimize collisions as much as possible, which will imply that most of our buckets are either empty or store just a single item. This observation allows us to make a slight change to our implementation so that, if a bucket $A[i]$ stores just a single item (k, e), we can simply have $A[i]$ point directly to the item (k, e) rather than to a sequence-based dictionary holding only the one item. We leave the details of this space optimization to an exercise (C-8.4).

In Figure 8.5, we give an illustration of a simple hash table that uses the division compression function and separate chaining to resolve collisions.

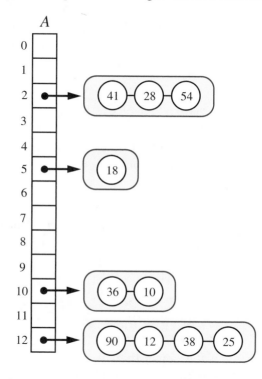

Figure 8.5: Example of a hash table of size 13, storing 10 integer keys, with collisions resolved by the chaining method. The compression map in this case is $h(k) = k \bmod 13$.

Assuming that we are using a good hash function for holding the n items of our dictionary in a bucket array of capacity N, we expect each bucket to be of size $\lceil n/N \rceil$. This parameter, which is called the **load factor** of the hash table, should therefore be bounded by a small constant, preferably below 1. For, given a good hash function, the expected running time of operations findElement, insertItem, and removeElement in a dictionary implemented with a hash table that uses this function is $O(\lceil n/N \rceil)$. Thus, we can implement the standard dictionary operations to run in $O(1)$ expected time, provided we know that n is $O(N)$.

Open Addressing

The separate chaining rule has many nice properties, such as allowing for simple implementations of dictionary operations, but it nevertheless has one slight disadvantage: it requires the use of an auxiliary data structure—a list, vector, or sequence—to hold items with colliding keys as a log file. We can handle collisions in other ways besides using the separate chaining rule, however. In particular, if space is of a premium (for example, if we are writing a program for a small hand-held device), then we can use the alternative approach of always storing each item directly in a bucket, at most one item per bucket. This approach saves space because no auxiliary structures are employed, but it requires a bit more complexity to deal with collisions. There are several methods for implementing this approach, which we discuss next. These methods are collectively referred to as *open addressing* schemes, which require that the load factor is always at most 1, that is, $n \leq N$, and that items are stored only in the bucket array itself.

Linear Probing

A simple open addressing collision-handling strategy is *linear probing*. In this strategy, if we try to insert an item (k, e) into a bucket $A[i]$ that is already occupied, where $i = h(k)$, then we try next at $A[(i+1) \bmod N]$. If $A[(i+1) \bmod N]$ is occupied, then we try $A[(i+2) \bmod N]$, and so on, until we find an empty bucket in A that can accept the new item. Once this bucket is located, we simply insert the item (k, e) here. Of course, using this collision resolution strategy requires that we change the implementation of the findElement(k) operation. In particular, to perform such a search we must examine consecutive buckets, starting from $A[h(k)]$, until we either find an item with key equal to k or we find an empty bucket (in which case the search is unsuccessful). (See Figure 8.6.)

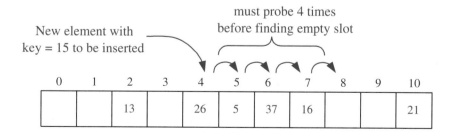

Figure 8.6: An insertion into a hash table using linear probing to resolve collisions. Here we use the compression map $h(k) = k \bmod 11$.

The operation removeElement(k) is more complicated than this, however. Indeed, to fully implement this method, we should restore the contents of the bucket array to look as though the item with key k was never inserted in its bucket $A[i]$ in the first place. Although performing such a restoration is certainly possible, it requires that we shift items down in buckets above $A[i]$, while not shifting others in this group (namely, the items that are already in their correct location). A typical way we can get around this difficulty is to replace the deleted item with a special "deactivated item" object. This object must be marked in some way so that we can immediately detect when it is occupying a given bucket. With this special marker possibly occupying buckets in our hash table, we modify our search algorithm for removeElement(k) or findElement(k), so that the search for a key k should skip over deactivated items and continue probing until reaching the desired item or an empty bucket. But our algorithm for the insertItem(k,e) should instead stop at a deactivated item and replace it with the new item to be inserted.

Linear probing saves space, but it complicates removals. Even with the use of the deactivated item object, the linear-probing collision-handling strategy suffers from an additional disadvantage. It tends to cluster the items of the dictionary into contiguous runs, which causes searches to slow down considerably.

Quadratic Probing

Another open addressing strategy, known as *quadratic probing*, involves iteratively trying the buckets $A[(i+f(j)) \bmod N]$, for $j = 0,1,2,\ldots$, where $f(j) = j^2$, until finding an empty bucket. As with linear probing, the quadratic probing strategy complicates the removal operation, but it does avoid the kinds of clustering patterns that occur with linear probing. Nevertheless, it creates its own kind of clustering, called *secondary clustering*, where the set of filled array cells "bounces" around the array in a fixed pattern. If N is not chosen as a prime, then the quadratic probing strategy may not find an empty bucket in A even if one exists. In fact, even if N is prime, this strategy may not find an empty slot, if the bucket array is at least half full; we explore the cause of this type of clustering in an exercise (C-8.7).

Double Hashing

Another open addressing strategy that does not cause clustering of the kind produced by linear probing or the kind produced by quadratic probing is the *double hashing* strategy. In this approach, we choose a secondary hash function, h', and if h maps some key k to a bucket $A[i]$, with $i = h(k)$, that is already occupied, then we iteratively try the buckets $A[(i+f(j)) \bmod N]$ next, for $j = 1,2,3,\ldots$, where $f(j) = j \cdot h'(k)$. In this scheme, the secondary hash function is not allowed to evaluate to zero; a common choice is $h'(k) = q - (k \bmod q)$, for some prime number

$q < N$. Also, N should be a prime. Moreover, we should choose a secondary hash function that will attempt to minimize clustering as much as possible.

These *open addressing* schemes save some space over the separate chaining method, but they are not necessarily faster. In experimental and theoretical analyses, the chaining method is either competitive or faster than the other methods, depending on the load factor of the bucket array. So, if memory space is not a major issue, the collision-handling method of choice seems to be separate chaining. Still, if memory space is in short supply, then one of these open addressing methods might be worth implementing, provided our probing strategy minimizes the clustering that can occur from open addressing.

8.3.6 A Java Hash Table Implementation

In Code Fragments 8.1–8.2, we show major portions of a LinearProbingHashTable class that implements the dictionary ADT using a hash table with linear probing to resolve collisions. This code fragment includes the main dictionary methods (we leave the rest to Exercise R-8.9).

The main design elements of the Java class LinearProbingHashTable are as follows:

- We maintain in instance variables the size, n, of the dictionary, and the capacity, N, of the bucket array, A.
- We use a *hash comparator* h to compare keys and to compute the hash function of a key. The hash comparator ADT (implemented as interface Hash-Comparator) provides methods isComparable(k) (which checks if a key can be tested for equality), isEqualTo(k_1, k_2) (which tests the equality of two keys), and hashValue(k) (which returns the hash function of a key).
- We define a sentinel, AVAILABLE, as a marker for deactivated items.
- A hash comparator and (optionally) an integer specifying the capacity of the bucket array are provided to the constructors.
- If the number of items, n, is equal to A's capacity, N, and one tries to insert a new item, exception HashTableFullException is thrown.
- The following auxiliary methods are used:
  - available(i), which tests if $A[i]$ is referencing the AVAILABLE sentinel
  - empty(i), which tests if $A[i]$ is empty
  - key(i), which returns the key of the item in $A[i]$
  - element(i), which returns the element in $A[i]$
  - check(k), which checks if the key k is comparable according to the hash comparator, and otherwise throws exception InvalidKeyException.

```
public class LinearProbingHashTable implements Dictionary {

  /** Marker for deactivated buckets */
  private static Item AVAILABLE = new Item(null, null);
  /** number of items in the dictionary */
  private int n = 0;
  /** capacity of the bucket array */
  private int N;
  /** bucket array */
  private Item[] A;
  /** hash comparator */
  private HashComparator h;

  /** constructor providing the hash comparator */
  public LinearProbingHashTable(HashComparator hc) {
    h = hc;
    N = 1023; // default capacity
    A = new Item[N];
  }

  /** constructor providing the hash comparator and the capacity
    * of the bucket array */
  public LinearProbingHashTable(HashComparator hc, int bN) {
    h = hc;
    N = bN;
    A = new Item[N];
  }

  // auxiliary methods
  private boolean available(int i) { return (A[i] == AVAILABLE); }
  private boolean empty(int i) { return (A[i] == null); }
  private Object key(int i) { return A[i].key(); }
  private Object element(int i) { return A[i].element(); }
  private void check(Object k) {
    if (!h.isComparable(k))
      throw new InvalidKeyException("Invalid key.");
  }
```

Code Fragment 8.1: Portions of class LinearProbingHashTable implementing the dictionary ADT using a hash table with linear probing to resolve collisions. (Continues in Code Fragment 8.2.)

```
/** helper search method */
private int findItem(Object key) throws InvalidKeyException {
  check(key);
  int i = h.hashValue(key) % N; // division method compression map
  int j = i;
  do {
    if (empty(i))  return −1;  // item is not found
    if (available(i))   i = (i + 1) % N; // bucket is deactivated
    else if (h.isEqualTo(key(i), key)) // we have found our item
      return i;
    else  // we must keep looking
      i = (i + 1) % N;
  } while (i != j);
  return −1;  // item is not found
}
// methods  of the dictionary ADT
public Object findElement (Object key) throws InvalidKeyException {
  int i = findItem(key); // helper method for finding a key
  if (i < 0) return Dictionary.NO_SUCH_KEY;
  return element(i);
}
public void insertItem (Object key, Object element) throws InvalidKeyException {
  check(key);
  int i = h.hashValue(key) % N; // division method compression map
  int j = i; // remember where we are starting
  do {
    if (empty(i) || available(i)) {  // this slot is available
      A[i] = new Item(key, element);
      n++;
      return;
    }
    i = (i + 1) % N; // check next slot
  } while (i != j); // repeat until we return to start
  throw new HashTableFullException("Hash table is full.");
}
public Object removeElement (Object key) throws InvalidKeyException {
  int i = findItem(key); // find this key first
  if (i <0) return Dictionary.NO_SUCH_KEY; // nothing to remove
  Object toReturn = element(i);
  A[i] = AVAILABLE; // mark this slot as deactivated
  n−−;
  return toReturn;
}
```

Code Fragment 8.2: Portions of class LinearProbingHashTable implementing the dictionary ADT using a hash table with linear probing to resolve collisions. (Continued from Code Fragment 8.1.)

8.3.7   Load Factors and Rehashing

In all of the hash table schemes described above, we should desire that the load factor, $\lambda = \lceil n/N \rceil$, be kept below 1. Experiments and average-case analyses suggest that we should maintain $\lambda < 0.5$ for the open addressing schemes and we should maintain $\lambda < 0.9$ for separate chaining. Indeed, as we explore in Exercise C-8.7, some open addressing schemes can start to fail when $\lambda \geq 0.5$. Although the details of an average-case analysis of hashing are beyond the scope of this book, its probabilistic basis is quite intuitive. If our hash function is good, then we expect the hash function values to be uniformly distributed in the range $[0, N-1]$. Thus, to store n items in our dictionary, the expected number of keys in a bucket would be $\lceil n/N \rceil$, which is $O(1)$ if n is $O(N)$.

With separate chaining, as λ gets very close to 1, the probability of a collision also approaches 1, which adds overhead to our operations, since we must revert to linear-time, sequence-based methods in buckets that have collisions. Of course, in the worst case, a poor hash function could map every item to the same bucket, which would result in linear-time performance for all dictionary operations, but this is very unlikely.

With open addressing, on the other hand, as the load factor λ grows beyond 0.5 and starts approaching 1, clusters of items in the bucket array start to grow as well. These clusters cause the probing strategies to "bounce around" the bucket array for a considerable amount of time before they can finish. At the limit, when λ is close to 1, all dictionary operations have linear expected running times, since in this case we expect to encounter a linear number of occupied buckets before finding one of the few remaining empty cells.

Thus, keeping the load factor below a certain threshold is vital for open addressing schemes and is also of concern with the separate chaining method. If the load factor of a hash table goes significantly above the specified threshold, then it is common to require that the table be resized (to regain the specified load factor) and all the objects inserted into this new table. Indeed, if we let our hash table become full, some implementations, including the Java example given in Code Fragment 8.1, may crash. When rehashing to a new table, it is a good requirement for the new array's size to be at least double the previous size. Once we have allocated this new bucket array, we must define a new hash function to go with it (possibly computing new parameters, as in the MAD method). Given this new hash function, we then reinsert every item from the old array into the new array using this new hash function. This process is known as *rehashing*.

Even with periodic rehashing, a hash table is an efficient means of implementing an unordered dictionary. Indeed, if we always double the size of the table with each rehashing operation, then we can amortize the cost of rehashing all the elements in the table against the time used to insert them in the first place. The analysis of this rehashing process is similar to that used to analyze vector growth. (See Section 5.1.3.) Each rehashing will generally scatter the elements throughout the new bucket array. Thus, while being effective for an unordered dictionary, the hash table is not a good choice for implementing an ordered dictionary.

8.4   The Ordered Dictionary ADT

In an ordered dictionary, we wish to perform the usual dictionary operations, but also maintain an order relation for the keys in our dictionary. We can use a comparator to provide the order relation among keys, and, as we will see, use of such an ordering helps to efficiently implement the dictionary ADT. In addition, an ordered dictionary also supports the following methods beyond those included in the generic dictionary ADT:

closestKeyBefore(k): Return the key of the item with largest key less than or equal to k.
Input: Object (key); *Output:* Object (key).

closestElemBefore(k): Return the element for the item with largest key less than or equal to k.
Input: Object (key); *Output:* Object (element).

closestKeyAfter(k): Return the key of the item with smallest key greater than or equal to k.
Input: Object (key); *Output:* Object (key).

closestElemAfter(k): Return the element for the item with smallest key greater than or equal to k.
Input: Object (key); *Output:* Object (element).

Each of these methods returns the special NO_SUCH_KEY object if no item in the dictionary satisfies the query.

The ordered nature of the above operations makes the use of a log file or a hash table inappropriate for implementing the dictionary, for neither of these data structures maintains any ordering information for the keys in the dictionary. Indeed, hash tables achieve their best search speeds when their keys are distributed almost at random. Thus, we should consider new dictionary implementations when dealing with ordered dictionaries.

8.5   Look-Up Tables

If a dictionary D is ordered, we can store its items in a vector S by nondecreasing order of the keys. (See Figure 8.7.) We specify that S is a vector, rather than a general sequence, for the ordering of the keys in the vector S allows for faster searching than would be possible had S been, say, a linked list. We refer to this ordered vector implementation of a dictionary D as a **look-up table**. We contrast this implementation with the log-file implementation, which uses an unordered sequence to implement the dictionary.

0	1	2	3	4	5	6	7	8	9	10
4	6	9	12	15	16	18	28	34		

Figure 8.7: Realization of a dictionary D by means of a look-up table. We show only the keys for this dictionary, so as to highlight its ordered vector implementation.

The space requirement of the look-up table is $\Theta(n)$, which is similar to the log file, assuming we grow and shrink the array supporting the vector S to keep the size of this array proportional to the number of items in S. Unlike a log file, however, performing updates in a look-up table takes a considerable amount of time. In particular, performing the insertItem(k, e) operation in a look-up table requires $O(n)$ time in the worst case, since we need to shift up all the items in the vector with key greater than k to make room for the new item (k, e). Similar observations apply to operations removeElement(k) and removeAllElements(k), since it takes $O(n)$ time in the worst case to shift all the items in the vector with key greater than k to close the "hole" left by the removed item (or items). The look-up table implementation is therefore inferior to the log file in terms of the worst-case running times of the dictionary update operations. Nevertheless, we can perform the operations findElement and findAllElements much faster in a look-up table.

8.5.1   Binary Search

A significant advantage of using an array-based vector S to implement an ordered dictionary D with n items is that accessing an element of S by its **rank** takes $O(1)$ time. We recall from Section 5.1 that the rank of an element in a vector is the number of elements preceding it. Thus, the first element in S has rank 0, and the last element has rank $n - 1$.

The elements in S are the items of dictionary D, and since S is ordered, the item at rank i has a key no smaller than keys of the items at ranks $0, \ldots, i - 1$, and no larger than keys of the items at ranks $i + 1, \ldots, n - 1$. This observation allows us to quickly "home in" on a search key k using a variant of the children's game "high-low." We call an item I of D a **candidate** if, at the current stage of the search, we cannot rule out that I has key equal to k. The algorithm maintains two parameters, low and high, such that all the candidate items have rank at least low and at most high in S. Initially, low $= 0$ and high $= n - 1$, and we let key(i) denote the key at rank i, which has elem(i) as its element. We then compare k to the key of the median candidate, that is, the item with rank

$$\text{mid} = \lfloor (\text{low} + \text{high})/2 \rfloor.$$

We consider three cases:

- If $k = \text{key}(\text{mid})$, then we have found the item we were looking for, and the search terminates successfully returning elem(mid).
- If $k < \text{key}(\text{mid})$, then we recur on the first half of the vector, that is, on the range of ranks from low to mid $- 1$.
- If $k > \text{key}(\text{mid})$, we recur on the range of ranks from mid $+ 1$ to high.

This search method is called **binary search**, and is given in pseudo-code in Code Fragment 8.3. Operation findElement(k) on an n-item dictionary implemented with a vector S consists of calling BinarySearch$(S, k, 0, n - 1)$.

Algorithm BinarySearch$(S, k, \text{low}, \text{high})$:

    Input: An ordered vector S storing n items, whose keys are accessed with method key(i) and whose elements are accessed with method elem(i); a search key k; and integers low and high

    Output: An element of S with key k and rank between low and high, if such an element exists, and otherwise the special element NO_SUCH_KEY

    if low $>$ high **then**
        return NO_SUCH_KEY
    else
        mid $\leftarrow \lfloor (\text{low} + \text{high})/2 \rfloor$
        if $k = \text{key}(\text{mid})$ **then**
            return elem(mid)
        else if $k < \text{key}(\text{mid})$ **then**
            return BinarySearch$(S, k, \text{low}, \text{mid} - 1)$
        else
            return BinarySearch$(S, k, \text{mid} + 1, \text{high})$

Code Fragment 8.3: Binary search in an ordered vector.

We illustrate the binary search algorithm in Figure 8.8.

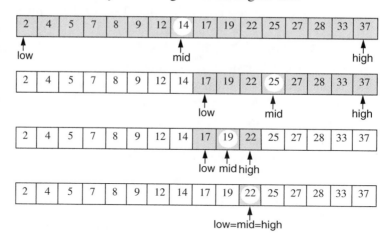

Figure 8.8: Example of a binary search to perform operation findElement(22), in a dictionary with integer keys, implemented with an array-based ordered vector. For simplicity, we show the keys stored in the dictionary but not the elements.

Considering the running time of binary search, we observe that a constant number of primitive operations are executed at each recursive call of method Binary-Search. Hence, the running time is proportional to the number of recursive calls performed. A crucial fact is that with each recursive call the number of candidate items still to be searched in the sequence S is given by the value

$$high - low + 1.$$

Moreover, the number of remaining candidates is reduced by at least one half with each recursive call. Specifically, from the definition of mid the number of remaining candidates is either

$$(mid - 1) - low + 1 = \left\lfloor \frac{low + high}{2} \right\rfloor - low \leq \frac{high - low + 1}{2}$$

or

$$high - (mid + 1) + 1 = high - \left\lfloor \frac{low + high}{2} \right\rfloor \leq \frac{high - low + 1}{2}.$$

Initially, the number of candidate items is n; after the first call to BinarySearch, it is at most $n/2$; after the second call, it is at most $n/4$; and so on. In general, after the ith call to BinarySearch, the number of candidate items remaining is at most $n/2^i$. In the worst case (unsuccessful search), the recursive calls stop when there are no more candidate items. Hence, the maximum number of recursive calls performed, is the smallest integer m such that

$$n/2^m < 1.$$

In other words (recalling that we omit a logarithm's base when it is 2), $m > \log n$. Thus, we have

$$m = \lfloor \log n \rfloor + 1,$$

which implies that BinarySearch($S, k, 0, n-1$), and hence method findElement runs in $O(\log n)$ time.

There is a simple variation of binary search that performs findAllElements(k) in time $O(\log n + s)$, where s is the number of elements in the iterator returned. The details are left as an exercise (C-8.3).

Thus, we can use a look-up table to perform fast dictionary searches, but using a look-up table for lots of dictionary updates would take a considerable amount of time. For this reason, the primary application for look-up tables is situations where we expect few updates to the dictionary but many searches. Such a situation could arise, for example, in an ordered list of English words we use to order entries in an encyclopedia or help file.

Table 8.3 compares the running times of the methods of a dictionary realized by either a log file or a look-up table. A log file allows for fast insertions but slow searches and removals, whereas a look-up table allows for fast searches but slow insertions and removals. Incidentally, although we don't explicitly discuss it, we note that a sorted sequence implemented with a doubly linked list would be slow in performing almost all the dictionary operations. (See Exercise R-8.1.)

Method	Log File	Look-Up Table
size, isEmpty	$O(1)$	$O(1)$
keys, elements	$O(n)$	$O(n)$
findElement	$O(n)$	$O(\log n)$
findAllElements	$\Theta(n)$	$O(\log n + s)$
insertItem	$O(1)$	$O(n)$
removeElement	$O(n)$	$O(n)$
removeAllElements	$\Theta(n)$	$O(n)$

Table 8.3: Comparison of the running times of the methods of a dictionary realized by means of a log file or a look-up table, which can also be viewed as implementations using an unsorted or sorted sequence, respectively. We denote the number of items in the dictionary at the time a method is executed with n, and the size of the iterator returned by operations findAllElements and removeAllElements with s.

As we explore next, it is possible to build a hierarchy of linked-list look-up tables to allow for both fast searching and fast updates.

8.6 Skip Lists

An interesting data structure for efficiently realizing the ordered dictionary ADT is the *skip list*. This data structure makes random choices in arranging the items in such a way that search and update times are $O(\log n)$ *on average*, where n is the number of items in the dictionary. Interestingly, the notion of average time complexity used here does not depend on the probability distribution of the keys in the input. Instead, it depends on the use of a random-number generator in the implementation of the insertions to help decide where to place the new item. The running time is averaged over all possible outcomes of the random numbers used when inserting items.

Because they are used extensively in computer games, cryptography, and computer simulations, methods that generate numbers that can be viewed as random numbers are built into most modern computers. Some methods, called *pseudorandom number generators*, generate random-like numbers deterministically, starting with an initial number called a *seed*. Other methods use hardware devices to extract "true" random numbers from nature. In any case, we will assume that our computer has access to numbers that are sufficiently random for our analysis.

The main advantage of using *randomization* in data structure and algorithm design is that the structures and methods that result are usually simple and efficient. We can devise a simple randomized data structure, called the skip list, which the same logarithmic time bounds for searching as is achieved by the binary searching algorithm. Nevertheless, the bounds are *expected* for the skip list, while they are *worst-case* bounds for binary searching in a look-up table. On the other hand, skip lists are much faster than look-up tables for dictionary updates.

A *skip list* S for dictionary D consists of a series of lists $\{S_0, S_1, \ldots, S_h\}$. Each list S_i stores a subset of the items of D sorted by a nondecreasing key plus items with two special keys, denoted $-\infty$ and $+\infty$, where $-\infty$ is smaller than every possible key that can be inserted in D and $+\infty$ is larger than every possible key that can be inserted in D. In addition, the lists in S satisfy the following:

- List S_0 contains every item of dictionary D (plus the special items with keys $-\infty$ and $+\infty$).
- For $i = 1, \ldots, h - 1$, list S_i contains (in addition to $-\infty$ and $+\infty$) a randomly generated subset of the items in list S_{i-1}.
- List S_h contains only $-\infty$ and $+\infty$.

An example of a skip list is shown in Figure 8.9. It is customary to visualize a skip list S with list S_0 at the bottom and lists $S_1, \ldots, S_h$ above it. Also, we refer to h as the *height* of skip list S.

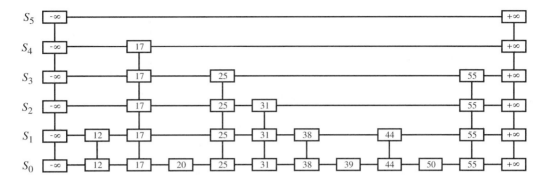

Figure 8.9: Example of a skip list.

Intuitively, the lists are set up so that S_{i+1} contains more or less every other item in S_i. As we shall see in the details of the insertion method, the items in S_{i+1} are chosen at random from the items in S_i by picking each item from S_i to also be in S_{i+1} with probability $1/2$. That is, in essence, we "flip a coin" for each item in S_i and place that item in S_{i+1} if the coin comes up "heads." Thus, we expect S_1 to have about $n/2$ items, S_2 to have about $n/4$ items, and, in general, S_i to have about $n/2^i$ items. In other words, we expect the height h of S to be about $\log n$. The halving of the number of items from one list to the next is not enforced as an explicit property of skip lists, however. Instead, randomization is used.

Using the position abstraction used for lists and trees, we view a skip list as a two-dimensional collection of positions arranged horizontally into **levels** and vertically into **towers**. Each level is a list S_i and each tower contains positions storing the same item across consecutive lists. The positions in a skip list can be traversed using the following operations:

after(p): Return the position following p on the same level.

before(p): Return the position preceding p on the same level.

below(p): Return the position below p in the same tower.

above(p): Return the position above p in the same tower.

We conventionally assume that the above operations return a **null** position if the position requested does not exist. Without going into the details, we note that we can easily implement a skip list by means of a linked structure such that the above traversal methods each take $O(1)$ time, given a skip-list position p. Such a linked structure is essentially a collection of h doubly linked lists aligned at towers, which are also doubly linked lists.

8.6.1 Searching

The skip list structure allows for simple dictionary search algorithms. In fact, all of the skip list search algorithms are based on an elegant SkipSearch method that takes a key k and finds the item in a skip list S with the largest key (which is possibly $-\infty$) that is less than or equal to k. Suppose we are given such a key k. We begin the SkipSearch method by setting a position variable p to the top-most, left position in the skip list S. That is, p is set to the position of the special item with key $-\infty$ in S_h. We then perform the following steps (see Figure 8.10):

1. If $S.$below(p) is null, then the search terminates—we are **at the bottom** and have located the largest item in S with key less than or equal to the search key k. Otherwise, we **drop down** to the next lower level in the present tower by setting $p \leftarrow S.$below(p).

2. Starting at position p, we move p forward until it is at the right-most position on the present level such that key$(p) \leq k$. We call this the **scan forward** step. Note that such a position always exists, since each level contains the special keys $+\infty$ and $-\infty$. In fact, after we perform the scan forward for this level, p may remain where it started. In any case, we then repeat the previous step.

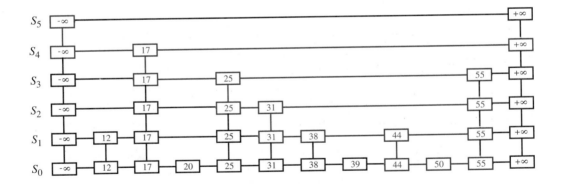

Figure 8.10: Example of a search in a skip list. The positions visited when searching for key 50 are highlighted in blue.

We give a pseudo-code description of the skip-list search algorithm, SkipSearch, in Code Fragment 8.4. Given this method, it is now easy to implement the operation findElement(k)—we simply perform $p \leftarrow$ SkipSearch(k) and test whether or not key$(p) = k$. If these two keys are equal, we return $p.$element; otherwise, we return the sentinel NO_SUCH_KEY.

Algorithm SkipSearch(k):

   Input: A search key k

   Output: Position p in S such that the item at p has the largest key less than or equal to k

   Let p be the top-most, left position of S (which should have at least 2 levels).

   while below(p) $\neq$ **null do**

      $p \leftarrow$ below(p)   {drop down}

      while key(after(p)) $\leq k$ **do**

         Let $p \leftarrow$ after(p)   {scan forward}

   return p.

Code Fragment 8.4: Algorithm for searching in a skip list S.

As it turns out, the expected running time of algorithm SkipSearch is $O(\log n)$. We postpone the justification of this fact, however, until after we discuss the implementation of the update methods for skip lists.

8.6.2 Update Operations

Another feature of the skip list data structure is that, besides having an elegant search algorithm, it also provides simple algorithms for dictionary updates.

Insertion

The insertion algorithm for skip lists uses randomization to decide how many references to the new item (k,e) should be added to the skip list. We begin the insertion of a new item (k,e) into a skip list by performing a SkipSearch(k) operation. This gives us the position p of the bottom-level item with the largest key less than or equal to k (note that p may be the position of the special item with key $-\infty$). We then insert (k,e) in this bottom-level list immediately after position p. After inserting the new item at this level, we "flip" a coin. That is, we call a method random() that returns a number between 0 and 1, and if that number is less than $1/2$, then we consider the flip to have come up "heads"; otherwise, we consider the flip to have come up "tails." If the flip comes up tails, then we stop here. If the flip comes up heads, on the other hand, then we backtrack to the previous (next higher) level and insert (k,e) in this level at the appropriate position. We again flip a coin; if it comes up heads, we go to the next higher level and repeat. Thus, we continue to insert the new item (k,e) in lists until we finally get a flip that comes up tails. We link together all the references to the new item (k,e) created in this process to create the *tower* for (k,e).

We give the pseudo-code for this insertion algorithm for a skip list S in Code Fragment 8.5 and we illustrate this algorithm in Figure 8.11. Our insertion algorithm uses an operation insertAfterAbove$(p,q,(k,e))$ that inserts a position storing the item (k,e) after position p (on the same level as p) and above position q, returning the position r of the new item (and setting internal references so that after, before, above, and below methods will work correctly for p, q, and r).

Algorithm SkipInsert(k,e):

    Input: Item (k,e)

    Output: None

    $p \leftarrow$ SkipSearch(k)

    $q \leftarrow$ insertAfterAbove$(p,\textbf{null},(k,e))$ {we are at the bottom level}

    while random$() < 1/2$ **do**

        while above$(p) = \textbf{null}$ **do**

            $p \leftarrow$ before(p) {scan backward}

        $p \leftarrow$ above(p) {jump up to higher level}

        $q \leftarrow$ insertAfterAbove$(p,q,(k,e))$ {insert new item}

Code Fragment 8.5: Insertion in a skip list, assuming random$()$ returns a random number between 0 and 1, and we never insert past the top level.

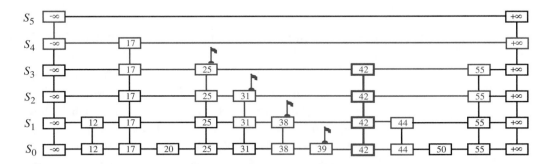

Figure 8.11: Insertion of an element with key 42 into the skip list of Figure 8.9. We assume that the random "coin flips" for the new item came up heads three times in a row, followed by tails. The positions visited are highlighted in blue. The positions inserted to hold the new item are drawn with thick lines, and the positions preceding them are flagged.

The expected running time of the insertion algorithm is $O(\log n)$, which we show in Section 8.6.3.

Removal

Like the search and insertion algorithms, the removal algorithm for a skip list S is quite simple. In fact, it is even easier than the insertion algorithm. Namely, to perform a removeElement(k) operation, we begin by performing a search for the given key k. If a position p with key k is not found, then we return the NO_SUCH_KEY element. Otherwise, if a position p with key k is found (on the bottom level), then we remove all the positions above p, which are easily accessed by using above operations to climb up the tower of this item in S starting at position p. The removal algorithm is illustrated in Figure 8.12 and a detailed description of it is left as an exercise. As we show in the next subsection, the running time for removal in a skip list is expected to be $O(\log n)$.

Before we give this analysis, however, there are some minor improvements to the skip list data structure we would like to discuss. First, we don't actually need to store references to items at the levels of the skip list above 0, because all that is needed at these levels are references to keys. Second, we don't actually need the above method. In fact, we don't need the before method either. We can perform item insertion and removal in strictly a top-down, scan-forward fashion, thus saving space for "up" and "prev" references. We explore the details of this optimization in an exercise. Neither of these optimizations improve the asymptotic performance of skip lists by more than a constant factor, but these improvements can, nevertheless, be meaningful in practice. In fact, experimental evidence suggests that optimized skip lists are faster in practice than AVL trees and other balanced search trees, which are discussed in Chapter 9.

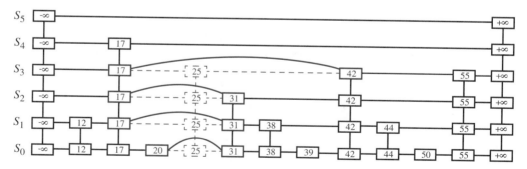

Figure 8.12: Removal of the item with key 25 from the skip list of Figure 8.11. The positions visited after the search for the position of S_0 holding the item are highlighted in blue. The positions removed are drawn with dashed lines.

The expected running time of the removal algorithm is $O(\log n)$, which we show in Section 8.6.3.

Maintaining the Top-most Level

A skip-list S must maintain a reference to the top-most, left position in S as an instance variable, and must have a policy for any insertion that wishes to continue inserting a new item past the top level of S. There are two possible courses of action we can take, both of which have their merits.

One possibility is to restrict the top level, h, to be kept at some fixed value that is a function of n, the number of elements currently in the dictionary (from the analysis we will see that $h = \max\{10, 2\lceil \log n \rceil\}$ is a reasonable choice, and picking $h = 3\lceil \log n \rceil$ is even safer). Implementing this choice means that we must modify the insertion algorithm to stop inserting a new item once we reach the top-most level (unless $\lceil \log n \rceil < \lceil \log(n+1) \rceil$, in which case we can now go at least one more level, since the bound on the height is increasing).

The other possibility is to let an insertion continue inserting a new element as long it keeps getting heads returned from the random number generator. As we show in the analysis of skip lists, the probability that an insertion will go to a level that is more than $O(\log n)$ is very low, so this design choice should also work.

Either choice will still result in our being able to perform element search, insertion, and removal in expected $O(\log n)$ time, however, which we show in the next section.

8.6.3 A Probabilistic Analysis of Skip Lists ⋆

As we have shown above, skip lists provide a simple implementation of an ordered dictionary. In terms of worst-case performance, however, skip lists are not a superior data structure. In fact, if we don't officially prevent an insertion from continuing significantly past the current highest level, then the insertion algorithm can go into what is almost an infinite loop (it is not actually an infinite loop, however, since the probability of having a fair coin repeatedly come up heads forever is 0). Moreover, we cannot infinitely add elements to a list without eventually running out of memory. In any case, if we terminate item insertion at the highest level h, then the **worst-case** running time for performing the findElement, insertItem, and removeElement operations in a skip list S with n items and height h is $O(n+h)$. This worst-case performance occurs when the tower of every item reaches level $h-1$, where h is the height of S. However, this event has very low probability. Judging from this worst case, we might conclude that the skip list structure is strictly inferior to the other dictionary implementations discussed earlier in this chapter. But this would not be a fair analysis, for this worst-case behavior is a gross overestimate.

⋆We use a star (⋆) to indicate sections containing material more advanced than the material in the rest of the chapter; this material can be considered optional in a first reading.

Because the insertion step involves randomization, a more honest analysis of skip lists involves a bit of probability. At first, this might seem like a major undertaking, for a complete and thorough probabilistic analysis could require deep mathematics (and, indeed, there are several such deep analyses that have appeared in data structure and algorithm literature). Fortunately, such an analysis is not necessary to understand the expected asymptotic behavior of skip lists. The informal and intuitive probabilistic analysis we give below uses only basic concepts of probability theory.

Let us begin by determining the expected value of the height h of S (assuming that we do not terminate insertions early). The probability that a given item is stored in a position at level i is equal to the probability of getting i consecutive heads when flipping a coin, that is, this probability is $1/2^i$. Hence, the probability P_i that level i has at least one item is at most

$$P_i \leq \frac{n}{2^i},$$

for the probability that any one of n different events occurs is, at most, the sum of the probabilities that each occurs.

The probability that the height h of S is larger than i is equal to the probability that level i has at least one item, that is, it is no more than P_i. This means that h is larger than, say, $3 \log n$ with probability at most

$$P_{3 \log n} \leq \frac{n}{2^{3 \log n}} = \frac{n}{n^3} = \frac{1}{n^2}.$$

More generally, given a constant $c > 1$, h is larger than $c \log n$ with probability at most $1/n^{c-1}$. That is, the probability that h is smaller than or equal to $c \log n$ is at least $1 - 1/n^{c-1}$. Thus, with high probability, the height h of S is $O(\log n)$.

Consider the running time of a search in skip list S, and recall that such a search involves two nested **while** loops. The inner loop performs a scan forward on a level of S as long as the next key is no greater than the search key k, and the outer loop drops down to the next level and repeats the scan forward iteration. Since the height h of S is $O(\log n)$ with high probability, the number of drop-down steps is $O(\log n)$ with high probability.

So we have yet to bound the number of scan-forward steps we make. Let n_i be the number of keys examined while scanning forward at level i. Observe that, after the key at the starting position, each additional key examined in a scan-forward at level i cannot also belong to level $i + 1$. If any of these items were on the previous level, we would have encountered them in the previous scan-forward step. Thus, the probability that any key is counted in n_i is $1/2$. Therefore, the expected value of n_i is exactly equal to the expected number of times we must flip a fair coin before it comes up heads. This expected value is 2. Hence, the expected amount of time spent scanning forward at any level i is $O(1)$. Since S has $O(\log n)$ levels with high probability, a search in S takes the expected time $O(\log n)$. By a similar analysis, we can show that the expected running time of an insertion or a removal is $O(\log n)$.

Finally, let us turn to the space requirement of a skip list S. As we observed above, the expected number of items at level i is $n/2^i$, which means that the expected total number of items in S is

$$\sum_{i=0}^{h} \frac{n}{2^i} = n \sum_{i=0}^{h} \frac{1}{2^i} < 2n.$$

Hence, the expected space requirement of S is $O(n)$.

Table 8.4 summarizes the performance of a dictionary realized by a skip list.

Operation	Time
size, isEmpty	$O(1)$
keys, elements	$O(n)$
findElement, insertItem, removeElement	$O(\log n)$ (expected)
findAllElements, removeAllElements	$O(\log n + s)$ (expected)

Table 8.4: Performance of a dictionary implemented with a skip list. We denote the number of items in the dictionary at the time the operation is performed with n, and the size of the iterator returned by operations findAllElements and removeAllElements with s. The expected space requirement is $O(n)$.

8.7   Supporting Locators in a Dictionary ⋆

As we did for priority queues, we can also use the locator pattern (Section 7.4) in the context of dictionaries. In the dictionary ADT, locators offer additional functionality for both unordered and ordered dictionaries. In an unordered dictionary, locators allow for a remove method that need not begin with an implicit search, but can instead be immediately given a locator to the item being removed. Likewise, locators in an ordered dictionary allow us to refer to items before and after some specified item.

Locator-Based Dictionary Methods

We can extend the set of operations for a dictionary D with methods that refer to locators. First, we add methods akin to those defined for priority queues, such as insert(k,e), remove(ℓ), replaceElement(ℓ,e), and replaceKey(ℓ,k), with the same meanings of the operations as given in Section 7.4.1.

Next, we define the following specific locator-based methods for a dictionary:

find(k): Return a locator to an item with key k, or a special locator NO_SUCH_KEY if no such item exists.
Input: Object (key); *Output:* Locator.

findAll(k): Return an iterator of locators to all items with key k.
Input: Object (key); *Output:* Iterator (of locators).

Finally, we define the following specialized locator-based methods for ordered dictionaries:

before(ℓ): Return a locator to an item whose key is the largest key in D smaller than ℓ.key$()$.
Input: Locator; *Output:* Locator.

after(ℓ): Return a locator to an item whose key is the smallest key in D larger than ℓ.key$()$.
Input: Locator; *Output:* Locator.

closestBefore(k): Return a locator to an item whose key is the largest key in D smaller than or equal to k.
Input: Object; *Output:* Locator.

closestAfter(k): Return a locator to an item whose key is the smallest key in D greater than or equal to k.
Input: Object; *Output:* Locator.

first$()$: Return a locator to an item with smallest key in D.
Input: None; *Output:* Locator.

last$()$: Return a locator to an item with largest key in D.
Input: None; *Output:* Locator.

The above methods return the special locator BOUNDARY_VIOLATION if no locator to an item can be returned because an access before the item with smallest key, or past the item with largest key is attempted. For example, this occurs when calling before(first) or after(last).

Key-Based Containers

As abstract data types, priority queues and dictionaries share the notions of storing key-element items, support the locator pattern, and have several common methods.

They are special cases of a more general ADT called ***key-based container***, which is a container of key-element items that are accessed via key-based methods.

Recalling the notion of inspectable container (see Section 5.6), we can define the following Java interfaces for key-based containers, whose inheritance diagram is shown in Figure 8.13: InspectableContainer, InspectableKeyBasedContainer, KeyBasedContainer, InspectablePriorityQueue, PriorityQueue, InspectableDictionary, Dictionary, InspectableOrderedDictionary, and OrderedDictionary.

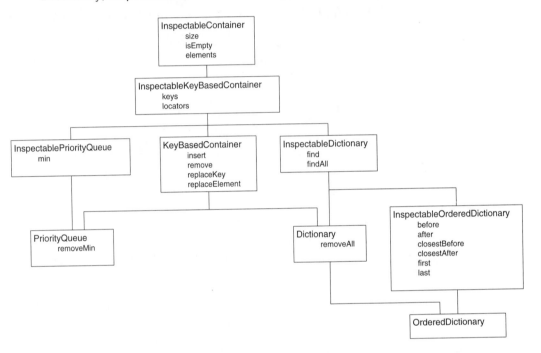

Figure 8.13: Inheritance hierarchy for ADTs representing key-based containers. Only locator-based access and update methods are shown.

Implementing Locator-Based Dictionary Methods

We can extend the dictionary implementations based on hash tables, log files, lookup tables, and skip lists discussed in this chapter with an approach similar to that used to extend the implementations of priority queues in Section 7.4.2. Namely, we can realize a locator by extending the key-element item object with a position reference. While the locators always stay attached to the items (indeed, they store the items), we have to keep track of the positions where the items are placed, and update the position references in the locators. We leave these extensions as exercises.

8.8 Exercises

Reinforcement

R-8.1 Briefly describe how an ordered sequence implemented as a doubly linked list could be used to implement a dictionary D, and analyze the running time of the fundamental methods of the dictionary ADT.

R-8.2 Assuming that an ordered dictionary D is implemented with an ordered sequence, describe how to implement the following operations in $O(1)$ time:

minElement(): Return the element of an item of D with smallest key.
Input: None; ***Output:*** Object.

maxElement(): Return the element of an item of D with the largest key.
Input: None; ***Output:*** Object.

Argue why your implementation of these operations runs in $O(1)$ time, independent of whether the sequence is itself implemented with an array or a linked list.

R-8.3 What would be a good hash code for a vehicle identification that is a string of numbers and letters of the form "9X9XX99X9XX999999," where a "9" represents a digit and an "X" represents a letter?

R-8.4 Draw the 11-item hash table that results from using the hash function

$$h(i) = (2i + 5) \bmod 11,$$

to hash the keys 12, 44, 13, 88, 23, 94, 11, 39, 20, 16, and 5, assuming collisions are handled by chaining.

R-8.5 What is the result of the previous exercise, assuming collisions are handled by linear probing?

R-8.6 Show the result of Exercise R-8.4, assuming collisions are handled by quadratic probing, up to the point where the method fails because no empty slot is found.

R-8.7 What is the result of Exercise R-8.4 assuming collisions are handled by double hashing using a secondary hash function $h'(k) = 7 - (k \bmod 7)$?

R-8.8　Give a pseudo-code description of an insertion into a hash table that uses quadratic probing to resolve collisions, assuming we also use the trick of replacing deleted items with a special "deactivated item" object.

R-8.9　Give Java code fragments describing implementations of the findAllElements and removeAllElements methods that could be included in the hash table implementation of Code Fragment 8.1.

R-8.10　Explain how to modify the Java code fragment given in Code Fragment 8.1, so that the implementation uses rehashing instead of crashing.

R-8.11　Show the result of rehashing the hash table shown in Figure 8.5 into a table of size 19 using the new hash function $h(k) = 2k \bmod 19$.

R-8.12　What is the worst-case running time for inserting n items into an initially empty hash table, where collisions are resolved by chaining? What if each sequence is stored in sorted order?

R-8.13　Explain why a hash table is not suited to implement the ordered dictionary ADT.

R-8.14　Draw an example skip list that results from performing the following sequence of operations on the skip list shown in Figure 8.12: removeElement(38), insertItem(48,x), insertItem(24,y), removeElement(55). Assume the coin flips for the first insertion yield two heads followed by tails, and those for the second insertion yield three heads followed by tails.

R-8.15　Give a pseudo-code description of the removeElement dictionary operation, assuming the dictionary is implemented by a skip-list structure.

Creativity

C-8.1　Suppose we are given two ordered dictionaries S and T, each with n items, and that S and T are implemented by means of array-based ordered sequences. Describe an $O(\log^2 n)$-time algorithm for finding the kth smallest key in the union of the keys from S and T (assuming no duplicates).

C-8.2★　Give an $O(\log n)$-time solution for the previous problem.

C-8.3　Design a variation of binary search for performing findAllElements(k) in an ordered dictionary implemented with an ordered array, and show that it runs in time $O(\log n + s)$, where n is the number of elements in the dictionary and s is the size of the iterator returned.

C-8.4 Describe the changes that must be made in the pseudo-code descriptions of the fundamental dictionary methods when we implement a dictionary with a hash table such that collisions are handled via separate chaining, but we add the space optimization that if a bucket stores just a single item, then we simply have the bucket reference that item directly.

C-8.5 The hash table dictionary implementation requires that we find a prime number between a number M and a number $2M$. Implement a method for finding such a prime by using the *sieve algorithm*. In this algorithm, we allocate a $2M$ cell Boolean array A, such that cell i is associated with the integer i. We then initialize the array cells to all be "true" and we "mark off" all the cells that are multiples of 2, 3, 5, 7, and so on. This process can stop after it reaches a number larger than $\sqrt{2M}$. (Hint: Consider a bootstrapping method for finding the primes up to $\sqrt{2M}$.)

C-8.6 Give the pseudo-code description for performing a removal from a hash table that uses linear probing to resolve collisions where we do not use a special marker to represent deleted elements. That is, we must rearrange the contents of the hash table so that it appears that the removed item was never inserted in the first place.

C-8.7 The quadratic probing strategy has a clustering problem that relates to the way it looks for open slots when a collision occurs. Namely, when a collision occurs at bucket $h(k)$, we check $A[(h(k) + f(j)) \bmod N]$, for $f(j) = j^2$, using $j = 1, 2, \ldots, N - 1$.

  a. Show that $f(j) \bmod N$ will assume at most $(N + 1)/2$ distinct values, for N prime, as j ranges from 1 to $N - 1$. As a part of this justification, note that $f(R) = f(N - R)$ for all R.

  b. A better strategy is to choose a prime N such that N is congruent to 3 modulo 4 and then to check the buckets $A[(h(k) \pm j^2) \bmod N]$ as j ranges from 1 to $(N - 1)/2$, alternating between addition and subtraction. Show that this alternate type of quadratic probing is guaranteed to check every bucket in A.

C-8.8 Show that the methods above(p) and before(p) are not actually needed to efficiently implement a dictionary using a skip list. That is, we can implement item insertion and removal in a skip list using a strictly top-down, scan-forward approach, without ever using the above or before methods. (Hint: In the insertion algorithm, first repeatedly flip the coin to determine the level where you should start inserting the new item.)

C-8.9⋆ Assuming a ordered dictionary D is implemented as an unordered sequence, describe how to implement the following operation:

> locAtRank(r): Return a locator to an item (k,e) of D, such that D has exactly r items with key less than k.
> **Input:** Integer; **Output:** Locator.

What is the worst-case running time of this method?

C-8.10⋆ Describe how to implement the locator-based method before(ℓ) as well as the locator-based method closestBefore(k) in a dictionary realized using an ordered sequence. Do the same using an unordered sequence implementation. What are the running times of these methods?

C-8.11⋆ Repeat the previous exercise using a skip list. What are the expected running times of the two locator-based methods in your implementation?

C-8.12 Suppose that each row of an $n \times n$ array A consists of 1's and 0's such that, in any row of A, all the 1's come before any 0's in that row. Assuming A is already in memory, describe a method running in $O(n \log n)$ time (not $O(n^2)$ time!) for counting the number of 1's in A.

C-8.13 Describe an efficient ordered dictionary structure for storing n elements that have an associated set of $k < n$ keys that come from a total order. That is, the set of keys is smaller than the number of elements. Your structure should perform all the ordered dictionary operations in $O(\log k + s)$ expected time, where s is the number of elements returned.

C-8.14 Describe an efficient unordered dictionary structure for storing n elements that have an associated set of $k < n$ keys that have distinct hash codes. That is, the set of keys is smaller than the number of elements. Your structure should be able to perform all the ordered dictionary operations in $O(1+s)$ expected time, where s is the number of elements returned.

C-8.15 Describe an efficient data structure for implementing the *bag* ADT, which supports a method add(e), for adding an element e to the bag, and a method remove(), which removes an arbitrary element in the bag. Show that both of these methods can be done in $O(1)$ time.

C-8.16⋆ Describe how to modify the skip list data structure to support the method atRank(i), which returns the position of the element in the "bottom" list S_0 at rank i, for $i \in [0, n-1]$. Show that your implementation of this method runs in $O(\log n)$ expected time.

Projects

P-8.1 Implement a class that implements the dictionary ADT by adapting the java.util.Hashtable class.

P-8.2 Implement a class that realizes the Comparator ADT so as to be able to compare objects that are numeric strings (see Section 11.1). In this case, the character strings should be interpreted as numbers in some base, such as base 2 (binary strings) or base 10 (decimal numbers). In addition to the comparator operations, the StringNumberComparator should support a method setBase(b) that takes a positive integer less than or equal to 10 as the base for the numeric strings to be compared.

P-8.3 Implement the dictionary ADT with a hash table that handles collisions with separate chaining (do not adapt the built-in java.util.Hashtable class of Java).

P-8.4 Implement the methods of the ordered dictionary ADT using an ordered sequence.

P-8.5 Implement the methods of the ordered dictionary ADT using a skip list.

P-8.6 Extend the previous project by providing a graphical animation of the skip list operations. Visualize how items move up the skip list during insertions and are linked out of the skip list during removals. Also, in a search operation, visualize the scan-forward and drop-down actions.

P-8.7 Implement a dictionary that supports locator-based methods by means of an ordered sequence.

P-8.8 Perform a comparative analysis that studies the collision rates for various hash codes for character strings, such as various polynomial hash codes for different values of the parameter a. Use a hash table to determine collisions, but only count collisions where different strings map to the same hash code (not if they map to the same location in this hash table). Test these hash codes on text files found on the Internet.

P-8.9 Perform a comparative analysis as in the previous exercise but for 10-digit telephone numbers instead of character strings.

Chapter Notes

Interestingly, the binary search algorithm was first published in 1946, but was not published in a fully correct form until 1962. For further discussions on the lessons to be learned from this history, please see the discussions in Knuth's book [60] and the papers by Bentley [12] and Levisse [65].

Skip lists were introduced by Pugh [84]. Our analysis of skip lists is a simplification of a presentation given in the book by Motwani and Raghavan [79]. In addition, our discussion of universal hashing is also a simplification of a presentation given in that book. The reader interested in other probabilistic constructions for supporting the dictionary ADT (including more information about universal hashing) is referred to the text by Motwani and Raghavan [79]. For a more in-depth analysis of skip lists, the reader is referred to papers on skip lists that have appeared in the data structures literature [57, 81, 82]. Exercise C-8.7 was contributed by James Lee.

Chapter

9

Search Trees

Contents

People like choices. We like to have different ways of solving the same problem, so that we can explore different trade-offs and efficiencies. This chapter is devoted to the exploration of different ways of solving a problem we discussed in an earlier chapter—the implementation of an ordered dictionary (Chapter 8). Namely, we study several alternative data structures based on trees for realizing ordered dictionaries.

We begin this chapter by discussing binary search trees, in Section 9.1, and how they support a simple tree-based implementation of an ordered dictionary, but do not guarantee efficient worst-case performance. Nevertheless, they form the basis of many tree-based dictionary implementations, and we discuss several in this chapter. One of the classic implementations is the AVL tree, presented in Section 9.2, which is a binary search tree that achieves logarithmic-time search and update operations.

In Section 9.3, we introduce the concept of a multi-way search tree, which is an ordered tree where each internal node can store several items and have several children. A multi-way search tree is a generalization of the binary search tree studied in Section 9.1, and like the binary search tree, it can be specialized into an efficient data structure for dictionaries by imposing additional constraints. One of the advantages of using these multi-way trees is that they often require fewer internal nodes than binary search trees to store items. But, just as with binary search trees, multi-way trees require additional methods to make them efficient for all dictionary methods.

Section 9.4 is devoted to the discussion of $(2,4)$ trees, which are also known as 2-4 trees or 2-3-4 trees. These are multi-way search trees, such that all the external nodes have the same depth and each node stores 1, 2, or 3 keys and has 2, 3, or 4 children, respectively. The advantage of these trees is that they have algorithms for inserting and removing keys that are simple and intuitive. Update operations rearrange a $(2,4)$ tree by means of natural operations that split and merge "nearby" nodes or transfer keys between them. A $(2,4)$ tree storing n items uses $O(n)$ space and supports searches, insertions, and removals in $O(\log n)$ worst-case time.

We present red-black trees in Section 9.5. These are binary search trees whose nodes are colored "red" and "black" in such a way that the coloring scheme guarantees logarithmic height. There is a simple, yet illuminating, correspondence between red-black and $(2,4)$ trees. Using this correspondence, we motivate and provide intuition for the somewhat more complex algorithms for insertion and removal in red-black trees, which are based on rotations and recolorings. Like an AVL tree, a red-black tree storing n items uses $O(n)$ space and supports searches, insertions, and removals in $O(\log n)$ worst-case time. The advantage that a red-black tree achieves over an AVL tree is that it can be restructured after an insertion or removal with only $O(1)$ rotations (although at the expense of more complex operations).

Finally, in Section 9.6, we discuss external searching, that is, searching in external memory (which will usually be a disk). We introduce a type of multi-way tree called the B-tree and we show how it can be used to store and search items so as to minimize the number of input-output (I/O) operations.

There are admittedly quite a few kinds of search trees discussed in this chapter, and we recognize that a reader or instructor with limited time might be interested in studying only selected topics. For this reason, in Figure 9.1, we show the conceptual dependencies between the sections in this chapter. Thus, for example, a reader can focus on binary search trees and then study AVL trees, (2,4) trees (possibly along with red-black trees as well), and/or external searching.

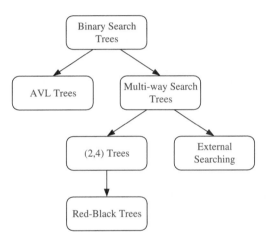

Figure 9.1: Dependencies between the sections in this chapter.

Since all of the data structures discussed in this chapter implement the ordered dictionary ADT, let us briefly review its fundamental methods before we begin:

- findElement(k): Return an element of an item with key k, if it exists.
- findAllElements(k): Return an iterator of all elements with keys equal to k.
- insertItem(k,e): Insert an item with element e and key k.
- removeElement(k): Remove an item with key k, if it exists, and return its element.
- removeAllElements(k): Remove all items with key k, and return an iterator of their elements.

Methods findElement and removeElement return NO_SUCH_KEY if k is not found. The ordered dictionary ADT also includes the search methods closestKeyBefore(k), closestElemBefore(k), closestKeyAfter(k), and closestElemAfter(k), but their performance is similar to that for findElement. So we will be focusing in this chapter on findElement as the primary search operation in an ordered dictionary.

9.1   Binary Search Trees

Binary trees are an excellent data structure for storing the items of an ordered dictionary. As we have seen in Section 6.3.4, a ***binary search tree*** is a binary tree T such that each internal node v of T stores an item (k, e) of a dictionary D, and

- Keys stored at nodes in the left subtree of v are less than or equal to k.
- Keys stored at nodes in the right subtree of v are greater than or equal to k.

The external nodes of T do not store any key or element of D, and serve only as "placeholders." We can even allow these external nodes to be **null** or references to a NULL_NODE object, so long as we have a positional wrapper for any external node that identifies the parent of that node. Nevertheless, to simplify the discussions in this chapter, we assume that external nodes are actual nodes of the tree T; they just happen not to store anything.

No matter how we represent empty external nodes, the important property of a binary search tree is that it represent an ordered dictionary. That is, a binary search tree should hierarchically represent an ordering of its keys, using relationships between parent and children. Specifically. it is easy to verify that an inorder traversal (Section 6.3.4) of a binary search tree T visits the keys of its dictionary in nondecreasing order. (See Figure 9.2a.)

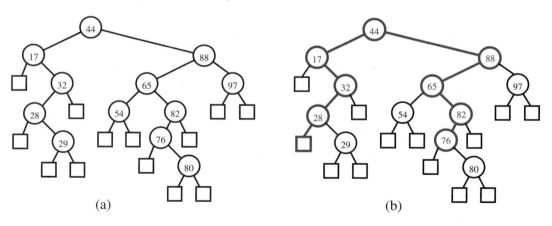

(a)   (b)

Figure 9.2: (a) A binary search tree T representing an ordered dictionary D with integer keys; (b) nodes of T visited when executing operations findElement(76) (successful) and findElement(25) (unsuccessful) on D. For simplicity, we show the keys but not the elements of D.

9.1.1 Searching

To perform operation findElement(k) in a dictionary D that is represented with a binary search tree T, we view the tree T as a decision tree (recall Figure 6.5). In this case, the question asked at each internal node v of T is whether the search key k is less than, equal to, or greater than the key stored at node v, denoted with key(v). If the answer is "smaller," then the search continues in the left subtree. If the answer is "equal," then the search terminates successfully. If the answer is "greater," then the search continues in the right subtree. Finally, if we reach an external node, then the search terminates unsuccessfully. (See Figure 9.2b.)

In Code Fragment 9.1, we give a recursive method TreeSearch, based on the above strategy for searching in a binary search tree T. Given a search key k and a node v of T, method TreeSearch returns a node (position) w of the subtree $T(v)$ of T rooted at v, such that one of the following two cases occurs:

- w is an internal node of $T(v)$ that stores key k.
- w is an external node of $T(v)$, all the internal nodes of $T(v)$ that precede w in the inorder traversal have keys smaller than k, and all the internal nodes of $T(v)$ that follow w in the inorder traversal have keys greater than k.

Thus, method findElement(k) can be performed on dictionary D by calling the method TreeSearch(k, T.root()) on T. Let w be the node of T returned by this call of the TreeSearch method. If node w is internal, we return the element stored at w; otherwise, if w is external, then we return NO_SUCH_KEY.

Algorithm TreeSearch(k, v):
    Input: A search key k, and a node v of a binary search tree T
    Output: A node w of the subtree $T(v)$ of T rooted at v, such that either w is an
        internal node storing key k or w is the external node where an item with key
        k would belong if it existed

    if v is an external node **then**
        return v
    if $k = $ key(v) **then**
        return v
    else if $k < $ key(v) **then**
        return TreeSearch(k, T.leftChild(v))
    else
        {we know $k > $ key(v)}
        return TreeSearch(k, T.rightChild(v))

        Code Fragment 9.1: Recursive search in a binary search tree.

Analysis of Binary Tree Searching

The analysis of the worst-case running time of searching in a binary search tree T is simple. Algorithm TreeSearch is recursive and executes a constant number of primitive operations for each recursive call. Each recursive call of TreeSearch is made on a child of the previous node. That is, TreeSearch is called on the nodes of a path of T that starts from the root and goes down one level at a time. Thus, the number of such nodes is bounded by $h + 1$, where h is the height of T. In other words, since we spend $O(1)$ time per node encountered in the search, method findElement on dictionary D runs in $O(h)$ time, where h is the height of the binary search tree T used to implement D. (See Figure 9.3.)

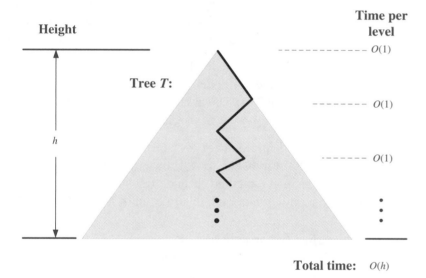

Figure 9.3: Illustrating the running time of searching in a binary search tree. The figure uses standard visualization shortcuts of viewing a binary search tree as a big triangle and a path from the root as a zig-zag line.

We can also show that a variation of the above algorithm performs operation findAllElements(k) in time $O(h + s)$, where s is the number of elements in the iterator returned. However, this method is slightly more complicated, and the details are left as an exercise (C-9.1).

Admittedly, the height h of T can be as large as n, but we expect that it is usually much smaller. Indeed, we will show how to maintain an upper bound of $O(\log n)$ on the height of a search tree T in Section 9.2. Before we describe such a scheme, however, let us describe implementations for dictionary update methods.

9.1.2 Update Operations

Binary search trees allow implementations of the insertItem and removeElement operations using algorithms that are fairly straightforward, but not trivial.

Insertion

To perform the operation insertItem(k, e) on a dictionary D implemented with a binary search tree T, we start by calling the method TreeSearch$(k, T.\text{root}())$ on T. Let w be the node returned by TreeSearch.

- If w is an external node (no item with key k is stored in T), we replace w with a new internal node storing the item (k, e) and two external children, by means of operation expandExternal(w) on T (see Section 6.3.1). Note that w is the appropriate place to insert an item with key k.
- If w is an internal node (another item with key k is stored at w), we call TreeSearch$(k, \text{rightChild}(w))$ (or, equivalently, TreeSearch$(k, \text{leftChild}(w))$) and recursively apply the algorithm to the node returned by TreeSearch.

The above insertion algorithm eventually traces a path from the root of T down to an external node, which gets replaced with a new internal node accommodating the new item. Hence, an insertion adds the new item at the "bottom" of the search tree T. An example of insertion into a binary search tree is shown in Figure 9.4.

The analysis of the insertion algorithm is analogous to that for searching. The number of nodes visited is proportional to the height h of T in the worst case. Also, assuming a linked structure implementation for T (see Section 6.4.2), we spend $O(1)$ time at each node visited. Thus, method insertItem runs in $O(h)$ time.

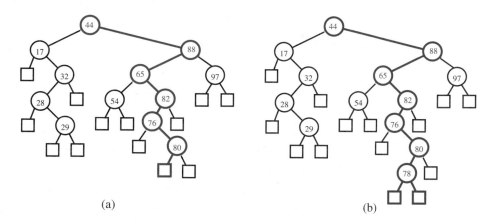

(a)   (b)

Figure 9.4: Insertion of an item with key 78 into the search tree of Figure 9.2. Finding the position to insert is shown in (a), and the resulting tree is shown in (b).

Removal

The implementation of the removeElement(k) operation on a dictionary D implemented with a binary search tree T is a bit more complex, since we do not wish to create any "holes" in the tree T. The operation starts out simple enough, since we begin by executing algorithm TreeSearch$(k, T.\text{root}())$ on T to find a node storing key k. If TreeSearch returns an external node, then there is no element with key k in dictionary D, and we return the special element NO_SUCH_KEY and we are done. If TreeSearch returns an internal node w instead, then w stores an item we wish to remove.

We distinguish two cases (of increasing difficulty):

- If one of the children of node w is an external node, say node z, we simply remove w and z from T by means of operation removeAboveExternal(z) on T. This operation (see also Figure 6.13 and Section 6.4.2) restructures T by replacing w with the sibling of z, removing both w and z from T. This case is illustrated in Figure 9.5.
- If both children of node w are internal nodes, we cannot simply remove the node w from T, since this would create a "hole" in T. Instead, we proceed as follows (see Figure 9.6):
  - We find the first internal node y that follows w in an inorder traversal of T. Node y is the left-most internal node in the right subtree of w, and is found by going first to the right child of w and then down T from there, following left children. Also, the left child x of y is the external node that immediately follows node w in the inorder traversal of T.
  - We save the element stored at w in a temporary variable t, and move the item of y into w. This action has the effect of removing the former item stored at w.
  - We remove nodes x and y from T by means of operation removeAboveExternal(x) on T. This action replaces y with x's sibling, and removes both x and y from T.
  - We return the element previously stored at w, which we had saved in the temporary variable t.

The analysis of the removal algorithm is analogous to that of the insertion and search algorithms. We spend $O(1)$ time at each node visited, and, in the worst case, the number of nodes visited is proportional to the height h of T. Thus, in a dictionary D implemented with a binary search tree T, the removeElement method runs in $O(h)$ time, where h is the height of T.

We can also show that a variation of the above algorithm performs operation removeAllElements(k) in time $O(h + s)$, where s is the number of elements in the iterator returned. The details are left as an exercise (C-9.2).

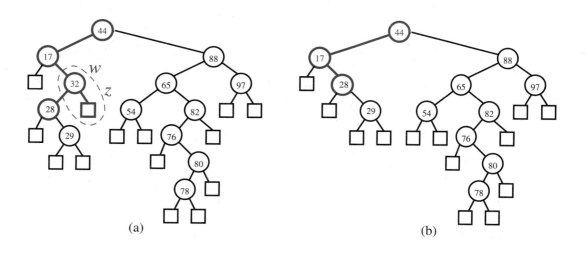

Figure 9.5: Removal from the binary search tree of Figure 9.4b, where the key to remove (32) is stored at a node (*w*) with an external child: (a) before the removal; (b) after the removal.

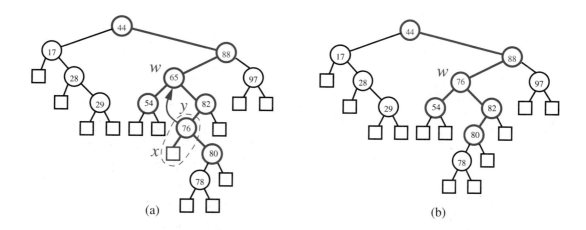

Figure 9.6: Removal from the binary search tree of Figure 9.4b, where the key to remove (65) is stored at a node whose children are both internal: (a) before the removal; (b) after the removal.

Best-case versus Worst-case

A binary search tree T is an efficient implementation of an ordered dictionary with n items but only if the height of T is small. In the best case, T has height h such that $h = \lceil \log(n+1) \rceil$, which yields logarithmic-time performance for all the dictionary operations. In the worst case, however, T has height n; hence, it looks and feels like an ordered sequence. Such a worst-case configuration arises, for example, if we insert a set of keys in increasing or decreasing order. (See Figure 9.7.)

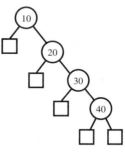

Figure 9.7: Example of a binary search tree with linear height, obtained by inserting keys in increasing order.

9.1.3   Java Implementation

We describe a binary search tree class, BinarySearchTree, which stores key-element pairs of class Item (shown again in Code Fragment 9.2) as the elements stored at the positions (nodes) of its underlying binary tree. The code for BinarySearchTree is shown in Code Fragments 9.3 through 9.5. Note that the underlying binary tree T is used only through the BinaryTree interface, where we assume that Binary-Tree includes also methods expandExternal and removeAboveExternal (see Section 6.4.2). Thus, class BinarySearchTree is independent from the specific implementation of the binary tree, and it takes advantage of code reuse.

The auxiliary method findPosition, based on the TreeSearch algorithm, is invoked by the findElement, insertItem, and removeElement methods. The instance variable actionPos stores the position where the most recent search, insertion or removal ended. This instance variable is not necessary to the implementation of a binary search tree, but is useful to classes that will extend BinarySearchTree (see Code Fragments 9.8–9.9 and 9.12–9.13) to identify the position where the previous search, insertion, or removal has taken place. Position actionPos has the intended meaning provided it is used right after executing methods findElement, insertItem, and removeElement.

```
public class Item {
  private Object key, elem;
  protected Item (Object k, Object e) {
    key = k;
    elem = e;
  }
  public Object key() { return key; }
  public Object element() { return elem; }
  public void setKey(Object k) { key = k; }
  public void setElement(Object e) { elem = e; }
}
```

Code Fragment 9.2: Class for the key-element pairs stored in a dictionary (same as the class of Code Fragment 7.2).

```
/** Realization of a dictionary by means of a binary search tree */
public class BinarySearchTree implements Dictionary  {
  Comparator C;  // comparator
  BinaryTree T; // binary tree
  protected Position actionPos; // insertion position or parent of removed position

  public BinarySearchTree(Comparator c)  {
    C = c;
    T = (BinaryTree) new NodeBinaryTree();
  }

  // auxiliary methods:
  /** Extract the key of the item at a given node of the tree. */
  protected Object key(Position position)  {
    return ((Item) position.element()).key();
  }
  /** Extract the element of the item at a given node of the tree. */
  protected Object element(Position position)  {
    return ((Item) position.element()).element();
  }
  /** Check whether a given key is valid. */
  protected void checkKey(Object key) throws InvalidKeyException {
    if(!C.isComparable(key))
      throw new InvalidKeyException("Key "+key+" is not comparable");
  }
}
```

Code Fragment 9.3: Class BinarySearchTree. (Continues in Code Fragment 9.4.)

```java
/** Auxiliary method used by removeElement. */
protected void swap(Position swapPos, Position remPos){
  T.replaceElement(swapPos, remPos.element());
}
/** Auxiliary method used by findElement, insertItem, and removeElement. */
protected Position findPosition(Object key, Position pos) {
  if (T.isExternal(pos))
    return pos; // key not found and external node reached returned
  else {
    Object curKey = key(pos);
    if(C.isLessThan(key, curKey))
      return findPosition(key, T.leftChild(pos));
    else if(C.isGreaterThan(key, curKey)) // search in left subtree
      return findPosition(key, T.rightChild(pos)); // search in right subtree
    else
      return pos; // return internal node where key is found
  }
}


// methods of the dictionary ADT
public int size()  {
  return (T.size() − 1) / 2;
}


public boolean isEmpty() {
  return T.size() == 1;
}


public Object findElement(Object key) throws InvalidKeyException {
  checkKey(key); // may throw an InvalidKeyException
  Position curPos = findPosition(key, T.root());
  actionPos = curPos; // node where the search ended
  if (T.isInternal(curPos))
    return element(curPos);
  else
    return NO_SUCH_KEY;
}
```

Code Fragment 9.4: Class BinarySearchTree, continued from Code Fragment 9.3. (Continues in Code Fragment 9.5.)

```
public void insertItem(Object key, Object element)
  throws InvalidKeyException {
  checkKey(key); // may throw an InvalidKeyException
  Position insPos = T.root();
  do {
    insPos = findPosition(key, insPos);
    if (T.isExternal(insPos))
      break;
    else // the key already exists
      insPos = T.rightChild(insPos);
  } while (true);
  T.expandExternal(insPos);
  Item newItem = new Item(key, element);
  T.replaceElement(insPos, newItem);
  actionPos = insPos; // node where the new item was inserted
}

public Object removeElement(Object key) throws InvalidKeyException {
  Object toReturn;
  checkKey(key); // may throw an InvalidKeyException
  Position remPos = findPosition(key, T.root());
  if(T.isExternal(remPos)) {
    actionPos = remPos; // node where the search ended unsuccessfully
    return NO_SUCH_KEY;
  }
  else{
    toReturn = element(remPos); // element to be returned
    if (T.isExternal(T.leftChild(remPos)))
      remPos = T.leftChild(remPos);
    else if (T.isExternal(T.rightChild(remPos)))
      remPos = T.rightChild(remPos);
    else { // key is at a node with internal children
      Position swapPos = remPos; // find node for swapping items
      remPos = T.rightChild(swapPos);
      do
        remPos = T.leftChild(remPos);
      while (T.isInternal(remPos));
      swap(swapPos, T.parent(remPos));
    }
    actionPos = T.sibling(remPos); // sibling of the leaf to be removed
    T.removeAboveExternal(remPos);
    return toReturn;
  }
}
}
```

Code Fragment 9.5: Class BinarySearchTree, continued from Code Fragment 9.4.

9.1.4   Performance

The performance of a dictionary implemented with a binary search is summarized in the following proposition and in Table 9.1.

Proposition 9.1: *A binary search tree T with height h for n key-element items uses $O(n)$ space and executes the dictionary ADT operations with the following running times. Operations* size *and* isEmpty *each take $O(1)$ time. Operations* findElement, *insertItem, and* removeElement *each take time $O(h)$ time. Operations* findAllElements *and* removeAllElements *each take $O(h+s)$ time, where s is the size of the iterators returned.*

Method	Time
size, isEmpty	$O(1)$
findElement, insertItem, removeElement	$O(h)$
findAllElements, removeAllElements	$O(h+s)$

Table 9.1: Running times of the main methods of a dictionary realized by a binary search tree. We denote with h the current height of the tree and with s the size of the iterators returned by findAllElements and removeAllElements. The space usage is $O(n)$, where n is the number of items stored in the dictionary.

Note that the running time of search and update operations in a binary search tree varies dramatically depending on the tree's height. We can nevertheless take comfort that, on average, a binary search tree with n keys generated from a random series of insertions and removals of keys has expected height $O(\log n)$. Such a statement requires careful mathematical language to precisely define what we mean by a random series of insertions and removals, and sophisticated probability theory to justify; hence, its justification is beyond the scope of this book. Thus, we can be content knowing that random update sequences give rise to binary search trees that have logarithmic height on average, but, keeping in mind their poor worst-case performance, we should also take care in using standard binary search trees in applications where updates are not random.

Caution

The relative simplicity of their dictionary implementation, combined with good average-case performance, make binary search trees a rather attractive dictionary data structure in applications where the keys inserted and removed follow a random pattern and occasionally slow response time is acceptable. There are, however, applications where it is essential to have a dictionary with fast worst-case search and update time. The data structures presented in the next sections address this need.

9.2 AVL Trees

In the previous section, we discussed what should be an efficient dictionary data structure, but the worst-case performance it achieves for the various operations is linear time, which is no better than the performance of sequence-based dictionary implementations (such as log files and look-up tables discussed in Chapter 8). In this section, we describe a simple way of correcting this problem so as to achieve logarithmic time for all the fundamental dictionary operations.

Definition

The simple correction is to add a rule to the binary search tree definition that will maintain a logarithmic height for the tree. The rule we consider in this section is the following ***height-balance property***, which characterizes the structure of a binary search tree T in terms of the heights of its internal nodes (recall from Section 6.2.2 that the height of a node v in a tree is the length of a longest path from v to an external node):

Height-Balance Property: For every internal node v of T, the heights of the children of v can differ by at most 1.

Any binary search tree T that satisfies this property is said to be an ***AVL tree***, which is a concept named after the initials of its inventors: Adel'son-Vel'skii and Landis. An example of an AVL tree is shown in Figure 9.8.

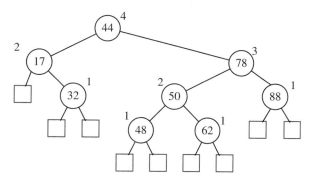

Figure 9.8: An example of an AVL tree. The keys are shown inside the nodes, and the heights are shown next to the nodes.

An immediate consequence of the height-balance property is that a subtree of an AVL tree is itself an AVL tree. The height-balance property has also the important consequence of keeping the height small, as shown in the following proposition.

Proposition 9.2: *The height of an AVL tree T storing n items is $O(\log n)$.*

Justification: Instead of trying to find an upper bound on the height of an AVL tree directly, it turns out to be easier to work on the "inverse problem" of finding a lower bound on the minimum number of internal nodes $n(h)$ of an AVL tree with height h. We will show that $n(h)$ grows at least exponentially, that is, $n(h)$ is $\Omega(c^h)$ for some constant $c > 1$. From this, it will be an easy step to derive that the height of an AVL tree storing n keys is $O(\log n)$.

To start with, notice that $n(1) = 1$ and $n(2) = 2$, because an AVL tree of height 1 must have at least one internal node and an AVL tree of height 2 must have at least two internal nodes. Now, for $h \geq 3$, an AVL tree with height h and the minimum number of nodes is such that both its subtrees are AVL trees with the minimum number of nodes: one with height $h-1$ and the other with height $h-2$. Taking the root into account, we obtain the following formula that relates $n(h)$ to $n(h-1)$ and $n(h-2)$, for $h \geq 3$:

$$n(h) = 1 + n(h-1) + n(h-2). \tag{9.1}$$

At this point, the reader familiar with the properties of Fibonacci progressions (Section 2.2.3 and Exercise C-3.12) will already see that $n(h)$ is a function exponential in h. For the rest of the readers, we will proceed with our reasoning.

Formula 9.1 implies that $n(h)$ is a strictly increasing function of h. Thus, we know that $n(h-1) > n(h-2)$. Replacing $n(h-1)$ with $n(h-2)$ in Formula 9.1 and dropping the 1, we get, for $h \geq 3$,

$$n(h) > 2 \cdot n(h-2). \tag{9.2}$$

Formula 9.2 indicates that $n(h)$ at least doubles each time h increases by 2, which intuitively means that $n(h)$ grows exponentially. To show this fact in a formal way, we apply Formula 9.2 repeatedly, yielding the following series of inequalities:

$$
\begin{aligned}
n(h) \;&>\; 2 \cdot n(h-2) \\
&>\; 4 \cdot n(h-4) \\
&>\; 8 \cdot n(h-6) \\
&\;\;\vdots \\
&>\; 2^i \cdot n(h-2i). \tag{9.3}
\end{aligned}
$$

That is, $n(h) > 2^i \cdot n(h-2i)$, for any integer i, such that $h - 2i \geq 1$. Since we already know the values of $n(1)$ and $n(2)$, we pick i so that $h - 2i$ is equal to either 1 or 2. That is, we pick

$$i = \left\lceil \frac{h}{2} \right\rceil - 1.$$

By substituting the above value of i in formula 9.3, we obtain, for $h \geq 3$,

$$
\begin{aligned}
n(h) \;&>\; 2^{\lceil \frac{h}{2} \rceil - 1} \cdot n\left(h - 2\left\lceil \frac{h}{2} \right\rceil + 2\right) \\
&\geq\; 2^{\lceil \frac{h}{2} \rceil - 1} n(1) \\
&\geq\; 2^{\frac{h}{2} - 1}.
\end{aligned}
\tag{9.4}
$$

By taking logarithms of both sides of formula 9.4, we obtain

$$
\log n(h) \;>\; \frac{h}{2} - 1,
$$

from which we get

$$
h \;<\; 2\log n(h) + 2,
\tag{9.5}
$$

which implies that an AVL tree storing n keys has height at most $2\log n + 2$. ∎

By Proposition 9.2 and the analysis of binary search trees given in Section 9.1, the operations findElement and findAllElements, in a dictionary implemented with an AVL tree, run in time $O(\log n)$ and $O(\log n + s)$, respectively, where n is the number of items in the dictionary and s is the size of the iterator returned by findAllElements. The important issue remaining is to show how to maintain the height-balance property of an AVL tree after an insertion or removal.

9.2.1 Update Operations

The insertion and removal operations for AVL trees are similar to those for binary search trees, but with AVL trees we must perform additional computations.

Insertion

An insertion in an AVL tree T begins as in an insertItem operation described in Section 9.1.2 for a (simple) binary search tree. Recall that this operation always inserts the new item at a node w in T that was previously an external node, and it makes w become an internal node with operation expandExternal. That is, it adds two external node children to w. This action may violate the height-balance property, however, for some nodes increase their heights by one. In particular, node w, and possibly some of its ancestors, increase their heights by one. Therefore, let us describe how to restructure T to restore its height balance.

Given the binary search tree T, we say that a node v of T is ***balanced*** if the absolute value of the difference between the heights of the children of v is at most 1, and we say that it is ***unbalanced*** otherwise. Thus, the height-balance property characterizing AVL trees is equivalent to saying that every internal node is balanced.

Suppose that T satisfies the height-balance property, and hence is an AVL tree, prior to our inserting the new item. As we have mentioned, after performing the operation expandExternal(w) on T, the heights of some nodes of T, including w, increase. All such nodes are on the path of T from w to the root of T, and these are the only nodes of T that may have just become unbalanced. (See Figure 9.9a.) Of course, if this happens, then T is no longer an AVL tree; hence, we need a mechanism to fix the "unbalance" that we have just caused.

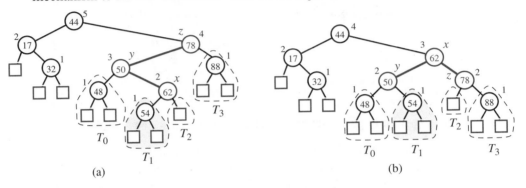

(a)   (b)

Figure 9.9: An example insertion of an element with key 54 in the AVL tree of Figure 9.8: (a) after adding a new node for key 54, the nodes storing keys 78 and 44 become unbalanced; (b) a trinode restructuring restores the height-balance property. We show the heights of nodes next to them, and we identify the nodes x, y, and z.

We restore the balance of the nodes in the binary search tree T by a simple "search-and-repair" strategy. In particular, let z be the first node we encounter in going up from w toward the root of T such that z is unbalanced. (See Figure 9.9a.) Also, let y denote the child of z with higher height (and note that y must be an ancestor of w). Finally, let x be the child of y with higher height (and if there is a tie, choose x to be an ancestor of w). Note that node x could be equal to w and x is a grandchild of z. Since z became unbalanced because of an insertion in the subtree rooted at its child y, the height of y is 2 greater than its sibling. We now rebalance the subtree rooted at z by calling the ***trinode restructuring*** method, restructure(x), described in Code Fragment 9.6 and illustrated in Figures 9.9 and 9.10. A trinode restructure temporarily renames the nodes x, y, and z as a, b, and c, so that a precedes b and b precedes c in an inorder traversal of T. There are four possible ways of mapping x, y and z to a, b, and c, as shown in Figure 9.10, which are unified into one case by our relabeling. The trinode restructure then replaces z with the node called b, makes the children of this node be a and c, and makes the children of a and c be the four previous children of x, y, and z (other than x and y) while maintaining the inorder relationships of all the nodes in T.

Algorithm restructure(x):

> **Input:** A node x of a binary search tree T that has both a parent y and a grandparent z
>
> **Output:** Tree T after a trinode restructuring (which corresponds to a single or double rotation) involving nodes x, y, and z

1: Let (a, b, c) be a left-to-right (inorder) listing of the nodes x, y, and z, and let (T_0, T_1, T_2, T_3) be a left-to-right (inorder) listing of the four subtrees of x, y, and z not rooted at x, y, or z.

2: Replace the subtree rooted at z with a new subtree rooted at b.

3: Let a be the left child of b and let T_0 and T_1 be the left and right subtrees of a, respectively.

4: Let c be the right child of b and let T_2 and T_3 be the left and right subtrees of c, respectively.

Code Fragment 9.6: The trinode restructure operation in a binary search tree.

The modification of a tree T caused by a trinode restructure operation is often called a **rotation**, because of the geometric way we can visualize the way it changes T. If $b = y$ (see Code Fragment 9.6), the trinode restructure method is called a **single rotation**, for it can be visualized as "rotating" y over z. (See Figure 9.10a and b.) Otherwise, if $b = x$, the trinode restructure operation is called a **double rotation**, for it can be visualized as first "rotating" x over y and then over z. (See Figure 9.10c and d, and Figure 9.9.) Some computer researchers treat these two kinds of rotations as separate methods, each with two symmetric types; we have chosen, however, to unify these four types of rotations into a single trinode restructure operation. No matter how we view it, however, note that the trinode restructure method modifies parent-child relationships of $O(1)$ nodes in T, while preserving the inorder traversal ordering of all the nodes in T.

In addition to its order-preserving property, a trinode restructuring changes the heights of nodes in T, so as to restore balance. Recall that we execute the method restructure(x) because z, the grandparent of x, is unbalanced. Moreover, this unbalance is due to one of the children of x now having too large a height relative to the height of z's other child. As a result of a rotation, we move up the "tall" child of x while pushing down the "short" child of z. Thus, after performing restructure(x), all the nodes in the subtree now rooted at the node we called b are balanced. (See Figure 9.10.) Thus, we restore the height-balance property **locally** at the nodes x, y, and z. In addition, since after performing the new item insertion the subtree rooted at b replaces the one formerly rooted at z, which was taller by one unit, all the ancestors of z that were formerly unbalanced become balanced. (See Figure 9.9.) (The justification of this fact is left as Exercise C-9.11.) Therefore, this one restructuring also restores the height-balance property **globally**.

(a)

(b)

(c)

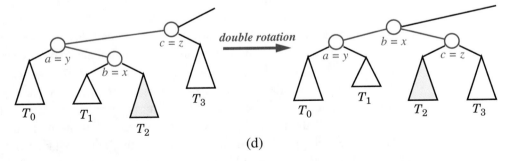

(d)

Figure 9.10: Schematic illustration of a trinode restructure operation (Code Fragment 9.6). Parts (a) and (b) show a single rotation, and parts (c) and (d) show a double rotation.

Removal

As was the case for the insertItem dictionary operation, we begin the implementation of the removeElement dictionary operation on an AVL tree T by using the algorithm for performing this operation on a regular binary search tree. The added difficulty in using this approach with an AVL tree is that it may violate the height-balance property. In particular, after removing an internal node with operation removeAboveExternal and elevating one of its children into its place, there may be an unbalanced node in T on the path from the parent w of the previously removed node to the root of T. (See Figure 9.11a.) In fact, there can be one such unbalanced node at most. (The justification of this fact is left as Exercise C-9.10.)

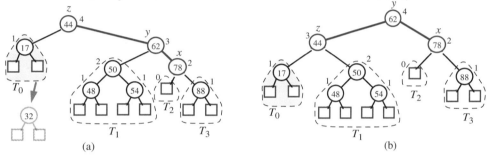

Figure 9.11: Removal of the element with key 32 from the AVL tree of Figure 9.8: (a) after removing the node storing key 32, the root becomes unbalanced; (b) a (single) rotation restores the height-balance property.

As with insertion, we use trinode restructuring to restore balance in the tree T. In particular, let z be the first unbalanced node encountered going up from w toward the root of T. Also, let y be the child of z with larger height (note that node y is the child of z that is not an ancestor of w), and let x be a child of y with largest height. The choice of x may not be unique, since the subtrees of y may have the same height. In any case, we then perform a restructure(x) operation, which restores the height-balance property *locally*, at the subtree that was formerly rooted at z and is now rooted at the node we temporarily called b. (See Figure 9.11b.)

Unfortunately, this trinode restructuring may reduce the height of the subtree rooted at b by 1, which may cause an ancestor of b to become unbalanced. Thus, a single trinode restructuring does not necessarily restore the height-balance property globally after a removal. So, after rebalancing z, we continue walking up T looking for unbalanced nodes. If we find another, we perform a restructure operation to restore its balance, and continue marching up T looking for more, all the way to the root. Still, since the height of T is $O(\log n)$, where n is the number of items, by Proposition 9.2, $O(\log n)$ trinode restructurings are sufficient to restore the height-balance property.

9.2.2   Java Implementation

Let us now turn to the implementation details and analysis of using an AVL tree T with n internal nodes to implement an ordered dictionary of n items. The insertion and removal algorithms for T require that we are able to perform trinode restructurings and determine the difference between the heights of two sibling nodes. Regarding restructurings, we should extend the collection of operations of the binary tree ADT by adding the method restructure. It is easy to see that a restructure operation can be performed in $O(1)$ time if T is implemented with a linked structure (Section 6.4.2), which would not be the case with a vector (Section 6.4.1). Thus, we prefer a linked structure for representing an AVL tree.

Regarding height information, we can explicitly store the height of each internal node, v, in the node itself. Alternatively, we can store the *balance factor* of v at v, which is defined as the height of the left child of v minus the height of the right child of v. Thus, the balance factor of v is always equal to -1, 0, or 1, except during an insertion or removal, when it may become *temporarily* equal to -2 or $+2$. During the execution of an insertion or removal, the heights and balance factors of $O(\log n)$ nodes are affected and can be maintained in $O(\log n)$ time.

In Code Fragments 9.7–9.9, we show a Java implementation of a dictionary realized with an AVL tree. Class AVLItem, shown in Code Fragment 9.7, extends the Item class used to represent a key-element item of a binary search tree. It defines an additional instance variable height, representing the height of the node. Class AVLTree, shown in full in Code Fragments 9.8 and 9.9, extends BinarySearchTree (Code Fragments 9.3–9.5). The constructor of AVLTree executes the superclass's constructor first, and then assigns a RestructurableNodeBinaryTree to T, which is a class that implements the binary tree ADT, and in addition supports method restructure for performing trinode restructurings (its implementation is left as Exercise P-9.3). Class AVLTree inherits methods size, isEmpty, findElement, findAllElements, and removeAllElements from its superclass BinarySearchTree, but overrides methods insertItem and removeElement.

Method insertItem (Code Fragment 9.9) begins by calling the superclass's insertItem method, which inserts the new item and assigns the insertion position (node storing key 54 in Figure 9.9) to instance variable actionPos. The auxiliary method rebalance is then used to traverse the path from the insertion position to the root. This traversal updates the heights of all the nodes visited, and performs a trinode restructuring if necessary. Similarly, method removeElement (Code Fragment 9.9) begins by calling the superclass's removeElement method, which performs the removal of the item and assigns the position replacing the deleted one to instance variable actionPos. The auxiliary method rebalance is then used to traverse the path from the removed position to the root.

```
public class AVLItem extends Item  {
  int height;
  AVLItem(Object k, Object e, int h)  {
    super(k, e);
    height = h;
  }
  public int height()  { return height; }
  public int setHeight(int h)  {
    int oldHeight = height;
    height = h;
    return oldHeight;
  }
}
```

Code Fragment 9.7: Class implementing a node of an AVL tree. The height of the node in the tree is stored as an instance variable.

```
/** Realization of a dictionary by means of an AVL tree. */
public class AVLTree extends BinarySearchTree implements Dictionary  {
  public AVLTree(Comparator c)  {
    super(c);
    T = new RestructurableNodeBinaryTree();
  }
  private int height(Position p)  {
    if(T.isExternal(p))
      return 0;
    else
      return ((AVLItem) p.element()).height();
  }
  private void setHeight(Position p)  { // called only if p is internal
    ((AVLItem) p.element()).setHeight(1+Math.max(height(T.leftChild(p)),
                                              height(T.rightChild(p))));
  }
  private boolean isBalanced(Position p)  {
    // test whether node p has balance factor between -1 and 1
    int bf = height(T.leftChild(p)) − height(T.rightChild(p));
    return ((−1 <= bf) &&  (bf <= 1));
  }
  private Position tallerChild(Position p)  {
    // return a child of p with height no smaller than that of the other child
    if(height(T.leftChild(p)) >= height(T.rightChild(p)))
      return T.leftChild(p);
    else
      return T.rightChild(p);
  }
}
```

Code Fragment 9.8: Constructor and auxiliary methods of class AVLTree.

```
/**
 * Auxiliary method called by insertItem and removeElement.
 * Traverses the path of T from the given node to the root. For
 * each node zPos encountered, recomputes the height of zPos and
 * performs a trinode restructuring if zPos is unbalanced.
 */
private void rebalance(Position zPos) {
  while (!T.isRoot(zPos)) {
    zPos = T.parent(zPos);
    setHeight(zPos);
    if (!isBalanced(zPos)) {
      // perform a trinode restructuring
      Position xPos = tallerChild(tallerChild(zPos));
      zPos = ((RestructurableNodeBinaryTree) T).restructure(xPos);
      setHeight(T.leftChild(zPos));
      setHeight(T.rightChild(zPos));
      setHeight(zPos);
    }
  }
}

// methods of the dictionary ADT

/** Overrides the corresponding method of the parent class. */
public void insertItem(Object key, Object element)
    throws InvalidKeyException  {
  super.insertItem(key, element); // may throw an InvalidKeyException
  Position zPos = actionPos; // start at the insertion position
  T.replaceElement(zPos, new AVLItem(key, element, 1));
  rebalance(zPos);
}

/** Overrides the corresponding method of the parent class. */
public Object removeElement(Object key)
    throws InvalidKeyException {
  Object toReturn = super.removeElement(key);
                      // may throw an InvalidKeyException
  if(toReturn != NO_SUCH_KEY) {
    Position zPos = actionPos; // start at the removal position
    rebalance(zPos);
  }
  return toReturn;
}
```

Code Fragment 9.9: Auxiliary method rebalance and dictionary methods insertItem and removeElement of class AVLTree.

9.2.3 Performance

We summarize the analysis of the AVL tree as follows. Operations findElement, insertItem, and removeElement visit the nodes along a root-to-leaf path of T, plus, possibly, their siblings, and spend $O(1)$ time per node. Thus, since the height of T is $O(\log n)$ by Proposition 9.2, each of the above operations takes $O(\log n)$ time. We leave the implementation and analysis of operations findAllElements and removeAllElements as interesting exercises. In Table 9.2, we summarize the performance of a dictionary implemented with an AVL tree. We illustrate this performance in Figure 9.12.

Operation	Time
size, isEmpty	$O(1)$
findElement, insertItem, removeElement	$O(\log n)$
findAllElements, removeAllElements	$O(\log n + s)$

Table 9.2: Performance of an n-element dictionary realized by an AVL tree, where s denotes the size of the iterators returned by findAllElements and removeAllElements. The space usage is $O(n)$.

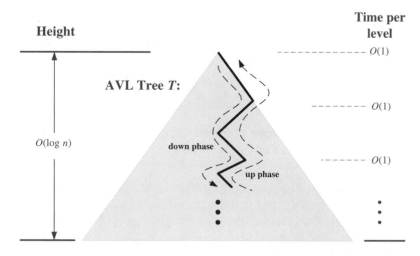

Figure 9.12: Illustrating the running time of searches and updates in an AVL tree. The time performance is $O(1)$ per level, broken into a down phase, which typically involves searching, and an up phase, which typically involves updating height values and performing local trinode restructurings (rotations).

9.3 Multi-Way Search Trees

Some of the data structures we discuss in this chapter are multi-way trees, that is, trees with internal nodes that have two or more children. In this section, we describe how multi-way trees can be used as search trees, including how multi-way trees store items and how we can perform search operations in multi-way search trees. Recall that the *items* that we store in a search tree are pairs of the form (k,x), where k is the *key* and x is the element associated with the key. However, we do not discuss how to perform updates in multi-way search trees now, for the details for update methods depend on additional properties we might wish to maintain for multi-way trees, which we discuss in Sections 9.4 and 9.6.

Definition

Let v be a node of an ordered tree. We say that v is a *d-node* if v has d children. We define a *multi-way search tree* to be an ordered tree T that has the following properties (which are illustrated in Figure 9.13a):

- Each internal node of T has at least two children. That is, each internal node is a d-node, where $d \geq 2$.
- Each internal node of T stores a collection of items of the form (k,x), where k is a key and x is an element.
- Each d-node v of T, with children $v_1, \ldots, v_d$, stores $d-1$ items $(k_1,x_1), \ldots,$ (k_{d-1},x_{d-1}), where $k_1 \leq \cdots \leq k_{d-1}$.
- Let us conventionally define $k_0 = -\infty$ and $k_d = +\infty$. For each item (k,x) stored at a node in the subtree of v rooted at v_i, $i = 1, \ldots, d$, we have that $k_{i-1} \leq k \leq k_i$.

That is, if we think of the set of keys stored at v as including the special fictitious keys $k_0 = -\infty$ and $k_d = +\infty$, then a key k stored in the subtree of T rooted at a child node v_i must be "in between" two keys stored at v. This simple viewpoint gives rise to the rule that a node with d children stores $d-1$ regular keys, and it also forms the basis of the algorithm for searching in a multi-way search tree.

By the above definition, the external nodes of a multi-way search do not store any items and serve only as "placeholders." Thus, we view a binary search tree (Section 9.1) as a special case of a multi-way search tree, where each internal node stores one item and has two children. At the other extreme, a multi-way search tree may have only a single internal node storing all the items. In addition, while the external nodes could be **null** or references to a NULL_NODE object, we make the simplifying assumption here that they are actual nodes that don't store anything.

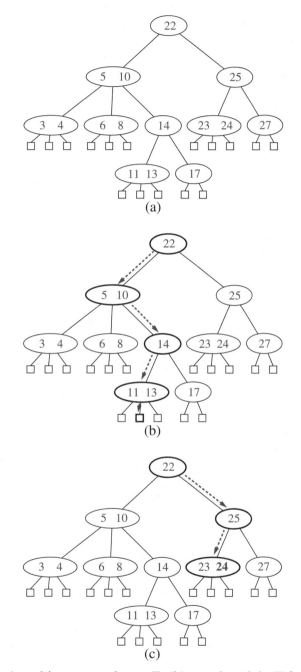

Figure 9.13: (a) A multi-way search tree T; (b) search path in T for key 12 (unsuccessful search); (c) search path in T for key 24 (successful search).

Whether internal nodes of a multi-way tree have two children or many, however, there is an interesting relationship between the number of items and the number of external nodes.

Proposition 9.3: *A multi-way search tree storing n items has $n+1$ external nodes.*

We leave the justification of this proposition as an exercise (C-9.14).

Searching in a Multi-Way Tree

Given a multi-way search tree T, searching for an element with key k is simple. We perform such a search by tracing a path in T starting at the root. (See Figure 9.13b and c.) When we are at a d-node v during this search, we compare the key k with the keys $k_1, \dots, k_{d-1}$ stored at v. If $k = k_i$ for some i, the search is successfully completed. Otherwise, we continue the search in the child v_i of v such that $k_{i-1} < k < k_i$. (Recall that we consider $k_0 = -\infty$ and $k_d = +\infty$.) If we reach an external node, then we know that there is no item with key k in T, and the search terminates unsuccessfully.

Data Structures for Multi-Way Search Trees

In Section 6.4, we discuss different ways of representing general trees. Each of these representations can also be used for multi-way search trees. In fact, in using a general multi-way tree to implement a multi-way search tree, the only additional information that we need to store at each node is the set of items (including keys) associated with that node. That is, we need to store with v a reference to some container or collection object that stores the items for v.

Recall that when we use a binary tree to represent an ordered dictionary D, we simply store a reference to a single item at each internal node. In using a multi-way search tree T to represent D, we must store a reference to the ordered set of items associated with v at each internal node v of T. This reasoning may at first seem like a circular argument, since we need a representation of an ordered dictionary to represent an ordered dictionary. We can avoid any circular arguments, however, by using the ***bootstrapping*** technique, where we use a previous (less advanced) solution to a problem to create a new (more advanced) solution. In this case, bootstrapping consists of representing the ordered set associated with each internal node using a dictionary data structure that we have previously constructed (for example, a look-up table based on an ordered vector, as shown in Section 8.5). In particular, assuming we already have a way of implementing ordered dictionaries, we can realize a multi-way search tree by taking a tree T and storing such a dictionary at each d-node v of T.

The dictionary we store at each node v is known as a ***secondary*** data structure, for we are using it to support the bigger, ***primary*** data structure. We denote the dictionary stored at a node v of T as $D(v)$. The items we store in $D(v)$ will allow us to find which child node to move to next during a search operation. Specifically, for each node v of T, with children $v_1, \ldots, v_d$ and items $(k_1, x_1), \ldots, (k_{d-1}, x_{d-1})$, we store in the dictionary $D(v)$ the items $(k_1, x_1, v_1), (k_2, x_2, v_2), \ldots, (k_{d-1}, x_{d-1}, v_{d-1})$, $(+\infty, null, v_d)$. That is, an item (k_i, x_i, v_i) of dictionary $D(v)$ has key k_i and element (x_i, v_i). Note that the last item stores the special key $+\infty$.

With the above realization of a multi-way search tree T, processing a d-node v while searching for an element of T with key k can be done by performing a search operation to find the item (k_i, x_i, v_i) in $D(v)$ with smallest key greater than or equal to k, such as in the closestElemAfter(k) operation (see Section 8.4). We distinguish two cases:

- If $k < k_i$, then we continue the search by processing child v_i. (Note that if the special key $k_d = +\infty$ is returned, then k is greater than all the keys stored at node v, and we continue the search processing child v_d).

- Otherwise ($k = k_i$), then the search terminates successfully.

Consider the space requirement for the above realization of a multi-way search tree T storing n items. By Proposition 9.3, using any of the common realizations of ordered dictionaries (Chapter 8) for the secondary structures of the nodes of T, the overall space requirement for T is $O(n)$.

Consider next the time spent answering a search in T. The time spent at a d-node v of T during a search depends on how we realize the secondary data structure $D(v)$. If $D(v)$ is realized with an vector-based sorted sequence (that is, a look-up table), then we can process v in $O(\log d)$ time. If instead $D(v)$ is realized using an unsorted sequence (that is, a log file), then processing v takes $O(d)$ time. Let d_{max} denote the maximum number of children of any node of T, and let h denote the height of T. The search time in a multi-way search tree is either $O(h d_{max})$ or $O(h \log d_{max})$, depending on the specific implementation of the secondary structures at the nodes of T (the dictionaries $D(v)$). If d_{max} is a constant, the running time for performing a search is $O(h)$, irrespective of the implementation of the secondary structures.

Thus, the prime efficiency goal for a multi-way search tree is to keep the height as small as possible, that is, we want h to be a logarithmic function of n, the number of total items stored in the dictionary. A search tree with logarithmic height, such as this, is called a ***balanced search tree***. We discuss next in this chapter a balanced search tree that caps d_{max} at 4.

9.4 (2,4) Trees

A multi-way search tree that keeps the secondary data structures stored at each node small and also keeps the primary multi-way tree balanced is the $(2,4)$ tree, which is sometimes called 2-4 tree or 2-3-4 tree. This data structure achieves these goals by maintaining two simple properties (see Figure 9.14):

Size Property: Every node has at most four children.

Depth Property: All the external nodes have the same depth.

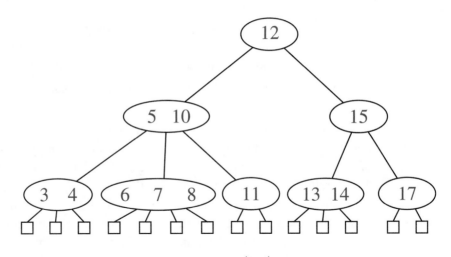

Figure 9.14: A $(2,4)$ tree.

Again, we assume that external nodes are empty and, for the sake of simplicity, we describe our search and update methods assuming that external nodes are real nodes, although this latter requirement is not strictly needed.

Enforcing the size property for $(2,4)$ trees keeps the nodes in the multi-way search tree simple. It also gives rise to the alternative name "2-3-4 tree," since it implies that each internal node in the tree has 2, 3, or 4 children. Another implication of this rule is that we can represent the dictionary $D(v)$ stored at each internal node v using a vector, and still achieve $O(1)$-time performance for all operations (since $d_{max} = 4$). The depth property, on the other hand, enforces an important bound on the height of a $(2,4)$ tree.

Proposition 9.4: *The height of a* $(2,4)$ *tree storing* n *items is* $\Theta(\log n)$.

Justification: Let h be the height of a $(2,4)$ tree T storing n items. We justify the proposition by showing that the claims

$$\frac{1}{2}\log(n+1) \leq h \qquad\qquad (9.6)$$

and

$$h \leq \log(n+1) \qquad\qquad (9.7)$$

are true.

To justify these claims note first that, by the size property, we can have at most 4 nodes at depth 1, at most 4^2 nodes at depth 2, and so on. Thus, the number of external nodes in T is at most 4^h. Likewise, by the depth property and the definition of a $(2,4)$ tree, we must have at least 2 nodes at depth 1, at least 2^2 nodes at depth 2, and so on. Thus, the number of external nodes in T is at least 2^h. In addition, by Proposition 9.3, the number of external nodes in T is $n+1$. Therefore, we obtain

$$2^h \leq n+1$$

and

$$n+1 \leq 4^h.$$

Taking the logarithm in base 2 of each of the above terms, we get that

$$h \leq \log(n+1)$$

and

$$\log(n+1) \leq 2h,$$

which justifies our claims (9.6 and 9.7).   ■

Proposition 9.4 states that the size and depth properties are sufficient for keeping a multi-way tree balanced (Section 9.3). Moreover, this proposition implies that performing a search in a $(2,4)$ tree takes $O(\log n)$ time and that the specific realization of the secondary structures at the nodes is not a crucial design choice, since the maximum number of children d_{max} is a constant (4). We can, for example, use the simplest previous ordered dictionary implementation for each secondary structure—a vector-based look-up table.

9.4.1 Update Operations

Maintaining the size and depth properties requires some effort after performing insertions and removals in a $(2,4)$ tree, however. We discuss these operations next.

Insertion

To insert a new item (k,x), with key k, into a $(2,4)$ tree T, we first perform a search for k. Assuming that T has no element with key k, this search terminates unsuccessfully at an external node z. Let v be the parent of z. We insert the new item into node v and add a new child w (an external node) to v on the left of z. That is, we add item (k,x,w) to the dictionary $D(v)$.

Our insertion method preserves the depth property, since we add a new external node at the same level as existing external nodes. Nevertheless, it may violate the size property. Indeed, if a node v was previously a 4-node, then it may become a 5-node after the insertion, which causes the tree T to no longer be a $(2,4)$ tree. This type of violation of the size property is called an **overflow** at node v, and it must be resolved in order to restore the properties of a $(2,4)$ tree. Let $v_1,\ldots,v_5$ be the children of v, and let $k_1,\ldots,k_4$ be the keys stored at v. To remedy the overflow at node v, we perform a **split** operation on v as follows (see Figure 9.15):

- Replace v with two nodes v' and v'', where
    - v' is a 3-node with children v_1,v_2,v_3 storing keys k_1 and k_2
    - v'' is a 2-node with children v_4,v_5 storing key k_4.

- If v was the root of T, create a new root node u; else, let u be the parent of v.
- Insert key k_3 into u and make v' and v'' children of u, so that if v was child i of u, then v' and v'' become children i and $i+1$ of u, respectively.

We show a sequence of insertions in a $(2,4)$ tree in Figure 9.16.

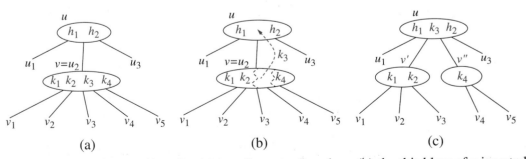

Figure 9.15: A node split: (a) overflow at a 5-node v; (b) the third key of v inserted into the parent u of v; (c) node v replaced with a 3-node v' and a 2-node v''.

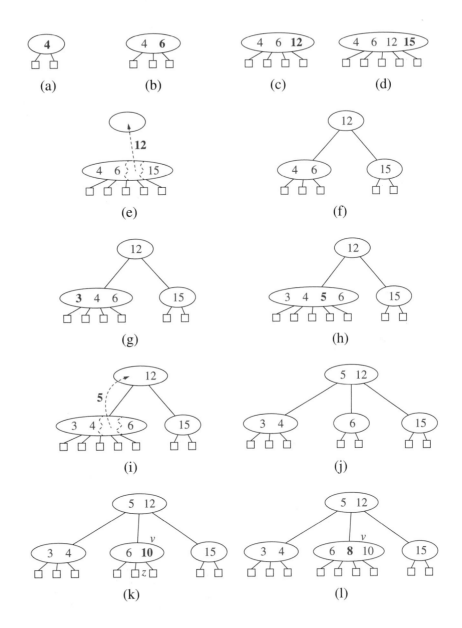

Figure 9.16: A sequence of insertions into a $(2,4)$ tree: (a) initial tree with one item; (b) insertion of 6; (c) insertion of 12; (d) insertion of 15, which causes an overflow; (e) split, which causes the creation of a new root node; (f) after the split; (g) insertion of 3; (h) insertion of 5, which causes an overflow; (i) split; (j) after the split; (k) insertion of 10; (l) insertion of 8.

Analysis of Insertion in a $(2,4)$ Tree

A split operation affects a constant number of nodes of the tree and $O(1)$ items stored at such nodes. Thus, it can be implemented to run in $O(1)$ time.

As a consequence of a split operation on node v, a new overflow may occur at the parent u of v. If such an overflow occurs, it triggers in turn a split at node u. (See Figure 9.17.) A split operation either eliminates the overflow or propagates it into the parent of the current node. Hence, the number of split operations is bounded by the height of the tree, which is $O(\log n)$ by Proposition 9.4. Therefore, the total time to perform an insertion in a $(2,4)$ tree is $O(\log n)$.

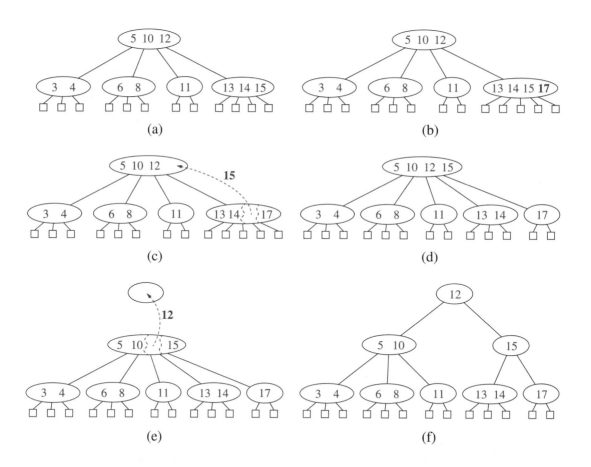

Figure 9.17: An insertion in a $(2,4)$ tree that causes a cascading split: (a) before the insertion; (b) insertion of 17, causing an overflow; (c) a split; (d) after the split a new overflow occurs; (e) another split, creating a new root node; (f) final tree.

Removal

Let us now consider the removal of an item with key k from a $(2,4)$ tree T. We begin such an operation by performing a search in T for an item with key k. Removing such an item from a $(2,4)$ tree can always be reduced to the case where the item to be removed is stored at a node v whose children are external nodes. Suppose, for instance, that the item with key k that we wish to remove is stored in the ith item (k_i, x_i) at a node z that has only internal-node children. In this case, we swap the item (k_i, x_i) with an appropriate item that is stored at a node v with external-node children as follows (Figure 9.18d):

1. We find the right-most internal node v in the subtree rooted at the ith child of z, noting that the children of node v are all external nodes.
2. We swap the item (k_i, x_i) at z with the last item of v.

Once we ensure that the item to remove is stored at a node v with only external-node children (because either it was already at v or we swapped it into v), we simply remove the item from v (that is, from the dictionary $D(v)$) and remove the ith external node of v.

Removing an item (and a child) from a node v as described above preserves the depth property, for we always remove an external node child from a node v with only external-node children. However, in removing such an external node we may violate the size property at v. Indeed, if v was previously a 2-node, then it becomes a 1-node with no items after the removal (Figure 9.18d and e), which is not allowed in a $(2,4)$ tree. This type of violation of the size property is called an ***underflow*** at node v. To remedy an underflow, we check whether an immediate sibling of v is a 3-node or a 4-node. If we find such a sibling w, then we perform a ***transfer*** operation, in which we move a child of w to v, a key of w to the parent u of v and w, and a key of u to v. (See Figure 9.18b and c.) If v has only one sibling, or if both immediate siblings of v are 2-nodes, then we perform a ***fusion*** operation, in which we merge v with a sibling, creating a new node v', and move a key from the parent u of v to v'. (See Figure 9.19e and f.)

A fusion operation at node v may cause a new underflow to occur at the parent u of v, which in turn triggers a transfer or fusion at u. (See Figure 9.19.) Hence, the number of fusion operations is bounded by the height of the tree, which is $O(\log n)$ by Proposition 9.4. If an underflow propagates all the way up to the root, then the root is simply deleted. (See Figure 9.19c and d.) We show a sequence of removals from a $(2,4)$ tree in Figures 9.18 and 9.19.

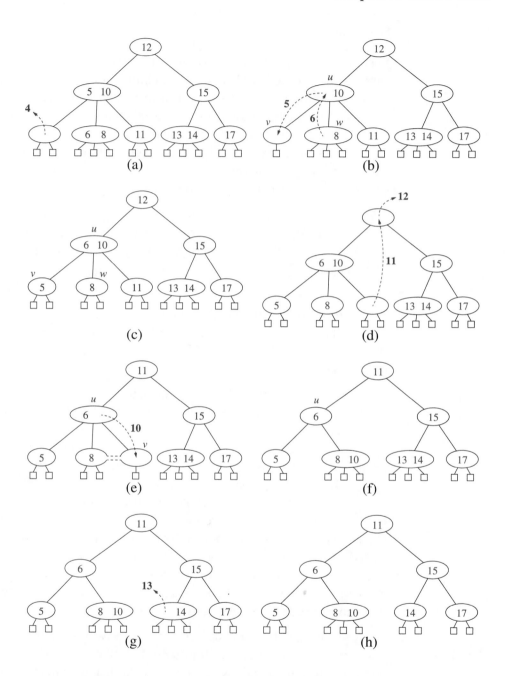

Figure 9.18: A sequence of removals from a $(2,4)$ tree: (a) removal of 4, causing an underflow; (b) a transfer operation; (c) after the transfer operation; (d) removal of 12, causing an underflow; (e) a fusion operation; (f) after the fusion operation; (g) removal of 13; (h) after removing 13.

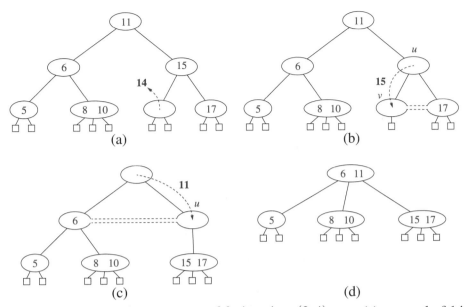

Figure 9.19: A propagating sequence of fusions in a $(2,4)$ tree: (a) removal of 14, which causes an underflow; (b) fusion, which causes another underflow; (c) second fusion operation, which causes the root to be removed; (d) final tree.

9.4.2 Performance

Table 9.3 summarizes the running times of the main operations of a dictionary realized with a $(2,4)$ tree. The time complexity analysis is based on the following:

- The height of a $(2,4)$ tree storing n items is $O(\log n)$, by Proposition 9.4.
- A split, transfer, or fusion operation takes $O(1)$ time.
- A search, insertion, or removal of an item visits $O(\log n)$ nodes.

Operation	Time
size, isEmpty	$O(1)$
findElement, insertItem, removeElement	$O(\log n)$
findAllElements, removeAllElements	$O(\log n + s)$

Table 9.3: Performance of an n-element dictionary realized by a $(2,4)$ tree, where s denotes the size of the iterators returned by findAllElements and removeAllElements. The space usage is $O(n)$.

Thus, $(2,4)$ trees provide for fast dictionary search and update operations. $(2,4)$ trees also have an interesting relationship to the data structure we discuss next.

9.5   Red-Black Trees

Although AVL Trees and $(2,4)$ trees have a number of nice properties, there are some dictionary applications for which they are not well suited. For instance, AVL trees may require many restructure operations (rotations) to be performed after an element removal, and $(2,4)$ trees may require many fusing or split operations to be performed after either an insertion or removal. The data structure we discuss in this section, the red-black tree, does not have these drawbacks, however, as it requires that only $O(1)$ structural changes be made after an update in order to stay balanced.

A *red-black tree* is a binary search tree (see Section 9.1) with nodes colored red and black in a way that satisfies the following properties:

Root Property: The root is black.

External Property: Every external node is black.

Internal Property: The children of a red node are black.

Depth Property: All the external nodes have the same *black depth*, which is defined as the number of black ancestors minus one.

An example of a red-black tree is shown in Figure 9.20.

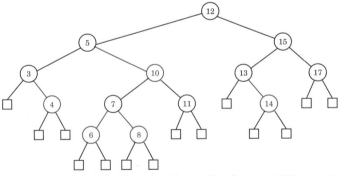

Figure 9.20: Red-black tree associated with the $(2,4)$ tree of Figure 9.14. Each external node of this red-black tree has 3 black ancestors; hence, it has black depth 3. We use the color blue instead of red. Also, we use the convention of giving an edge of the tree the same color as the child node.

As has been the convention in this chapter, we assume that items are stored in the internal nodes of a red-black tree, with the external nodes being empty placeholders. Also, we describe our algorithms assuming they are actual nodes, but we note in passing that at the expense of slightly more complicated search and update methods, external nodes could be **null** or references to a NULL_NODE object.

We can make the red-black tree definition more intuitive by noting an interesting correspondence between red-black and $(2,4)$ trees, as illustrated in Figure 9.21. Namely, given a red-black tree, we can construct a corresponding $(2,4)$ tree by merging every red node v into its parent and storing the item from v at its parent. Conversely, we can transform any $(2,4)$ tree into a corresponding red-black tree by coloring each node black and performing the following transformation for each internal node v:

- If v is a 2-node, then keep the (black) children of v as is.

- If v is a 3-node, then create a new red node w, give v's first two (black) children to w, and make w and v's third child be the two children of v.

- If v is a 4-node, then create two new red nodes w and z, give v's first two (black) children to w, give v's last two (black) children to z, and make w and z be the two children of v.

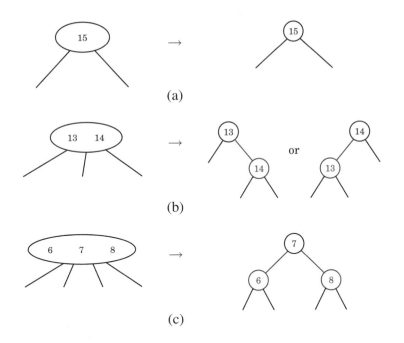

Figure 9.21: Correspondence between a $(2,4)$ tree and a red-black tree: (a) 2-node; (b) 3-node; (c) 4-node.

The correspondence between $(2,4)$ trees and red-black trees provides important intuition that we will use in our discussion of how to perform updates in red-black trees. In fact, the update algorithms for red-black trees are mysteriously complex without this intuition.

Proposition 9.5: *The height of a red-black tree storing n items is* $O(\log n)$.

Justification: Let T be a red-black tree storing n items, and let h be the height of T. We justify this proposition by establishing the following fact:

$$\log(n+1) \leq h \leq 2\log(n+1).$$

Let d be the common black depth of all the external nodes of T. Let T' be the $(2,4)$ tree associated with T, and let h' be the height of T'. We know that $h' = d$. Hence, by Proposition 9.4, $d = h' \leq \log(n+1)$. By the internal node property, $h \leq 2d$. Thus, we obtain $h \leq 2\log(n+1)$. The other inequality, $\log(n+1) \leq h$, follows from Proposition 6.10 and the fact that T has n internal nodes. ∎

We assume that a red-black tree is realized with a linked structure for binary trees (Section 6.4.2), in which we store a dictionary item and a color indicator at each node. Thus the space requirement for storing n keys is $O(n)$. The algorithm for searching in a red-black tree T is the same as that for a standard binary search tree (Section 9.1). Thus, searching in a red-black tree takes $O(\log n)$ time.

9.5.1 Update Operations

Performing the update operations in a red-black tree is similar to that of a binary search tree, except that we must additionally restore the color properties.

Insertion

Consider now the insertion of an element x with key k into a red-black tree T, keeping in mind the correspondence between T and its associated $(2,4)$ tree T' and the insertion algorithm for T'. The insertion algorithm initially proceeds as in a binary search tree (Section 9.1.2). Namely, we search for k in T until we reach an external node of T, and we replace this node with an internal node z, storing (k,x) and having two external-node children. If z is the root of T, we color z black, else we color z red. We also color the children of z black. This action corresponds to inserting (k,x) into a node of the $(2,4)$ tree T' with external children. In addition, this action preserves the root, external and depth properties of T, but it may violate the internal property. Indeed, if z is not the root of T and the parent v of z is red, then we have a parent and a child (namely, v and z) that are both red. Note that by the root property, v cannot be the root of T, and by the internal property (which was previously satisfied), the parent u of v must be black. Since z and its parent are red, but z's grandparent u is black, we call this violation of the internal property a ***double red*** at node z.

To remedy a double red, we consider two cases.

Case 1: *The Sibling* **w** *of* **v** *is Black*. (See Figure 9.22.) In this case, the double red denotes the fact that we have created in our red-black tree T a malformed replacement for a corresponding 4-node of the $(2,4)$ tree T', which has as its children the four black children of u, v, and z. Our malformed replacement has one red node (v) that is the parent of another red node (z), while we want it to have the two red nodes as siblings instead. To fix this problem, we perform a ***trinode restructuring*** of T. The trinode restructuring is done by the operation restructure(z), which consists of the following steps (see again Figure 9.22; this operation is also discussed in Section 9.2):

- Take node z, its parent v, and grandparent u, and temporarily relabel them as a, b, and c, in left-to-right order, so that a, b, and c will be visited in this order by an inorder tree traversal.
- Replace the grandparent u with the node labeled b, and make nodes a and c the children of b, keeping inorder relationships unchanged.

After performing the restructure(z) operation, we color b black and we color a and c red. Thus, the restructuring eliminates the double red problem.

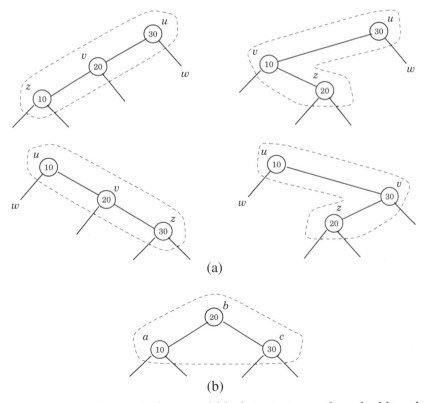

(a)

(b)

Figure 9.22: Restructuring a red-black tree to remedy a double red: (a) the four configurations for u, v, and z before restructuring; (b) after restructuring.

Case 2: *The Sibling* **w** *of* **v** *is Red.* (See Figure 9.23.) In this case, the double red
denotes an overflow in the corresponding $(2,4)$ tree T. To fix the problem,
we perform the equivalent of a split operation. Namely, we do a ***recoloring***:
we color v and w black and their parent u red (unless u is the root, in which
case, it is colored black). It is possible that, after such a recoloring, the
double red problem reappears, albeit higher up in the tree T, since u may
have a red parent. If the double red problem reappears at u, then we repeat
the consideration of the two cases at u. Thus, a recoloring either eliminates
the double red problem at node z, or propagates it to the grandparent u of z.
We continue going up T performing recolorings until we finally resolve the
double red problem (with either a final recoloring or a trinode restructuring).
Thus, the number of recolorings caused by an insertion is no more than half
the height of tree T, that is, no more than $\log(n+1)$ by Proposition 9.5.

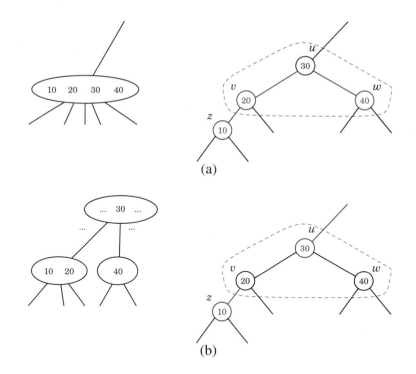

Figure 9.23: Recoloring to remedy the double red problem: (a) before recoloring
and the corresponding 5-node in the associated $(2,4)$ tree before the split; (b) after
the recoloring (and corresponding nodes in the associated $(2,4)$ tree after the split).

Figures 9.24 and 9.25 show a sequence of insertion operations in a red-black
tree.

The cases for insertion imply an interesting property for red-black trees. Namely, since the Case 1 action eliminates the double-red problem with a single trinode restructuring and the Case 2 action performs no restructuring operations, at most one restructuring is needed in a red-black tree insertion. By the above analysis and the fact that a restructuring or recoloring takes $O(1)$ time, we have the following:

Proposition 9.6: *The insertion of a key-element item in a red-black tree storing n items can be done in $O(\log n)$ time and requires at most $O(\log n)$ recolorings and one trinode restructuring (a restructure operation).*

Removal

Suppose now that we are asked to remove an item with key k from a red-black tree T. Removing such an item initially proceeds as for a binary search tree (Section 9.1.2). First, we search for a node u storing such an item. If node u does not have an external child, we find the internal node v following u in the inorder traversal of T, move the item at v to u, and perform the removal at v. Thus, we may consider only the removal of an item with key k stored at a node v with an external child w. Also, as we did for insertions, we keep in mind the correspondence between red-black tree T and its associated $(2,4)$ tree T' (and the removal algorithm for T').

To remove the item with key k from a node v of T with an external child w we proceed as follows. Let r be the sibling of w and x be the parent of v. We remove nodes v and w, and make r a child of x. If v was red (hence r is black) or r is red (hence v was black), we color r black and we are done. If, instead, r is black and v was black, then, to preserve the depth property, we give r a fictitious **double black** color. We now have a color violation, called the double black problem. A double black in T denotes an underflow in the corresponding $(2,4)$ tree T'. Recall that x is the parent of the double black node r. To remedy the double-black problem at r, we consider three cases.

Case 1: *The Sibling* **y** *of* **r** *is Black and has a Red Child* **z**. (See Figure 9.26.)
Resolving this case corresponds to a transfer operation in the $(2,4)$ tree T'. We perform a **trinode restructuring** by means of operation restructure(z). Recall that the operation restructure(z) takes the node z, its parent y, and grandparent x, labels them temporarily left to right as a, b, and c, and replaces x with the node labeled b, making it the parent of the other two. (See also the description of restructure in Section 9.2.) We color a and c black, give b the former color of x, and color r black. This trinode restructuring eliminates the double black problem. Hence, at most one restructuring is performed in a removal operation in this case.

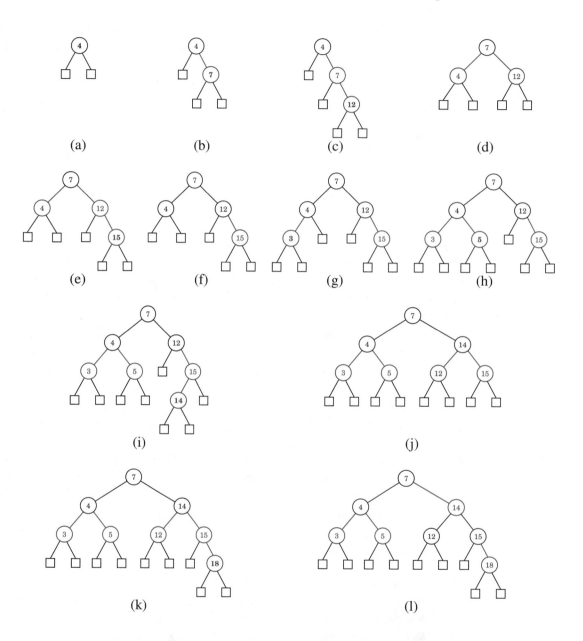

Figure 9.24: A sequence of insertions in a red-black tree: (a) initial tree; (b) insertion of 7; (c) insertion of 12, which causes a double red; (d) after restructuring; (e) insertion of 15, which causes a double red; (f) after recoloring (the root remains black); (g) insertion of 3; (h) insertion of 5; (i) insertion of 14, which causes a double red; (j) after restructuring; (k) insertion of 18, which causes a double-red; (l) after recoloring. (Continued in Figure 9.25.)

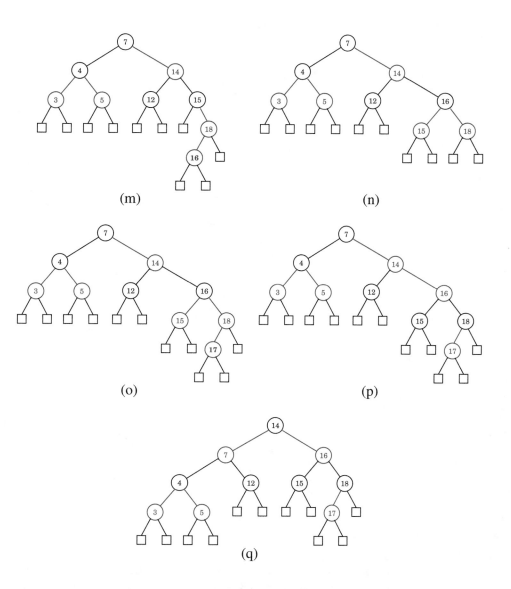

Figure 9.25: A sequence of insertions in a red-black tree (continued from Figure 9.24): (m) insertion of 16, which causes a double red; (n) after restructuring; (o) insertion of 17, which causes a double red; (p) after recoloring there is again a double red, to be handled by a restructuring; (q) after restructuring.

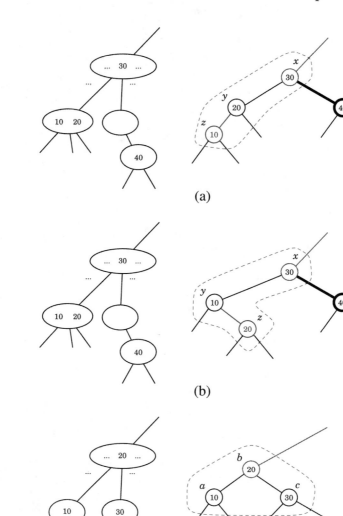

Figure 9.26: Restructuring of a red-black tree to remedy the double black problem: (a) and (b) configurations before the restructuring, where r is a right child and the associated nodes in the corresponding $(2,4)$ tree before the transfer (two other symmetric configurations where r is a left child are possible); (c) configuration after the restructuring and the associated nodes in the corresponding $(2,4)$ tree after the transfer. The grey color for node x in parts (a) and (b) and for node b in part (c) denotes the fact that this node may be colored either red or black.

Case 2: *The Sibling* **y** *of* **r** *is Black and Both Children of* **y** *are Black*. (See Figures 9.27 and 9.28.) Resolving this case corresponds to a fusion operation in the corresponding $(2,4)$ tree T'. We do a ***recoloring***; we color r black, we color y red, and, if x is red, we color it black (Figure 9.27); otherwise, we color x ***double black*** (Figure 9.28). Hence, after this recoloring, the double black problem may reappear at the parent x of r. (See Figure 9.28.) That is, this recoloring either eliminates the double black problem or propagates it into the parent of the current node. We then repeat a consideration of these three cases at the parent. Thus, since Case 1 performs a trinode restructuring operation and stops (and, as we will soon see, Case 3 is similar), the number of recolorings caused by a removal is no more than $\log(n+1)$.

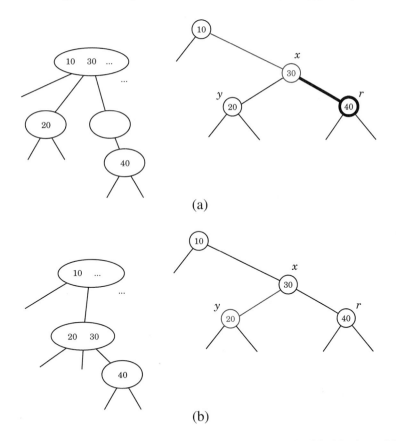

Figure 9.27: Recoloring of a red-black tree that fixes the double black problem: (a) before the recoloring and corresponding nodes in the associated $(2,4)$ tree before the fusion (other similar configurations are possible); (b) after the recoloring and corresponding nodes in the associated $(2,4)$ tree after the fusion.

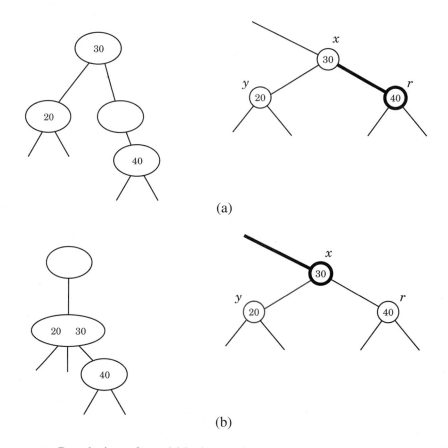

(a)

(b)

Figure 9.28: Recoloring of a red-black tree that propagates the double black problem: (a) configuration before the recoloring and corresponding nodes in the associated $(2,4)$ tree before the fusion (other similar configurations are possible); (b) configuration after the recoloring and corresponding nodes in the associated $(2,4)$ tree after the fusion.

Case 3: *The Sibling* **y** *of* **r** *is Red.* (See Figure 9.29.) In this case, we perform an *adjustment* operation, as follows. If y is the right child of x, let z be the right child of y; otherwise, let z be the left child of y. Execute the trinode restructure operation restructure(z), which makes y the parent of x. Color y black and x red. An adjustment corresponds to choosing a different representation of a 3-node in the $(2,4)$ tree T'. After the adjustment operation, the sibling of r is black, and either Case 1 or Case 2 applies, with a different meaning of x and y. Note that if Case 2 applies, the double-black problem cannot reappear. Thus, to complete Case 3 we make one more application of either Case 1 or Case 2 above and we are done. Therefore, at most one adjustment is performed in a removal operation.

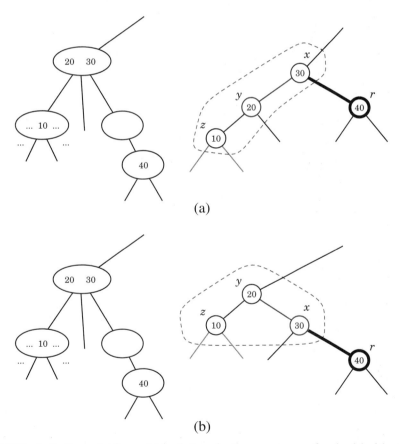

(a)

(b)

Figure 9.29: Adjustment of a red-black tree in the presence of a double black problem: (a) configuration before the adjustment and corresponding nodes in the associated $(2,4)$ tree (a symmetric configuration is possible); (b) configuration after the adjustment with the same corresponding nodes in the associated $(2,4)$ tree.

From the above algorithm description, we see that the tree updating needed after a removal involves an upward march in the tree T, while performing at most a constant amount of work (in a restructuring, recoloring, or adjustment) per node. Thus, since any changes we make at a node in T during this upward march takes $O(1)$ time (because it affects a constant number of nodes), we have the following:

Proposition 9.7: *The algorithm for removing an item from a red-black tree with* n *items takes* $O(\log n)$ *time and performs* $O(\log n)$ *recolorings and at most one adjustment plus one additional trinode restructuring. Thus, it performs at most two* restructure *operations.*

In Figures 9.30 and 9.31, we show a sequence of removal operations on a red-black tree. We illustrate Case 1 restructurings in Figure 9.30c and d. We illustrate Case 2 recolorings at several places in Figures 9.30 and 9.31. Finally, in Figure 9.31i and j, we show an example of a Case 3 adjustment.

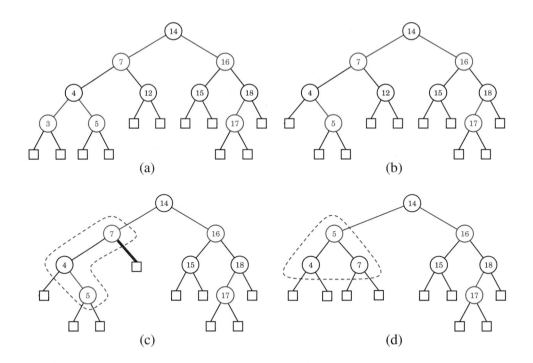

Figure 9.30: Sequence of removals from a red-black tree: (a) initial tree; (b) removal of 3; (c) removal of 12, causing a double black (handled by restructuring); (d) after restructuring.

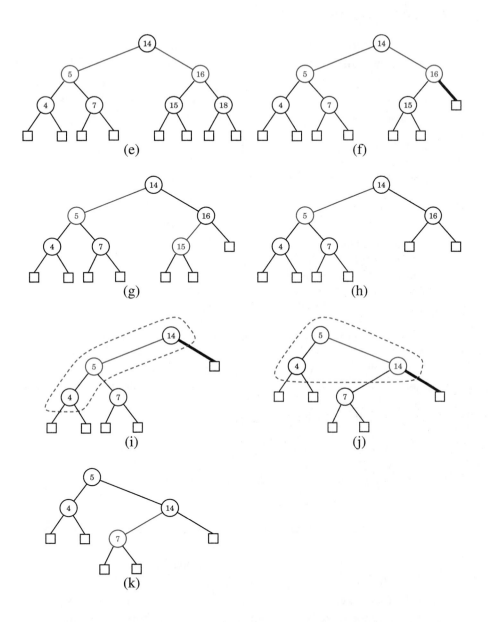

Figure 9.31: Sequence of removals in a red-black tree (continued): (e) removal of 17; (f) removal of 18, causing a double black (handled by recoloring); (g) after recoloring; (h) removal of 15; (i) removal of 16, causing a double black (handled by an adjustment); (j) after the adjustment the double black needs to be handled by a recoloring; (k) after the recoloring.

9.5.2   Java Implementation

In Code Fragments 9.10–9.13, we show portions of a Java implementation of a dictionary realized by means of a red-black tree. Class RBTItem, shown in Code Fragment 9.10, extends the Item class used to represent a key-element item of a binary search tree. It defines an additional instance variable isRed, representing the color of the node, and methods to set and return it.

```java
public class RBTItem extends Item  {
  private boolean isRed;
  public RBTItem(Object k, Object elem, boolean color)  {
    super(k, elem);
    isRed = color;
  }
  public boolean isRed()  {return isRed;}
  public void makeRed()  {isRed = true;}
  public void makeBlack()  {isRed = false;}
  public void setColor(boolean color)  {isRed = color;}
}
```

Code Fragment 9.10: Class implementing a node of a red-black tree.

```java
/** Realization of a dictionary by means of a red-black tree. */
public class RBTree extends BinarySearchTree implements Dictionary  {
  static boolean Red = true;
  static boolean Black = false;

  public RBTree(Comparator C)  {
    super(C);
    T = new RestructurableNodeBinaryTree();
  }
```

Code Fragment 9.11: Instance variables and constructor of class RBTree.

Class RBTree, partially shown in Code Fragments 9.11–9.13, extends BinarySearchTree (Code Fragments 9.3–9.5). As in class AVLTree, the constructor of RBTree executes first the superclass's constructor, and then assigns to T a RestructurableNodeBinaryTree, which is a class that implements the binary tree ADT, and, in addition, supports the method restructure for performing trinode restructurings (rotations); its implementation is left as an exercise (P-9.3). Class RBTree inherits methods size, isEmpty, findElement, findAllElements, and removeAllElements from BinarySearchTree but overrides methods insertItem and removeElement. Several auxiliary methods of class RBTree are not shown.

```
      public void insertItem(Object key, Object element)
         throws InvalidKeyException  {
         super.insertItem(key, element); // may throw an InvalidKeyException
         Position posZ = actionPos; // start at the insertion position
         T.replaceElement(posZ, new RBTItem(key, element, Red));
         if (T.isRoot(posZ))
            setBlack(posZ);
         else
            remedyDoubleRed(posZ);
      }

      protected void remedyDoubleRed(Position posZ)  {
         Position posV = T.parent(posZ);
         if (T.isRoot(posV))
            return;
         if (!isPosRed(posV))
            return;
         // we have a double red: posZ and posV
         if (!isPosRed(T.sibling(posV)))  { // Case 1: trinode restructuring
            posV = ((RestructurableNodeBinaryTree) T).restructure(posZ);
            setBlack(posV);
            setRed(T.leftChild(posV));
            setRed(T.rightChild(posV));
          }
         else  { // Case 2: recoloring
            setBlack(posV);
            setBlack(T.sibling(posV));
            Position posU = T.parent(posV);
            if (T.isRoot(posU))
               return;
            setRed(posU);
            remedyDoubleRed(posU);
         }
      }
```

Code Fragment 9.12: Dictionary method insertItem and auxiliary method remedy-DoubleRed of class RBTree.

Methods insertItem (Code Fragment 9.12) and removeElement (Code Fragment 9.13) call the corresponding methods of the superclass first and then rebalance the tree by calling auxiliary methods to perform rotations along the path from the update position (given by the instance variable actionPos inherited from the superclass) to the root.

```
public Object removeElement(Object key)  throws InvalidKeyException {
  Object toReturn = super.removeElement(key);
  Position posR = actionPos;
  if (toReturn != NO_SUCH_KEY) {
    if (wasParentRed(posR) || T.isRoot(posR) || isPosRed(posR))
      setBlack(posR);
    else
      remedyDoubleBlack(posR);
  }
  return toReturn;
}
protected void remedyDoubleBlack(Position posR) {
  Position posX, posY, posZ;
  boolean oldColor;
  posX = T.parent(posR);
  posY = T.sibling(posR);
  if (!isPosRed(posY))  {
    posZ = redChild(posY);
    if (hasRedChild(posY))  { // Case 1: trinode restructuring
      oldColor = isPosRed(posX);
      posZ = ((RestructurableNodeBinaryTree) T).restructure(posZ);
      setColor(posZ, oldColor);
      setBlack(posR);
      setBlack(T.leftChild(posZ));
      setBlack(T.rightChild(posZ));
      return;
    }
    setBlack(posR);
    setRed(posY);
    if (!isPosRed(posX))  { // Case 2: recoloring
      if (!T.isRoot(posX))
        remedyDoubleBlack(posX);
      return;
    }
    setBlack(posX);
    return;
  } // Case 3: adjustment
  if (posY == T.rightChild(posX))
    posZ = T.rightChild(posY);
  else
    posZ = T.leftChild(posY);
  ((RestructurableNodeBinaryTree)T).restructure(posZ);
  setBlack(posY);
  setRed(posX);
  remedyDoubleBlack(posR);
}
```

Code Fragment 9.13: Method removeElement and its auxiliary method.

9.5.3   Performance

Table 9.4 summarizes the running times of the main operations of a dictionary realized by means of a red-black tree. We illustrate the justification for these bounds in Figure 9.32.

Operation	Time
size, isEmpty	$O(1)$
findElement, insertItem, removeElement	$O(\log n)$
findAllElements, removeAllElements	$O(\log n + s)$

Table 9.4: Performance of an n-element dictionary realized by a red-black tree, where s denotes the size of the iterators returned by findAllElements and removeAllElements. The space usage is $O(n)$.

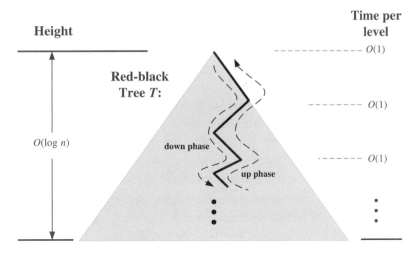

Figure 9.32: Illustrating the running time of searches and updates in a red-black tree. The time performance is $O(1)$ per level, broken into a down phase, which typically involves searching, and an up phase, which typically involves recolorings and performing local trinode restructurings (rotations).

Thus, a red-black tree achieves logarithmic worst-case running times for both searching and updating in a dictionary. The red-black tree data structure is slightly more complicated than its corresponding $(2,4)$ tree. Even so, a red-black tree has a conceptual advantage that only a constant number of trinode restructurings are ever needed to restore the balance in a red-black tree after an update.

9.6   External Searching ⋆

In this section, we study the problem of implementing an ordered dictionary for a large collection of items that do not fit in main memory. One of the main applications of large dictionaries is in database systems. When data cannot be held in main memory, it must be stored in **external memory**, which is usually a disk. The time to access information on a disk is so much slower than the time used to transfer that information, so data items on a disk are usually grouped into contiguous sections called **blocks**. We refer to these secondary-memory blocks as **disk blocks**. Likewise, we refer to the transfer of a block between secondary memory and main memory as a **disk transfer**. Even though we use this terminology, the search techniques we discuss in this section apply also when the main memory is the CPU cache and the secondary memory is the main (RAM) memory, for cache lines are also collected into blocks.

There is a great time difference that exists between main memory accesses and disk accesses, equal to several orders of magnitude for many systems. Thus, the main goal of maintaining a dictionary in external memory is to minimize the number of disk transfers needed to perform a query or update. In fact, the difference in speed between disk and internal memory is so great that we should be willing to perform a considerable number of internal-memory accesses if they allow us to avoid a few disk transfers. Let us, therefore, analyze the performance of dictionary implementations by counting the number of disk transfers each would require to perform the standard dictionary search and update operations. We refer to this count as the **I/O complexity** of the algorithms involved.

Let us consider first the simple dictionary realizations that use a sequence to store the items. If the sequence is implemented as an unsorted doubly linked list, that is, a list-based log file, then insertions can be performed with $O(1)$ transfers each, but removals and searching requires $\Theta(n)$ transfers in the worst case, where n is the number of items in the dictionary, since each link hop we perform could access a different block. This search time can be improved to $O(n/B)$ transfers (using a method we explore in Exercise C-9.19), where B denotes the number of nodes of the list that can fit into a block, but this is still poor performance. We could alternately implement the sequence using a sorted vector, that is, a look-up table. In this case, a search performs $O(\log_2 n)$ transfers, using the binary search algorithm, which is a nice improvement. But this solution requires $\Theta(n/B)$ transfers to implement an insert or remove operation in the worst case, for we may have to access all the blocks holding the array to move elements up or down. Thus, sequence-based implementations of a dictionary are not efficient from an external memory standpoint.

Since these simple implementations are I/O inefficient, then perhaps we should consider the logarithmic-time strategies that use balanced binary trees (such as AVL trees or red-black trees) or other search structures with logarithmic average-case query and update times (such as skip lists). These methods store the dictionary items at the nodes of a binary tree or a graph (for skip lists). Typically, each node accessed for a query or update in one of these structures will be in a different block. Thus, these methods typically require $O(\log_2 n)$ transfers to perform a query or update operation. This is pretty good, but we can do much better. In particular, we describe in the remainder of this section how to perform dictionary query and update operations using only $O(\log_B n)$, that is, $O(\log n / \log B)$, transfers, where B is much larger than 2.

To improve the external-memory performance of the dictionary implementations discussed above we should be willing to perform up to $O(B)$ internal-memory accesses to avoid a single disk transfer, where B denotes the size of a disk block. The hardware and software that drives the disk performs this many internal-memory accesses just to bring a block into internal memory, and, even then, this is only a small part of the cost of a disk transfer. Thus, $O(B)$ high-speed, internal-memory accesses are a small price to pay to avoid a time-consuming disk transfer.

9.6.1 (a,b) Trees

To reduce the importance of the performance difference between internal-memory accesses and external-memory accesses for searching, we can represent our dictionary using a multi-way search tree (Section 9.3). This approach gives rise to a generalization of the $(2,4)$ tree data structure to a structure known as the (a,b) tree.

An (a,b) tree is a multi-way search tree such that each node has between a and b children and stores between $a-1$ and $b-1$ items. The algorithms for searching, inserting, and removing elements in an (a,b) tree are straightforward generalizations of the corresponding ones for $(2,4)$ trees. The advantage of generalizing $(2,4)$ trees to (a,b) trees is that a generalized class of trees provides a flexible search structure, where the size of the nodes and the running time of the various dictionary operations depends on the parameters a and b. By setting the parameters a and b appropriately with respect to the size of disk blocks, we can derive a data structure that achieves good external-memory performance.

An (a,b) **tree**, where a and b are integers, such that $2 \le a \le (b+1)/2$, is a multi-way search tree T with the following additional restrictions:

Size Property: Each internal node has at least a children, unless it is the root, and has at most b children.

Depth Property: All the external nodes have the same depth.

Proposition 9.8: *The height of an* (a,b) *tree storing* n *items is* $\Omega(\log n/\log b)$ *and* $O(\log n/\log a)$.

Justification: Let T be an (a,b) tree storing n elements, and let h be the height of T. We justify the proposition by establishing the following bounds on h:

$$\frac{1}{\log b}\log(n+1) \le h \le \frac{1}{\log a}\log\frac{n+1}{2}+1.$$

By the size and depth properties, the number n'' of external nodes of T is at least $2a^{h-1}$ and at most b^h. By Proposition 9.3, $n'' = n+1$. Thus

$$2a^{h-1} \le n+1 \le b^h.$$

Taking the logarithm in base 2 of each term, we get

$$(h-1)\log a+1 \le \log(n+1) \le h\log b.$$

                                                                               ■

We recall that in a multi-way search tree T, each node v of T holds a secondary structure $D(v)$, which is itself a dictionary (Section 9.3). If T is an (a,b) tree, then $D(v)$ stores at most b items. Let $f(b)$ denote the time for performing a search in a $D(v)$ dictionary. The search algorithm in an (a,b) tree is exactly like the one for multi-way search trees given in Section 9.3. Hence, searching in an (a,b) tree T with n items takes $O(\frac{f(b)}{\log a}\log n)$ time. Note that if b is a constant (and thus a is also), then the search time is $O(\log n)$, independent of the specific implementation of the secondary structures.

The main application of (a,b) trees is for dictionaries stored in external memory (for example, on a disk or CD-ROM). Namely, to minimize disk accesses, we select the parameters a and b so that each tree node occupies a single disk block (so that $f(b) = 1$ if we wish to simply count block transfers). Providing the right a and b values in this context gives rise to a data structure known as the B-tree, which we will describe shortly. Before we describe this structure, however, let us discuss how insertions and removals are handled in (a,b) trees.

Update Operations

The insertion algorithm for an (a,b) tree is similar to that for a $(2,4)$ tree. An overflow occurs when an item is inserted into a b-node v, which becomes an illegal $(b+1)$-node. (Recall that a node in a multi-way tree is a d-node if it has d children.) To remedy an overflow, we split node v by moving the median item of v

into the parent of v and replacing v with a $\lceil (b+1)/2 \rceil$-node v' and a $\lfloor (b+1)/2 \rfloor$-node v''. We can now see the reason for requiring $a \leq (b+1)/2$ in the definition of an (a,b) tree. Note that as a consequence of the split, we need to build the secondary structures $D(v')$ and $D(v'')$.

Removing an element from an (a,b) tree is also similar to what was done for $(2,4)$ trees. An underflow occurs when a key is removed from an a-node v, distinct from the root, which causes v to become an illegal $(a-1)$-node. To remedy an underflow, we either perform a transfer with a sibling of v that is not an a-node or we perform a fusion of v with a sibling that is an a-node. The new node w resulting from the fusion is a $(2a-1)$-node. Here, we see another reason for requiring $a \leq (b+1)/2$. Note that as a consequence of the fusion, we need to build the secondary structure $D(w)$.

Table 9.5 shows the performance of a dictionary realized with an (a,b) tree.

Method	Time
findElement	$O\left(\dfrac{f(b)}{\log a} \log n\right)$
insertItem	$O\left(\dfrac{g(b)}{\log a} \log n\right)$
removeElement	$O\left(\dfrac{g(b)}{\log a} \log n\right)$

Table 9.5: Time bounds for methods of a dictionary realized by an (a,b) tree. Only the fundamental methods are shown. We let n denote the number of elements in the dictionary. The space usage is $O(n)$.

The time bounds in Table 9.5 are based on the following assumptions and facts:

- The (a,b) tree T is realized using the data structure described in Section 9.3, and the secondary structure of the nodes of T support search in $f(b)$ time, and split and fusion operations in $g(b)$ time, for some functions $f(b)$ and $g(b)$, which can be made to be $O(1)$ when we are only counting disk transfers.
- The height of an (a,b) tree storing n elements is $O((\log n)/(\log a))$, by Proposition 9.8.
- A search visits $O((\log n)/(\log a))$ nodes on a path between the root and an external node, and spends $f(b)$ time per node.
- A transfer operation takes $f(b)$ time.
- A split or fusion operation takes $g(b)$ time and builds a secondary structure of size $O(b)$ for the new node(s) created.
- An insertion or removal of an element visits $O((\log n)/(\log a))$ nodes on a path between the root and an external node, and spends $g(b)$ time per node.

9.6.2 B-Trees

A version of the (a,b) tree data structure, which is the best known method for maintaining a dictionary in external memory, is known as the "B-tree." (See Figure 9.33.) A **B-tree of order** d is an (a,b) tree with $a = \lceil d/2 \rceil$ and $b = d$. Since we discussed the standard dictionary query and update methods for (a,b) trees above, we restrict our discussion here to the I/O complexity of B-trees.

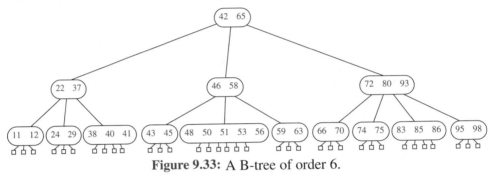

Figure 9.33: A B-tree of order 6.

An important property of B-trees is that we can choose d so that the d children references and the $d-1$ keys stored at a node can all fit into a single disk block, implying that d is $\Theta(B)$. This choice also allows us to assume that a and b are $\Theta(B)$ in the analysis of the search and update operations on (a,b) trees. Thus, $f(b)$ and $g(b)$ are both $O(1)$, for each time we access a node to perform a search or an update operation, we need only perform a single disk transfer.

As we have already observed above, each search or update requires that we examine at most $O(1)$ nodes for each level of the tree. Therefore, any dictionary search or update operation on a B-tree requires only $O(\log_{\lceil d/2 \rceil} n)$, that is, $O(\log n / \log B)$, disk transfers. For example, an insert operation proceeds down the B-tree to locate the node in which to insert the new item. If the node would **overflow** (to have $d+1$ children) because of this addition, then this node is **split** into two nodes that have $\lfloor (d+1)/2 \rfloor$ and $\lceil (d+1)/2 \rceil$ children, respectively. This process is then repeated at the next level up, and will continue for at most $O(\log_B n)$ levels.

Likewise, if a remove operation results in a node **underflow** (to have $\lceil d/2 \rceil - 1$ children), then we move references from a sibling node with at least $\lceil d/2 \rceil + 1$ children or we need to perform a **fusion** operation of this node with its sibling (and repeat this computation at the parent). As with the insert operation, this will continue up the B-tree for at most $O(\log_B n)$ levels. The requirement that each internal node have at least $\lceil d/2 \rceil$ children implies that each disk block used to support a B-tree is at least half full. Thus, we have the following:

Proposition 9.9: *A B-tree with n items has I/O complexity $O(\log_B n)$ for search or update operation, and uses $O(n/B)$ blocks, where B is the size of a block.*

9.7 Exercises

Reinforcement

R-9.1 Insert, into an initially empty binary search tree items, items with the following keys (in this order): 30, 40, 24, 58, 48, 26, 11, 13. Draw the tree after each insertion.

R-9.2 Suppose that the methods of class BinarySearchTree, shown in Code Fragments 9.3 through 9.5, are used to perform the updates showin in Figures 9.4, 9.5, and 9.6. What is the node referenced by the instance variable actionPos after each update?

R-9.3 A certain Professor Amongus claims that the order in which a fixed set of elements is inserted into a binary search tree does not matter—the same tree results every time. Give a small example that proves Professor Amongus wrong.

R-9.4 Professor Amongus claims he has a "patch" to his claim from the previous exercise, namely, that the order in which a fixed set of elements is inserted into an AVL tree does not matter—the same AVL tree results every time. Give a small example that proves that Professor Amongus is still wrong.

R-9.5 Is the rotation done in Figure 9.9 a single or a double rotation? What about the rotation in Figure 9.11?

R-9.6 Draw the AVL tree resulting from the insertion of an item with key 52 into the AVL tree of Figure 9.11b.

R-9.7 Draw the AVL tree resulting from the removal of the item with key 62 from the AVL tree of Figure 9.11b.

R-9.8 Explain why performing a rotation in an n-node binary tree represented using a sequence takes $\Omega(n)$ time.

R-9.9 Is the multi-way search tree of Figure 9.13a a $(2,4)$ tree? Justify your answer.

R-9.10 An alternative way of performing a split at a node v in a $(2,4)$ tree is to partition v into v' and v'', with v' being a 2-node and v'' being a 3-node. Which of the keys k_1, k_2, k_3, or k_4 do we store at v's parent in this case? Why?

R-9.11 Professor Amongus claims that a $(2,4)$ tree storing a set of items will always have the same structure, regardless of the order in which the items are inserted. Show that Professor Amongus is wrong.

R-9.12 Consider the following sequence of keys:

$$(5, 16, 22, 45, 2, 10, 18, 30, 50, 12, 1).$$

Consider the insertion of items with this set of keys in the order given into:

a. An initially empty $(2,4)$ tree T'
b. An initially empty red-black tree T''.

Draw T' and T'' after each insertion.

R-9.13 Draw four different red-black trees that correspond to the same $(2,4)$ tree using the correspondence rules described in the chapter.

R-9.14 For each of the following statements about red-black trees, determine whether it is true or false. If you think it is true, provide a justification. If you think it is false, give a counterexample.

a. A subtree of a red-black tree is itself a red-black tree.
b. The sibling of an external node is either external or it is red.
c. Given a red-black tree T, there is an unique $(2,4)$ tree T' associated with T.
d. Given a $(2,4)$ tree T, there is a unique red-black tree T' associated with T.

R-9.15 Draw an example red-black tree that is not an AVL tree. Your tree should have at least 6 nodes, but no more than 16.

R-9.16 Consider a tree T storing 100,000 items. What is the worst-case height of T in the following cases?

a. T is an AVL tree.
b. T is a $(2,4)$ tree.
c. T is a red-black tree.
d. T is a binary search tree.

R-9.17 Describe, in detail, the insertion and removal algorithms for an (a,b) tree.

R-9.18 Suppose T is a multi-way tree such that each internal node has at least five and at most eight children. For what values of a and b is T a valid (a,b) tree?

R-9.19 For what values of d is the tree T of the previous exercise an order-d B-tree?

R-9.20 Draw the order-7 B-tree resulting from inserting the following keys (in this order) into an initially empty tree T:

$$(4, 40, 23, 50, 11, 34, 62, 78, 66, 22, 90, 59, 25, 72, 64, 77, 39, 12).$$

R-9.21 Show each level of recursion in performing a four-way merge-sort of the sequence given in the previous exercise.

Creativity

C-9.1 Design a variation of algorithm TreeSearch for performing the operation findAllElements(k) in an ordered dictionary implemented with a binary search tree T, and show that it runs in time $O(h+s)$, where h is the height of T and s is the size of the iterator returned.

C-9.2 Describe how to perform the operation removeAllElements(k) in an ordered dictionary implemented with a binary search tree T, and show that this method runs in time $O(h+s)$, where h is the height of T and s is the size of the iterator returned.

C-9.3 Draw an example of an AVL tree such that a single removeElement operation could require $\Theta(\log n)$ trinode restructurings (or rotations) from a leaf to the root in order to restore the height-balance property. (Use triangles to represent subtrees that are not affected by this operation.)

C-9.4 Show how to perform operation removeAllElements(k) in a dictionary implemented with an AVL tree in time $O(s \log n)$, where n is the number of elements in the dictionary at the time the operation is performed and s is the size of the iterator returned by the operation.

C-9.5 If we maintain a reference to the position of the left-most internal node of an AVL tree, then operation first can be performed in $O(1)$ time. Describe how the implementation of the other dictionary methods needs to be modified to maintain a reference to the left-most position.

C-9.6$\star$ Show that any n-node binary tree can be converted to any other n-node binary tree using $O(n)$ rotations.   (Hint: Show that $O(n)$ rotations suffice to convert any binary tree into a *left chain*, where each internal node has an external right child.)

C-9.7 Let D be an ordered dictionary with n items implemented by means of an AVL tree. Show how to implement the following operation on D in time $O(\log n + s)$, where s is the size of the iterator returned:

findAllInRange(k_1, k_2): Return an iterator of all the elements in D with key k such that $k_1 \leq k \leq k_2$.
Input: Objects; *Output:* Iterator.

C-9.8★ Let D be an ordered dictionary with n items implemented with an AVL tree. Show how to implement the following method for D in time $O(\log n)$:

countAllInRange(k_1, k_2): Compute and return the number of items in D with key k such that $k_1 \leq k \leq k_2$.
Input: Objects; *Output:* Integer.

Note that this method returns a single integer.   (Hint: You will need to extend the AVL tree data structure, adding a new field to each internal node and the ways of maintaining this field during updates.)

C-9.9 Show that the nodes that become unbalanced in an AVL tree after operation expandExternal is performed, within the execution of an insertItem operation, may be nonconsecutive on the path from the newly inserted node to the root.

C-9.10 Show that at most one node in an AVL tree becomes unbalanced after operation removeAboveExternal is performed within the execution of a removeElement dictionary operation.

C-9.11 Show that at most one trinode restructure operation (which corresponds to one single or double rotation) is needed to restore balance after any insertion in an AVL tree.

C-9.12 Let T and U be $(2, 4)$ trees storing n and m items, respectively, such that all the items in T have keys less than the keys of all the items in U. Describe an $O(\log n + \log m)$ time method for *joining* T and U into a single tree that stores all the items in T and U (destroying the old versions of T and U).

C-9.13 Repeat the previous problem for red-black trees T and U.

C-9.14 Justify Proposition 9.3.

C-9.15 The Boolean indicator used to mark nodes in a red-black tree as being "red" or "black" is not strictly needed. Describe a scheme for implementing a red-black tree without adding any extra space to standard binary search tree nodes. How does your scheme affect the running times for searching and updating a red-black tree?

C-9.16 Let T be a red-black tree storing n items, and let k be the key of an item in T. Show how to construct from T, in $O(\log n)$ time, two red-black trees T' and T'', such that T' contains all the keys of T less than k, and T'' contains all the keys of T greater than k. This operation destroys T.

C-9.17 Show that the nodes of any AVL tree T can be colored "red" and "black" so that T becomes a red-black tree.

C-9.18 The **mergeable heap** ADT consists of operations insert(k,x), remove(k), unionWith(h), and minElement(), where the unionWith(h) operation performs a union of the mergeable heap h with the present one, destroying the old versions of both. Describe a concrete implementation of the mergeable heap ADT that achieves $O(\log n)$ performance for all its operations. For simplicity, you may assume that all keys in existing mergeable heaps are distinct, although this is not strictly necessary.

C-9.19 Show how to implement a dictionary in external memory using an unordered sequence so that updates require only $O(1)$ transfers and updates require $O(n/B)$ transfers in the worst case, where n is the number of elements and B is the number of list nodes that can fit into a disk block. (Hint: Consider an alternate linked list implementation that uses "fat" nodes.)

C-9.20 Change the rules that define red-black trees so that each red-black tree T has a corresponding $(4,8)$ tree, and vice versa.

C-9.21 Describe a modified version of the B-tree insertion algorithm so that each time we create an overflow because of a split of a node v, we redistribute keys among all of v's siblings such that each sibling holds roughly the same number of keys (possibly cascading the split up to the parent of v). What is the minimum fraction of each block that will always be filled using this scheme?

C-9.22 Suppose that instead of having the node-search function $f(d) = 1$ in an order-d B-tree T, we instead have $f(d) = \log d$. What does the asymptotic running time of performing a search in T now become?

C-9.23 Describe how to use a B-tree to implement the queue ADT so that the total number of disk transfers needed to process a sequence of n enqueue and dequeue operations is $O(n/B)$.

C-9.24 Another possible external-memory dictionary implementation is to use a skip list, but to collect in individual blocks consecutive groups of $O(B)$ nodes on any level in the skip list. In particular, we define an **order-d B-skip list** to be such a representation of a skip list structure, where each block contains at least $\lceil d/2 \rceil$ list nodes and at most d list nodes. Let us also choose d in this case to be the maximum number of list nodes from a level of a skip list that can fit into one block. Describe how we should modify the skip-list insertion and removal algorithms for a B-skip list so that the expected height of the structure is $O(\log n / \log B)$.

C-9.25 Suppose we are given a sequence S of n elements with integer keys such that some items in S are colored "blue" and some elements in S are colored "red." In addition, say that a red element e **pairs** with a blue element f if they have the same key value. Describe an efficient external-memory algorithm for finding all the red-blue pairs in S. How many disk transfers does your algorithm perform?

Projects

P-9.1 Extend class BinarySearchTree, shown in Code Fragments 9.3 through 9.5, to support the methods of the ordered dictionary ADT (see Section 8.4).

P-9.2 Extend class BinarySearchTree, shown in Code Fragments 9.3 through 9.5, to support the locator-based methods of the ordered dictionary ADT (see Section 8.7).

P-9.3 Implement a class RestructurableNodeBinaryTree that supports the methods of the binary tree ADT, plus a method restructure for performing a rotation operation. This class is a component of the implementation of an AVL tree given in Section 9.2.2.

P-9.4 Implement the methods of the ordered dictionary ADT using an AVL tree.

P-9.5 Implement a dictionary that supports locator-based methods by means of an AVL tree.

P-9.6 Write a Java class that implements all the methods of an ordered dictionary given in Chapter 8 using a $(2,4)$ tree.

P-9.7 Write a Java class that can take any red-black tree and convert it into its corresponding $(2,4)$ tree and can take any $(2,4)$ tree and convert it into its corresponding red-black tree.

P-9.8   Write a Java class that implements all the methods of a dictionary given in Chapter 8 by means of a red-black tree.

P-9.9   Form a three-programmer team and have each member implement a different one of the previous three projects. Perform extensive experimental studies to compare the speed of these three implementations. Try to design three sets of experiments such that each favors a different implementation.

P-9.10 Write a Java class that implements all the methods of a dictionary given in Chapter 8 by means of an (a, b) tree, where a and b are integer constants.

P-9.11 Implement the B-tree data structure, assuming a block size of $1,000$ and that keys are integers. Test the number of "disk transfers" needed to process a sequence of dictionary operations.

Chapter Notes

Some of the data structures discussed in this chapter are extensively covered by Knuth in his *Sorting and Searching* book [60], and by Mehlhorn in [73]. AVL trees are due to Adel'son-Vel'skii and Landis [1], who invented this class of balanced search trees in 1962. Binary search trees, AVL trees, and hashing are described in Knuth's *Sorting and Searching* [60] book. Average-height analyses for binary search trees can be found in the books by Aho, Hopcroft, and Ullman [5] and Cormen, Leiserson, and Rivest [25]. The handbook by Gonnet and Baeza-Yates [41] contains a number of theoretical and experimental comparisons among dictionary implementations. Aho, Hopcroft, and Ullman [4] discuss $(2, 3)$ trees, which are similar to $(2, 4)$ trees. Red-black trees were defined by Bayer [10]. Variations and interesting properties of red-black trees are presented in a paper by Guibas and Sedgewick [46]. The reader interested in learning more about different balanced tree data structures is referred to the books by Mehlhorn [73] and Tarjan [92], and the book chapter by Mehlhorn and Tsakalidis [76]. Knuth [60] is excellent additional reading that includes early approaches to balancing trees.

   B-trees were invented by Bayer and McCreight [11], and Comer [24] provides a very nice overview of this data structure. The books by Mehlhorn [73] and Samet [85] also have nice discussions about B-trees and their variants. Aggarwal and Vitter [2] study the I/O complexity of sorting and related problems, establishing upper and lower bounds, including the lower bound for sorting given in this chapter. The reader interested in further study of I/O-efficient algorithms is encouraged to examine the survey paper of Vitter [95].

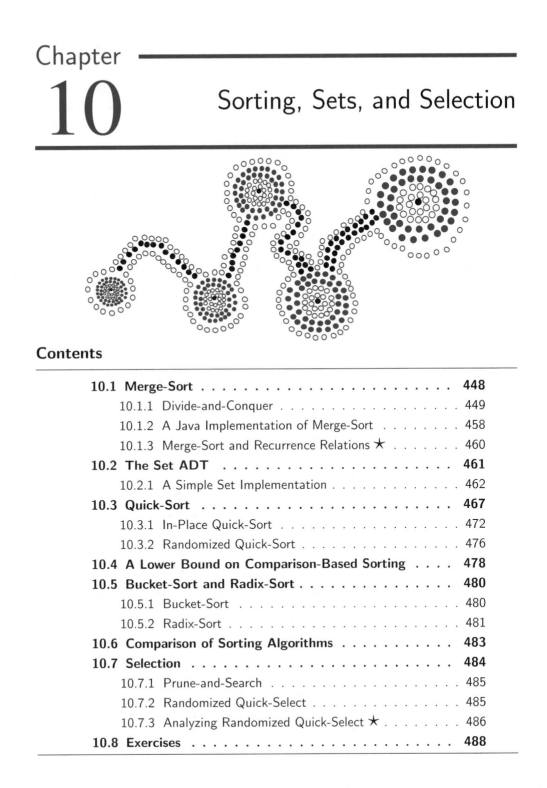

Chapter 10

Sorting, Sets, and Selection

Contents

The Second Law of Thermodynamics suggests that Nature tends toward disorder. Humans, on the other hand, prefer order. Indeed, there are several advantages to keeping data in order. For example, the binary search algorithm, discussed in Section 8.2, works correctly only for an ordered vector. Since computers are intended to be tools for humans, we devote this chapter to the study of sorting algorithms and their applications. We recall that the sorting problem is defined as follows. Let S be a sequence of n elements that can be compared to each other according to a total order relation, that is, it is always possible to compare two elements of S to see which is larger or smaller, or if the two of them are equal. We want to rearrange S in such a way that the elements appear in increasing order (or in nondecreasing order if there are equal elements in S).

We have already presented several sorting algorithms in the previous chapters. In particular, in Section 7.1.2, we presented a simple sorting scheme, which is called PriorityQueueSort, that consists of inserting elements into a priority queue and then extracting them in nondecreasing order, by means of a series of removeMin operations. If the priority queue is implemented by means of a sequence, then PriorityQueueSort runs in $O(n^2)$ time and corresponds to the sorting method known as either insertion-sort or selection-sort, depending on whether the sequence realizing the priority queue is kept ordered or not (Section 7.2.3). If instead the priority queue is implemented by means of a heap (Section 7.3), then PriorityQueueSort runs in $O(n\log n)$ time and corresponds to the sorting method known as heap-sort (Section 7.3.4).

In this chapter, we present four other sorting algorithms, called ***merge-sort***, ***quick-sort***, ***bucket-sort***, and ***radix-sort***. We also introduce the ***set*** abstract data type and show how the merge technique used in the merge-sort algorithm can be used in the implementation of its methods. Throughout this chapter, we assume that a total order relation is defined over the elements to be sorted. If this relation is induced by a comparator (Section 7.1.4), we assume that a comparison test takes $O(1)$ time.

10.1   Merge-Sort

We have already seen the power of recursion to describe algorithms in an elegant manner. (See, for example, the tree traversal techniques presented in Chapter 6.) In this section, we present a sorting technique, called ***merge-sort***, which can be described in a simple and compact way using recursion. This algorithm is also based on our using an algorithmic design pattern called ***divide-and-conquer***, which is both powerful and general.

10.1.1 Divide-and-Conquer

Merge-sort is based on an algorithmic design pattern called ***divide-and-conquer***. The divide-and-conquer paradigm can be described in general terms as consisting of the following three steps:

1. ***Divide:*** If the input size is smaller than a certain threshold (say, one or two elements), solve the problem directly using a straightforward method and return the solution so obtained. Otherwise, divide the input data into two or more disjoint subsets.
2. ***Recur:*** Recursively solve the subproblems associated with the subsets.
3. ***Conquer:*** Take the solutions to the subproblems and "merge" them into a solution to the original problem.

The merge-sort algorithm applies the divide-and-conquer technique to the sorting problem.

Using Divide-and-Conquer for Sorting

Recall that in the sorting problem we are given a collection of n objects, typically stored in a list, vector, array, or sequence, together with some comparator defining a total order on these objects, and we are asked to produce an ordered representation of these objects. For the sake of generality, we focus on the version of the sorting problem that takes a sequence S of objects as input and returns S in sorted order. Specializations to other linear structures, such as lists, vectors, or arrays, are straightforward and left as exercises (R-10.3 and R-10.12). For the problem of sorting a sequence S with n elements, the three divide-and-conquer steps are as follows:

1. ***Divide:*** If S has zero or one element, return S immediately; it is already sorted. Otherwise (S has at least two elements), remove all the elements from S and put them into two sequences, S_1 and S_2, each containing about half of the elements of S; that is, S_1 contains the first $\lceil n/2 \rceil$ elements of S, and S_2 contains the remaining $\lfloor n/2 \rfloor$ elements.
2. ***Recur:*** Recursively sort sequences S_1 and S_2.
3. ***Conquer:*** Put back the elements into S by merging the sorted sequences S_1 and S_2 into a sorted sequence.

In reference to the divide step, we recall that the notation $\lceil x \rceil$ indicates the ***ceiling*** of x, that is, the smallest integer m, such that $x \leq m$. Similarly, the notation $\lfloor x \rfloor$ indicates the ***floor*** of x, that is, the largest integer k, such that $k \leq x$.

We can visualize an execution of the merge-sort algorithm by means of a binary tree T, called the ***merge-sort tree***. Each node of T represents a recursive invocation (or call) of the merge-sort algorithm. We associate with each node v of T the sequence S that is processed by the invocation associated with v. The children of node v are associated with the recursive calls that process the subsequences S_1 and S_2 of S. The external nodes of T are associated with individual elements of S, corresponding to instances of the algorithm that make no recursive calls.

Figure 10.1 summarizes an execution of the merge-sort algorithm by showing the input and output sequences processed at each node of the merge-sort tree. The step-by-step evolution of the merge-sort tree is shown in Figures 10.2 through 10.5.

This algorithm visualization in terms of the merge-sort tree helps us analyze the running time of the merge-sort algorithm. In particular, since the size of the input sequence roughly halves at each recursive call of merge-sort, the height of the merge-sort tree is about $\log n$ (recall that the base of log is 2 if omitted).

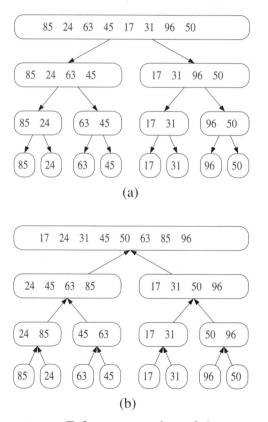

Figure 10.1: Merge-sort tree T for an execution of the merge-sort algorithm on a sequence with 8 elements: (a) input sequences processed at each node of T; (b) output sequences generated at each node of T.

Figure 10.2: Visualization of an execution of merge-sort. Each node of the tree represents a recursive call of merge-sort. The nodes drawn with dashed lines represent calls that have not been made yet. The node drawn with thick lines represents the current call. The empty nodes drawn with thin lines represent completed calls. The remaining nodes (drawn with thin lines and not empty) represent calls that are waiting for a child invocation to return).

Figure 10.3: (Continued from Figure 10.2.) Visualization of an execution of merge-sort. Note the conquer step performed in (h).

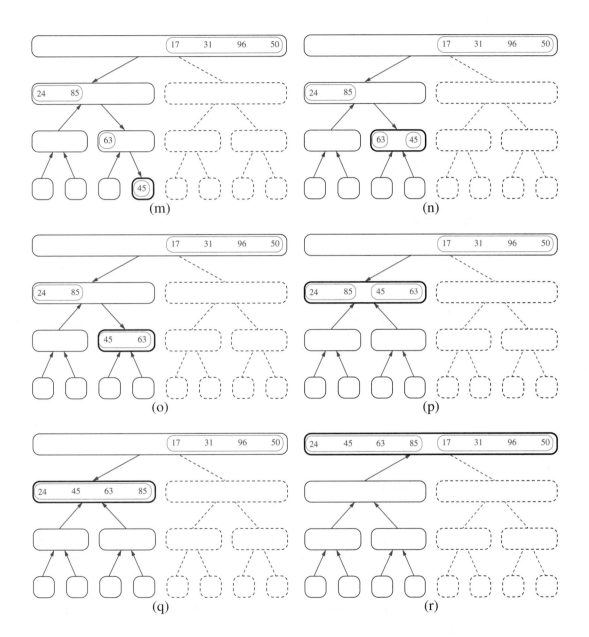

Figure 10.4: (Continued from Figure 10.3.) Visualization of an execution of merge-sort. Note the conquer steps performed in (o) and (q).

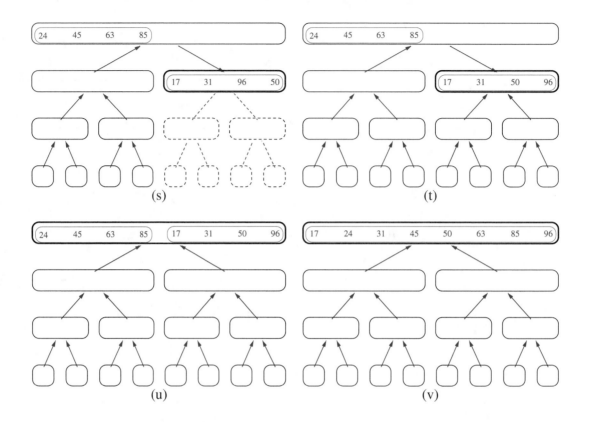

Figure 10.5: (Continued from Figure 10.4.) Visualization of an execution of merge-sort. Several invocations are omitted between (s) and (t). Note the conquer steps performed in (t) and (v).

Proposition 10.1: *The merge-sort tree associated with an execution of merge-sort on a sequence of size n has height $\lceil \log n \rceil$.*

We leave the justification of Proposition 10.1 as a simple exercise (R-10.1). We will use this proposition to analyze the running time of the merge-sort algorithm.

Having given an overview of merge-sort and an illustration of how it works, let us consider each of the steps of this divide-and-conquer algorithm in more detail. The divide and recur steps of the merge-sort algorithm are simple; dividing a sequence of size n involves separating it at the element with rank $\lceil n/2 \rceil$, and the recursive calls simply involve passing these smaller sequences as parameters. The difficult step is the conquer step, which merges two sorted sequences into a single sorted sequence. Thus, before we present our analysis of merge-sort, we need to say more about how this is done.

Merging Two Sorted Sequences

Algorithm merge, in Code Fragment 10.1, merges two sorted sequences, S_1 and S_1, by iteratively removing a smallest element from one of these two and adding it to the end of the output sequence, S, until one of these two sequences is empty, at which point we copy the remainder of the other sequence to the output sequence.

We analyze the running time of the merge algorithm by making some simple observations. Let n_1 and n_2 be the number of elements of S_1 and S_2, respectively. Also, let us assume that the sequences S_1, S_2, and S are implemented so that access to, insertion into, and deletion from their first and last positions each take $O(1)$ time. This is the case for implementations based on circular arrays or doubly linked lists (Section 5.3). Algorithm merge has three **while** loops. Because of our assumptions, the operations performed inside each loop take $O(1)$ time each. The key observation is that during each iteration of one of the loops, one element is removed from either S_1 or S_2. Since no insertions are performed into S_1 or S_2, this observation implies that the overall number of iterations of the three loops is $n_1 + n_2$. Thus, the running time of algorithm merge is $O(n_1 + n_2)$, as we summarize:

Proposition 10.2: *Merging two sorted sequences S_1 and S_2 takes $O(n_1 + n_2)$ time, where n_1 is the size of S_1 and n_2 is the size of S_2.*

Algorithm merge(S_1, S_2, S):

   Input: Sequences S_1 and S_2 sorted in nondecreasing order, and an empty sequence S

   Output: Sequence S containing the elements from S_1 and S_2 sorted in nondecreasing order, with sequences S_1 and S_2 becoming empty

   while S_1 is not empty **and** S_2 is not empty **do**

     if S_1.first().element() $\leq$ S_2.first().element() **then**

       { move the first element of S_1 at the end of S }

       S.insertLast(S_1.remove(S_1.first()))

     else

       { move the first element of S_2 at the end of S }

       S.insertLast(S_2.remove(S_2.first()))

   { move the remaining elements of S_1 to S }

   while S_1 is not empty **do**

     S.insertLast(S_1.remove(S_1.first()))

   { move the remaining elements of S_2 to S }

   while S_2 is not empty **do**

     S.insertLast(S_2.remove(S_2.first()))

Code Fragment 10.1: Algorithm merge for merging two sorted sequences.

We show an example execution of algorithm merge in Figure 10.6.

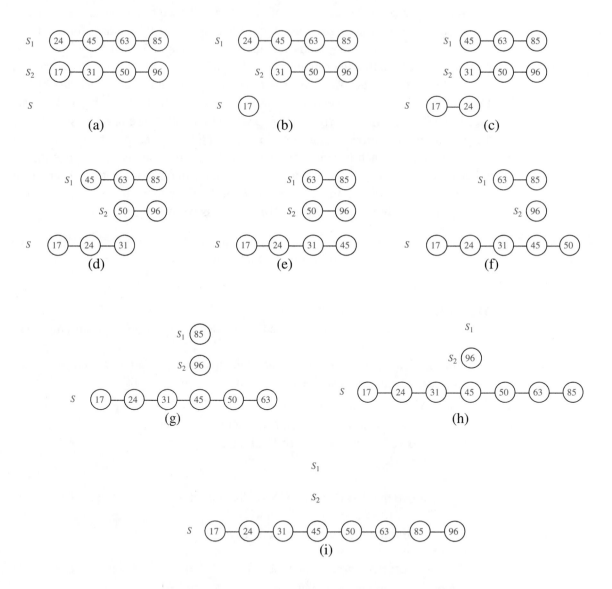

Figure 10.6: Example of execution of algorithm merge shown in Code Fragment 10.1.

The Running Time of Merge-Sort

Now that we have given the details of the merge-sort algorithm and we have analyzed the running time of the crucial merge algorithm used in the conquer step, let us analyze the running time of the entire merge-sort algorithm, assuming it is given an input sequence of n elements. For simplicity, we restrict our attention to the case where n is a power of 2. We leave it to an exercise (R-10.4) to show that the result of our analysis also holds when n is not a power of 2.

As we did in the analysis of the merge algorithm, we assume that the input sequence S and the auxiliary sequences S_1 and S_2, created by each recursive call of merge-sort, are implemented in such a way that access to, insertion into, and deletion from the first and last positions of the sequence each take $O(1)$ time. This is the case for the implementations based on a circular array and a doubly linked list (Section 5.3), or if we use one of these data structures directly.

As we mentioned earlier, we analyze the merge-sort procedure by referring to the merge-sort tree T. (Recall Figures 10.2 through 10.5.) We call the ***time spent at a node*** v of T the running time of the recursive call associated with v, excluding the time taken waiting for the recursive calls associated with the children of v to terminate. In other words, the time spent at node v includes the running times of the divide and conquer steps, but excludes the running time of the recur step. We have already observed that the details of the divide step are straightforward; this step runs in time proportional to the size of the sequence for v. Also, as shown in Proposition 10.2, the conquer step, which consists of merging two sorted subsequences, also takes linear time. That is, letting i denote the depth of node v, the time spent at node v is $O(n/2^i)$, since the size of the sequence handled by the recursive call associated with v is equal to $n/2^i$.

Looking at the tree T more globally, as shown in Figure 10.7, we see that, given our definition of "time spent at a node," the running time of merge-sort is equal to the sum of the times spent at the nodes of T. Observe that T has exactly 2^i nodes at depth i. This simple observation has an important consequence, for it implies that the overall time spent at all the nodes of T at depth i is $O(2^i \cdot n/2^i)$, which is $O(n)$. By Proposition 10.1, the height of T is $\lceil \log n \rceil$. Thus, since the time spent at each of the $\lceil \log n \rceil + 1$ levels of T is $O(n)$, we have the following result:

Proposition 10.3: *Algorithm merge-sort sorts a sequence of size n in $O(n \log n)$ time in the worst case.*

In other words, the merge-sort algorithm asymptotically matches the fast running time of the heap-sort algorithm.

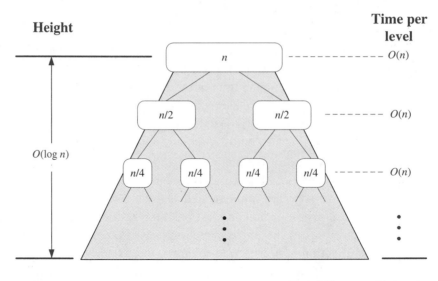

Total time: $O(n \log n)$

Figure 10.7: A visual time analysis of the merge-sort tree T. Each node is shown labeled with the size of its subproblem.

10.1.2 A Java Implementation of Merge-Sort

In Code Fragment 10.2, we show a complete Java implementation of the merge-sort algorithm. The mergeSort method is recursive and calls method merge to perform the conquer step. A comparator (see Section 7.1.4) is used to decide the relative order of two elements in the merge method.

In this implementation, the input sequence, S, and the auxiliary sequences, S1 and S2, are modified by insertions and deletions only at the head and tail. Hence, each such update takes $O(1)$ time in a sequence implemented with a doubly linked list or with an array used in a circular fashion (see Table 5.4). This is the case for the class NodeSequence (see Code Fragment 5.12) used for the auxiliary sequences.

Hence, for a sequence S of size n, method mergeSort(S, c) runs in time $O(n \log n)$ provided the following two conditions are satisfied:

1. S is implemented with a doubly linked list or with an array used in a circular fashion.

2. Comparator c can compare two elements of S in $O(1)$ time.

```
/**
 * Sort the elements of sequence S in nondecreasing order according
 * to comparator c, using the merge-sort algorithm.
 **/
public static void mergeSort (Sequence S, Comparator c) {
  int n = S.size();
  // a sequence with 0 or 1 element is already sorted
  if (n < 2) return;
  // divide
  int i = n;
  Sequence S1 = new NodeSequence();
  do { // move the first n/2 elements to S1
    S1.insertLast(S.remove(S.first()));
    i−−;
  } while (i > n/2);
  Sequence S2 = new NodeSequence();
  do { // move the remaining n/2 elements to S2
    S2.insertLast(S.remove(S.first()));
    i−−;
  } while (i > 0); // sequence S is now empty
  // recur
  mergeSort(S1,c);
  mergeSort(S2,c);
  //conquer
  merge(S1,S2,c,S);
}


/**
 * Merge two sorted sequences, S1 and S2, into a sorted sequence S.
 **/
public static void merge(Sequence S1, Sequence S2, Comparator c, Sequence S) {
  while(!S1.isEmpty() && !S2.isEmpty())
    if(c.isLessThanOrEqualTo(S1.first().element(), S2.first().element()))
      S.insertLast(S1.remove(S1.first()));
    else
      S.insertLast(S2.remove(S2.first()));
  while(!S1.isEmpty()) // move the remaining elements of S1
    S.insertLast(S1.remove(S1.first()));
  while(!S2.isEmpty()) // move the remaining elements of S2
    S.insertLast(S2.remove(S2.first()));
}
```

Code Fragment 10.2: Methods mergeSort and merge implementing the merge-sort algorithm.

10.1.3 Merge-Sort and Recurrence Relations ⋆

There is another way to justify that the running time of the merge-sort algorithm is $O(n \log n)$ (Proposition 10.3). Namely, there is a justification that deals more directly with the recursive nature of the merge-sort algorithm. In this section, we present such an analysis of the running time of merge-sort, and in so doing introduce the mathematical concept of a *recurrence relation*.

Let the function $t(n)$ denote the worst-case running time of merge-sort on an input sequence of size n. Since merge-sort is recursive, we can characterize function $t(n)$ by means of the following equalities, where function $t(n)$ is recursively expressed in terms of itself, as follows:

$$t(n) = \begin{cases} b & \text{if } n \leq 1 \\ t(\lceil n/2 \rceil) + t(\lfloor n/2 \rfloor) + cn & \text{otherwise} \end{cases}$$

where $b \geq 1$ and $c \geq 1$ are constants. A characterization of a function such as the one above is called a *recurrence relation*, since the function appears on both the left- and right-hand sides of the equal sign. Although such a characterization is correct and accurate, what we really desire is a big-Oh type of characterization of $t(n)$ that does not involve the function $t(n)$ itself (that is, we want a *closed-form* characterization of $t(n)$).

In order to provide a closed-form characterization of $t(n)$, let us restrict our attention to the case when n is a power of 2 (we leave as an exercise the problem of showing that our asymptotic characterization still holds in the general case). In this case, we can simplify the definition of $t(n)$ to

$$t(n) = \begin{cases} b & \text{if } n \leq 1 \\ 2t(n/2) + cn & \text{otherwise} \end{cases}$$

but, even so, we must still try to characterize this recurrence equation in a closed-form way. One way to do this is to iteratively apply this equation, assuming n is relatively large. For example, after one more application of this equation we can write a new recurrence for $t(n)$ as follows:

$$\begin{aligned} t(n) &= 2(2t(n/2^2) + (cn/2)) + cn \\ &= 2^2 t(n/2^2) + 2(cn/2) + cn \\ &= 2^2 t(n/2^2) + 2cn. \end{aligned}$$

If we apply the equation again, we get

$$t(n) = 2^3 t(n/2^3) + 3cn.$$

At this point, we see a pattern emerging, so that after applying this equation i times we get

$$t(n) = 2^i t(n/2^i) + icn.$$

The issue that remains, then, is to determine when to stop this process. To see when to stop, recall that we switch to the closed form $t(n) = b$ when $n \leq 1$, which will occur when $2^i = n$. In other words, this will occur when $i = \log n$. Making this substitution, then, yields

$$\begin{aligned}
t(n) &= 2^{\log n} t(n/2^{\log n}) + (\log n)cn \\
&= nt(1) + cn \log n \\
&= nb + cn \log n.
\end{aligned}$$

That is, we get an alternative justification of the fact that $t(n)$ is $O(n \log n)$.

In the next section we show how sorting and the merge algorithm can be used to implement an abstract data type for sets.

10.2 The Set ADT

In this section, we introduce the **set** ADT. A **set** is a container of distinct objects. That is, there are no duplicate elements in a set, and there is no explicit notion of keys or even an order. Even so, we include our discussion of sets here in a chapter on sorting, because sorting can play a vital role in efficient implementations of the operations of the set ADT.

First, we recall the mathematical definitions of the **union**, **intersection**, and **subtraction** of two sets A and B:

$$\begin{aligned}
A \cup B &= \{x : x \in A \text{ or } x \in B\}, \\
A \cap B &= \{x : x \in A \text{ and } x \in B\}, \\
A - B &= \{x : x \in A \text{ and } x \notin B\}.
\end{aligned}$$

Example 10.4: *Most Internet search engines store, for each word x in their dictionary database, a set, $W(x)$, of Web pages that contain x, where each Web page is identified by a unique Internet address. When presented with a query for a word x, such a search engine need only return the Web pages in the set $W(x)$, sorted according to some proprietary priority ranking of page "importance." But when presented with a two-word query for words x and y, such a search engine must first compute the intersection $W(x) \cap W(y)$, and then return the Web pages in the resulting set sorted by priority. Many search engines use the algorithm described in this section to perform this intersection.*

The fundamental methods of the set ADT, acting on a set A, are as follows:

union(B): Replace A with the union of A and B, that is, execute $A \leftarrow A \cup B$.
Input: Set; *Output:* None.

intersect(B): Replace A with the intersection of A and B, that is, execute $A \leftarrow A \cap B$.
Input: Set; *Output:* None.

subtract(B): Replace A with the difference of A and B, that is, execute $A \leftarrow A - B$.
Input: Set; *Output:* None.

We have defined the operations union, intersect, and subtract above so that they modify the contents of the set A involved. Alternatively, we could have defined these methods so that they not modify A but instead return a new set.

The java.util package includes a Set interface. It maintains the property that a set can contain no duplicate entries and it includes methods similar to those defined above. We show the correspondence between the methods of our minimalistic set ADT and the methods of the java.util.Set interface in Table 10.1.

Set ADT Methods	java.util.Set **Methods**
union(B)	addAll(Collection B)
intersect(B)	retainAll(Collection B)
subtract(B)	removeAll(Collection B)

Table 10.1: Correspondence between methods of the set ADT and of the java.util.Set interface. The latter supports several other methods as well.

10.2.1 A Simple Set Implementation

One of the simplest ways of implementing a set is to store its elements in an ordered sequence. Indeed, this implementation preference is implicit in the interface java.util.SortedSet, which extends java.util.Set and imposes an ordering on the contents of the set. Even if a comparator is not provided, the elements themselves may have a natural order relation defined on them. In general, it should always be possible to impose an order on the elements. For example, we could use the memory addresses of the objects. Therefore, let us consider implementing the set ADT with an ordered sequence (we consider other implementations in several exercises).

We implement each of the three fundamental set operations using a generic version of the merge algorithm that takes, as input, two sorted sequences representing the input sets and constructs a sequence representing the output set, be it the union, intersection, or subtraction of the input sets. The ordering for the two sequences can be based on any consistent ordering rule (that is, a total order), provided the same ordering rule is used for the two sets on which we wish to perform a union, intersection, or subtraction. We describe the generic merge algorithm in detail in Code Fragment 10.3.

Algorithm genericMerge(A, B):

    Input: Sets represented by sorted sequences A and B

    Output: Set represented by a sorted sequence C

    {We won't destroy A and B}

    let A' be a copy of A

    let B' be a copy of B

    while A' and B' are not empty **do**

        $a \leftarrow A'.\text{first}()$

        $b \leftarrow B'.\text{first}()$

        if $a < b$ **then**

            aIsLess(a, C)

            $A'.\text{removeFirst}()$

        else if $a = b$ **then**

            bothAreEqual(a, b, C)

            $A'.\text{removeFirst}()$

            $B'.\text{removeFirst}()$

        else

            bIsLess(b, C)

            $B'.\text{removeFirst}()$

    while A' is not empty **do**

        $a \leftarrow A'.\text{first}()$

        aIsLess(a, C)

        $A'.\text{removeFirst}()$

    while B' is not empty **do**

        $b \leftarrow B'.\text{first}()$

        bIsLess(b, C)

        $B'.\text{removeFirst}()$

Code Fragment 10.3: Generic merge algorithm, parametrized by methods aIsLess, bothAreEqual, and bIsLess, which determine the composition of the set C. Note that this algorithm does not modify the input sequences.

The generic merge method iteratively examines and compares the current elements a and b of sequences A and B, respectively, and finds out whether $a < b$, $a = b$, or $a > b$. Then, based on the outcome of this comparison, it determines whether it should copy one or none of the elements a and b to the end of the output sequence C. This determination is made based on the particular operation we are performing, be it a union, intersection, or subtraction.

For example, in a union operation, we copy the smaller of a and b to the output sequence, and, if they are equal, we copy just one (say a). This approach ensures that we will copy each element that is in one of the two sets, but we will not create duplicate entries. We specify the copy actions to perform using the *auxiliary methods* aIsLess, bothAreEqual, and bIsLess, which we define depending on the operation we wish to perform.

Generic Merging as a Template Method Pattern

The generic merge algorithm is based on the *template method pattern* (see Section 6.3.5). The template method pattern is a software engineering design pattern describing a generic computation mechanism that can be specialized by redefining certain steps. In this case we describe a method that merges two sequences into one and can be specialized by the behavior of three abstract methods.

Code Fragment 10.4 shows the class Merger providing a Java implementation of the generic merge algorithm. To convert the generic Merger class into useful classes, we must extend it with classes that redefine the three auxiliary methods, aIsLess, bothAreEqual, and bIsLess. We show how each of the operations of union, intersection, and subtraction can be easily described in terms of these methods in Code Fragment 10.5. The auxiliary methods are redefined so that the template method merge performs the following actions:

- In class UnionMerger, merge copies every element from A and B into C, but does not duplicate any element.
- In class IntersectMerger, merge copies every element that is in both A and B into C, but "throws away" any elements that is in one set but not in the other. In class SubtractMerger, merge copies every element that is in A but not in B into C.

We could also consider extending the set ADT, by adding methods such as insert and remove, for inserting and removing elements of a set. Such methods could be implemented in our sorted sequence approach by simple scans of the sequence representing a set, which can easily be done in $O(n)$ time, as we explore in an exercise (R-10.7).

```
/** Generic merge for sorted sequences. */
public abstract class Merger {
  private Object a, b;                    // current elements in A and B
  private ObjectIterator iterA, iterB;   // iterators for A and B
  /** Generic merge template method */
  public void merge(Sequence A, Sequence B, Comparator comp, Sequence C) {
    iterA = A.elements();
    iterB = B.elements();
    boolean aExists = advanceA();  // Boolean test if there is a current a
    boolean bExists = advanceB();  // Boolean test if there is a current b
    while (aExists && bExists) {   // Main loop for merging a and b
      if (comp.isLessThan(a, b)) {
        aIsLess(a, C);  aExists = advanceA();
      }
      else if (comp.isEqualTo(a, b)) {
        bothAreEqual(a, b, C);
        aExists = advanceA();  bExists = advanceB();
      } else {
        bIsLess(b, C);  bExists = advanceB();
      }
    }
    while (aExists) { aIsLess(a, C); aExists = advanceA(); }
    while (bExists) { bIsLess(b, C); bExists = advanceB(); }
  }
  // auxiliary methods to be specialized by subclasses
  protected void aIsLess(Object a, Sequence C) { }
  protected void bothAreEqual(Object a, Object b, Sequence C) { }
  protected void bIsLess(Object b, Sequence C) { }
  // helper methods
  private boolean advanceA() {
    if (iterA.hasNext()) {
      a = iterA.nextObject();
      return true;
    }
    return false;
  }
  private boolean advanceB() {
    if (iterB.hasNext()) {
      b = iterB.nextObject();
      return true;
    }
    return false;
  }
}
```

Code Fragment 10.4: Class Merger implementing the generic merge algorithm.

```java
/** Class specializing the generic merge template to union two sets */
public class UnionMerger extends Merger {
  protected void aIsLess(Object a, Sequence C) {
    C.insertLast(a);     // add a
  }
  protected void bothAreEqual(Object a, Object b, Sequence C) {
    C.insertLast(a);     // add a (but not its duplicate b)
  }
  protected void bIsLess(Object b, Sequence C) {
    C.insertLast(b);   // add b
  }
}

/** Class specializing the generic merge template to intersect two sets */
public class IntersectMerger extends Merger {
  protected void aIsLess(Object a, Sequence C) { }
  protected void bothAreEqual(Object a, Object b, Sequence C) {
    C.insertLast(a);     // add a (but not its duplicate b)
  }
  protected void bIsLess(Object b, Sequence C) { }
}

/** Class specializing the generic merge template to subtract two sets */
public class SubtractMerger extends Merger {
  protected void aIsLess(Object a, Sequence C) {
    C.insertLast(a);     // add a
  }
  protected void bothAreEqual(Object a, Object b, Sequence C) { }
  protected void bIsLess(Object b, Sequence C) { }
}
```

Code Fragment 10.5: Classes extending the Merger class by specializing the auxiliary methods to perform set union, intersection, and subtraction, respectively.

Performance of Generic Merging

Let us analyze the running time of the generic merge algorithm. At each iteration of one of the loops, an element is removed from A, B, or both. Assuming that comparisons take $O(1)$ time, and that each call to an auxiliary method takes $O(1)$ time, the total running time of genericMerge(A,B) is $O(n_A + n_B)$, where n_A is the size of A and n_B is the size of B; that is, merging takes time proportional to the number of elements involved. Thus, we have the following:

Proposition 10.5: *The set ADT can be implemented with an ordered sequence and a generic merge scheme that supports operations* union, intersect, *and* subtract *in $O(n)$ time, where n denotes the sum of sizes of the sets involved.*

10.3 Quick-Sort

The next sorting algorithm we discuss is called ***quick-sort***. Like merge-sort, this algorithm is also based on the ***divide-and-conquer*** paradigm, but it uses this technique in a somewhat opposite manner, as all the hard work is done ***before*** the recursive calls.

High-Level Description of Quick-Sort

The quick-sort algorithm sorts a sequence S using a simple recursive approach. The main idea is to apply the divide-and-conquer technique, whereby we divide S into subsequences, recur to sort each subsequence, and then combine the sorted subsequences by a simple concatenation. In particular, the quick-sort algorithm consists of the following three steps (see Figure 10.8):

1. ***Divide:*** If S has at least two elements (nothing needs to be done if S has zero or one element), select a specific element x from S, which is called the ***pivot***. As is common practice, choose the pivot x to be the last element in S. Remove all the elements from S and put them into three sequences:

   - L, storing the elements in S less than x
   - E, storing the elements in S equal to x
   - G, storing the elements in S greater than x.

   Of course, if the elements of S are all distinct, then E holds just one element—the pivot itself.

2. ***Recur:*** Recursively sort sequences L and G.
3. ***Conquer:*** Put back the elements into S in order by first inserting the elements of L, then those of E, and finally those of G.

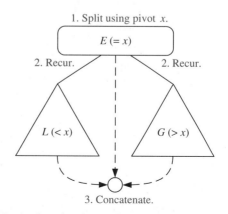

Figure 10.8: A visual schematic of the quick-sort algorithm.

Like merge-sort, the execution of quick-sort can be visualized by means of a binary recursion tree, called the **quick-sort tree**. Figure 10.9 summarizes an execution of the quick-sort algorithm by showing the input and output sequences processed at each node of the quick-sort tree. The step-by-step evolution of the quick-sort tree is shown in Figures 10.10, 10.11, and 10.12.

Unlike merge-sort, however, the height of the quick-sort tree associated with an execution of quick-sort is linear in the worst case. This happens, for example, if the sequence consists of n distinct elements and is already sorted. Indeed, in this case, the standard choice of the pivot as the largest element yields a subsequence L of size $n - 1$, while subsequence E has size 1 and subsequence G has size 0. At each invocation of quick-sort on subsequence L, the size decreases by 1. Hence, the height of the quick-sort tree is $n - 1$.

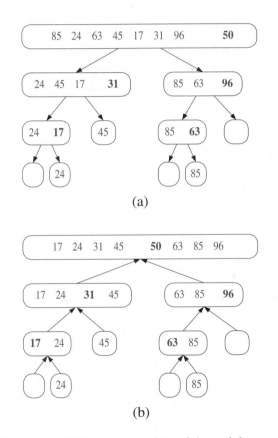

Figure 10.9: Quick-sort tree T for an execution of the quick-sort algorithm on a sequence with 8 elements: (a) input sequences processed at each node of T; (b) output sequences generated at each node of T. The pivot used at each level of the recursion is shown in bold.

Figure 10.10: Visualization of quick-sort. Each node of the tree represents a recursive call. The nodes drawn with dashed lines represent calls that have not been made yet. The node drawn with thick lines represents the running invocation. The empty nodes drawn with thin lines represent terminated calls. The remaining nodes represent suspended calls (that is, active invocations that are waiting for a child invocation to return). Note the divide steps performed in (b), (d), and (f). (Continues in Figure 10.11.)

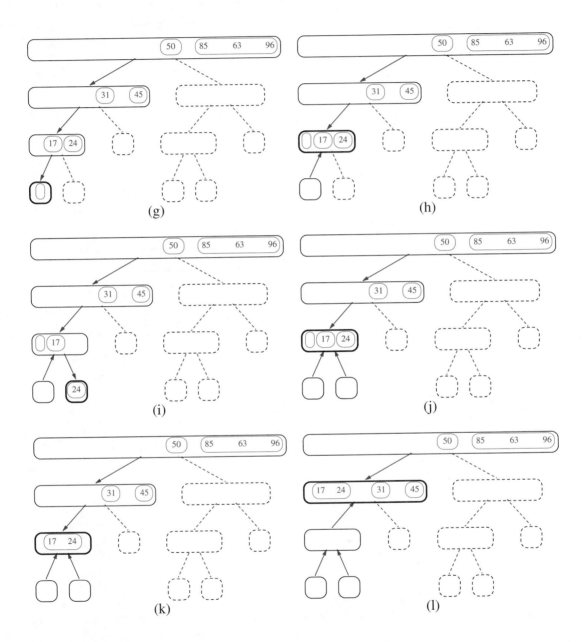

Figure 10.11: (Continued from Figure 10.10.) Visualization of an execution of quick-sort. Note the conquer step performed in (k).

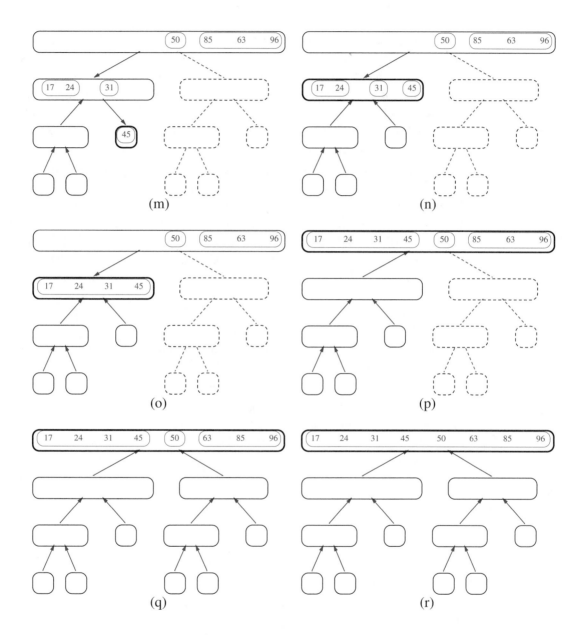

Figure 10.12: (Continued from Figure 10.11.) Visualization of an execution of quick-sort. Several invocations between (p) and (q) have been omitted. Note the conquer steps performed in (o) and (r).

10.3.1 In-Place Quick-Sort

Recall from Section 7.3.4 that a sorting algorithm is ***in-place*** if it uses only a constant amount of memory in addition to that needed for the objects being sorted themselves. The merge-sort algorithm, as we have described it above, is not in-place, and making it be in-place requires a more complicated merging method than the one we discuss in Section 10.1.1. In-place sorting is not inherently difficult, however. For, as with heap-sort, quick-sort can be adapted to be in-place.

Performing the quick-sort algorithm in-place requires a bit of ingenuity, however, for we must use the input sequence itself to store the subsequences for all the recursive calls. We show algortitm inPlaceQuickSort, which performs in-place quick-sort, in Code Fragment 10.6. Algorithm inPlaceQuickSort assumes that the inpt sequence, S, has distinct elements. The reason for this restriction is explored in Exercise R-10.11. The extension to the general case is discussed in Exercise C-10.7. The algorithm accesses the elements of the input sequence, S, with rank-based methods. Hence, it runs efficiently provided S is implemented with an array.

Algorithm inPlaceQuickSort(S, a, b):

   Input: Sequence S of distinct elements; integers a and b

   Output: Sequence S with elements originally from ranks from a to b, inclusive, sorted in nondecreasing order from ranks a to b

   if $a \geq b$ **then return**   {empty subrange}
   $p \leftarrow S.\text{elemAtRank}(b)$ {pivot}
   $l \leftarrow a$ {will scan rightward}
   $r \leftarrow b - 1$ {will scan leftward}
   while $l \leq r$ **do**
      {find an element larger than the pivot}
      while $l \leq r$ **and** $S.\text{elemAtRank}(l) \leq p$ **do**
         $l \leftarrow l + 1$
      {find an element smaller than the pivot}
      while $r \geq l$ **and** $S.\text{elemAtRank}(r) \geq p$ **do**
         $r \leftarrow r - 1$
      if $l < r$ **then**
         $S.\text{swapElements}(S.\text{atRank}(l), S.\text{atRank}(r))$
   {put the pivot into its final place}
   $S.\text{swapElements}(S.\text{atRank}(l), S.\text{atRank}(b))$
   {recursive calls}
   inPlaceQuickSort($S, a, l - 1$)
   inPlaceQuickSort($S, l + 1, b$)

Code Fragment 10.6: In-place quick-sort for a sequence implemented with an array.

In-place quick-sort modifies the input sequence using swapElements operations and does not explicitly create subsequences. Indeed, a subsequence of the input sequence is implicitly represented by a range of positions specified by a left-most rank *l* and a right-most rank *r*. The divide step is performed by scanning the sequence simultaneously from *l* forward and from *r* backward, swapping pairs of elements that are in reverse order, as shown in Figure 10.13. When these two indices "meet," subsequences *L* and *G* are on opposite sides of the meeting point. The algorithm completes by recursing on these two subsequences.

In-place quick-sort reduces the running time, caused by the creation of new sequences and the movement of elements between them, by a constant factor. We show a Java version of in-place quick-sort in Code Fragment 10.7.

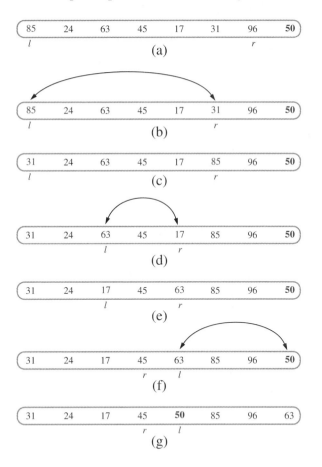

Figure 10.13: Divide step of in-place quick-sort. Index *l* scans the sequence from left to right, and index *r* scans the sequence from right to left. A swap is performed when *l* is at an element larger than the pivot and *r* is at an element smaller than the pivot. A final swap with the pivot completes the divide step.

```java
/**
 * Sort the elements of sequence S in nondecreasing order according
 * to comparator c, using the quick-sort algorithm. Most of the work
 * is done by the auxiliary recursive method quickSortStep.
 **/
public static void quickSort (Sequence S, Comparator c) {
  if (S.size() < 2)
    return; // a sequence with 0 or 1 element is already sorted
  quickSortStep(S, c, 0, S.size()-1); // recursive sort method
}

/**
 * Sort in nondecreasing order the elements of sequence S between
 * ranks leftBound and rightBound, using a recursive, in-place,
 * implementation of the quick-sort algorithm.
 **/
private static void quickSortStep (Sequence S, Comparator c,
                          int leftBound, int rightBound ) {
  if (leftBound >= rightBound)
    return;
  Object pivot = S.atRank(rightBound).element();
  int leftIndex = leftBound;       // will scan rightward
  int rightIndex = rightBound-1; // will scan leftward
  while (leftIndex <= rightIndex) {
    // scan rightward to find an element larger than the pivot
    while ( (leftIndex <= rightIndex) &&
        c.isLessThanOrEqualTo(S.atRank(leftIndex).element(), pivot) )
      leftIndex++;
    // scan leftward to find an element smaller than the pivot
    while ( (rightIndex >= leftIndex) &&
        c.isGreaterThanOrEqualTo(S.atRank(rightIndex).element(), pivot) )
      rightIndex--;
    if (leftIndex < rightIndex) // both elements were found
      S.swapElements(S.atRank(leftIndex), S.atRank(rightIndex));
  } // the loop continues until the indices cross
  // place the pivot by swapping it with the element at leftIndex
  S.swapElements(S.atRank(leftIndex), S.atRank(rightBound));
  // the pivot is now at leftIndex, so recur on both sides of it
  quickSortStep(S, c, leftBound, leftIndex-1);
  quickSortStep(S, c, leftIndex+1, rightBound);
}
```

Code Fragment 10.7: Java implementation of in-place quick-sort. It is assumed that the input sequence is implemented with an array and that it has distinct elements.

Unfortunately, the above implementation of quick-sort is, technically speaking, not quite in-place, as it still requires more than a constant amount of additional space. Of course, we are using no additional space for the subsequences, and we are using only a constant amount of additional space for local variables (such as *l* and *r*). So, where does this additional space come from? It comes from the recursion, for, recalling Section 4.1.3, we note that we need space for a stack proportional to the depth of the recursion tree for quick-sort, which is at least $\log n$ and at most $n - 1$. In order to make quick-sort truly in-place, we must implement it nonrecursively (and not use a stack). The key detail for such an implementation is that we need an in-place way of determining the bounds for the left and right boundaries of the "current" subsequence. Such a scheme is not too difficult, however, and we leave the details of this implementation to an exercise (C-10.5).

Running Time of Quick-Sort

We can analyze the running time of quick-sort with the same technique used for merge-sort in Section 10.1.1. Namely, we identify the time spent at each node of the quick-sort tree T (Figures 10.10, 10.11, and 10.12), and we sum up the running times for all the nodes.

The divide step and the conquer step of quick-sort are easy to implement in linear time. Thus, the time spent at a node v of T is proportional to the ***input size*** $s(v)$ of v, defined as the size of the sequence handled by the invocation of quick-sort associated with node v. Since subsequence E has at least one element (the pivot), the sum of the input sizes of the children of v is at most $s(v) - 1$.

Given a quick-sort tree T, let s_i denote the sum of the input sizes of the nodes at depth i in T. Clearly, $s_0 = n$, since the root r of T is associated with the entire sequence. Also, $s_1 \leq n - 1$, since the pivot is not propagated to the children of r. Consider next s_2. If both children of r have nonzero input size, then $s_2 = n - 3$. Otherwise (one child of the root has zero size, the other has size $n - 1$), $s_2 = n - 2$. Thus, $s_2 \leq n - 2$. Continuing this line of reasoning, we obtain that $s_i \leq n - i$. As observed in Section 10.3, the height of T is $n - 1$ in the worst case. Thus, the worst-case running time of quick-sort is

$$O\left(\sum_{i=0}^{n-1} s_i\right), \quad \text{which is} \quad O\left(\sum_{i=0}^{n-1}(n-i)\right) \quad \text{that is,} \quad O\left(\sum_{i=1}^{n} i\right).$$

By Proposition 3.4, $\sum_{i=1}^{n} i$ is $O(n^2)$. Thus, quick-sort runs in $O(n^2)$ worst-case time.

Given its name, we would expect quick-sort to run quickly. However, the above quadratic bound indicates that quick-sort is slow in the worst case. Paradoxically, this worst-case behavior occurs for problem instances when sorting should be easy—if the sequence is already sorted. Moreover, one can show that quick-sort performs poorly even if the sequence is "almost" sorted.

Going back to our analysis, note that the best case for quick-sort on a sequence of distinct elements occurs when subsequences L and G happen to have roughly the same size. Indeed, in this case we save one pivot at each internal node and make two equal-sized calls for its children. Thus, we save 1 pivot at the root, 2 at level 1, 2^2 at level 2, and so on. That is, in the best case, we have

$$
\begin{aligned}
s_0 &= n \\
s_1 &= n-1 \\
s_2 &= n-(1+2) = n-3 \\
&\vdots \\
s_i &= n-(1+2+2^2+\cdots+2^{i-1}) = n-(2^i-1) \\
&\vdots
\end{aligned}
$$

Thus, in the best case, T has height $O(\log n)$ and quick-sort runs in $O(n\log n)$ time; we leave the justification of this fact as an exercise (R-10.10).

The informal intuition behind the expected behavior of quick-sort is that at each invocation the pivot will probably divide the input sequence about equally. Thus, we expect the average running time quick-sort to be similar to the best-case running time, that is, $O(n\log n)$. We will see in the next section that introducing randomization makes quick-sort behave exactly as described above.

10.3.2 Randomized Quick-Sort

One common method for analyzing quick-sort is to assume that the pivot will always divide the sequence almost equally. We feel such an assumption would presuppose knowledge about the input distribution that is typically not available, however. For example, we would have to assume that we will rarely be given "almost" sorted sequences to sort, which are actually common in many applications. Fortunately, this assumption is not needed in order for us to match our intuition to quick-sort's behavior.

Since the goal of the partition step of the quick-sort method is to divide the sequence S almost equally, let us introduce randomization into the algorithm and pick as the pivot a ***random element*** of the input sequence. This variation of quick-sort is called ***randomized quick-sort***. The following proposition shows that the expected running time of randomized quick-sort on a sequence with n elements is $O(n\log n)$. This expectation is taken over all the possible random choices the algorithm makes, and is independent of any assumptions about the distribution of the possible input sequences the algorithm is likely to be given.

Proposition 10.6: *The expected running time of randomized quick-sort on a se-quence of size n is $O(n \log n)$.*

Justification: We make use of a simple fact from probability theory:

> *The expected number of times that a fair coin must be flipped until it shows "heads" k times is 2k.*

Consider now a single recursive invocation of randomized quick-sort, and let m denote the size of the input sequence for this invocation. Say that this invocation is "good" if the pivot chosen is such that subsequences L and G have size at least $m/4$ and at most $3m/4$ each. Thus, since the pivot is chosen uniformly at random and there are $m/2$ pivots for which this invocation is good, the probability that an invocation is good is $1/2$ (the same as the probability a coin comes up heads).

If a node v of the quick-sort tree T, as shown in Figure 10.14, is associated with a "good" recursive call, then the input sizes of the children of v are each at most $3s(v)/4$ (which is the same as $(s(v)/(4/3))$). If we take any path in T from the root to an external node, then the length of this path is at most the number of invocations that have to be made (at each node on this path) until achieving $\log_{4/3} n$ good invocations. Applying the probabilistic fact reviewed above, the expected number of invocations we must make until this occurs is $2\log_{4/3} n$. Thus, the expected length of any path from the root to an external node in T is $O(\log n)$. Recalling that the time spent at each level of T is $O(n)$, the expected running time of randomized quick-sort is $O(n \log n)$. ∎

Actually, by using powerful facts from probability, we can show that the running time of randomized quick-sort is $O(n \log n)$ with high probability. We leave this analysis as an exercise (C-10.7) for the more mathematically inclined reader.

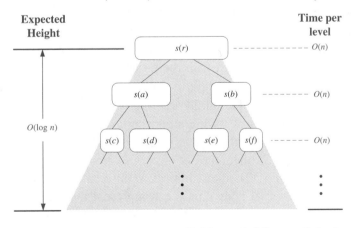

Total expected time: $O(n \log n)$

Figure 10.14: A visual time analysis of the quick-sort tree T.

10.4   A Lower Bound on Comparison-Based Sorting

Recapping our discussions on sorting to this point, we have described several methods with either a worst-case or expected running time of $O(n \log n)$ on an input sequence of size n. These methods include merge-sort and quick-sort, described in this chapter, as well as heap-sort, described in Section 7.3.4. A natural question to ask, then, is whether it is possible to sort any faster than in $O(n \log n)$ time.

In this section, we show that if the computational primitive used by a sorting algorithm is the comparison of two elements, then this is the best we can do—comparison-based sorting has an $\Omega(n \log n)$ worst-case lower bound on its running time. (Recall the notation $\Omega(\cdot)$ from Section 3.6.2.) To focus on the main cost of comparison-based sorting, let us only count the comparisons that a sorting algorithm performs. Since we want to derive a lower bound, this will be sufficient.

Suppose we are given a sequence $S = (x_0, x_1, \ldots, x_{n-1})$ that we wish to sort, and assume that all the elements of S are distinct (this is not a restriction since we are deriving a lower bound). Each time a sorting algorithm compares two elements x_i and x_j (that is, it asks, "is $x_i < x_j$?"), there are two outcomes: "yes" or "no." Based on the result of this comparison, the sorting algorithm may perform some internal calculations (which we are not counting here) and will eventually perform another comparison between two other elements of S, which again will have two outcomes. Therefore, we can represent a comparison-based sorting algorithm with a decision tree T (recall Example 6.4). That is, each internal node v in T corresponds to a comparison and the edges from node v' to its children correspond to the computations resulting from either a "yes" or "no" answer (see Figure 10.15).

It is important to note that the hypothetical sorting algorithm in question probably has no explicit knowledge of the tree T. We simply use T to represent all the possible sequences of comparisons that a sorting algorithm might make, starting from the first comparison (associated with the root) and ending with the last comparison (associated with the parent of an external node) just before the algorithm terminates its execution.

Each possible initial ordering, or ***permutation***, of the elements in S will cause our hypothetical sorting algorithm to execute a series of comparisons, traversing a path in T from the root to some external node. Let us associate with each external node v in T, then, the set of permutations of S that cause our sorting algorithm to end up in v. The most important observation in our lower-bound argument is that each external node v in T can represent the sequence of comparisons for at most one permutation of S. The justification for this claim is simple: if two different permutations P_1 and P_2 of S are associated with the same external node, then there are at least two objects x_i and x_j, such that x_i is before x_j in P_1 but x_i is after x_j

in P_2. At the same time, the output associated with v must be a specific reordering of S, with either x_i or x_j appearing before the other. But if P_1 and P_2 both cause the sorting algorithm to output the elements of S in this order, then that implies there is a way to trick the algorithm into outputting x_i and x_j in the wrong order. Since this cannot be allowed by a correct sorting algorithm, each external node of T must be associated with exactly one permutation of S. We use this property of the decision tree associated with a sorting algorithm to prove the following result:

Proposition 10.7: *The running time of any comparison-based algorithm for sorting an n-element sequence is $\Omega(n \log n)$ in the worst case.*

Justification: The running time of a comparison-based sorting algorithm must be greater than or equal to the height of the decision tree T associated with this algorithm, as described above. (See Figure 10.15.) By the above argument, each external node in T must be associated with one permutation of S. Moreover, each permutation of S must result in a different external node of T. The number of permutations of n objects is $n! = n(n-1)(n-2)\cdots 2 \cdot 1$. Thus, T must have at least $n!$ external nodes. By Proposition 6.10, the height of T is at least $\log(n!)$. This immediately justifies the proposition, because there are at least $n/2$ terms that are greater than or equal to $n/2$ in the product $n!$; hence

$$\log(n!) \ge \log\left(\frac{n}{2}\right)^{\frac{n}{2}} = \frac{n}{2}\log\frac{n}{2},$$

which is $\Omega(n \log n)$. ∎

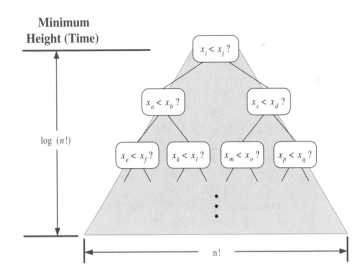

Figure 10.15: Visualizing the lower bound for comparison-based sorting.

10.5 Bucket-Sort and Radix-Sort

In the previous section, we show that $\Omega(n \log n)$ time is necessary, in the worst case, to sort an n-element sequence with a comparison-based sorting algorithm. A natural question to ask, then, is whether there are other kinds of sorting algorithms that can be designed to run asymptotically faster than $O(n \log n)$ time. Interestingly, such algorithms exist, but they require special assumptions about the input sequence to be sorted. Even so, such scenarios often arise in practice, so discussing them is worthwhile. In this section, we consider the problem of sorting a sequence of items, each a key-element pair.

10.5.1 Bucket-Sort

Consider a sequence S of n items whose keys are integers in the range $[0, N-1]$, for some integer $N \geq 2$, and suppose that S should be sorted according to the keys of the items. In this case, it is possible to sort S in $O(n+N)$ time. It might seem surprising, but this implies, for example, that if N is $O(n)$, then we can sort S in $O(n)$ time. Of course, the crucial point is that, because of the restrictive assumption about the format of the elements, we can avoid using comparisons.

The main idea is to use an algorithm called **bucket-sort**, which is not based on comparisons, but on using keys as indices into a bucket array B that has entries from 0 to $N-1$. An item with key k is placed in the "bucket" $B[k]$, which itself is a sequence (of items with key k). After inserting each item of the input sequence S into its bucket, we can put the items back into S in sorted order by enumerating the contents of the buckets $B[0], B[1], \ldots, B[N-1]$ in order. We describe the bucket-sort algorithm in Code Fragment 10.8.

Algorithm bucketSort(S):

    Input: Sequence S of items with integer keys in the range $[0, N-1]$
    Output: Sequence S sorted in nondecreasing order of the keys

    let B be an array of N sequences, each of which is initially empty
    for each item x in S **do**
        let k be the key of x
        remove x from S and insert it at the end bucket (sequence) $B[k]$
    for $i \leftarrow 0$ to $N-1$ **do**
        for each item x in sequence $B[i]$ **do**
            remove x from $B[i]$ and insert it at the end of S

Code Fragment 10.8: Bucket-sort.

It is easy to see that bucket-sort runs in $O(n+N)$ time and uses $O(n+N)$ space. Hence, bucket-sort is efficient when the range N of values for the keys is small compared to the sequence size n, say $N = O(n)$ or $N = O(n\log n)$. Still, its performance deteriorates as N grows compared to n.

An important property of the bucket-sort algorithm is that it works correctly even if there are many different elements with the same key. Indeed, we described it in a way that anticipates such occurrences.

Stable Sorting

When sorting key-element items, an important issue is how equal keys are handled. Let $S = ((k_0,e_0),\dots,(k_{n-1},e_{n-1}))$ be a sequence of items. We say that a sorting algorithm is **stable** if, for any two items (k_i,e_i) and (k_j,e_j) of S, such that $k_i = k_j$ and (k_i,e_i) precedes (k_j,e_j) in S before sorting (that is, $i < j$), item (k_i,e_i) also precedes item (k_j,e_j) after sorting. Stability is important for a sorting algorithm because applications may want to preserve the initial ordering of elements with the same key.

Our informal description of bucket-sort in Code Fragment 10.8 does not guarantee stability. This is not inherent in the bucket-sort method itself, however, for we can easily modify our description to make bucket-sort stable, while still preserving its $O(n+N)$ running time. Indeed, we can obtain a stable bucket-sort algorithm by always removing the *first* element from sequence S and from the sequences $B[i]$ during the execution of the algorithm.

10.5.2 Radix-Sort

One of the reasons that stable sorting is so important is that it allows the bucket-sort approach to be applied to more general contexts than to sort integers. Suppose, for example, that we want to sort items that are pairs (k,l), where k and l are integers in the range $[0,N-1]$, for some integer $N \geq 2$. In a context such as this, it is natural to define an ordering on these items using the **lexicographical** (dictionary) convention, where $(k_1,l_1) < (k_2,l_2)$ if $k_1 < k_2$ or if $k_1 = k_2$ and $l_1 < l_2$ (Section 7.1.4). This is a pair-wise version of the lexicographic comparison function, usually applied to equal-length character strings (and it easily generalizes to tuples of d numbers for $d > 2$).

The **radix-sort** algorithm sorts a sequence of pairs such as S, by applying a stable bucket-sort on the sequence twice; first using one component of the pair as the ordering key and then using the second component. But which order is correct? Should we first sort on the k's (the first component) and then on the l's (the second component), or should it be the other way around?

Before we answer this question, we consider the following example.

Example 10.8: *Consider the following sequence S:*

$$S = ((3,3),(1,5),(2,5),(1,2),(2,3),(1,7),(3,2),(2,2)).$$

If we sort S stably on the first component, then we get the sequence

$$S_1 = ((1,5),(1,2),(1,7),(2,5),(2,3),(2,2),(3,3),(3,2)).$$

If we then stably sort this sequence S_1 using the second component, then we get the sequence

$$S_{1,2} = ((1,2),(2,2),(3,2),(2,3),(3,3),(1,5),(2,5),(1,7)),$$

which is not exactly a sorted sequence. On the other hand, if we first stably sort S using the second component, then we get the sequence

$$S_2 = ((1,2),(3,2),(2,2),(3,3),(2,3),(1,5),(2,5),(1,7)).$$

If we then stably sort sequence S_2 using the first component, then we get the sequence

$$S_{2,1} = ((1,2),(1,5),(1,7),(2,2),(2,3),(2,5),(3,2),(3,3)),$$

which is indeed sequence S lexicographically ordered.

So, from this example, we are led to believe that we should first sort using the second component and then again using the first component. This intuition is exactly right. By first stably sorting by the second component and then again by the first component, we guarantee that if two elements are equal in the second sort (by the first component), then their relative order in the starting sequence (which is sorted by the second component) is preserved. Thus, the resulting sequence is guaranteed to be sorted lexicographically every time. We leave to a simple exercise (R-10.14) the determination of how this approach can be extended to triples and other d-tuples of numbers. We can summarize this section as follows:

Proposition 10.9: *Let S be a sequence of n key-element items, each of which has a key $(k_1, k_2, \ldots, k_d)$, where k_i is an integer in the range $[0, N-1]$ for some integer $N \geq 2$. We can sort S lexicographically in time $O(d(n+N))$ using radix-sort.*

As important as it is, sorting is not the only interesting problem dealing with a total order relation on a set of elements. There are some applications, for example, that do not require an ordered listing of an entire set, but nevertheless call for some amount of ordering information about the set. Before we study such a problem (called "selection"), let us step back and briefly compare all of the sorting algorithms we have studied so far.

10.6 Comparison of Sorting Algorithms

At this point, it might be useful for us to take a breath and consider all the algorithms we have studied in this book to sort an n-element sequence. We have studied several methods, such as bubble-sort, insertion-sort, and selection-sort, that have $O(n^2)$-time behavior in the average and worst case. We have also studied several methods with $O(n\log n)$-time behavior, including heap-sort, merge-sort, and quick-sort. Finally, we have studied a special class of sorting algorithms, namely, the bucket-sort and radix-sort methods, that run in linear time for certain types of keys. Certainly, the bubble-sort and selection-sort algorithms are poor choices in any application, since they run in $\Theta(n^2)$ time even in the best case. But, of the remaining sorting algorithms, which is the best?

As with many things in life, there is no clear "best" sorting algorithm from the remaining candidates. The sorting algorithm best suited for a particular application depends on several properties of that application. We can offer some guidance and observations, therefore, based on the known properties of the "good" sorting algorithms:

- If implemented well, the running time of **insertion-sort** is $O(n+k)$, where k is the number of inversions (that is, the number of pairs of elements out of order). Thus, insertion-sort is an excellent algorithm for sorting small sequences (say, less than 50 elements), because insertion-sort is simple to program, and small sequences necessarily have few inversions. Also, insertion-sort is quite effective for sorting sequences that are already "almost" sorted. By "almost," we mean that the number of inversions is small. But the $O(n^2)$-time performance of insertion-sort makes it a poor choice outside of these special contexts.

- **Merge-sort**, on the other hand, runs in $O(n\log n)$ time in the worst case, which is optimal for comparison-based sorting methods. Still, experimental studies have shown that, since it is difficult to make merge-sort run in-place, the overheads needed to implement merge-sort make it less attractive than the in-place implementations of heap-sort and quick-sort for sequences that can fit entirely in a computer's main memory area. Even so, merge-sort is an excellent algorithm for situations where the input cannot all fit into main memory, but must be stored in blocks on an external memory device, such as a disk. In these contexts, the way that merge-sort processes runs of data in long merge streams makes the best use of all the data brought into main memory in a block from disk. Thus, for external memory sorting, the merge-sort algorithm tends to minimize the total number of disk reads and writes needed, which makes the merge-sort algorithm superior in such contexts.

- Experimental studies have shown that if an input sequence can fit entirely in main memory, then the in-place versions of quick-sort and heap-sort run faster than merge-sort. In fact, quick-sort tends, on average, to beat heap-sort in these tests. So, *quick-sort* is an excellent choice as a general-purpose, in-memory sorting algorithm. Indeed, it is included in the qsort sorting utility provided in C language libraries. Still, its $O(n^2)$ time worst-case performance makes quick-sort a poor choice in real-time applications where we must make guarantees on the time needed to complete a sorting operation.
- In real-time scenarios where we have a fixed amount of time to perform a sorting operation and the input data can fit into main memory, the *heap-sort* algorithm is probably the best choice. It runs in $O(n\log n)$ worst-case time and can easily be made to execute in-place.
- Finally, if our application involves sorting by integer keys or d-tuples of integer keys, then *bucket-sort* or *radix-sort* is an excellent choice, for it runs in $O(d(n+N))$ time, where $[0, N-1]$ is the range of integer keys (and $d = 1$ for bucket sort). Thus, if $d(n+N)$ is "below" $n\log n$ (formally, $d(n+N)$ is $o(n\log n)$ using the little-oh notation from Section 3.6.2), then this sorting method should run faster than even quick-sort or heap-sort.

Thus, our study of all these different sorting algorithms provides us with a versatile collection of sorting methods in our algorithm engineering "toolbox."

10.7   Selection

There are a number of applications in which we are interested in identifying a single element in terms of its rank relative to an ordering of the entire set. Examples include identifying the minimum and maximum elements, but we may also be interested in, say, identifying the *median* element, that is, the element such that half of the other elements are smaller and the remaining half are larger. In general, queries that ask for an element with a given rank are called *order statistics*.

In this section, we discuss the general order-statistic problem of selecting the kth smallest element from an unsorted collection of n comparable elements. This is known as the *selection* problem. Of course, we can solve this problem by sorting the collection and then indexing into the sorted sequence at rank k. Using the best comparison-based sorting algorithms, this approach would take $O(n\log n)$ time, which is obviously an overkill for the cases where $k = 1$ or $k = n$ (or even $k = 2$, $k = 3$, $k = n-1$, or $k = n-5$), because we can easily solve the selection problem for these values of k in $O(n)$ time. Thus, a natural question to ask is whether we can achieve an $O(n)$ running time for all values of k (including the interesting case of finding the median, where $k = \lfloor n/2 \rfloor$).

10.7.1 Prune-and-Search

This may come as a small surprise, but we can indeed solve the selection problem in $O(n)$ time for any value of k. Moreover, the technique we use to achieve this result involves an interesting algorithmic design pattern. This design pattern is known as ***prune-and-search*** or ***decrease-and-conquer***. In applying this design pattern, we solve a given problem that is defined on a collection of n objects by pruning away a fraction of the n objects and recursively solving the smaller problem. When we have finally reduced the problem to one defined on a constant-sized collection of objects, then we solve the problem using some brute-force method. Returning back from all the recursive calls completes the construction. In some cases, we can avoid using recursion, in which case we simply iterate the prune-and-search reduction step until we can apply a brute-force method and stop. Incidentally, the binary search method described in Section 8.5.1 is an example of the prune-and-search design pattern.

10.7.2 Randomized Quick-Select

In applying the prune-and-search pattern to the selection problem, we can design a simple and practical method, called ***randomized quick-select***, for finding the kth smallest element in an unordered sequence of n elements on which a total order relation is defined. Randomized quick-select runs in $O(n)$ ***expected*** time, taken over all possible random choices made by the algorithm, and this expectation does not depend whatsoever on any randomness assumptions about the input distribution. We note though that randomized quick-select runs in $O(n^2)$ time in the ***worst-case*** time, the justification of which is left as an exercise (R-10.17). We also provide an exercise (C-10.23) for modifying randomized quick-select to get a ***deterministic*** selection algorithm that runs in $O(n)$ ***worst-case*** time. The existence of this deterministic algorithm is mostly of theoretical interest, however, since the constant factor hidden by the big-Oh notation is relatively large in this case.

Suppose we are given an unsorted sequence S of n comparable elements together with an integer $k \in [1, n]$. At a high level, the quick-select algorithm for finding the kth smallest element in S is similar in structure to the randomized quick-sort algorithm described in Section 10.3.2. We pick an element x from S at random and use this as a "pivot" to subdivide S into three subsequences L, E, and G, storing the elements of S less than x, equal to x, and greater than x, respectively. This is the prune step. Then, based on the value of k, we then determine which of these sets to recur on. Randomized quick-select is described in Code Fragment 10.9.

Algorithm quickSelect(S,k):

    Input: Sequence S of n comparable elements, and an integer $k \in [1,n]$

    Output: The kth smallest element of S

    if $n = 1$ **then**

        return the (first) element of S.

    pick a random element x of S

    remove all the elements from S and put them into three sequences:

- L, storing the elements in S less than x
- E, storing the elements in S equal to x
- G, storing the elements in S greater than x.

    if $k \leq |L|$ **then**

        quickSelect(L,k)

    else if $k \leq |L| + |E|$ **then**

        return x {each element in E is equal to x}

    else

        quickSelect($G, k - |L| - |E|$)   {note the new selection parameter}

Code Fragment 10.9: Randomized quick-select algorithm.

10.7.3   Analyzing Randomized Quick-Select ⋆

We mentioned above that the randomized quick-select algorithm runs in expected $O(n)$ time. Fortunately, justifying this claim requires only the simplest of probabilistic arguments. The main probabilistic fact that we use is the ***linearity of expectation***. This fact states that if X and Y are random variables and c is a number, then

$$E(X+Y) = E(X) + E(Y)$$

and

$$E(cX) = cE(X),$$

where we use $E(\mathcal{Z})$ to denote the expected value of the expression $\mathcal{Z}$.

Let $t(n)$ denote the running time of randomized quick-select on a sequence of size n. Since the randomized quick-select algorithm depends on the outcome of random events, its running time, $t(n)$, is a random variable. We are interested in bounding $E(t(n))$, the expected value of $t(n)$. Say that a recursive invocation of randomized quick-select is "good" if it partitions S, so that the size of L and G is at most $3n/4$. Clearly, a recursive call is good with probability $1/2$. Let $g(n)$ denote the number of consecutive recursive invocations (including the present one) before getting a good invocation. Then

$$t(n) \leq bn \cdot g(n) + t(3n/4),$$

where $b \geq 1$ is a constant (to account for the overhead of each call). We are, of course, focusing on the case where n is larger than 1, for we can easily characterize in a closed form that $t(1) = b$. Applying the linearity of expectation property to the general case, then, we get

$$E\left(t(n)\right) \leq E\left(bn \cdot g(n) + t(3n/4)\right) = bn \cdot E\left(g(n)\right) + E\left(t(3n/4)\right).$$

Since a recursive call is good with probability $1/2$, and whether a recursive call is good or not is independent of its parent call being good, the expected value of $g(n)$ is the same as the expected number of times we must flip a fair coin before it comes up "heads." This implies that $E(g(n)) = 2$. Thus, if we let $T(n)$ be a shorthand notation for $E(t(n))$ (the expected running time of the randomized quick-select algorithm), then we can write the case for $n > 1$ as

$$T(n) \leq T(3n/4) + 2bn.$$

As with the merge-sort recurrence relation, we would like to convert this relation into a closed form. To do this, let us again iteratively apply this equation assuming n is large. So, for example, after two iterative applications, we get

$$T(n) \leq T((3/4)^2 n) + 2b(3/4)n + 2bn.$$

At this point, we see that the general case is

$$T(n) \leq 2bn \cdot \sum_{i=0}^{\lceil \log_{4/3} n \rceil} (3/4)^i.$$

In other words, the expected running time of randomized quick-select is $2bn$ times the sum of a geometric progression whose base is a positive number less than 1. Thus, by Proposition 3.3 on geometric summations, we obtain the result that $T(n)$ is $O(n)$. To summarize, we have:

Proposition 10.10: *The expected running time of randomized quick-select on a sequence of size n is $O(n)$.*

As we mentioned earlier, there is a variation of quick-select that does not use randomization and runs in $O(n)$ worst-case time. Exercise C-10.23 walks the interested reader through the design and analysis of this algorithm.

10.8   Exercises

Reinforcement

R-10.1 Give a complete justification of Proposition 10.1.

R-10.2 In the merge-sort tree shown in Figures 10.2 through 10.5, some edges are drawn as arrows. What is the meaning of a downward arrow? How about an upward arrow?

R-10.3 Give a pseudo-code description of merge-sort that takes an array as its input and output, rather than a general sequence. (Note: You will probably need to use an auxiliary array as a "buffer.")

R-10.4 Show that the running time of the merge-sort algorithm on an n-element sequence is $O(n \log n)$, even when n is not a power of 2.

R-10.5 Suppose we are given two n-element sorted sequences A and B that should not be viewed as sets (that is, A and B may contain duplicate entries). Describe an $O(n)$-time method for computing a sequence representing the set $A \cup B$ (with no duplicates).

R-10.6 Show that $(X - A) \cup (X - B) = X - (A \cap B)$, for any three sets X, A, and B.

R-10.7 Provide pseudo-code descriptions for performing the insert and remove methods of the set ADT assuming we use sorted sequences to implement sets.

R-10.8 Suppose we modify the deterministic version of the quick-sort algorithm so that, instead of selecting the last element in an n-element sequence as the pivot, we choose the element at rank $\lfloor n/2 \rfloor$. What is the running time of this version of quick-sort on a sequence that is already sorted?

R-10.9 Consider again the modification of the deterministic version of the quick-sort algorithm so that, instead of selecting the last element in an n-element sequence as the pivot, we choose the element at rank $\lfloor n/2 \rfloor$. Describe the kind of sequence that would cause this version of quick-sort to run in $\Theta(n^2)$ time.

R-10.10 Show that the best-case running time of quick-sort on a sequence of size n with distinct elements is $O(n \log n)$.

R-10.11 Suppose that algorithm inPlaceQuickSort (Code Fragment 10.6) is executed on a sequence with duplicate elements. Show that, in this case, the algorithm correctly sorts the input sequence, but the result of the divide step may differ from the high-level description given in Section 10.3 and may result in inefficiencies. In particular, what happens in the partition step when there are elements equal to the pivot? Is the sequence E (storing the elements equal to the pivot) actually computed? Does the algorithm recur on the subsequences L and R, or on some other subsequences? What is the running time of the algorithm if all the elements of the input sequence are equal?

R-10.12 Give a pseudo-code description of the in-place version of quick-sort that is specialized to take an array as input, rather than a general sequence, and return that same array as output.

R-10.13 Which, if any, of the algorithms bubble-sort, heap-sort, merge-sort, and quick-sort are stable?

R-10.14 Describe a radix-sort method for lexicographically sorting a sequence S of triplets (k, l, m), where k, l, and m are integers in the range $[0, N-1]$, for some $N \geq 2$. How could this scheme be extended to sequences of d-tuples $(k_1, k_2, \ldots, k_d)$, where each k_i is an integer in the range $[0, N-1]$?

R-10.15 Is the bucket-sort algorithm in-place? Why or why not?

R-10.16 Give a pseudo-code description of an in-place quick-select algorithm.

R-10.17 Show that the worst-case running time of quick-select on an n-element sequence is $\Omega(n^2)$.

Creativity

C-10.1 Show how to implement method equals(B) on a set A (which tests whether $A = B$) in $O(|A| + |B|)$ time by means of a concrete class extending the Merger class, assuming A and B are implemented with sorted sequences.

C-10.2 Give a concrete class extending the Merger class for computing $A \oplus B$, which is the set of elements that are in A or B, but not in both.

C-10.3 Suppose that we implement the set ADT by representing each set using a balanced search tree. Describe and analyze algorithms for each of the methods in the set ADT.

C-10.4 Let A be a collection of objects. Describe an efficient method for converting A into a set. That is, remove all duplicates from A. What is the running time of this method?

C-10.5 Consider sets whose elements are (or can be mapped to) integers in the range $[0, N-1]$. A popular scheme for representing a set A of this type is by means of a Boolean vector, B, where we say that x is in A if and only if $B[x] = $ **true**. Since each cell of B can be represented with a single bit, B is sometimes referred to as a *bit vector*. Describe efficient algorithms for performing the union, intersection, and subtraction methods of the set ADT assuming this representation. What are the running times of these methods?

C-10.6★ Describe a nonrecursive, in-place version of the quick-sort algorithm. The algorithm should still be based on the same divide-and-conquer approach. (Hint: Think about how to "mark" the left and right boundaries of the current subsequence before making a recursive call from this one.)

C-10.7 Modify Algorithm inPlaceQuickSort (Code Fragment 10.6) to handle the general case efficiently when the input sequence, S, may have duplicate keys.

C-10.8★ Show that randomized quick-sort runs in $O(n \log n)$ time with probability $1 - 1/n^2$. (Hint: Use the *Chernoff bound* that states that if we flip a coin k times, then the probability that we get fewer than $k/16$ heads is less than $2^{-k/8}$.)

C-10.9 Suppose we are given a sequence S of n elements, each of which is colored red or blue. Assuming S is represented as an array, give an in-place method for ordering S so that all the blue elements are listed before all the red elements. Can you extend your approach to three colors?

C-10.10 Suppose we are given an n-element sequence S such that each element in S represents a different vote for class president, where each vote is given as an integer representing the student ID of the chosen candidate. Without making any assumptions about who is running or even how many candidates there are, design an $O(n \log n)$-time algorithm to see who wins the election S represents, assuming the candidate with the most votes wins.

C-10.11 Consider the voting problem from the previous exercise, but now suppose that we know the number $k < n$ of candidates running. Describe an $O(n \log k)$-time algorithm for determining who wins the election.

C-10.12 Show that any comparison-based sorting algorithm can be made to be stable, without affecting the asymptotic running time of this algorithm. (Hint: Change the way elements are compared with each other.)

C-10.13 Suppose we are given two sequences A and B of n elements, possibly containing duplicates, on which a total order relation is defined. Describe an efficient algorithm for determining if A and B contain the same set of elements (possibly in different orders). What is the running time of this method?

C-10.14 Suppose we are given a sequence S of n elements, each of which is an integer in the range $[0, n^2 - 1]$. Describe a simple method for sorting S in $O(n)$ time. (Hint: Think of alternate ways of viewing the elements.)

C-10.15 Let $S_1, S_2, \ldots, S_k$ be k different sequences whose elements have integer keys in the range $[0, N - 1]$, for some parameter $N \geq 2$. Describe an algorithm running in $O(n + N)$ time for sorting all the sequences (not as a union), where n denotes the total size of all the sequences.

C-10.16 Suppose we are given a sequence S of n elements, on which a total order relation is defined. Describe an efficient method for determining whether there are two equal elements in S. What is the running time of your method?

C-10.17 Let S be a sequence of n elements on which a total order relation is defined. An **inversion** in S is a pair of elements x and y such that x appears before y in S but $x > y$. Describe an algorithm running in $O(n \log n)$ time for determining the **number** of inversions in S. (Hint: Try to modify the merge-sort algorithm to solve this problem.)

C-10.18 Let S be a sequence of n elements on which a total order relation is defined. Describe a comparison-based method for sorting S in $O(n + k)$ time, where k is the number of inversions in S (recall the definition of inversion from the previous problem). (Hint: Think of an in-place version of the insertion-sort algorithm that, after an linear-time preprocessing step, only swaps elements that are inverted.)

C-10.19 Give a sequence of n integers with $\Omega(n^2)$ inversions. (Recall the definition of inversion from Exercise C-10.17.)

C-10.20 Let A and B be two sequences of n integers each. Given an integer m, describe an $O(n \log n)$-time algorithm for determining if there is an integer a in A and an integer b in B such that $m = a + b$.

C-10.21 Given a sequence S of n comparable elements, describe an efficient method for finding the $\lceil \sqrt{n} \rceil$ items whose rank in S is closest to that of the median. What is the running time of your method?

C-10.22 Bob has a set A of n nuts and a set B of n bolts, such that each nut in A has a unique matching bolt in B. Unfortunately, the nuts in A all look the same, and the bolts in B all look the same as well. The only kind of a comparison that Bob can make is to take a nut-bolt pair (a,b), such that $a \in A$ and $b \in B$, and test it to see if the threads of a are larger, smaller, or a perfect match with the threads of b. Describe an efficient algorithm for Bob to match up all of his nuts and bolts. What is the running time of this algorithm, in terms of nut-bolt tests that Bob must make?

C-10.23 This problem deals with the modification of the quick-select algorithm so as to make it deterministic yet still run in $O(n)$ time on an n-element sequence. The idea is to modify the way we choose the pivot so that it is chosen deterministically, not randomly, as follows:

> Partition the set S into $\lceil n/5 \rceil$ groups of size 5 each (except possibly for one group). Sort each little set and identify the median element in this set. From this set of $\lceil n/5 \rceil$ "baby" medians, apply the selection algorithm recursively to find the median of the baby medians. Use this element as the pivot and proceed as in the quick-select algorithm.

Show that this deterministic method runs in $O(n)$ time by answering the following questions (please ignore floor and ceiling functions if that simplifies the mathematics, for the asymptotics are the same either way):

a. How many baby medians are less than or equal to the chosen pivot? How many are greater than or equal to the pivot?

b. For each baby median less than or equal to the pivot, how many other elements are less than or equal to the pivot? Is the same true for those greater than or equal to the pivot?

c. Argue why the method for finding the deterministic pivot and using it to partition S takes $O(n)$ time.

d. Based on these estimates, write a recurrence relation that bounds the worst-case running time $t(n)$ for this selection algorithm (note that in the worst case there are two recursive calls—one to find the median of the baby medians and one to then recur on the larger of L and G).

e. Using this recurrence relation, show by induction that $t(n)$ is $O(n)$.

C-10.24 Show how a deterministic $O(n)$-time selection algorithm can be used to design a quick-sort-like sorting algorithm that runs in $O(n \log n)$ *worst-case* time on an n-element sequence.

C-10.25 Given an unsorted sequence S of n comparable elements, and an integer k, give an $O(n \log k)$ expected-time algorithm for finding the $O(k)$ elements that have rank $\lceil n/k \rceil$, $2\lceil n/k \rceil$, $3\lceil n/k \rceil$, and so on.

Projects

P-10.1 Implement a nonrecursive version of the merge-sort algorithm. Perform a series of benchmarking time trials to test whether this method does indeed run in $O(n \log n)$ time, and write a short report describing the code and the results of these trials.

P-10.2 Design and implement a stable version of the bucket-sort algorithm for sorting a sequence of n elements with integer keys taken from the range $[0, N-1]$, for $N \geq 2$. The algorithm should run in $O(n+N)$ time. Perform a series of benchmarking time trials to test whether this method does indeed run in this time, for various values of n and N, and write a short report describing the code and the results of these trials.

P-10.3 Implement merge-sort and deterministic quick-sort and perform a series of benchmarking tests to see which one is faster. Your tests should include sequences that are very "random" looking, as well as ones that are "almost" sorted. Write a short report describing the code and the results of these trials.

P-10.4 Implement deterministic and randomized versions of the quick-sort algorithm and perform a series of benchmarking tests to see which one is faster. Your tests should include sequences that are very "random" looking as well as ones that are "almost" sorted. Write a short report describing the code and the results of these trials.

P-10.5 Implement an in-place version of insertion-sort and an in-place version of quick-sort. Perform benchmarking tests to determine the range of values of n where quick-sort is on average better than insertion-sort.

P-10.6 Design and implement an animation for one of the sorting algorithms described in this chapter. Your animation should illustrate the key properties of this algorithm in an intuitive manner, and should be annotated with text or sound so as to explain this algorithm to someone unfamiliar with it. Write a short report describing this animation.

P-10.7 Implement the randomized quick-sort and quick-select algorithms. Design a series of benchmarking tests to test the relative speed of solving the selection problem either directly, by the quick-select method, or indirectly, by first sorting via the quick-sort method and then returning the element at the requested rank. Write a short report describing the code and the results of these trials.

P-10.8 Implement an extended set ADT that includes the methods union(B), intersect(B), subtract(B), size(), isEmpty(), plus the methods equals(B), contains(e), insert(e), and remove(e) with obvious meaning. You may use any representation you wish for sets, but your implementation must guarantee that no set contains any duplicate entries. Use a comparator, passed as an argument to a constructor, to test equality of elements.

Chapter Notes

Knuth's classic text on *Sorting and Searching* [60] contains an extensive history of the sorting problem and algorithms for solving it, starting with the census card sorting machines of the late 19th century. Huang and Langston [51] describe how to merge two sorted lists in-place in linear time. Our set ADT is derived from the set ADT of Aho, Hopcroft, and Ullman [5]. The standard quick-sort algorithm is due to Hoare [48]. A tighter analysis of randomized quick-sort can be found in the book by Motwani and Raghavan [79]. Gonnet and Baeza-Yates [41] provide experimental comparisons and theoretical analyses of a number of different sorting algorithms. The term "prune-and-search" comes originally from the computational geometry literature (such as in the work of Clarkson [22] and Megiddo [71, 72]). The term "decrease-and-conquer" is from Levitin [66].

Chapter
11

Text Processing

Document processing is rapidly becoming one of the dominant functions of computers. Computers are used to edit documents, to search documents, to transport documents over the Internet, and to display documents on printers and computer screens. Web "surfing" and Web searching are becoming significant and important computer applications, and many of the key computations in all of this document processing involve character strings and string pattern matching. For example, the Internet document formats HTML and XML are primarily text formats, with added tags for multimedia content. Making sense of the many terabytes of information on the Internet requires a considerable amount of text processing.

In this chapter, we study several of the fundamental text processing algorithms for quickly performing important string operations. We pay particular attention to algorithms for string searching and pattern matching, since these can often be computational bottlenecks in many document-processing applications. We also study some fundamental data structure and algorithmic issues involved in text processing, as well.

The progression of topics studied in this chapter continues to follow our abstract data type approach. The terminology and notation for the string ADT, which is used in this chapter, is defined in Section 11.1. It turns out that representing a string as an array of characters is quite simple and efficient, so we don't spend a lot of attention on string representations. Nevertheless, the string ADT includes an interesting method for string pattern matching, and we study pattern matching algorithms in Section 11.2. In Section 11.3 we study the trie data structure, which is a tree-based structure that allows for fast searching in a collection of strings. We study an important text processing problem in Section 11.4, namely, the problem of compressing a document of text so that it fits more efficiently in storage or can be transmitted more efficiently over a network. We study another text processing problem in Section 11.5, which deals with how we can measure the similarity between two documents. All of these problems are topics that arise often in Internet computations, such as Web crawlers, search engines, document distribution, and information retrieval.

In addition to having interesting applications, the topics of this chapter also highlight some important algorithmic design patterns. In particular, in the section on pattern matching, we discuss the ***brute-force method***, which is often inefficient but has wide applicability. For text compression we study the ***greedy method***, which often allows us to approximate solutions to hard problems, and for some problems (such as in text compression) actually gives rise to optimal algorithms. Finally, in discussing text similarity, we introduce the ***dynamic programming*** design pattern, which can be applied in some special instances to solve a problem in polynomial time that appears at first to require exponential time to solve.

11.1 String Operations

At the heart of algorithms for processing text are methods for dealing with character strings. Character strings can come from a wide variety of sources, including scientific, linguistic, and Internet applications. Indeed, the following are examples of such strings:

$$P = \text{"CGTAAACTGCTTTAATCAAACGC"}$$
$$R = \text{"U.S. Men Win Soccer World Cup!"}$$
$$S = \text{"http://www.wiley.com/college/cs2java/"}.$$

The first string, P, comes from DNA applications, the last string, S, is the Internet address (URL) for the Web site that accompanies this book, and the middle string, R, is a fictional news headline. In this section, we present some of the useful operations that are supported by the string ADT for processing strings such as these.

Several of the typical string processing operations involve breaking large strings into smaller strings. In order to be able to speak about the pieces that result from such operations, we use the term ***substring*** of an m-character string P to refer to a string of the form $P[i]P[i+1]P[i+2]\cdots P[j]$, for some $0 \le i \le j \le m-1$, that is, the string formed by the characters in P from index i to index j, inclusive. Technically, this means that a string is actually a substring of itself (taking $i = 0$ and $j = m-1$), so if we want to rule this out as a possibility, we must restrict the definition to ***proper*** substrings, which require that either $i > 0$ or $j < m-1$. To simplify the notation for referring to substrings, let us use $P[i..j]$ to denote the substring of P from index i to index j, inclusive. That is,

$$P[i..j] = P[i]P[i+1]\cdots P[j].$$

We use the convention that if $i > j$, then $P[i..j]$ is equal to the ***null string***, which has length 0. In addition, in order to distinguish some special kinds of substrings, let us refer to any substring of the form $P[0..i]$, for $0 \le i \le m-1$, as a ***prefix*** of P, and any substring of the form $P[i..m-1]$, for $0 \le i \le m-1$, as a ***suffix*** of P. For example, if we again take P to be the string of DNA given above, then "CGTAA" is a prefix of P, "CGC" is a suffix of P, and "TTAATC" is a (proper) substring of P. Note that the null string is a prefix and a suffix of any other string.

String operations come in two flavors: those that modify the string they act on and those that simply return information about the string without actually modifying it. Java makes this distinction precise by defining the String class to represent ***immutable strings***, which cannot be modified, and the StringBuffer class to represent ***mutable strings***, which can be modified.

11.1.1 The Java String Class

The main operations of the Java String class are listed below:

length(): Return the length, n, of S.
Input: None; *Output:* **int**.

charAt(i): Return the character at index i in S.
Input: **int**; *Output:* **char**.

startsWith(Q): Determine if Q is a prefix of S.
Input: String; *Output:* **boolean**.

endsWith(Q): Determine if Q is a suffix of S.
Input: String; *Output:* **boolean**.

substring(i, j): Return the substring $S[i, j]$.
Input: **int** (i) and **int** (j); *Output:* String.

concat(Q): Return the concatenation of S and Q, that is, $S + Q$.
Input: String; *Output:* String.

equals(Q): Determine if Q is equal to S.
Input: String; *Output:* **boolean**.

indexOf(Q): If Q is a substring of S, return the index of the beginning of the first occurrence of Q in S, else return -1.
Input: String; *Output:* **int**.

This collection forms the typical operations for immutable strings.

Example 11.1: *Consider the following set of operations, which are performed on the string $S =$ "abcdefghijklmnop":*

Operation	*Output*
length()	16
charAt(5)	'f'
concat("qrs")	"abcdefghijklmnopqrs"
endsWith("javapop")	**false**
equals("abcdefghijklmnop")	**true**
indexOf("ghi")	6
startsWith("abcd")	**true**
substring(4,9)	"efghij"

With the exception of the indexOf(Q) method, which we discuss in Section 11.2, all the above methods are easily implemented simply by representing the string as an array of characters, which is the standard String implementation in Java.

11.1.2 The Java StringBuffer Class

The main methods of the Java StringBuffer class are listed below:

append(Q): Return $S + Q$, replacing S with $S + Q$.
Input: String; *Output:* StringBuffer.

insert(i, Q): Return and update S to be the string obtained by inserting Q inside S starting at index i.
Input: String; *Output:* StringBuffer.

reverse(): Reverse and return the string S.
Input: None; *Output:* StringBuffer.

setCharAt(i, ch): Set the character at index i in S to be ch.
Input: **int** (i) and **char** (ch); *Output:* None.

charAt(i): Return the character at index i in S.
Input: **int**; *Output:* **char**.

Error conditions occur when the index i is out of the bounds of the indices of the string. With the exception of the charAt method, most of the methods of the String class are not immediately available to a StringBuffer object S in Java.

Caution | Fortunately, the Java StringBuffer class provides a toString() method that returns a String version of S, which can be used to access String methods.

Example 11.2: *Consider the following sequence of operations, which are performed on the mutable string that is initially* $S =$ `"abcdefghijklmnop"`:

Operation	S
append*("qrs")*	`"abcdefghijklmnopqrs"`
insert*(3,"xyz")*	`"abcxyzdefghijklmnopqrs"`
reverse*()*	`"srqponmlkjihgfedzyxcba"`
setCharAt*(7,'W')*	`"srqponmWkjihgfedzyxcba"`

Incidentally, we have not given an exhaustive listing of all methods supported by String and StringBuffer objects in Java, but the methods included above should be sufficient for most applications, such as use in instance variables. Thus, let us view the methods of the String class as defining an immutable string ADT, and let us view the methods of the StringBuffer as adding to this ADT to define a mutable string ADT.

11.2   Pattern Matching Algorithms

In the classic ***pattern matching*** problem on strings, we are given a ***text*** string T of length n and a ***pattern*** string P of length m, and want to find whether P is a substring of T. The notion of a "match" is that there is a substring of T starting at some index i that matches P, character by character, so that $T[i] = P[0]$, $T[i+1] = P[1]$, ..., $T[i+m-1] = P[m-1]$. That is, $P = T[i..i+m-1]$. Thus, the output from a pattern matching algorithm could either be some indication that the pattern P does not exist in T or an integer indicating the starting index in T of a substring matching P. This is exactly the computation performed by the indexOf method of the Java String interface. Alternatively, one may want to find all the indices where a substring of T matching P begins.

To allow for fairly general notions of a character string, we typically do not restrict the characters in T and P to explicitly come from a well-known character set, like the ASCII or Unicode character sets. Instead, we typically use the general symbol Σ to denote the character set, or ***alphabet***, from which characters in T and P can come. This alphabet Σ can, of course, be a subset of the ASCII or Unicode character sets, but it could also be something more general and is even allowed to be infinite, like positive integers. Nevertheless, since most document processing algorithms are used in applications where the underlying character set is finite, we usually assume that the size of the alphabet Σ, denoted with $|\Sigma|$, is a fixed finite constant.

In this section, we present three pattern matching algorithms (with increasing levels of difficulty).

11.2.1   Brute Force

The ***brute force*** algorithmic design pattern is a powerful technique for algorithm design when we have something we wish to search for or when we wish to optimize some function. In applying this technique in a general situation we typically enumerate all possible configurations of the inputs involved and pick the best of all these enumerated configurations.

Brute-Force Pattern Matching

In applying this technique to design the ***brute-force pattern matching*** algorithm, we derive what is probably the first algorithm that we might think of for solving the pattern matching problem—we simply test all the possible placements of P relative to T. This algorithm, shown in Code Fragment 11.1, is quite simple.

Algorithm BruteForceMatch(T, P):

    Input: Strings T (text) with n characters and P (pattern) with m characters

    Output: Starting index of the first substring of T matching P, or an indication that P is not a substring of T

    for $i \leftarrow 0$ **to** $n - m$ {for each candidate index in T} **do**
        $j \leftarrow 0$
        while $(j < m$ **and** $T[i + j] = P[j])$ **do**
            $j \leftarrow j + 1$
        if $j = m$ **then**
            return i
    return "There is no substring of T matching P."

Code Fragment 11.1: Brute-force pattern matching.

The brute-force pattern matching algorithm could not be simpler. It consists of two nested loops, with the outer loop indexing through all possible starting indices of the pattern in the text, and the inner loop indexing through each character of the pattern, comparing it to its potentially corresponding character in the text. Thus, the correctness of the brute-force pattern matching algorithm follows immediately from this exhaustive search approach.

Performance

The running time of brute-force pattern matching in the worst case is not good, however, because, for each candidate index in T, we can perform up to m character comparisons to discover that P does not match T at the current index. Referring to Code Fragment 11.1, we see that the outer for-loop is executed at most $n - m + 1$ times, and the inner loop is executed at most m times. Thus, the running time of the brute-force method is $O((n - m + 1)m)$, which is simplified as $O(nm)$. Thus, in the worst case, when n and m are roughly equal, this algorithm has a quadratic running time.

Example 11.3: *Suppose we are given the text string*

$$T = \texttt{"abacaabaccabacabaabb"}$$

and the pattern string

$$P = \texttt{"abacab"}.$$

In Figure 11.1 we illustrate the execution of the brute-force pattern matching algorithm on T and P.

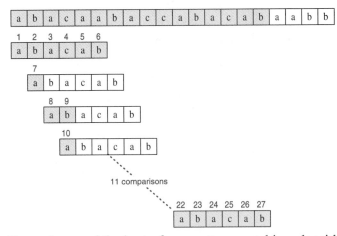

Figure 11.1: Example run of the brute-force pattern matching algorithm. The algorithm performs 27 character comparisons, indicated above with numerical labels.

11.2.2   The Boyer-Moore Algorithm

At first, we might feel that it is always necessary to examine every character in T in order to locate a pattern P as a substring. But this is not always the case, for the **Boyer-Moore** (**BM**) pattern matching algorithm, which we study in this section, can sometimes avoid comparisons between P and a sizable fraction of the characters in T. The only caveat is that, whereas the brute-force algorithm can work even with a potentially unbounded alphabet, the BM algorithm assumes the alphabet is of fixed, finite size. It works the fastest when the alphabet is moderately sized and the pattern is relatively long. Thus, the BM algorithm is ideal for searching words in documents. In this section, we describe a simplified version of the original algorithm by Boyer and Moore.

The main idea of the BM algorithm is to improve the running time of the brute-force algorithm by adding two potentially time-saving heuristics. Roughly stated, these heuristics are as follows:

Looking-Glass Heuristic: When testing a possible placement of P against T, begin the comparisons from the end of P and move backward to the front of P.

Character-Jump Heuristic: During the testing of a possible placement of P against T, a mismatch of text character $T[i] = c$ with the corresponding pattern character $P[j]$ is handled as follows. If c is not contained anywhere in P, then shift P completely past $T[i]$ (for it cannot match any character in P). Otherwise, shift P until an occurrence of character c in P gets aligned with $T[i]$.

We will formalize these heuristics shortly, but at an intuitive level, they work as an integrated team. The looking-glass heuristic sets up the other heuristic to allow us to avoid comparisons between P and whole groups of characters in T. In this case at least, we can get to the destination faster by going backwards, for if we encounter a mismatch during the consideration of P at a certain location in T, then we are likely to avoid lots of needless comparisons by significantly shifting P relative to T using the character-jump heuristic. The character-jump heuristic pays off big if it can be applied early in the testing of a potential placement of P against T.

Let us therefore get down to the business of defining how the character-jump heuristics can be integrated into a string pattern matching algorithm. To implement this heuristic, we define a function $\text{last}(c)$ that takes a character c from the alphabet and characterizes how far we may shift the pattern P if a character equal to c is found in the text that does not match the pattern. In particular, we define $\text{last}(c)$ as

- If c is in P, $\text{last}(c)$ is the index of the last (right-most) occurrence of c in P. Otherwise, we conventionally define $\text{last}(c) = -1$.

If characters can be used as indices in arrays, then the last function can be easily implemented as a look-up table. We leave the method for computing this table in $O(m + |\Sigma|)$ time, given P, as a simple exercise (R-11.6). This last function will give us all the information we need to perform the character-jump heuristic.

In Code Fragment 11.2, we show the BM pattern matching algorithm.

Algorithm $\text{BMMatch}(T, P)$:

> *Input:* Strings T (text) with n characters and P (pattern) with m characters
> *Output:* Starting index of the first substring of T matching P, or an indication that P is not a substring of T

> compute function last
> $i \leftarrow m - 1$
> $j \leftarrow m - 1$
> **repeat**
>   **if** $P[j] = T[i]$ **then**
>   **if** $j = 0$ **then**
>   **return** i {a match!}
>   **else**
> $i \leftarrow i - 1$
> $j \leftarrow j - 1$
>   **else**
> $i \leftarrow i + m - \min(j, 1 + \text{last}(T[i]))$ { jump step }
> $j \leftarrow m - 1$
> **until** $i > n - 1$
> **return** "There is no substring of T matching P."

Code Fragment 11.2: The Boyer-Moore pattern matching algorithm.

The jump step is illustrated in Figure 11.2. In Figure 11.3, we illustrate the execution of the Boyer-Moore pattern matching algorithm on a similar input string as in Example 11.3.

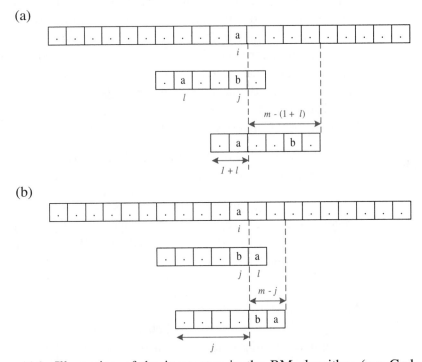

Figure 11.2: Illustration of the jump step in the BM algorithm (see Code Fragment 11.2), where we use the notation $l = \text{last}(T[i])$. We distinguish two cases: (a) $1 + l \leq j$, where we shift the pattern by $j - l$ units; (b) $j < 1 + l$, where we shift the pattern by one unit.

The correctness of the BM pattern matching algorithm follows from the fact that each time the method makes a shift, it is guaranteed not to "skip" over any possible matches. For $\text{last}(c)$ is the location of the *last* occurrence of c in P.

The worst-case running time of the BM algorithm is $O(nm + |\Sigma|)$. Namely, the computation of the last function takes time $O(m + |\Sigma|)$ and the actual search for the pattern takes $O(nm)$ time in the worst case, the same as the brute-force algorithm. An example of a text-pattern pair that achieves the worst case is

$$T = \overbrace{aaaaaa \cdots a}^{n}$$
$$P = b\overbrace{aa \cdots a}^{m-1}.$$

The worst-case performance, however, is unlikely to be achieved for English text.

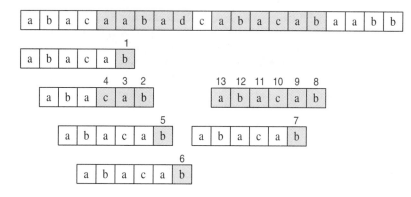

The last(c) function:

c	a	b	c	d
last(c)	4	5	3	−1

Figure 11.3: An illustration of the BM pattern matching algorithm. The algorithm performs 13 character comparisons, which are indicated with numerical labels.

Indeed, the BM algorithm is often able to skip over large portions of the text. (See Figure 11.4.) There is experimental evidence that on English text, the average number of comparisons done per text character is approximately 0.24 for a five-character pattern string. The payoff is not as great for binary strings or for very short patterns, however, in which case the KMP algorithm, discussed in Section 11.2.3, or, for very short patterns, the brute-force algorithm, may be better.

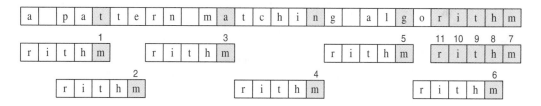

Figure 11.4: Execution of the Boyer-Moore algorithm on an English text and pattern, where a significant speedup is achieved. Note that not all text characters are examined.

A Java implementation of the BM pattern matching algorithm is shown in Code Fragment 11.3.

```
/** Simplified version of the Boyer-Moore (BM) algorithm, which uses
 * only the looking-glass and character-jump heuristics.
 * @return Index of the beginning of the leftmost substring of the text
 * matching the pattern, or -1 if there is no match.  */
public static int BMmatch (String text, String pattern) {
  int[] last = buildLastFunction(pattern);
  int n = text.length();
  int m = pattern.length();
  int i = m −1;
  if (i > n − 1)
    return −1; // no match if pattern is longer than text
  int j = m − 1;
  do {
    if (pattern.charAt(j) == text.charAt(i))
      if (j == 0)
        return i; // match
      else { // looking-glass heuristic: proceed right-to-left
        i−−;
        j−−;
      }
    else { // character jump heuristic
      i = i + m − Math.min(j, 1 + last[text.charAt(i)]);
      j = m − 1;
    }
  } while (i <= n − 1);
  return −1; // no match
}
/** Computation of the auxiliary function used in the BM algorithm.
 * @return Array of size 128 storing the index of the last
 * occurrence of each ASCII character in the pattern.  */
public static int[] buildLastFunction (String pattern) {
  int[] last = new int[128]; // assume ASCII character set
  for (int i = 0; i < 128; i++) {
    last[i] = −1; // initialize array
  }
  for (int i = 0; i < pattern.length(); i++) {
    last[pattern.charAt(i)] = i; // implicit cast to integer ASCII code
  }
  return last;
}
```

Code Fragment 11.3: Java implementation of the BM pattern matching algorithm. The algorithm is expressed by two static methods: method BMmatch performs the matching and calls the auxiliary method buildLastFunction to compute the last function, expressed by an array indexed by the ASCII code of the character. Method BMmatch indicates the absence of a match by returning the conventional value −1.

We have actually presented a simplified version of the Boyer-Moore (BM) algorithm. The original BM algorithm achieves running time $O(n + m + |\Sigma|)$ by using an alternative shift heuristic to the partially matched text string, whenever it shifts the pattern more than the character-jump heuristic. This alternative shift heuristic is based on applying the main idea from the Knuth-Morris-Pratt pattern matching algorithm, which we discuss next.

11.2.3 The Knuth-Morris-Pratt Algorithm

In studying the worst-case performance of the brute-force and BM pattern matching algorithms on specific instances of the problem, such as that given in Example 11.3, we should notice a major inefficiency. Specifically, we may perform many comparisons while testing a potential placement of the pattern against the text, yet if we discover a pattern character that does not match in the text, then we throw away all the information gained by these comparisons and start over again from scratch with the next incremental placement of the pattern. The Knuth-Morris-Pratt (or "KMP") algorithm, discussed in this section, avoids this waste of information and, in so doing, it achieves a running time of $O(n + m)$, which is optimal in the worst case. That is, in the worst case any pattern matching algorithm will have to examine all the characters of the text and all the characters of the pattern at least once.

The Failure Function

The main idea of the KMP algorithm is to preprocess the pattern string P so as to compute a ***failure function*** f that indicates the proper shift of P so that, to the largest extent possible, we can reuse previously performed comparisons. Specifically, the failure function $f(j)$ is defined as the length of the longest prefix of P that is a suffix of $P[1..j]$ (note that we did ***not*** put $P[0..j]$ here). We also use the convention that $f(0) = 0$. Later, we will discuss how to compute the failure function efficiently. The importance of this failure function is that it "encodes" repeated substrings inside the pattern itself.

Example 11.4: *Consider the pattern string $P =$ "abacab" from Example 11.3. The Knuth-Morris-Pratt (KMP) failure function $f(j)$ for the string P is as shown in the following table:*

j	0	1	2	3	4	5
$P[j]$	a	b	a	c	a	b
$f(j)$	0	0	1	0	1	2

The KMP pattern matching algorithm, shown in Code Fragment 11.4, incrementally processes the text string T comparing it to the pattern string P. Each time there is a match, we increment the current indices. On the other hand, if there is a mismatch and we have previously made progress in P, then we consult the failure function to determine the new index in P where we need to continue checking P against T. Otherwise (there was a mismatch and we are at the beginning of P), we simply increment the index for T (and keep the index variable for P at its beginning). We repeat this process until we find a match of P in T or the index for T reaches n, the length of T (indicating that we did not find the pattern P in T).

Algorithm KMPMatch(T, P):

   Input: Strings T (text) with n characters and P (pattern) with m characters

   Output: Starting index of the first substring of T matching P, or an indication that P is not a substring of T

   $f \leftarrow$ KMPFailureFunction(P)   {construct the failure function f for P}
   $i \leftarrow 0$
   $j \leftarrow 0$
   while $i < n$ **do**
      if $P[j] = T[i]$ **then**
         if $j = m - 1$ **then**
            return $i - m + 1$ {a match!}
         $i \leftarrow i + 1$
         $j \leftarrow j + 1$
      else if $j > 0$ {no match, but we have advanced in P} **then**
         $j \leftarrow f(j - 1)$ {j indexes just after prefix of P that must match}
      else
         $i \leftarrow i + 1$
   return "There is no substring of T matching P."

Code Fragment 11.4: The KMP pattern matching algorithm.

The main part of the KMP algorithm is the while-loop, which performs a comparison between a character in T and a character in P each iteration. Depending upon the outcome of this comparison, the algorithm either moves on to the next characters in T and P, consults the failure function for a new candidate character in P, or starts over with the next index in T. The correctness of this algorithm follows from the definition of the failure function. Any comparisons that are skipped are actually unnecessary, for the failure function guarantees that all the ignored comparisons are redundant—they would involve comparing the same matching characters over again.

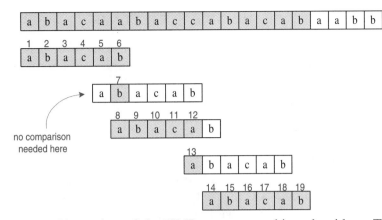

Figure 11.5: An illustration of the KMP pattern matching algorithm. The failure function *f* for this pattern is given in Example 11.4. The algorithm performs 19 character comparisons, which are indicated with numerical labels.

In Figure 11.5, we illustrate the execution of the KMP pattern matching algorithm on the same input strings as in Example 11.3. Note the use of the failure function to avoid redoing one of the comparisons between a character of the pattern and a character of the text. Also note that the algorithm performs fewer overall comparisons than the brute-force algorithm run on the same strings (Figure 11.1).

Performance

Excluding the computation of the failure function, the running time of the KMP algorithm is clearly proportional to the number of iterations of the while-loop. For the sake of the analysis, let us define $k = i - j$. Intuitively, k is the total amount by which the pattern P has been shifted with respect to the text T. Note that throughout the execution of the algorithm, we have $k \leq n$. One of the following three cases occurs at each iteration of the loop.

- If $T[i] = P[j]$, then i increases by 1, and k does not change, since j also increases by 1.
- If $T[i] \neq P[j]$ and $j > 0$, then i does not change and k increases by at least 1, since in this case k changes from $i - j$ to $i - f(j-1)$, which is an addition of $j - f(j-1)$, which is positive because $f(j-1) < j$.
- If $T[i] \neq P[j]$ and $j = 0$, then i increases by 1 and k increases by 1, since j does not change.

Thus, at each iteration of the loop, either i or k increases by at least 1 (possibly both); hence, the total number of iterations of the while-loop in the KMP pattern matching algorithm is at most $2n$. Achieving this bound, of course, assumes that we have already computed the failure function for P.

Constructing the KMP Failure Function

To construct the failure function, we use the method shown in Code Fragment 11.5, which is a "bootstrapping" process quite similar to the KMPMatch algorithm. We compare the pattern to itself as in the KMP algorithm. Each time we have two characters that match, we set $f(i) = j + 1$. Note that since we have $i > j$ throughout the execution of the algorithm, $f(j - 1)$ is always defined when we need to use it.

Algorithm KMPFailureFunction(P):

    Input: String P (pattern) with m characters

    Output: The failure function f for P, which maps j to the length of the longest prefix of P that is a suffix of $P[1..j]$

    $i \leftarrow 1$

    $j \leftarrow 0$

    $f(0) \leftarrow 0$

    while $i < m$ **do**

      if $P[j] = P[i]$ **then**

        {we have matched $j + 1$ characters}

        $f(i) \leftarrow j + 1$

        $i \leftarrow i + 1$

        $j \leftarrow j + 1$

      else if $j > 0$ **then**

        {j indexes just after a prefix of P that must match}

        $j \leftarrow f(j - 1)$

      else

        {we have no match here}

        $f(i) \leftarrow 0$

        $i \leftarrow i + 1$

Code Fragment 11.5: Computation of the failure function used in the KMP pattern matching algorithm. Note how the algorithm uses the previous values of the failure function to efficiently compute new values.

Algorithm KMPFailureFunction runs in $O(m)$ time. Its analysis is analogous to that of algorithm KMPMatch. Thus, we have:

Proposition 11.5: *The Knuth-Morris-Pratt algorithm performs pattern matching on a text string of length n and a pattern string of length m in $O(n + m)$ time.*

A Java implementation of the KMP pattern matching algorithm is shown in Code Fragment 11.6.

```
public static int KMPmatch(String text, String pattern) {
  int n = text.length();
  int m = pattern.length();
  int[] fail = computeFailFunction(pattern);
  int i = 0;
  int j = 0;
  while (i < n) {
    if (pattern.charAt(j) == text.charAt(i)) {
      if (j == m − 1)
        return i − m + 1; // match
      i++;
      j++;
    }
    else if (j > 0)
      j = fail[j − 1];
    else
      i++;
  }
  return −1; // no match
}
public static int[] computeFailFunction(String pattern) {
  int[] fail = new int[pattern.length()];
  fail[0] = 0;
  int m = pattern.length();
  int j = 0;
  int i = 1;
  while (i < m) {
    if (pattern.charAt(j) == pattern.charAt(i)) { // j + 1 characters match
      fail[i] = j + 1;
      i++;
      j++;
    }
    else if (j > 0) // j follows a matching prefix
      j = fail[j − 1];
    else { // no match
      fail[i] = 0;
      i++;
    }
  }
  return fail;
}
```

Code Fragment 11.6: Java implementation of the KMP pattern matching algorithm. The algorithm is expressed by two static methods: method KMPmatch performs the matching and calls the auxiliary method computeFailFunction to compute the failure function, expressed by an array. Method KMPmatch indicates the absence of a match by returning the conventional value −1.

11.3 Tries

The pattern matching algorithms presented in the previous section speed up the search in a text by preprocessing the pattern (to compute the failure function in the KMP algorithm or the last function in the BM algorithm). In this section, we take a complementary approach, namely, we present string searching algorithms that preprocess the text. This approach is suitable for applications where a series of queries is performed on a fixed text, so that the initial cost of preprocessing the text is compensated by a speedup in each subsequent query (for example, a Web site that offers pattern matching in Shakespeare's *Hamlet* or a search engine that offers Web pages on the *Hamlet* topic).

A ***trie*** (pronounced "try") is a tree-based data structure for storing strings in order to support fast pattern matching. The main application for tries is in information retrieval. Indeed, the name "trie" comes from the word "re*trie*val." In an information retrieval application, such as a search for a certain DNA sequence in a genomic database, we are given a collection S of strings, all defined using the same alphabet. The primary query operations that tries support are pattern matching and ***prefix matching***. The latter operation involves being given a string X, and looking for all the strings in S that contain X as a prefix.

11.3.1 Standard Tries

Let S be a set of s strings from alphabet Σ such that no string in S is a prefix of another string. A ***standard trie*** for S is an ordered tree T with the following properties (see Figure 11.6):

- Each node of T, except the root, is labeled with a character of Σ.
- The ordering of the children of an internal node of T is determined by a canonical ordering of the alphabet Σ.
- T has s external nodes, each associated with a string of S, such that the concatenation of the labels of the nodes on the path from the root to an external node v of T yields the string of S associated with v.

Thus, a trie T represents the strings of S with paths from the root to the external nodes of T. Note the importance of assuming that no string in S is a prefix of another string. This ensures that each string of S is uniquely associated with an external node of T. We can always satisfy this assumption by adding a special

Caution

character that is not in the original alphabet Σ at the end of each string.

An internal node in a standard trie T can have anywhere between 1 and d children, where d is the size of the alphabet. There is an edge going from the root r to

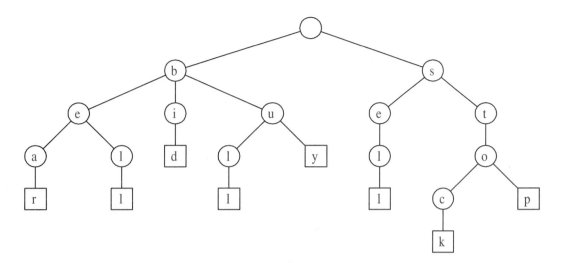

Figure 11.6: Standard trie for the strings {bear, bell, bid, bull, buy, sell, stock, stop}.

one of its children for each character that is first in some string in the collection S. In addition, a path from the root of T to an internal node v at depth i corresponds to an i-character prefix $X[0..i-1]$ of a string X of S. In fact, for each character c that can follow the prefix $X[0..i-1]$ in a string of the set S, there is a child of v labeled with character c. In this way, a trie concisely stores the common prefixes that exist among a set of strings.

If there are only two characters in the alphabet, then the trie is essentially a binary tree, although some internal nodes may have only one child (that is, it may be an improper binary tree). In general, if there are d characters in the alphabet, then the trie will be a multi-way tree where each internal node has between 1 and d children. In addition, there are likely to be several internal nodes in a standard trie that have fewer than d children. For example, the trie shown in Figure 11.6 has several internal nodes with only one child. We can implement a trie with a tree storing characters at its nodes.

The following proposition provides some important structural properties of a standard trie:

Proposition 11.6: *A standard trie storing a collection S of s strings of total length n from an alphabet of size d has the following properties:*

- *Every internal node of T has at most d children*
- *T has s external nodes*
- *The height of T is equal to the length of the longest string in S*
- *The number of nodes of T is $O(n)$.*

The worst case for the number of nodes of a trie occurs when no two strings share a common nonempty prefix; that is, except for the root, all internal nodes have one child.

A trie T for a set S of strings can be used to implement a dictionary whose keys are the strings of S. Namely, we perform a search in T for a string X by tracing down from the root the path indicated by the characters in X. If this path can be traced and terminates at an external node, then we know X is in the dictionary. For example, in the trie in Figure 11.6, tracing the path for "bull" ends up at an external node. If the path cannot be traced or the path can be traced but terminates at an internal node, then X is not in the dictionary. In the example in Figure 11.6, the path for "bet" cannot be traced and the path for "be" ends at an internal node. Neither such word is in the dictionary. Note that in this implementation of a dictionary, single characters are compared instead of the entire string (key). It is easy to see that the running time of the search for a string of size m is $O(dm)$, where d is the size of the alphabet. Indeed, we visit at most $m + 1$ nodes of T and we spend $O(d)$ time at each node. For some alphabets, we may be able to improve the time spent at a node to be $O(1)$ or $O(\log d)$ by using a dictionary of characters implemented in a hash table or look-up table. However, since d is a constant in most applications, we can stick with the simple approach that takes $O(d)$ time per node visited.

From the above discussion, it follows that we can use a trie to perform a special type of pattern matching, called *word matching*, where we want to determine whether a given pattern matches one of the words of the text exactly. (See Figure 11.7.) Word matching differs from standard pattern matching since the pattern cannot match an arbitrary substring of the text, but only one of its words. Using a trie, word matching for a pattern of length m takes $O(dm)$ time, where d is the size of the alphabet, independent of the size of the text. If the alphabet has constant size (as is the case for text in natural languages and DNA strings), a query takes $O(m)$ time, proportional to the size of the pattern. A simple extension of this scheme supports prefix matching queries. However, arbitrary occurrences of the pattern in the text (for example, the pattern is a proper suffix of a word or spans two words) cannot be efficiently performed.

To construct a standard trie for a set S of strings, we can use an incremental algorithm that inserts the strings one at a time. Recall the assumption that no string of S is a prefix of another string. To insert a string X into the current trie T, we first try to trace the path associated with X in T. Since X is not already in T and no string in S is a prefix of another string, we will stop tracing the path at an *internal* node v of T before reaching the end of X. We then create a new chain of node descendents of v to store the remaining characters of X. The time to insert X is $O(dm)$, where m is the length of X and d is the size of the alphabet. Thus, constructing the entire trie for set S takes $O(dn)$ time, where n is the total length of the strings of S.

(a)

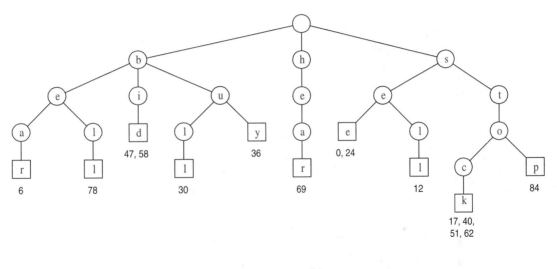

(b)

Figure 11.7: Word matching and prefix matching with a standard trie: (a) text to be searched; (b) standard trie for the words in the text (articles and prepositions, which are also known as *stop words*, excluded), with external nodes augmented with indications of the word positions.

There is a potential space inefficiency in the standard trie that has prompted the development of the *compressed trie*, which is also known (for historical reasons) as the *Patricia trie*. Namely, there are potentially a lot of nodes in the standard trie that have only one child, and the existence of such nodes is a waste. We discuss the compressed trie next.

11.3.2 Compressed Tries

A *compressed trie* is similar to a standard trie but it ensures that each internal node in the trie has at least two children. It enforces this rule by compressing chains of single-child nodes into individual edges. (See Figure 11.8.) Let T be a standard trie. We say that an internal node v of T is *redundant* if v has one child and is not the root. For example, the trie of Figure 11.6 has eight redundant nodes. Let us also say that a chain of $k \geq 2$ edges,

$$(v_0, v_1)(v_1, v_2) \cdots (v_{k-1}, v_k),$$

is *redundant* if

- v_i is redundant for $i = 1, \ldots, k-1$
- v_0 and v_k are not redundant.

We can transform T into a compressed trie by replacing each redundant chain $(v_0, v_1) \cdots (v_{k-1}, v_k)$ of $k \geq 2$ edges into a single edge (v_0, v_k), relabeling v_k with the concatenation of the labels of nodes $v_1, \ldots, v_k$.

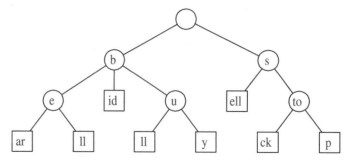

Figure 11.8: Compressed trie for the strings {bear, bell, bid, bull, buy, sell, stock, stop}. Compare this with the standard trie shown in Figure 11.6.

Thus, nodes in a compressed trie are labeled with strings, which are substrings of strings in the collection, rather than with individual characters. The advantage of a compressed trie over a standard trie is that the number of nodes of the compressed trie is proportional to the number of strings and not to their total length, as shown in the following proposition (compare with Proposition 11.6).

Proposition 11.7: *A compressed trie storing a collection S of s strings from an alphabet of size d has the following properties:*

- *Every internal node of T has at least two children and most d children*
- *T has s external nodes*
- *The number of nodes of T is O(s).*

The attentive reader may wonder whether the compression of paths provides any significant advantage, since it is offset by a corresponding expansion of the node labels. Indeed, a compressed trie is truly advantageous only when it is used as an *auxiliary* index structure over a collection of strings already stored in a primary structure, and is not required to actually store all the characters of the strings in the collection.

Suppose, for example, that the collection S of strings is an array of strings $S[0]$, $S[1]$, ..., $S[s-1]$. Instead of storing the label X of a node explicitly, we represent it implicitly by a triplet of integers (i, j, k), such that $X = S[i][j..k]$; that is, X is the substring of $S[i]$ consisting of the characters from the jth to the kth included. (See the example in Figure 11.9. Also compare with the standard trie of Figure 11.7.)

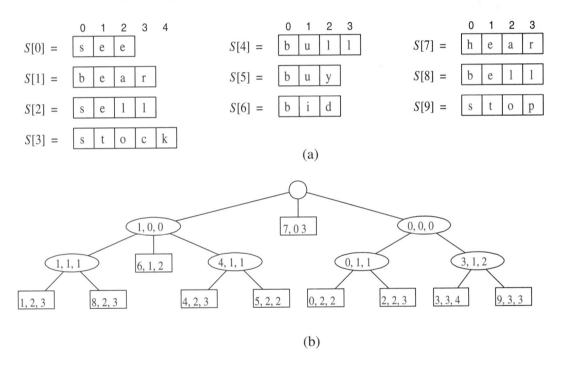

Figure 11.9: (a) Collection S of strings stored in an array. (b) Compact representation of the compressed trie for S.

This additional compression scheme allows us to reduce the total space for the trie itself from $O(n)$ for the standard trie to $O(s)$ for the compressed trie, where n is the total length of the strings in S and s is the number of strings in S. We must still store the different strings in S, of course, but we nevertheless reduce the space for the trie. In the next section, we present an application where the collection of strings can also be stored compactly.

11.3.3 Suffix Tries

One of the primary applications for tries is for the case when the strings in the collection S are all the suffixes of a string X. Such a trie is called the *suffix trie* (also known as a *suffix tree* or *position tree*) of string X. For example, Figure 11.10a shows the suffix trie for the eight suffixes of string "minimize." For a suffix trie, the compact representation presented in the previous section can be further simplified. Namely, the label of each vertex is a pair (i, j) indicating the string $X[i..j]$. (See Figure 11.10b.) To satisfy the rule that no suffix of X is a prefix of another suffix, we can add a special character, denoted with $, that is not in the original alphabet Σ at the end of X (and thus to every suffix). That is, if string X has length n, we build a trie for the set of n strings $X[i..n-1]\$$, for $i = 0, \ldots, n-1$.

Saving Space

Using a suffix trie allows us to save space over a standard trie by using several space compression techniques, including those used for the compressed trie.

The advantage of the compact representation of tries now becomes apparent for suffix tries. Since the total length of the suffixes of a string X of length n is

$$1 + 2 + \cdots + n = \frac{n(n+1)}{2},$$

storing all the suffixes of X explicitly would take $O(n^2)$ space. Even so, the suffix trie represents these strings implicitly in $O(n)$ space, as formally stated in the following proposition.

Proposition 11.8: *The compact representation of a suffix trie T for a string X of length n uses $O(n)$ space.*

Construction

We can construct the suffix trie for a string of length n with an incremental algorithm like the one given in Section 11.3.1. This construction takes $O(dn^2)$ time because the total length of the suffixes is quadratic in n. However, the (compact) suffix trie for a string of length n can be constructed in $O(n)$ time with a specialized algorithm, different from the one for general tries. This linear-time construction algorithm is fairly complex, however, and is not reported here. Still, we can take advantage of the existence of this fast construction algorithm when we want to use a suffix trie to solve other problems.

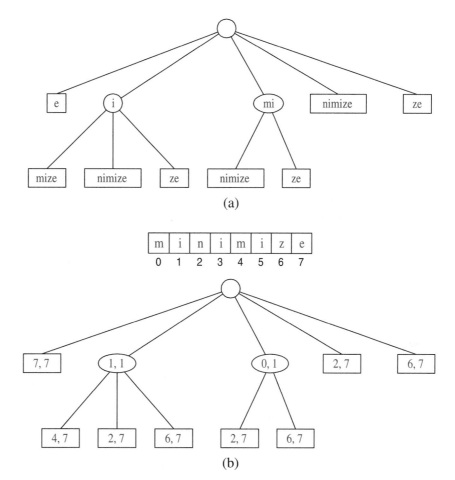

Figure 11.10: (a) Suffix trie T for the string $X = $ ''minimize''. (b) Compact representation of T, where pair (i, j) denotes $X[i..j]$.

Using a Suffix Trie

The suffix trie T for a string X can be used to efficiently perform pattern matching queries on text X. Namely, we can determine whether a pattern P is a substring of X by trying to trace a path associated with P in T. P is a substring of X if and only if such a path can be traced. The details of the pattern matching algorithm are given in Code Fragment 11.7, which assumes the following additional property on the labels of the nodes in the compact representation of the suffix trie:

> If node v has label (i, j) and Y is the string of length y associated with the path from the root to v (included), then $X[j - y + 1..j] = Y$.

This property ensures that we can easily compute the start index of the pattern in the text when a match occurs.

Algorithm suffixTrieMatch(T,P):

   Input: Compact suffix trie T for a text X and pattern P

   Output: Starting index of a substring of X matching P or an indication that P
      is not a substring of X

   $p \leftarrow P$.length() { length of suffix of the pattern to be matched }

   $j \leftarrow 0$ { start of suffix of the pattern to be matched }

   $v \leftarrow T$.root()

   repeat

      $f \leftarrow$ **true** { flag indicating that no child was successfully processed }

      for each child w of v **do**

         $i \leftarrow$ start(v)

         if $P[j] = T[i]$ **then**

            { process child w }

            $x \leftarrow$ end(w) $- i + 1$

            if $p \leq x$ **then**

               { suffix is shorter than or of the same length of the node label }

               if $P[j..j+p-1] = X[i..i+p-1]$ **then**

                  return $i - j$ { match }

               else

                  return "P is not a substring of X"

            else

               { suffix is longer than the node label }

               if $P[j..j+x-1] = X[i..i+x-1]$ **then**

                  $p \leftarrow p - x$ { update suffix length }

                  $j \leftarrow j + x$ { update suffix start index }

                  $v \leftarrow w$

                  $f \leftarrow$ **false**

                  break out of the **for** loop

   until f **or** T.isExternal(v)

   return "P is not a substring of X"

Code Fragment 11.7: Pattern matching with a suffix trie. We denote the label of a node v with (start(v), end(v)), that is, the pair of indices specifying the substring of the text associated with v.

The correctness of algorithm suffixTrieMatch follows from the fact that we search down the trie T, matching characters of the pattern P one at a time until one of the following events occurs:

- We completely match the pattern P
- We get a mismatch (caught by the termination of the for-loop without a break out)
- We are left with characters of P still to be matched after processing an external node.

Let m be the size of pattern P and d be the size of the alphabet. In order to determine the running time of algorithm suffixTrieMatch, we make the following observations:

- We process at most $m + 1$ nodes of the trie
- Each node processed has at most d children
- At each node v processed, we perform at most one character comparison for each child w of v to determine which child of v needs to be processed next (which may possibly be improved by using a fast dictionary to index the children of v)
- We perform at most m character comparisons overall in the processed nodes
- We spend $O(1)$ time for each character comparison.

Performance

We conclude that algorithm suffixTrieMatch performs pattern matching queries in $O(dm)$ time (and would possibly run even faster if we used a dictionary to index children of nodes in the suffix trie). Note that the running time does not depend on the size of the text X. Also, the running time is linear in the size of the pattern, that is, it is $O(m)$, for a constant-size alphabet. Hence, suffix tries are suited for repetitive pattern matching applications, where a series of pattern matching queries is performed on a fixed text.

We summarize the results of this section in the following proposition.

Proposition 11.9: *Let X be a text string with n characters from an alphabet of size d. We can perform pattern matching queries on X in $O(dm)$ time, where m is the length of the pattern, with the suffix trie of X, which uses $O(n)$ space and can be constructed in $O(dn)$ time.*

We explore another application of tries in the next subsection.

11.3.4   Search Engines

The World Wide Web contains a huge collection of text documents (Web pages). Information about these pages are gathered by a program called a ***Web crawler***, which then stores this information in a special dictionary database. A Web ***search engine*** allows users to retrieve relevant information from this database, thereby identifying relevant pages on the Web containing given keywords. In this section, we present a simplified model of a search engine.

Inverted Files

The core information stored by a search engine is a dictionary, called an ***inverted index*** or ***inverted file***, storing key-value pairs (w, L), where w is a word and L is a collection of pages containing word w. The keys (words) in this dictionary are called ***index terms*** and should be a set of vocabulary entries and proper nouns as large as possible. The elements in this dictionary are called ***occurrence lists*** and should cover as many Web pages as possible.

We can efficiently implement an inverted index with a data structure consisting of:

1. An array storing the occurrence lists of the terms (in no particular order).
2. A compressed trie for the set of index terms, where each external node stores the index of the occurrence list of the associated term.

The reason for storing the occurrence lists outside the trie is to keep the size of the trie data structure sufficiently small to fit in internal memory. Instead, because of their large total size, the occurrence lists have to be stored on disk.

With our data structure, a query for a single keyword is similar to a word matching query (see Section 11.3.1). Namely, we find the keyword in the trie and we return the associated occurrence list.

When multiple keywords are given and the desired output are the pages containing ***all*** the given keywords, we retrieve the occurrence list of each keyword using the trie and return their intersection. To facilitate the intersection computation, each occurrence list should be implemented with a sequence sorted by address or with a dictionary (see, for example, the generic merge computation discussed in Section 10.2).

In addition to the basic task of returning a list of pages containing given keywords, search engines provide an important additional service by ***ranking*** the pages returned by relevance. Devising fast and accurate ranking algorithms for search engines is a major challenge for computer researchers and electronic commerce companies.

11.4 Text Compression

In this section, we consider another text processing application, *text compression*. In this problem, we are given a string X defined over some alphabet, such as the ASCII or Unicode character sets, and we want to efficiently encode X into a small binary string Y (using only the characters 0 and 1). Text compression is useful in any situation where we are communicating over a low-bandwidth channel, such as a modem line or infrared connection, and we wish to minimize the time needed to transmit our text. Likewise, text compression is also useful for storing collections of large documents more efficiently, so as to allow for a fixed-capacity storage device to contain as many documents as possible.

The method for text compression explored in this section is the *Huffman code*. Standard encoding schemes, such as the ASCII and Unicode systems, use fixed-length binary strings to encode characters (with 7 bits in the ASCII system and 16 in the Unicode system). A Huffman code, on the other hand, uses a variable-length encoding optimized for the string X. The optimization is based on the use of character *frequencies*, where we have, for each character c, a count $f(c)$ of the number of times c appears in the string X. The Huffman code saves space over a fixed-length encoding by using short code-word strings to encode high-frequency characters and long code-word strings to encode low-frequency characters.

To encode the string X, we convert each character in X from its fixed-length code word to its variable-length code word, and we concatenate all these code words in order to produce the encoding Y for X. In order to avoid ambiguities, we insist that no code word in our encoding is a prefix of another code word in our encoding. Such a code is called a *prefix code*, and it simplifies the decoding of Y in order to get back X. (See Figure 11.11.) Even with this restriction, the savings produced by a variable-length prefix code can be significant, particularly if there is a wide variance in character frequencies (as is the case for natural language text in almost every spoken language).

Huffman's algorithm for producing an optimal variable-length prefix code for X is based on the construction of a binary tree T that represents the code. Each node in T, except the root, represents a bit in a code word, with each left child representing a "0" and each right child representing a "1." Each external node v is associated with a specific character, and the code word for that character is defined by the sequence of bits associated with the nodes in the path from the root of T to v. (See Figure 11.11.) Each external node v has a *frequency* $f(v)$, which is simply the frequency in X of the character associated with v. In addition, we give each internal node v in T a frequency, $f(v)$, that is the sum of the frequencies of all the external nodes in the subtree rooted at v.

(a)

Character	a	b	d	e	f	h	i	k	n	o	r	s	t	u	v
Frequency	9	5	1	3	7	3	1	1	1	4	1	5	1	2	1	1

(b)

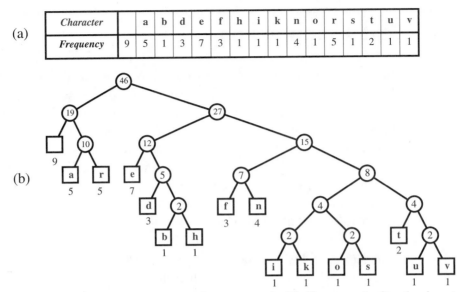

Figure 11.11: An illustration of an example Huffman code for the input string $X =$ "a fast runner need never be afraid of the dark": (a) frequency of each character of X; (b) Huffman tree T for string X. The code for a character c is obtained by tracing the path from the root of T to the external node where c is stored, and associating a left child with 0 and a right child with 1. For example, the code for "a" is 010, and the code for "f" is 1100.

11.4.1 The Huffman Coding Algorithm

The Huffman coding algorithm begins with each of the d distinct characters of the string X to encode being the root node of a single-node binary tree. The algorithm proceeds in a series of rounds. In each round, the algorithm takes the two binary trees with the smallest frequencies and merges them into a single binary tree. It repeats this process until only one tree is left. (See Code Fragment 11.8.)

Each iteration of the while-loop in Huffman's algorithm can be implemented in $O(\log d)$ time using a priority queue represented with a heap. In addition, each iteration takes two nodes out of Q and adds one in, a process that will be repeated $d - 1$ times before exactly one node is left in Q. Thus, this algorithm runs in $O(n + d \log d)$ time. Although a full justification of this algorithm's correctness is beyond our scope here, we note that its intuition comes from a simple idea—any optimal code can be converted into an optimal code in which the code words for the two lowest-frequency characters, a and b, differ only in their last bit. Repeating the argument for a string with a and b replaced by a character c, gives the following:

Proposition 11.10: *Huffman's algorithm constructs an optimal prefix code for a string of length n with d distinct characters in $O(n + d \log d)$ time.*

Algorithm Huffman(X):

    Input: String X of length n with d distinct characters
    Output: Coding tree for X

    Compute the frequency $f(c)$ of each character c of X.
    Initialize a priority queue Q.
    for each character c in X **do**
        Create a single-node binary tree T storing c.
        Insert T into Q with key $f(c)$.
    while Q.size() > 1 **do**
        $f_1 \leftarrow Q$.minKey()
        $T_1 \leftarrow Q$.removeMin()
        $f_2 \leftarrow Q$.minKey()
        $T_2 \leftarrow Q$.removeMin()
        Create a new binary tree T with left subtree T_1 and right subtree T_2.
        Insert T into Q with key $f_1 + f_2$.
    return tree Q.removeMin()

Code Fragment 11.8: Huffman coding algorithm.

11.4.2 The Greedy Method

Huffman's algorithm for building an optimal encoding is an example application of an algorithmic design pattern called the ***greedy method***. This design pattern is applied to optimization problems, where we are trying to construct some structure while minimizing or maximizing some property of that structure.

The general formula for the greedy method pattern is almost as simple as that for the brute-force method. In order to solve a given optimization problem using the greedy method, we proceed by a sequence of choices. The sequence starts from some well-understood starting condition, and computes the cost for that initial condition. The pattern then asks that we iteratively make additional choices by identifying the decision that achieves the best cost improvement from all of the choices that are currently possible. This approach does not always lead to an optimal solution.

But there are several problems that it does work for, and such problems are said to possess the ***greedy-choice*** property. This is the property that a global optimal condition can be reached by a series of locally optimal choices (that is, choices that are each the current best from among the possibilities available at the time), starting from a well-defined starting condition. The problem of computing an optimal variable-length prefix code is just one example of a problem that possesses the greedy-choice property.

11.5 Text Similarity Testing

A common text processing problem, which arises in genetics and software engineering, is to test the similarity between two text strings. In a genetics application, the two strings could correspond to two strands of DNA, which could, for example, come from two individuals, who we will consider genetically related if they have a long subsequence common to their respective DNA sequences. Likewise, in a software engineering application, the two strings could come from two versions of source code for the same program, and we may wish to determine which changes were made from one version to the next. Indeed, determining the similarity between two strings is considered such a common operation that the Unix/Linux operating systems come with a program, called `diff`, for comparing text files.

11.5.1 The Longest Common Subsequence Problem

There are several different ways we can define the similarity between two strings. Even so, we can abstract a simple, yet common, version of this problem using character strings and their subsequences. Given a string $X = x_0 x_1 x_2 \cdots x_{n-1}$, a **subsequence** of X is any string that is of the form $x_{i_1} x_{i_2} \cdots x_{i_k}$, where $i_j < i_{j+1}$; that is, it is a sequence of characters that are not necessarily contiguous but are nevertheless taken in order from X. For example, the string *AAAG* is a subsequence of the string *CGATAATTGAGA*. Note that the concept of **subsequence** of a string is different from the one of **substring** of a string, defined in Section 11.1.

Caution

Problem Definition

The specific text similarity problem we address here is the **longest common subsequence** (LCS) problem. In this problem, we are given two character strings, $X = x_0 x_1 x_2 \cdots x_{n-1}$ and $Y = y_0 y_1 y_2 \cdots y_{m-1}$, over some alphabet (such as the alphabet $\{A, C, G, T\}$ common in computational genetics) and are asked to find a longest string S that is a subsequence of both X and Y.

One way to solve the longest common subsequence problem is to enumerate all subsequences of X and take the largest one that is also a subsequence of Y. Since each character of X is either in or not in a subsequence, there are potentially 2^n different subsequences of X, each of which requires $O(m)$ time to determine whether it is a subsequence of Y. Thus, this brute-force approach yields an exponential algorithm that runs in $O(2^n m)$ time, which is very inefficient. In this section, we discuss how to use an algorithmic design pattern called **dynamic programming** to solve the longest common subsequence problem much faster than this.

11.5.2 Dynamic Programming

There are few algorithmic techniques that can take problems that seem to require exponential time and produce polynomial-time algorithms to solve them. Dynamic programming is one such technique. In addition, the algorithms that result from applications of the dynamic programming technique are usually quite simple— often needing little more than a few lines of code to describe some nested loops for filling in a table.

The dynamic programming technique is used primarily for *optimization* problems, where we wish to find the "best" way of doing something. Often the number of different ways of doing that "something" is exponential, so a brute-force search for the best is computationally infeasible for all but the smallest problem sizes. We can apply the dynamic programming technique in such situations, however, if the problem has a certain amount of structure that we can exploit. This structure involves the following three components:

Simple Subproblems: There has to be some way of repeatedly breaking the global optimization problem into subproblems. Moreover, there should be a simple way of defining subproblems with just a few indices, like i, j, k, and so on.

Subproblem Optimization: An optimal solution to the global problem must be a composition of optimal subproblem solutions. We should not be able to find a globally optimal solution that contains suboptimal subproblems.

Subproblem Overlap: Optimal solutions to unrelated subproblems can contain subproblems in common.

Having given the general components of a dynamic programming algorithm, we next show how to apply it to the longest common subsequence problem.

11.5.3 Applying Dynamic Programming to the LCS Problem

We can solve the longest common subsequence problem much faster than exponential time using the dynamic programming technique. As mentioned above, one of the key components of the dynamic programming technique is the definition of simple subproblems that satisfy the subproblem optimization and subproblem overlap properties.

Recall that in the LCS problem, we are given two character strings, X and Y, of length n and m, respectively, and are asked to find a longest string S that is a subsequence of both X and Y. Since X and Y are character strings, we have a natural set of indices with which to define subproblems—indices into the strings X

Figure 11.12: The two cases in the longest common subsequence algorithm: (a) $x_i = y_j$; (b) $x_i \neq y_j$. Note that the algorithm stores only the $L[i, j]$ values, not the matches.

and Y. Let us define a subproblem, therefore, as that of computing the value $L[i, j]$, which we will use to denote the length of a longest string that is a subsequence of both $X[0..i] = x_0x_1x_2\ldots x_i$ and $Y[0..j] = y_0y_1y_2\ldots y_j$. This definition allows us to rewrite $L[i, j]$ in terms of optimal subproblem solutions. This definition depends on which of two cases we are in. (See Figure 11.12.)

- $x_i = y_j$. In this case, we have a match between the last character of $X[0..i]$ and the last character of $Y[0..j]$. We claim that this character belongs to a longest common subsequence of $X[0..i]$ and $Y[0..j]$. To justify this claim, let us suppose it is not true. There has to be some longest common subsequence $x_{i_1}x_{i_2}\ldots x_{i_k} = y_{j_1}y_{j_2}\ldots y_{j_k}$. If $x_{i_k} = x_i$ or $y_{j_k} = y_j$, then we get the same sequence by setting $i_k = i$ and $j_k = j$. Alternately, if $x_{j_k} \neq x_i$, then we can get an even longer common subsequence by adding x_i to the end. Thus, a longest common subsequence of $X[0..i]$ and $Y[0..j]$ ends with x_i. Therefore, we set

$$L[i, j] = L[i - 1, j - 1] + 1 \quad \text{if } x_i = y_j.$$

- $x_i \neq y_j$. In this case, we cannot have a common subsequence that includes both x_i and y_j. That is, we can have a common subsequence end with x_i or one that ends with y_j (or possibly neither), but certainly not both. Therefore, we set

$$L[i, j] = \max\{L[i - 1, j], L[i, j - 1]\} \quad \text{if } x_i \neq y_j.$$

In order to make both of these equations make sense in the boundary cases when $i = 0$ or $j = 0$, we assign $L[i, -1] = 0$ for $i = -1, 0, 1, \ldots, n - 1$ and $L[-1, j] = 0$ for $j = -1, 0, 1, \ldots, m - 1$.

The above definition of $L[i, j]$ satisfies subproblem optimization, for we cannot have a longest common subsequence without also having longest common subsequences for the subproblems. Also, it uses subproblem overlap, because a subproblem solution $L[i, j]$ can be used in several other problems (namely, the problems $L[i + 1, j]$, $L[i, j + 1]$, and $L[i + 1, j + 1]$).

The LCS Algorithm

Turning this definition of $L[i,j]$ into an algorithm is actually quite straightforward. We initialize an $(n+1) \times (m+1)$ array, L, for the boundary cases when $i=0$ or $j=0$. Namely, we initialize $L[i,-1] = 0$ for $i = -1, 0, 1, \ldots, n-1$ and $L[-1,j] = 0$ for $j = -1, 0, 1, \ldots, m-1$. (This is a slight abuse of notation, since in reality, we would have to index the rows and columns of L starting with 0.) Then, we iteratively build up values in L until we have $L[n-1,m-1]$, the length of a longest common subsequence of X and Y. We give a pseudo-code description of how this approach results in a dynamic programming solution to the longest common subsequence (LCS) problem in Code Fragment 11.9.

Algorithm LCS(X,Y):

> *Input:* Strings X and Y with n and m elements, respectively
>
> *Output:* For $i = 0, \ldots, n-1$, $j = 0, \ldots, m-1$, the length $L[i,j]$ of a longest string that is a subsequence of both the string $X[0..i] = x_0 x_1 x_2 \cdots x_i$ and the string $Y[0..j] = y_0 y_1 y_2 \cdots y_j$
>
> **for** $i \leftarrow -1$ **to** $n-1$ **do**
> > $L[i,-1] \leftarrow 0$
>
> **for** $j \leftarrow 0$ **to** $m-1$ **do**
> > $L[-1,j] \leftarrow 0$
>
> **for** $i \leftarrow 0$ **to** $n-1$ **do**
> > **for** $j \leftarrow 0$ **to** $m-1$ **do**
> > > **if** $x_i = y_j$ **then**
> > > > $L[i,j] \leftarrow L[i-1,j-1] + 1$
> > >
> > > **else**
> > > > $L[i,j] \leftarrow \max\{L[i-1,j], L[i,j-1]\}$
>
> **return** array L

Code Fragment 11.9: Dynamic programming algorithm for the LCS problem.

Performance

The running time of the algorithm of Code Fragment 11.9 is easy to analyze, for it is dominated by two nested for-loops, with the outer one iterating n times and the inner one iterating m times. Since the if-statement and assignment inside the loop each requires $O(1)$ primitive operations, this algorithm runs in $O(nm)$ time. Thus, the dynamic programming technique can be applied to the longest common subsequence problem to improve significantly over the exponential-time brute-force solution to the LCS problem.

Algorithm LCS (Code Fragment 11.9) computes the length of the longest common subsequence (stored in $L[n-1,m-1]$), but not the subsequence itself. As shown in the following proposition, a simple postprocessing step can extract the longest common subsequence from the array L returned by algorithm.

Proposition 11.11: *Given a string X of n characters and a string Y of m characters, we can find the longest common subsequence of X and Y in $O(nm)$ time.*

Justification: Algorithm LCS computes $L[n-1,m-1]$, the ***length*** of a longest common subsequence, in $O(nm)$ time. Given the table of $L[i,j]$ values, constructing a longest common subsequence is straightforward. One method is to start from $L[n,m]$ and work back through the table, reconstructing a longest common subsequence from back to front. At any position $L[i,j]$, we can determine whether $x_i = y_j$. If this is true, then we can take x_i as the next character of the subsequence (noting that x_i is ***before*** the previous character we found, if any), moving next to $L[i-1,j-1]$. If $x_i \neq y_j$, then we can move to the larger of $L[i,j-1]$ and $L[i-1,j]$. (See Figure 11.13.) We stop when we reach a boundary cell (with $i=-1$ or $j=-1$). This method constructs a longest common subsequence in $O(n+m)$ additional time. ■

L	-1	0	1	2	3	4	5	6	7	8	9	10	11
-1	0	0	0	0	0	0	0	0	0	0	0	0	0
0	0	0	1	1	1	1	1	1	1	1	1	1	1
1	0	0	1	1	2	2	2	2	2	2	2	2	2
2	0	0	1	1	2	2	2	3	3	3	3	3	3
3	0	1	1	1	2	2	2	3	3	3	3	3	3
4	0	1	1	1	2	2	2	3	3	3	3	3	3
5	0	1	1	1	2	2	2	3	4	4	4	4	4
6	0	1	1	2	2	3	3	3	4	4	5	5	5
7	0	1	1	2	2	3	4	4	4	4	5	5	6
8	0	1	1	2	3	3	4	5	5	5	5	5	6
9	0	1	1	2	3	4	4	5	5	5	6	6	6

```
               0 1 2 3 4 5 6 7 8 9 10 11
           Y=C G A T A A T T G A G A

           X=G T T C C T A A T A
             0 1 2 3 4 5 6 7 8 9
```

Figure 11.13: Illustration of the algorithm for constructing a longest common subsequence from the array L.

11.6 Exercises

Reinforcement

R-11.1 How many nonempty prefixes of the string $P =$ "aaabbaaa" are also suffixes of P?

R-11.2 Draw a figure illustrating the comparisons done by the brute-force pattern matching algorithm for the case when the text is "aaabaadaabaaa" and the pattern is "aabaaa".

R-11.3 Repeat the previous problem for the BM pattern matching algorithm, not counting the comparisons made to compute the $last(c)$ function.

R-11.4 Repeat the previous problem for the KMP pattern matching algorithm, not counting the comparisons made to compute the failure function.

R-11.5 Compute a table representing the last function used in the BM pattern matching algorithm for the pattern string

"the quick brown fox jumped over a lazy cat"

assuming the following alphabet (which starts with the space character):

$$\Sigma = \{ \,,a,b,c,d,e,f,g,h,i,j,k,l,m,n,o,p,q,r,s,t,u,v,w,x,y,z\}.$$

R-11.6 Assuming that the characters in alphabet Σ can be enumerated and can index arrays, give an $O(m + |\Sigma|)$ time method for constructing the last function from an m-length pattern string P.

R-11.7 Compute a table representing the KMP failure function for the pattern string "cgtacgttcgtac".

R-11.8 Draw a standard trie for the following set of strings:

$\{$abab, baba, ccccc, bbaaaa, caa, bbaacc, cbcc, cbca$\}$.

R-11.9 Draw a compressed trie for the set of strings given in Exercise R-11.8.

R-11.10 Draw the compact representation of the suffix trie for the string

"minimize minime".

R-11.11 What is the longest prefix of the string "cgtacgttcgtacg" that is also a suffix of this string?

R-11.12 Draw the frequency array and Huffman tree for the following string:

"dogs do not spot hot pots or cats".

R-11.13 Show the longest common subsequence array L for the two strings

$$X = \text{"skullandbones"}$$

$$Y = \text{"lullabybabies"}.$$

What is a longest common subsequence between these strings?

Creativity

C-11.1 Give an example of a text T of length n and a pattern P of length m that force the brute-force pattern matching algorithm to have a running time that is $\Omega(nm)$.

C-11.2 Give a justification of why the KMPFailureFunction method (Code Fragment 11.5) runs in $O(m)$ time on a pattern of length m.

C-11.3 Show how to modify the KMP string pattern matching algorithm so as to find *every* occurrence of a pattern string P that appears as a substring in T, while still running in $O(n+m)$ time. (Be sure to catch even those matches that overlap.)

C-11.4 Let T be a text of length n, and let P be a pattern of length m. Describe an $O(n+m)$-time method for finding the longest prefix of P that is a substring of T.

C-11.5 Say that a pattern P of length m is a **circular** substring of a text T of length n if there is an index $0 \leq i < m$, such that $P = T[n-m+i..n-1] + T[0..i-1]$, that is, if P is a (normal) substring of T or P is equal to the concatenation of a suffix of T and a prefix of T. Give an $O(n+m)$-time algorithm for determining whether P is a circular substring of T.

C-11.6 The KMP pattern matching algorithm can be modified to run faster on binary strings by redefining the failure function as

$$f(j) = \text{the largest } k < j \text{ such that } P[0..k-2]\widehat{p}_k \text{ is a suffix of } P[1..j],$$

where $\widehat{p}_k$ denotes the complement of the kth bit of P. Describe how to modify the KMP algorithm to be able to take advantage of this new failure function and also give a method for computing this failure function. Show that this method makes at most n comparisons between the text and the pattern (as opposed to the $2n$ comparisons needed by the standard KMP algorithm given in Section 11.2.3).

C-11.7 Modify the simplified BM algorithm presented in this chapter using ideas from the KMP algorithm so that it runs in $O(n+m)$ time.

C-11.8 Show how to perform prefix matching queries using a suffix trie.

C-11.9 Give an efficient algorithm for deleting a string from a standard trie and analyze its running time.

C-11.10 Give an efficient algorithm for deleting a string from a compressed trie and analyze its running time.

C-11.11 Describe an algorithm for constructing the compact representation of a suffix trie and analyze its running time.

C-11.12 Let T be a text string of length n. Describe an $O(n)$-time method for finding the longest prefix of T that is a substring of the reversal of T.

C-11.13 Describe an efficient algorithm to find the longest palindrome that is a suffix of a string T of length n. Recall that a *palindrome* is a string that is equal to its reversal. What is the running time of your method?

C-11.14 Given a sequence $S = (x_0, x_1, x_2, \ldots, x_{n-1})$ of numbers, describe an $O(n^2)$-time algorithm for finding a longest subsequence $T = (x_{i_0}, x_{i_1}, x_{i_2}, \ldots, x_{i_{k-1}})$ of numbers, such that $i_j < i_{j+1}$ and $x_{i_j} > x_{i_{j+1}}$. That is, T is a longest decreasing subsequence of S.

C-11.15 Define the *edit distance* between two strings X and Y of length n and m, respectively, to be the number of edits that it takes to change X into Y. An edit consists of a character insertion, a character deletion, or a character replacement. For example, the strings `"algorithm"` and `"rhythm"` have edit distance 6. Design an $O(nm)$-time algorithm for computing the edit distance between X and Y.

C-11.16 Design a greedy algorithm for making change after someone buys some candy costing x cents and the customer gives the clerk \$1. Your algorithm should try to minimize the number of coins returned.

    a. Show that your greedy algorithm returns the minimum number of coins if the coins have denominations \$0.25, \$0.10, \$0.05, and \$0.01.

    b. Give a set of denominations for which your algorithm may not return the minimum number of coins. Include an example where your algorithm fails.

C-11.17 Anna has just won a contest that allows her to take n pieces of candy out of a candy store for free. Anna is old enough to realize that some candy is expensive, costing dollars per piece, while other candy is cheap, costing pennies per piece. The jars of candy are numbered $0, 1, \ldots, m-1$, so that jar j has n_j pieces in it, with a price of c_j per piece. Design an $O(n+m)$-time algorithm that allows Anna to maximize the value of the pieces of candy she takes for her winnings. Show that your algorithm produces the maximum value for Anna.

C-11.18 Let three integer arrays, A, B, and C, be given, each of size n. Given an arbitrary integer x, design an $O(n^2 \log n)$-time algorithm to determine if there exist numbers $a \in A$, $b \in B$, and $c \in C$, such that $x = a+b+c$. (Hint: Use brute force first to enumerate all pairs (a,b) such that $a \in A$ and $b \in B$.)

C-11.19⋆ Give an $O(n^2)$-time algorithm for the previous problem.

Projects

P-11.1 Perform an experimental analysis, using documents found on the Internet, of the efficiency (number of character comparisons performed) of the brute-force and KMP pattern matching algorithms for varying-length patterns.

P-11.2 Perform an experimental analysis, using documents found on the Internet, of the efficiency (number of character comparisons performed) of the brute-force and BM pattern matching algorithms for varying-length patterns.

P-11.3 Perform an experimental comparison of the relative speeds of the brute-force, KMP, and BM pattern matching algorithms. Document the time taken for coding up each of these algorithms as well as their relative running times on documents found on the Internet that are then searched using varying-length patterns.

P-11.4 Implement a compression and decompression scheme that is based on Huffman coding.

P-11.5 Create a class that implements a standard trie for a set of ASCII strings. The class should have a constructor that takes as argument a list of strings, and the class should have a method that tests whether a given string is stored in the trie.

P-11.6 Create a class that implements a compressed trie for a set of ASCII strings. The class should have a constructor that takes as argument a list of strings, and the class should have a method that tests whether a given string is stored in the trie.

P-11.7 Create a class that implements a prefix trie for an ASCII string. The class should have a constructor that takes as argument a string and a method for pattern matching on the string.

P-11.8 Implement the simplified search engine described in Section 11.3.4 for the pages of a small Web site. Use all the words in the pages of the site as index terms, excluding stop words such as articles, prepositions, and pronouns.

P-11.9 Implement a search engine for the pages of a small Web site by adding a page-ranking feature to the simplified search engine described in Section 11.3.4. Your page-ranking feature should return the most relevant pages first. Use all the words in the pages of the site as index terms, excluding stop words, such as articles, prepositions, and pronouns.

Chapter Notes

The KMP algorithm is described by Knuth, Morris, and Pratt in their journal article [62], and Boyer and Moore describe their algorithm in a journal article published the same year [16]. In their article, however, Knuth *et al.* [62] also prove that the BM algorithm runs in linear time. More recently, Cole [23] shows that the BM algorithm makes at most $3n$ character comparisons in the worst case, and this bound is tight. All of the algorithms discussed above are also discussed in the book chapter by Aho [3], albeit in a more theoretical framework, including the methods for regular-expression pattern matching. The reader interested in further study of string pattern matching algorithms is referred to the book by Stephen [88] and the book chapters by Aho [3] and Crochemore and Lecroq [27].

The trie was invented by Morrison [78] and is discussed extensively in the classic *Sorting and Searching* book by Knuth [60]. The name "Patricia" is short for "Practical Algorithm to Retrieve Information Coded in Alphanumeric" [78]. McCreight [69] shows how to construct suffix tries in linear time. An introduction to the field of information retrieval, which includes a discussion of search engines for the Web is provided in the book by Baeza-Yates and Ribeiro-Neto [8].

Chapter

12

Graphs

Contents

Greek mythology tells of an elaborate labyrinth that was built to house the monstrous part bull, part man Minotaur. This labyrinth was so complex that neither beast nor human could escape it. No human, that is, until the Greek hero, Theseus, with the help of the king's daughter, Ariadne, decided to implement one of the algorithms discussed in this chapter. Theseus fastened a ball of thread to the door of the labyrinth and unwound it as he traversed the twisting passages in search of the monster. Theseus obviously knew about good algorithm design, for, after finding and defeating the beast, Theseus easily followed the string back out of the labyrinth to the loving arms of Ariadne.

Being able to determine which objects, such as labyrinth passages, are connected to which other objects may not always be as vitally important as it was in this story, but it is nevertheless fundamental. Connectivity information is present, for example, in city maps, where the objects are roads, and also in the routing tables for the Internet, where the objects are computers. Connectivity information is also present in the parent-child relationships defined by a binary tree, where the objects are tree nodes. Indeed, connectivity information can be defined by all kinds of relationships that exist between pairs of objects. The topic we study in this chapter—*graphs*—is therefore focused on representations and algorithms for dealing efficiently with such relationships. That is, a graph is a set of objects, called vertices, together with a collection of pairwise connections between them. By the way, this notion of a "graph" should not be confused with bar charts and function plots, as these kinds of "graphs" are unrelated to the topic of this chapter.

Graphs have applications in a host of different domains, including mapping (in geographic information systems), transportation (in road and flight networks), electrical engineering (in circuits), and computer networking (in the connections of the Internet). Because applications for graphs are so widespread and diverse, people have developed a great deal of terminology to describe different components and properties of graphs. Fortunately, since most graph applications are relatively recent developments, this terminology is fairly intuitive.

We therefore begin this chapter by reviewing much of this terminology and presenting the graph ADT, including some elementary properties of graphs. Having given the graph ADT, we then present, in Section 12.2, three main data structures for representing graphs. As with trees, traversals are important computations for graphs, and we discuss such computations in Section 12.3. We discuss directed graphs in Section 12.4, where relationships have a given direction. This topic is not addressed in subsequent sections, however, so readers or instructors with limited time may skip Section 12.4. In Sections 12.5 through 12.7 we discuss weighted graphs, where connections have a cost or distance associated with them. While weighted connections could be directed, in these sections we study the well-known shortest path and minimum spanning tree problems for undirected graphs.

12.1 The Graph Abstract Data Type

Viewed abstractly, a *graph* G is simply a set V of *vertices* and a collection E of pairs of vertices from V, called *edges*. Thus, a graph is a way of representing connections or relationships between pairs of objects from some set V. Incidentally, some books use different terminology for graphs and refer to what we call vertices as *nodes* and what we call edges as *arcs*. We use the terms "vertices" and "edges."

Edges in a graph are either *directed* or *undirected*. An edge (u, v) is said to be *directed* from u to v if the pair (u, v) is ordered, with u preceding v. An edge (u, v) is said to be *undirected* if the pair (u, v) is not ordered. Undirected edges are sometimes denoted with set notation, as $\{u, v\}$, but for simplicity we use the pair notation (u, v), noting that in the undirected case (u, v) is the same as (v, u). Graphs are typically visualized by drawing the vertices as ovals or rectangles and the edges as segments or curves connecting pairs of ovals and rectangles. The following are some examples of directed and undirected graphs.

Example 12.1: *We can visualize collaborations among the researchers of a certain discipline by constructing a graph whose vertices are associated with the researchers themselves, and whose edges connect pairs of vertices associated with researchers who have coauthored a paper or book. (See Figure 12.1.) Such edges are undirected because coauthorship is a* **symmetric** *relation; that is, if A has coauthored something with B, then B necessarily has coauthored something with A.*

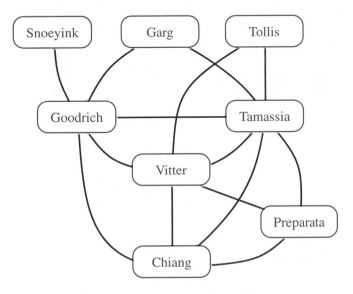

Figure 12.1: Graph of coauthorships among some authors.

Example 12.2: *We can associate with an object-oriented program a graph whose vertices represent the classes defined in the program, and whose edges indicate inheritance between classes. There is an edge from a vertex v to a vertex u if the class for v extends the class for u. Such edges are directed because the inheritance relation only goes in one direction (that is, it is* **asymmetric***).*

If all the edges in a graph are undirected, then we say the graph is an ***undirected graph***. Likewise, a ***directed graph***, also called a ***digraph***, is a graph whose edges are all directed. A graph that has both directed and undirected edges is often called a ***mixed graph***. Note that an undirected or mixed graph can be converted into a directed graph by replacing every undirected edge (u,v) by the pair of directed edges (u,v) and (v,u). It is often useful, however, to keep undirected and mixed graphs represented as they are, for such graphs have several applications, such as that of the following example.

Example 12.3: *A city map can be modeled by a graph whose vertices are intersections or dead-ends, and whose edges are stretches of streets without intersections. This graph has both undirected edges, which correspond to stretches of two-way streets, and directed edges, which correspond to stretches of one-way streets. Thus, in this way, a graph modeling a city map is a mixed graph.*

Example 12.4: *Physical examples of graphs are present in the electrical wiring and plumbing networks of a building. Such networks can be modeled as graphs, where each connector, fixture, or outlet is viewed as a vertex, and each uninterrupted stretch of wire or pipe is viewed as an edge. Such graphs are actually components of much larger graphs, namely the local power and water distribution networks. Depending on the specific aspects of these graphs that we are interested in, we may consider their edges as undirected or directed, for, in principle, water can flow in a pipe and current can flow in a wire in either direction.*

The two vertices joined by an edge are called the ***end vertices*** of the edge. The end vertices of an edge are also known as the ***endpoints*** of that edge. If an edge is directed, its first endpoint is its ***origin*** and the other is the ***destination*** of the edge.

Two vertices are said to be ***adjacent*** if they are endpoints of the same edge. An edge is said to be ***incident*** on a vertex if the vertex is one of the edge's endpoints. The ***outgoing edges*** of a vertex are the directed edges whose origin is that vertex. The ***incoming edges*** of a vertex are the directed edges whose destination is that vertex. The ***degree*** of a vertex v, denoted $\deg(v)$, is the number of incident edges of v. The ***in-degree*** and ***out-degree*** of a vertex v are the number of the incoming and outgoing edges of v, and are denoted $\mathrm{indeg}(v)$ and $\mathrm{outdeg}(v)$, respectively.

Example 12.5: *We can study air transportation by constructing a graph G, called a* **flight network**, *whose vertices are associated with airports, and whose edges are associated with flights. (See Figure 12.2.) In graph G, the edges are directed because a given flight has a specific travel direction (from the origin airport to the destination airport). The endpoints of an edge e in G correspond respectively to the origin and destination for the flight corresponding to e. Two airports are adjacent in G if there is a flight that flies between them, and an edge e is incident upon a vertex v in G if the flight for e flies to or from the airport for v. The outgoing edges of a vertex v correspond to the outbound flights from v's airport, and the incoming edges correspond to the inbound flights to v's airport. Finally, the in-degree of a vertex v of G corresponds to the number of inbound flights to v's airport, and the out-degree of a vertex v in G corresponds to the number of outbound flights.*

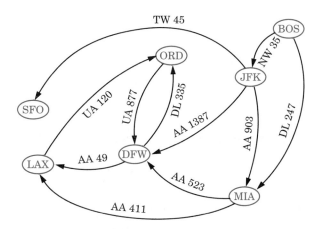

Figure 12.2: Example of a directed graph representing a flight network. The endpoints of edge UA 120 are LAX and ORD; hence, LAX and ORD are adjacent. The in-degree of DFW is 3, and the out-degree of DFW is 2.

The definition of a graph refers to the group of edges as a ***collection***, not a ***set***, thus allowing for two undirected edges to have the same end vertices, and for two directed edges to have the same origin and the same destination. Such edges are called ***parallel edges*** or ***multiple edges***. Parallel edges can be in a flight network (Example 12.5), in which case multiple edges between the same pair of vertices could indicate different flights operating on the same route at different times of the day. Another special type of edge is one that connects a vertex to itself. Namely, we say that an edge (undirected or directed) is a ***self-loop*** if its two endpoints coincide. A self-loop may occur in a graph associated with a city map (Example 12.3), where it would correspond to a "circle" (a curving street that returns to its starting point).

With few exceptions, like those mentioned above, graphs do not have parallel edges or self-loops. Such graphs are said to be *simple*. Thus, we can usually say that the edges of a simple graph are a *set* of vertex pairs (and not just a collection). Throughout this chapter, we shall assume that a graph is simple unless otherwise

| Caution |

specified. This assumption simplifies the presentation of data structures and algorithms for graphs. Extending the results of this chapter to general graphs that admit self-loops and/or parallel edges is straightforward, though the details can be tedious.

We explore, in the propositions that follow, a few important properties of degrees and the number of edges in a graph. These properties relate the number of vertices and edges to each other and to the degrees of the vertices in a graph.

Proposition 12.6: *If G is a graph with m edges, then*

$$\sum_{v \in G} deg(v) = 2m.$$

Justification: An edge (u,v) is counted twice in the above summation; once by its endpoint u and once by its endpoint v. Thus, the total contribution of the edges to the degrees of the vertices is twice the number of edges.   ■

Proposition 12.7: *If G is a directed graph with m edges, then*

$$\sum_{v \in G} indeg(v) \; = \; \sum_{v \in G} outdeg(v) = m.$$

Justification: In a directed graph, an edge (u,v) contributes one unit to the out-degree of its origin u and one unit to the in-degree of its destination v. Thus, the total contribution of the edges to the out-degrees of the vertices is equal to the number of edges, and similarly for the out-degrees.   ■

Proposition 12.8: *Let G be a simple graph with n vertices and m edges. If G is undirected, then $m \leq n(n-1)/2$, and if G is directed, then $m \leq n(n-1)$.*

Justification: Suppose that G is undirected. Since no two edges can have the same endpoints and there are no self-loops, the maximum degree of a vertex in G is $n-1$ in this case. Thus, by Proposition 12.6, $2m \leq n(n-1)$. Now suppose that G is directed. Since no two edges can have the same origin and destination, and there are no self-loops, the maximum in-degree of a vertex in G is $n-1$ in this case. Thus, by Proposition 12.7, $m \leq n(n-1)$.   ■

Put another way, this last proposition states that a simple graph with n vertices has $O(n^2)$ edges.

A *path* of a graph is a sequence of alternating vertices and edges that starts at a vertex and ends at a vertex such that each edge is incident to its predecessor and successor vertex. A *cycle* is a path such that its start and end vertices are the same. We say that a path is *simple* if each vertex in the path is distinct, and we say that a cycle is *simple* if each vertex in the cycle is distinct, except for the first and last one. A *directed path* is a path such that all the edges are directed and are traversed along their direction. A *directed cycle* is defined similarly. For example, in the flight network of Figure 12.2, (BOS, NW 35, JFK, AA 1387, DFW) is a directed simple path, and (LAX, UA 120, ORD, UA 877, DFW, AA 49, LAX) is a directed simple cycle.

Example 12.9: *Given a graph G representing a city map (see Example 12.3), we can model a couple driving from their home to dinner at a recommended restaurant as traversing a path though G. If they know the way, and don't accidentally go through the same intersection twice, then they traverse a simple path in G. Likewise, we can model the entire trip the couple takes, from their home to the restaurant and back, as a cycle. If they go home from the restaurant in a completely different way than how they went, not even going through the same intersection twice, then their entire round trip is a simple cycle. Finally, if they travel along one-way streets for their entire trip, then we can model their night out as a directed cycle.*

A *subgraph* of a graph G is a graph H whose vertices and edges are subsets of the vertices and edges of G, respectively. For example, in the flight network of Figure 12.2, vertices BOS, JFK, and MIA, and edges AA 903 and DL 247 form a subgraph. A *spanning subgraph* of G is a subgraph of G that contains all the vertices of the graph G. A graph is *connected* if, for any two vertices, there is a path between them. If a graph G is not connected, its maximal connected subgraphs are called the *connected components* of G. A *forest* is a graph without cycles. A *tree* is a connected forest, that is, a connected graph without cycles. Note that this definition of a tree is somewhat different from the one given in Chapter 6. Namely, in the context of graphs, a tree has no root. Whenever there is ambiguity, the trees of Chapter 6 should be referred to as *rooted trees*, while the trees of this chapter should be referred to as *free trees*. The connected components of a forest are (free) trees. A *spanning tree* of a graph is a spanning subgraph that is a (free) tree.

Caution

Example 12.10: *Perhaps the most talked about graph today is the Internet, which can be viewed as a graph whose vertices are computers and whose (undirected) edges are communication connections between pairs of computers on the Internet. The computers and the connections between them in a single domain, like wiley.com, form a subgraph of the Internet. If this subgraph is connected, then two* *users on computers in this domain can send e-mail to one another without having their information packets ever leave their domain. Suppose the edges of this subgraph form a spanning tree. This implies that, if even a single connection goes down (for example, because someone pulls a communication cable out of the back of a computer in this domain), then this subgraph will no longer be connected.*

There are a number of simple properties of trees, forests, and connected graphs. We explore a few of them in the following proposition.

Proposition 12.11: *Let G be an undirected graph with n vertices and m edges. Then we have the following:*

- *If G is connected, then $m \geq n - 1$.*
- *If G is a tree, then $m = n - 1$.*
- *If G is a forest, then $m \leq n - 1$.*

We leave the justification of this proposition as an exercise (C-12.1).

12.1.1   Graph Methods

As an abstract data type, a graph is a positional container of elements that are stored at the graph's vertices and edges. Namely, the **positions** in a graph are its vertices and edges. Hence, we can store elements in a graph at either its edges or its vertices (or both). In terms of a Java implementation, this implies that we can define Vertex and Edge interfaces that each extend the Position interface. Recall that a position has an element() method, which returns the element that is stored at this position. We also use specialized iterators for vertices and edges, called VertexIterator and EdgeIterator, respectively.

Since a graph is a positional container (Section 6.1.3), the graph ADT supports the methods size(), isEmpty(), elements(), positions(), replaceElement(p, o), and swapElements(p, q), where p and q denote positions, and o denotes an object (that is, an element).

Graphs are a much richer abstract data type than we have discussed in previous chapters. Their richness derives mostly from the different kinds of objects that help define a graph, such as vertices and edges. So as to present the methods for the graph ADT in as organized a way as possible, we divide the graph methods into three main categories: general methods, methods dealing with directed edges, and methods for updating and modifying graphs. In addition, in order to simplify the presentation, we denote with v a vertex position, with e an edge position, and with o an object (element) stored at a vertex or edge. Also, we do not discuss error conditions that may occur.

General Methods

We begin by describing the fundamental methods for a graph, which ignore the direction of the edges. Each of the following methods returns global information about a graph G:

numVertices(): Return the number of vertices in G.

numEdges(): Return the number of edges in G.

vertices(): Return an iterator of the vertices of G.

edges(): Return an iterator of the edges of G.

Unlike a tree (which has a root), a graph has no special vertex. Hence, we have a method that returns an arbitrary vertex of the graph:

aVertex(): Return a vertex of G.

The following accessor methods take vertex and edge positions as arguments:

degree(v): Return the degree of v.

adjacentVertices(v): Return an iterator of the vertices adjacent to v.

incidentEdges(v): Return an iterator of the edges incident upon v.

endVertices(e): Return an array of size 2 storing the end vertices of e.

opposite(v, e): Return the endpoint of edge e distinct from v.

areAdjacent(v, w): Return whether vertices v and w are adjacent.

Methods Dealing with Directed Edges

When we allow for some or all the edges in a graph to be directed, then there are several additional methods we should include in the graph ADT. We begin with some methods for dealing specifically with directed edges.

directedEdges(): Return an iterator of all directed edges.

undirectedEdges(): Return an iterator of all undirected edges.

destination(e): Return the destination of the directed edge e.

origin(e): Return the origin of the directed edge e.

isDirected(e): Return true if and only if the edge e is directed.

In addition, the existence of directed edges require that we have ways of relating vertices and edges in terms of directions:

inDegree(v): Return the in-degree of v.

outDegree(v): Return the out-degree of v.

inIncidentEdges(v): Return an iterator of all the incoming edges to v.

outIncidentEdges(v): Return an iterator of all the outgoing edges from v.

inAdjacentVertices(v): Return an iterator of all the vertices adjacent to v along incoming edges to v.

outAdjacentVertices(v): Return an iterator of all the vertices adjacent to v along outgoing edges from v.

Methods for Updating Graphs

We can also allow for update methods that add or delete edges and vertices:

insertEdge(v, w, o): Insert and return an undirected edge between vertices v and w, storing the object o at this position.

insertDirectedEdge(v, w, o): Insert and return a directed edge from vertex v to vertex w, storing the object o at this position.

insertVertex(o): Insert and return a new (isolated) vertex storing the object o at this position.

removeVertex(v): Remove vertex v and all its incident edges.

removeEdge(e): Remove edge e.

makeUndirected(e): Make edge e undirected.

reverseDirection(e): Reverse the direction of directed edge e.

setDirectionFrom(e, v): Make edge e directed away from vertex v.

setDirectionTo(e, v): Make edge e directed into vertex v.

There are admittedly a lot of methods in the graph ADT. The number of methods is to a certain extent unavoidable, however, since graphs are such rich structures. Graphs support two kinds of positions—vertices and edges—and even then allow for edges to be either directed or undirected. We need to have different methods for accessing and updating all these different positions, as well as dealing with the relationships that can exist between these different positions.

12.2 Data Structures for Graphs

There are several ways to realize the graph ADT with a concrete data structure. In this section, we discuss three popular approaches, usually referred to as the *edge list* structure, the *adjacency list* structure, and the *adjacency matrix*. In all the three representations, we use a container (a list or vector, for example) to store the vertices of the graph. Regarding the edges, there is a fundamental difference between the first two structures and the latter. The edge list structure and the adjacency list structure only store the edges actually present in the graph, while the adjacency matrix stores a placeholder for every pair of vertices (whether there is an edge between them or not). As we will explain in this section, this difference implies that, for a graph G with n vertices and m edges, an edge list or adjacency list representation uses $O(n+m)$ space, whereas an adjacency matrix representation uses $O(n^2)$ space.

12.2.1 The Edge List Structure

The *edge list* structure is possibly the simplest, though not the most efficient, representation of a graph G. In this representation, a vertex v of G storing an element o is explicitly represented by a vertex object. All such vertex objects are stored in a container V, which would typically be a list, vector, or dictionary. If we represent V as a vector, for example, then we would naturally think of the vertices as being numbered. If we represent V as a dictionary, on the other hand, then we would naturally think of each vertex as being identified by a key that we associate with it. It is also useful for this dictionary to support the locator pattern (see Section 8.7). Note that the elements of container V are the vertex positions of graph G.

Vertex Objects

The vertex object for a vertex v storing element o has instance variables for

- A reference to o
- Counters for the number of incident undirected edges, incoming directed edges, and outgoing directed edges
- A reference to the position (or locator) of the vertex-object in container V.

The distinguishing feature of the edge list structure is not how it represents vertices, however, but the way in which it represents edges. In this structure, an edge e of G storing an element o is explicitly represented by an edge object. The edge objects are stored in a container E, which would typically be a list, vector, or dictionary (possibly supporting the locator pattern).

Edge Objects

The edge object for an edge e storing element o has instance variables for

- A reference to o
- A Boolean indicator of whether e is directed or undirected
- References to the vertex objects in V associated with the endpoint vertices of e (if the edge e is undirected) or to the origin and destination vertices of e (if the edge e is directed)
- A reference to the position (or locator) of the edge-object in container E.

A schematic illustration of the edge list structure for a directed graph G is shown in Figure 12.3.

The Edge List

The reason this structure is called the *edge list* structure is that the simplest and most common implementation of the container E is with a list. Even so, in order to be able to conveniently search for specific objects associated with edges, we may wish to implement E with a dictionary, in spite of our calling this the "edge list." We may also wish to implement the container V as a dictionary for the same reason. Still, in keeping with tradition, we call this structure the edge list structure.

The main feature of the edge list structure is that it provides direct access from edges to the vertices they are incident upon. This allows us to define simple algorithms for implementing the different edge-based methods of the graph ADT (for example, methods endVertices, origin, and destination). We can simply access the appropriate components of the given edge object to implement each such method.

Nevertheless, the "inverse" operation—that of accessing the edges that are incident upon a vertex—requires an exhaustive inspection of all the edge objects in container E. That is, in order to determine which edges are incident to a vertex v we must examine all the edges in the edge list and check, for each one, if it happens to be incident to v. Thus, for example, method incidentEdges(v) runs in time proportional to the number of edges in the graph, not in time proportional to the degree of vertex v. In fact, even to check if two vertices v and w are adjacent, by the areAdjacent(v,w) method, requires that we search the entire edge list looking for the edge (v,w) or (w,v). Moreover, since removing a vertex involves removing all of its incident edges, the method removeVertex also requires a complete search of the edge list, E.

(a)

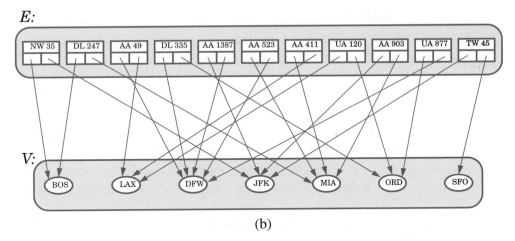

(b)

Figure 12.3: (a) A directed graph G; (b) schematic representation of the edge list structure for G. To avoid clutter, we do not show the following fields of the vertex objects: the three counters for the incident edges and the reference to the position (or locator) of the vertex-object in container V. Also, we do not show the following fields of the edge objects: the Boolean direction indicator and the reference to the position (or locator) of the edge-object in container E. Finally, we visualize the elements stored in the vertex and edge objects with the element names, instead of with actual references to the element objects.

Performance

Table 12.1 summarizes the performance of the edge-list implementation of a graph.

Operation	Time
size, isEmpty, replaceElement, swapElements	$O(1)$
numVertices, numEdges, aVertex	$O(1)$
vertices	$O(n)$
edges, directedEdges, undirectedEdges	$O(m)$
elements, positions	$O(n+m)$
endVertices, opposite, origin, destination, isDirected, degree, inDegree, outDegree	$O(1)$
incidentEdges, inIncidentEdges, outIncidentEdges, adjacentVertices, inAdjacentVertices, outAdjacentVertices, areAdjacent	$O(m)$
insertVertex, insertEdge, insertDirectedEdge, removeEdge, makeUndirected, reverseDirection, setDirectionFrom, setDirectionTo	$O(1)$
removeVertex	$O(m)$

Table 12.1: Running times of methods of a graph implemented with an edge list, where V and E are realized with linked lists. The space used is $O(n+m)$, where n is the number of vertices and m is the number of edges.

Details for selected methods of the graph ADT are as follows:

- Methods numVertices(), numEdges(), and size() are implemented in $O(1)$ time by returning V.size(), E.size(), and V.size() $+ E$.size(), respectively.
- The counters stored with each vertex object allow us to perform, in constant time, methods degree, inDegree, and outDegree.
- Methods vertices() and edges() are implemented by calling V.elements() and E.elements(), respectively.
- We implement iterators directedEdges() and undirectedEdges() by calling E.elements() and only returning those edges that are of the correct type.
- Since the containers V and E are lists implemented with a doubly linked list, we can insert vertices, and insert and remove edges, in $O(1)$ time.
- Methods incidentEdges, inIncidentEdges, outIncidentEdges, adjacentVertices, inAdjacentVertices, outAdjacentVertices, and areAdjacent all take $O(m)$ time, for to determine which edges are incident upon a vertex v we must inspect all edges.
- The update method removeVertex(v) takes $O(m)$ time, since it requires that we inspect all the edges to find and remove those incident upon v.

12.2.2   The Adjacency List Structure

The ***adjacency list*** structure for a graph G extends the edge list structure, adding extra information that supports direct access to the incident edges (and thus to the adjacent vertices) of each vertex. While the edge list structure views the edge-vertex incidence relation only from the point of view of the edges, the adjacency list structure considers it from both viewpoints. This symmetric approach allows us to use the adjacency list structure to implement a number of vertex methods of the graph ADT much faster than what is possible with the edge list structure, even though these two representations both use an amount of space proportional to the number of vertices and edges in the graph. The adjacency list structure includes all the structural components of the edge list structure plus the following:

- The vertex object v holds a reference to a container $I(v)$, called the ***incidence container***, that stores references to the edges incident on v. If directed edges are allowed, then we partition $I(v)$ into $I_{in}(v)$, $I_{out}(v)$, and $I_{un}(v)$, which respectively store the in-coming, out-going, and undirected edges incident to v.
- The edge object for an edge (u,v) holds references to the positions (or locators) of the edge in the incidence containers $I(u)$ and $I(v)$.

The Adjacency List

Traditionally, the incidence container $I(v)$ for a vertex v is realized by means of a list, which is why we call this way of representing a graph the ***adjacency list*** structure. Still, there may be some contexts where we wish to represent an incidence container $I(v)$ as, say, a dictionary or a priority queue, so let us stick with thinking of $I(v)$ as a generic container of edge objects. If we want to support a graph representation that can represent a graph G potentially containing both directed and undirected edges, then we have, for each vertex, three incidence containers, $I_{in}(v)$, $I_{out}(v)$, and $I_{un}(v)$, that store references to the edge objects associated with the directed incoming, directed outgoing, and undirected edges incident on v, respectively.

The adjacency list structure provides direct access both from the edges to the vertices and from the vertices to their incident edges. Being able to provide access between vertices and edges in both directions allows us to speed up the performance of a number of the graph methods by using an adjacency list structure instead of an edge list structure. We illustrate the adjacency list structure of a directed graph in Figure 12.4. For a vertex v, the space used by the incidence container of v is proportional to the degree of v, that is, it is $O(\deg(v))$. Thus, by Proposition 12.6, the space requirement of the adjacency list structure is $O(n+m)$.

(a)

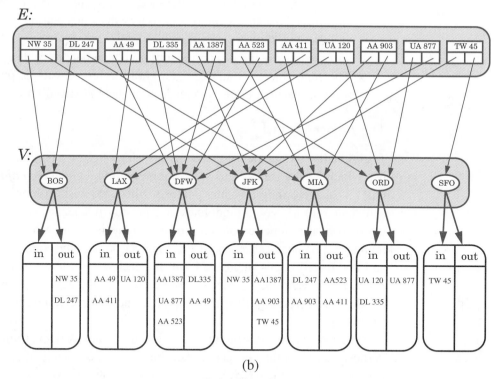

(b)

Figure 12.4: (a) A directed graph G; (b) schematic representation of the adjacency list structure of G. As in Figure 12.3, we do not show various fields of the vertex and edge objects, and we visualize the elements of containers with names instead of objects. Also, we only show the incidence containers for directed edges, since there are no undirected edges in this graph.

Performance

Table 12.2 summarizes the performance of the adjacency list representation of a graph, assuming that V, E, and the incident structures are all implemented with linked lists.

Note that all of the methods of the graph ADT that can be implemented with the edge list structure in $O(1)$ time can also be implemented in $O(1)$ time for the adjacency list structure using essentially the same algorithms. In addition, the adjacency list structure provides improved running time for the following methods:

- The methods that return iterators of incident edges or adjacent vertices for a vertex v can be constructed in time proportional to their size, that is, in $O(\deg(v))$ time.
- Method areAdjacent(u, v) can be performed by inspecting either the incidence container of u or that of v. By choosing the smaller of the two, we get $O(\min(\deg(u), \deg(v)))$ running time.
- Method removeVertex(v) requires the inspection of the incidence container of v, and thus takes $O(\deg(v))$ time.

Operation	Time
size, isEmpty, replaceElement, swapElements	$O(1)$
numVertices, numEdges, aVertex	$O(1)$
vertices	$O(n)$
edges, directedEdges, undirectedEdges	$O(m)$
elements, positions	$O(n+m)$
endVertices, opposite, origin, destination, isDirected, degree, inDegree, outDegree	$O(1)$
incidentEdges(v), inIncidentEdges(v), outIncidentEdges(v), adjacentVertices(v), inAdjacentVertices(v), outAdjacentVertices(v)	$O(\deg(v))$
areAdjacent(u, v)	$O(\min(\deg(u), \deg(v)))$
insertVertex, insertEdge, insertDirectedEdge, removeEdge, makeUndirected, reverseDirection, setDirectionFrom, setDirectionTo	$O(1)$
removeVertex(v)	$O(\deg(v))$

Table 12.2: Running times for the methods of a graph implemented with an adjacency list structure such that containers V and E and the incidence containers are realized with lists, which are in turn implemented with doubly linked lists. We denote with n and m the number of vertices and edges of the graph, respectively. The space used is $O(n+m)$.

As we will see in future sections, the improvement of an adjacency list over an edge list is quite useful, for the adjacency list structure allows us to perform several iterator methods for a vertex v in $O(\deg(v))$ time, as opposed to the $O(m)$ time performance for the edge list structure. Note that we can further improve the running time of the areAdjacent(u,v) method if we implement the container E with a fast dictionary whose keys are pairs of vertices; we explore this approach in further detail in an exercise (C-12.4).

12.2.3 The Adjacency Matrix Structure

Like the adjacency list structure, the ***adjacency matrix*** representation of a graph also extends the edge-structure with an additional component. In this case, we augment the edge list with a matrix (a two-dimensional array) A that allows us to determine adjacencies between pairs of vertices in constant time. As we shall see, achieving this speedup comes at a price in the space usage of the data structure.

In the adjacency matrix representation, we think of the vertices as being the integers in the set $\{0, 1, \ldots, n-1\}$ and the edges as being pairs of such integers. This allows us to store references to edges in the cells of a two-dimensional $n \times n$ array A. Specifically, the adjacency matrix representation extends the edge list structure as follows (see Figure 12.5):

- A vertex object v also stores a distinct integer key in the range $0, 1, \ldots, n-1$, called the ***index*** of v. To simplify the discussion, we may refer to the vertex with index i simply as "vertex i."

- We keep a two-dimensional $n \times n$ array A such that the cell $A[i, j]$ holds a reference to the edge object e that goes from the vertex with index i to the vertex with index j, if such an edge exists. If the edge e, connecting vertices i and j, is undirected, then we store references to e in both $A[i, j]$ and $A[j, i]$. If there is no edge from vertex i to vertex j, then $A[i, j]$ references the null object (or some other indicator that this cell is associated with no edge).

The adjacency matrix A allows us to perform the method areAdjacent(v, w) in $O(1)$ time. We achieve this performance by accessing the vertices v and w to determine their respective indices i and j, and then testing whether or not the cell $A[i, j]$ references the null object. This performance achievement is counteracted by an increase in the space usage, however, which is now $O(n^2)$, and in the running time of other methods. For example, the vertex methods, such as incidentEdges, adjacentVertices, inAdjacentVertices, and outAdjacentVertices, now require that we examine an entire row or column of array A, which takes $O(n)$ time. Moreover, any vertex insertions or deletions now require creating a whole new array A, of larger or smaller size, respectively, which takes time $O(n^2)$.

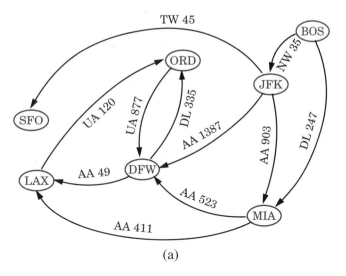

(a)

0	1	2	3	4	5	6
BOS	DFW	JFK	LAX	MIA	ORD	SFO

(b)

	0	1	2	3	4	5	6
0	Ø	Ø	NW 35	Ø	DL 247	Ø	Ø
1	Ø	Ø	Ø	AA 49	Ø	DL 335	Ø
2	Ø	AA 1387	Ø	Ø	AA 903	Ø	TW 45
3	Ø	Ø	Ø	Ø	Ø	UA 120	Ø
4	Ø	AA 523	Ø	AA 411	Ø	Ø	Ø
5	Ø	UA 877	Ø	Ø	Ø	Ø	Ø
6	Ø	Ø	Ø	Ø	Ø	Ø	Ø

(c)

Figure 12.5: Schematic representation of the adjacency matrix structure: (a) a directed graph G; (b) a numbering of the vertices in G; (c) the adjacency matrix A for G.

Performance

Table 12.3 summarizes the performance of the adjacency matrix implementation of a graph. From this table we observe that the adjacency list structure is superior to the adjacency matrix in space, and is superior in time for all methods except for the areAdjacent method.

Operation	Time
size, isEmpty, replaceElement, swapElements	$O(1)$
numVertices, numEdges, aVertex	$O(1)$
vertices	$O(n)$
edges, directedEdges, undirectedEdges	$O(m)$
elements, positions	$O(n+m)$
endVertices, opposite, origin, destination, isDirected, degree, inDegree, outDegree	$O(1)$
incidentEdges, inIncidentEdges, outIncidentEdges, adjacentVertices, inAdjacentVertices, outAdjacentVertices	$O(n)$
areAdjacent	$O(1)$
insertEdge, insertDirectedEdge, removeEdge, makeUndirected, reverseDirection, setDirectionFrom, setDirectionTo	$O(1)$
insertVertex, removeVertex	$O(n^2)$

Table 12.3: Running times of the methods of a graph implemented with an adjacency matrix. We denote with n and m the number of vertices and edges of the graph, respectively. The space used is $O(n^2)$.

Historically, the adjacency matrix was the first representation used for graphs. We should not find this fact surprising, however, for the adjacency matrix has a natural appeal as a mathematical structure (for example, an undirected graph has a symmetric adjacency matrix). The adjacency list structure came later, with its natural appeal in computing due to its faster methods for most algorithms (many algorithms do not use method areAdjacent) and its space efficiency.

Most of the graph algorithms we examine in this book will run efficiently when acting upon a graph stored using the adjacency list representation. In some cases, however, a trade-off occurs, where graphs with few edges are most efficiently processed with an adjacency list structure and graphs with many edges are most efficiently processed with an adjacency matrix structure.

Next, we explore a fundamental kind of algorithmic operation that we might wish to perform on a graph—traversing the edges and the vertices of that graph.

12.3 Graph Traversal

A *traversal* is a systematic procedure for exploring a graph by examining all of its vertices and edges. A traversal is efficient if it visits all the vertices and edges in time proportional to their number, that is, in linear time. In this section and the next, we consider two efficient traversals of undirected graphs, called depth-first search and breadth-first search, respectively. In Section 12.4.1, we extend these techniques to traversals of directed graphs.

12.3.1 Depth-First Search

The first traversal algorithm we consider is *depth-first search* (DFS) in an undirected graph. Depth-first search is useful for performing a number of computations on graphs, including finding a path from one vertex to another, determining whether or not a graph is connected, and computing a spanning tree of a connected graph. In this section, we explain how DFS works and how it can be used.

Depth-first search in an undirected graph G is analogous to wandering in a labyrinth with a string and a can of paint without getting lost. We begin at a specific starting vertex s in G, which we initialize by fixing one end of our string to s and painting s as "visited." The vertex s is now our "current" vertex—call our current vertex u. We then traverse G by considering an (arbitrary) edge (u, v) incident to the current vertex u. If the edge (u, v) leads us to an already visited (that is, painted) vertex v, we immediately return to vertex u. If, on the other hand, (u, v) leads to an unvisited vertex v, then we unroll our string, and go to v. We then paint v as "visited," and make it the current vertex, repeating the above computation. Eventually, we will get to a "dead-end," that is, a current vertex u such that all the edges incident on u lead to vertices already visited. Thus, taking any edge incident on u will cause us to return to u. To get out of this impasse, we roll our string back up, backtracking along the edge that brought us to u, going back to a previously visited vertex v. We then make v our current vertex and repeat the above computation for any edges incident upon v that we have not looked at before. If all of v's incident edges lead to visited vertices, then we again roll up our string and backtrack to the vertex we came from to get to v, and repeat the procedure at that vertex. Thus, we continue to backtrack along the path that we have traced so far until we find a vertex that has yet unexplored edges, take one such edge, and continue the traversal. The process terminates when our backtracking leads us back to the start vertex s, and there are no more unexplored edges incident on s. This simple process traverses the edges of G in an elegant, systematic way. (See Figure 12.6.)

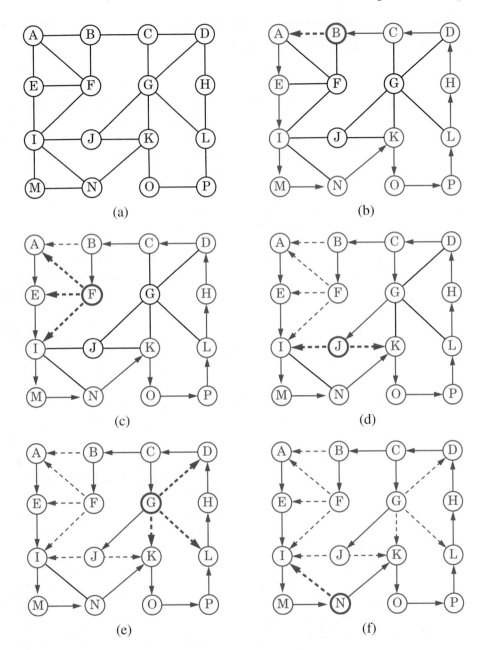

Figure 12.6: Example of depth-first search traversal on a graph starting at vertex *A*. Discovery edges are shown with solid lines and back edges are shown with dashed lines: (a) input graph; (b) path of discovery edges traced from A until back edge (B,A) is hit; (c) reaching F, which is a dead end; (d) after backtracking to C, resuming with edge (C,G), and hitting another dead end, J; (e) after backtracking to G; (f) after backtracking to N.

We can visualize a DFS traversal by orienting the edges along the direction in which they are explored during the traversal, distinguishing the edges used to discover new vertices, called *discovery edges*, or *tree edges*, from those that lead to already visited vertices, called *back edges*. (See Figure 12.6f.) In the analogy above, discovery edges are the edges where we unroll our string when we traverse them, and back edges are the edges where we immediately return without unrolling any string. As we will see, the discovery edges form a spanning tree of the connected component of the starting vertex s. We call the edges not in this tree "back edges" because, assuming that the tree is rooted at the start vertex, each such edge leads back from a vertex in this tree to one of its ancestors in the tree.

The pseudo-code for a DFS traversal starting at a vertex v follows our analogy with string and paint. We use recursion to implement the string analogy, and we assume that we have a mechanism (the paint analogy) to determine if a vertex or edge has been explored or not, and to label the edges as discovery edges or back edges. This mechanism will require additional space and may affect the running time of the algorithm. A pseudo-code description of the recursive DFS algorithm is given in Code Fragment 12.1.

Algorithm DFS(G, v):

    Input: A graph G and a vertex v of G

    Output: A labeling of the edges as discovery edges and back edges

  for all edges e in G.incidentEdges(v) **do**

    if edge e is unexplored **then**

      $w \leftarrow G$.opposite(v, e)

      if vertex w is unexplored **then**

        label e as a discovery edge

        recursively call DFS(G, w)

      else

        label e as a back edge

Code Fragment 12.1: The DFS algorithm.

There are a number of observations that we can make about the depth-first search algorithm, many of which derive from the way the DFS algorithm partitions the edges of the undirected graph G into two groups, the discovery edges and the back edges. For example, since back edges always connect a vertex v to a previously visited vertex u, each back edge implies a cycle in G, consisting of the discovery edges from u to v plus the back edge (u, v).

Proposition 12.12, which follows, identifies some other important properties of the depth-first search traversal method.

Proposition 12.12: *Let G be an undirected graph on which a DFS traversal starting at a vertex s has been performed. Then:*

- *The traversal visits all vertices in the connected component of s*
- *The discovery edges form a spanning tree of the connected component of s.*

Justification: The justification for why we visit all the vertices in the connected component of s is based upon a simple contradiction argument. Suppose there is at least one vertex v in s's connected component not visited, and let w be the first unvisited vertex on some path from s to v (of course, we may have $v = w$). Since w is the first unvisited vertex on this path, it has a neighbor u that was visited. But when we visited u, we must have considered the edge (u, w); hence, it cannot be correct that w is unvisited. Therefore, there are no unvisited vertices in s's connected component.

Since we only mark edges when we go to unvisited vertices, we will never form a cycle with discovery edges, that is, discovery edges form a tree. Moreover, this is a spanning tree because, as we have just seen, the depth-first search visits each vertex in the connected component of s.   ■

In terms of its running time, depth-first search is an efficient method for traversing a graph. Note that DFS is called exactly once on each vertex, and that every edge is examined exactly twice, once from each of its end vertices. Thus, if n_s vertices and m_s edges are in the connected component of vertex s, a DFS starting at s runs in $O(n_s + m_s)$ time, provided the following conditions are satisfied:

- The graph is represented by a data structure with the following performance bounds:
  - method incidentEdges(v) takes $O(\text{degree}(v))$ time
  - methods hasNext() and nextEdge() of the EdgeIterator returned by incidentEdges(v) each take $O(1)$ time
  - method opposite(v, e) takes $O(1)$ time.

  The adjacency list structure satisfies the above properties, but the adjacency matrix structure does not.
- We have a way to "mark" a vertex or edge as explored, and to test if a vertex or edge has been explored in $O(1)$ time. One way to do such marking is to extend the functionality of positions, as discussed below. Another way is to use an auxiliary hash table to store the explored vertices and edges. This scheme satisfies the condition in the probabilistic sense, because a hash table supports the mark (insert) and test (find) operations in $O(1)$ *expected* time (see Section 8.3).

The Decorator Pattern

Marking the explored vertices in a DFS traversal is an example of the ***decorator*** software engineering design pattern. This pattern is used to add attributes or "decorations" to existing objects. Each attribute is identified by a specific decoration object, a, which acts as a kind of key identifying this attribute. Intuitively, the attribute a is the "name" of the decoration, and we then allow this attribute to take on different values for the different objects that are decorated with a attributes. The use of decorations is motivated by the need of some algorithms and data structures to add extra variables, or temporary scratch data, to objects that do not normally have such variables. Hence, a decoration is an (attribute, value) pair that can be dynamically attached to an object. For example, nodes in an AVL tree or red-black tree could be decorated with height or color attributes. In our DFS example, we would like to have "decorable" vertices and edges with an ***explored*** attribute and a Boolean value. We can realize the decorator pattern for all positional containers by adding the following methods to the position ADT:

has(a): Tests whether the position has attribute a.

get(a): Returns the value of attribute a.

set(a, x): Sets to x the value of attribute a.

destroy(a): Removes attribute a and its associated value.

The above methods can be implemented by storing at each position a dictionary of the attributes and their values for that position. By Proposition 12.12 and the above discussion, we can solve a number of interesting problems for an undirected graph, as summarized below.

Proposition 12.13: *Let G be a graph with n vertices and m edges represented with an adjacency list structure. A DFS traversal of G can be performed in $O(n+m)$ time. Also, there exist $O(n+m)$-time algorithms based on DFS for the following problems:*

- *Testing whether G is connected*
- *Computing a spanning tree of G, if G is connected*
- *Computing the connected components of G*
- *Computing a path between two given vertices of G, or reporting that no such path exists*
- *Computing a cycle in G, or reporting that G has no cycles.*

The justification of Proposition 12.13 is based on algorithms that use the depth-first search algorithm or a slightly modified versions of the DFS algorithm as subroutines. We explore the details in some interesting, but not too difficult, exercises.

A Generic DFS Implementation in Java

In Code Fragments 12.2–12.4, we show a Java implementation of a generic depth-first search traversal by means of a class DFS whose behavior can be specialized for a particular application by redefining method execute, which activates the computation, and the following methods, which are called at various times by the recursive template method dfsTraversal.

- initResult(): called at the beginning of the execution of dfsTraversal.
- startVisit(Vertex v): also called at the beginning of the execution of dfsTraversal.
- traverseDiscovery(Edge e, Vertex v): called when a discovery edge e out of v is traversed.
- traverseBack(Edge e, Vertex v): called when a back edge e out of v is traversed.
- isDone(): called to determine whether to end the traversal early.
- finishVisit(Vertex v): called when all the incident edges of v have been traversed.
- result(): called to return the output of dfsTraversal.

Using the Template Method Pattern for DFS

Our generic depth-first search traversal is based on the template method pattern (see Section 6.3.5), which describes a generic computation mechanism that can be specialized by redefining certain steps.

The mechanism used to identify the vertices and edges that have been already visited (explored) during the traversal is encapsulated in the calls to methods isVisited, visit, and unVisit. Our implementation (see Code Fragment 12.4) assumes that the vertex and edge positions support the decorator pattern. Alternatively, we can set up a dictionary of positions and store the visited vertices and edges in it.

For us to do anything interesting with the dfsTraversal, we must extend the DFS class and redefine some of the auxiliary methods of Code Fragment 12.3 to do something nontrivial. This approach conforms to the template method pattern, for these methods specialize the behavior of the template method dfsTraversal.

Code Fragments 12.5–12.7 illustrate some interesting uses of the dfsTraversal method in classes that extend DFS. Class ConnectivityTesterDFS (Code Fragment 12.5), for instance, tests whether the graph is connected. It counts the vertices reachable by a DFS traversal starting at a vertex and compares this number with the total number of vertices of the graph.

```
/** Generic depth first search traversal of a graph using the template
 * method pattern.  A subclass should override various methods to add
 * functionality to this traversal.  */
public abstract class DFS {
  /** The graph being traversed. */
  protected InspectableGraph G;
  /** The result of the traversal. */
  protected Object visitResult;
  /** Perform a depth first search traversal.
   * @param g Input graph.
   * @param start Start vertex of the traversal.
   * @param info Auxiliary information (to be used by subclasses).
   */
  public Object execute(InspectableGraph g, Vertex start, Object info) {
    G = g;
    for (PositionIterator pos = G.positions(); pos.hasNext(); )
      unVisit(pos.nextPosition());
    return null;
  }
  /**
   * Recursive template method for a generic DFS traversal.
   * @param v Start vertex of the traversal.
   */
  protected Object dfsTraversal(Vertex v) {
    initResult();
    startVisit(v);
    visit(v);
    for (EdgeIterator inEdges = G.incidentEdges(v); inEdges.hasNext(); ) {
      Edge nextEdge = inEdges.nextEdge();
      if (!isVisited(nextEdge)) { // found an unexplored edge, explore it
        visit(nextEdge);
        Vertex w = G.opposite(v, nextEdge);
        if (!isVisited(w)) { // w is unexplored, this is a discovery edge
          traverseDiscovery(nextEdge, v);
          if (!isDone())
            visitResult = dfsTraversal(w);
        }
        else // w is explored, this is a back edge
          traverseBack(nextEdge, v);
      }
    }
    finishVisit(v);
    return result();
  }
```

Code Fragment 12.2: Instance variables and template method dfsTraversal of class DFS, which performs a generic DFS traversals of a graph. (Continued in Code Fragment 12.3.)

```
/** Auxiliary methods for specializing a generic DFS */
protected void initResult() {} // Initializes result (called first)
protected void startVisit(Vertex v) {} // Called when we first visit v
protected void finishVisit(Vertex v) {} // Called when we finish with v
protected void traverseDiscovery(Edge e, Vertex from) {} // Discovery edge
protected void traverseBack(Edge e, Vertex from) {} // Back edge
protected boolean isDone() { return false; } // Is DFS done early?
protected Object result() { return new Object(); } // The result of the DFS
```

Code Fragment 12.3: Auxiliary methods for specializing the template method dfs-Traversal of class DFS (Code Fragment 12.2).

```
/** Attribute and its two values for the visit status of positions. */
protected static Object STATUS = new Object(); // The status attribute
protected static Object VISITED = new Object(); // Visited value
protected static Object UNVISITED = new Object(); // Unvisited value
/** Mark a position as visited.     */
protected void visit(Position p) { p.set(STATUS, VISITED); }
/** Mark a position as unvisited.     */
protected void unVisit(Position p) { p.set(STATUS, UNVISITED); }
/** Test if a position has been visited. */
protected boolean isVisited(Position p) { return (p.get(STATUS) == VISITED); }
```

Code Fragment 12.4: Methods visit, unVisit, and isVisited of class DFS (Code Fragment 12.2) implemented using decorable positions.

```
/** This class specializes DFS to determine whether the graph is connected. */
public class ConnectivityTesterDFS extends DFS {
  protected int reached;
  public Object execute(InspectableGraph g, Vertex start, Object info) {
    super.execute(g, start, info);
    reached = 0;
    if (!G.isEmpty()) {
      Vertex v = G.aVertex();
      dfsTraversal(v);
    }
    return (new Boolean(reached == G.numVertices()));
  }
  public void startVisit(Vertex v) { reached++; }
}
```

Code Fragment 12.5: Specialization of class DFS to test if the graph is connected.

Class FindPathDFS (Code Fragment 12.6) finds a path between a pair of given start and target vertices. It performs a depth-first search traversal beginning at the start vertex. We maintain the path of discovery edges from the start vertex to the current vertex. When we encounter an unexplored vertex, we add it to the end of the path, and when we finish processing a vertex, we remove it from the path. The traversal is terminated when the target vertex is encountered, and the path is returned as an iterator of vertices. Note that the path found by this class consists of discovery edges.

```
/** This class specializes DFS to find a path between the start vertex
 * and a given target vertex. */
public class FindPathDFS extends DFS {
  protected Sequence path;
  protected boolean done;
  protected Vertex target;
  /** @param info target vertex of the path
   * @return Iterator of the vertices in a path from the start vertex
   * to the target vertex, or an empty iterator if no such path
   * exists in the graph */
  public Object execute(InspectableGraph g, Vertex start, Object info) {
    super.execute(g, start, info);
    path = new NodeSequence();
    done = false;
    target = (Vertex) info; // target vertex is stored in info parameter
    dfsTraversal(start);
    return new VertexIteratorAdapter(path.elements());
  }
  protected void startVisit(Vertex v) {
    path.insertLast(v);
    if (v == target)
      done = true;
  }
  protected void finishVisit(Vertex v) {
    if (!done)
      path.remove(path.last());
  }
  protected boolean isDone() {
    return done;
  }
}
```

Code Fragment 12.6: Specialization of class DFS to find a path between the start vertex and a target vertex. The auxiliary class VertexIteratorAdapter provides an adapter from a sequence to a vertex iterator.

Class FindCycleDFS (Code Fragment 12.7) finds a cycle in the connected component of a given vertex *v*, by performing a depth-first search traversal from *v* that terminates when a back edge is found. It returns a (possibly empty) iterator of the cycle formed by the found back edge.

```
/** Specialize DFS to find a cycle in connected component of start vertex. */
public class FindCycleDFS extends DFS {
  protected Sequence cycle; // sequence of edges of the cycle
  protected boolean done;
  protected Vertex cycleStart, target;
  /** @return Iterator of edges of a cycle in the component of start vertex */
  public Object execute(InspectableGraph g, Vertex start, Object info) {
    super.execute(g, start, info);
    cycle = new NodeSequence();
    done = false;
    dfsTraversal(start);
    if (!cycle.isEmpty() && start != cycleStart) {
      PositionIterator pos = cycle.positions();
      while (pos.hasNext()) { // remove the edges from start to cycleStart
        Position p = pos.nextPosition();
        Edge e = (Edge) p.element();
        cycle.remove(p);
        if (g.areIncident(cycleStart, e)) break;
      }
    }
    return new EdgeIteratorAdapter(cycle.elements());
  }
  protected void finishVisit(Vertex v) {
    if ((!cycle.isEmpty()) && (!done)) cycle.remove(cycle.last());
  }
  protected void traverseDiscovery(Edge e, Vertex from) {
    if (!done) cycle.insertLast(e);
  }
  protected void traverseBack(Edge e, Vertex from) {
    if (!done) {
      cycle.insertLast(e); // back edge e creates a cycle
      cycleStart = G.opposite(from, e);
      done = true;
    }
  }
  protected boolean isDone() {  return done; }
}
```

Code Fragment 12.7: Specialization of class DFS to find a cycle in the connected component of the start vertex. The auxiliary class EdgeIteratorAdapter provides an adapter from a sequence to an edge iterator.

12.3.2 Breadth-First Search

In this section, we consider the ***breadth-first search*** (BFS) traversal algorithm. Like DFS, BFS traverses a connected component of a graph, and in so doing defines a useful spanning tree. BFS is less "adventurous" than DFS, however. Instead of wandering the graph, BFS proceeds in rounds and subdivides the vertices into *levels*. BFS can also be thought of as a traversal using a string and paint, with BFS unrolling the string in a more conservative manner.

BFS starts at vertex s, which is at level 0 and defines the "anchor" for our string. In the first round, we let out the string the length of one edge and we visit all the vertices we can reach without unrolling the string any farther. In this case, we visit, and paint as "visited," the vertices adjacent to the start vertex s—these vertices are placed into level 1. In the second round, we unroll the string the length of two edges and we visit all the new vertices we can reach without unrolling our string any farther. These new vertices, which are adjacent to level 1 vertices and not previously assigned to a level, are placed into level 2, and so on. The BFS traversal terminates when every vertex has been visited.

Pseudo-code for a BFS starting at a vertex s is shown in Code Fragment 12.8. We use auxiliary space to label edges, mark visited vertices, and store containers associated with levels. That is, the containers L_0, L_1, L_2, and so on, store the nodes that are in level 0, level 1, level 2, and so on. These containers could, for example, be implemented as queues. They also allow BFS to be nonrecursive.

Algorithm BFS(s):

    initialize container L_0 to contain vertex s
    $i \leftarrow 0$
    while L_i is not empty **do**
        create container L_{i+1} to initially be empty
        for each vertex v in L_i **do**
            for each edge e incident on v **do**
                if edge e is unexplored **then**
                    let w be the other endpoint of e
                    if vertex w is unexplored **then**
                        label e as a discovery edge
                        insert w into L_{i+1}
                else
                    label e as a cross edge
      $i \leftarrow i+1$

Code Fragment 12.8: The BFS algorithm.

We illustrate a BFS traversal in Figure 12.7.

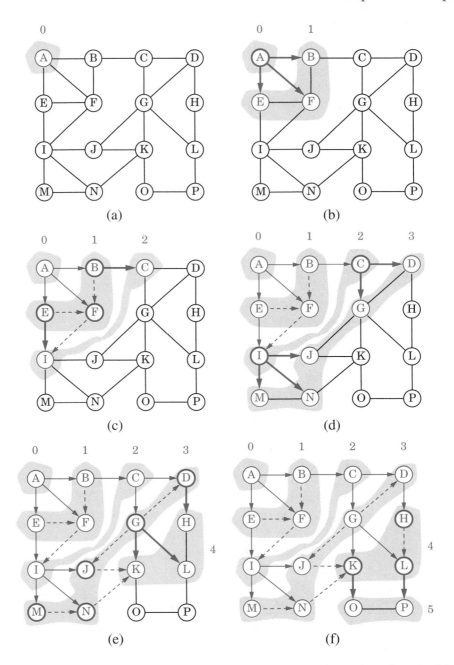

Figure 12.7: Example of breadth-first search traversal, where the edges incident on a vertex are explored by the alphabetical order of the adjacent vertices. The discovery edges are shown with solid lines and the cross edges are shown with dashed lines: (a) graph before the traversal; (b) discovery of level 1; (c) discovery of level 2; (d) discovery of level 3; (e) discovery of level 4; (f) discovery of level 5.

One of the nice properties of the BFS approach is that, in performing the BFS traversal, we can label each vertex by the length of a shortest path (in terms of the number of edges) from the start vertex s. In particular, if vertex v is placed into level i by a BFS starting at vertex s, then the length of a shortest path from s to v is i.

As with DFS, we can visualize the BFS traversal by orienting the edges along the direction in which they are explored during the traversal, and by distinguishing the edges used to discover new vertices, called ***discovery edges***, from those that lead to already visited vertices, called ***cross edges***. (See Figure 12.7f.) As with the DFS, the discovery edges form a spanning tree, which in this case we call the BFS tree. We do not call the nontree edges "back edges" in this case, however, for none of them connects a vertex to one of its ancestors. Every nontree edge connects a vertex v to another vertex that is neither v's ancestor nor its descendent.

The BFS traversal algorithm has a number of interesting properties, some of which we explore in the proposition that follows.

Proposition 12.14: *Let G be an undirected graph on which a BFS traversal starting at vertex s has been performed. Then*

- *The traversal visits all vertices in the connected component of s.*
- *The discovery-edges form a spanning tree T, which we call the BFS tree, of the connected component of s.*
- *For each vertex v at level i, the path of the BFS tree T between s and v has i edges, and any other path of G between s and v has at least i edges.*
- *If (u,v) is an edge that is not in the BFS tree, then the level numbers of u and v differ by at most 1.*

We leave the justification of this proposition as an exercise (C-12.13). The analysis of the running time of BFS is similar to the one of DFS, which implies the following.

Proposition 12.15: *Let G be a graph with n vertices and m edges represented with the adjacency list structure. A BFS traversal of G takes $O(n+m)$ time. Also, there exist $O(n+m)$-time algorithms based on BFS for the following problems:*

- *Testing whether G is connected*
- *Computing a spanning tree of G, if G is connected*
- *Computing the connected components of G*
- *Given a start vertex s of G, computing, for every vertex v of G, a path with the minimum number of edges between s and v, or reporting that no such path exists.*
- *Computing a cycle in G, or reporting that G has no cycles.*

Comparing BFS and DFS

By Proposition 12.15, the BFS traversal can do everything we claimed for the DFS traversal. There are a number of interesting differences between these two methods, however, and there are, in fact, a number of tasks that each can do better than the other. The BFS traversal is better at finding shortest paths in a graph (where distance is measured by the number of edges). Also, it produces a spanning tree such that all the nontree edges are cross edges. The DFS traversal is better for answering complex connectivity questions, such as determining if every pair of vertices in a graph can be connected by two disjoint paths. Also, it produces a spanning tree such that all the nontree edges are back edges. These properties only hold for undirected graphs, however. Nevertheless, as we explore in the next section, there are a number of interesting properties for the directed analogues of DFS and BFS.

12.4   Directed Graphs

In this section, we consider issues that are specific to directed graphs. Recall that a directed graph, which is also known as a *digraph*, is a graph whose edges are all directed.

Reachability

One of the most fundamental issues with directed graphs is the notion of *reachability*, which deals with determining where we can get to in a directed graph. A traversal in a directed graph always goes along directed paths, that is, paths where all the edges are traversed according to their respective directions. Given vertices u and v of a digraph $\vec{G}$, we say that u *reaches* v (and v is *reachable* from u) if $\vec{G}$ has a directed path from u to v. We also say that a vertex v reaches an edge (w,z) if v reaches the origin vertex w of the edge.

A digraph $\vec{G}$ is *strongly connected* if for any two vertices u and v of $\vec{G}$, u reaches v and v reaches u. A *directed cycle* of $\vec{G}$ is a cycle where all the edges are traversed according to their respective directions. (Note that $\vec{G}$ may have a cycle consisting of two edges with opposite direction between the same pair of vertices.) A digraph $\vec{G}$ is *acyclic* if it has no directed cycles. (See Figure 12.8 for some examples.)

The *transitive closure* of a digraph $\vec{G}$ is the digraph $\vec{G}^*$ such that the vertices of $\vec{G}^*$ are the same as the vertices of $\vec{G}$, and $\vec{G}^*$ has an edge (u,v), whenever $\vec{G}$ has a directed path from u to v. That is, we define $\vec{G}^*$ by starting with the digraph $\vec{G}$ and adding in an extra edge (u,v) for each u and v such that v is reachable from u (and there isn't already an edge (u,v) in $\vec{G}$).

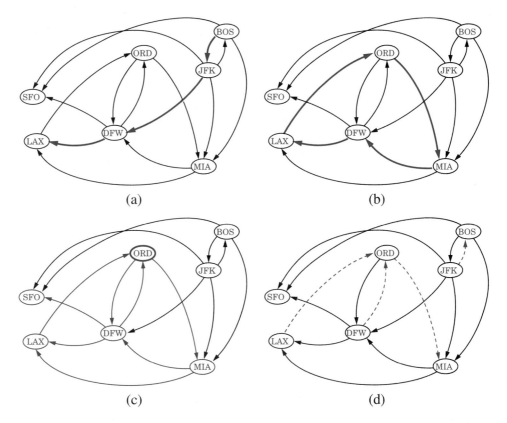

Figure 12.8: Examples of reachability in a digraph: (a) a directed path from BOS to LAX is drawn in blue; (b) a directed cycle (ORD, MIA, DFW, LAX, ORD) is shown in blue; its vertices induce a strongly connected subgraph; (c) the subgraph of the vertices and edges reachable from ORD is shown in blue; (d) removing the dashed blue edges gives an acyclic digraph.

Interesting problems that deal with reachability in a digraph $\vec{G}$ include the following:

- Given vertices u and v, determine whether u reaches v.
- Find all the vertices of $\vec{G}$ that are reachable from a given vertex s.
- Determine whether $\vec{G}$ is strongly connected.
- Determine whether $\vec{G}$ is acyclic.
- Compute the transitive closure $\vec{G}^*$ of $\vec{G}$.

In the remainder of this section, we explore some efficient algorithms for solving these problems.

12.4.1 Traversing a Digraph

As with undirected graphs, we can explore a digraph in a systematic way with methods akin to the depth-first search (DFS) and breadth-first search (BFS) algorithms defined previously for undirected graphs (Sections 12.3.1 and 12.3.2). Such explorations can be used, for example, to answer reachability questions. The directed depth-first search and breadth-first search methods we develop in this section for performing such explorations are very similar to their undirected counterparts. In fact, the only real difference is that the directed depth-first search and breadth-first search methods only traverse edges according to their respective directions.

The directed version of DFS starting at a vertex v can be described by the recursive algorithm in Code Fragment 12.9. (See Figure 12.9.)

Algorithm DirectedDFS(v):

    Mark vertex v as visited.

    for each outgoing edge (v, w) of v **do**

        if vertex w has not been visited **then**

            Recursively call DirectedDFS(w).

Code Fragment 12.9: The DirectedDFS algorithm.

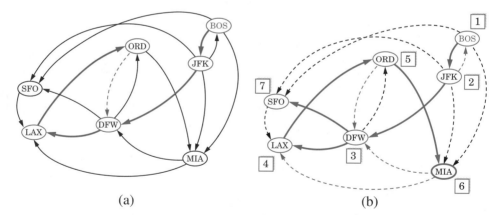

(a)   (b)

Figure 12.9: An example of a DFS in a digraph: (a) intermediate step, where, for the first time, an already visited vertex (DFW) is reached; (b) the completed DFS. The tree edges are shown with solid blue lines, the back edges are shown with dashed blue lines, and the forward and cross edges are shown with dashed black lines. The order in which the vertices are visited is indicated by a label next to each vertex. The edge (ORD,DFW) is a back edge, but (DFW,ORD) is a forward edge. Edge (BOS,SFO) is a forward edge, and (SFO,LAX) is a cross edge.

A DFS on a digraph $\vec{G}$ partitions the edges of $\vec{G}$ reachable from the starting vertex into *tree edges* or *discovery edges*, which lead us to discover a new vertex, and *nontree edges*, which take us to a previously visited vertex. The tree edges form a tree rooted at the starting vertex, called the *depth-first search* tree, and there are three kinds of nontree edges:

- **back edges**, which connect a vertex to an ancestor in the DFS tree
- **forward edges**, which connect a vertex to a descendent in the DFS tree
- **cross edges**, which connect a vertex to a vertex that is neither its ancestor nor its descendent.

Refer back to Figure 12.9b to see an example of each type of nontree edge.

Proposition 12.16: *Let $\vec{G}$ be a digraph. Depth-first search on $\vec{G}$ starting at a vertex s visits all the vertices of $\vec{G}$ that are reachable from s. Also, the DFS tree contains directed paths from s to every vertex reachable from s.*

Justification: Let V_s be the subset of vertices of $\vec{G}$ visited by DFS starting at vertex s. We want to show that V_s contains s and every vertex reachable from s belongs to V_s. Suppose now, for the sake of a contradiction, that there is a vertex w reachable from s that is not in V_s. Consider a directed path from s to w, and let (u,v) be the first edge on such a path taking us out of V_s, that is, u is in V_s but v is not in V_s. When DFS reaches u, it explores all the outgoing edges of u, and thus must reach also vertex v via edge (u,v). Hence, v should be in V_s, and we have obtained a contradiction. Therefore, V_s must contain every vertex reachable from s. ∎

Analyzing the running time of the directed DFS method is analogous to that for its undirected counterpart. In particular, a recursive call is made for each vertex exactly once, and each edge is traversed exactly once (from its origin). Hence, if n_s vertices and m_s edges are reachable from vertex s, a directed DFS starting at s runs in $O(n_s + m_s)$ time, provided the digraph is represented with a data structure that supports constant-time vertex and edge methods. The adjacency list structure satisfies this requirement, for example.

By Proposition 12.16, we can use DFS to find all the vertices reachable from a given vertex, and hence to find the transitive closure of $\vec{G}$. That is, we can perform a DFS, starting from each vertex v of $\vec{G}$, to see which vertices w are reachable from v, adding an edge (v,w) to the transitive closure for each such w. Likewise, by repeatedly traversing digraph $\vec{G}$ with a DFS, starting in turn at each vertex, we can easily test whether $\vec{G}$ is strongly connected. Namely, $\vec{G}$ is strongly connected if each DFS visits all the vertices of $\vec{G}$.

Thus, we may immediately derive the proposition that follows.

Proposition 12.17: *Let $\vec{G}$ be a digraph with n vertices and m edges. The following problems can be solved by an algorithm that traverses $\vec{G}$ n times using DFS, runs in $O(n(n+m))$ time, and uses $O(n)$ auxiliary space:*

- *Computing, for each vertex v of $\vec{G}$, the subgraph reachable from v*
- *Testing whether $\vec{G}$ is strongly connected*
- *Computing the transitive closure $\vec{G}^*$ of $\vec{G}$.*

Testing for Strong Connectivity

Actually, we can determine if a directed graph $\vec{G}$ is strongly connected much faster than this, just using two depth-first searches. We begin by performing a DFS of our directed graph $\vec{G}$ starting at an arbitrary vertex s. If there is any vertex of $\vec{G}$ that is not visited by this DFS, and is not reachable from s, then the graph is not strongly connected. So, if this first DFS visits each vertex of $\vec{G}$, then we reverse all the edges of $\vec{G}$ (using the reverseDirection method) and perform another DFS starting at s in this "reverse" graph. If every vertex of $\vec{G}$ is visited by this second DFS, then the graph is strongly connected, for each of the vertices visited in this DFS can reach s. Since this algorithm makes just two DFS traversals of $\vec{G}$, it runs in $O(n+m)$ time.

Directed Breadth-First Search

As with DFS, we can extend breadth-first search (BFS) to work for directed graphs. The algorithm still visits vertices level by level and partitions the set of edges into *tree edges* (or *discovery edges*), which together form a directed *breadth-first search* tree rooted at the start vertex, and *nontree edges*. Unlike the directed DFS method, however, the directed BFS method only leaves two kinds of nontree edges: *back edges*, which connect a vertex to one of its ancestors, and *cross edges*, which connect a vertex to another vertex that is neither its ancestor nor its descendent. There are no forward edges, which is a fact we explore in an exercise (C-12.9).

12.4.2 Transitive Closure

In this section, we explore an alternative technique for computing the transitive closure of a digraph. Let $\vec{G}$ be a digraph with n vertices and m edges. We compute the transitive closure of $\vec{G}$ in a series of rounds. We initialize $\vec{G}_0 = \vec{G}$. We also arbitrarily number the vertices of $\vec{G}$ as $v_1, v_2, \ldots, v_n$. We then begin the computation of the rounds, beginning with round 1. In a generic round k, we construct digraph $\vec{G}_k$ starting with $\vec{G}_k = \vec{G}_{k-1}$ and adding to $\vec{G}_k$ the directed edge (v_i, v_j) if digraph $\vec{G}_{k-1}$ contains both the edges (v_i, v_k) and (v_k, v_j). In this way, we will enforce a simple rule embodied in the proposition that follows.

Proposition 12.18: *For* $i = 1, \ldots, n$, *digraph* $\vec{G}_k$ *has an edge* (v_i, v_j) *if and only if digraph* $\vec{G}$ *has a directed path from* v_i *to* v_j, *whose intermediate vertices (if any) are in the set* $\{v_1, \ldots, v_k\}$. *In particular,* $\vec{G}_n$ *is equal to* $\vec{G}^*$, *the transitive closure of* $\vec{G}$.

Proposition 12.18 suggests a simple algorithm for computing the transitive closure of $\vec{G}$ that is based on the series of rounds we described above. This algorithm is known as the ***Floyd-Warshall algorithm***, and its pseudo-code is given in Code Fragment 12.10. From this pseudo-code, we can easily analyze the running time of the Floyd-Warshall algorithm assuming that the data structure representing G supports methods areAdjacent and insertDirectedEdge in $O(1)$ time. The main loop is executed n times and the inner loop considers each of $O(n^2)$ pairs of vertices, performing a constant-time computation for each one. Thus, the total running time of the Floyd-Warshall algorithm is $O(n^3)$.

Algorithm FloydWarshall($\vec{G}$):
    Input: A digraph $\vec{G}$ with n vertices
    Output: The transitive closure $\vec{G}^*$ of $\vec{G}$

    let $v_1, v_2, \ldots, v_n$ be an arbitrary numbering of the vertices of $\vec{G}$
    $\vec{G}_0 \leftarrow \vec{G}$
    for $k \leftarrow 1$ to n **do**
        $\vec{G}_k \leftarrow \vec{G}_{k-1}$
        for each i, j in $\{1, \ldots, n\}$ with $i \neq j$ and $i, j \neq k$ **do**
            if both edges (v_i, v_k) and (v_k, v_j) are in $\vec{G}_{k-1}$ **then**
                add edge (v_i, v_j) to $\vec{G}_k$ (if it is not already present)
    return $\vec{G}_n$

Code Fragment 12.10: Pseudo-code for the Floyd-Warshall algorithm. This algorithm computes the transitive closure $\vec{G}^*$ of G by incrementally computing a series of digraphs $\vec{G}_0, \vec{G}_1, \ldots, \vec{G}_n$, where for $k = 1, \ldots, n$.

This description is actually an example of an algorithmic design pattern known as dynamic programming, which is discussed in more detail in Section 11.5.2. From the above description and analysis we may immediately derive the following proposition.

Proposition 12.19: *Let* $\vec{G}$ *be a digraph with* n *vertices, and let* $\vec{G}$ *be represented by a data structure that supports lookup and update of adjacency information in* $O(1)$ *time. Then the Floyd-Warshall algorithm computes the transitive closure* $\vec{G}^*$ *of* $\vec{G}$ *in* $O(n^3)$ *time.*

We illustrate an example run of the Floyd-Warshall algorithm in Figure 12.10.

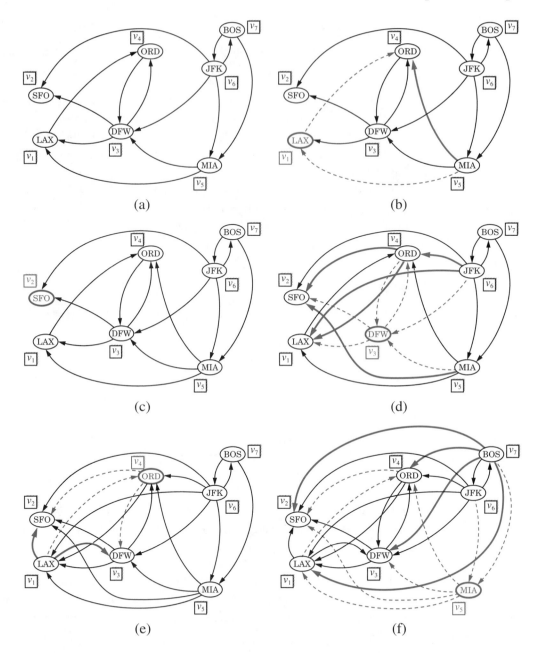

Figure 12.10: Sequence of digraphs computed by the Floyd-Warshall algorithm: (a) initial digraph $\vec{G} = \vec{G}_0$ and numbering of the vertices; (b) digraph $\vec{G}_1$; (c) $\vec{G}_2$; (d) $\vec{G}_3$; (e) $\vec{G}_4$; (f) $\vec{G}_5$. Note that $\vec{G}_5 = \vec{G}_6 = \vec{G}_7$. If digraph $\vec{G}_{k-1}$ has the edges (v_i, v_k) and (v_k, v_j), but not the edge (v_i, v_j), in the drawing of digraph $\vec{G}_k$, we show edges (v_i, v_k) and (v_k, v_j) with dashed blue lines, and edge (v_i, v_j) with a thick blue line.

Performance of the Floyd-Warshall Algorithm

The running time of the Floyd-Warshall algorithm might appear to be slower than performing a DFS of a directed graph from each of its vertices, but this depends upon the representation of the graph. If a graph is represented using an adjacency matrix, then running the DFS method once on a directed graph $\vec{G}$ takes $O(n^2)$ time (we explore the reason for this in an exercise). Thus, running DFS n times takes $O(n^3)$ time, which is no better than a single execution of the Floyd-Warshall algorithm, but the Floyd-Warshall algorithm would be much simpler to implement. Nevertheless, if the graph is represented using an adjacency list structure, then running the DFS algorithm n times would take $O(n(n+m))$ time to compute the transitive closure. Even so, if the graph is **dense**, that is, if it has $\Theta(n^2)$ edges, then this approach still runs in $O(n^3)$ time and is more complicated than a single instance of the Floyd-Warshall algorithm. The only case where repeatedly calling the DFS method is better is when the graph is not dense and is represented using an adjacency list structure.

12.4.3 Directed Acyclic Graphs

Directed graphs without directed cycles are encountered in many applications. Such a digraph is often referred to as a **directed acyclic graph**, or **DAG**, for short. Applications of such graphs include the following:

- Inheritance between classes of a Java program
- Prerequisites between courses of a degree program
- Scheduling constraints between the tasks of a project.

Example 12.20: *In order to manage a large project, it is convenient to break it up into a collection of smaller tasks. The tasks, however, are rarely independent, because scheduling constraints exist between them. (For example, in a house building project, the task of ordering nails obviously precedes the task of nailing shingles to the roof deck.) Clearly, scheduling constraints cannot have circularities, because they would make the project impossible. (For example, in order to get a job you need to have work experience, but in order to get work experience you need to have a job.) The scheduling constraints impose restrictions on the order in which the tasks can be executed. Namely, if a constraint says that task a must be completed before task b is started, then a must precede b in the order of execution of the tasks. Thus, if we model a feasible set of tasks as vertices of a directed graph, and we place a directed edge from v to w whenever the task for v must be executed before the task for w, then we define a directed acyclic graph.*

The above example motivates the following definition. Let $\vec{G}$ be a digraph with n vertices. A ***topological ordering*** of $\vec{G}$ is an ordering $v_1, \ldots, v_n$ of the vertices of $\vec{G}$ such that for every edge (v_i, v_j) of $\vec{G}$, $i < j$. That is, a topological ordering is an ordering such that any directed path in $\vec{G}$ traverses vertices in increasing order. (See Figure 12.11.) Note that a digraph may have more than one topological ordering.

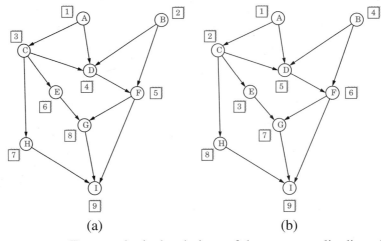

(a)   (b)

Figure 12.11: Two topological orderings of the same acyclic digraph.

Proposition 12.21: *$\vec{G}$ has a topological ordering if and only if it is acyclic.*

Justification: The necessity (the "only if" part of the statement) is easy to demonstrate. Suppose $\vec{G}$ is topologically ordered. Assume, for the sake of a contradiction, that $\vec{G}$ has a cycle consisting of edges $(v_{i_0}, v_{i_1}), (v_{i_1}, v_{i_2}), \ldots, (v_{i_{k-1}}, v_{i_0})$. Because of the topological ordering, we must have $i_0 < i_1 < \cdots < i_{k-1} < i_0$, which is clearly impossible. Thus, $\vec{G}$ must be acyclic.

We now argue the sufficiency of the condition (the "if" part of the statement). Suppose $\vec{G}$ is acyclic. We will give an algorithmic description of how to build a topological ordering for $\vec{G}$. Since $\vec{G}$ is acyclic, $\vec{G}$ must have a vertex with no incoming edges (that is, with in-degree 0). Let v_1 be such a vertex. Indeed, if v_1 did not exist, then in tracing a directed path from an arbitrary start vertex we would eventually encounter a previously visited vertex, thus contradicting the acyclicity of $\vec{G}$. If we remove v_1 from $\vec{G}$, together with its outgoing edges, the resulting digraph is still acyclic. Hence, the resulting digraph also has a vertex with no incoming edges, and we let v_2 be such a vertex. By repeating this process until the digraph becomes empty, we obtain an ordering $v_1, \ldots, v_n$ of the vertices of $\vec{G}$. Because of the above construction, if (v_i, v_j) is an edge of $\vec{G}$, then v_i must be deleted before v_j can be deleted, and thus $i < j$. Thus, $v_1, \ldots, v_n$ is a topological ordering.
∎

Proposition 12.21's justification suggests an algorithm (Code Fragment 12.11), called ***topological sorting***, for computing a topological ordering of a digraph.

Algorithm TopologicalSort($\vec{G}$):

> ***Input:*** A digraph $\vec{G}$ with n vertices.
>
> ***Output:*** A topological ordering $v_1, \ldots, v_n$ of $\vec{G}$.
>
> Let S be an initially empty stack.
> **for** each vertex u of $\vec{G}$ **do**
> > Let incounter(u) be the in-degree of u.
> > **if** incounter(u) $= 0$ **then**
> > > S.push(u)
>
> $i \leftarrow 1$
> **while** S is not empty **do**
> > $u \leftarrow S$.pop()
> > Let u be vertex number i in the topological ordering.
> > $i \leftarrow i + 1$
> > **for** each outgoing edge (u, w) of u **do**
> > > incounter(w) $\leftarrow$ incounter(w) $- 1$
> > > **if** incounter(w) $= 0$ **then**
> > > > S.push(w)

Code Fragment 12.11: Pseudo-code for the topological sorting algorithm. (We show an example application of this algorithm in Figure 12.12.)

Proposition 12.22: *Let $\vec{G}$ be a digraph with n vertices and m edges. The topological sorting algorithm runs in $O(n + m)$ time using $O(n)$ auxiliary space, and either computes a topological ordering of $\vec{G}$ or fails to number some vertices, which indicates that $\vec{G}$ has a directed cycle.*

Justification: The initial computation of in-degrees and setup of the incounter variables can be done with a simple traversal of the graph, which takes $O(n + m)$ time. We use the decorator pattern to associate counter attributes with the vertices. Say that a vertex u is ***visited*** by the topological sorting algorithm when u is removed from the stack S. A vertex u can be visited only when incounter(u) $= 0$, which implies that all its predecessors (vertices with outgoing edges into u) were previously visited. As a consequence, any vertex that is on a directed cycle will never be visited, and any other vertex will be visited exactly once. The algorithm traverses all the outgoing edges of each visited vertex once, so its running time is proportional to the number of outgoing edges of the visited vertices. Therefore, the algorithm runs in $O(n + m)$ time. Regarding the space usage, observe that the stack S and the incounter variables attached to the vertices use $O(n)$ space. ∎

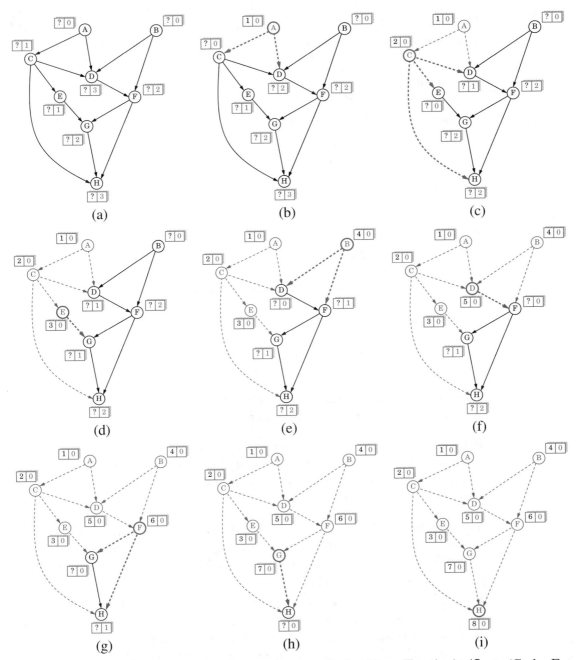

Figure 12.12: Example of a run of algorithm TopologicalSort (Code Fragment 12.11): (a) initial configuration; (b–i) after each while-loop iteration. The vertex labels show the vertex number and the current incounter value. The edges traversed are shown with dashed blue arrows. Thick lines denote the vertex and edges examined in the current iteration.

As a side effect, the topological sorting algorithm of Code Fragment 12.11 also tests whether the input digraph $\vec{G}$ is acyclic. Indeed, if the algorithm terminates without ordering all the vertices, then the subgraph of the vertices that have not been ordered must contain a directed cycle. (See Figure 12.13.)

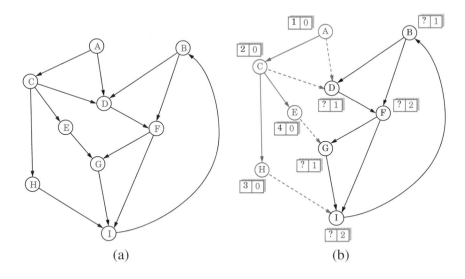

(a)   (b)

Figure 12.13: Detecting a directed cycle: (a) input digraph; (b) after algorithm TopologicalSort (Code Fragment 12.11) terminates, the subgraph of the vertices with undefined number contains a directed cycle.

Next we present an application of directed graph traversal in Java.

12.4.4 Application: Garbage Collection in Java ★

In some languages, like C and C++, the memory space for objects must be explicitly allocated and deallocated by the programmer. This memory-allocation duty is often overlooked by beginning programmers, and, when done incorrectly, it can even be the source of frustrating programming errors for experienced programmers. Thus, the designers of other languages, like Java, place the burden of memory management on the run-time environment. A Java programmer does not have to explicitly deallocate the memory for some object when its life is over. Instead, the *garbage collector* mechanism deallocates the memory for such objects.

Recall that in Java the memory for most objects is allocated from the memory heap (see Section 4.2.3). In addition, the running threads in a Java program (see Section 4.2.4) store the current space for their instance variables on their respective Java stacks (see Section 4.1.3). Since the instance variables in the Java stacks can refer to objects in the memory heap, all the variables and objects in the Java stacks of running threads are called *root objects*. All those objects that can be reached by following object references that start from a root object are called *live objects*. The live objects are the active objects currently being used by the running program; these objects should *not* be deallocated. For example, a running Java program may store in a variable a reference to a sequence S that is implemented using a doubly linked list. The reference variable to S is a root object, while the object for S is a live object, as are all the node objects that are referenced from this object and all the elements that are referenced from these node objects.

From time to time, the Java virtual machine (JVM) may notice that the available free space in the memory heap is becoming scarce. At such times, the JVM will probably elect to reclaim the space that is being used for objects that are no longer live. This reclamation process is known as *garbage collection*. There are several different algorithms for garbage collection, but one of the most used is the *mark-sweep algorithm*. Therefore, let us consider the steps that we would need to implement to design a Java virtual machine that uses mark-sweep garbage collection algorithm.

The Mark-Sweep Algorithm

In the mark-sweep garbage collection algorithm, we associate with each object a "mark" bit that identifies if that object is live or not. When we determine at some point that garbage collection is needed, we suspend all other running threads and clear all of the mark bits of objects currently allocated in the memory heap. We then trace through the Java stacks of the currently running threads and we mark as "live" all of the (root) objects in these stacks. We must then determine all of the other live objects—the ones that are reachable from the root objects. To do this efficiently, we should use the directed-graph version of the depth-first search traversal. In this case, each object in the memory heap is viewed as a vertex in a directed graph, and the reference from one object to another is viewed as an edge. By performing a directed DFS from each root object, we can correctly identify and mark each live object. This process is known as the "mark" phase. Once this process has completed, we then scan through the memory heap and reclaim any space that is being used for an object that has not been marked. This scanning process is known as the "sweep" phase, and when it completes, we resume running the suspended threads. Thus, the mark-sweep garbage collection algorithm will reclaim unused space in time proportional to the number of live objects and their references plus the size of the memory heap.

Performing DFS In-place

The mark-sweep algorithm is an effective way of reclaiming unused space in the memory heap, but there is an important issue we must face during the mark phase. Since we are probably reclaiming memory space at a time when free memory is scarce, we must take special care not to use much extra space during the garbage collection itself. The trouble is that the DFS algorithm, as we have described it, can use as much extra space as there are vertices in the graph. In the case of garbage collection, the vertices in our graph are the objects in the memory heap. We probably don't have this much memory to use, so our only alternative is to find a way to perform DFS in-place rather than recursively, that is, we must perform DFS using only a constant amount of additional storage. Fortunately, it is possible to perform DFS in-place.

The main idea for performing DFS in-place is to simulate the recursion stack using the edges of the graph (which in the case of garbage collection correspond to object references). Whenever we traverse an edge from a visited vertex v to a new vertex w, we change the edge (v, w) stored in v's adjacency list to point back to v's parent in the DFS tree. When we return back to v (simulating the return from the "recursive" call at w), we can now switch the edge we modified to point back to w as it did before. Of course, we need to have some way of identifying which edge we need to change back. One possibility is to number the references going out of v as 1, 2, and so on, and store, in addition to the mark bit (which we are using for the "visited" tag in our DFS), a count identifier that tells us which edges we have modified.

Using a count identifier of course requires an extra word of storage per object. This extra word can be avoided in some implementations, however. For example, many implementations of the Java virtual machine represent an object as a composition of a reference with a type identifier (which indicates if this object is an Integer or Vector or some other type) and as a reference to the other objects or data fields for this object. Since the type reference is always supposed to be the first element of the composition in such implementations, we can use this reference to "mark" the edge we changed when leaving an object v and going to some object w in our DFS. We simply swap the reference at v that refers to the type of v with the reference at v that refers to w. When we return to v, we can quickly identify the edge (v, w) we changed, because it will be the first reference in the composition for v, and the position of the reference to v's type will tell us the place were this edge belongs in v's adjacency list. Thus, whether we use this edge-swapping trick or a count identifier, we can implement DFS in-place without affecting its asymptotic running time.

12.5 Weighted Graphs

As we saw in Section 12.3.2, the breadth-first search strategy can be used to find a shortest path from some starting vertex to every other vertex in a connected graph. This approach makes sense in cases where each edge is as good as any other, but there are many situations where this approach is not appropriate. For example, we might be using a graph to represent a computer network (such as the Internet), and we might be interested in finding the fastest way to route a data packet between two computers. In this case, it is probably not appropriate for all the edges to be equal to each other, for some connections in a computer network are typically much faster than others (for example, some edges might represent slow phone-line connections while others might represent high-speed, fiber-optic connections). Likewise, we might want to use a graph to represent the roads between cities, and we might be interested in finding the fastest way to travel cross-country. In this case, it is again probably not appropriate for all the edges to be equal to each other, for some inter-city distances will likely be much larger than others. Thus, it is natural to consider graphs whose edges are not weighted equally.

A *weighted graph* is a graph that has a numeric (for example, integer) label $w(e)$ associated with each edge e, called the *weight* of edge e. We show an example of a weighted graph in Figure 12.14.

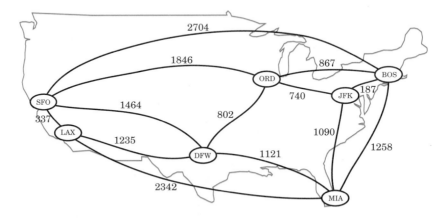

Figure 12.14: A weighted graph whose vertices represent major U.S. airports and whose edge weights represent distances in miles. This graph has a path from JFK to LAX of total weight 2,777 (going through ORD and DFW). This is the minimum weight path in the graph from JFK to LAX.

In the remaining sections of this chapter, we study weighted graphs.

12.6 Shortest Paths

Let G be a weighted graph. The **length** (or weight) of a path is the sum of the weights of the edges of P. That is, if $P = ((v_0, v_1), (v_1, v_2), \ldots, (v_{k-1}, v_k))$, then the length of P, denoted $w(P)$, is defined as

$$w(P) = \sum_{i=0}^{k-1} w((v_i, v_{i+1})).$$

The **distance** from a vertex v to a vertex u in G, denoted $d(v, u)$, is the length of a minimum length path (also called **shortest path**) from v to u, if such a path exists.

People often use the convention that $d(v, u) = +\infty$ if there is no path at all from v to u in G. Even if there is a path from v to u in G, the distance from v to u may not be defined, however, if there is a cycle in G whose total weight is negative. For example, suppose vertices in G represent cities, and the weights of edges in G represent how much money it costs to go from one city to another. If someone were willing to actually pay us to go from say JFK to ORD, then the "cost" of the edge (JFK,ORD) would be negative. If someone else were willing to pay us to go from ORD to JFK, then there would be a negative-weight cycle in G and distances would no longer be defined. That is, anyone can now build a path (with cycles) in G from any city A to another city B that first goes to JFK and then cycles as many times as he or she likes from JFK to ORD and back, before going on to B. The existence of such paths allows us to build arbitrarily low negative-cost paths (and in this case make a fortune in the process). But distances cannot be arbitrarily low negative numbers. Thus, any time we use edge weights to represent distances, we must be careful not to introduce any negative-weight cycles.

Suppose we are given a weighted graph G, and we are asked to find a shortest path from some vertex v to each other vertex in G, viewing the weights on the edges as distances. In this section, we explore efficient ways of finding all such shortest paths, if they exist. The first algorithm we discuss is for the simple, yet common, case when all the edge weights in G are nonnegative (that is, $w(e) \geq 0$ for each edge e of G); hence, we know in advance that there are no negative-weight cycles in G. Recall that the special case of computing a shortest path when all weights are 1 was solved with the BFS traversal algorithm presented in Section 12.3.2.

There is an interesting approach for solving this **single-source** problem based on the **greedy method** design pattern (Section 11.4.2). Recall that in this pattern we solve the problem at hand by repeatedly selecting the best choice from among those available in each iteration. This paradigm can often be used in situations where we are trying to optimize some cost function over a collection of objects. We can add objects to our collection, one at a time, always picking the next one that optimizes the function from among those yet to be chosen.

12.6.1   Dijkstra's Algorithm

The main idea in applying the greedy method pattern to the single-source shortest-path problem is to perform a "weighted" breadth-first search starting at v. In particular, we can use the greedy method to develop an algorithm that iteratively grows a "cloud" of vertices out of v, with the vertices entering the cloud in order of their distances from v. Thus, in each iteration, the next vertex chosen is the vertex outside the cloud that is closest to v. The algorithm terminates when no more vertices are outside the cloud, at which point we have a shortest path from v to every other vertex of G. This approach is a simple, but nevertheless powerful, example of the greedy method design pattern.

A Greedy Method for Finding Shortest Paths

Applying the greedy method to the single-source, shortest-path problem, results in an algorithm known as ***Dijkstra's algorithm***. When applied to other graph problems, however, the greedy method may not necessarily find the best solution (such as in the so-called ***traveling salesman problem***, in which we wish to find the shortest path that visits all the vertices in a graph exactly once). Nevertheless, there are a number of situations in which the greedy method allows us to compute the best solution. In this chapter, we discuss two such situations: computing shortest paths and constructing a minimum spanning tree.

In order to simplify the description of Dijkstra's algorithm, we assume, in the following, that the input graph G is undirected (that is, all its edges are undirected) and simple (that is, it has no self-loops and no parallel edges). Hence, we denote the edges of G as unordered vertex pairs (u, z).

| Caution |

In Dijkstra's algorithm for finding shortest paths, the cost function we are trying to optimize in our application of the greedy method is also the function that we are trying to compute—the shortest path distance. This may at first seem like circular reasoning until we realize that we can actually implement this approach by using a "bootstrapping" trick, consisting of using an approximation to the distance function we are trying to compute, which in the end will be equal to the true distance.

Edge Relaxation

Let us define a label $D[u]$ for each vertex u in V, which we use to approximate the distance in G from v to u. The meaning of these labels is that $D[u]$ will always store the length of the best path we have found ***so far*** from v to u. Initially, $D[v] = 0$ and $D[u] = +\infty$ for each $u \neq v$, and we define the set C, which is our "***cloud***" of vertices, to initially be the empty set $\emptyset$. At each iteration of the algorithm, we select a vertex u not in C with smallest $D[u]$ label, and we pull u into C. In the very first iteration we will, of course, pull v into C. Once a new vertex u is pulled into C, we then update the label $D[z]$ of each vertex z that is adjacent to u and is outside of C, to reflect the fact that there may be a new and better way to get to z via u. This update operation is known as a ***relaxation*** procedure, for it takes an old estimate and checks if it can be improved to get closer to its true value. (A metaphor for why we call this a relaxation comes from a spring that is stretched out and then "relaxed" back to its true resting shape.) In the case of Dijkstra's algorithm, the relaxation is performed for an edge (u, z) such that we have computed a new value of $D[u]$ and wish to see if there is a better value for $D[z]$ using the edge (u, z). The specific edge relaxation operation is as follows:

Edge Relaxation:

$$\textbf{if } D[u] + w((u,z)) < D[z] \textbf{ then}$$
$$D[z] \leftarrow D[u] + w((u,z))$$

We give the pseudo-code for Dijkstra's algorithm in Code Fragment 12.12. Note that we use a priority queue Q to store the vertices outside of the cloud C.

Algorithm ShortestPath(G, v):

  Input: A simple undirected weighted graph G with nonnegative edge weights, and a distinguished vertex v of G.

  Output: A label $D[u]$, for each vertex u of G, such that $D[u]$ is the length of a shortest path from v to u in G

  Initialize $D[v] \leftarrow 0$ and $D[u] \leftarrow +\infty$ for each vertex $u \neq v$.

  Let a priority queue Q contain all the vertices of G using the D labels as keys.

  while Q is not empty **do**

    {pull a new vertex u into the cloud}

    $u \leftarrow Q$.removeMin()

    for each vertex z adjacent to u such that z is in Q **do**

      {perform the ***relaxation*** procedure on edge (u, z)}

      if $D[u] + w((u,z)) < D[z]$ **then**

        $D[z] \leftarrow D[u] + w((u,z))$

        Change to $D[z]$ the key of vertex z in Q.

  return the label $D[u]$ of each vertex u

Code Fragment 12.12: Dijkstra's algorithm for the single-source shortest path problem.

We illustrate several iterations of Dijkstra's algorithm in Figures 12.15 and 12.16.

Figure 12.15: An execution of Dijkstra's algorithm on a weighted graph. The start vertex is BWI. A box next to each vertex v stores the label $D[v]$. The symbol $\bullet$ is used instead of $+\infty$. The edges of the shortest-path tree are drawn as thick blue arrows, and for each vertex u outside the "cloud" we show the current best edge for pulling in u with a solid blue line.

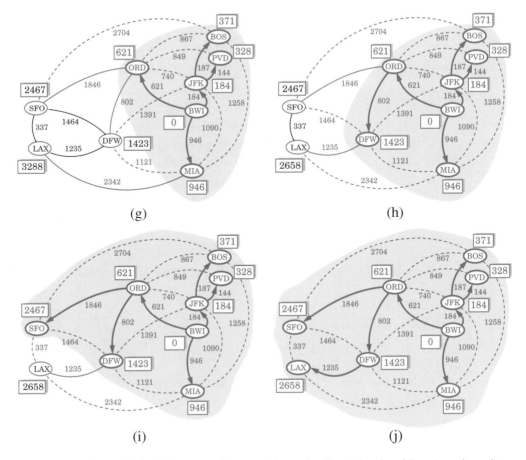

Figure 12.16: An example execution of Dijkstra's algorithm (continued).

Why It Works

The interesting, and possibly even a little surprising, aspect of the Dijkstra algorithm is that, at the moment a vertex u is pulled into C, its label $D[u]$ stores the correct length of a shortest path from v to u. Thus, when the algorithm terminates, it will have computed the shortest-path distance from v to every vertex of G. That is, it will have solved the single-source shortest path problem.

It is probably not immediately clear why Dijkstra's algorithm correctly finds the shortest path from the start vertex v to each other vertex u in the graph. Why is it that the distance from v to u is equal to the value of the label $D[u]$ at the time vertex u is pulled into the cloud C (which is also the time u is removed from the priority queue Q)? The answer to this question depends on there being no negative-weight edges in the graph, for it allows the greedy method to work correctly, as we show in the proposition that follows.

Proposition 12.23: *In Dijkstra's algorithm, whenever a vertex u is pulled into the cloud, the label $D[u]$ is equal to $d(v,u)$, the length of a shortest path from v to u.*

Justification: Suppose that $D[t] > d(v,t)$ for some vertex t in V, and let u be the *first* vertex the algorithm pulled into the cloud C (that is, removed from Q) such that $D[u] > d(v,u)$. There is a shortest path P from v to u (for otherwise $d(v,u) = +\infty = D[u]$). Let us therefore consider the moment when u is pulled into C, and let z be the first vertex of P (when going from v to u) that is not in C at this moment. Let y be the predecessor of z in path P (note that we could have $y = v$). (See Figure 12.17.) We know, by our choice of z, that y is already in C at this point. Moreover, $D[y] = d(v,y)$, since u is the *first* incorrect vertex. When y was pulled into C, we tested (and possibly updated) $D[z]$ so that we had at that point

$$D[z] \le D[y] + w((y,z)) = d(v,y) + w((y,z)).$$

But since z is the next vertex on the shortest path from v to u, this implies that

$$D[z] = d(v,z).$$

But we are now at the moment when we are picking u, not z, to join C; hence,

$$D[u] \le D[z].$$

It should be clear that a subpath of a shortest path is itself a shortest path. Hence, since z is on the shortest path from v to u,

$$d(v,z) + d(z,u) = d(v,u).$$

Moreover, $d(z,u) \ge 0$ because there are no negative-weight edges. Therefore,

$$D[u] \le D[z] = d(v,z) \le d(v,z) + d(z,u) = d(v,u).$$

But this contradicts the definition of u; hence, there can be no such vertex u. ∎

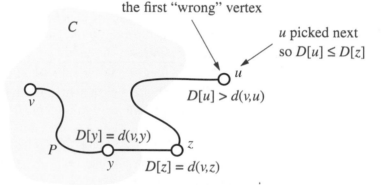

the first "wrong" vertex

C

u picked next
so $D[u] \le D[z]$

u

$D[u] > d(v,u)$

v

$D[y] = d(v,y)$

P

z

y

$D[z] = d(v,z)$

Figure 12.17: A schematic illustration for the justification of Proposition 12.23.

The Running Time of Dijkstra's Algorithm

In this section, we analyze the time complexity of Dijkstra's algorithm. We denote with n and m, the number of vertices and edges of the input graph G, respectively. We assume that the edge weights can be added and compared in constant time. Because of the high level of the description we gave for Dijkstra's algorithm in Code Fragment 12.12, analyzing its running time requires that we give more details on its implementation. Specifically, we should indicate the data structures used and how they are implemented.

Let us first assume that we are representing the graph G using an adjacency list structure. This data structure allows us to step through the vertices adjacent to u during the relaxation step in time proportional to their number. It still does not settle all the details for the algorithm, however, for we must say more about how to implement the other principle data structure in the algorithm—the priority queue Q.

An efficient implementation of the priority queue Q uses a heap (see Section 7.3). This allows us to extract the vertex u with smallest D label (call to the removeMin method) in $O(\log n)$ time. As noted in the pseudo-code, each time we update a $D[z]$ label we need to update the key of z in the priority queue. If Q is implemented as a heap, then this key update can, for example, be done by first removing and then inserting z with its new key. If our priority queue Q supports the locator pattern (see Section 7.4), then we can easily implement such key updates in $O(\log n)$ time, since a locator for vertex z would allow Q to have immediate access to the item storing z in the heap (see Section 7.4). Assuming this implementation of Q, Dijkstra's algorithm runs in $O((n+m)\log n)$ time.

Referring back to Code Fragment 12.12, the details of the running-time analysis are as follows:

- Inserting all the vertices in Q with their initial key value can be done in $O(n \log n)$ time by repeated insertions, or in $O(n)$ time using bottom-up heap construction (see Section 7.3.5).
- At each iteration of the **while** loop, we spend $O(\log n)$ time to remove vertex u from Q, and $O(\text{degree}(v)\log n)$ time to perform the relaxation procedure on the edges incident on u.
- The overall running time of the **while** loop is

$$\sum_{v \in G}(1 + \text{degree}(v))\log n,$$

which is $O((n+m)\log n)$ by Proposition 12.6.

Note that if we wish to express the running time as a function of n only, then it is $O(n^2 \log n)$ in the worst case.

An Alternative Implementation for Dijkstra's Algorithm

Let us now consider an alternative implementation for the priority queue Q using an unsorted sequence. This, of course, requires that we spend $\Omega(n)$ time to extract the minimum element, but it allows for very fast key updates, provided Q supports the locator pattern (Section 7.4). Specifically, we can implement each key update done in a relaxation step in $O(1)$ time—we simply change the key value once we locate the item in Q to update. Hence, this implementation results in a running time that is $O(n^2 + m)$, which can be simplified to $O(n^2)$ since G is simple.

Comparing the Two Implementations

We have two choices for implementing the priority queue in Dijkstra's algorithm: a locator-based heap implementation, which yields $O((n+m)\log n)$ running time, and a locator-based unsorted sequence implementation, which yields an $O(n^2)$-time algorithm. Since both implementations would be fairly simple to code up, they are about equal in terms of the programming sophistication needed. These two implementations are also about equal in terms of the constant factors in their worst-case running times. Looking only at these worst-case times, we prefer the heap implementation when the number of edges in the graph is small (that is, when $m < n^2/\log n$), and we prefer the sequence implementation when the number of edges is large (that is, when $m > n^2/\log n$).

Proposition 12.24: *Given a simple undirected weighted graph G with n vertices and m edges, such that the weight of each edge is nonnegative, and a vertex v of G, Dijkstra's algorithm computes the distance from v to all other vertices of G in $O((n+m)\log n)$ worst-case time, or, alternatively, in $O(n^2)$ worst-case time.*

In Exercise R-12.16, we explore how to modify Dijkstra's algorithm to output a tree T rooted at v, such that the path in T from v to a vertex u is a shortest path in G from v to u.

Programming Dijkstra's Algorithm in Java

Having given a pseudo-code description of Dijkstra's algorithm, let us now present Java code for performing Dijkstra's algorithm, assuming we are given an undirected graph with positive integer weights. We express the algorithm by means of an abstract class Dijkstra (Code Fragments 12.13–12.15), which declares the abstract method weight(e) to extract the weight of edge e. Class Dijkstra is meant to be extended by subclasses that implement method weight(e). See, for example, class MyDijkstra shown in Code Fragment 12.16.

```
/** Dijkstra's algorithm for the single-source shortest path problem
  * in an undirected graph whose edges have integer weights. Classes
  * extending ths abstract class must define the weight(e) method,
  * which extracts the weight of an edge. */
public abstract class Dijkstra {
  /** Execute Dijkstra's algorithm.  */
  public void execute(InspectableGraph g, Vertex source) {
    graph = g;
    dijkstraVisit(source);
  }
  /** Attribute for vertex distances. */
  protected Object DIST = new Object();
  /** Set the distance of a vertex. */
  protected void setDist(Vertex v, int d) {
    v.set(DIST, new Integer(d));
  }
  /** Get the distance of a vertex from the source vertex. This method
    * returns the length of a shortest path from the source to u after
    * method execute has been called.  */
  public int getDist(Vertex u) {
    return ((Integer) u.get(DIST)).intValue();
  }
  /** This abstract method must be defined by subclasses.
    * @return weight of edge e. */
  protected abstract int weight(Edge e);
  /** Infinity value. */
  public static final int INFINITE = Integer.MAX_VALUE;
  /** Input graph. */
  protected InspectableGraph graph;
  /** Auxiliary priority queue. */
  protected PriorityQueue Q;
```

Code Fragment 12.13: Class Dijkstra implementing Dijkstra's algorithm. (Continued in Code Fragments 12.14 and 12.15.)

The main computation of Dijkstra's algorithm is performed by method dijkstraVisit. A priority queue Q supporting locator-based methods (Section 7.4.1) is used. We insert a vertex u into Q with method insert, which returns the locator of u in Q. We "attach" to u its locator in Q by means of method setLoc, and we retrieve the locator of u by means of method getLoc. Note that associating locators to the vertices is an instance of the decorator design pattern (Section 12.3.1). Instead of using an additional data structure for the labels $D[u]$, we exploit the fact that $D[u]$ is the key of vertex u in Q, and thus $D[u]$ can be retrieved given the locator of u in Q. Changing the label of a vertex z to d in the relaxation procedure corresponds to calling method replaceKey(ℓ, d), where ℓ is the locator of z in Q.

```
/** The actual execution of Dijkstra's algorithm.
 * @param v source vertex.  */
protected void dijkstraVisit (Vertex v) {
  // initialize the priority queue Q and store all the vertices in it
  Q = new ArrayHeap(new IntegerComparator());
  for (VertexIterator vertices = graph.vertices(); vertices.hasNext();) {
    Vertex u = vertices.nextVertex();
    int u_dist;
    if (u==v)
      u_dist = 0;
    else
      u_dist = INFINITE;
    // setDist(u, u_dist);
    Locator u_loc = Q.insert(new Integer(u_dist), u);
    setLoc(u, u_loc);
  }
  // grow the cloud, one vertex at a time
  while (!Q.isEmpty()) {
    // remove from Q and insert into cloud a vertex with minimum distance
    Locator u_loc = Q.min();
    Vertex u = getVertex(u_loc);
    int u_dist = getDist(u_loc);
    Q.remove(u_loc); // remove u from the priority queue
    setDist(u, u_dist); // the distance of u is final
    destroyLoc(u); // remove the locator associated with u
    if (u_dist == INFINITE)
      continue; // unreachable vertices are not processed
    // examine all the neighbors of u and update their distances
    for (EdgeIterator edges = graph.incidentEdges(u); edges.hasNext();) {
      Edge e = edges.nextEdge();
      Vertex z = graph.opposite(u,e);
      if (hasLoc(z)) { // check that z is in Q, i.e., it is not in the cloud
        int e_weight = weight(e);
        Locator z_loc = getLoc(z);
        int z_dist = getDist(z_loc);
        if ( u_dist + e_weight < z_dist ) // relaxation of edge e = (u,z)
          Q.replaceKey(z_loc, new Integer(u_dist + e_weight));
      }
    }
  }
}
```

Code Fragment 12.14: Method dijkstraVisit of class Dijkstra.

```
/** Attribute for vertex locators in the priority queue Q. */
protected Object LOC = new Object();
/** Check if there is a locator associated with a vertex. */
protected boolean hasLoc(Vertex v) {
  return v.has(LOC);
}
/** Get the locator in Q of a vertex. */
protected Locator getLoc(Vertex v) {
  return (Locator) v.get(LOC);
}
/** Associate with a vertex its locator in Q. */
protected void setLoc(Vertex v, Locator l) {
  v.set(LOC, l);
}
/** Remove the locator associated with a vertex. */
protected void destroyLoc(Vertex v) {
  v.destroy(LOC);
}
/** Get the vertex associated with a locator. */
protected Vertex getVertex(Locator l) {
  return (Vertex) l.element();
}
/** Get the distance of a vertex given its locator in Q. */
protected int getDist(Locator l) {
  return ((Integer) l.key()).intValue();
}
```

Code Fragment 12.15: Auxiliary methods of class Dijkstra. They assume that the vertices of the graph are decorable.

```
/** A specialization of class Dijkstra that extracts edge weights from
  * decorations.  */
public class MyDijkstra extends Dijkstra {
  /** Attribute for edge weights. */
  protected Object WEIGHT;
  /** Constructor that sets the weight attribute. */
  public MyDijkstra(Object weight_attribute) {
    WEIGHT = weight_attribute;
  }
  /** The edge weight is stored in attribute WEIGHT of the edge. */
  public int weight(Edge e) {
    return ((Integer) e.get(WEIGHT)).intValue();
  }
}
```

Code Fragment 12.16: Class MyDijkstra that extends Dijkstra and provides a concrete implementation of method weight(e).

12.7 Minimum Spanning Trees

Suppose we wish to connect all the computers in a new office building using the least amount of cable. We can model this problem using a weighted graph G whose vertices represent the computers, and whose edges represent all the possible pairs (u, v) of computers, where the weight $w((v, u))$ of edge (v, u) is equal to the amount of cable needed to connect computer v to computer u. Rather than computing a shortest path tree from some particular vertex v, we are interested instead in finding a (free) tree T that contains all the vertices of G and has the minimum total weight over all such trees. Methods for finding such a tree are the focus of this section.

Problem Definition

Given a weighted undirected graph G, we are interested in finding a tree T that contains all the vertices in G and minimizes the sum

$$w(T) = \sum_{(v,u) \in T} w((v, u)).$$

A tree, such as this, that contains every vertex of a connected graph G is said to be a *spanning tree*, and the problem of computing a spanning tree T with smallest total weight is known as the *minimum spanning tree* (or *MST*) problem.

The development of efficient algorithms for the minimum spanning tree problem predates the modern notion of computer science itself. In this section, we discuss two algorithms for solving the MST problem. These algorithms are all classic applications of the *greedy method*, which, as was discussed briefly in the previous section, is based on choosing objects to join a growing collection by iteratively picking an object that minimizes some cost function. The first algorithm we discuss is Kruskal's algorithm, which "grows" the MST in clusters by considering edges in order of their weights. The second algorithm we discuss is the Prim-Jarník algorithm, which grows the MST from a single root vertex, much in the same way as Dijkstra's shortest-path algorithm.

Caution

As in Section 12.6.1, in order to simplify the description the algorithms, we assume, in the following, that the input graph G is undirected (that is, all its edges are undirected) and simple (that is, it has no self-loops and no parallel edges). Hence, we denote the edges of G as unordered vertex pairs (u, z).

Before we discuss the details of these algorithms, however, let us give a crucial fact about minimum spanning trees that forms the basis of the algorithms.

A Crucial Fact about Minimum Spanning Trees

The two MST algorithms we discuss are based on the greedy method, which in this case depends crucially on the following fact. (See Figure 12.18.)

e Belongs to a Minimum Spanning Tree

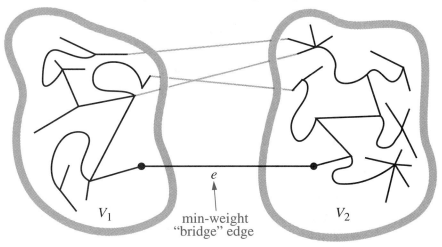

Figure 12.18: An illustration of the crucial fact about minimum spanning trees.

Proposition 12.25: *Let G be a weighted connected graph, and let V_1 and V_2 be a partition of the vertices of G into two disjoint nonempty sets. Furthermore, let e be an edge in G with minimum weight from among those with one endpoint in V_1 and the other in V_2. There is a minimum spanning tree T that has e as one of its edges.*

Justification: Let T be a minimum spanning tree of G. If T does not contain edge e, the addition of e to T must create a cycle. Therefore, there is some edge f of this cycle that has one endpoint in V_1 and the other in V_2. Moreover, by the choice of e, $w(e) \leq w(f)$. If we remove f from $T \cup \{e\}$, we obtain a spanning tree whose total weight is no more than before. Since T was a minimum spanning tree, this new tree must also be a minimum spanning tree. ∎

In fact, if the weights in G are distinct, then the minimum spanning tree is unique; we leave the justification of this less crucial fact as an exercise (C-12.17). In addition, note that Proposition 12.25 remains valid even if the graph G contains negative-weight edges or negative-weight cycles, unlike the algorithms we presented for shortest paths.

12.7.1   Kruskal's Algorithm

The reason Proposition 12.25 is so important is that it can be used as the basis for building a minimum spanning tree. In Kruskal's algorithm, it is used to build the minimum spanning tree in clusters. Initially, each vertex is in its own cluster all by itself. The algorithm then considers each edge in turn, ordered by increasing weight. If an edge e connects two different clusters, then e is added to the set of edges of the minimum spanning tree, and the two clusters connected by e are merged into a single cluster. If, on the other hand, e connects two vertices that are already in the same cluster, then e is discarded. Once the algorithm has added enough edges to form a spanning tree, it terminates and outputs this tree as the minimum spanning tree.

We give pseudo-code for Kruskal's MST algorithm in Code Fragment 12.17 and we show the working of this algorithm in Figures 12.19, 12.20, and 12.21.

Algorithm Kruskal(G):

    Input: A simple connected weighted graph G with n vertices and m edges

    Output: A minimum spanning tree T for G

  for each vertex v in G **do**

    Define an elementary cluster $C(v) \leftarrow \{v\}$.

  Initialize a priority queue Q to contain all edges in G, using the weights as keys.

  $T \leftarrow \emptyset$ {T will ultimately contain the edges of the MST}

  while T has fewer than $n - 1$ edges **do**

    $(u, v) \leftarrow Q.\text{removeMin}()$

    Let $C(v)$ be the cluster containing v, and let $C(u)$ be the cluster containing u.

    if $C(v) \neq C(u)$ **then**

      Add edge (v, u) to T.

      Merge $C(v)$ and $C(u)$ into one cluster, that is, union $C(v)$ and $C(u)$.

  return tree T

      Code Fragment 12.17: Kruskal's algorithm for the MST problem.

As mentioned before, the correctness of Kruskal's algorithm follows from the crucial fact about minimum spanning trees, Proposition 12.25. Each time Kruskal's algorithm adds an edge (v, u) to the minimum spanning tree T, we can define a partitioning of the set of vertices V (as in the proposition) by letting V_1 be the cluster containing v and letting V_2 contain the rest of the vertices in V. This clearly defines a disjoint partitioning of the vertices of V and, more importantly, since we are extracting edges from Q in order by their weights, e must be a minimum-weight edge with one vertex in V_1 and the other in V_2. Thus, Kruskal's algorithm always adds a valid minimum spanning tree edge.

(a)

(b)

(c)

(d)

(e)

(f)

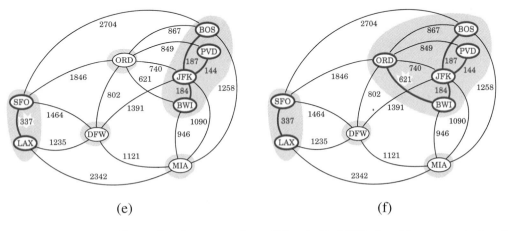

Figure 12.19: Example of an execution of Kruskal's MST algorithm on a graph with integer weights. We show the clusters as shaded regions and we highlight the edge being considered in each iteration. (Continued in Figure 12.20.)

(g)

(h)

(i)

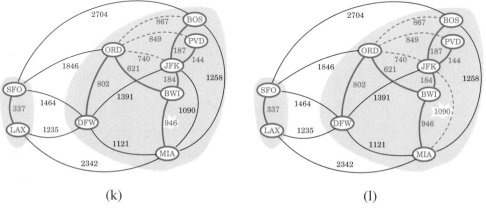

(j)

(k)

(l)

Figure 12.20: An example of an execution of Kruskal's MST algorithm (continued). Rejected edges are shown dashed. (Continued in Figure 12.21.)

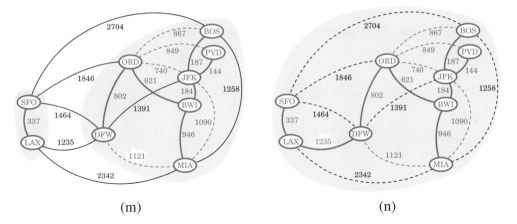

(m)   (n)

Figure 12.21: Example of an execution of Kruskal's MST algorithm (continued). The edge considered in (n) merges the last two clusters, which concludes this execution of Kruskal's algorithm.

The Running Time of Kruskal's Algorithm

In this section, we analyze the time complexity of Kruskal's algorithm. We denote the number of vertices and edges of the input graph G with n and m, respectively. We assume that the edge weights can be compared in constant time. Because of the high level of the description we gave for Kruskal's algorithm in Code Fragment 12.17, analyzing its running time requires that we give more details on its implementation. Specifically, we should indicate the data structures used and how they are implemented.

We implement the priority queue Q using a heap. Thus, we can initialize Q in $O(m \log m)$ time by repeated insertions, or in $O(m)$ time using bottom-up heap construction (see Section 7.3.5). In addition, at each iteration of the **while** loop, we can remove a minimum-weight edge in $O(\log m)$ time, which actually is $O(\log n)$, since G is simple.

We represent each cluster C with an unordered list of vertices, which could, for example, be implemented with a linked list. Also, we store with each vertex v a reference to its cluster $C(v)$. With this representation, testing whether $C(u) \neq C(v)$ takes $O(1)$ time. When we need to merge two clusters, $C(u)$ and $C(v)$, we move the elements of the ***smaller*** cluster into the larger one and update the cluster references of the vertices in the smaller cluster. Since we can simply add the elements of the smaller cluster at the end of the list for the larger cluster, merging two clusters takes time proportional to the size of the smaller cluster. That is, merging clusters $C(u)$ and $C(v)$ takes $O(\min\{|C(u)|, |C(v)|\})$ time.

Proposition 12.26: *Consider an execution of Kruskal's algorithm on a graph with n vertices, where clusters are represented with sequences and with cluster references at each vertex. The total time spent merging clusters is $O(n\log n)$.*

Justification: We observe that each time a vertex is moved to a new cluster, the size of the cluster containing the vertex at least doubles. Let $t(v)$ be the number of times that vertex v is moved to a new cluster. Since the maximum cluster size is n,

$$t(v) \le \log n.$$

The total time spent merging clusters in Kruskal's algorithm can be obtained by summing up the work done on each vertex, which is proportional to

$$\sum_{v \in G} t(v) \le n\log n.$$

■

Using Proposition 12.26 and arguments similar to those used in the analysis of Dijkstra's algorithm, we conclude that the total running time of Kruskal's algorithm is $O((n+m)\log n)$, which can be simplified as $O(m\log n)$ since G is simple and connected.

Proposition 12.27: *Given a simple connected weighted graph G with n vertices and m edges, Kruskal's algorithm constructs a minimum spanning tree for G in $O(m\log n)$ time.*

12.7.2 The Prim-Jarník Algorithm

In the Prim-Jarník algorithm, we grow a minimum spanning tree from a single cluster starting from some "root" vertex v. The main idea is similar to that of Dijkstra's algorithm. We begin with some vertex v, defining the initial "cloud" of vertices C. Then, in each iteration, we choose a minimum-weight edge $e = (v, u)$, connecting a vertex v in the cloud C to a vertex u outside of C. The vertex u is then brought into the cloud C and the process is repeated until a spanning tree is formed. Again, the crucial fact about minimum spanning trees comes to play, for by always choosing the smallest-weight edge joining a vertex inside C to one outside C, we are assured of always adding a valid edge to the MST.

To efficiently implement this approach, we can take another cue from Dijkstra's algorithm. We maintain a label $D[u]$ for each vertex u outside the cloud C, so that $D[u]$ stores the weight of the best current edge for joining u to the cloud C.

Algorithm PrimJarnik(G):

    Input: A weighted connected graph G with n vertices and m edges

    Output: A minimum spanning tree T for G

  Pick any vertex v of G

  $D[v] \leftarrow 0$

  for each vertex $u \neq v$ **do**

    $D[u] \leftarrow +\infty$

  Initialize $T \leftarrow \emptyset$.

  Initialize a priority queue Q with an item $((u, \text{null}), D[u])$ for each vertex u, where (u, null) is the element and $D[u])$ is the key.

  while Q is not empty **do**

    $(u, e) \leftarrow Q.\text{removeMin}()$

    Add vertex u and edge e to T.

    for each vertex z adjacent to u such that z is in Q **do**

      {perform the relaxation procedure on edge (u, z)}

      if $w((u, z)) < D[z]$ **then**

        $D[z] \leftarrow w((u, z))$

        Change to $(z, (u, z))$ the element of vertex z in Q.

        Change to $D[z]$ the key of vertex z in Q.

  return the tree T

Code Fragment 12.18: The Prim-Jarník algorithm for the MST problem.

These labels allow us to reduce the number of edges that we must consider in deciding which vertex is next to join the cloud. We give the pseudo-code in Code Fragment 12.18.

Let n and m denote the number of vertices and edges of the input graph G, respectively. The implementation issues for the Prim-Jarník algorithm are similar to those for Dijkstra's algorithm. If we implement the priority queue Q as a heap that supports the locator-based priority queue methods (see Section 7.4), we can extract the vertex u in each iteration in $O(\log n)$ time. In addition, we can update each $D[z]$ value in $O(\log n)$ time, as well, which is a computation considered at most once for each edge (u, z). The other steps in each iteration can be implemented in constant time. Thus, the total running time is $O((n+m) \log n)$, which is $O(m \log n)$. Hence, we can summarize as follows:

Proposition 12.28: *Given a simple connected weighted graph G with n vertices and m edges, the Prim-Jarník algorithm constructs a minimum spanning tree for G in $O(m \log n)$ time.*

We illustrate the Prim-Jarník algorithm in Figures 12.22 and 12.23.

(a)

(b)

(c)

(d)

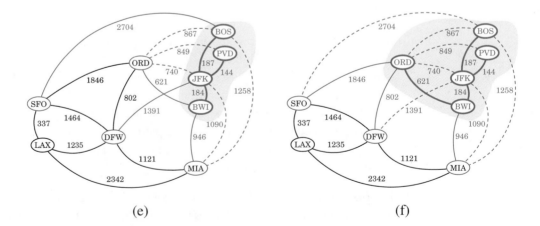

(e)

(f)

Figure 12.22: An illustration of the Prim-Jarník algorithm. (Continued in Figure 12.23.)

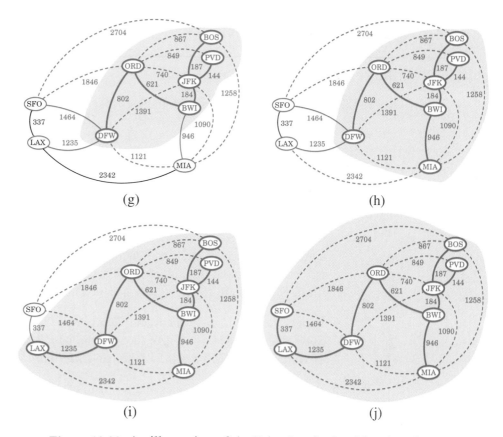

Figure 12.23: An illustration of the Prim-Jarník algorithm (continued).

A Comparison of the Above MST Algorithms

Although each of the above algorithms for computing minimum spanning trees has the same worst-case running time, each one achieves this running time using different data structures and different approaches to building the minimum spanning tree.

Concerning auxiliary data structures, Kruskal's algorithm uses a priority queue, to store edges, and a collection of sets, implemented with lists, to store clusters. The Prim-Jarník algorithm uses only a priority queue, to store vertex-edge pairs. Thus, from an ease of programming viewpoint, the Prim-Jarník algorithm is preferable. Indeed, the Prim-Jarník algorithm is so similar to Dijkstra's algorithm that an implementation of Dijkstra's algorithm could be converted into an implementation for the Prim-Jarník algorithm without much effort.

In terms of the constant factors, the two algorithms are fairly similar in that they both have relatively small constant factors in their asymptotic running times.

12.8 Exercises

Reinforcement

R-12.1 Draw a simple undirected graph G that has 12 vertices, 18 edges, and 3 connected components. Why would it be impossible to draw G with 3 connected components if G had 66 edges?

R-12.2 Let G be a simple connected graph with n vertices and m edges. Explain why $O(\log m)$ is $O(\log n)$.

R-12.3 Draw a simple connected directed graph with 8 vertices and 16 edges such that the in-degree and out-degree of each vertex is 2. Show that there is a single (nonsimple) cycle that includes all the edges of your graph, that is, you can trace all the edges in their respective directions without ever lifting your pencil. (Such a cycle is called an ***Euler tour***.)

R-12.4 Repeat the previous problem and then remove one edge from the graph. Show that now there is a single (nonsimple) path that includes all the edges of your graph. (Such a path is called an ***Euler path***.)

R-12.5 Bob loves foreign languages and wants to plan his course schedule for the following years. He is interested in the following nine language courses: LA15, LA16, LA22, LA31, LA32, LA126, LA127, LA141, and LA169. The course prerequisites are:

- LA15: (none)
- LA16: LA15
- LA22: (none)
- LA31: LA15
- LA32: LA16, LA31
- LA126: LA22, LA32
- LA127: LA16
- LA141: LA22, LA16
- LA169: LA32.

Find the sequence of courses that allows Bob to satisfy all the prerequisites.

R-12.6 Suppose we represent a graph G having n vertices and m edges with the edge list structure. Why, in this case, does the insertVertex method run in $O(1)$ time while the removeVertex method runs in $O(m)$ time?

R-12.7 Let G be a graph whose vertices are the integers 1 through 8, and let the adjacent vertices of each vertex be given by the table below:

vertex	adjacent vertices
1	(2, 3, 4)
2	(1, 3, 4)
3	(1, 2, 4)
4	(1, 2, 3, 6)
5	(6, 7, 8)
6	(4, 5, 7)
7	(5, 6, 8)
8	(5, 7)

Assume that, in a traversal of G, the adjacent vertices of a given vertex are returned in the same order as they are listed in the above table.

a. Draw G.
b. Give the sequence of vertices of G visited using a DFS traversal starting at vertex 1.
c. Give the sequence of vertices visited using a BFS traversal starting at vertex 1.

R-12.8 Would you use the adjacency list structure or the adjacency matrix structure in each of the following cases? Justify your choice.

a. The graph has 10,000 vertices and 20,000 edges, and it is important to use as little space as possible.
b. The graph has 10,000 vertices and 20,000,000 edges, and it is important to use as little space as possible.
c. You need to answer the query areAdjacent as fast as possible, no matter how much space you use.

R-12.9 Explain why the DFS traversal runs in $\Theta(n^2)$ time on an n-vertex simple graph that is represented with the adjacency matrix structure.

R-12.10 Draw the transitive closure of the directed graph shown in Figure 12.2.

R-12.11 Compute a topological ordering for the directed graph drawn with solid edges in Figure 12.8d.

R-12.12 Can we use a queue instead of a stack as an auxiliary data structure in the topological sorting algorithm shown in Code Fragment 12.11?

R-12.13 Draw a simple, connected, weighted graph with 8 vertices and 16 edges, each with unique edge weights. Identify one vertex as a "start" vertex and illustrate a running of Dijkstra's algorithm on this graph.

R-12.14 Show how to modify the pseudo-code for Dijkstra's algorithm for the case when the graph may contain parallel edges and self-loops.

R-12.15 Show how to modify the pseudo-code for Dijkstra's algorithm for the case when the graph is directed and we we want to compute shortest *directed paths* from the source vertex to all the other vertices.

R-12.16 Show how to modify the pseudo-code for Dijkstra's algorithm to not only output the distance from v to each vertex in G, but also to output a tree T rooted at v, such that the path in T from v to a vertex u is actually a shortest path in G from v to u.

R-12.17 There are eight small islands in a lake, and the state wants to build seven bridges to connect them so that each island can be reached from any other one via one or more bridges. The cost of constructing a bridge is proportional to its length. The distances between pairs of islands are given in the following table.

	1	2	3	4	5	6	7	8
1	–	240	210	340	280	200	345	120
2	–	–	265	175	215	180	185	155
3	–	–	–	260	115	350	435	195
4	–	–	–	–	160	330	295	230
5	–	–	–	–	–	360	400	170
6	–	–	–	–	–	–	175	205
7	–	–	–	–	–	–	–	305
8	–	–	–	–	–	–	–	–

Find which bridges to build so that the total construction cost is minimum.

R-12.18 Draw a simple, connected, undirected, weighted graph with 8 vertices and 16 edges, each with unique edge weights. Illustrate the execution of Kruskal's algorithm on this graph. (Note that there is only one minimum spanning tree for this graph.)

R-12.19 Repeat the previous problem for the Prim-Jarník algorithm.

R-12.20 Consider the unsorted sequence implementation of the priority queue Q used in Dijkstra's algorithm. What is, in this case, the best-case running time of Dijkstra's algorithm $\Omega(n^2)$ on an n-vertex graph? (Hint: Consider the size of Q each time the minimum element is extracted.)

R-12.21 Describe the meaning of the graphical conventions used in Figure 12.6 illustrating a DFS traversal. What do the colors blue and black refer to? What do the arrows signify? How about thick lines and dashed lines?

R-12.22 Repeat Exercise R-12.21 for Figure 12.7 illustrating a BFS traversal.

R-12.23 Repeat Exercise R-12.21 for Figure 12.9 illustrating a directed DFS traversal.

R-12.24 Repeat Exercise R-12.21 for Figure 12.10 illustrating the Floyd-Warshall algorithm.

R-12.25 Repeat Exercise R-12.21 for Figure 12.12 illustrating the topological sorting algorithm.

R-12.26 Repeat Exercise R-12.21 for Figures 12.15 and 12.16 illustrating Dijkstra's algorithm.

R-12.27 Repeat Exercise R-12.21 for Figures 12.19 and 12.21 illustrating Kruskal's algorithm.

R-12.28 Repeat Exercise R-12.21 for Figures 12.22 and 12.23 illustrating the Prim-Jarník algorithm.

Creativity

C-12.1 Justify Proposition 12.11.

C-12.2 Describe the details of an $O(n+m)$ time algorithm for computing *all* the connected components of an undirected graph G with n vertices and m edges.

C-12.3 Let T be the spanning tree rooted at the start vertex produced by the depth-first search of a connected, undirected graph G. Argue why every edge of G, not in T, goes from a vertex in T to one of its ancestors, that is, it is a *back edge*. (Hint: Suppose that such a nontree edge is a cross edge, and argue based upon the order the DFS visits the end vertices of this edge.)

C-12.4 Suppose we wish to represent an n-vertex graph G using the edge list structure, assuming that we identify the vertices with the integers in the set $\{0, 1, \ldots, n-1\}$. Describe how to implement the container E to support $O(\log n)$-time performance for the areAdjacent method. How are you implementing the method in this case?

C-12.5 Tamarindo University and many other schools worldwide are doing a joint project on multimedia. A computer network is built to connect these schools using communication links that form a free tree. The schools decide to install a file server at one of the schools to share data among all the schools. Since the transmission time on a link is dominated by the link setup and synchronization, the cost of a data transfer is proportional to the number of links used. Hence, it is desirable to choose a "central" location for the file server. Given a free tree T and a node v of T, the *eccentricity* of v is the length of a longest path from v to any other node of T. A node of T with minimum eccentricity is called a *center* of T.

    a. Design an efficient algorithm that, given an n-node free tree T, computes a center of T.

    b. Is the center unique? If not, how many distinct centers can a free tree have?

C-12.6 Show that, if T is a BFS tree produced for a connected graph G, then, for each vertex v at level i, the path of T between s and v has i edges, and any other path of G between s and v has at least i edges. (Hint: Justify this by induction on the length of a shortest path from the start vertex.)

C-12.7 The time delay of a long-distance call can be determined by multiplying a small fixed constant by the number of communication links on the telephone network between the caller and callee. Suppose the telephone network of a company named RT&T is a free tree. The engineers of RT&T want to compute the maximum possible time delay that may be experienced in a long-distance call. Given a free tree T, the *diameter* of T is the length of a longest path between two nodes of T. Give an efficient algorithm for computing the diameter of T.

C-12.8 A company named RT&T has a network of n switching stations connected by m high-speed communication links. Each customer's phone is directly connected to one station in his or her area. The engineers of RT&T have developed a prototype video-phone system that allows two customers to see each other during a phone call. In order to have acceptable image quality, however, the number of links used to transmit video signals between the two parties cannot exceed 4. Suppose that RT&T's network is represented by a graph. Design an efficient algorithm that computes, for each station, the set of stations it can reach using no more than 4 links.

C-12.9 Explain why there are no forward nontree edges with respect to a BFS tree constructed for a directed graph. (Hint: Suppose there is such an edge and show why it would not be a nontree edge.)

C-12.10 An independent set of an undirected graph $G = (V,E)$ is a subset I of V such that no two vertices in I are adjacent. That is, if $u, v \in I$, then $(u,v) \notin E$. A *maximal independent set* M is an independent set such that, if we were to add any additional vertex to M, then it would not be independent any more. Every graph has a maximal independent set. (Can you see this? This question is not part of the exercise, but it is worth thinking about.) Give an efficient algorithm that computes a maximal independent set for a graph G. What is this method's running time?

C-12.11 An *Euler tour* of a directed graph $\vec{G}$ with n vertices and m edges is a cycle that traverses each edge of $\vec{G}$ exactly once according to its direction. Such a tour always exists if $\vec{G}$ is connected and the in-degree equals the out-degree of each vertex in $\vec{G}$. Describe an $O(n+m)$-time algorithm for finding an Euler tour of such a digraph $\vec{G}$.

C-12.12 Let G be an undirected graph G with n vertices and m edges. Describe an $O(n+m)$-time algorithm for traversing each edge of G exactly once in each direction.

C-12.13 Justify Proposition 12.14.

C-12.14 Give an example of an n-vertex simple graph G that causes Dijkstra's algorithm to run in $\Omega(n^2 \log n)$ time when its implemented with a heap for the priority queue.

C-12.15 Give an example of a weighted directed graph $\vec{G}$ with negative-weight edges, but no negative-weight cycle, such that Dijkstra's algorithm incorrectly computes the shortest-path distances from some start vertex v.

C-12.16 Consider the following greedy strategy for finding a shortest path from vertex *start* to vertex *goal* in a given connected graph.

    1: Initialize *path* to *start*.
    2: Initialize *VisitedVertices* to {*start*}.
    3: If *start=goal*, return *path* and exit. Otherwise, continue.
    4: Find the edge (*start,v*) of minimum weight such that v is adjacent to *start* and v is not in *VisitedVertices*.
    5: Add v to *path*.
    6: Add v to *VisitedVertices*.
    7: Set *start* equal to v and go to step 3.

Does this greedy strategy always find a shortest path from *start* to *goal*? Either explain intuitively why it works, or give a counter example.

C-12.17 Show that if all the weights in a connected weighted graph G are distinct, then there is exactly one minimum spanning tree for G.

C-12.18 Design an efficient algorithm for finding a *longest* directed path from a vertex s to a vertex t of an acyclic weighted digraph $\vec{G}$. Specify the graph representation used and any auxiliary data structures used. Also, analyze the time complexity of your algorithm.

C-12.19 Suppose you are given a diagram of a telephone network, which is a graph G whose vertices represent switching centers, and whose edges represent communication lines between two centers. The edges are marked by their bandwidth. The bandwidth of a path is the bandwidth of its lowest bandwidth edge. Give an algorithm that, given a diagram and two switching centers a and b, will output the maximum bandwidth of a path between a and b.

C-12.20 NASA wants to link n stations spread over the country using communication channels. Each pair of stations has a different bandwidth available, which is known a priori. NASA wants to select $n-1$ channels (the minimum possible) in such a way that all the stations are linked by the channels and the total bandwidth (defined as the sum of the individual bandwidths of the channels) is maximum. Give an efficient algorithm for this problem and determine its worst-case time complexity. Consider the weighted graph $G = (V, E)$, where V is the set of stations and E is the set of channels between the stations. Define the weight $w(e)$ of an edge $e \in E$ as the bandwidth of the corresponding channel.

C-12.21 Suppose you are given a *timetable*, which consists of:

- A set $\mathcal{A}$ of n airports, and for each airport $a \in \mathcal{A}$, a minimum connecting time $c(a)$
- A set $\mathcal{F}$ of m flights, and the following, for each flight $f \in \mathcal{A}$:
  - Origin airport $a_1(f) \in \mathcal{A}$
  - Destination airport $a_2(f) \in \mathcal{A}$
  - Departure time $t_1(f)$
  - Arrival time $t_2(f)$.

Describe an efficient algorithm for the flight scheduling problem. In this problem, we are given airports a and b, and a time t, and we wish to compute a sequence of flights that allows one to arrive at the earliest possible time in b when departing from a at or after time t. Minimum connecting times at intermediate airports should be observed. What is the running time of your algorithm as a function of n and m?

C-12.22 Let $\vec{G}$ be a weighted digraph with n vertices. Design a variation of Floyd-Warshall's algorithm for computing the lengths of the shortest paths from every vertex to every other vertex. Your algorithm should run in $O(n^3)$ time.

C-12.23 As your reward for saving the Kingdom of Bigfunnia from the evil monster, "Exponential Asymptotic," the king has given you the opportunity to earn a big reward. Behind the castle there is a maze, and along each corridor of the maze there is a bag of gold coins. The amount of gold in each bag varies. You will be given the opportunity to walk through the maze, picking up bags of gold. You may enter only through the door marked "ENTER" and exit through the door marked "EXIT." (These are distinct doors.) While in the maze you may not retrace your steps. Each corridor of the maze has an arrow painted on the wall. You may only go down the corridor in the direction of the arrow. There is no way to traverse a "loop" in the maze. You will receive a map of the maze, including the amount of gold in and the direction of each corridor. Describe an algorithm to help you pick up the most gold.

C-12.24 Suppose we are given a directed graph $\vec{G}$ with n vertices, and let M be the $n \times n$ adjacency matrix corresponding to $\vec{G}$.

    a. Let the product of M with itself (M^2) be defined, for $1 \le i, j \le n$, as follows:

$$M^2(i,j) = M(i,1) \odot M(1,j) \oplus \cdots \oplus M(i,n) \odot M(n,j),$$

where "$\oplus$" is the Boolean **or** operator and "$\odot$" is Boolean **and**. Given this definition, what does $M^2(i,j) = 1$ imply about the vertices i and j? What if $M^2(i,j) = 0$?

    b. Suppose M^4 is the product of M^2 with itself. What do the entries of M^4 signify? How about the entries of $M^5 = (M^4)(M)$? In general, what information is contained in the matrix M^p?

    c. Now suppose that $\vec{G}$ is weighted and assume the following:

        1: for $1 \le i \le n, M(i,i) = 0$.
        2: for $1 \le i, j \le n, M(i,j) = weight(i,j)$ if $(i,j) \in E$.
        3: for $1 \le i, j \le n, M(i,j) = \infty$ if $(i,j) \notin E$.

Also, let M^2 be defined, for $1 \le i, j \le n$, as follows:

$$M^2(i,j) = \min\{M(i,1) + M(1,j), \ldots, M(i,n) + M(n,j)\}.$$

If $M^2(i,j) = k$, what may we conclude about the relationship between vertices i and j?

Projects

P-12.1 Write a class implementing a simplified graph ADT that has only methods relevant to undirected graphs and does not include update methods, using the adjacency matrix structure. Your class should include a constructor method that takes two containers (for example, sequences)—a container V of vertex elements and a container E of pairs of vertex elements—and produces the graph G that these two containers represent.

P-12.2 Implement the simplified graph ADT described in Project P-12.1, using the adjacency list structure.

P-12.3 Implement the simplified graph ADT described in Project P-12.1, using the edge list structure.

P-12.4 Extend the class of Project P-12.2 to support update methods.

P-12.5 Extend the class of Project P-12.2 to support all the methods of the graph ADT (including methods for directed edges).

P-12.6 Implement a generic BFS traversal using the template method pattern.

P-12.7 Implement the topological sorting algorithm.

P-12.8 Implement the Floyd-Warshall transitive closure algorithm.

P-12.9 Design an experimental comparison of repeated DFS traversals versus the Floyd-Warshall algorithm for computing the transitive closure of a digraph.

P-12.10 Implement Kruskal's algorithm assuming that the edge weights are integers.

P-12.11 Implement the Prim-Jarník algorithm assuming that the edge weights are integers.

P-12.12 Perform an experimental comparison of two of the minimum spanning tree algorithms discussed in this chapter (Kruskal and Prim-Jarník). Develop an extensive set of experiments to test the running times of these algorithms using randomly generated graphs.

Chapter Notes

The depth-first search method is a part of the "folklore" of computer science, but Hopcroft and Tarjan [49, 91] are the ones who showed how useful this algorithm is for solving several different graph problems. Knuth [59] discusses the topological sorting problem. The simple linear-time algorithm that we describe for determining if a directed graph is strongly connected is due to Kosaraju. The Floyd-Warshall algorithm appears in a paper by Floyd [35] and is based upon a theorem of Warshall [97]. The mark-sweep garbage collection method we describe is one of many different algorithms for performing garbage collection. We encourage the reader interested in further study of garbage collection to examine the book by Jones [54]. To learn about different algorithms for drawing graphs, please see the book chapter by Tamassia [89], the annotated bibliography of Di Battista *et al.* [29], or the book by Di Battista *et al.* [30]. The first known minimum spanning tree algorithm is due to Barůvka [9], and was published in 1926. The Prim-Jarník algorithm was first published in Czech by Jarník [53] in 1930 and in English in 1957 by Prim [83]. Kruskal published his minimum spanning tree algorithm in 1956 [63]. The reader interested in further study of the history of the minimum spanning tree problem is referred to the paper by Graham and Hell [44]. The current asymptotically fastest minimum spanning tree algorithm is a randomized method of Karger, Klein, and Tarjan [55] that runs in $O(m)$ expected time.

Dijkstra [31] published his single-source, shortest path algorithm in 1959. The reader interested in further study of graph algorithms is referred to the books by Ahuja, Magnanti, and Orlin [6], Cormen, Leiserson, and Rivest [25], Even [33], Gibbons [39], Mehlhorn [74], and Tarjan [92], and the book chapter by van Leeuwen [94]. Incidentally, the running time for the Prim-Jarník algorithm, and also that of Dijkstra's algorithm, can actually be improved to be $O(n \log n + m)$ by implementing the queue Q with either of two more sophisticated data structures, the "Fibonacci Heap" [37] or the "Relaxed Heap" [32]. The reader interested in these implementations is referred to the papers that describe the implementation of these structures, and how they can be applied to the shortest-path and minimum spanning tree problems.

Appendix

A — Useful Mathematical Facts

In this appendix we give several useful mathematical facts. We begin with some combinatorial definitions and facts.

Logarithms and Exponents

The logarithm function is defined as

$$\log_b a = c \quad \text{if} \quad a = b^c.$$

The following identities hold for logarithms and exponents:

1. $\log_b ac = \log_b a + \log_b c$
2. $\log_b a/c = \log_b a - \log_b c$
3. $\log_b a^c = c\log_b a$
4. $\log_b a = (\log_c a)/\log_c b$
5. $b^{\log_c a} = a^{\log_c b}$
6. $(b^a)^c = b^{ac}$
7. $b^a b^c = b^{a+c}$
8. $b^a / b^c = b^{a-c}$

In addition, we have the following:

Proposition A.1: *If $a > 0$, $b > 0$, and $c > a + b$, then*

$$\log a + \log b \le 2\log c - 2.$$

The **natural logarithm** function $\ln x = \log_e x$, where $e = 2.71828\ldots$, is the value of the following progression:

$$e = 1 + \frac{1}{1!} + \frac{1}{2!} + \frac{1}{3!} + \cdots.$$

In addition,

$$e^x = 1 + \frac{x}{1!} + \frac{x^2}{2!} + \frac{x^3}{3!} + \cdots$$

$$\ln(1+x) = x - \frac{x^2}{2!} + \frac{x^3}{3!} - \frac{x^4}{4!} + \cdots.$$

There are a number of useful inequalities relating to these functions (which derive from these definitions).

Proposition A.2: *If $x > -1$,*

$$\frac{x}{1+x} \leq \ln(1+x) \leq x.$$

Proposition A.3: *For $0 \leq x < 1$,*

$$1 + x \leq e^x \leq \frac{1}{1-x}.$$

Proposition A.4: *For any two positive real numbers x and n,*

$$\left(1 + \frac{x}{n}\right)^n \leq e^x \leq \left(1 + \frac{x}{n}\right)^{n+x/2}.$$

Integer Functions and Relations

The "floor" and "ceiling" functions are defined respectively as follows:

1. $\lfloor x \rfloor$ = the largest integer less than or equal to x.
2. $\lceil x \rceil$ = the smallest integer greater than or equal to x.

The **modulus** function is defined for integers $a \geq 0$ and $b > 0$ as

$$a \bmod b = a - \left\lfloor \frac{a}{b} \right\rfloor b.$$

The **factorial** function is defined as

$$n! = 1 \cdot 2 \cdot 3 \cdot \cdots \cdot (n-1)n.$$

The binomial coefficient is

$$\binom{n}{k} = \frac{n!}{k!(n-k)!},$$

which is equal to the number of different **combinations** one can define by choosing k different items from a collection of n items (where the order does not matter). The name "binomial coefficient" derives from the **binomial expansion**:

$$(a+b)^n = \sum_{k=0}^{n} \binom{n}{k} a^k b^{n-k}.$$

We also have the following relationships.

Proposition A.5: *If* $0 \le k \le n$, *then*

$$\left(\frac{n}{k}\right)^k \le \binom{n}{k} \le \frac{n^k}{k!}.$$

Proposition A.6 (Stirling's Approximation):

$$n! = \sqrt{2\pi n}\left(\frac{n}{e}\right)^n\left(1 + \frac{1}{12n} + \varepsilon(n)\right),$$

where $\varepsilon(n)$ *is* $O(1/n^2)$.

The ***Fibonacci progression*** is a numeric progression such that $F_0 = 0$, $F_1 = 1$, and $F_n = F_{n-1} + F_{n-2}$ for $n \ge 2$.

Proposition A.7: *If* F_n *is defined by the Fibonacci progression, then* F_n *is* $\Theta(g^n)$, *where* $g = (1 + \sqrt{5})/2$ *is the so-called* **golden ratio**.

Summations

There are a number of useful facts about summations.

Proposition A.8: *Factoring summations:*

$$\sum_{i=1}^{n} af(i) = a\sum_{i=1}^{n} f(i),$$

provided a *does not depend upon* i.

Proposition A.9: *Reversing the order:*

$$\sum_{i=1}^{n}\sum_{j=1}^{m} f(i,j) = \sum_{j=1}^{m}\sum_{i=1}^{n} f(i,j).$$

One special form of summation is a ***telescoping sum***:

$$\sum_{i=1}^{n}(f(i) - f(i-1)) = f(n) - f(0),$$

which arises often in the amortized analysis of a data structure or algorithm.

The following are some other facts about summations that arise often in the analysis of data structures and algorithms.

Proposition A.10:

$$\sum_{i=1}^{n} i = \frac{n(n+1)}{2}.$$

Proposition A.11:

$$\sum_{i=1}^{n} i^2 = \frac{n(n+1)(2n+1)}{6}.$$

Proposition A.12: *If $k \geq 1$ is an integer constant, then*

$$\sum_{i=1}^{n} i^k \text{ is } \Theta(n^{k+1}).$$

Another common summation is the **geometric sum**

$$\sum_{i=0}^{n} a^i,$$

for any fixed real number $0 < a \neq 1$.

Proposition A.13:

$$\sum_{i=0}^{n} a^i = \frac{1 - a^{n+1}}{1 - a}$$

for any real number $0 < a \neq 1$.

Proposition A.14:

$$\sum_{i=0}^{\infty} a^i = \frac{1}{1 - a}$$

for any real number $0 < a < 1$.

There is also a combination of the two common forms, called the **linear exponential** summation, which has the following expansion:

Proposition A.15: *For $0 < a \neq 1$, and $n \geq 2$,*

$$\sum_{i=1}^{n} ia^i = \frac{a - (n+1)a^{(n+1)} + na^{(n+2)}}{(1-a)^2}.$$

The nth **harmonic number** H_n is defined as

$$H_n = \sum_{i=1}^{n} \frac{1}{i}.$$

Proposition A.16: *If H_n is the nth harmonic number, then H_n is $\ln n + \Theta(1)$.*

Basic Probability

We review some basic facts from probability theory. The most basic is that any statement about a probability is defined upon a ***sample space*** S, which is defined as the set of all possible outcomes from some experiment. We leave the terms "outcomes" and "experiment" undefined in any formal sense.

Example A.17: *Consider an experiment that consists of the outcome from flipping a coin five times. This sample space has 2^5 different outcomes, one for each different ordering of possible flips that can occur.*

Sample spaces can also be infinite, as the following example illustrates.

Example A.18: *Consider an experiment that consists of flipping a coin until it comes up heads. This sample space is infinite, with each outcome being a sequence of i tails followed by a single flip that comes up heads, for $i \in \{1, 2, 3, \ldots\}$.*

A ***probability space*** is a sample space S together with a probability function Pr that maps subsets of S to real numbers in the interval $[0, 1]$. It captures mathematically the notion of the probability of certain "events" occurring. Formally, each subset A of S is called an ***event***, and the probability function Pr is assumed to possess the following basic properties with respect to events defined from S:

1. $\Pr(\emptyset) = 0$.
2. $\Pr(S) = 1$.
3. $0 \leq \Pr(A) \leq 1$, for any $A \subseteq S$.
4. If $A, B \subseteq S$ and $A \cap B = \emptyset$, then $\Pr(A \cup B) = \Pr(A) + \Pr(B)$.

Two events A and B are ***independent*** if

$$\Pr(A \cap B) = \Pr(A) \cdot \Pr(B).$$

A collection of events $\{A_1, A_2, \ldots, A_n\}$ is ***mutually independent*** if

$$\Pr(A_{i_1} \cap A_{i_2} \cap \cdots \cap A_{i_k}) = \Pr(A_{i_1}) \Pr(A_{i_2}) \cdots \Pr(A_{i_k}).$$

for any subset $\{A_{i_1}, A_{i_2}, \ldots, A_{i_k}\}$.

The ***conditional probability*** that an event A occurs, given an event B, is denoted as $\Pr(A|B)$, and is defined as the ratio

$$\frac{\Pr(A \cap B)}{\Pr(B)},$$

assuming that $\Pr(B) > 0$.

An elegant way for dealing with events is in terms of ***random variables***. Intuitively, random variables are variables whose values depend upon the outcome of some experiment. Formally, a ***random variable*** is a function X that maps outcomes from some sample space S to real numbers. An ***indicator random variable*** is a random variable that maps outcomes to the set $\{0, 1\}$. Often in data structure and algorithm analysis we use a random variable X to characterize the running time of a randomized algorithm. In this case, the sample space S is defined by all possible outcomes of the random sources used in the algorithm.

We are most interested in the typical, average, or "expected" value of such a random variable. The ***expected value*** of a random variable X is defined as

$$\mathbf{E}(X) = \sum_x x \Pr(X = x),$$

where the summation is defined over the range of X (which in this case is assumed to be discrete).

Proposition A.19 (The Linearity of Expectation): *Let X and Y be two arbitrary random variables. Then*

$$\mathbf{E}(X + Y) = \mathbf{E}(X) + \mathbf{E}(Y).$$

Example A.20: *Let X be a random variable that assigns the outcome of the roll of two fair dice to the sum of the number of dots showing. Then $\mathbf{E}(X) = 7$.*

Justification: *To justify this claim, let X_1 and X_2 be random variables corresponding to the number of dots on each die. Thus, $X_1 = X_2$ (i.e., they are two instances of the same function) and $\mathbf{E}(X) = \mathbf{E}(X_1 + X_2) = \mathbf{E}(X_1) + \mathbf{E}(X_2)$. Each outcome of the roll of a fair die occurs with probability $1/6$. Thus*

$$\mathbf{E}(X_i) = \frac{1}{6} + \frac{2}{6} + \frac{3}{6} + \frac{4}{6} + \frac{5}{6} + \frac{6}{6} = \frac{7}{2},$$

for $i = 1, 2$. Therefore, $E(X) = 7$.   ■

Two random variables X and Y are ***independent*** if

$$\Pr(X = x | Y = y) = \Pr(X = x),$$

for all real numbers x and y.

Proposition A.21: *If two random variables X and Y are independent, then*

$$\mathbf{E}(XY) = \mathbf{E}(X)\mathbf{E}(Y).$$

Example A.22: *Let X be a random variable that assigns the outcome of a roll of two fair dice to the product of the number of dots showing. Then $E(X) = 49/4$.*

Justification: Let X_1 and X_2 be random variables denoting the number of dots on each die. The variables X_1 and X_2 are clearly independent; hence

$$E(X) = E(X_1 X_2) = E(X_1)E(X_2) = (7/2)^2 = 49/4.$$

∎

Useful Mathematical Techniques

To determine whether a function is little-oh or little-omega of another, it is sometimes helpful to apply the following rule.

Proposition A.23 (L'Hôpital's Rule): *If we have $\lim_{n\to\infty} f(n) = +\infty$ and we have $\lim_{n\to\infty} g(n) = +\infty$, then $\lim_{n\to\infty} f(n)/g(n) = \lim_{n\to\infty} f'(n)/g'(n)$, where $f'(n)$ and $g'(n)$ respectively denote the derivatives of $f(n)$ and $g(n)$.*

In deriving an upper or lower bound for a summation, it is often useful to *split a summation* as follows:

$$\sum_{i=1}^{n} f(i) = \sum_{i=1}^{j} f(i) + \sum_{i=j+1}^{n} f(i).$$

Another useful technique is to **bound a sum by an integral**. If f is a nondecreasing function, then, assuming the following terms are defined,

$$\int_{a-1}^{b} f(x)\,dx \le \sum_{i=a}^{b} f(i) \le \int_{a}^{b+1} f(x)\,dx.$$

There is a general form of recurrence relation that arises in the analysis of divide-and-conquer algorithms:

$$T(n) = aT(n/b) + f(n),$$

for constants $a \ge 1$ and $b > 1$.

Proposition A.24: *Let $T(n)$ be defined as above. Then*

1. *If $f(n)$ is $O(n^{\log_b a - \varepsilon})$, for some constant $\varepsilon > 0$, then $T(n)$ is $\Theta(n^{\log_b a})$.*
2. *If $f(n)$ is $\Theta(n^{\log_b a} \log^k n)$, for a fixed nonnegative integer $k \ge 0$, then $T(n)$ is $\Theta(n^{\log_b a} \log^{k+1} n)$.*
3. *If $f(n)$ is $\Omega(n^{\log_b a + \varepsilon})$, for some constant $\varepsilon > 0$, and if $af(n/b) \le cf(n)$, then $T(n)$ is $\Theta(f(n))$.*

This proposition is known as the **master method** for characterizing divide-and-conquer recurrence relations asymptotically.

Bibliography

[1] G. M. Adel'son-Vel'skii and Y. M. Landis, "An algorithm for the organization of information," *Doklady Akademii Nauk SSSR*, vol. 146, pp. 263–266, 1962. English translation in *Soviet Math. Dokl.*, **3**, 1259–1262.

[2] A. Aggarwal and J. S. Vitter, "The input/output complexity of sorting and related problems," *Commun. ACM*, vol. 31, pp. 1116–1127, 1988.

[3] A. V. Aho, "Algorithms for finding patterns in strings," in *Handbook of Theoretical Computer Science* (J. van Leeuwen, ed.), vol. A. Algorithms and Complexity, pp. 255–300, Amsterdam: Elsevier, 1990.

[4] A. V. Aho, J. E. Hopcroft, and J. D. Ullman, *The Design and Analysis of Computer Algorithms*. Reading, MA: Addison-Wesley, 1974.

[5] A. V. Aho, J. E. Hopcroft, and J. D. Ullman, *Data Structures and Algorithms*. Reading, MA: Addison-Wesley, 1983.

[6] R. K. Ahuja, T. L. Magnanti, and J. B. Orlin, *Network Flows: Theory, Algorithms, and Applications*. Englewood Cliffs, NJ: Prentice Hall, 1993.

[7] K. Arnold and J. Gosling, *The Java Programming Language*. The Java Series, Reading, Mass.: Addison-Wesley, 1996.

[8] R. Baeza-Yates and B. Ribeiro-Neto, *Modern Information Retrieval*. Reading, Mass.: Addison-Wesley, 1999.

[9] O. Baruvka, "O jistem problemu minimalnim," *Praca Moravske Prirodovedecke Spolecnosti*, vol. 3, pp. 37–58, 1926. (in Czech).

[10] R. Bayer, "Symmetric binary B-trees: Data structure and maintenance," *Acta Informatica*, vol. 1, no. 4, pp. 290–306, 1972.

[11] R. Bayer and McCreight, "Organization of large ordered indexes," *Acta Inform.*, vol. 1, pp. 173–189, 1972.

[12] J. L. Bentley, "Programming pearls: Writing correct programs," *Communications of the ACM*, vol. 26, pp. 1040–1045, 1983.

[13] J. L. Bentley, "Programming pearls: Thanks, heaps," *Communications of the ACM*, vol. 28, pp. 245–250, 1985.

[14] G. Booch, *Object-Oriented Analysis and Design with Applications*. Redwood City, CA: Benjamin/Cummings, 1994.

[15] C. B. Boyer and U. C. Merzbach, *A History of Mathematics*. New York: John Wiley & Sons, Inc., 2nd ed., 1991.

[16] R. S. Boyer and J. S. Moore, "A fast string searching algorithm," *Communications of the ACM*, vol. 20, no. 10, pp. 762–772, 1977.

[17] G. Brassard, "Crusade for a better notation," *SIGACT News*, vol. 17, no. 1, pp. 60–64, 1985.

[18] T. Budd, *An Introduction to Object-Oriented Programming*. Reading, Mass.: Addison-Wesley, 1991.

[19] M. Campione and H. Walrath, *The Java Tutorial: Programming for the Internet*. Reading, Mass.: Addison Wesley, 1996.

[20] L. Cardelli and P. Wegner, "On understanding types, data abstraction and polymorphism," *ACM Computing Surveys*, vol. 17, no. 4, pp. 471–522, 1985.

[21] S. Carlsson, "Average case results on heapsort," *BIT*, vol. 27, pp. 2–17, 1987.

[22] K. L. Clarkson, "Linear programming in $O(n3^{d^2})$ time," *Inform. Process. Lett.*, vol. 22, pp. 21–24, 1986.

[23] R. Cole, "Tight bounds on the complexity of the Boyer-Moore pattern matching algorithm," *SIAM Journal on Computing*, vol. 23, no. 5, pp. 1075–1091, 1994.

[24] D. Comer, "The ubiquitous B-tree," *ACM Comput. Surv.*, vol. 11, pp. 121–137, 1979.

[25] T. H. Cormen, C. E. Leiserson, and R. L. Rivest, *Introduction to Algorithms*. Cambridge, MA: MIT Press, 1990.

[26] G. Cornell and C. S. Horstmann, *Core Java*. Mountain View, CA: SunSoft Press, 1996.

[27] M. Crochemore and T. Lecroq, "Pattern matching and text compression algorithms," in *The Computer Science and Engineering Handbook* (A. B. Tucker, Jr., ed.), ch. 8, pp. 162–202, CRC Press, 1997.

[28] S. A. Demurjian, Sr., "Software design," in *The Computer Science and Engineering Handbook* (A. B. Tucker, Jr., ed.), ch. 108, pp. 2323–2351, CRC Press, 1997.

[29] G. Di Battista, P. Eades, R. Tamassia, and I. G. Tollis, "Algorithms for drawing graphs: an annotated bibliography," *Comput. Geom. Theory Appl.*, vol. 4, pp. 235–282, 1994.

[30] G. Di Battista, P. Eades, R. Tamassia, and I. G. Tollis, *Graph Drawing: Algorithms for Geometric Representations of Graphs*. Englewood Cliffs, NJ: Prentice Hall, 1998.

[31] E. W. Dijkstra, "A note on two problems in connexion with graphs," *Numerische Mathematik*, vol. 1, pp. 269–271, 1959.

[32] J. R. Driscoll, H. N. Gabow, R. Shrairaman, and R. E. Tarjan, "Relaxed heaps: An alternative to Fibonacci heaps with applications to parallel computation.," *Commun. ACM*, vol. 31, pp. 1343–1354, 1988.

[33] S. Even, *Graph Algorithms*. Potomac, Maryland: Computer Science Press, 1979.

[34] D. Flanagan, *Java in a Nutshell*. O'Reilly, 3rd ed., 1999.

[35] R. W. Floyd, "Algorithm 97: Shortest path," *Communications of the ACM*, vol. 5, no. 6, p. 345, 1962.

[36] R. W. Floyd, "Algorithm 245: Treesort 3," *Communications of the ACM*, vol. 7, no. 12, p. 701, 1964.

[37] M. Fredman and R. E. Tarjan, "Fibonacci heaps and their uses in improved network optimization problems," *J. ACM*, vol. 34, pp. 596–615, 1987.

[38] E. Gamma, R. Helm, R. Johnson, and J. Vlissides, *Design Patterns: Elements of Reusable Object-Oriented Software*. Reading, Mass.: Addison-Wesley, 1995.

[39] A. M. Gibbons, *Algorithmic Graph Theory*. Cambridge, UK: Cambridge University Press, 1985.

[40] A. Goldberg and D. Robson, *Smalltalk-80: The Language*. Reading, Mass.: Addison-Wesley, 1989.

[41] G. H. Gonnet and R. Baeza-Yates, *Handbook of Algorithms and Data Structures in Pascal and C*. Reading, Mass.: Addison-Wesley, 1991.

[42] G. H. Gonnet and J. I. Munro, "Heaps on heaps," *SIAM Journal on Computing*, vol. 15, no. 4, pp. 964–971, 1986.

[43] M. T. Goodrich, M. Handy, B. Hudson, and R. Tamassia, "Accessing the internal organization of data structures in the JDSL library," in *Proc. Workshop on Algorithm Engineering and Experimentation* (M. T. Goodrich and C. C. McGeoch, eds.), vol. 1619 of *Lecture Notes Comput. Sci.*, pp. 124–139, Springer-Verlag, 1999.

[44] R. L. Graham and P. Hell, "On the history of the minimum spanning tree problem," *Annals of the History of Computing*, vol. 7, no. 1, pp. 43–57, 1985.

[45] R. L. Graham, D. E. Knuth, and O. Patashnik, *Concrete Mathematics*. Reading, Mass.: Addison-Wesley, 1989.

[46] L. J. Guibas and R. Sedgewick, "A dichromatic framework for balanced trees," in *Proc. 19th Annu. IEEE Sympos. Found. Comput. Sci.*, Lecture Notes Comput. Sci., pp. 8–21, Springer-Verlag, 1978.

[47] Y. Gurevich, "What does $O(n)$ mean?," *SIGACT News*, vol. 17, no. 4, pp. 61–63, 1986.

[48] C. A. R. Hoare, "Quicksort," *The Computer Journal*, vol. 5, pp. 10–15, 1962.

[49] J. E. Hopcroft and R. E. Tarjan, "Efficient algorithms for graph manipulation," *Communications of the ACM*, vol. 16, no. 6, pp. 372–378, 1973.

[50] C. S. Horstmann, *Computing Concepts in Java*. New York: John Wiley, and Sons, 1998.

[51] B. Huang and M. Langston, "Practical in-place merging," *Communications of the ACM*, vol. 31, no. 3, pp. 348–352, 1988.

[52] J. JáJá, *An Introduction to Parallel Algorithms*. Reading, Mass.: Addison-Wesley, 1992.

[53] V. Jarnik, "O jistem problemu minimalnim," *Praca Moravske Prirodovedecke Spolecnosti*, vol. 6, pp. 57–63, 1930. (in Czech).

[54] R. E. Jones, *Garbage Collection: Algorithms for Automatic Dynamic Memory Management*. John Wiley and Sons, 1996.

[55] D. R. Karger, P. Klein, and R. E. Tarjan, "A randomized linear-time algorithm to find minimum spanning trees," *Journal of the ACM*, vol. 42, pp. 321–328, 1995.

[56] R. M. Karp and V. Ramachandran, "Parallel algorithms for shared memory machines," in *Handbook of Theoretical Computer Science* (J. van Leeuwen, ed.), pp. 869–941, Amsterdam: Elsevier/The MIT Press, 1990.

[57] P. Kirschenhofer and H. Prodinger, "The path length of random skip lists," *Acta Informatica*, vol. 31, pp. 775–792, 1994.

[58] D. E. Knuth, *Fundamental Algorithms*, vol. 1 of *The Art of Computer Programming*. Reading, MA: Addison-Wesley, 1st ed., 1968.

[59] D. E. Knuth, *Fundamental Algorithms*, vol. 1 of *The Art of Computer Programming*. Reading, MA: Addison-Wesley, 2nd ed., 1973.

[60] D. E. Knuth, *Sorting and Searching*, vol. 3 of *The Art of Computer Programming*. Reading, MA: Addison-Wesley, 1973.

[61] D. E. Knuth, "Big omicron and big omega and big theta," in *SIGACT News*, vol. 8, pp. 18–24, 1976.

[62] D. E. Knuth, J. H. Morris, Jr., and V. R. Pratt, "Fast pattern matching in strings," *SIAM Journal on Computing*, vol. 6, no. 1, pp. 323–350, 1977.

[63] J. B. Kruskal, Jr., "On the shortest spanning subtree of a graph and the traveling salesman problem," *Proc. Amer. Math. Soc.*, vol. 7, pp. 48–50, 1956.

[64] N. G. Leveson and C. S. Turner, "An investigation of the Therac-25 accidents," *IEEE Computer*, vol. 26, no. 7, pp. 18–41, 1993.

[65] R. Levisse, "Some lessons drawn from the history of the binary search algorithm," *The Computer Journal*, vol. 26, pp. 154–163, 1983.

[66] A. Levitin, "Do we teach the right algorithm design techniques?," in *30th ACM SIGCSE Symp. on Computer Science Education*, pp. 179–183, 1999.

[67] T. Lindholm and F. Yellin, *The Java Virtual Machine Specification*. Reading, Mass.: Addison-Wesley, 1997.

[68] B. Liskov and J. Guttag, *Abstraction and Specification in Program Development*. Cambridge, Mass./New York: The MIT Press/McGraw-Hill, 1986.

[69] E. M. McCreight, "A space-economical suffix tree construction algorithm," *Journal of Algorithms*, vol. 23, no. 2, pp. 262–272, 1976.

[70] C. J. H. McDiarmid and B. A. Reed, "Building heaps fast," *Journal of Algorithms*, vol. 10, no. 3, pp. 352–365, 1989.

[71] N. Megiddo, "Linear-time algorithms for linear programming in R^3 and related problems," *SIAM J. Comput.*, vol. 12, pp. 759–776, 1983.

[72] N. Megiddo, "Linear programming in linear time when the dimension is fixed," *J. ACM*, vol. 31, pp. 114–127, 1984.

[73] K. Mehlhorn, *Data Structures and Algorithms 1: Sorting and Searching*, vol. 1 of *EATCS Monographs on Theoretical Computer Science*. Heidelberg, Germany: Springer-Verlag, 1984.

[74] K. Mehlhorn, *Data Structures and Algorithms 2: Graph Algorithms and NP-Completeness*, vol. 2 of *EATCS Monographs on Theoretical Computer Science*. Heidelberg, Germany: Springer-Verlag, 1984.

[75] K. Mehlhorn and S. Näher, *LEDA: a Platform for Combinatorial and Geometric Computing*. Cambridge, UK: Cambridge University Press, 1999.

[76] K. Mehlhorn and A. Tsakalidis, "Data structures," in *Handbook of Theoretical Computer Science* (J. van Leeuwen, ed.), vol. A. Algorithms and Complexity, pp. 301–341, Amsterdam: Elsevier, 1990.

[77] M. H. Morgan, *Vitruvius: The Ten Books on Architecture*. New York: Dover Publications, Inc., 1960.

[78] D. R. Morrison, "PATRICIA—practical algorithm to retrieve information coded in alphanumeric," *Journal of the ACM*, vol. 15, no. 4, pp. 514–534, 1968.

[79] R. Motwani and P. Raghavan, *Randomized Algorithms*. New York, NY: Cambridge University Press, 1995.

[80] D. R. Musser and A. Saini, *STL Tutorial and Reference Guide: C++ Programming with the Standard Template Library*. Reading, Mass.: Addison-Wesley, 1996.

[81] T. Papadakis, J. I. Munro, and P. V. Poblete, "Average search and update costs in skip lists," *BIT*, vol. 32, pp. 316–332, 1992.

[82] P. V. Poblete, J. I. Munro, and T. Papadakis, "The binomial transform and its application to the analysis of skip lists," in *Proceedings of the European Symposium on Algorithms (ESA)*, pp. 554–569, 1995.

[83] R. C. Prim, "Shortest connection networks and some generalizations," *Bell Syst. Tech. J.*, vol. 36, pp. 1389–1401, 1957.

[84] W. Pugh, "Skip lists: a probabilistic alternative to balanced trees," *Commun. ACM*, vol. 33, no. 6, pp. 668–676, 1990.

[85] H. Samet, *The Design and Analysis of Spatial Data Structures*. Reading, MA: Addison-Wesley, 1990.

[86] R. Schaffer and R. Sedgewick, "The analysis of heapsort," *Journal of Algorithms*, vol. 15, no. 1, pp. 76–100, 1993.

[87] R. Sedgewick and P. Flajolet, *An Introduction to the Analysis of Algorithms*. Reading, Mass.: Addison-Wesley, 1996.

[88] G. A. Stephen, *String Searching Algorithms*. World Scientific Press, 1994.

[89] R. Tamassia, "Graph drawing," in *Handbook of Discrete and Computational Geometry* (J. E. Goodman and J. O'Rourke, eds.), ch. 44, pp. 815–832, Boca Raton, FL: CRC Press LLC, 1997.

[90] R. Tarjan and U. Vishkin, "An efficient parallel biconnectivity algorithm," *SIAM J. Comput.*, vol. 14, pp. 862–874, 1985.

[91] R. E. Tarjan, "Depth first search and linear graph algorithms," *SIAM Journal on Computing*, vol. 1, no. 2, pp. 146–160, 1972.

[92] R. E. Tarjan, *Data Structures and Network Algorithms*, vol. 44 of *CBMS-NSF Regional Conference Series in Applied Mathematics*. Philadelphia, PA: Society for Industrial and Applied Mathematics, 1983.

[93] A. B. Tucker, Jr., *The Computer Science and Engineering Handbook*. CRC Press, 1997.

[94] J. van Leeuwen, "Graph algorithms," in *Handbook of Theoretical Computer Science* (J. van Leeuwen, ed.), vol. A. Algorithms and Complexity, pp. 525–632, Amsterdam: Elsevier, 1990.

[95] J. S. Vitter, "Efficient memory access in large-scale computation," in *Proc. 8th Sympos. Theoret. Aspects Comput. Sci.*, Lecture Notes Comput. Sci., Springer-Verlag, 1991.

[96] J. S. Vitter and P. Flajolet, "Average-case analysis of algorithms and data structures," in *Algorithms and Complexity* (J. van Leeuwen, ed.), vol. A of *Handbook of Theoretical Computer Science*, pp. 431–524, Amsterdam: Elsevier, 1990.

[97] S. Warshall, "A theorem on boolean matrices," *Journal of the ACM*, vol. 9, no. 1, pp. 11–12, 1962.

[98] J. W. J. Williams, "Algorithm 232: Heapsort," *Communications of the ACM*, vol. 7, no. 6, pp. 347–348, 1964.

[99] M. R. Williams, *A History of Computing Technology*. Prentice-Hall, Inc., 1985.

[100] D. Wood, *Data Structures, Algorithms, and Performance*. Reading, Mass.: Addison-Wesley, 1993.

Index